STUART YORKSHIRE

PLACES AND PEOPLE

J.T. Cliffe

Published by Northern Heritage Publications
an imprint of Jeremy Mills Publishing Limited

113 Lidget Street
Lindley
Huddersfield
West Yorkshire
HD3 3JR

www.jeremymillspublishing.co.uk

First published 2013
Text © J. T. Cliffe
Images © as attributed

ISBN: 978-1-906600-79-2

The moral right of J. T. Cliffe to be identified as the author of this work has been asserted.

All rights reserved. No part of this book may be reproduced in any form or by any means without prior permission in writing from the publisher.

Cover image:
Portrait of Thomas Fairfax, 3rd Baron Fairfax of Cameron by William Faithbourne after Robert Walker
© National Portrait Gallery, London

Contents

Acknowledgements	v
Abbreviations used in the Notes	vii
Introduction	1
York	9
The East Riding	15
The North Riding	129
The West Riding	273
Appendix	483
Select Bibliography	487
Index of Subjects	491
Index of Persons	495

Acknowledgements

FOR THIS STUDY I have drawn extensively on manuscript sources, both official records and private papers. As regards the latter category I should like to express my gratitude to the owners of family muniments which have been deposited in libraries and record offices and in particular the Duke of Norfolk, Lord Hotham, Lady Herries of Terregles, Sir Ian Macdonald, Mr Simon Cunliffe-Lister and the Trustees of the Wharncliffe Estate.

I also wish to thank the custodians of manuscript collections for the assistance which I have received: the British Library and the Public Record Office (now called The National Archives); the House of Lords Library; the Trustees of Dr Williams's Library, London; the Bodleian Library, Oxford; the Borthwick Institute of Historical Research, York; the Brotherton Library, University of Leeds; the East Riding of Yorkshire Archives Service; the Hull University Archives; the North Yorkshire County Record Office; the Department of Manuscripts and Special Collections, University of Nottingham; the Nottinghamshire and Southwell Diocesan Record Office; the Head of Leisure Services, Sheffield City Council; the West Yorkshire Archive Service, Bradford, Kirklees and Leeds; and the Yorkshire Archaeological Society Library.

The Wentworth Woodhouse Muniments have been accepted in lieu of Inheritance Tax by H M Government and allocated to Sheffield City Council.

The maps were prepared to my specifications by Catherine D'Alton and Elanor McBay of the Department of Geography, University College London.

I am particularly indebted to Gordon Forster of the University of Leeds and the late Professor Austin Woolrych of the University of Lancaster for their valuable advice and continuing encouragement during the course of what proved to be a long haul undertaking.

Finally, I must record my gratitude for the impressive contribution made by Meg Lewis who typed the early drafts of the work when it was still in an embryonic state and Jenny Chaplin who undertook the bulk of the typing and saw it through to the end.

Abbreviations used in the Notes

BIHR	Borthwick Institute of Historical Research, University of York
BL	British Library
C.2	Public Record Office, Chancery Proceedings, Series I
C.3	Public Record Office, Chancery Proceedings, Series II
C.5-10	Public Record Office, Chancery Proceedings, Six Clerks' Series
C.22	Public Record Office, Chancery Depositions
C.33	Public Record Office, Chancery, Entry Books of Decrees and Orders
C.38	Public Record Office, Chancery, Reports and Certificates
C.54	Public Record Office, Chancery, Close Rolls
CJ	*Commons Journals*
CRS	*Catholic Record Society Publications*
CSP Dom	*Calendar of State Papers Domestic*, Public Record Office
E.134	Public Record Office, Court of Exchequer, Depositions
E.178	Public Record Office, Court of Exchequer, Special Commissions
HMC	Historical Manuscripts Commission
PRO	Public Record Office
S.P.19	Public Record Office, State Papers Domestic, Committee for the Advance of Money
S.P.23	Public Record Office, State Papers Domestic, Committee for Compounding
STAC 8	Public Record Office, Star Chamber Proceedings, James I and Charles I
VCH	*Victoria County History*
Wards 5	Public Record Office, Court of Wards, Feodaries' Surveys

Wards 9	Public Record Office, Court of Wards, Miscellaneous Books
Wards 13	Public Record Office, Court of Wards, Pleadings
WYAS	West Yorkshire Archive Service
YAJ	*Yorkshire Archaeological Journal*
YAS	Yorkshire Archaeological Society
YASRS	*Yorkshire Archaeological Society Record Series*
YPRS	*Yorkshire Parish Record Society Publications*

NOTE: The Public Record Office is now known as The National Archives.

Portrait of Thomas Wentworth, Earl of Stafford by Sir Antony Van Dyck
Private Collection © Courtauld Institute of Art

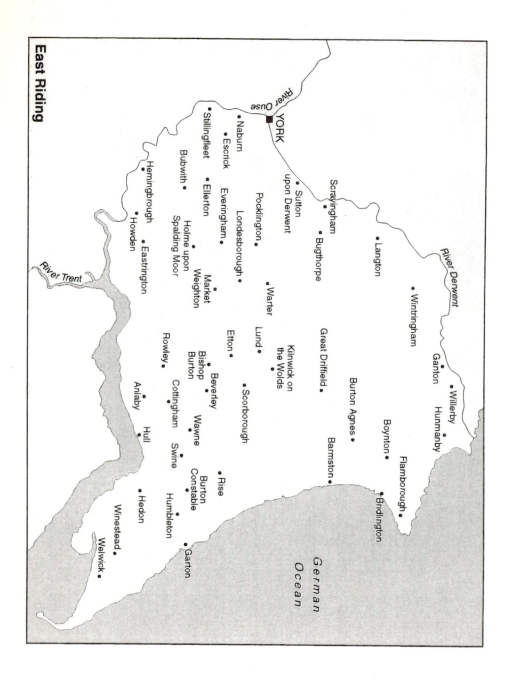

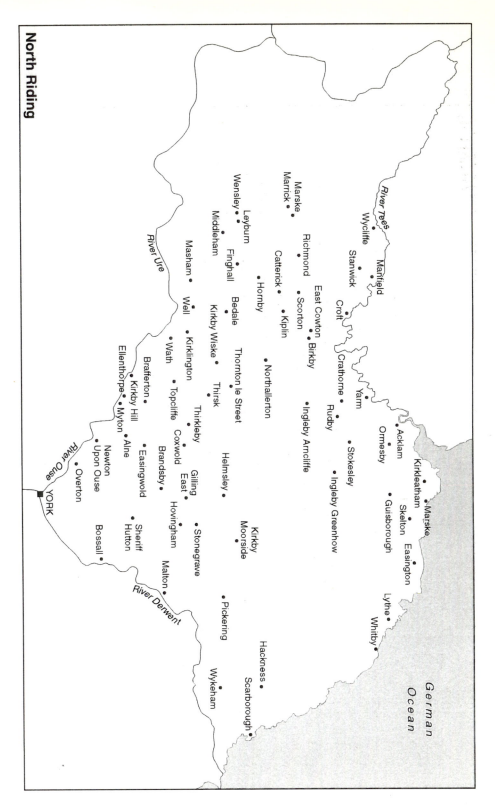

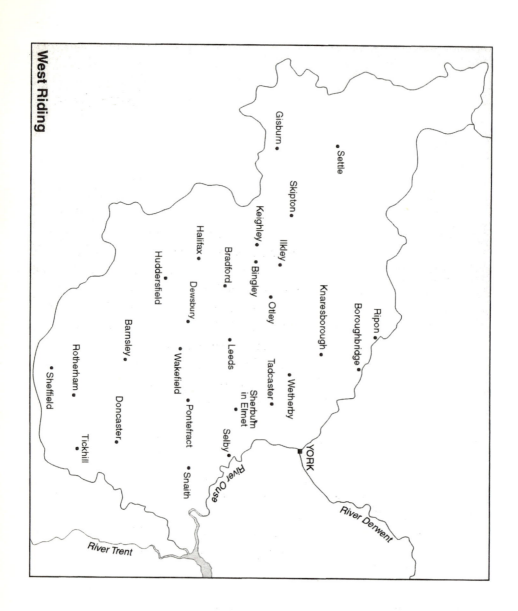

Introduction

AS WILLIAM CAMDEN observed in his *Britannia*, which originally appeared in 1586, Yorkshire was by far the largest county in England.[1] This point had been graphically illustrated seven years earlier when Christopher Saxton, who was himself a Yorkshireman, had published the very first atlas of the counties of England and Wales. Stretching from the Pennines to the German Ocean (as the North Sea was then called), Yorkshire contained some 3,700,000 acres while the West Riding alone was of greater extent than Devon, the next county in size. At the same time visitors from other parts of England were impressed not only by the sheer scale of the county but by the rich diversity of its landscape. Camden wrote that 'If in one place the soil be of a stony, sandy, barren nature, yet in another it is pregnant and fruitful; and so if it be naked and exposed in one part we find it cloathed and sheltered with great store of wood in another; Nature using an Allay and mixture, that the entire County, by this variety of parts, might seem more pleasing and beautiful'.[2]

In his *History of the Worthies of England* Thomas Fuller expressed the view that 'though other counties have more of the warm sun' Yorkshire 'hath as much as any of God's (corporal) blessings'.[3] The county was well watered by such rivers as the Aire, the Calder, the Derwent, the Don, the Humber, the Ouse, the Swale and the Wharfe. The rivers, or floods as he called them, figured prominently in Michael Drayton's poetical description of Yorkshire:

> But that wherein the world her greatness most may see,
> And that which doth this Shire before the rest prefer,

---

1   Edmund Gibson, *Camden's Britannia, Newly Translated into English, With Large Additions and Improvements* (1695), 706.
2   *Ibid*, 706.
3   Fuller, *The Worthies of England* (ed. J. Freeman) (1952), 634. This work was first published in 1662.

Is of so many Floods, and great, that rise from her,
Except some silly few out of her verge that flow,
So near to other Shires, that it is hard to know,
If that their springs be hers, or others them divide.[4]

Generally, there was an abundance of wood and stone for building work. The North Riding had deposits of lead and coal in that part of the region known as Richmondshire and alum at Guisborough, Mulgrave and elsewhere in Cleveland. Coal measures were to be found in many places in the West Riding which also had considerable resources of lead and ironstone. Only the East Riding lacked such bounty: 'coal-finders' who searched for coal seams there were forced to admit defeat. Like the North Riding, however, the East Riding profited from the great profusion and variety of fish in the waters of the German Ocean.

Given the size of the county there was never any serious possibility that the ridings would become merely a historical relic. They had their own deputy lieutenants, justices of the peace and subsidy commissioners and they provided at least the well-to-do with a genuine sense of community. Before the time of the Civil War the Lord Lieutenant of Yorkshire (who was also the Lord President of the Council in the North) had responsibility for military matters throughout the county but after the Restoration it was judged necessary for each riding to have its own Lord Lieutenant. Within the ridings there were administrative divisions known as wapentakes which were comparable to the hundreds in other counties. These were regarded as convenient units for such purposes as the levying of taxes.

The Diocese of York covered most of Yorkshire together with Nottinghamshire while the Bishop of Chester had jurisdiction over the Deanery of Richmond. In all, there were some 560 parishes in Yorkshire. A number of these parishes were very extensive and in addition to the parish churches had public chapels or chapels of ease which served the needs of outlying communities. During the course of the seventeenth century some new chapels were built, often on the initiative of the more Puritan-minded parishioners.

In the latter part of the century it was generally considered that the county had 48 market towns besides York: eight in the East Riding, 15 in the North Riding and 25 in the West Riding. A number of villages were also entitled to hold markets and fairs by virtue of medieval charters, though in some cases at least these rights were no longer being exercised.[5] While many towns enjoyed borough status only ten had corporations which had been formally constituted by royal decree: Beverley, Doncaster, Hedon, Hull, Leeds, Pontefract, Richmond, Ripon, Scarborough and York. Except for Doncaster and

---

4   The complete version of Drayton's *Poly-Olbion* from which this extract is drawn first appeared in 1622.
5   K. L. McCutcheon, *Yorkshire Fairs and Markets, Thoresby Society*, xxxix (1940).

Leeds each of these corporate towns had the right to elect two MPs. In 1640 the number of parliamentary representatives for the county and its boroughs was increased from 26 to 30.

Modern estimates suggest that the total population of Yorkshire amounted to some 300,000 at the beginning of the seventeenth century and that by the 1670s it may possibly have exceeded 400,000 despite the ravages of war and pestilence.[6] The largest towns were York, Leeds and Hull but no town appears to have had more than 12,000 inhabitants.

At the top of the social hierarchy were the nobility and gentry who between them governed the county. In 1640 there were ten aristocratic families seated in Yorkshire while the landed gentry consisted of over 600 families. Basically, it was the gentry who provided the sheriffs, deputy lieutenants, justices of the peace and MPs but as a class they embraced wide variations in income. At one extreme there were 73 families with estates worth £1000 a year or more; at the other there was a much larger group of families with incomes of £100 a year or less.[7] In 1588 a Yorkshire squire, James Ryther, wrote of his fellow gentry that 'Their moste unyversall exersize is huntinge' and added that for this reason the county was full of parks and chases 'greatly stored with red and fallowe deer, with conyes, hares, fesannts, partridges and whatsoever beastes or foules for game or use'.[8]

Most of the inhabitants of Yorkshire were dependent, either directly or indirectly, on agriculture for their livelihood. There was nevertheless a substantial amount of industrial activity, particularly in the West Riding. The manufacture of cloth in the towns and parishes of Leeds, Halifax, Wakefield and Bradford and other places in the same general area provided employment for many thousands of men, women and children. In 1639 a report on the food situation in the wapentake of Agbrigg and Morley (which broadly corresponded to the main clothing region) emphasised that above two-thirds of the division 'doe consist of tradeing, and for the rest the Corne that doth growe on itt is not able to sustaine itt …. for butter and cheese they are weekly supplyed from Ripon, Knaresborough and other places 30 miles of'.[9] As Clarendon would later point out, such towns as Leeds, Halifax and Bradford, 'depending wholly upon clothiers', enthusiastically supported the cause of Parliament in the Civil War.[10]

Coalmining was carried on in many parts of the West Riding. While visiting Castleford in 1697 Celia Fiennes noted that 'all the Country is full of Coale and the pitts

---

6 A. G. Dickens, 'The Extent and Character of Recusancy in Yorkshire, 1604', *YAJ*, xxxvii (1951), 32. J. D. Purdy, *Yorkshire Hearth Tax Returns (Studies in Regional and Local History, No. 7, University of Hull)* (1991), 123.

7 J. T. Cliffe, *The Yorkshire Gentry* (1969), 5, 25, 28.

8 BL, Lansdowne MSS 119, fols. 114, 115.

9 PRO, SP Dom, Charles I, S.P. 16/cdxiv/125.

10 Edward Earl of Clarendon, *The History of the Rebellion and Civil Wars in England* (ed. W. D. Macray) (1888), ii, 464.

are so thick in the roads that it is hazardous to travell for strangers'.[11] The industry was mainly in the hands of the country gentry who owned most of the land which contained coal deposits. In the reign of Charles I over 40 West Riding squires were engaged in mining operations, though these were generally limited in scope.

At Kirkstall, near Leeds, the Saviles of Howley Hall manufactured iron on an impressive scale and further south there were iron mills belonging to the Wortleys and other gentry families. In Sheffield and the surrounding villages a multitude of forges produced a wide range of cutlery and tools for which the town had long been famous.

Besides cloth and cutlery Yorkshire had other commodities which were much in demand beyond its boundaries. These included alum, lead, pins, spurs from Ripon and knitted stockings from Wensleydale and Doncaster. In addition, Yorkshire horses had a national reputation. Thomas Fuller was of the opinion that 'Yorkshire doth breed the best race of English horses, whose keeping commonly in steep and stony ground bringeth them to firmness of footing and hardness of hoof'.[12]

Packhorses or wagons might be used for the consignment of goods but in an age of poor road communications there was also a significant amount of freight movement on some rivers such as the Ouse which linked York with the Humber estuary. Visitors from the south were amazed by the number of stone bridges in Yorkshire which were meticulously recorded in John Ogilby's pioneering route maps of 1675[13] but they were far from complimentary about the roads on which they were forced to travel. Various factors were responsible for the problems encountered on the roads: the steep hills which were particularly difficult to negotiate in bad weather; the damage caused by wagons and coaches; and the reluctance of local communities to carry out essential maintenance. John Taylor the Water Poet related that in September 1639 he left Wortley with a guide 'and rode to Hallifax 16 miles, the ways were so rocky, stony, boggy and mountaynous that it was a day's journey to ride so short a way'.[14] To make matters worse, the Yorkshire miles were much longer than the statute mile which had been adopted as the standard measure in most parts of the kingdom. This disparity was clearly irksome to Celia Fiennes who also noted, with wry amusement, that in Yorkshire the ordinary people 'do not esteem it uphill unless so steep as a house or precipice; they say it's good levell gate all along, when it may be there are severall great hills to pass'.[15]

While travellers deplored the state of the roads there were some compensations. In the major towns there were often many inns which met with their approval and food was generally cheap and plentiful. Yorkshire ale was highly regarded for its strength and quality and in 1675 Thomas Baskerville thought it worth recording that 'They have

---

11 C. Morris (ed.), *The Journeys of Celia Fiennes* (1949), 94.
12 Thomas Fuller, *The Worthies of England* (ed. J. Freeman) (1952), 636-7.
13 John Ogilby, *Britannia* (1675). In his maps he noted both stone and wooden bridges.
14 John Taylor, *Part of this Summer's Travels* (1640), 26.
15 Morris, *op.cit.*, 93.

good wine in York, especially claret and sack'.[16] In most parts of Yorkshire it was customary when serving ale or wine to provide some food free of charge, though this practice was apparently in decline in the closing years of the seventeenth century.[17]

In a petition seeking the establishment of a university at York which was drawn up in 1641 it was said that 'we have been looked upon as rude and barbarous people'.[18] If there was such a perception it probably owed much to the geographical remoteness of Yorkshire and accounts of its turbulent past rather than to first-hand experience. In James Ryther's opinion the common people were by nature courteous and tractable, 'using more reverence and regard to straungers that passe amonge them' than those who lived nearer to the Court.[19] In the course of the seventeenth century there was a spectacular growth in the amount of educational provision for boys and some schools were linked to Cambridge colleges through the establishment of scholarships for their pupils. By 1660 Yorkshire could boast of having no fewer than 144 public grammar schools, most of which were reasonably well endowed.[20] Three-quarters of all the market towns had their own free schools, as did many villages. In addition, there were private schools which were often run by parish clergy as a means of supplementing their income. Some of the gentry employed resident tutors but in the main their sons were taught at public grammar schools within the county. After this initial schooling most Protestant squires with incomes of £500 a year or more sent their eldest sons to university or the inns of court and often to both; and a growing number of young men went over to the Continent to complete their education.[21]

The endowment of free grammar schools was generally the work of private benefactors who included landowners, merchants, clothiers and clergymen together with some rich widows. The same social groups were also largely responsible for a great outpouring of charitable giving in the field of poor relief. This took two principal forms: the donation of money for general purposes and the founding of hospitals or almshouses. At the beginning of the seventeenth century there were already a considerable number of almshouses, some of which were medieval in origin, but by the end of the century many more had come into existence. At that stage over 50 towns and villages had almshouses; and in some towns such as York and Hull there were numerous foundations of this kind. In all, these establishments housed at least 1000 inmates.[22]

---

16 HMC, *Thirteenth Report*, Appendix, part ii, 313. For inns see the Appendix.
17 Morris, *op. cit.*, 220.
18 G. W. Johnson (ed.), *The Fairfax Correspondence* (1848), ii, 278.
19 BL, Lansdowne MSS 119, fo. 115.
20 W. K. Jordan, *The Charities of Rural England 1480-1660* (1961), 348.
21 J. T. Cliffe, *The Yorkshire Gentry* (1969), Chapter IV.
22 Jordan, *op.cit.*, 252-82 (with additions to his figures covering the period from 1661 to the end of the century).

In the main the spread of Protestant influences after the Elizabethan church settlement of 1559 was a relatively slow process in Yorkshire. In 1577 Edwin Sandys the new Archbishop of York wrote of the Catholics within his diocese that 'a more stiffe necked, wilfull or obstinate people did I never knowe or heare of: doubtlesse they are reconciled to Rome and sworne to the pope. They will abide no conference, neither give eare to any doctrine or persuasion'. Five years later Thomas Lord Burghley and other members of the Council in the North reported that the inhabitants of Yorkshire were 'for the greater part inclined to popery'.[23] The persecution of Catholics was at its most severe during the period 1580 to 1620 and as a result many of them either turned their backs on the Old Religion or resorted to outward conformity. While the total numbers were declining there was an increase in recusancy after 1620 which was due partly to the Crown's policy of greater leniency and partly to the efforts of the missionary priests. In 1625 Sir Thomas Hoby told the House of Commons that in Yorkshire the recusants were 'doubled if not trebled since this connivency'. In the North Riding (which was the most Catholic of the three ridings) 'there were 1200 convicted five yeares since, now 2400'.[24] On the eve of the Civil War the total number of recusants in Yorkshire was of the order of 3500 and this figure appears to have remained more or less constant in the latter part of the century.[25]

The Yorkshire Catholics were heavily dependent on the leadership and patronage of the country gentry who for this reason were specially targeted by the authorities. In 1604 there were 254 gentry families which were wholly or partly Catholic. By 1642 this figure had fallen to 163 but they were still a significant minority.[26] In many respects the recusant gentry who remained fully committed to the Church of Rome were a community within a community. They had their Catholic servants, their own priests who either lived with them or regularly visited them and their own lawyers, agents and doctors. Their children were educated by private tutors or at clandestine schools and many were sent to Continental seminaries, monasteries and convents.

The advance of Protestantism had been particularly striking in the more industrialised parts of the West Riding. To judge from an official survey undertaken in 1604 there were few parishes in those areas which had any sizeable grouping of Catholics who defied the penal laws.[27] At an early stage such towns as Bradford, Halifax, Leeds, Sheffield and Wakefield began to fall under the influence of Puritanism with its emphasis on godly preaching, plain forms of public worship and strict moral standards. This was largely the work of Puritan ministers and schoolmasters who received active support and

---

23 PRO, SP Dom, Elizabeth I, S.P.12/cxvii/23. HMC, *Hatfield MSS* 12, 232.
24 *Camden Society*, New Series, vi (1873), 25.
25 This is based on the calculations of Hugh Aveling in his works on Catholicism in the East, North and West Ridings and York. These are listed in the Select Bibliography.
26 J. T. Cliffe, *The Yorkshire Gentry* (1969), 186, 189.
27 E. Peacock (ed.), *A List of the Roman Catholics in the County of York in 1604* (1872).

encouragement from the wealthier members of the community. Significantly, many of the Yorkshire ministers who were deprived of their livings after the Restoration were the sons of clothiers and other inhabitants of this industrial region. Elsewhere in the county the only other towns where Puritanism assumed real importance were Beverley and Hull, the two major centres of commerce in the East Riding.

Beyond the towns there were country gentry with Puritan sympathies who acted as patrons of godly ministers either by presenting them to livings in their gift or employing them as domestic chaplains. They took the view that the Church of England was in urgent need of reform and deplored what they regarded as the repressive policy of Richard Neile the Laudian Archbishop of York. Such families were particularly numerous in the West Riding. In his autobiography Adam Martindale, a Puritan minister, wrote that during the Civil War he was invited to serve five congregations in Cheshire but 'I had much more inclination to goe into the West-riding of Yorkshire. The noble spirit of the gentrie and others in those parts was very attractive'.[28]

During the latter part of the century there were various separatist groups which had emerged from the religious melting pot of the Interregnum. These included the Presbyterians, the Independents or Congregationalists, the Baptists and the Quakers. As a result of Charles II's Declaration of Indulgence of 1672 a considerable number of Yorkshire dissenting ministers secured licences authorising them to conduct services in their own houses. This declaration was soon withdrawn but following the passage of the Act of Toleration in 1689 many nonconformist chapels and meeting houses were established within the county. In October of that year it was reported that in the North Riding there were as many as 81 Quaker meeting houses.[29]

Few counties were so heavily involved in the Civil War as Yorkshire. Initially there was some hope that the county could be insulated from the war but a treaty of neutrality which was negotiated at Rothwell proved to be short-lived. In September 1642 a group of royalist gentry invited the Earl of Newcastle to bring his army into Yorkshire with a view to preserving the county in peace and safety.[30] In December Newcastle arrived at York and by July 1643 he had gained control of virtually the whole shire. The Hull garrison, however, managed to hold out and Newcastle's offensive in the West Riding had led many of the inhabitants of the clothing towns and villages to take up arms under the banner of Sir Thomas Fairfax.[31] The following year the decisive battle of Marston Moor completely reversed the situation.[32]

---

28 *Chetham Society*, iv (1845), 76.
29 *North Riding Records*, vii (1889), 102-3.
30 Margaret Duchess of Newcastle, *The Life of William Cavendish Duke of Newcastle* (ed. Sir Charles Firth) (1907), 188-91.
31 For the resistance of the West Riding towns see A. J. Hopper, *"The Readiness of the People": The Formation and Emergence of the Army of the Fairfaxes, 1642-3* (University of York, Borthwick Paper No. 92) (1997).
32 See P. R. Newman, *The Battle of Marston Moor 1644* (1981).

Among the Yorkshire gentry the royalists outnumbered the parliamentarians by two to one. Often there was a close association between religious and political loyalties: many Catholics joined the king while many Puritans were thoroughly committed to the cause of Parliament. At the same time a substantial proportion of the gentry, both Protestants and Catholics, declined to throw in their lot with either party but preferred to wait on events.[33]

The Civil War resulted in a major disruption of trade and industry within the county. Inevitably, given the number of battles and sieges, there was a heavy loss of life, though comprehensive figures are lacking. Among the royalist officers who died while in arms were Henry Viscount Dunbar, Sir Ralph Hansby, Sir Ingram Hopton, Sir Richard Hutton, Sir Thomas Metham, Sir William Pennyman, Sir John Ramsden and Sir William Savile. On the parliamentarian side the dead included Sir William Fairfax (a kinsman of Thomas Lord Fairfax), Sir Henry Foulis, Arthur Beckwith and William Lister (the eldest son of Sir William Lister) while Sir John Hotham and his son John were both executed as traitors to the cause. In York and such towns as Bradford, Leeds, Pontefract and Scarborough there was extensive damage to buildings and even churches and schools fell victim to artillery fire. In the rural areas a number of manor-houses were destroyed or badly damaged while many others were pillaged. At the same time the royalists in particular were apt to support themselves by looting whole villages. In the later stages of the Civil War a severe outbreak of the plague added substantially to the death toll. In October 1645 it was said that 'the contagious infection of plague and pestilence has generally overspredd the whole Westridinge'. Between March and December the outbreak accounted for no fewer than 1325 fatalities in Leeds alone.[34] The combination of war and pestilence caused widespread misery and hardship among all classes but it was the poor who were most vulnerable. For them starvation was an imminent danger.

Even when hostilities had fully ceased the process of economic recovery proved to be very slow. For the rest of the century the West Riding woollen industry remained largely in the doldrums, not only because of the effects of the Civil War but also on account of such factors as intensive competition in overseas markets. Eventually, in the early years of the eighteenth century, the rapid expansion of the worsted industry ushered in a new era of prosperity.[35]

---

33 J. T. Cliffe, *The Yorkshire Gentry* (1969), 336-8.
34 *YAJ*, xv (1900), 451-9. *VCH, Yorkshire*, iii, 458.
35 H. Heaton, *The Yorkshire Woollen and Worsted Industries* (1920), 214, 248-51, 257-9.

York

'TO YORK, THE second citty of England, fairely wall'd, of a circular forme, water'd by the brave river Ouse' (John Evelyn, 1654). 1672: 2124 households. The principal streets included Bootham, Coney Street, Goodramgate, Micklegate, Pavement, Peaseholme Green, Petergate, Skeldergate and Walmgate. 1676: 3806 persons aged 16 or more, including 86 recusants and 161 Protestant dissenters. The total population at this time was probably of the order of 12,000.

York's importance as a regional capital owed much to the fact that it was the seat of an archbishop. The Archbishop of York was responsible for a province which embraced eight counties and over 1000 parishes.

The Council in the North, which governed the region beyond the Trent, was based at York along with the ecclesiastical court known as the Northern High Commission. The King's Manor, near Bootham Bar, served as the residence of the Lord President of the Council in the North. The Council had judicial as well as administrative functions and offered private litigants a convenient alternative to the courts at Westminster. The Northern High Commission, for its part, had a key role in the periodic campaigns against Catholicism. In 1641 both these bodies were abolished by the Long Parliament.

The assizes for the whole county were held at York and prisoners were housed in a goal within the precincts of the castle.

The city had enjoyed the status of a county since 1396 and had its own sheriffs and justices of the peace. The county included the wapentake of the Ainsty which was administered by bailiffs acting on behalf of the sheriffs.

The corporation of York consisted of a lord mayor and aldermen, a recorder, two sheriffs, the 'twenty-four' (who were former sheriffs) and a common council. During the course of the 17th century a number of royal charters were issued which confirmed or varied the powers of the corporation.

Market rights had been formally granted in 1316. The city had various markets, including the Thursday market, the Pavement market, the malt market, the leather market and two fish markets. From the reign of Charles II onwards there was a separate butter market.

Fairs were held in the Thursday market and the Horsefair. A royal charter of 1632 made provision for a new annual fair.

York had some small-scale industries, in particular textile manufacture and leather working. In the main, however, its economy was dependent on the activities of its merchants who engaged in both regional and overseas trade. The Ouse was navigable as far as York and it provided access for shipping to the Humber.

In religion the city was overwhelmingly Protestant. During the early seventeenth century there were growing Puritan influences which were reflected in the choice of city preachers and even some of the parish clergy. In the latter part of the century Protestant nonconformity was more in evidence but the Presbyterians, Independents, Baptists and Quakers were no more than a small minority.

The city was steadily growing in popularity as a social centre. Some county families owned town houses and many more chose to winter in York. Among the social activities were dancing, music and theatrical entertainment. In 1629 the Crown approved the formation of a company of players, to be known as His Majesty's servants for the city of York, who were to present 'all the usual stage plays'.

By 1660 there was a regular coach service between York and London.

York is 'both pleasant, large, and strong, adorn'd with fine buildings (both publick and private) populous, rich, and an Arch-bishop's See. The river Ure, which now takes the name Ouse, runs gently .... through this City, and so divides it into two parts, joyn'd by a Stone-bridge which has one of the largest Arches that ever I saw .... Towards the North-east .... stands the Cathedral, dedicated to St Peter, a magnificent and curious fabrick' (William Camden).

'It hath a large fayre wall, with 8 gates, and many Towers and Bulwarkes that fence it in; and for the Inhabitants 28 Churches to serve God in' (visitors to York, 1634).

'A faire lardge cittie. Twenty six churches in it. One whereof, the minster, is a very goodly edifice and exceeding lardge, and for lightsomenesse much excells Paulls .... The king hath a meane pallace here .... The people are affable and free hearted, yet vaine glorious, and love to bee praised' (John Aston, 1639).

'The wall about it, and a castle where a garrison is constantly kept, is in good reparation. In this castle is a large and spacious hall new built, where they keep the assizes for this great shire'. The cathedral is 'the greatest now standing .... in general the whole town is old timber buildings and must have a purgation by fire if ever it arise in beauty like Northampton or London' (Thomas Baskerville, 1675).

York 'makes but a meane appearance, the Streetes are narrow and not of any length, save one which you enter of from the bridge .... the houses are very low and as indifferent as in any Country town .... there are a great many pretty Churches, 16 in number, but the Minster is a noble building .... the Minster is very large and fine of stone, carv'd all the outside, 3 high towers above the Leads' (Celia Fiennes, 1697).

In 1604 there was a severe outbreak of the plague which resulted in many deaths. Further outbreaks followed in 1631 and 1645.

In September 1640 Charles I convened a Great Council of Peers at York for the purpose of considering ways and means of ending the incursion of the Scottish rebels.

In March 1642 the king returned to York and for the next six months it was in effect the royal capital. On 3 June he addressed a crowd estimated at between 60,000 and 80,000 on Heworth Moor in an attempt to further his plan for raising an army. The response was generally favourable though there were some men who dissented.

After the king's departure in August 1642 York had a succession of royalist governors who included Sir William Savile and Sir Thomas Glemham. In June 1644 the city came under siege but the parliamentarians withdrew on hearing that Prince Rupert was approaching with a large army. Immediately after the battle of Marston Moor the siege was resumed and on 16 July Sir Thomas Glemham surrendered.

At the beginning of the siege the royalists set fire to houses in the suburbs in order to deny cover to the parliamentarian troops. During the actual fighting many buildings within the city were damaged and breaches were made in the walls.

In February 1660 Thomas Lord Fairfax held a meeting in York which resulted in a petition calling for a free Parliament.

During the years 1660 to 1689 the Crown kept a small garrison in York under the command of a military governor who resided in the King's Manor. Sir John Reresby, who was appointed governor in 1682, wrote that 'York was at that time one of the most factious towns of the kingdome'. In 1679 James Duke of York had met with a cool reception when visiting the city and there was strong support for the proposal to exclude him from the succession on account of his Catholicism.

In 1694 many houses in High Ousegate were destroyed in a fire.

In 1696 a new Mint was established in York. It was housed in the King's Manor.

Churches The Minster of St Peter: Norman, Early English, Decorated and Perpendicular.

'The minster, I believe, is the biggest building in England' (Abraham de la Pryme, 1686).

The cathedral emerged largely unscathed from the Civil War and the religious upheaval which followed it. In 1659, however, some damage was caused by a strong wind.

During the period between the Civil War and the Restoration four Puritan ministers took it in turn to preach in the Minster.

Before the Reformation there had been 42 parish churches in York but in the course of the 16th century a number of parishes had been amalgamated.

On the eve of the Civil War York had 22 parish churches, together with several churches which had no parochial status. Their architecture ranged in date from the Norman period to the early 16th century.

During the siege of 1644 seven of these churches were damaged: St Cuthbert, St Denys, St Lawrence, St Maurice, St Nicholas, St Olave and St Sampson. St Lawrence and St Nicholas were virtually destroyed but the former was partly rebuilt in 1669. The other five churches were all eventually restored.

In 1674 a Quaker meeting house was established in Friargate.

An Independent chapel was built in St Saviourgate in 1692 and registered for worship the following year. Dame Sarah Hewley provided an allowance for the minister and in 1707 arranged for this to be put on a permanent footing after her death. The chapel was also used by a Presbyterian congregation.

Castle The keep known as Clifford's Tower had been erected in the 13th century. Early on in the Civil War it was repaired and garrisoned by the royalists. In the siege of 1644 it was damaged by cannon fire.

In 1684 the interior was gutted when a fire caused the magazine to explode.

The King's Manor The manor had been largely rebuilt around the beginning of the 16th century and extended by Henry Earl of Huntingdon, the Lord President of the Council in the North, in the reign of Elizabeth. In the early 17th century two of his successors, Edmund Lord Sheffield and Thomas Lord Wentworth, made further improvements.

The manor sustained some damage during the siege of 1644. When Sir John Reresby took over as military governor in 1682 he found it in a ruinous condition and spent between £3000 and £4000 on its restoration.

Schools St Peter's School had been in existence in the 12th century and possibly much earlier. By a royal grant of 1557 it had been endowed as a free grammar school and formally placed under the control of the Dean and Chapter of York. New premises had also been provided for the school through the conversion of the old Bootham Hospital.

Since its buildings were damaged during the siege of 1644 it was decided to move the school to the Bedern on the east side of the Minster.

In 1547 Archbishop Holgate had obtained royal approval for the foundation of a free grammar school open to all boys in England. Archbishop Holgate's School, as it was called, was initially sited within the cathedral close.

There were other schools in the 17th century, including a Catholic boarding school for girls which was established in 1686.

Almshouses At the beginning of the 17th century York had a number of hospitals which were medieval in origin: these included St Catherine's Hospital, St Thomas's Hospital, Trinity Hospital (which was administered by the Merchant Adventurers of York) and similar institutions which belonged to the Company of Cordwainers and the

Merchant Taylors. In 1633 William Hart provided Trinity Hospital with an additional endowment for the support of 10 poor widows.

In his will (1609) Sir Robert Watter (or Walters), a wealthy merchant, referred to the hospital he had established in Chapel Row, George Street. At that time it had 12 occupants.

Agar's Hospital in Monkgate was founded by Alderman Thomas Agar, a tanner who had served as lord mayor. In his will (1631) he left a rent-charge of £20 a year for the support of six poor widows.

During the reign of Charles I Sir Arthur Ingram built a large hospital in Bootham and in his will (1640) settled lands worth £50 a year as an endowment. The hospital provided accommodation for 10 poor widows.

Ann Middleton, the widow of a York merchant, gave direction in her will (1655) that the sum of £2000 should be employed on building and endowing a hospital. It was intended that this hospital (which was duly built) should house up to 20 widows of York freemen.

During the reign of Charles II Edith Darke and Ann Wright founded almshouses of more modest capacity.

Prisons Besides the county gaol there were two prisons belonging to the corporation: the sheriffs' prison and the mayor's prison which was used mainly for the confinement of debtors. Both these prisons were situated on the Ouse bridge which also had shops and houses built on it.

St George's House was a house of correction and part of St Anthony's Hall was used for the same purpose. Here vagrants and minor offenders were kept under restraint and set to work.

Inns There were many inns in York. The Talbot in Petergate was described in 1639 as 'a very faire inne' while Celia Fiennes considered the Angel in Coney Street to be the best inn in the city. Other inns included the George, which was also in Coney Street, the Bell, the Dragon and the Swan. In 1639 the landlord of the Dragon was the York postmaster, Francis Housman.

According to a survey of 1686 the inns of York had 483 beds for guests and stabling for 800 horses.

Town houses In the reign of Charles I the owners of town houses in York included Henry Lord Dunbar, Thomas Lord Fauconberg, Sir John Bourchier, Sir John Goodricke, Sir Richard Hawksworth, Sir John Mallory and Sir Henry Slingsby.

The largest private residence in the city was the mansion built by Sir Arthur Ingram near the Minster which was completed about 1630. In 1665 his grandson Henry Lord Irwin was taxed on no fewer than 35 hearths.

In 1634 some visitors who were admitted to Sir Arthur's house gazed in wonder at 'his store of massie Plate, rich Hangings, lively Pictures and Statues, rich £150 pearle

Glasses, fayre stately £500 Organ, and other rich Furniture'. In the extensive grounds Sir Arthur had fish tanks, a pheasantry, a tennis court and a large bowling green.

(*CSP Dom, 1629-31*, 59. *CSP Dom, 1631-33*, 109-10. L. G. Wickham Legg, *A Relation of A Short Survey of 26 Counties* (1904), 20, 21. *Memoirs of Sir John Reresby* (ed. A. Browning and others) (1991) 191, 264, 268-9, 273, 283, 336-7. W. K. Jordan, *The Charities of Rural England 1480-1660* (1961), 268, 272-3, 275, 279, 282, 301, 311, 343. Sir Thomas Widdrington, *Analecta Eboracensia* (ed. C. Caine) (1897). Francis Drake, *Eboracum* (1736). C. B. Knight, *A History of the City of York* (2nd edition, 1944). P. Wenham, *The Great and Close Siege of York, 1644* (1970). A. Stacpoole and others (eds.), *The Noble City of York* (1972). G. E. Aylmer and R. Cant (eds.), *A History of York Minster* (1977). C. Galley, *The Demography of Early Modern Towns: York in the Sixteenth and Seventeenth Centuries* (1998). A. Raine, *History of St Peter's School, York* (1926).)

The East Riding

THE EAST RIDING justices of the peace usually held their quarter sessions at Beverley and Pocklington.

There were three parliamentary boroughs: Beverley, Hedon and Hull.

ACKLAM — Buckrose

A village to the north-east of York. The parish of Acklam included the hamlets of Barthorpe and Leavening. 1672: 74 households in Acklam cum Leavening.

The Bulmers of Leavening were minor gentry who had disposed of their whole estate by the time of the Civil War and were dependent on an annuity of £30 for their sustenance.

Church St John Baptist: Norman in origin.

The parish was subject to the peculiar jurisdiction of the Chancellor of York. (*YASRS*, xviii (1895), 79.)

ALDBROUGH — Holderness

A village to the south of Hornsea and a coastal parish which included the hamlets of Bewick, Carlton, East Newton, Etherdwick, Fosham, Ringbrough and Tansterne and part of West Newton. 1672: 87 households in Aldbrough and East Newton, 9 in Carlton and Fosham and 16 in West Newton. 1676: 300 persons aged 16 or more, including 30 recusants and 50 Protestant dissenters (parish).

The eastern side of the parish was under constant threat from coastal erosion.

The inhabitants of the parish included a number of minor gentry families: Greene of Etherdwick, Michelburne of Carlton, More of Bewick and Thorpe of Aldbrough.

In 1627 the common lands in Carlton were the subject of an enclosure agreement which resulted in the division of some 490 acres between the two main proprietors, Thomas Michelburne and Leonard Gill. Subsequently, in 1651, the freeholders of Etherdwick followed their example.

The Protestant dissenters of 1676 may have been mainly Quakers. During the late 17th century there were occasional Quaker meetings at Aldbrough.

Church St Bartholomew: Norman, Early English, Decorated and Perpendicular.

In his will (1663) Robert Towry settled considerable property for the augmentation of the church living and the relief of the poor of the parish.

School From the 1680s a schoolmaster was employed under the provisions of the Towry Charity.

ANLABY   Hull Shire

A village to the west of Hull which was partly in the parish of Hessle but mainly in the parish of Kirk Ella. 1673: 31 households.

School There was a private school at Anlaby shortly after the Restoration. The master was probably Joseph Wilson, a Presbyterian divine who had settled in Anlaby following his ejection from the living of Hessle in 1660.

Principal family Legard of Anlaby Hall. Estate revenue: £700 a year (1663).

Robert Legard (1582-1648) sent three of his sons to be educated at Sidney Sussex, Cambridge which was regarded by Archbishop Laud as a nursery of Puritanism.

His son Christopher (c.1602-1661) joined the garrison at Hull after the Long Parliament appointed his kinsman Sir John Hotham as governor of the town. In July 1642, some weeks before the formal declaration of war, royalist troops pillaged Anlaby Hall and drove away horses, sheep and cattle. During the war he served as a lieutenant colonel in the parliamentarian army and (like his father) as a member of the East Riding committee. In 1648 Parliament awarded him the sum of £5000, partly as compensation for his losses, and noted that he and his family had been the first to suffer at the hands of the royalists.

His eldest son Charles, who was a parliamentary captain, had no male issue and the estate eventually passed to a younger son, Robert (c.1636-1721). He was a barrister and for many years one of the Masters in Chancery. In 1682 he was knighted.

Anlaby Hall The house was rebuilt in the course of the 17th century. A brick building of two storeys.

In 1673 there were 10 taxable hearths.

(East Riding of Yorkshire Archives Service, Legard of Anlaby MSS. BL, Thomason Tracts 669 f.6 (53). Sir James Digby Legard, *The Legards of Anlaby and Ganton* (1926).)

ARGAM   Dickering

A decayed village situated to the north-west of Bridlington. The village had been depopulated in the Middle Ages and by 1632 there was only one cottage which was still inhabited while the parish church of St John Baptist had been demolished.

The small parish contained no other centre of population yet the church authorities continued to institute and induct ministers to a living which was said to be worth £40 a year.

(M. W. Beresford, *'The Lost Villages of Yorkshire'*, *YAJ*, xxxviii (1955), 50.)

ATWICK   Holderness

A coastal village to the north of Hornsea. There was no other village within the parish. 1672: 25 households (township of Atwick). 1676: 100 persons aged 16 or more (parish).

In 1627 there were 15 Catholic recusants in the parish but only one was reported in the 1676 census return.

Church St Lawrence: Norman in origin.

AUGHTON   Harthill

A village to the north-east of Selby. The parish of Aughton included the village of East Cottingwith which had a dependent chapel and the hamlet of Laytham. 1672: 44 households in Aughton, 40 in East Cottingwith and 19 in Laytham cum Foggathorpe. (Foggathorpe was in the parish of Bubwith).

During his travels Roger Dodsworth the antiquary noted that Aughton, which had been the principal seat of the Aske family, had recently been sold to a neighbouring squire, Sir Hugh Bethell of Ellerton. John Aske (c.1565-1605) had inherited an estate worth over £1500 a year but little remained at the time of his death. Richard his son and heir became a barrister of the Inner Temple and served as a member of the prosecution team at the trial of Charles I.

The moated house of the Askes appears to have been demolished before the time of the Civil War.

Church All Saints: Norman, Early English and Perpendicular.

School During the reign of Charles I William Alder the Puritan vicar of Aughton kept a private school.

(YASRS, xxxiv (1904), 164, C.2/James I/A4/56. C.2/James I/A7/12.)

BAINTON   Harthill

A village to the south-west of Great Driffield. The parish of Bainton included the village of Neswick. 1672: 46 households in Bainton and 25 in Neswick. 1676: 160 persons aged 16 or more (parish).
Church St Andrew: Decorated.
(S. L. Ollard, *Bainton Church and Parish: Some Notes on Their History* (2nd edition, 1934).)

BARMBY MOOR   Harthill

A village to the west of Pocklington. The parish of Barmby Moor included the village of Fangfoss which had a medieval chapel. Fangfoss had once been an independent parish but in 1568 the two parishes had been united. 1672: 79 households in Barmby Moor and 25 in Fangfoss.
Church St Catherine: Norman in origin.
The parish was subject to the peculiar jurisdiction of a Prebendary of York.

BARMSTON   Holderness

A coastal village south of Bridlington. The parish of Barmston included part of the chapelry of Ulcome. 1672: 33 households (township of Barmston). 1676: 60 persons aged 16 or more, including 10 Protestant dissenters (parish of Barmston).

In 1626 three ships ran aground at Barmston and the villagers helped themselves to the merchandise on board. The government therefore instructed Sir Matthew Boynton of Barmston and Sir Henry Griffith of Burton Agnes to take possession of the goods and keep them in safe custody until further notice. Shortly afterwards Henry Viscount Dunbar began legal proceedings against Sir Matthew and some of his servants who had been collecting 'peeces of timber of broken shippes' on Barmston sands. Lord Dunbar claimed that as lord of the manor of Holderness he had good title to all wrecks within the manor of Barmston and Boynton finally acknowledged his right.
Church All Saints: Norman and Perpendicular.
School In the 1630s there was a private school at Barmston. The master, Mr Wilson,

may be identified as George Wilson, a Puritan who was ejected from his living of Easingwold in 1662.

Principal family Boynton of Barmston Hall (and later of Burton Agnes Hall) (baronetcy 1619). Estate revenue: £3000 a year (1636); £2600 a year (1654).

The Boyntons were one of the leading Puritan families in Yorkshire.

Sir Francis Boynton (1561-1617) added to his estate, partly by purchase and partly by marrying an heiress.

His son Sir Matthew (1591-1647) sometimes resided at Roxby in the North Riding where he built a house.

In 1629 he was commended by his friend Sir John Hotham for his 'affection to religion' while in 1643 he was described in a royalist newspaper as 'a declared Anabaptist'. Some years later a nonconformist divine wrote that he was 'a Religious Gentleman that gave much Countenance and Shelter to the Puritans' and was unable to stomach the Laudian innovations.

By 1635 he was so concerned about the state of religion that he began to make plans, in conjunction with his friend Sir William Constable, for emigrating to New England. In 1636 he was in correspondence with John Winthrop the younger on such matters as the provision of a house for his 'greate ffamilie', the welfare and employment of the servants he had sent over as an advance guard and the management of the herds of cattle and other livestock in which he had invested a considerable amount of money. The following year, however, he had a change of heart. Towards the end of 1637 he sold some of his outlying property but settled the bulk of his estate on trustees. In July 1638 he secured a pass authorising him to travel to the Low Countries with his wife and family. They finally joined Sir William Constable and his wife at Arnhem in Holland where they were able to participate in the kind of religious worship which suited their needs.

Sir Matthew returned to England after the Long Parliament began to sit. On the outbreak of the Civil War he took up arms for Parliament, along with his sons Francis, Matthew and John. In January 1643 he defeated a royalist force at Guisborough and in July 1645 he captured Scarborough Castle. For two years he served as governor of Scarborough Castle and was then succeeded by his son Matthew who, however, changed sides in 1648.

Sir Francis Boynton (1619-1695), who was a parliamentarian colonel, inherited a heavily encumbered estate. Portions amounting to over £12,000 had to be raised for the benefit of his many brothers and sisters and his stepmother had a large jointure. In 1649 Dame Katherine, who had soon remarried, agreed to release her jointure lands to him in return for a cash payment of £12,000. Between 1649 and 1653 he sold substantial property in the North Riding but in 1654 his fortunes took a turn for the better when he succeeded to the Yorkshire estate of his uncle Sir Henry Griffith of Burton Agnes. After the death of Sir Henry's widow he sold the Staffordshire lands which she had held as her jointure.

Sir Francis continued to live at Barmston Hall where he dispensed generous hospitality. Burton Agnes Hall was assigned to his son William (1641-1689) and by the end of the century had become the family's principal seat.

In June 1685, at the time of the Monmouth Rebellion, the government gave order for the arrest of Sir Francis and his son William who were considered to be disaffected.

Barmston Hall A moated Elizabethan mansion. It was designed by Sir Thomas Boynton (d.1581) and completed by his son Sir Francis who built the middle part in 1598.

In 1672 there were 10 taxable hearths.

(Hull University Archives, Wickham-Boynton MSS. C.V. Collier, *An Account of the Boynton Family* (1914). J. T. Cliffe, *The Yorkshire Gentry* (1969), 273-4, 306-8, 310-11, 332-3. Dr Williams's Library, Morrice MSS, J, no pagination. C.33/215/ fo.576 and 235/fo.259.)

BEEFORD   Holderness

A village to the east of Great Driffield. The parish of Beeford included the hamlets of Dunnington and Lissett, both of which had medieval chapels. 1672: 83 households in Beeford and 17 in Lissett. 1676: 400 persons aged 16 or more (parish).

John Neile, who was presented to the rectory of Beeford in 1637, enjoyed a number of preferments through the patronage of his uncle Archbishop Neile of York. A man of royalist sympathies, he was deprived of all his sources of income during the Civil War.

In 1650 the inhabitants of Beeford complained to the magistrates about the financial burden occasioned by the great number of poor people in the parish. As a result the inhabitants of Dunnington and Lissett were ordered to contribute to Beeford's poor rates.

In 1669 it was reported that a substantial number of Quakers had been meeting at a house in Lissett.

Church St Leonard: Norman, Early English and Perpendicular.

(John Walker, *Sufferings of the Clergy* (1714), part 2, 83-4. G. C. F. Forster, *The East Riding Justices of the Peace in the Seventeenth Century* (1973), 49.)

BEMPTON   Dickering

A village to the north of Bridlington. There was no other village within the parish. 1672: 79 households in Bempton and Buckton. (Buckton was in the parish of Bridlington).

The parish of Bempton extended as far as the coast where the massive chalk cliffs provided a home for large colonies of sea birds.

Church St Michael: Norman, Early English and Decorated.

School In 1619 there was an unlicensed schoolmaster resident in Bempton.
(E. H. Rudkin, *Bempton cum Newsholme cum Buckton* (1853).)

BESSINGBY   Dickering

A small village to the south-west of Bridlington. There was no other centre of population within the parish. 1672: 25 households in Bessingby and Easton. (The neighbouring hamlet of Easton was in the parish of Bridlington). 1676: 80 persons aged 16 or more (parish).
Church St Mary Magdalene: Norman in origin.
The minister was a perpetual curate with a meagre stipend.
Schools Christopher Bradley, who was presented to the living in 1637, was granted a licence to teach.
There was also a school at Bessingby in the later years of the 17th century.

BEVERLEY   Harthill

A market town and parliamentary borough. As the main quarter sessions town it was in effect the capital of the East Riding. The parish of St John of Beverley included the villages and hamlets of Storkhill, Thearne, Tickton, Weel and Woodmansey. 1672: 584 households in Beverley town and 36 in Woodmansey and Beverley Park. The main streets which featured in the hearth tax return of 1672 were Flemingate, Hengate, Highgate, Keldgate, Lairgate and Walkergate. 1676: 1500 persons aged 16 or more (Beverley parishes).
'The town is nothing so famous or populous as I presume it has formerly been' (Ralph Thoresby, 1682).
Beverley is 'large and handsome …. It is above a mile in length, being of late much improv'd in its buildings; and has pleasant springs running quite through it. It is more especially beautified with two stately Churches' (Edmund Gibson, 1695).
'Beverly …. is a very fine town for its size …. there are 3 or 4 large Streetes well pitch'd, bigger than any in Yorke …. there are 3 markets, one for Beasts, another for Corne and another for Fish …. the town is serv'd with water, by wells walled up round or rather in a Square …. there are many of these wells in all the streetes' (Celia Fiennes, 1697).
New houses erected in the course of the 17th century were usually built of brick.
The town had been formally incorporated by a charter of 1573 which was confirmed in 1628. The corporation consisted of a mayor, governors and burgesses together with a recorder and a town clerk. In a charter of 1685 the name of governor was changed to

that of alderman.

Beverley had formerly been an important clothing town but in the 17th century there was no longer any large-scale industrial activity. 'The principal trade of the town is making Malt, Oat-meal, and Tann'd-leather; but the poor people mostly support themselves by working of Bone-lace' (Edmund Gibson, 1695).

Markets were held on Wednesdays and Saturdays and there were also a number of annual fairs. 'In this town we saw many shops shut up, which are used by the Londoners when they come hither to a fair' (Thomas Baskerville, 1675). 'They have several Fairs; but one more especially remarkable, beginning about nine days before Ascension-day, and kept in a street …. call'd Londoner-street. For then the Londoners bring down their Wares, and furnish the Country-Tradesmen by whole-sale' (Edmund Gibson, 1695).

Beverley was a popular place of resort for the local gentry. A number of gentry families owned town houses at one time or another, among them the Gees, Hildyards, Remingtons, St Quintins and Wartons.

A potentially important factor in the religious life of the town was the right of the corporation to nominate the curate in charge of the Minster and to appoint the master of the public grammar school. During the early 17th century there were a number of Puritan ministers and schoolmasters. In 1676 it was reported that there were 122 Protestant dissenters in the town and neighbourhood.

In 1604 and 1610 the town suffered from outbreaks of the plague.

At the beginning of the Civil War parliamentarian troops drove out the small royalist garrison which the king had left at Beverley. In the autumn of 1643 the royalists plundered the town after a bitter struggle with a garrison force which was in the process of pulling out. For the rest of the war, however, Beverley remained largely undisturbed, mainly on account of the commanding presence of the garrison at Hull.

In 1662 the government was informed that there had been a riotous assembly in the Minster over the choice of a new curate. Those involved were supporters of Joseph Wilson, a Puritan minister nominated by the corporation. In the event the church authorities put in their own nominee.

In 1676 a violent storm caused considerable damage to the Minster and the church of St Mary.

Churches St John of Beverley (the Minster): Early English, Decorated and Perpendicular.

'The Minster has been a fine building, all stone, carv'd on the outside with Figures and Images, and more than 100 pedestalls that remaine where Statues has stood' (Celia Fiennes, 1697).

St Mary: Norman, Early English, Decorated and Perpendicular.

There were two other churches, St Martin and St Nicholas. In 1667 it was decided that the livings of St Mary and St Nicholas should be united; and the decaying church of St Nicholas was then demolished.

Schools In 1552 the burgesses of Beverley petitioned the Crown for a free grammar school. They claimed that the town had no educational facilities of any kind though the medieval school was still apparently in existence. As a result of this petition the Crown made funds available from confiscated Minster lands and a grammar school was duly established. A new schoolhouse was built and furnished during the years 1606 to 1610 with most of the expenditure being met by public subscription.

'There is a very good free schoole for boys, they say the best in England for learning and care, which makes it fill'd with Gentlemens Sons besides the free Schollars from all parts' (Celia Fiennes, 1697).

Towards the end of the 17th century a charity school was founded for the purpose of teaching young children to read and make bone-lace.

Almshouses Several medieval hospitals had been taken over by the corporation for use as almshouses.

In 1636 Thwaites Fox, a baker, founded a hospital for four poor widows.

Michael Warton of Beverley Park, who died in 1688, left the sum of £1000 for the establishment of almshouses for six poor widows. These were built the following year by his executors and were described in 1695 as the largest of the six hospitals in Beverley.

Prisons The East Riding house of correction was located at Beverley. In addition, there were two municipal prisons and a prison belonging to the manor of Beverley.

Inns The town had a number of inns, including the Bell, the George, the Talbot and the White Horse.

Principal family Warton of Beverley Park. Estate revenue: £3000 a year (1640).

The Wartons were descended from Tudor merchants. During the course of the 17th century they grew very rich, partly through their businesslike approach to estate management and partly through advantageous marriages. On the eve of the Civil War they owned property in Lincolnshire, Middlesex and London in addition to their main estate in Yorkshire.

Sir Michael Warton (1575-1655) was a ward of the Crown in his youth. While serving as sheriff of Yorkshire in 1617 he announced that there were plans for imprisoning all recusants and pulling down their houses. This fabrication infuriated the government and as a result he spent some time in the Fleet prison.

During the early 17th century there was a Catholic strain in the family, though neither Sir Michael nor his son Michael (1593-1645) was ever convicted of recusancy. In the reign of Charles I the wives of both men were indicted as recusants.

The Wartons had held leases of the Crown manor of Beverley, including the park, since 1573. In 1627 Sir Michael bought the manor for the modest sum of £3593. According to his own account it was worth £1197 a year over and above the fee-farm rent which he paid.

In August 1642 it was said that he had lent the king £20,000; and in a further show of loyalty he signed the Yorkshire Engagement of February 1643. In 1645 he claimed that the war had cost him £30,000 through the destruction of his houses, goods, tenements and woods.

After some delay his son Michael, who was an MP, finally took up arms for the king and was killed while defending Scarborough Castle.

Michael Warton (1623-1688) also joined the royalist army but deserted (as he put it) after the battle of Marston Moor. He took on responsibility for managing his grandfather's affairs and set about the task of restoring and improving the estate. He was an efficient landlord who farmed on a commercial scale and through his efforts the family became even more prosperous than before.

According to Abraham de la Pryme he was considered to be the richest gentleman in England with an estimated income of £15,000 a year.

His son Sir Michael (c.1648-1725), who was the last of the line, inherited his philanthropic instincts. During his lifetime he distributed a total of £6000 for charitable purposes.

Beverley Park The Wartons apparently lived at first in a former hunting lodge which had been restored in 1548. In 1632 Sir Michael Warton's residence was called Beverley High Lodge.

The house was destroyed or badly damaged in the Civil War. Significantly, Michael Warton (1623-1688) lived mainly in Beverley where he had a large town house. In the latter part of his life, however, he built a two-storeyed mansion in the park which was called the New Lodge.

(G. Oliver, *The History and Antiquities of the Town and Minster of Beverley* (1829). G. Poulson, *Beverlac, or the Antiquities and History of the Town of Beverley* (1829). I. and E. Hall, *Historic Beverley* (1973). YAS Library, Archer-Houblon Collection. BIHR, High Commission Act Books, RVI/A25, no foliation and RVII/A18/fo.91.)

BIRDSALL   Buckrose

A village to the south-east of Malton. There was no other village within the parish. 1672: 70 households (township of Birdsall).

Birdsall was the birthplace of Henry Burton (1579-1648), a radical preacher and pamphleteer who was an implacable enemy of the bishops. In 1637 he was severely punished for delivering what were termed seditious sermons.

The Sothebys of Birdsall, who owned the manor, were enterprising landlords who considered the open field system to be a major constraint on good husbandry.

In the reign of James I Thomas Sotheby was busily engaged in enclosing activities. Later on it was estimated that they had resulted in an increase of £110 a year in his estate revenue.

In 1635 Sir Arthur Ingram of Temple Newsam bought the impropriate rectory of Birdsall for £2450. During the Commonwealth period it was reported that the rectory was worth £168 a year and that the minister was allowed only £10 a year.

In 1665 Robert Sotheby and Francis Thorpe, who also owned property in Birdsall, approached Henry Ingram, Viscount Irwin with proposals for the wholesale division and enclosure of the common lands, including the glebe lands belonging to the rectory. Lord Irwin's initial response was encouraging and draft articles were accordingly prepared. In a Chancery suit of 1668 it was said that Sotheby had recently enclosed nearly 200 acres of ground in the common fields and meadows. Four years later, however, he and Thorpe began legal proceedings against the Ingrams over their failure to implement the enclosure agreement. In reply the Ingrams took the line that it was unlikely that Lord Irwin, who had died in 1666, had formally approved the document but indicated that they were ready to proceed with the scheme if it could be established that it would be of benefit to them.

Of the 70 households in 1672 no fewer than 39 were declared exempt from the hearth tax on grounds of poverty.

Church St Mary: Norman and Decorated. Some work was apparently undertaken in 1601.

Birdsall Hall A two-storeyed Elizabethan house of a type which has been associated with Robert Smythson.

In 1672 Robert Sotheby was taxed on 10 hearths.

(C.5/558/45. C10/118/89. *East Riding Antiquarian Society Transactions*, ii (1894), 65.)

BISHOP BURTON   Harthill

A village to the west of Beverley. 1672: 67 households.

Church All Saints: Early English and Decorated.

Almshouses In 1615 Ralph Hansby, a Catholic gentleman, built almshouses for two poor unmarried men and one poor woman.

Principal family Gee of High Hall. Estate revenue: £1100 a year (1653).

Sir William Gee (1561-1611) was a lawyer who served as Secretary of the Council in the North from 1604 till his death. In 1603 he bought the manor of Bishop Burton for £2300.

A man with a Puritan cast of mind, he believed that he was numbered among the elect. He was said to have had a 'revered opinion' of William Perkins the Calvinist theologian and to have taken great delight in reading his books. In his will (1611) he expressed his gratitude to Jesus Christ who 'hath given me knowledge of the true religion and of the vanitie and falshoud of the antichristian religion of Rome as well by the pure preaching of his holie word and reading of good bookes .... as also by the wonders within my tyme he hath done for his church'. He left the sum of £26 13s 4d a year for an able preacher to deliver two sermons every Sunday at Bishop Burton and nominated Thomas Micklethwaite, a Puritan divine, as the first lecturer.

During the early 17th century the family sustained two successive minorities which left them exposed to the financial exactions of the Court of Wards.

When William Gee (1625-1678) succeeded his father in 1626 the estate was heavily burdened with the jointures of his grandmother Dame Mary who lived on until 1649 and his mother Frances who subsequently married Sir Philip Stapleton the future parliamentarian.

Gee does not appear to have been a combatant in the Civil War but he was named in 1645 as a member of the East Riding parliamentary committee and in 1648 as one of the Yorkshire commissioners for the settling of the national militia. Perhaps as a reaction to the Cromwellian revolution he eventually decided to spend some time on the Continent. In 1653 he took as his second wife Mary Spencer, the daughter of a Kent royalist who was then living in exile in Brussels. In the marriage settlement (which in 1662 was the subject of litigation) he agreed, among other things, that he would buy lands in southern England for the benefit of any children they might have.

His son William (c.1648-1714) was a Whig politician. At the time of the Monmouth Rebellion in 1685 he was one of a number of 'disaffected and suspicious persons' who were arrested and kept under restraint at Hull. He later went over to Holland where he was apparently involved in preparations for William of Orange's invasion of England.

High Hall A two-storey mansion built by Sir William Gee between 1603 and 1611. In 1672 there were 20 taxable hearths.

William Gee (c.1648-1714) probably made alterations to the house.

The Wartons of Beverley Park had a secondary house in Bishop Burton which they had inherited from Ralph Hansby.

(Hull University Archives, Gee (Watt) of Bishop Burton MSS. BIHR, York Registry, will of Sir William Gee, 2 November 1611. C.7/465/40. C.33/219/fo.19. D. Neave, 'High and Low Halls, Bishop Burton', *Georgian Society for East Yorkshire*, no. 6 (1979).)

BISHOP WILTON Harthill

A village to the east of York. The parish of Bishop Wilton included the villages of Bolton, which had a dependent chapel, and Youlthorpe with Gowthorpe. 1672: 94 households in Bishop Wilton, 25 in Bolton and 20 in Youlthorpe with Gowthorpe.

During the reign of Charles I Bishop Wilton had a Puritan vicar, John Plaxton. In 1660 he was forced out of his living of Scrayingham on account of his nonconformity.

Church St Edith: Norman, Decorated and Perpendicular.

The parish was subject to the peculiar jurisdiction of the Treasurer of York Minster.

Principal family Hildyard of Bishop Wilton Hall. Estate revenue: £600 a year (1632).

The Bishop Wilton estate was built up by William Hildyard (c.1540-1608), a lawyer resident in York, and his son Sir William (1577-1632) who inherited some property there from his father-in-law Ralph Hansby. Among their holdings were two manors known as the Bishop's manor and the Treasurer's or prebendal manor.

In 1618 Sir William began Star Chamber proceedings against a number of men who he claimed were conspiring to kill him on account of his activities as a magistrate. Among other things, they had lain in wait for him near his house and had attacked his servants.

Sir William was drawn into the controversy over Charles I's forced loan scheme. In April 1627 the Privy Council was informed that he had failed to attend meetings with his fellow loan commissioners or to signify his willingness to contribute. As a result he was required to appear before the Council but managed to escape imprisonment.

In an Exchequer case of 1630 the Court heard that he had been planning to carry out a wholesale enclosure of Bishop Wilton and that as an essential preliminary he had been attempting to gain possession of some lands belonging to Anne Lister the plaintiff. Besides offering £1500 for this property he had also sought to persuade her tenants to give their consent to his enclosure scheme. These approaches, however, had proved abortive and it is unlikely that he was able to proceed very far with his plans in the brief period before his death.

Sir William left no male issue and his estate descended to his three daughters. Elizabeth was married to Richard Darley who promptly bought the share of her sister Mary. The family mansion had been included in Elizabeth's share and the Darleys took up residence there.

Bishop Wilton Hall In 1672 Richard Darley was taxed on 12 hearths.

(Hull University Archives, Sykes MSS. C.8/39/50. STAC 8/180/15. PRO, State Papers Domestic, S.P.16/lx/52. *Acts of the Privy Council, January-August 1627*, 277. E.134/5 and 6 Charles I/Hilary 19.)

BOYNTON   Dickering

A village to the west of Bridlington. 1672: 31 households (township of Boynton).

Church St Andrew: Perpendicular.

School In 1685 the vicar, William Kenyon, secured a licence to teach and for some years ran a private school.

Principal family Strickland of Boynton Hall (baronetcy 1641). Estate revenue £1500 a year (1631). Stone quarrying at Easton.

The Stricklands lived at Boynton from 1549 until 1950. They were a major Puritan family whose religious radicalism can be dated back to the early years of Elizabeth's reign when William Strickland was one of the principal advocates of church reform in the House of Commons.

Walter Strickland (d.1636) was a leading patron of Puritan ministers. At the time of his death he owned four impropriate benefices and had a reversionary interest in another two, Boynton and Wintringham. In 1660 there was a dispute over the right of presentation to the living of Boynton.

When the forced loan scheme was launched in 1627 Strickland refused to pay his assessment. Subsequently he delayed payment of his knighthood composition.

His son Sir William (1596-1673) was described by Roger Morrice, a nonconformist minister, as 'a publick Professor of Religion, and one that openly avowed it, and that to the uttermost of his power Sheltered and Protected the Strictest professors thereof'.

Writing to Strafford in 1639 he observed that his lordship had been 'pleased to acknowledge me as a partaker of your bloode, as being descended of a Wentworthe, in which respecte …. nothing shall be more visible then that my veines are filled with your bloode, which is but reserved to be employed in your service'. Even so, he did not feel able to vote against Strafford's attainder in April 1641.

In the Civil War he took up arms for Parliament at an early stage and was appointed a member of the East Riding committee but he was mainly occupied with his duties as an MP. In March 1643 it was reported that goods worth over £4000 had been taken from Boynton Hall by royalist troops and he later declared in a Chancery suit that all his deeds had been lost during the war.

His brother Walter served as the Long Parliament's ambassador to Holland between 1642 and 1648.

As an MP in the Commonwealth period Sir William spoke out against the Quakers who in his view were 'all levellers against magistracy and propriety'. He was also disturbed by the refusal of some men to pay tithes, arguing that 'The same levelling principle will lay waste properties and deny rents upon the same accounts they do tithes'.

In 1657 he and his brother Walter were chosen to serve as peers in Cromwell's Upper House.

His son Sir Thomas (1639-1684) was characterised by Roger Morrice as 'a serious person' who 'gave much Countenance to Religion and vigerously endeavoured a further Reformation'. Shortly after his father's death he took in a Presbyterian minister, James Calvert, as chaplain and tutor to his sons. In 1683 Sir John Cochrane and his son, who were suspected of complicity in the Rye House Plot, sought refuge with their relatives at Boynton Hall. Calvert helped them to escape to Holland and found himself in trouble with the authorities as a result. The local magistrates, however, exonerated Sir Thomas, describing him as a 'melancholy distracted man'.

Sir William Strickland (1665-1724), who succeeded his father while still a minor, fell under suspicion at the time of the Monmouth Rebellion. In June 1685 James II instructed the East Riding deputy lieutenants to arrest and disarm him as a disaffected person.

Boynton Hall A gabled Elizabethan house built of brick. In 1672 Sir William Strickland was taxed on 23 hearths.

(BL, Egerton MSS 2645, fols. 241, 243. C.8/138/139. Dr Williams's Library, Morrice MSS, J, no pagination. Sheffield Archives, Wentworth Woodhouse Collection, Strafford Letters, xviii, letter of Sir William Strickland, 3 February 1638/9. Thomas Burton, *Diary of Thomas Burton* (ed. J. T. Rutt) (1828), i, 169 and ii, 166.)

BRANDESBURTON   Holderness

A village to the north-east of Beverley. There was no other village within the parish. 1672: 85 households (township of Brandesburton). 1676: 200 persons aged 16 or more (parish).

In 1286 Brandesburton had been granted the right to hold a weekly market and an annual fair. In the 17th century the main function of the fair was the sale of cattle, sheep and horses.

In the reign of Charles I the freeholders entered into an agreement for the enclosure of the common fields and the exchange of strips. This was formally endorsed in a Chancery decree of 1633.

At Brandesburton 'we could get no accomodation at a Publick house, it being a sad poore thatch'd place and only 2 or 3 sorry Ale-houses' (Celia Fiennes, 1697).

Church St Mary: Norman, Early English and Perpendicular.
Schools The curate was keeping a school in 1640.

Robert Steele, who was rector of Brandesburton in the years 1661 to 1688, set up a private school which attracted pupils from outside the parish. These included a son of Sir Hugh Bethell of Rise.

(PRO, Chancery Decrees, C.78/605.)

BRANTINGHAM   Howdenshire/Harthill

A small village to the west of Hull. The extensive parish of Brantingham included Blacktoft and Ellerker, both of which had dependent chapels, Scalby and Thorpe Brantingham. 1672: 22 households in Brantingham, 44 in Blacktoft, 55 in Ellerker, 23 in Scalby and 10 in Thorpe Brantingham.

Blacktoft, on the north bank of the River Ouse, was a considerable distance from Brantingham. In a Commonwealth survey of benefices the commissioners described its church as a parochial chapel and added that it was impossible to secure the services of a minister as the salary was so meagre.

Church All Saints: Early English.

The parish was subject to the peculiar jurisdiction of the Dean and Chapter of Durham.

(J. G. Hall, *A History of South Cave and of Other Parishes in the East Riding of the County of York* (1892).)

BRIDLINGTON   Dickering

A market town with harbour facilities used by cargo ships and fishing vessels. In the 17th century it was usually called 'Burlington'. The extensive parish of Bridlington included a number of villages and hamlets. 1672: 232 households in Bridlington Old Town, 120 in Bridlington Quay, 79 in Buckton and Bempton, 23 in Grindale, 3 in Hilderthorpe, 53 in Sewerby and Marton and 25 in Speeton. Grindale and Speeton had medieval chapels while Bempton was a separate parish (see separate entry for Bempton). 1676: 500 persons aged 16 or more, including 30 Protestant dissenters (parish of Bridlington but possibly excluding the chapelries of Grindale and Speeton).

Bridlington Priory was an Augustinian foundation established in the 12th century and dissolved in 1538. Many of the monastic buildings were immediately pulled down but the nave was retained for use as a parish church.

The town had a Saturday market and an annual fair. During the 17th century the fair was usually held on 10 October. In 1667 it was said that the inhabitants were 'a very Industrious people, and much addicted to sea trafficke' and that they now owned some 40 'trade ships'.

In 1630 the manor of Bridlington was bought by a group of well-to-do residents and in 1636 it was formally placed under the control of a body of feoffees who assumed responsibility for the government of the town.

According to Ralph Thoresby the streets of Bridlington were 'well paved' through the generosity of William Hustler, a wealthy draper and landowner who died in 1644.

When Queen Henrietta Maria landed at the Quay in February 1643, bringing with her supplies for the royalist army, the town was bombarded by parliamentary ships. Generally, however, there was little military activity in or around Bridlington during the Civil War.

From time to time the town came under threat from foreign vessels. In 1666 Dutch ships mounted an attack and it was probably as a direct result of this episode that a new fort was built the following year.

Major reconstructions of the piers were carried out in 1643, 1664 and 1697. In December 1663 a violent storm caused such severe damage that it was estimated that £4000 would need to be spent on the restoration work.

Church St Mary: Norman, Early English, Decorated and Perpendicular.

Schools The grammar school had been founded in 1563 or possibly earlier. In the 17th century the masters included Christopher Wallis (who left in 1637 to become master of St Peter's School, York) and Francis Holdsworth.

In what was apparently a re-foundation of the existing school William Hustler built a new schoolhouse and in 1637 settled a rent-charge of £40 a year for the maintenance of a master and usher. The declared intention was to provide free instruction 'in the art of grammar'.

During the reign of Charles I there was also a private school in Bridlington.

In 1671 William Bower founded a school for teaching poor children to card and spin wool and knit stockings.

(J. S. Purvis, *Bridlington Charters, Court Rolls and Papers XVI*[th] *to XIX*[th] *Century* (1926). H. E. Ingram, *The Manor of Bridlington and its Lords Feoffees* (1977). W. K. Jordan, *The Charities of Rural England 1480-1660* (1961).)

BUBWITH   Harthill

A village to the north-east of Selby. The extensive parish of Bubwith included a number of villages and hamlets. 1672: 60 households in Bubwith and Harlthorpe, 22 in Breighton, 19 in Foggathorpe and Laytham, 11 in Gribthorpe and Willitoft and 44 in Spaldington. Laytham was in the parish of Aughton. 1676: 369 persons aged 16 or more, including 35 recusants (parish).

Bubwith was one of the more Catholic parishes in the East Riding, particularly in the early 17th century. There were 66 recusants in 1615 and 56 in 1637.

Church All Saints: Norman, Early English and Perpendicular.

Principal families (1) Aykroyd of Foggathorpe Hall. Estate revenue: £570 a year (1628).

Henry Aykroyd (c.1574-1628) was granted a coat of arms in 1614. In a series of Star Chamber suits he was accused of various offences, including kidnapping and committing perjury before the Council in the North.

His son John (1614-1673) was made a ward of the Crown in 1628. In the Civil War he appears to have avoided any commitment to either side.

He was the last of the Aykroyds to feature in the parish register of Bubwith. At his death he had no surviving male issue and the estate passed to his nephew John Aykroyd, the son of a London draper, who was probably an absentee landlord.

(2) Vavasour of Spaldington Hall. Estate revenue: £1200 a year (1659 and 1680).

In the reign of Elizabeth the family had been largely Catholic but Sir John Vavasour (c.1580-1641) and his successors were Protestants.

Sir John quarrelled with his wife, Dame Mary, and she eventually left him. In 1617 the Northern High Commission ruled that he should allow her £50 a year while they were living apart and that he should have custody of their children. He subsequently informed the Commission he was willing to have her back despite her extravagance but in 1625 she was still refusing to return home.

In 1636 he was involved in litigation with Marmaduke Dolman who held a lease of the rectory of Bubwith from the Dean and Chapter of York. Dolman related that in recent years Sir John had been making large-scale enclosures in Spaldington and that by intermixing grounds within the parishes of Aughton and Bubwith had put in jeopardy some of the tithe payments due to him.

His son Peter (1607-1659) apparently took no part in the Civil War but from 1649 onwards he was one of the East Riding commissioners who were responsible for levying money for military purposes. In 1651 some men attempted to force their way into Spaldington Hall in the belief that he was harbouring a royalist but he denied the allegation and they went away empty-handed.

On the death of his son Thomas (1636-1680) the male line expired. The estate then passed to Sir Ralph Assheton of Middleton in Lancashire who had married his daughter Mary.

Foggathorpe Hall A moated house which may have been Tudor in origin. In 1672 John Aykroyd was taxed on 11 hearths.

Spaldington Hall An Elizabethan mansion which was mainly the work of Peter Vavasour who in his will (1573) bequeathed to his half-brother Edward 'such thinges which are provided for the fynishing of the buildinges' at Spaldington.

In 1672 there were 14 taxable hearths.

(STAC 8/53/14; 58/10; and 69/7. Wards 5/49. C.10/4/143. *YPRS*, xcix (1935). BIHR, High Commission Act Book, RVII/AB9/fols.174, 343, 352, 376. C.3/400/107. C.5/635/29. C33/314/fols.491-2. *Surtees Society*, cxxi (1912), 65.)

BUGTHORPE   Buckrose

A village between Stamford Bridge and Great Driffield. There was no other village within the parish. 1672: 45 households (township of Bugthorpe).

Church St Andrew: Norman, Decorated and Perpendicular.

The parish was subject to the peculiar jurisdiction of a Prebendary of York.

School Bugthorpe had a school from 1624 onwards.

Principal family Payler of Thoralby Hall (baronetcy 1642). Estate revenue: £1000 a year (1640); £2000 a year (1693).

Edward Payler (c.1582-1647) was the son of a lawyer who served as the Queen's Attorney in the North. He secured employment as an assistant to William Watkinson of Thoralby, who was clerk of the assizes for the Northern Circuit, and married his daughter Ann. Watkinson had no other children and in his will (1612) he left his whole estate, subject to his wife's jointure, to his daughter and son-in-law. The estate included the manor of Thoralby where he had been busily engaged in enclosing activities. Many years later it was said that before his marriage Payler had not owned a single foot of land in all England.

In the reign of Charles I he purchased the Crown manor of Skirpenbeck and acquired a long lease of the prebend of Bugthorpe.

The grant of a baronetcy in June 1642 was part of a campaign aimed at winning support for the king. When signing the Yorkshire Engagement of February 1643 Sir Edward undertook to contribute £300 in support of the royalist cause but this appears to have been the extent of his involvement in the war. His executors subsequently claimed that 'he was a party in no esteem with the king's party' in Yorkshire; and it was also deposed that he had never been in arms for the king and that he had been 'much plundered and abused' by the royalists.

To judge from his choice of friends he may have had Puritan sympathies. In his will (1647) he expressed a wish to be buried in Bugthorpe church but gave direction that there should be no funeral ceremony.

Sir Edward outlived his son Watkinson and was succeeded by his grandson who was also called Watkinson. Sir Watkinson (c.1636-1704) remained largely inactive when serving as an MP in the reign of Charles II but was nevertheless regarded as an opponent of the Court. At the time of the Monmouth Rebellion in 1685 the East Riding deputy lieutenants were instructed to arrest him as a man who was disaffected.

In 1693 his son Watkinson married a rich widow, Dame Mary Stoughton, who had a jointure worth £500 a year from her previous marriage.

Thoralby Hall The house had probably been built by William Watkinson.

In 1672 Sir Watkinson Payler was taxed on 15 hearths.

(E.134/7 Charles I/Easter 12. BL, Harleian MSS 6288, fols.74-7, 84. S.P.19/ cxxi/76, 81. C.33/315/fols.221-2, 625.)

BURNBY   Harthill

A hamlet situated to the south-east of Pocklington. There was no other centre of population within the parish. 1672: 29 households (township of Burnby). 1676: 40 persons aged 16 or more (parish).

Church St Giles: Norman and Early English.

BURSTWICK CUM SKECKLING   Holderness

A village to the east of Hedon. The parish of Burstwick included the hamlets of Camerton and Ryhill. 1672: 65 households in Burstwick and 35 in Camerton and Ryhill. 1676: 250 persons aged 16 or more (parish).

Church All Saints: mainly Decorated and Perpendicular.

School John Catlyn, who served as vicar of Burstwick during the years 1670 to 1678, was also master of Hull Grammar School until his dismissal in 1676 which was occasioned by the difficulty he experienced in combining the two appointments. Subsequently he kept a private school at Burstwick.

Principal family Appleyard of Burstwick Garth. Estate revenue: £800 a year (1640).

Following his father's death Thomas Appleyard (1581-c.1660) became a ward of the Crown. Through his second marriage he acquired a valuable estate in Lincolnshire which remained in his possession until the death of his wife.

During the Civil War period the parliamentary committee in Lincolnshire sequestered this property on the grounds that he had consorted with the royalist party. He claimed, however, that he had always been a loyal supporter of Parliament. In contrast his son Matthew, who had formerly been a soldier of fortune, fought valiantly for the king and attained the rank of colonel. In 1645 he was knighted as a reward for his services.

Although Sir Matthew (c.1607-1670) had been born a younger son he eventually inherited the Yorkshire estate. In 1660 he was appointed collector of customs at Hull.

Burstwick Garth The mansion house of the Appleyards (which was sometimes called the Long House) had probably been built in the early 16th century. In 1672 it had 12 hearths.

(J. Lawson, *The Endowed Grammar Schools of East Yorkshire, East Yorkshire Local History Society* No. 14 (1962), 19-20. Wards 5/49. S.P.23/lxii/348-9.)

BURTON AGNES   Dickering

A village to the south-west of Bridlington. The parish of Burton Agnes included a number of villages. 1672: 48 households in Burton Agnes, 70 in Gransmoor and Harpham, 28 in Haisthorpe and 26 in Thornholme. 1676: 450 persons aged 16 or more (parish).

Church St Martin: Norman, Early English and Perpendicular.

School Burton Agnes had a free grammar school which had been founded in 1563. During the reign of Charles I there was a school at Harpham.

Principal families (1) Griffith of Burton Agnes Hall (baronetcy 1627). Estate revenue: £2200 a year (1640); £1700 a year (1654).

The Griffiths had lived at Burton Agnes since the mid-15th century. Besides their Yorkshire estate they had property in Lincolnshire and Staffordshire.

Sir Henry Griffith (1558-1620) originally planned to settle in Staffordshire but in the end he decided to build a new house for himself at Burton Agnes.

In 1618 he was a dedicatee, along with his neighbour William St Quintin of Harpham, of a work entitled *Milke for Babes, or a North-Countrie Catechisme, made plaine and easy to the capacitie of the countrie people*. The author was William Crashaw, the

Puritan vicar of Burton Agnes. In the epistle dedicatory he urged them to continue the godly exercise of catechising within their own families and to ensure that their tenants were fully involved. 'This', he stressed, 'will make our Sermons at home, and our Exercises abroad, much more profitable and effectuall, your Servants and Tenants more faithfull to God, and more serviceable to your selves'.

At 3 a.m. on 14 October 1620 (when Sir Henry was on his deathbed) his son Henry, who was still a minor, married Mary Willoughby in the parish church of Burton Agnes. The unusual timing was dictated by the family's determination to avoid the financial exactions of the Court of Wards. On hearing of Sir Henry's death the Court instructed its local officials to survey his lands but in 1621 it accepted that the marriage was valid and that the wardship should therefore be discharged.

Sir Henry Griffith (1603-1654) purchased the manor of Flamborough in 1636 but on the eve of the Civil War he was heavily in debt. As a deputy lieutenant he was well equipped to serve as one of the king's commissioners of array in the summer of 1642. When hostilities began his strong royalist sympathies led him to sign the Yorkshire Engagement of February 1643 and to take up arms as the colonel of a regiment. He eventually surrendered in July 1644 and was required to pay a substantial fine. In 1650 he sold the manor of Flamborough.

Sir Henry had no issue by either of his marriages and following his death the estate descended to his nephew Sir Francis Boynton of Barmston, subject to the jointure settled on his wife (see under Barmston).

(2) St Quintin of Harpham Hall (and later of Scampston Hall) (baronetcy 1642). Estate revenue: £1000 a year (1630).

George St Quintin (c.1555-1612) was a Catholic who conformed in the latter part of his life. His daughter Alice eloped with the butler, Robert Frankish. Despite the scandal which had been created her brother Sir William (1579-1649) took pity on her when she was left a widow and helped to support her until she married again.

One of Sir William's brothers was a convicted recusant but he himself was the first Protestant head of the family. Through his marriage to an heiress he added considerably to the estate. During the 1630s his major enclosing activities in Harpham brought him into conflict with Sir Henry Griffith. The Privy Council was informed that his enclosures were causing great damage to many of the king's subjects and that he was refusing to desist. In the light of this report the Council gave order that he should be arrested and brought to London for questioning.

In the Civil War Sir William and his son Henry both served as members of the East Riding parliamentary committee.

In his will (1649) Sir William described himself as of Beverley and it seems likely that Harpham Hall had been destroyed in the war. A hearth tax return of 1672 reveals that his son Sir Henry (1606-1695) was then living at Beverley and that Harpham Hall no longer existed. The following year he took advantage of Charles II's Declaration of

Indulgence to secure a licence permitting him to use his mansion house in Beverley for Presbyterian worship.

By 1684 the St Quintins had a new country seat, Scampston Hall, in the extreme north of the riding.

Burton Agnes Hall A gabled mansion of red brick built by Sir Henry Griffith between 1601 and 1610. The architect was Robert Smythson.

The hall 'is all built with Brick .... it stands on a pretty ascent, we enter under a Gate house built with 4 large towers into a Court .... in the middle is a Bowling green palisado'd round .... out of an entry you come into a very lofty good Hall .... the parlour and drawing-roome are well proportion'd roomes .... there is a noble gallery over all with large windows on the sides .... out of which you view the whole Country round, and discover the shipps under saile though at a good distance' (Celia Fiennes, 1697).

(Hull University Archives, Wickham-Boynton MSS. Wards 5/39. Wards 9/94/fo.564. C.8/94/20. PRO, Privy Council Office Registers, PC2/44/fols. 12, 75.)

BURTON CONSTABLE   Holderness

Burton Constable, which was in the parish of Swine, was usually linked with the neighbouring hamlet of West Newton for fiscal purposes. 1672: 16 households (West Newton, including Burton Constable).

Principal family Constable of Burton Constable Hall (peerage as Viscount Dunbar, 1620). Estate revenue: £2400 a year (1640). Number of servants: 22 (1660).

The Constables had moved from Halsham to Burton Constable about the beginning of the 16th century. Halsham remained their burial place.

Sir Henry Constable (c.1550-1607) had a recusant wife but he was himself a Church Papist.

His son Sir Henry (c.1588-1645), who acquired the title of Viscount Dunbar, blew hot and cold in matters of religion. In 1607, shortly after his father's death, he emerged as a recusant but within a few months he had conformed. Eventually, in 1630, he was convicted of recusancy and required to pay a composition rent of £300 a year. In a petition to the king he complained that this was much greater than he was 'able to undergoe, his debts and other great charges considered'. No doubt through the intercession of his friends at Court the king ruled that it should be reduced to £250 a year but the northern commissioners were slow to comply.

Constable's growing financial problems appear to have been partly due to his love of gaming. In 1636 it was reported that he had lost £3000 at a single sitting. By the time of the Civil War his debts amounted to some £17,000 and he decided to set aside half his estate revenue with the aim of discharging them.

In the Civil War he took up arms for the king, fought at the battle of Marston Moor and died of wounds received at the siege of Scarborough. As the second Viscount his son John (c.1615-1668) inherited an encumbered estate which was to remain under sequestration throughout the Interregnum. He and his son Robert (c.1647-1714) who succeeded him were both Catholics.

Robert the third Viscount managed to secure a royal pardon in 1671 after killing a man by striking him on the head with a rapier. In 1687 it was said that his wife Mary had given birth to a child by her father confessor and that Lord Dunbar was adamant that it was not his.

Burton Constable Hall A two-storeyed Elizabethan mansion built of brick.

In a survey of the estate in 1578 it was noted that the hall was an ancient building to which Sir John Constable had made an addition of a greater beauty on the north side. Sir John died in 1579 and about 20 years later the house was largely rebuilt by his son Sir Henry (c.1550-1607).

Burton Constable Hall was the largest country house in the East Riding: in 1672 it had 40 taxable hearths.

According to the survey of 1578 the park contained 384 acres and was well stocked with red and fallow deer.

(East Riding of Yorkshire Archives Service, Burton Constable MSS. *CRS*, liii (1961), 321, 407-8, 420-1. Barbara English, *The Great Landowners of East Yorkshire 1530-1910* (1990).)

BURTON FLEMING   Dickering

A village situated to the north-west of Bridlington which was often called North Burton in the 17th century. There was no other village within the parish. 1672: 50 households (township of Burton Fleming). 1676: 90 persons aged 16 or more (parish).

In a Commonwealth survey of benefices the commissioners took the view that the church at North Burton was a chapel belonging to the parish of Hunmanby.

Church St Cuthbert: Norman and Perpendicular.

The minister was a perpetual curate with a modest stipend.

BURTON PIDSEA   Holderness

A village to the north-east of Hedon. There was no other village within the parish. 1672: 65 households (township of Burton Pidsea).

During the latter part of the 17th century the inhabitants included a number of Quakers.

Church St Peter: Early English, Decorated and Perpendicular. A major renovation project had been completed in 1542.

The parish was subject to the peculiar jurisdiction of the Dean and Chapter of York.

BURYTHORPE   Buckrose

A village to the south of Malton. There was no other centre of population within the parish. 1672: 20 households (township of Burythorpe). 1676: 53 persons aged 16 or more (parish).

During the 1650s the freeholders enclosed the common lands. This was said to have seriously impaired the value of the church living.

Church All Saints: Norman in origin.

CARNABY   Dickering

A village to the south-west of Bridlington. The parish of Carnaby included the chapelries of Auburn and Fraisthorpe. Auburn was a decayed hamlet which had suffered much from coastal erosion. 1672: 48 households in Carnaby and 37 in Fraisthorpe with Auburn. 1676: 100 persons aged 16 or more (parish).

In 1299 Carnaby had been granted the right to hold a weekly market and an annual fair.

The manor of Carnaby and all the patronage rights within the parish belonged to the Stricklands of Boynton, a major Puritan family who were anxious to promote the spread of godly preaching. In 1637 Sir William Strickland presented Peter Clark to the living of Carnaby and the following year he recruited Enoch Sinclair to serve as curate of Auburn with Fraisthorpe. Clark, who was a native of Beverley, had been a fellow of St John's College, Cambridge. In 1643 he was appointed a member of the Westminster Assembly of Divines. Eventually, in 1648, he took over the living of Kirby Underdale where he remained until his ejection for nonconformity in 1662.

Church St John Baptist: Norman, Decorated and Perpendicular.

For much of the 17th century the church was in a poor state of repair. Restoration work was put in hand in 1680.

(A. G. Matthews, *Calamy Revised* (1934), 118, 443.)

CATTON   Harthill/Ouse and Derwent

Twin villages, High and Low Catton, lying to the east of York. The parish of Catton, which straddled the River Derwent, included several villages and hamlets. 1672: 75

households in High and Low Catton, 23 in Kexby, 18 in Stamford Bridge East and 16 in Stamford Bridge West and Scoreby. 1676: 360 persons aged 16 or more (parish).

The River Derwent flows through Stamford Bridge 'which from a battel fought there is also called Battle-bridge' (William Camden).

Some 400 acres of common pasture in Low Catton were enclosed about the beginning of the 17th century.

'The Derwent ….is apt to overflow the banks, and lay all the neighbouring meadows a-float' (William Camden). In 1619 the Court of Wards was informed that the estate of the Beaumonts of High Catton suffered much 'by the overflowing of waters, sanding of meaddowes and drownding of the Arrable, so that many yeares a great parte of the … .Cropp and profytts are lost theireby'.

Church All Saints, Low Catton: Early English and Perpendicular.

In 1676 the church was said to be in a ruinous condition.

(Wards 5/49.)

CATWICK   Holderness

A village situated between Beverley and Hornsea. There was no other village or hamlet in the parish. 1672: 33 households. 1676: 80 persons aged 16 or more.

Church St Michael: Norman and Perpendicular.

CHERRY BURTON   Harthill

A village to the north-west of Beverley. There was no other village within the parish. 1672: 58 households (township of Cherry Burton). 1676: 90 persons aged 16 or more (parish).

The Gees of Bishop Burton purchased the manor of Cherry Burton in 1605. As patrons of the living they had a marked preference for godly preaching ministers.

In the first half of the 17th century Cherry Burton had two Puritan rectors: Samuel Culverwell who was minister from 1579 to 1613 and Thomas Micklethwaite who served the cure from 1613 until his ejection for nonconformity in 1662. The latter was said to have been famous for his piety, gravity, prudence and learning. He was sufficiently well regarded to be appointed a member of the Westminster Assembly of Divines. His son Sir John (1612-1682) was a distinguished physician who had inherited his religious principles.

In 1683 the rector, John Johnson, calculated that of 146 families which had resided in Cherry Burton since 1562 over a hundred were either extinct or had moved elsewhere.

On Sunday 12 February 1688 there was a 'mighty pulsation of the earth, or Earthquake which resembled the sound of a canon, with a rumbling noise going before it, which lasted but a moment of time. It caused buildings to shake, and the earth to tremble or shake.'

When James Deane was buried in 1691 he was described in the parish register as 'the Ringleader and first founder of the Separatists in this parish'.

Church St Michael: Norman or Early English.

(A. G. Matthews, *Calamy Revised* (1934), 349. *YPRS*, xv (1903), 28-9, 30, 46, 50.)

COTTINGHAM   Harthill

A large village near Hull. The parish of Cottingham included the village and chapelry of Skidby and part of the village of Willerby. 1672: 288 households in Cottingham and 41 in Skidby. 1676: 1000 persons aged 16 or more, including 700 Protestant dissenters (parish of Cottingham).

Cottingham had a weekly market and a Martinmas fair. In 1672 the main streets included Hallgate, Newgate and Finkle Street.

In William Camden's time the ruins of a castle were still visible.

In 1638 Cottingham was afflicted by the plague.

On the outbreak of the Civil War the rector, Edward Gibson, sought refuge with the army of the Earl of Newcastle but the inhabitants of Cottingham seem generally to have favoured the cause of Parliament. In August 1643 many of them fled to Hull as a royalist force approached and some men were enlisted by the parliamentary garrison. The royalists plundered most of the houses in Cottingham and took away horses, cattle and sheep. They also seized the plate in the parish church, 'carrying themselves more like Turks and pagans than like Christians'.

In the latter part of the century the parish was a stronghold of nonconformity and had both Presbyterian and Independent congregations.

Churches St Mary: Decorated and Perpendicular. In 1700 Abraham de la Pryme described the church as 'very larg, beautifull and handsom'.

By 1692 the village had a Presbyterian chapel.

School Several schoolmasters were licensed to teach in Cottingham during the course of the 17th century.

John Wardell of Hull Bank, who died in 1676, built a small schoolhouse in the churchyard and provided an endowment of £5 a year.

Almshouses According to Abraham de la Pryme's account Wardell was in the process of building almshouses for six poor people at the time of his death but had made no arrangements for their financial support.

(A. G. Matthews, *Walker Revised* (1988), 393. HMC, *Seventh Report*, Appendix, 567. C. Overton, *The History of Cottingham* (1861).)

COWLAM   Buckrose

A remote hamlet situated between Malton and Bridlington. The parish of Cowlam had no other centres of population. 1672: 14 households. 1676: 40 persons aged 16 or more.

In 1713 it was reported that Cowlam no longer had any houses nor any inhabitants except for two shepherds.

Church St Mary: Norman in origin.

By 1713 the chancel was in a dilapidated condition.

DRYPOOL   Holderness

A hamlet situated near Hull at the confluence of the Rivers Hull and Humber. Drypool was a chapelry in the parish of Swine until the mid-17th century when it became an independent parish. 1672: 14 households in Drypool and 12 in Southcoates.

In a Commonwealth survey of benefices the commissioners observed that the parochial chapel at Drypool had been without a minister for over four years. They recommended that it should be made a separate parish as it was five miles from Swine.

There had been a ferry at Drypool since at least the 14th century.

Church St Peter: Norman in origin.

(*East Riding Antiquarian Society Transactions*, iv (1896), 52.)

DUNNINGTON   Ouse and Derwent

A village to the east of York. The parish of Dunnington included part of the hamlet of Grimston. 1672: 74 households in Dunnington and 14 in Grimston. 1676: 200 persons aged 16 or more (parish).

In the reign of Charles I Dunnington had both a Puritan rector, Henry Ayscough (who had been instituted in 1610), and a Puritan curate, Christopher Richardson.

Church St Nicholas: Norman, Decorated and Perpendicular.

School Christopher Richardson, who graduated from Trinity College, Cambridge in 1637, served as a schoolmaster as well as Ayscough's assistant.

(R. A. Marchant, *The Puritans and the Church Courts in the Diocese of York, 1560-1642* (1960), 226-7, 272.)

EASINGTON
Holderness

A village near the southern tip of Holderness. The parish included the hamlet of Out Newton which had a medieval chapel, though in the Commonwealth period this was described as 'much decayed'. 1672: 91 households in Easington and 14 in Out Newton.

In the Middle Ages some hamlets within the parish had disappeared into the sea.

George Fox the founder of the Quaker sect noted in his journal that in 1651 he visited Robert Overton at Easington Hall 'and had a great meetinge of the prime of the people of that Country'. Colonel Overton (1609-1679) was a political and religious radical who had served with distinction in the parliamentarian army. In 1660 he was arrested and imprisoned in the Tower of London.

In 1676 it was reported that there were 15 recusants in the parish.

Church All Saints: Norman, Early English, Decorated and Perpendicular.

School In 1604 there was an unlicensed schoolmaster at Easington.

(N. Penney (ed.), *The Journal of George Fox* (1911), i, 32.)

EASTRINGTON
Howdenshire

A village to the north-east of Howden. The parish of Eastrington included several villages. 1672: 73 households in Eastrington, 30 in Bellasize, 61 in Gilberdike and 20 in Portington and Cavil.

Church St Michael: Norman, Decorated, Perpendicular and early 17th century.

The chancel collapsed in 1632 and was rebuilt the same year at the expense of Sir Michael Warton of Beverley Park.

The parish was subject to the peculiar jurisdiction of the Dean and Chapter of Durham.

Principal family Monckton of Cavil Hall. Estate revenue: £500 a year (1640); £700 a year (1658); £1000 a year (1666).

The Moncktons were one of the most ardent royalist families in the East Riding. In the summer of 1642 Sir Philip Monckton (1574-1646) and his son Sir Francis (c.1602-1657) helped to muster troops for the king as commissioners of array. Sir Francis lent £200 to the king, signed the Yorkshire Engagement of February 1643 and joined the garrison at York. His son Sir Philip (c.1622-1679) took part in the battles of Marston Moor and Naseby and was badly wounded at Rowton Heath. In 1648 he was again in arms and was taken prisoner at the battle of Willoughby in Lincolnshire. He was allowed to go abroad but had returned by 1651. During the Interregnum he was heavily involved in royalist plots and in 1655 was arrested and imprisoned. Following his release he joined Thomas Lord Fairfax in the Yorkshire rising which began in December 1659.

In 1666 he finally gained possession of some landed property worth £200 a year which his mother had inherited.

Sir Philip was no stranger to controversy. He fell out with Lord Chancellor Clarendon who described him as mad and unfit for any employment. In May 1670 it was alleged that as sheriff of Yorkshire he was deliberately favouring men who were known to be disaffected.

In 1676 he was imprisoned for writing what was said to be a 'seditious and scandalous letter' which defamed the Crown and the Privy Council but he was eventually released on bail.

His son Robert (c.1660-1722) settled in Holland during the reign of James II and in 1688 came over with William of Orange.

Cavil Hall The house was probably Tudor in origin. During the Civil War it was abandoned by the Moncktons who feared that it would be attacked by troops from the parliamentarian garrison at Hull.

After the Restoration it suffered a decline in status. Sir Philip Monckton lived mainly at South Newbald where he had obtained a lease from the Dean and Chapter of York while his son Robert settled at Hodroyd Hall in the West Riding which he had acquired by marriage.

In 1672 Cavil Hall had 11 taxable hearths.

Portington Hall A two-storeyed Elizabethan house of brick which belonged to the Portingtons, a minor gentry family.

In 1672 Henry Portington was taxed on two houses in Portington. One house (presumably Portington Hall) had nine hearths while the other, which was described as 'his old house', had seven.

(Nottingham University Library, Galway of Serlby MSS. E. Peacock (ed.), *The Monckton Papers* (1884). BL, Lansdowne MSS 988, fo.316. C.6/328/14.)

ELLERTON   Harthill

A village near the River Derwent in the south-west of the riding. 1672: 56 households (township of Ellerton). 1676: 112 persons aged 16 or more (parish of Ellerton).

Church St Mary: Early English with later features.

When Ellerton Priory was dissolved in 1536 the nave of its church was converted for parochial purposes.

Almshouses In his will (1610) Sir Hugh Bethell gave direction that the six occupants of the almshouses which he was founding should be chosen from the oldest and poorest inhabitants of Ellerton and made provision for their support.

Principal family Bethell of Ellerton Hall (and Alne Hall, North Riding). Estate revenue: £1200 a year (1660).

Sir Hugh Bethell (c.1552-1611) held the appointment of Crown Surveyor in the East Riding and was also clerk of the peace there. At the time of his death he was the owner of a substantial landed estate which included the manors of Ellerton Pickering and Ellerton Priory. Although he married three times he left only a daughter, Grisel, and the greater part of the estate passed to his nephew Sir Walter Bethell (c.1580-1623) who also acquired the office of Crown Surveyor.

Sir Hugh's widow, Dame Jane, had the manor of Ellerton Pickering as her jointure. In 1612 she married a Hertfordshire gentleman, George Butler, with whom she lived at Ellerton Hall. During the reign of Charles I Butler was engaged in enclosing activities on the wastes of Ellerton.

For many years the Bethells resided at Alne. In July 1627 the commissioners for the forced loan reported that Dame Mary Bethell, the widow of Sir Walter, had refused to pay her assessment, claiming that she had no money and a large number of children to bring up. During the Laudian era she attended the conventicles held by John Birchall, a Puritan divine, in the house of the Dean of York.

Her son Sir Hugh (1605-1663) appears to have been heavily influenced by her views on religion. In February 1642 he signed a Yorkshire petition which called for the removal of 'scandalous ministers' and 'ceremonial burdens' in church services. In the Civil War he took the side of Parliament while remaining largely inactive. His brothers Henry and Walter displayed greater commitment and the latter served as a captain in the New Model Army. Another brother, Slingsby, held republican views.

In 1649 Sir Hugh was involved in litigation with a distant kinsman, Nathaniel Bethell, who claimed unsuccessfully that he was the rightful heir to the Bethell estates. By 1655 he had moved from Alne to Ellerton. In that year he complained in a Chancery suit that he had been wrongfully arrested over a debt of £400.

When Charles II issued his Declaration of Indulgence in 1672 the Bethells secured a licence authorising them to use Alne Hall for nonconformist worship.

Following the death of Walter Bethell (1628-1673) the estate passed to a junior branch of the family. In his will (1693) William Bethell left £50 for the benefit of such poor people of Ellerton 'as shall not have any Releife by the Hospitall'. This was to be invested in land and the resultant income used for the distribution of bread every Sunday after morning service in the parish church.

Ellerton Hall The house was probably built by Sir Hugh Bethell (c.1552-1611), though George Butler apparently carried out some work in the 1630s.

In 1672 Walter Bethell was taxed on 12 hearths.

(C.9/2/34. C.10/21/12 and 413/130. C.22/30/46.)

ELLOUGHTON   Harthill

A village to the west of Hull. The parish of Elloughton, which extended to the north bank of the Humber, included the hamlets of Brough and Wauldby, which had a dependent chapel. 1672: 70 households in Elloughton with Brough and 5 in Wauldby.

In the early 17th century Elloughton had two Puritan ministers: Jeremiah Collier, who served as vicar from 1617 to 1622, and Valentine Mason, who held the living from 1623 to 1639.

There was a ferry at Brough which conveyed passengers between Yorkshire and Lincolnshire. In 1629 it was said that the amount of traffic was too modest to be profitable.

In the late 17th century there was a Quaker burial ground in Elloughton.

Church St Mary: Norman, Early English and Perpendicular.

The parish was subject to the peculiar jurisdiction of a Prebendary of York.

School There was a schoolmaster at Elloughton in 1602.

(J. G. Hall, *A History of South Cave and of Other Parishes in the East Riding of the County of York* (1892). R. A. Marchant, *The Puritans and the Church Courts in the Diocese of York, 1560-1642* (1960), 239, 263.)

ELVINGTON   Ouse and Derwent

A village on the River Derwent to the east of York. There was no other village within the parish. 1672: 48 households (township of Elvington). 1676: 100 persons aged 16 or more (parish).

In 1646 Sir Roger Jaques bought the former Crown manor of Elvington and made it his country seat. He was a merchant who had served as Lord Mayor of York in 1639 and had subsequently embraced the royalist cause in the Civil War. After his death in 1653 he was succeeded by his son Roger (1628-1688) who seems to have preferred the life of a country squire.

From time to time Marmaduke Rawdon 'would goe to Elvington, five miles from Yorke, a lordship belonging to his nephew Squier Roger Jaques, closse by which runneth the river of Derwent, of which as lord of the manner he haith the royaltie of the fishinge. Here he tooke much pleasure to see them fish; the fishermen fishinge in little square leather bootes.... Here they catch good store of salmon, the river affordinge likewise exelent good pikes....and very good pearch' (Life of Marmaduke Rawdon, entry for 1656).

Church Holy Trinity: Norman in origin.

ESCRICK
Ouse and Derwent

A village to the east of Tadcaster. The parish of Escrick included the village of Deighton. 1672: 77 households in Escrick and 39 in Deighton. 1676: 270 persons aged 16 or more (parish of Escrick).

Church St Helen: Decorated.

Principal families (1) Howard of Escrick Hall (peerage as Baron Howard of Escrick, 1628). Estate revenue: £1000 a year (1640).

Edward Lord Howard (c.1600-1675), who was a younger son of Thomas Earl of Suffolk, inherited the manor of Escrick from his mother.

In the Civil War he was a staunch parliamentarian. He continued to sit in the House of Lords until its abolition in 1649 and was then elected MP for Carlisle.

In 1651 he was imprisoned and fined £10,000 for receiving bribes from wealthy royalists. He was released the following year.

In 1668 he agreed to sell the Escrick estate to Sir Henry Thompson (c.1625-1683), a York merchant, for £11,000. Although Thompson complained in a Chancery suit that the manor was encumbered the transaction was eventually completed.

(2) Robinson of Deighton Hall. Estate revenue: £800 a year (1640).

The Robinsons had bought the manor of Deighton in 1596 from the Aske family.

Sir Arthur Robinson (c.1575-1642), who was a London mercer, eventually took up residence at Deighton and before long was appointed to the commission of the peace. In 1632 he was pricked as sheriff of Yorkshire.

That same year he purchased the manor of Thornton Risborough in the North Riding and following his death this became the country seat of the senior branch of the family. In the Civil War his eldest son Luke (1610-1669) was a zealous parliamentarian who subsequently served as a member of the republican Council of State.

The manor of Deighton was settled on Sir Arthur's children by his second wife.

The Robinsons were a Puritan family and this may account for the fact that in 1641 Sir Arthur was presented for not receiving communion at his parish church of Escrick.

Arthur Robinson (1627-1681), who inherited the manor of Deighton in 1643, played little part in the public life of the county. According to his son the estate revenue amounted to a modest £300 a year in the reign of Charles II.

Escrick Hall According to the Howards Escrick Hall was 'a very good convenient house'. In 1672 Sir Henry Thompson was taxed on 17 hearths. His main country residence, however, was Marston Hall, near York.

Shortly after his death a new two-storeyed mansion was built at Escrick by his son Henry.

Deighton Hall In 1606 the hall which had been acquired by the Robinsons along with the manor was said to be a fair and large house which was fit for an esquire or gentleman. The Robinsons may, however, have commissioned some building work: in 1619 their house was described as 'fair and new built'.

In 1672 Arthur Robinson was taxed on 14 hearths.

(C.10/119/114 and 120/115 and 123. C.2/James I/A4/56 and A7/12. E.134/8 Charles 1/Trinity 10. C54/3215. C.10/483/227.)

ETTON   Harthill

A village to the north-west of Beverley. The township and parish of Etton were virtually identical. 1672: 67 households (township of Etton). 1676: 150 persons aged 16 or more (parish of Etton).

Church St Mary: Norman and Early English.

Principal family Anlaby of Etton Hall. Estate revenue: £600 a year (1630).

Thomas Anlaby (1566-1642) added considerably to the estate. During the reign of James I he was involved in a major dispute over the manorial rights in Etton. In a Star Chamber suit begun in 1620 he related that he and his ancestors had allowed the wastes, commons and moors of Etton to lie open for the benefit of the commoners without making any enclosures or improvements. Recently, however, he had permitted Marmaduke Harper, a poor man, to build a cottage for himself on waste ground but some of the inhabitants of Etton had almost immediately pulled it down. In taking this action they had enjoyed the full support of William Langdale of Langthorpe Hall who owned property in Etton. Langdale was a convicted recusant who had been travelling outside a five-mile radius of his house without a licence. In response one of the defendants claimed, without justification, that Anlaby had no manor within the township and suggested that he was seeking to establish a right to enclose or improve the commons.

John Anlaby (c.1595-1661), who succeeded his father as the Civil War was breaking out, served in the parliamentarian army first as a captain and then as a lieutenant-colonel and was also a member of the East Riding committee. Elected to the Long Parliament in 1647, he was named as one of the king's judges but took care to distance himself from their proceedings.

During the 1650s he was on close terms with the Quakers at a time when they were under attack in Parliament.

His son Thomas (c.1638-1672), who left only a daughter, sold the Etton estate in 1668 to a West Riding squire, John Eastoft of Eastoft.

Etton Hall There was a considerable amount of building work in the late 17th century, probably after John Eastoft's purchase of the estate. In 1672 there were 15 taxable hearths.

(STAC8/36/11. T. W. Hall, *Etton, an East Yorkshire Village* (1932).)

EVERINGHAM   Harthill

A village to the west of Weighton (Market Weighton). 1672: 56 households (township of Everingham). 1676: 176 persons aged 16 or more, including 34 recusants (parish of Everingham).

Church St Everilda: Early English.

Principal family Constable of Everingham Hall (and West Rasen Hall, Lincolnshire) (baronetcy 1642). Estate revenue: £1300 a year (1632); £2100 a year (1650); £2200 a year (1670); £1700 a year (1693). Number of servants: 26 (1662); 18 (1672).

The Constables were a major Catholic family who sent some of their children to Continental seminaries, monasteries and convents.

Sir Philip Constable (c.1550-1619) was a Church Papist who served as a member of the Council in the North. It appeared for a time that the family was drifting into Protestantism but this trend was reversed through the intervention of two Jesuit priests, James Sharpe and Richard Holtby. When Sir Philip's son William was admitted to the English College at Rome in 1613 he related that all the children (apart from one of his sisters) were Catholics and that his father had recently been converted as a result of Holtby's spiritual counsel. However, neither Sir Philip nor his eldest son Marmaduke was convicted of recusancy.

Marmaduke Constable (1574-1632) ran into financial difficulties and in 1627 sold all his North Riding property.

His son Sir Philip (1595-1664), who inherited a heavily encumbered estate, compounded for his recusancy in 1632 and was required to pay a rent of £250 a year to the Crown. In 1635 he employed Henry Paxton to carry out a survey of his manors of Everingham and Thorpe le Street. According to this survey the Everingham estate consisted of 2859 acres.

In the Civil War Sir Philip was branded as a delinquent for residing in the royalist garrison at Newark. His estate was sequestered and eventually put up for sale. With the help of John Rushworth the Constables managed to regain possession, though at a price. In 1660 their debts amounted to some £12,000.

Sir Marmaduke Constable (1619-1680) sought to overcome his financial problems through rent increases, enclosure and the sale of timber. During his frequent absences from home his wife, Dame Anne, helped to manage the estate along with the steward, George Constable. Despite a considerable amount of litigation in the reign of Charles II there was a steady improvement in the family fortunes.

Sir Marmaduke was a recusant like his father and had a resident chaplain. He was imprisoned during the Popish Plot controversy and after his release retired to Antwerp.

His son Sir Philip (1651-1706) paid heavily for his loyalty to the Catholic faith, particularly in view of allegations of treason. He was imprisoned in 1678, 1680, 1690 and 1696.

In the last decade of the 17th century he was faced with growing financial problems as a result of increases in direct taxation, a falling rent-roll and personal extravagance.

Everingham Hall An early Tudor mansion with an Elizabethan or Jacobean extension. Sir Philip Constable (c.1550-1619) was probably responsible for improving and enlarging the house.

Among the rooms listed in an inventory of 1575 were the hall, the parlour, the great chamber, the great and little galleries, the Duke of Norfolk's chamber and the armoury. There was also a chapel.

The house was damaged in the Civil War though not apparently to any serious extent.

In 1672 Sir Marmaduke Constable was taxed on 24 hearths.

The survey of 1635 refers to a park of 378 acres 'adioining to the house which hath sometimes been in many devisions but nowe lieth all togither'. In 1687 Sir Philip Constable was granted a licence authorising him to 'keep up' the park (which had existed for time out of mind) and to stock it with deer.

(Hull University Archives, Maxwell-Constable MSS. P. Roebuck, *Yorkshire Baronets 1640-1760* (1980).)

FILEY   Dickering

A fishing village which straddled the border between the East and North Ridings. For official purposes it was treated as being wholly within the East Riding. The parish of Filey included the hamlets of Gristhorpe and Lebberston, both of which were in the North Riding. 1672: 77 households (township of Filey). 1676: 248 persons aged 16 or more (parish).

Filey had been granted market rights in 1221 and 1240.

In 1619 the Court of Wards was told that the manor of Filey had provided Christopher Maltby its late owner with only a modest revenue: the pasture lands were 'moorish' and some of the cottages were untenanted while others were occupied by 'poore fishermen, soe as they are of verey small value.'

Sir John Buck of Hanby Grange in Lincolnshire acquired the rectory of Filey, which was said to be worth £300 a year, through his marriage to an heiress, Elizabeth Greene, in 1616. He had a house near the church but he usually resided in Lincolnshire. In 1623 it was alleged that he had 'no care' for the church and cure of souls and that his sole concern was to increase his income from the tithes.

Church St Oswald: Norman and Early English.

The church was in the North Riding but in the Commonwealth period it was considered appropriate to assign it to the East Riding.

(J. Cole, *History and Antiquities of Filey* (1828). W. S. Cortis, *History and Descriptive Guide to Filey* (1861). Wards 5/49. Wards 9/94/fo.750. C.6/15/17.)

FLAMBOROUGH   Dickering

A coastal village near Bridlington. 1672: 101 households (township of Flamborough). The inhabitants included fishermen as well as farmers and agricultural workers.

In 1674 Sir John Clayton built a lighthouse on Flamborough Head but the project was blighted by financial problems.

Church St Oswald: Norman with later medieval features.

By 1640 the steeple was no more than a stump and the cost of rebuilding it was considered to be prohibitive.

Restoration work on the interior was undertaken in 1632-3 and 1687.

School There are references to schoolmasters in the course of the 17th century.

Principal family Constable of Flamborough Hall (and Holme Hall, Holme upon Spalding Moor) (baronetcy 1611). Estate revenue: £1400 a year (1612); £750 a year (1630).

The estates of the Constable family had been forfeited to the Crown in 1537 when Sir Robert Constable was attainted and executed for participating in the Pilgrimage of Grace. In 1582 they had managed to recover the manors of Flamborough and Holme upon Spalding Moor, subject to the payment of a fee-farm rent.

Sir William Constable (1590-1655) was named after William Lord Burghley, the Queen's chief minister, who had consented to be his godfather. In 1608 he married Dorothy Fairfax, a sister of Ferdinando Fairfax the future parliamentarian general.

In 1614 he sold the manor of North Duffield, which he had inherited from his mother, for £9250. Even after this he continued to borrow heavily, apparently as the result of personal extravagance.

In 1627 he was arrested for refusing to contribute to the forced loan and spent several months in prison. Thomas Lord Wentworth, however, had a high regard for him and appointed him as one of his deputy lieutenants.

Sir William's financial situation became increasingly desperate and before long he had disposed of the rest of his estate. The manor of Holme was sold in 1634 and the manor of Flamborough in 1636. After the sale of the Holme estate it was leased back to him at a rent of £300 a year.

Sir William and his friend Sir Matthew Boynton planned to emigrate to New England. In the end they decided to go into exile in Holland and in June 1637 Constable and his wife crossed over. As members of the English Protestant congregation at Arnhem they enjoyed the kind of religious freedom which had been denied them under the Laudian regime.

By 1641 Sir William was back in England. When he appeared as a candidate in the Knaresborough by-election held in November he was described by an opponent as a Puritan who had spoken out against the Book of Common Prayer.

In the Civil War he was a distinguished parliamentarian commander who fought at the battle of Edgehill and later served as lieutenant general of the horse under Thomas Lord Fairfax.

In 1649 he was made a member of the Council of State and acted as one of the judges at the trial of the king.

In his will (1654) he gave direction that his funeral should be without ostentation. In the event he was buried in Westminster Abbey but his body was disinterred after the Restoration. He was the last of his line.

Subsequent owners Sir Henry Griffith of Burton Agnes bought the manor of Flamborough in 1636 and sold it in 1650 to Walter Strickland, a younger brother of Sir William Strickland of Boynton. He died without issue in 1671 and after the death of his widow the manor passed to the main branch of the family.

Flamborough Hall A fortified manor-house with a tower. A licence to crenellate had been obtained in 1351.

According to a Crown survey of 1573 the house was then in a ruinous condition: it had not simply been neglected but had been used as a source of building materials by some of the East Riding gentry. It would therefore have been necessary for the Constables to carry out major restoration work before taking up residence there towards the end of the 16th century.

In 1672 there were 12 taxable hearths.

(BL, Additional MSS 40,132 and 40,135 (Holme Hall MSS). Hull University Archives, Harford of Holme MSS. C.54/2746. J. T. Cliffe, *The Yorkshire Gentry* (1969), 293-4, 306-8. E.178/2564. F. Brearley, *A History of Flamborough* (1971).)

FOLKTON   Dickering

A village to the west of Filey. The parish of Folkton included the village of Flixton and the decayed hamlet of Flotmanby. 1672: 35 households in Folkton and Flotmanby and 36 in Flixton. 1676: 164 persons aged 16 or more (parish).

The Babthorpes of Osgodby, a major Catholic family, owned the manor of Flotmanby until 1633 when it was sold to Sir John Buck. It was the last remnant of a once great estate. (For the Babthorpes see the entry for Hemingbrough.)

During the years of persecution in James I's reign the Babthorpes sometimes retired to Flotmanby in the hope of escaping the attentions of the Northern High Commission. Since the whole household was Catholic this sometimes led to a temporary upsurge in the number of persons who were presented for recusancy in the parish. In the late 17th century, however, there is no evidence of any residual Catholicism.

Church St John Evangelist: Norman, Early English and Perpendicular.

In the Commonwealth period it was reported that the parish had no minister. (C.8/49/47.)

FOSTON ON THE WOLDS Dickering

A village to the south-east of Great Driffield. The parish of Foston included several villages. 1672: 39 households in Foston, 37 in Brigham and 40 in Gembling and Great Kelk. 1676: 180 persons aged 16 or more (parish).

Church St Andrew: Norman, Early English, Decorated and Perpendicular.
Schools There were schoolmasters at Gembling in 1662 and at Brigham in 1682.

FOXHOLES Dickering

A small Wolds village situated to the north-west of Bridlington. The parish of Foxholes included the hamlets of Boythorpe and Butterwick which had a medieval chapel. 1672: 20 households in Foxholes and 21 in Boythorpe and Butterwick. 1676: 100 persons aged 16 or more (parish).

Church St Mary: Norman in origin.
School In 1662 Edward Smith secured a licence to teach at Foxholes.

FRIDAYTHORPE Buckrose

A small village on the road between York and Great Driffield. There was no other village within the parish. 1672: 24 households (township of Fridaythorpe).

Francis Sherwood, a Puritan divine, was instituted as vicar of Fridaythorpe in 1637. He had previously been undermaster at Beverley School and in the years 1652 to 1669 he was the headmaster there.

Church St Mary: Norman and Early English.

The parish was subject to the peculiar jurisdiction of a Prebendary of York.

School Francis Sherwood may possibly have taken in pupils while vicar of Fridaythorpe.

(R. A. Marchant, *The Puritans and the Church Courts in the Diocese of York, 1560-1642* (1960), 277.)

FULFORD Ouse and Derwent

Twin villages, Gate Fulford and Water Fulford, situated to the south of York. Fulford was a chapelry within the parish of St Olave, York. 1672: 67 households (township of Fulford). 1676: 137 persons aged 16 or more, including 16 Protestant dissenters (chapelry).

Church St Oswald, Gate Fulford: Norman and Perpendicular.

FULL SUTTON   Harthill

A small village to the east of York. There was no other village within the parish. 1672: 23 households (township of Full Sutton). 1676: 40 persons aged 16 or more (parish).

The manor of Full Sutton belonged to the Dealtry family who were minor gentry with little prospect of moving up the social ladder. In a Chancery case of 1661 it was said that Francis Dealtry (1630-1653) had left an estate worth about £100 a year of which one-third had been assigned for his wife's jointure.

As owners of the patronage rights the Dealtrys were able to provide employment for some of the younger members of the family. In 1623 George Dealtry was presented to the living (which was worth £40 a year) while in 1662 his son William became the new rector of Full Sutton. In 1672, however, the advowson was sold.

Church St Mary: Early English.

(C.10/61/41.)

GANTON   Dickering

A village on the northern edge of the Wolds between Malton and Filey. There was no other village within the parish. 1672: 46 households in Ganton with Brompton. Brompton was a parish in the North Riding. 1676: 130 persons aged 16 or more (parish of Ganton).

Church St Nicholas: mainly Perpendicular.

Almshouses In 1616 John Legard settled property for the support of almshouses which he 'hath now lately from a godly, religious and charitable disposition .... founded and erected and buylded'. The object was to house four poor people who were to be 'very conformable to the Religion professed by the Church of England'.

Principal family Legard of Ganton Hall (baronetcy 1660). Estate revenue: £800 a year (1658).

The manor of Ganton had been bought by John Legard, a London merchant, in 1583.

John Legard (1576-1643), who was the founder of the almshouses, periodically added to the estate. During the Civil War he favoured the cause of Parliament and in February 1643 it was reported that he had been declared a traitor by the Earl of Newcastle. His second son Richard initially supported Parliament but he later served as a royalist captain.

John Legard (1631-1678), who succeeded his grandfather in December 1643, had been made a ward of the Crown after his father's death in 1638. The grant of a baronetcy in 1660 was probably in recognition of his loyalty to the king during the events leading up to the Restoration.

During the latter part of the century the Legards continued to engage in the piecemeal acquisition of land.

Ganton Hall A gabled Elizabethan house which had been built by the Lacys who were the previous owners of the estate. In 1583 it was described as 'new beylded, the walls of chalk-stone and covered with slayt'.

In 1672 there were 13 taxable hearths.

A deed of 1658 records the existence of two parks belonging to Ganton Hall.

(Sir James Digby Legard, *The Legards of Anlaby and Ganton* (1926). C.8/121/104. YAS Library, MD 241.)

GARTON   Holderness

A small village to the north-east of Hull and within a short distance of the coast. The parish of Garton included the hamlets of Grimston and Owstwick. 1672: 22 households in Garton and Grimston and 17 in Owstwick. 1676: 120 persons aged 16 or more (parish).

Church St Michael: Early English.

Principal family Grimston of Grimston Garth. Estate revenue: £1500 a year (1604); £1200 a year (1640); £1700 a year (1660).

According to some accounts the Grimstons had been seated at Grimston ever since the Norman Conquest.

Sir Marmaduke Grimston had a Catholic wife and may himself have been a Church Papist but his successors were conventional Protestants. At his death in 1604 he was heavily indebted to the Crown as the result of problems which he had encountered while serving as sheriff of Yorkshire. His widow, Dame Elizabeth, who had a jointure worth £500 a year, subsequently married Sir Henry Browne, an Oxfordshire squire. The rest of the estate passed to Sir Matthew's brother Thomas, who died without issue in 1617, and then to his nephew Marmaduke Grimston.

During the reign of James I the Grimstons were involved in litigation with Sir Henry Browne over the payment of the Crown debts and his management of the jointure lands.

Following the death of Marmaduke Grimston in 1623 his son William (1619-1664) became a ward of the Crown. At this point the estate was encumbered with no fewer than three jointures which absorbed most of the annual revenue.

In the summer of 1642 Grimston helped to raise troops for the king as one of his commissioners of array. In 1647 the parliamentary authorities decided that his estate should be sequestered and his goods sold. As a result he found it necessary to sell some land but by the time of the Restoration virtually all the property which had been assigned for jointures had come into his possession.

In 1665 his son William (1640-1711) began legal proceedings against a number of persons, including his stepmother and Sir Thomas Strickland of Thornton Bridge who was said to be the sole executor of his father's will. In particular, he alleged that they had taken possession of all the deeds and evidences relating to the estate, that they had refused to let him see the will and that they were seeking to deprive him of 'the benefitt and profitt of most parts of the premisses and share them amongst themselves'.

Grimston Garth The house was burnt down in the Civil War period. It was rebuilt by William Grimston (1619-1664), though apparently on a relatively modest scale: in 1672, for example, the new house had only seven taxable hearths.

There was a park adjoining the house.

(C.3/309/14. C.8/19/6. C.10/16/149 and 471/53.)

GARTON ON THE WOLDS   Dickering

A village to the north-west of Great Driffield. There was no other village within the parish. 1672: 47 households (township of Garton). 1676: 120 persons aged 16 or more (parish).

Church St Michael: Norman and Perpendicular.

GOODMANHAM   Harthill

A village in the neighbourhood of Market Weighton. In this little village 'there stood an Idol-Temple, in very great glory even in the Saxon times, which from the heathen Gods in it was then called God-mundingham, and now in the same sense, Godmanham' (William Camden). There was no other village within the parish. 1672: 29 households (township of Goodmanham). 1676: 120 persons aged 16 or more (parish).

Church All Saints: Norman, Decorated and Perpendicular.

The parish was subject to the peculiar jurisdiction of the Dean and Chapter of York.

School During the reign of Charles I William Ward, a man of Puritan sympathies, served as schoolmaster and later as curate at Goodmanham.

GOXHILL   Holderness

A hamlet to the south-west of Hornsea. There were no other centres of population in the parish. 1672: 13 households (township of Goxhill). 1676: 25 persons aged 16 or more (parish).

Church St Giles: Norman in origin.

GREAT DRIFFIELD   Harthill

A market town on the main road between York and Bridlington. The parish of Great Driffield included the hamlets of Elmswell and Little Driffield which had a medieval chapel. 1672: 147 households in Great Driffield, 12 in Elmswell and 12 in Little Driffield.

Great Driffield had a Thursday market while fairs were held at Little Driffield. Henry Best, who lived at Elmswell, wrote in 1642 that 'the First Fayre of note hereabouts is Little Driffield Faire on Easter Munday' and that there were other fairs there on the Monday in Whitsun week and on 8 September.

Church All Saints: mainly Early English.

The parish was subject to the peculiar jurisdiction of the Precentor of York.

Principal family Crompton of Great Driffield. Estate revenue: £600 a year (1630); £700 a year (1640).

Robert Crompton, who was employed as a clerk in the Alienation Office in London, eventually settled at Great Driffield and built up a considerable estate. His third wife, Ceziah, was a sister of Sir William Strickland, one of the leading Puritans in the riding, and he appears to have had similar religious inclinations.

One of his sons, John, was apprenticed to a York mercer but left him after a few years and married a maidservant in his father's household to his 'great displeasure and discomfort.'

In 1640 Sir Thomas Danby of Farnley, who owned the manors of Great and Little Driffield, began legal proceedings against Crompton and other inhabitants of the parish, alleging that they had managed to gain possession of some of his estate papers and were encroaching on his property.

The following year Crompton settled part of his estate on trustees who were all Puritan friends of his, among them Sir William Strickland, Sir Robert Barwick and Sir Thomas Remington.

Crompton appears to have played no part in the Civil War. At his death in 1646 he left a large personal estate which included some £3000 in cash. The funeral sermon was preached by a Puritan minister, Thomas Micklethwaite of Cherry Burton.

Shortly before the Civil War his eldest son Thomas married Mary Remington, a sister of Sir Thomas Remington. While the Stricklands and the Remingtons were zealous parliamentarians he took up arms for the king. During the Interregnum he was regarded by the authorities as a man of doubtful loyalty and was required to pay a decimation assessment of £32 a year.

The capital messuage occupied by the Cromptons in Great Driffield had 11 taxable hearths in 1672.

(D. Woodward (ed.), *The Farming and Memorandum Books of Henry Best of Elmswell, 1642* (1984), 117, 118. C.6/114/20. C.7/100/34. C.10/35/194. F. Ross, *Contributions Towards a History of Driffield* (1898).)

GREAT GIVENDALE   Harthill

A Wolds hamlet to the east of York. The parish of Great Givendale included Grimthorpe, Little Givendale and Millington which had a medieval chapel. 1672: 13 households in Great Givendale, one in Grimthorpe and 36 in Millington and Little Givendale.
   Church St John Evangelist: Norman and Decorated.
   There is a considerable degree of uncertainty about the dedication.
   The parish was subject to the peculiar jurisdiction of a Prebendary of York.

HALSHAM   Holderness

A village to the east of Hedon. There was no other village within the parish. 1672: 36 households. 1676: 110 persons aged 16 or more.
   The Constables of Burton Constable, who had formerly been seated at Halsham, owned the manor and the patronage rights and continued to use the church as their main burial place.
   Although the Constables were a Catholic family only eight recusants were reported in the census return of 1676. During the late 17th century there were occasional Quaker meetings at Halsham.
   Church All Saints: Norman, Early English, Decorated and Perpendicular.
   School In 1579 Sir John Constable founded a free grammar school with an endowment of £80 a year out of which the master was to be paid a stipend of £20 a year. The pupils were to be taught English grammar, writing and arithmetic.
   Almshouses Sir John also made provision for the establishment of almshouses accommodating eight poor men and two poor women. For their financial support he settled a rent-charge of £36 a year.
   (W. K. Jordan, *The Charities of Rural England 1480-1660* (1961), 263, 319, 353.)

HARSWELL   Harthill

A hamlet to the west of Market Weighton. In the rest of the parish there was probably a scattering of farms. 1672: 8 households (township of Harswell). 1676: 60 persons aged 16 or more (parish).
   The Slingsbys of Moor Monkton in the West Riding bought the manor of Harswell in 1605. During the course of the 17th century there was some decline in the annual rent yield which amounted to £336 in 1639 and £270 in 1686 and 1690.
   In the years 1623 to 1660 Harswell had a Puritan rector, Stephen Dockery.

In a Commonwealth survey of benefices the commissioners noted that Harswell was a small parish which was within less than a mile of Everingham. They therefore proposed that the two parishes should be united but in the event they retained their own separate identities.

Church St Peter: Norman in origin.

(YAS Library, Slingsby MSS, D5 and J1/7. *East Riding Antiquarian Society Transactions*, ii (1894), 38-9.)

HAYTON   Harthill

A village situated to the south of Pocklington and on the road between York and Market Weighton. The parish of Hayton included the village of Bielby where there was a medieval chapel. 1672: 45 households in Hayton and 41 in Bielby.

In the Commonwealth period it was proposed that the chapelry of Bielby should become an independent parish but this was not followed up.

Church St Martin: Norman and Decorated.

The parish was subject to the peculiar jurisdiction of the Dean of York.

School During the reign of Charles I and possibly later the vicar, Thomas Sugden, kept a private school. Among his pupils was the parliamentarian Sir Thomas Norcliffe of Langton.

Principal family Rudston of Hayton Hall (baronetcy 1642). Estate revenue: £500 a year (1641).

The Rudstons were a family whose sudden emergence from relative obscurity was a product of exceptional circumstances. In April 1642 Walter Rudston (c.1597-1650) entertained Charles I at Hayton Hall when he was on his way from York to Hull; and in August, shortly after the outbreak of war, he was made a baronet, mainly no doubt in an attempt to guarantee his loyalty.

During the war Sir Walter displayed little sense of commitment. In 1650 his estate was sequestered after it was discovered that he had signed the Yorkshire Engagement of February 1643 in which many of the gentry had pledged financial support for the royalist cause. In response he claimed that he had done so under duress and that he had always been well disposed towards Parliament. Following his death the family offered to compound for the estate and his son Sir Thomas (1639-1707) was required to pay a fine.

With the death of Sir Thomas the male line expired.

Hayton Hall Sir Thomas Rudston rebuilt the hall in the reign of Charles II.

In 1672 the house had 10 hearths.

(*Calendar, Committee for the Advance of Money*, 908, 930-1. *Calendar, Committee for Compounding*, 1742.)

HEDON
Holderness

A market town with port facilities to the east of Hull. Its church was a parochial chapel within the parish of Preston. 1672: 117 households (township of Hedon). 1676: 246 persons aged 16 or more (chapelry of Hedon).

From the Middle Ages onwards Hedon had been both a corporate town and a parliamentary borough. A royal charter of 1348 had conferred the right to elect a mayor, bailiffs and a coroner. The municipal buildings consisted of a town hall (which was rebuilt in 1683) and a prison.

A weekly market was held on Saturdays. In 1273 the town had been granted the right to hold a fair and in 1661 it secured approval for two fairs.

In the Long Parliament it was represented by two parliamentarian MPs, Sir William Strickland of Boynton and John Alured of Sculcoates, who were both zealous Puritans.

In 1657 a fire destroyed 42 houses and resulted in financial losses estimated at £4000. In a petition submitted to Cromwell in 1658 the mayor and corporation described Hedon as the chief market town in the area and urged him to authorise a collection for the relief of those affected.

Hedon was formerly 'a very considerable place by reason of merchants and shipping' but it is now 'so diminsh'd, partly by reason of its being too near Hull, and partly because the Haven is block'd up and useless, that it has not the least shew of that grandeur it pretends to have had …. At present the Town begins to flourish again' (William Camden).

Since the fire at Hedon 'the greatest part is rebuilt, and the town thereby render'd much more beautiful. Of late years they have grown in wealth more than formerly; which is suppos'd to be owing principally to the several Fairs procur'd for them' (Edmund Gibson, 1695).

Church St Augustine: Early English, Decorated and Perpendicular. One of the largest churches in the East Riding.

School Hedon had a grammar school as early as 1335. During the 17th century the educational provision appears to have been limited. In 1630 Henry Viscount Dunbar was served notice that the free school, of which he was patron, should be kept at Hedon 'at some convenient time'.

Almshouses In his will (1563) George Paynter, a Hull minister, made provision for the establishment of almshouses for three impotent men or women.

In 1616 Thomas Kirkeby, a tanner who had been three times mayor of Hedon, left property for the further support of Paynter's almshouses.

(*CSP Dom, 1657-8*, 285. W. K. Jordan, *The Charities of Rural England 1480-1660* (1961), 262, 269-70, 296. J. R. Boyle, *The Early History of the Town and Port of Hedon* (1895). G. R. Park, *The History of the Ancient Borough of Hedon* (1895). M. Craven, *A History of the Borough of Hedon* (1972).)

HELPERTHORPE   Buckrose

A hamlet to the east of Malton. There was no other centre of population within the parish. 1672: 18 households (township of Helperthorpe).

In a Commonwealth survey of benefices the commissioners suggested that as Helperthorpe and Weaverthorpe were only half a mile apart the two parishes should be united. In the event no formal change resulted from this proposal.

Church St Peter: Perpendicular.

The parish was subject to the peculiar jurisdiction of the Dean and Chapter of York. (*East Riding Antiquarian Society Transactions*, ii (1894), 62.)

HEMINGBROUGH   Ouse and Derwent

A village to the east of Selby. The extensive parish of Hemingbrough included a number of villages and hamlets. 1672: 71 households in Hemingbrough, 54 in Barlby, 13 in Brackenholme with Woodhall, 72 in Cliffe with Lund, 11 in Menthorpe with Bowthorpe, 25 in Osgodby and 37 in South Duffield.

The manor of Hemingbrough belonged to the Ingrams of Temple Newsam from 1614 onwards.

There were 54 recusants within the parish in 1600, 53 in 1615 and 51 in 1627.

Church St Mary: Early English, Decorated and Perpendicular. The spire, which had been erected in the 15th century, was reputed to be the tallest in northern England.

The parish was subject to the peculiar jurisdiction of the Dean and Chapter of Durham.

School An elementary school was founded in 1654.

Principal families (1) Babthorpe of Osgodby Hall. Estate revenue: £1300 a year (1603). Number of servants: 30 or more (1603).

The Babthorpes, who had acquired the manor of Osgodby about 1440, were one of the most prominent Catholic families in the riding. They had resident chaplains and sent some of their children to religious establishments on the Continent. The survival of Catholicism in the parish owed much to their power and influence.

Sir Ralph Babthorpe (1561-1618) was initially a Church Papist but eventually became a professed Catholic through the persuasion of his wife, Dame Grace, who was described by James Sharpe, one of their chaplains, as 'the pillar of religion' in the East Riding. In his recollections of the Yorkshire mission Sharpe wrote that at Osgodby Hall

> we were continually two priests, one to serve and order the house at home, the other to help those who are abroad .... Our house I might count rather as a religious house than otherwise .... we had all our servants Catholic. On

the Sundays we locked up the doors and all came to Mass, had our sermons, catechisms, and spiritual lessons every Sunday and holiday.

During the early part of James I's reign Sir Ralph and his son Sir William (1580-1635) were subjected to an intensive campaign of harassment by the Northern High Commission and found it necessary to lead a peripatetic life. In 1612 Sir Ralph and his wife sought refuge abroad. They finally settled at Louvain where he died of a stroke and Dame Grace became a nun in the convent of St Monica.

According to his mother Sir William Babthorpe was imprisoned for nearly a year and heavily fined after an episode in which two priests who were discovered in his house managed to escape. This plunged him into severe financial difficulties and between 1620 and 1633 he disposed of his whole estate. He then enlisted in the Spanish army in the Netherlands and was killed while fighting against the French.

The manor of Osgodby was sold in 1622 to Sir Guy Palmes of Lindley in the West Riding.

(2) Smith of Osgodby Hall. Estate revenue: £500 a year (1675).

In 1668 the manor of Osgodby was purchased by Sir Jeremiah Smith, a celebrated sea captain who had served in the Protectorate navy and was made admiral of the blue squadron in Charles II's reign.

After his death in 1675 the family soon went into decline. His son George died while still a young man and his grandson Harrison Smith (1676-1697) was an invalid who was called 'mad, lame Smith'. The latter was succeeded by his brother Jeremiah (1677-1714) who before long was heavily in debt. In 1704 the Court of Chancery ruled that his estate should be sold.

Osgodby Hall The house of the Babthorpes had probably been built in the late 15th century or the early Tudor period.

The Palmes family may have pulled down part of the house, perhaps to make it more convenient for a tenant to live there. In 1672 there were only five taxable hearths.

According to a local tradition Jeremiah Smith rebuilt the hall after a fire which occurred at the end of the century.

The park was apparently medieval in origin.

(T. Burton, *The History and Antiquities of the Parish of Hemingbrough* (1888). H. Aveling, *Post Reformation Catholicism in East Yorkshire 1558-1790* (1960), 33-4, 63. C.8/49/47. J. Morris (ed.), *The Troubles of Our Catholic Forefathers*, First Series (1872) and Third Series (1877). BIHR, High Commission Act Book, RVII/AB12/fols. 42, 47, 70, 105, 127, 142, 210, 273.)

HESLINGTON Ouse and Derwent

A village on the outskirts of York. There was no other village within the parish. 1672: 59 households (township of Heslington).

The Heskeths resided at Heslington Hall, an Elizabethan mansion built by Thomas Eynns who had been Secretary of the Council in the North. The most distinguished member of the family was Sir Thomas Hesketh (1548-1605), a barrister who served as Attorney of the Court of Wards and also sat in three Elizabethan Parliaments. In 1603 he was appointed a member of the Council in the North.

Despite the close proximity of Heslington to York the Heskeths appear to have maintained a neutral stance during the Civil War.

Church St Paul: probably Norman in origin.

The parish was subject to the peculiar jurisdiction of a Prebendary of York.

Almshouses Sir Thomas Hesketh bequeathed the sum of £50 to the poor of Heslington but it fell to his widow, Dame Julia, to implement his plan for the building of a hospital. Sir Thomas Hesketh's Hospital, as it was called, was formally established by a trust deed of 1630. It provided accommodation for nine poor people, one of whom was to act as master.

(W. K. Jordan, *The Charities of Rural England 1480-1660* (1961), 266.)

HESSLE Hull Shire

A large village situated to the west of Hull on the north bank of the River Humber. Some houses in the village were in the parish of Kirk Ella. The parish of Hessle included part of the village of Anlaby and the chapelry of Holy Trinity, Hull (which, however, acquired independent status in 1661). Anlaby is separately noticed. 1672: 98 households (township of Hessle). 1676: 300 persons aged 16 or more, including 8 recusants and 66 Protestant dissenters (parish).

There was a ferry operating between Hessle and Barton upon Humber on the Lincolnshire side of the river. Because of the tidal currents the crossing could sometimes be hazardous.

In the late 17th century there was some shipbuilding activity in Hessle.

Church All Saints: Early English, Decorated and Perpendicular.

The parish was subject to the peculiar jurisdiction of the Dean and Chapter of Durham.

(J. G. Hall, *A History of South Cave and of Other Parishes in the East Riding of the County of York* (1892).)

HILSTON
Holderness

A hamlet to the north-east of Hedon. There was no other centre of population within the parish. 1672: 5 households.

In 1607 the rector, Richard Marston, was ejected on account of his nonconformity. He was succeeded by Marmaduke Marchant who held the living from 1607 to 1660. In 1643 the Earl of Newcastle was informed that the 'factious and disloyall minister' of Hilston had forsaken his parish and fled to Hull.

Church St Margaret: Norman.

The church was one of the smallest parish churches in the wapentake of Holderness.

School During the reign of Charles I there was a private school at Hilston.

(R. A. Marchant, *The Puritans and the Church Courts in the Diocese of York, 1560-1642* (1960), 262. *YASRS*, lxi (1920), 155-6.)

HOLLYM
Holderness

A village situated in the most southerly part of Holderness. It had originally been a chapelry within the parish of Withernsea but in the early 17th century, when Withernsea lost its church (see below), it was decided that the chapel at Hollym should take on the role of parish church. 1672: 60 households in Hollym and 33 in Withernsea. 1676: 207 persons aged 16 or more, including 15 Protestant dissenters (parish).

In 1338 Withernsea had been granted the right to hold a weekly market and two annual fairs. In the 15th century, however, most of the village was engulfed by the sea.

In the reign of Charles I there was a rapid turnover of vicars of Hollym with Withernsea which may be attributable in some measure to the character of the patron, Sir John Hotham. Presentations to the living were made in 1632, 1634, 1637, 1640 and 1641. Two of the ministers instituted, Daniel Bushell and Leonard Conyers, resigned while in 1640 George Conyers may have been forced out to make way for the patron's younger son Charles. Henry Lathley, who succeeded Charles Hotham, was a royalist who was reported to have been in arms.

Churches St Nicholas, Hollym: Perpendicular.

St Nicholas, Withernsea: Perpendicular. The church was consecrated in 1488 and replaced a church sited on the coast (St Mary) which had been destroyed by the sea. In 1609 the roof was blown off and not long afterwards the tower was demolished. In the Commonwealth period it was reported that the church was 'very much decayed' to the extent that it would cost over £300 to restore it.

(R. A. Marchant, *The Puritans and the Church Courts in the Diocese of York, 1560-1642* (1960), 237, 255. A. G. Matthews, *Walker Revised* (1988), 395.)

HOLME ON THE WOLDS   Harthill

A small village to the north-west of Beverley. There was no other village within the parish. 1672: 22 households (township of Holme).

Church St Peter: Norman and Decorated.

The parish was subject to the peculiar jurisdiction of a Prebendary of York. The minister was a perpetual curate who received only £10 a year.

HOLME UPON SPALDING MOOR   Harthill

A large village to the south-west of Market Weighton. 1672: 176 households (township of Holme). 1676: 387 persons aged 16 or more (parish of Holme).

A charter of 1301 had conferred the right to hold a weekly market and an annual fair.

The manor belonged to the Constables of Flamborough until 1634 (for an account of the family see under Flamborough).

In 1621 a number of the inhabitants contributed money to a common fund for the purpose of financing a suit in the Court of Exchequer. The suit was brought against a landowner, Marmaduke Dolman of Millington, over an alleged encroachment on the commons of Holme.

A decade later Sir William Constable, who was the current lord of the manor, negotiated an enclosure agreement with the freeholders of Holme. The agreement allowed him to 'take, improve, enclose and kepe in severaltye' part of the moor called Arglam which contained about 60 acres.

Church All Saints: Early English, Decorated and Perpendicular.

Principal family Langdale of Holme Hall (peerage as Baron Langdale of Holme, 1658). Estate revenue: £1000 a year (1640); £1300 a year (1665).

Sir Marmaduke Langdale (1598-1661) bought the manor of Holme in 1634 for £6500. He then leased it back to Sir William Constable at a rent of £300 a year and continued to live at North Dalton. In all, he spent some £12,000 on the purchase of land during the reign of Charles I.

Before the time of the Civil War he acquired a reputation for political radicalism. In Wentworth's view he was 'a Person of ill affections .... to the Provinciall Power, if not to the Regall power'. In 1627 he was arrested and brought before the Privy Council after refusing to contribute to the forced loan. By 1639 he was heading the opposition to ship money in the East Riding but later that year he was pricked as sheriff of Yorkshire on Wentworth's recommendation. When a new ship money writ was issued in December 1639 he procrastinated for some months and only agreed to execute it after being threatened with Star Chamber proceedings.

The abrupt change in his political stance which occurred on the eve of the Civil War may have been due in part to his fear of militant Puritanism. In the summer of 1642 he helped to raise troops for the king as a commissioner of array and subsequently signed the Yorkshire Engagement of February 1643. As a royalist cavalry commander he performed with distinction at the battles of Marston Moor and Naseby and defeated a parliamentarian force at Melton Mowbray in 1645. He also played a leading part in the uprising of 1648 but was taken prisoner at the battle of Preston. Shortly afterwards he managed to escape and went abroad. During his lengthy exile he fought against the Turks, embraced the Catholic religion and became a close associate of the new king.

In 1650 John Lambert had a grant of his estate except for the manor of Holme which Sir William Constable held until his death.

Langdale finally settled at Holme in 1660. Although he was appointed Lord Lieutenant of the West Riding he received no financial reward for his loyal service and in April 1661 pleaded poverty when explaining why he would not be attending the coronation.

His son Marmaduke Lord Langdale (1628-1703), who was also a Catholic, kept a chaplain at Holme Hall.

In 1665 the king procured for him the rectory of Holme, worth £160 a year, which his father had sold to St John's College, Cambridge.

In 1687 James II made him governor of Hull but a year later he was arrested by the deputy governor who declared for the Prince of Orange. After spending some years in exile he was allowed to return home in 1698.

Holme Hall Following the attainder of Sir Robert Constable in 1537 the Holme estate was for many years in the hands of the Crown. In 1573 it was reported that Holme Hall had been stripped of lead and wood and was in a ruinous condition. On recovering their estates in 1582 the Constables must have embarked on a major building programme to make the house habitable once more.

In 1672 Lord Langdale was taxed on 16 hearths.

There are references to two parks belonging to the house: the Old and New Parks.

(E.134/19 James I/Trinity 5. BL, Additional MSS 40,132, 40,135, 40,136 and 41,168. Hull University Archives, Harford of Holme MSS. YAS Library, MD 287(b). Sheffield Archives, Wentworth Woodhouse Collection, Strafford Letters, x, 272. E.178/2564. F. H. Sunderland, *Marmaduke Lord Langdale* (1926).)

HOLMPTON   Holderness

A village situated near the east coast in the most southerly part of Holderness. The parish of Holmpton included only a small portion of the village which was mainly located within the parish of Hollym to the north. 1672: 42 households (village of Holmpton).

In 1669 it was reported that Quaker meetings were held in Holmpton.

Church St Nicholas: said to have been built (or rebuilt) in the early 14th century.

HORNSEA   Holderness

A coastal village with a small harbour. There was no other village within the parish. 1672: 97 households (township of Hornsea). 1676: 420 persons aged 16 or more (parishes of Hornsea and Long Riston).

Hornsea had been granted market rights in 1257 and the right to hold an annual fair in 1358. The inhabitants were mainly engaged in agriculture and fishing.

The problem of coastal erosion was so serious that in 1609 a special inquiry was held at Hornsea to consider the matter. One witness testified that to his personal knowledge no fewer than 39 houses had been lost to the sea. It was feared that the problem would become much worse unless a new pier was built or some other form of sea defence was introduced. In the event no action appears to have been taken, presumably on account of the cost implications.

'Not many years ago there was a small street adjoyning to the Sea, call'd Hornseybeck, which is now washt away except one or two houses' (Edmund Gibson, 1695).

Hornsea Mere was the most extensive lake in Yorkshire. 'A little overward from Hornsey is the Mere, a water pretty deep and always fresh, about a mile and a half long, and half a mile broad, well stor'd with the best Pikes, Perches and Eels' (Edmund Gibson, 1695). In the 17th century Hornsea Mere, with the fishing and fowling rights, belonged to the Constables of Wassand Hall.

Church St Nicholas: Early English and Perpendicular.

The church steeple, 'being a high broach or spire, is a notable Sea-mark; tho' now it is much fal'n to ruin, and the Inhabitants are scarce able to repair it' (Edmund Gibson, 1695).

School There was a schoolmaster at Hornsea in 1698.

(E.178/4813. G. Poulson, *The History and Antiquities of the Seigniory of Holderness* (1840-1), i, 317-18.)

HOTHAM   Harthill

A village to the south of Market Weighton. There was no other village within the parish. 1672: 49 households (township of Hotham). 1676: 124 persons aged 16 or more (parish).

For Hotham Hall see the entry for North Cave.

Church St Oswald: Norman and Early English.

HOWDEN　　　　　　　　　　　　　　　　　　　　　　　　**Howdenshire**

A market town in the south-west corner of the East Riding. 'Howden is a very pretty town, there being many fine houses in it and a pretty church' (Abraham de la Pryme, 1685). The parish of Howden included the villages and hamlets of Asselby, Barmby on the Marsh, Cotness, Kilpin, Knedlington, Laxton, Metham, Saltmarshe, Skelton and Yokefleet. 1672: 207 households in Howden, 60 in Asselby, 88 in Barmby on the Marsh and 256 in the rest of the parish.

The town had enjoyed the right to hold an annual fair since 1200.

The manor of Howden belonged to the Bishops of Durham. Their palace here was in a dilapidated state at the time of the Restoration but John Cosin, who became Bishop of Durham in 1660, carried out a major renovation programme.

There was a ferry across the River Ouse between Metham and Whitgift on the south bank.

Church St Peter and St Paul: Early English, Decorated and Perpendicular. One of the most imposing churches in the East Riding.

In 1630 it was declared unsafe for use. With the aid of voluntary contributions some repair work was undertaken in 1634 and 1635 but this was apparently limited in scope. In the Commonwealth period it was reported that 'There is a large Church, but the Chancel is extremely out of repair'.

In 1696 the roof and upper walls of the choir collapsed.

The parish was subject to the peculiar jurisdiction of the Dean and Chapter of Durham.

School A grammar school which had been established in the 14th century or earlier was housed in a building adjoining the church. Since it was never properly endowed it appears to have had a precarious existence.

In 1663 the churchwardens funded some repairs to the schoolhouse.

Thomas Reynolds, who was presented to the living of Howden in 1679, served as both vicar and schoolmaster.

Principal family Metham of Metham Hall. Estate revenue: £1500 a year (1640).

The Methams were a mainly Catholic family but Sir Thomas Metham (1575-1644) was regarded by some at least of his relatives as a Protestant. On the other hand, the House of Commons took the view in the 1620s that he was 'ill affected' in religion. In a Commons petition which was submitted to the king in 1626 it was alleged that he had never been known to receive communion and that his daughters had been brought up as papists. Despite such aspersions he served as a member of the Council in the North, a deputy lieutenant and a justice of the peace.

In 1638 Sir Edward Osborne, the Vice-President of the Council in the North, suggested to Lord Wentworth that Metham should be re-appointed as a deputy lieutenant in view of his 'abillityes and sufficiencye both of minde and fortune' and the fact that his 'affections stand well inclined'. In the event Wentworth accepted this advice.

Sir Thomas sold a considerable amount of property but was still heavily indebted on the eve of the Civil War. When making a settlement of his estate in 1636 he assigned certain lands to trustees with the intention that they should be sold if his heirs failed to carry out his wishes over the payment of debts and legacies.

In the Civil War he participated in various engagements as a royalist captain and in 1644 was slain at the battle of Marston Moor.

Following his death there was a partial break-up of the estate: some property descended to his grandson Robert Dolman while the trust lands were gradually sold. The bulk of the estate which remained was inherited by his nephew George Metham (1618-1672) who took up arms for the king after returning from abroad. He was subjected to severe financial penalties both as a royalist and an open Catholic. Towards the end of his life he moved from Metham to North Cave. In 1683 his son George built a new house at North Cave which he called Hotham Hall.

George Metham (1655-1716) was a Catholic but he appears to have lacked the commitment of his wife Magdalen who was imprisoned in 1685 for refusing to take the oaths of allegiance and supremacy.

Metham Hall A moated house which may have been largely medieval. After the family moved to North Cave it fell into decay.

In 1672 there were 16 taxable hearths.

(W. K. Jordan, *The Charities of Rural England 1480-1660* (1961), 304, 393. P. Saltmarshe, 'Some Howdenshire Villages', *East Riding Antiquarian Society Transac-tions*, xv and xvi (1909). John Rushworth, *Historical Collections* (1721), i, 393. Sheffield Archives, Wentworth Woodhouse Collection, Strafford Letters, xviii, Sir Edward Osborne to Lord Wentworth, 5 December 1638. T. Clarke, *History of the Church, Parish and Manor of Howden* (1850).)

HUGGATE   Harthill

A Wolds village situated between York and Great Driffield. There was no other village within the parish. 1673: 54 households (township of Huggate). 1676: 122 persons aged 16 or more (parish).

In 1649 Thomas Hood of Huggate was alleged to have spoken against Cromwell 'to the encouragement of the malignant party' and to have spread rumours of his defeat.

Church St Mary: Norman, Decorated and Perpendicular.

(G. C. F. Forster, *The East Riding Justices of the Peace in the Seventeenth Century* (1973), 42.)

HULL
Hull Shire

A market town and parliamentary borough which was of dual importance as a fortress and a major trading port. It was by far the largest town in the East Riding. 1673: 1378 households. 1676: 6000 persons aged 16 or more, including 500 Protestant dissenters (parish of Holy Trinity and parochial chapelry of St Mary).

For 'statly building, strong forts, rich fleets, resort of merchants and plenty of all things, 'tis without dispute the most celebrated Town in these parts' (William Camden).

Hull 'is a place of greate trade, and walled about and moted …. Itt haith severall block houses well furnist with ordnance towards the sea' (Life of Marmaduke Rawdon, entry for 1664).

Hull has 'walls and gate-houses …. well stored with guns'. It is 'very populous because of the great resort of shipping' (Thomas Baskerville, 1675).

'…. the buildings of Hull are very neate, good streets, it's a good tradeing town … We enter the town …. from the southward over two drawbridges and gates' (Celia Fiennes, 1697).

'The town is a very fine town, exceeding well governed, and kept in very great aw …. There is seven or eight hospitals in the town, and yet, for all that, the maintaining of the poor cost them about £1700 a year' (Abraham de la Pryme, 1698).

Hull had been given corporate status in a royal charter of 1440. The corporation consisted of a mayor and aldermen, a high steward, a recorder and a town clerk. A number of 16th and 17th century charters basically confirmed the rights conferred in the original charter.

The charter of 1440 had also granted Hull the status of a county (Hull Shire) with its own sheriff.

The economy of the town owed much to its overseas trade, particularly with the Baltic countries and the Netherlands. The main exports were hides and cloth produced in the West Riding while imports included timber, hemp, flax and iron. There was also a busy coastal trade which involved, among other things, the importation of coal from Newcastle and Sunderland.

Trinity House regulated shipping, provided Humber pilots and appointed the harbour-master.

The right to hold markets and fairs derived from a charter of 1299. The market days were Tuesday and Saturday.

Hull was an ultra-Protestant town with few Catholics. During the early 17th century Holy Trinity church and the public grammar school were key agents in the promotion of Puritan values. After the Restoration the town had a considerable number of nonconformists, including Presbyterians, Independents and Quakers, and some degree of rivalry was in evidence. Hull is 'a mighty factious town, there being people of all sects in it' (Abraham de la Pryme, 1695).

There were outbreaks of the plague in 1602-3, 1637-8 and 1644. Stringent precautions were taken to avoid further incursions.

Charles I was well aware of the military importance of Hull and not least the magazine there and in January 1642 was planning to put in the Earl of Newcastle as governor. Parliament, however, forestalled him by sending down Sir John Hotham with orders to take on that responsibility. In April Hotham refused to allow the king to enter the town and was declared guilty of treason. On the outbreak of the Civil War Hull became the main bastion of the parliamentary cause in Yorkshire and continued in that role throughout the war. In June 1643 Hotham was taken into custody on the grounds that he was planning to hand over the town to the royalists. He was replaced as governor by Ferdinando Lord Fairfax who successfully defended Hull when it came under siege in the autumn of 1643. At that stage the rest of Yorkshire was under royalist control. (For the Hothams see under Scorborough).

In 1676 North Bridge was rebuilt in order to facilitate the passage of ships along the River Hull.

In 1687 James II appointed Marmaduke Lord Langdale, a Catholic, as governor of the town. Towards the end of 1688, however, Lionel Copley the deputy governor staged a coup and declared for Prince William of Orange.

Churches Holy Trinity: Decorated and Perpendicular.

Known as the High Church because of its size, Holy Trinity was a parochial chapel within the parish of Hessle until the reign of Charles II. In 1661 the king agreed, in response to a Hull petition, that it should become a fully independent parish church.

'There is a good large Church in Hull .... I observ'd there their alter stood table-wise for the Communion just in the middle of the Chancell, as it was in the primitive tymes before Popery came in' (Celia Fiennes, 1697).

St Mary: Perpendicular. The west tower was rebuilt in 1697.

St Mary, which was known as the Low Church, was a parochial chapel within the parish of North Ferriby.

In the last decade of the 17th century two nonconformist chapels were built, one for Presbyterians and the other for Independents.

Schools Hull Grammar School, which dated from the 14th century, had originally been endowed by John Alcock, then Bishop of Worcester, in 1479 and had moved into new premises in 1583. Since the beginning of the 16th century it had been under the patronage of the corporation.

One of its most celebrated masters was Anthony Stevenson, a Puritan divine appointed by the corporation in 1633.

The only other school in the 17th century was Charity Hall, the corporation workhouse, where poor children were taught a trade and might also receive tuition in reading and writing. In the latter part of the century the boys wore blue coats.

Almshouses There were already a number of hospitals or almshouses at the beginning of the 17th century. The most notable of these were the Charterhouse or God's House which had been founded by Sir Michael de la Pole in 1378; the Trinity House hospital for poor and distressed seamen or their widows; and the hospital recently built by William Gee, a Hull merchant who had been mainly responsible for the rehousing of the grammar school.

In 1621 Thomas Ferries provided a substantial endowment for the Trinity House hospital and four years later built a hospital for 10 seamen's widows on an adjoining site. After his death the new hospital was taken over by Trinity House.

In his will (1640) Sir John Lister made provision for the establishment of almshouses for six poor men and six poor women and these were built in 1642.

During the latter part of the century further almshouses were founded by George Crowle, William Robinson and Joseph Ellis. In 1697 Trinity House assumed responsibility for Robinson's almshouses.

'In the town there is an hospitall that's called the Trinity House, for Seamens widdows, 30 is their Complement their allowance 16 pence per weeke and fewell' (Celia Fiennes, 1697).

Prisons Hull had two prisons, one for felons and the other, known as the 'burgess prison', for persons who were committed for lesser offences.

There was also a house of correction where able-bodied rogues and vagabonds were set to work.

Inns These included the George, the King's Head and the White Horse.

The town was noted for a particularly strong kind of ale which was called 'Hull cheese'.

(K. M. Stanewell (ed.), *Calendar of the Ancient Deeds ,Letters....in the Archives of the Corporation [of Hull]* (1951). J. J. Sheahan, *History of the Town and Port of Kingston upon Hull* (2nd edition, 1866). T. Tindall Wildridge (ed.), *The Hull Letters* (1886). B. N. Reckitt, *Charles I and Hull* (1952). J. Lawson, *A Town and Grammar School through Six Centuries: A History of Hull Grammar School against the Local Background* (1963). H. Calvert, *A History of Kingston upon Hull* (1978). E. Gillett and K. A. MacMahon, *A History of Hull* (1980).)

HUMBLETON   Holderness

A village to the north-east of Hedon. The parish of Humbleton included a number of villages and hamlets. 1672: 20 households in Humbleton, 8 in Danthorpe, 34 in Elstronwick, 23 in Fitling and 23 in Flinton and Etherdwick. 1676: 250 persons aged 16 or more (parish).

Church St Peter and St Paul: Decorated and Perpendicular with some 17th century restoration work.

Principal family Thompson of Humbleton Hall. Estate revenue: £500 a year (1640); £2500 a year (1670). Number of servants: 7 (1660).

The Thompsons purchased the Humbleton estate for £1620 in 1614.

Francis Thompson (c.1579-1657), who succeeded his father in 1637, was employed as a collector of customs dues in the port of Scarborough. In 1630 he bought Scarborough Castle with some adjoining land for £2200.

He and his son Stephen (1602-1677) were both fined for supporting the royalist cause in the Civil War. The latter claimed that he had assisted Parliament by providing money, horses and arms and that when he had fled to Scarborough in 1643 he was unaware that the governor, Sir Hugh Cholmley, had decided to switch sides. According to Cholmley's account, however, Thompson was initially 'verie much affected to the king's cause'.

In 1662 Stephen Thompson and his son William (1629-1692) handed over Scarborough Castle to the Crown and as compensation the fee-farm rent payable out of the manor of Humbleton was reduced to a nominal sum.

Before long the Thompsons found themselves accused of abducting a young heiress, Arabella Alleyn, who as the only child of an Essex squire had inherited an estate worth some £2000 a year. It was alleged that William Thompson, who had taken her over to France, intended to marry her to his son Francis when he was of riper years. In their defence the Thompsons maintained that they had undertaken to act as her guardians since they were distantly related to her and that the choice of a husband would be a matter for her alone. The Privy Council, however, had difficulty in accepting their story and in November 1666 it was reported that Stephen Thompson had been committed to the Tower for assisting his son in the execution of his plan. Despite the controversy which they had stirred up the Thompsons eventually achieved their objective: the young couple were married in 1669 and the family acquired a fortune in lands and goods.

During the Monmouth Rebellion of 1685 William and Francis Thompson were taken into custody as 'disaffected and suspicious persons'.

Humbleton Hall The house was probably built after the purchase of the estate in 1614.

There were 11 taxable hearths in 1672 and 12 in 1685.

(Hull University Archives, Hotham MSS. C.54/2837. *YASRS*, cliii (2000), 142. C.7/176/67. *CSP Dom, 1665-6*, 474; *1666-7*, 263; *1667*, 132; and *1668-9*, 387.)

HUNMANBY   Dickering

A large village to the south of Filey. The parish of Hunmanby included the village of Fordon (which had its own public chapel) as well as many scattered farmsteads. 1672:

167 households (township of Hunmanby). 1676: 800 persons aged 16 or more (parish of Hunmanby).

The principal manor in Hunmanby was known as the Lennox manor. Two other manors or reputed manors were called the Roos and Hamerton manors.

In 1605 there were 97 deaths from the plague.

In 1618 William Leppington, the owner of the Roos manor, secured the right to hold a market every Tuesday and two fairs a year.

Church All Saints: Norman and Early English with later features.

School In the reign of Charles I there was a school at Hunmanby which was located in the church.

Principal family Osbaldeston of Hunmanby Hall. Estate revenue: £350 a year (1626); £1000 a year (1666).

The Osbaldestons were a junior branch of the Osbaldeston family of Osbaldeston in Lancashire.

Sir Richard Osbaldeston (c.1590-1640) was a lawyer who served for a time as an official of the Council in the North. He was responsible for establishing the family at Hunmanby. In 1623 he bought the Hamerton manor and the impropriate rectory of Hunmanby from his brother-in-law Thomas Westroppe.

Because of his legal work he lived mainly at York until 1636 when he was appointed Attorney General in Ireland on the recommendation of Lord Deputy Wentworth. While in Ireland he acquired some property there.

His son William (1631-1707) does not appear to have been made a ward of the Crown on succeeding to the estate. In 1653 he married Anne Wentworth, one of the daughters and coheirs of Sir George Wentworth of Woolley, and through her he acquired property worth £200 a year, though only after litigation. Shortly after the Restoration he further increased his estate by purchasing the Roos manor in 1664 and the Lennox manor the following year.

As a magistrate he was actively engaged in the campaign against conventicles.

Hunmanby Hall A new house was built in the early 17th century, probably by Sir Richard Osbaldeston.

In 1672 William Osbaldeston was taxed on 11 hearths. Later in the century he substantially enlarged and improved the house. A three-storeyed classical mansion of brick.

(East Riding of Yorkshire Archives Service, Osbaldeston MSS. C.22/830/31. Lucy M. Owston, *Hunmanby, East Yorkshire, a Story of Ten Centuries* (1948).)

HUTTON CRANSWICK   Harthill

A village to the south of Great Driffield. Hutton and Cranswick were some distance apart and for administrative purposes were sometimes treated as two separate villages. The parish of Hutton Cranswick included the hamlets of Rotsea and Sunderlandwick. 1672: 43 households in Hutton, 85 in Cranswick, 6 in Rotsea and 9 in Sunderlandwick.

In 1310 Hutton Cranswick had been granted the right to hold a weekly market and an annual fair.

Church St Peter: Norman and Early English.

In the Commonwealth period it was reported that the impropriate rectory was worth £250 a year; that the parish currently had no minister; and that it lacked the means to support one.

(*East Riding Antiquarian Society Transactions*, ii (1894), 25-6.)

KEYINGHAM   Holderness

A village to the south-east of Hedon. There was no other village within the parish. 1672: 72 households (township of Keyingham). 1676: 100 persons aged 16 or more (parish).

Church St Nicholas: Norman in origin but mainly 13th century.

KILHAM   Dickering

A large Wolds village to the north-east of Great Driffield. There was no other inhabited village within the parish: Swaythorpe had once been a village but had been converted to pasture, perhaps in the early 16th century. 1672: 110 households (township of Kilham).

Since 1334 Kilham had enjoyed the right to hold a weekly market and two annual fairs; and in the 17th century it also had a number of shops which sold groceries and clothing. In 1642 Henry Best of Elmswell wrote that on All Saints day, 1 November, 'there is a faire att Killam to which greate store of suckinge foales and other younge foales are brought to bee sold. Here alsoe doe wee sell all our old horses after-that they are past doinge us service. All sorts of sheepe goe well of here, and especially olde Ewes and hoggs, soe that it is a rule for the country till the next springe'.

The Thompsons of Kilham, who were a merchant family, held the rectory on long leases from the Dean of York. Richard Thompson (c. 1583-1653) was part owner of several ships which operated out of Scarborough. In the Civil War he was forced to compound for his estate as a royalist delinquent. In his defence he claimed that at the beginning of the war he had sent three men and a dragoon horse for the service of Parliament and that more recently he had been acting as a collector of parliamentary assessments.

Church All Saints: Norman and Perpendicular.

The parish was subject to the peculiar jurisdiction of the Dean of York.

School In the early 17th century the manor of Kilham belonged to John Lord Darcy of Aston (see the entry for Aston, West Riding). In 1633 he founded a free grammar school at Kilham for the sons of poor families. Besides building a schoolhouse he made provision for the payment of a salary of £20 a year to the master and £10 a year to the usher.

(D. Woodward (ed.), *The Farming and Memorandum Books of Henry Best of Elmswell, 1642* (1984), 120. S.P.23/cxxv/507. W. K. Jordan, *The Charities of Rural England 1480-1660* (1961), 336.)

KILNSEA   Holderness

A coastal village at the southernmost extremity of Holderness. 'In the very tongue of this Promontory, where it draws towards a point and takes the name of Spurnhead, stands the village [of] Kellnsey' (William Camden). 1672: 38 households (township of Kilnsea).

Over the centuries the parish had suffered badly from coastal erosion and the hamlets of Hutton, Ravenser and Sunthorpe had completely disappeared.

The manor of Kilnsea belonged to the Angell family. In 1674 Justinian Angell, a London merchant, erected a lighthouse on Spurn Head. 'Upon the Spurn-head....is a Light-house built....by one Mr Justinian Angell of London, who had a Patent for it from Charles the second. But the Lord Dunbar claiming the ground, there arose a difference between them which is not yet ended. The Lights however are kept up; and in the year 1684 a Day-mark was also erected, being a Beacon with a barrel on the top of it' (Edmund Gibson, 1695).

Church St Helen: Norman in origin.

The value of the living was so modest that it often proved difficult to recruit a resident minister.

(G. de Boer, *A History of the Spurn Lighthouses*, East Yorkshire Local History Society No.24 (1968). C.7/282/8.)

KILNWICK ON THE WOLDS   Harthill

A village to the north of Beverley. The parish of Kilnwick included the village and chapelry of Beswick. 1672: 41 households in Kilnwick and 35 in Beswick.

During the 17th century the manor of Kilnwick changed hands relatively frequently and the various owners usually resided elsewhere.

Church All Saints: Norman and Early English.
School In the reign of Charles I there was a private school at Kilnwick.
Principal family Daniel of Beswick Hall. Estate revenue: £600 a year (1662).

Sir Ingleby Daniel (c.1575-1645) may have been a Church Papist. In 1632 he compounded for the recusancy of his wife, Dame Frances.

His son George (1616-1657) also married a Catholic, Elizabeth Ireland. He was a minor poet who wrote high-flown verse. During the Civil War he and his brother Thomas supported the royalist cause and in 1653 the republican authorities imposed a heavy fine.

Thomas Daniel, who inherited his brother's estate, was knighted in 1662. During the early years of Charles II's reign he served as a captain in the foot guards and held a command appointment at Dover.

In 1679 he was pricked as sheriff of Yorkshire.

Kilnwick Hall An Elizabethan or Jacobean house which was probably built by the Alfords of Meaux Abbey who owned the manor during the years 1571 to 1645.

Beswick Hall A gabled Elizabethan house of three storeys which was constructed of brick.

In 1653 it contained 'a hall, a kitchin and a Parlour wainscotted, a Buttery, two Cellars, a Larder and two other Roomes below staires, one Dyninge Roome and two chambers wainscotted, one other little Chamber and foure garretts over them covered with Tyle'. In the grounds there was a dovecote 'well stored'.

In 1672 Sir Thomas Daniel was taxed on 15 hearths.

(A. B. Grosart (ed.), *The Poems of George Daniel, Esq. of Beswick, Yorkshire (1616-1657)* (1878). S.P.23/58A/fo.278.)

KILNWICK PERCY   Harthill

A hamlet to the east of Pocklington. There was no other centre of population within the parish. 1672: 10 households (township of Kilnwick Percy).

In 1607 the minister, Martin Briggs, was in trouble with the ecclesiastical authorities for refusing to wear a surplice. Five years later Sir Francis Boynton presented him to the living of Barmston.

The Woods of Kilnwick Percy, who owned the manor, were noted for their philanthropy. Like his father before him Barney Wood left money for the relief of the poor not only in his own parish but in many neighbouring parishes. Wood had no issue and following his death in 1616 the estate descended to his great niece Mary who was promptly made a ward of the Crown.

In a Commonwealth survey of benefices the commissioners noted that the church had only a small congregation and suggested that the parish should be united with the adjoining parish of Pocklington. This proposal, however, was never implemented.

Church St Helen: Norman.

The parish was subject to the peculiar jurisdiction of the Dean of York.
(*East Riding Antiquarian Society Transactions*, ii (1894), 48.)

KIRBY GRINDALYTHE   Buckrose

A small village or hamlet situated to the south-east of Malton. The parish of Kirby Grindalythe included the hamlets of Duggleby and Thirkleby. 1672: 23 households in Kirby Grindalythe, 20 in Duggleby and 8 in Thirkleby.

Church St Andrew: Norman in origin but with some later medieval work.

Principal family Towry of Kirby Grindalythe Hall. Estate revenue: £500 a year (1629, 1641).

The Towrys owned the manor and the impropriate rectory together with the patronage rights. In 1622 George Towry joined with the other freeholders in an enclosure agreement which involved the division of the common lands and the redistribution of strips.

During the Civil War the Towrys appear to have remained uncommitted.

Kirby Grindalythe Hall In 1672 John Towry was taxed on eight hearths.
(Hull University Archives, Sykes MSS, DDSY/38.)

KIRBY UNDERDALE   Buckrose

A Wolds village to the north-east of York. Besides the village the parish of Kirby Underdale embraced a scattering of farmsteads. 1672: 30 households (township of Kirby Underdale). 1676: 144 persons aged 16 or more (parish).

Church All Saints: Norman and Early English.

School John Shelton, who was rector in the years 1639 to 1647, kept a private school which attracted pupils from outside the parish. He was a Puritan who styled himself pastor and who in the Civil War sided with Parliament.

Principal family Bourchier of Hanging Grimston Hall. Estate revenue: £500 a year (1620).

Sir John Bourchier (c.1570-1626) was a younger son of Sir Ralph Bourchier of Beningbrough Grange (North Riding) who settled on him one-half of the manor of Hanging Grimston. The other half descended in the main line.

Sir John was a London merchant and businessman who was heavily involved in the Yorkshire alum industry.

In 1619 he began legal proceedings against Lord William Howard over the ownership of certain lands in Hanging Grimston. In the course of this Chancery suit it was said that Sir John had caused several fields to be divided and enclosed with hedges and ditches.

By this time he was becoming heavily indebted, mainly as a result of expensive litigation, and in 1623 he sold his Hanging Grimston estate to Sir William Cokayne. The following year Cokayne complained in a Chancery suit that he had found many encumbrances but the sale was nevertheless confirmed.

In 1634 Richard Bourchier was lamenting that as a result of his father's misfortunes he was on the very brink of ruin and that he might even be forced to pawn his own and his wife's clothes.

Hanging Grimston Hall Sir Ralph Bourchier may have built a house after purchasing the manor in 1575.

In 1619 it was said that Sir John Bourchier 'hath caused a troughe or pipe of woode to be layd….for conveyeinge the Water' to his house.

(C.3/302/5 and 396/138. *Lords Journals*, iii, 179, 191-2. C.2/James I/C4/49. *HMC, Coke MSS*, ii, 72. W. R. Shepherd, *The History of Kirby Underdale* (1928).)

KIRKBURN   Harthill

A small Wolds village to the south-west of Great Driffield. The parish of Kirkburn included several hamlets. 1672: 24 households in Kirkburn, 4 in Eastburn, 19 in Southburn and 22 in Tibthorpe. 1676: 115 persons aged 16 or more (parish).

In 1371 Kirkburn had been granted the right to hold a weekly market and two annual fairs.

Eastburn had suffered from depopulation. In the reign of Charles I it was said that 'The town or village of the parish of Kirkburn did anciently consist of a great many messuages, cottages and dwelling houses'.

Church St Mary: Norman, Early English and Perpendicular.

(M. W. Beresford, 'The Lost Villages of Yorkshire', *YAJ*, xxxviii (1955), 53.)

KIRK ELLA   Hull Shire

A village to the west of Hull. Some houses in the village were within the parish of North Ferriby. The parish of Kirk Ella included parts of the villages of Anlaby, Swanland, West Ella and Willerby. Anlaby is separately noticed. 1672: 32 households in Kirk Ella, 13 in West Ella and 33 in Willerby. 1676: 260 persons aged 16 or more (parish).

In his will (1674) Francis Wright made provision for the distribution of bread to the poor on every Sunday after the sermon.

Church St Andrew: Norman in origin; Early English and Perpendicular.

(J. G. Hall, *A History of South Cave and of Other Parishes in the East Riding of the County of York* (1892).)

LANGTHORPE   Holderness

A hamlet within the parish of Swine. It had formerly been a grange belonging to Swine Priory.

Principal family Langdale of Langthorpe Hall (and Houghton Hall). Estate revenue: £740 a year (1653).

The Langdales were a family whose uncompromising loyalty to the Church of Rome had serious financial implications. Successive heads of the family were convicted recusants.

William Langdale (1579-1645) took up residence at Langthorpe after inheriting the estate of his great uncle Marmaduke Langdale of Dowthorpe who died in 1611.

In 1615 one of his servants, Thomas Jackson, was presented for teaching without a licence but it was claimed that he was 'a butler in the house and no schoolman'. Three years later he accompanied William Langdale's daughter Joyce on a journey which culminated in her admission to the English Benedictine nunnery at Brussels.

During the Civil War the Langdales were careful to avoid any degree of commitment to the royalist cause, perhaps because they felt overawed by the parliamentarian garrison at Hull. In 1652 William Langdale (1629-1684), who had recently inherited the estate, claimed in a petition which he submitted that he had always been well affected to Parliament. Even so, he forfeited two-thirds of his landed income on account of his recusancy and it was perhaps for this reason that he was granted a knighthood in 1660.

Sir William married four times. His third wife, Frances Tempest, was described as a person of great merit 'and well deserving from Sir William Langdale for her prudent management of his Estate and Discharge of his debts'. Their son Marmaduke had lands in Holderness worth £200 a year settled on him.

Philip Langdale, who was Sir William's eldest son, inherited Houghton Hall and an estate which was called the 'Wold lands'. In a Chancery suit of 1685 he claimed that his father had formally undertaken to settle his Holderness lands on him but Marmaduke Lord Langdale and other trustees had denied him access to the relevant deeds. In response the defendants maintained that there had been no such settlement. Langdale's mother, Ursula Stapleton, had been strongly opposed to the idea of assigning the Holderness lands to him on the grounds that they had been 'ill gotten'. Possibly her main source of concern was that some of the property acquired from Marmaduke Langdale of Dowthorpe had once belonged to Swine Priory.

The main branch of the family continued to live at Houghton Hall. In 1692 it was recorded in a Catholic list of chaplains that John May, who was aged about 70, usually resided with Philip Langdale at Houghton on the Wolds.

Langthorpe Hall The house was probably built or enlarged by William Langdale (1579-1645) after he had inherited the estate of Marmaduke Langdale in 1611.

In 1673 Sir William Langdale was taxed on 11 hearths.

('Genealogia Antiquae Famillae Langdalorum', *YAJ*, xi (1891). C.6/281/56. Hull University Archives, Harford of Holme MSS. *CRS*, ix (1911), 108-9.)

LANGTOFT   Dickering

A Wolds village to the north of Great Driffield. The parish of Langtoft included the hamlet of Cottam which had a medieval chapel. 1672: 57 households (township of Langtoft but possibly including Cottam).

In 1638 Langtoft was badly hit by the plague.

Church St Peter: Norman in origin; Early English, Decorated and Perpendicular. The parish was subject to the peculiar jurisdiction of a Prebendary of York.

LANGTON   Buckrose

A village to the south of Malton. The parish of Langton included the hamlet of Kennythorpe. 1672: 41 households in Langton and 17 in Kennythorpe and Thornthorpe. 1676: 120 persons aged 16 or more, including 20 Protestant dissenters (parish).

Church St Andrew: 13th century.

Principal family Norcliffe of Langton Hall (and Nunnington Hall, North Riding). Estate revenue: £2000 a year (1652).

Although the Norcliffes only received a coat of arms in 1606 they rapidly ascended into the higher reaches of the Yorkshire gentry.

Sir Thomas Norcliffe (c.1580-1628), who was a barrister of the Middle Temple, added considerably to the estate which he had inherited. In 1618 he bought the manor of Langton for £2400 and other property there, including Bulmer Hall, for £600. He preferred, however, to live at Nunnington where his father had acquired a long lease of the manor belonging to the Crown.

In 1623 he was reprimanded by the Privy Council following complaints by some of his fellow magistrates in the North Riding that he had acted in defiance of a decision taken in open sessions. Three years later he was chosen to serve as sheriff of Yorkshire.

His son Thomas (1618-1680) was made a ward of the Crown on succeeding to the estate. During the negotiations over the wardship it was claimed on his behalf that the lands were of small value 'for the greater parte thereof is upon the highe Woulds and Moores which are so barren that a greate quantity of it yeild but a small Rent'.

In 1631 his mother, Dame Katherine, married Sir John Hotham. After her death in 1634 the Hothams held on to the property which she had inherited from her father, Sir William Bamburgh of Howsham, and it was not until 1652 that Thomas Norcliffe, who had disputed their title, was able to gain possession. By this time it was worth £700 a year.

In 1639 Norcliffe married Dorothy Ingram, a widow with a substantial jointure, who would live on until 1686.

Norcliffe was knighted in April 1642 but this was not enough to guarantee his loyalty to the king. Perhaps because of his Puritan sympathies he took up arms on behalf of Parliament when the Civil War began and served for some years as a colonel in command of a regiment of horse. Among other exploits he played an important part in the storming of Leeds in January 1643.

In 1651 he entered into articles of agreement with the freeholders of Langton for the enclosure of the wastes.

In 1660 he was involved in litigation with Ranald Graham, the new owner of Nunnington, who claimed that he had committed great waste during his tenancy.

Dame Dorothy Norcliffe had the same kind of religious outlook as her husband. She provided financial support for one of the ministers ejected after the Restoration and during her widowhood employed another nonconformist divine as her chaplain. In addition she left the sum of £40 to the pastor of a Congregational church in Hull.

Langton Hall During the Commonwealth period Sir Thomas Norcliffe built a new house for himself at Langton. For this purpose he brought panelling, floors, doors, a staircase and a quantity of lead from Nunnington Hall which according to Ranald Graham had been left in a ruinous condition.

(East Riding of Yorkshire Archives Service, Howard-Vyse MSS. Wards 5/49. YAS Library, MD 237(c). C10/58/48.)

LECONFIELD   Harthill

A village to the north of Beverley. The parish of Leconfield, which extended eastwards to the River Hull, included the hamlet of Arram. 1672: 66 households (township of Leconfield). 1676: 100 persons aged 16 or more (parish).

In 1383 Leconfield had been granted the right to hold a weekly market and an annual fair.

The manor of Leconfield belonged to the Earls of Northumberland. It had formerly been their principal seat in Yorkshire but in the early years of the 17th century their fortified manor-house was demolished and their deer parks were converted into agricultural holdings.

In 1655 the inhabitants of Leconfield submitted a petition to the Lord Protector in which they sought an increase in financial support for their minister, William Mainprice, and his successors. In arguing their case they stressed that Leconfield was a large parish; that the impropriator's clear profits only amounted to £40 a year; and that they had never had any powerful preaching until Mainprice arrived. Of the 48 persons who joined in the petition half indicated their assent by a mark in place of a signature.

Church St Catherine: Saxon in origin; Early English and Decorated. In 1684 a new tower and porch were built, both of brick.

The minister was a stipendiary curate who had a salary of £25 a year.

School In the 1650s there was a private school at Leconfield.

(*CSP Dom, 1655*, 27.)

LEVEN   Holderness

A village situated between Beverley and Hornsea. The parish of Leven included the hamlet of Hempholme. 1672: 66 households in Leven and 17 in Hempholme. 1676: 170 persons aged 16 or more (parish).

In 1270 Leven had been granted the right to hold a weekly market and an annual fair.

At Hempholme there was a ferry which offered passage across the River Hull.

Church St Faith: Early English and Perpendicular.

LOCKINGTON   Harthill

A village situated between Beverley and Great Driffield. Only part of the village fell within the parish of Lockington; the rest was in the parish of Kilnwick. In a Commonwealth survey of benefices the commissioners noted that 'There are in Lockington about twentie houses belonging to the parish of Kilnwick'. The parish of Lockington also included part of the hamlet of Aike. 1672: 71 households in Lockington and 19 in Aike. 1676: 162 persons aged 16 or more (parish).

The rectory of Lockington was in the gift of the Remingtons of Lund, a family with Puritan sympathies. Henry Remington was presented in 1616, Robert Remington in 1639 and Richard Remington in 1647, in his case with the approval of Parliament. In 1627, when serving as perpetual curate of Whitby, Robert Remington had confessed before the Northern High Commission that he had been present on a number of occasions at conventicles and other unlawful meetings.

Church St Mary: Norman, Early English and Perpendicular.

School During the reign of Charles I William Barden kept a private school at Lockington.

(*East Riding Antiquarian Society Transactions*, ii (1894), 27. R. A. Marchant, *The Puritans and the Church Courts in the Diocese of York, 1560-1642* (1960), 270-1.)

LONDESBOROUGH   Harthill

A village to the north of Market Weighton. The parish of Londesborough included the hamlet of Easthorpe. 1672: 23 households in Londesborough and 12 in Easthorpe. 1676: 200 persons aged 16 or more (parish)

The Londesborough estate belonged to the Cliffords of Skipton Castle until the death of Henry Earl of Cumberland in 1643. It then passed to Richard Boyle, Earl of Cork (1612-1698) who had married his daughter Elizabeth. In 1664 he was created Earl of Burlington.

Church All Saints: Norman and Early English with a porch of 1678.

Almshouses Richard Earl of Burlington and his wife founded a hospital for 12 aged persons. It was built between 1677 and 1679.

Londesborough House Francis Clifford, later Earl of Cumberland, erected a three-storeyed house of stone in or about 1589.

In 1672 Richard Earl of Burlington was taxed on 22 hearths. During the late 1670s he considerably enlarged the house by adding two brick wings which were probably designed by Robert Hooke.

Hooke was also responsible for the design of new gardens in the same period.

The hall was approached through an avenue of trees.

In 1697 Celia Fiennes noted that she had passed by Londesborough House which 'stood in a bottom amongst trees; it look'd well and they say is well painted and good furniture'.

(D. Neave, *Londesborough* (1977). R. T. Spence, *Londesborough House and its Community 1590-1643* (ed. A. Hassell Smith), *East Yorkshire Local History Society*, No. 53 (2005).

LONG RISTON   Holderness

A village to the east of Beverley. The parish of Long Riston included part of the hamlet of Arnold. 1672: 39 households (township of Long Riston).

There was a formal link between the churches of Long Riston and Hornsea, though they were a considerable distance apart. In 1676 there was a joint census return which indicated that the two parishes contained 420 persons aged 16 or more.

Church St Margaret: Norman in origin.

LOWTHORPE Dickering

A village to the north-east of Great Driffield. There was no other village within the parish. 1672: 28 households (township of Lowthorpe). 1676: 100 persons aged 16 or more (parish).

In 1304 Lowthorpe had been granted the right to hold a weekly market and an annual fair.

In 1630 Thomas Peirson of Harpham (d.1641) and his son John bought the manor of Lowthorpe. John Peirson (c.1589-1665) settled at Lowthorpe and added considerably to the estate by purchasing the manors of Nafferton Lennox and Nafferton Constable. His son Matthew (c. 1651-1712), who acquired a knighthood in 1669, was said to have had a landed income of £1000 a year.

The Peirsons do not appear to have played an active part in the Civil War.

Church St Martin: Norman, Decorated and Perpendicular.

The minister was a perpetual curate who had only a modest stipend. (C.8/186/51. C.10/118/79. C.33/334, part 1/fo. 447.)

LUND Harthill

A village to the north of Beverley. 1672: 52 households (township of Lund). 1676: 170 persons aged 16 or more (parish of Lund).

Church All Saints: Perpendicular.

Principal family Remington of Lund Hall. Estate revenue: £800 a year (1670).

The Remingtons were a Puritan family and appear as such in a group portrait which was painted in 1647.

Richard Remington (1590-1649) was the son of a wealthy clergyman who was Archdeacon of the East Riding and a grandson of Matthew Hutton, Archbishop of York. In 1623 he bought the manor of Lund from a kinsman and made it his family seat.

During the Civil War he was a member of the East Riding parliamentary committee.

His son Sir Thomas (1611-1681) was knighted by Lord Deputy Wentworth in 1633 during a visit which he made to Dublin. In the Civil War he served as a parliamentarian captain and a member of the East Riding committee.

In a deed poll of 1669 he related that his father had instructed him to take steps to cut off the entail of his manors of Garrowby and Catfoss so that provision could be made for Sir Thomas's daughters and younger sons. In 1672 the manor of Catfoss was sold for £3100.

Lund Hall A two-storeyed 17th century mansion of red brick which was probably built by Richard Remington after his acquisition of the manor.

Sir Thomas Remington was taxed on 15 hearths in 1670 and 1675.

(PRO, Exchequer, Pipe Office, E.367/3102. East Riding of Yorkshire Archives Service, Bethell of Rise MSS.)

MAPPLETON   Holderness

A coastal village to the south of Hornsea. The parish of Mappleton included the hamlets of Great and Little Cowden and Rolston. 1672: 50 households in Mappleton and 36 in Great and Little Cowden. 1676: 340 persons aged 16 or more (parish).

Little Cowden suffered much from coastal erosion. In the latter part of the 17th century its medieval chapel disappeared into the sea.

Church All Saints: Norman, Early English and Perpendicular.

The parish was subject to the peculiar jurisdiction of the Archdeacon of the East Riding.

School There was a school at Mappleton in the mid-17th century.

MARFLEET   Holderness

A village situated to the east of Hull on the north bank of the River Humber. For many years Marfleet had been a chapelry dependent on the parish church of Paull. In a Commonwealth survey of benefices the commissioners described the chapel as formerly belonging to the church of Paull and recommended that it should become a parish church. It was granted full independent status at some point before 1706 and possibly by 1676 when the minister submitted a separate census return. 1672: 31 households (township of Marfleet). 1676: 65 persons aged 16 or more (chapelry or parish of Marfleet).

In his will (1670) Robert Harpham left £50 towards the cost of purchasing the great tithes of Marfleet which belonged to the Gees of Bishop Burton. The intention was to provide support for a preacher at Marfleet church.

Church St Giles: Norman in origin.

The church was subject to the peculiar jurisdiction of the Archdeacon of the East Riding.

The minister was a perpetual curate.

(*East Riding Antiquarian Society Transactions*, iv (1896), 50.)

MARKET WEIGHTON   Harthill

A market town to the west of Beverley which was called simply 'Weighton' in the 17th century. It was described by a visitor who lodged there as 'a little neate Thatch'd town of a mile long' (Celia Fiennes, 1697). The parish of Market Weighton included the village of Shipton which had a medieval chapel. 1672: 141 households in Market Weighton and 54 in Shipton.

A charter of 1311 had conferred the right to hold a weekly market and an annual fair. In 1642 Henry Best of Elmswell wrote that the fair was held on St Helen's day, 3 May.

Church All Saints: Early English, Decorated and Perpendicular.

The parish was subject to the peculiar jurisdiction of a Prebendary of York.

Schools There are references to a school at Market Weighton in 1592 and 1609.

In his will (which was proved in 1657) William Hide the Puritan minister of Market Weighton not only made generous provision for the relief of the poor of the parish but also founded a school for the village of Shipton.

(D. Woodward (ed.), *The Farming and Memorandum Books of Henry Best of Elmswell, 1642* (1984), 117. W. K. Jordan, *The Charities of Rural England 1480-1660* (1961), 249, 344, 382. J. V. Harwood, *Market Weighton: the Early History and Church* (1940). A. G. Fox and D. Stother, *A History of the Parish of Market Weighton and District* (1957).)

MIDDLETON ON THE WOLDS   Harthill

A village to the east of Pocklington. There was no other village within the parish. 1672: 50 households (township of Middleton). 1676: 130 persons aged 16 or more (parish).

The Kipling Cotes horse-races were apparently named after a farmhouse on the southern edge of the parish. In 1618 a group of major landowners, including both Catholics and Puritans, decided to stage an annual race meeting for 'the continueing of Neighbourhood and societie amongst the Noblemen and Gentlemen' of the county of York. In furtherance of this aim they contributed some £300 for the purchase of items of silver plate which were to be given as prizes. The races took place on the third Thursday in March and were run over a four-mile course.

Church St Andrew: Norman and Early English.

(C.8/89/160.)

MUSTON   Dickering

A village to the west of Filey. Thee was no other village within the parish. 1672: 57 households (township of Muston). 1676: 100 persons aged 16 or more (parish).

The common lands were divided and enclosed either in the early 17th century or shortly before.

Church All Saints: Norman in origin.

NABURN
Ouse and Derwent

A village on the River Ouse to the south of York. It was partly in the parish of Acaster Malbis, in the West Riding, and partly in the parish of St George, York. 1672: 38 households.

Church St Nicholas: a public chapel dating from the 14th century.

School There was a school at Naburn in 1600.

Principal family Palmes of Naburn Hall. Estate revenue: £450 a year (1641). Number of servants: 9 (1619).

The Palmes family had settled at Naburn in the 13th century. They remained strongly attached to the Catholic faith throughout the 17th century.

Sir George Palmes (1582-1654) was described as 'one of as ancient an house and as well allied in affinity as any gentleman in the country'. His father, whom he succeeded in 1619, had been a Church Papist but he rejected any form of compromise and suffered imprisonment and considerable financial loss as a result. His brother William was a Jesuit missioner.

In 1619 Sir George and his wife, his six children and his servants were all presented as recusants. Of his children George became a Benedictine monk while Ursula and Grace entered convents in the Spanish Netherlands. When George Palmes was admitted to the English College at Rome in 1637 he testified that all his friends and relatives were Catholics.

In the Civil War Sir George supported the king and took part in the defence of York in 1644. As a consequence his estate was sequestered.

William Palmes (1610-1674) eventually regained possession of the estate and in spite of the financial problems which he faced was able to keep it largely intact. In 1662 he and his wife were named as recusants. Later on he may have taken refuge in outward conformity but his son William (1639-1686) was indicted for recusancy on several occasions.

During the early 1690s George Palmes (1666-1732) had a chaplain, Dr George Witham, who was his brother-in-law.

Naburn Hall A gabled Elizabethan or Jacobean house of two storeys which had probably been built by John Palmes (c.1552-1619).

The unpretentious character of the house was a faithful reflection of the financial status of the family. In 1672 it had eight taxable hearths.

Bell Hall In 1662 Sir John Hewley, a lawyer resident in York, bought the Bell Hall property in Naburn. This included a house of about the same age as Naburn Hall which had nine taxable hearths in 1672.

In 1680 Sir John replaced it with a two-storeyed house of brick.

(Hull University Archives, Palmes of Naburn MSS. T. B. Trappes-Lomax, 'The Palmes Family of Naburn', *YAJ*, xl (1961).)

NAFFERTON
Dickering

A village to the north-east of Great Driffield. The parish of Nafferton included the hamlet of Pockthorpe and the village of Wansford where there was a dependent chapel. 1672: 102 households in Nafferton and Pockthorpe and 43 in Wansford. 1676: 220 persons aged 16 or more (parish).

In 1304 Wansford had been granted the right to hold a weekly market and an annual fair.

In a Commonwealth survey of benefices the commissioners suggested that the chapelry of Wansford should become a parish but this proposal was not acted upon.

Church All Saints: Norman, Decorated and Perpendicular.

School There were schoolmasters at Nafferton in the 1640s and in 1685.

NORTH CAVE
Harthill

A village situated to the west of Hull. The parish of North Cave included the villages of Drewton, Everthorpe and South Cliffe where there was a medieval chapel. 1672: 98 households in North Cave, 34 in Drewton and Everthorpe and 27 in South Cliffe. 1676: 356 persons aged 16 or more (parish).

The Methams owned the manor of North Cave and the tithes of North Cave, Drewton and Everthorpe and also had the patronage rights. (For an account of the Metham family see the entry for Howden.) Although they were in the main a Catholic family there is little evidence of recusancy in the parish during the course of the 17th century.

In 1628 Sir Thomas Metham secured a licence from the Crown which permitted him to enclose 500 acres within the parish for the purpose of creating a deer park.

William Brearcliffe, who was vicar of North Cave during the years 1606 to 1644, found himself in trouble with the ecclesiastical authorities in 1633 when he was accused of various acts of nonconformity, including the holding of conventicles in his house. Although he was undoubtedly a man of Puritan temperament the case was eventually abandoned through lack of firm evidence. In the Civil War he came out in favour of Parliament.

In the reign of Charles II the Methams moved from Metham to North Cave. They already had a large mansion at North Cave which in 1672 contained 26 hearths. In 1683, however, George Metham built a new two-storeyed house called Hotham Hall.

During the late 17th century there were Quaker meetings at North Cave and South Cliffe.

Church All Saints: Norman, Early English and Perpendicular. In 1318 the church had been described as newly built.

Schools In 1615 there was an unlicensed schoolmaster at North Cave.

James Tennant kept a school there during the 1620s. In 1627 he was ordained deacon.

John Seaman appears to have worked as a schoolmaster in North Cave before he became vicar of South Cave in 1638. One of his pupils was Christopher Nesse, a nonconformist divine and the author of various theological works, who was born at North Cave in 1621.

(J. G. Hall, *A History of South Cave and of Other Parishes in the East Riding of the County of York* (1892). *CSPDom, 1628-9*, 174. R. A. Marchant, *The Puritans and the Church Courts in the Diocese of York, 1560-1642* (1960), 102-5, 232-3.)

NORTH DALTON   Harthill

A Wolds village situated between Pocklington and Great Driffield. 1672: 57 households (township of North Dalton).

The Hungates had been squires of North Dalton for many years but in the reign of James I they experienced a sudden change of fortune. In 1615 William Hungate was killed in a duel with Philip Constable of Wassand. His opponent managed to secure a royal pardon but two years later was mortally wounded in another duel. Following his father's death Ralph Hungate was made a ward of the Crown. He was soon borrowing heavily and in 1623 he sold the manor and rectory of North Dalton to a London lawyer. Subsequently he took part in an expedition to the New World and, according to a Court of Wards decree, he perished 'in the River Wyapeco above the Falls in Guiana'.

Church All Saints: Norman, Early English and Perpendicular.

(*CSP Dom, 1611-1618*, 295. Hull University Archives, Langdale MSS, DDLA 19/74, 81.)

NORTH FERRIBY   Hull Shire

A village situated to the west of Hull on the north bank of the River Humber. Some houses in the village were in the parish of Kirk Ella. The parish of North Ferriby included the chapelry of St Mary, Hull and part of the village of Swanland. 1672: 33 households in North Ferriby and 35 in Swanland. 1676: 340 persons aged 16 or more, including 100 Protestant dissenters (parish). (There was a separate census return for the chapelry of St Mary, Hull which had some parochial functions.)

The Priory of North Ferriby, which had originally belonged to the Knights Templars, had been founded about 1200 and dissolved in 1536.

In 1604 a Catholic gentleman, Robert Dalton, had six recusants in his household. In the course of the 17th century there were occasional presentations for recusancy but the parish was overwhelmingly Protestant.

Churches All Saints: Early English, perhaps with later features.

In 1693 an Independent chapel was built in Swanland.

(J. G. Hall, *A History of South Cave and of Other Parishes in the East Riding of the County of York* (1892).)

NORTH FRODINGHAM   Holderness

A village to the south-east of Great Driffield. There was no other village within the parish. 1672: 85 households (township of North Frodingham). 1676: 120 persons aged 16 or more (parish).

In 1642 Henry Best of Elmswell wrote that on 29 June 'there is a Faire att Frodingham, att which Fatte beasts goe of indifferent well, and allsoe fatte younge Calves and horses'. He also observed that another fair was held there on 21 September.

Church St Helen: Norman in origin but mainly Decorated and Perpendicular.

(D. Woodward (ed.), *The Farming and Memorandum Books of Henry Best of Elmswell, 1642* (1984), 119-20.)

NORTH GRIMSTON   Buckrose

A small village to the south-east of Malton. There was no other village or hamlet within the parish. 1672: 26 households (township of North Grimston).

Church St Nicholas: Norman and Early English.

The parish was subject to the peculiar jurisdiction of a Prebendary of York.

NORTH NEWBALD   Harthill

A village to the south-east of Market Weighton. The parish of North Newbald included the adjoining hamlet of South Newbald. 1672: 68 households in North Newbald and 28 in South Newbald.

In 1348 North Newbald had been granted the right to hold a weekly market and an annual fair.

Church St Nicholas: Norman, Early English and Perpendicular.

The parish of North Newbald was subject to the peculiar jurisdiction of a Prebendary of York.

School There was a school at North Newbald in the reign of James I.

(J. G. Hall, *A History of South Cave and of Other Parishes in the East Riding of the County of York* (1892).)

NORTON   Buckrose

A village separated from Malton by the River Derwent. The parish of Norton included the hamlet of Welham. 1672: 43 households (Norton and Welham). 1676: 120 persons aged 16 or more (parish).

In 1672 no fewer than 20 of the 43 households were granted exemption from the hearth tax on grounds of poverty.

Church St Peter: Norman and Perpendicular.

The church was usually served by a curate who in the Commonwealth period was paid only £10 a year.

Principal family Hebblethwaite of Norton Hall. Estate revenue: £500 a year (1629).

Thomas Hebblethwaite (c.1582-1647), who was a barrister, inherited the Norton estate from a cousin and purchased further property, including the impropriate rectory of Norton.

He was elected to the Long Parliament as one of the members for Malton but by the end of 1642 he had ceased to attend and two years later he was formally deprived of his seat. Although he contributed £300 to the royalist cause he remained largely inactive and compounded for his estate as early as December 1644.

His elder son James (1607-1653) appears to have taken no part in the Civil War but the other son, Thomas, fought on the royalist side and was killed in an engagement at Manchester.

Sir Thomas Hebblethwaite (1628-1668) went abroad during the Interregnum and may have joined the exiled Court. Shortly before his death he procured a private act enabling him to sell part of his estate for the payment of debts and the raising of marriage portions. In his will (1668) he observed that the lands earmarked for his wife's jointure had fallen in value as a result of recent enclosures in Norton and Sutton.

Norton Hall In 1672 the Hebblethwaites were taxed on 17 hearths.

(N. A. Hudleston, *History of Malton and Norton* (1962). BL, Additional MSS 24,476, 57-9. S.P.23/clxxiii/53.)

NUNBURNHOLME   Harthill

A village to the east of Pocklington. The parish of Nunburnholme included the hamlet of Thorpe le Street which had a decaying medieval chapel. 1672: 35 households in Nunburnholme and 5 in Thorpe le Street. 1676: 88 persons aged 16 or more (parish).

Nunburnholme derived its name from a priory of Benedictine nuns which had been established there in the 12th century and dissolved in 1538.

In 1635 Philip Constable of Everingham commissioned Henry Paxton to carry out a survey of his manor of Thorpe le Street. According to the survey report the manor contained 650 acres, much of which was divided into closes. In all, there were eleven tenants, not all of whom lived in Thorpe.

Church All Hallows, then St James: Norman and Decorated.

The dedication was changed at some stage between 1536 and 1742.

The Archbishop of York was the patron of the living.

(M. C. F. Morris, *Nunburnholme: Its History and Antiquities* (1907). Hull University Archives, Maxwell-Constable MSS, DDEV/59/7.)

NUNKEELING   Holderness

A hamlet to the north-west of Hornsea. Although the parish church was in Nunkeeling the main centre of population in the parish was the village of Bewholme. 1672: 49 households in Bewholme with Arram (presumably including Nunkeeling). 1676: 80 persons aged 16 or more, including 24 recusants (parish).

Nunkeeling Priory, which was an establishment of Benedictine nuns, had been founded in 1152 and dissolved in 1540.

Nunkeeling was one of the most Catholic parishes in the East Riding, mainly through the influence of two of the leading families, the Creswells of Nunkeeling and the Acklams of Bewholme. There were 16 recusants in 1627, 21 in 1637 and 33 in 1667.

Church St Mary Magdalen and St Helen: Norman and Early English.

The minister was a perpetual curate who had only a modest stipend.

(H. Aveling, *Post Reformation Catholicism in East Yorkshire, 1558-1790* (1960), 68.)

OTTRINGHAM   Holderness

A village to the south-east of Hedon. There was no other village within the parish. 1672: 100 households (township of Ottringham). 1676: 126 persons aged 16 or more (parish).

The Cobbs of Ottringham had migrated from Norfolk to Yorkshire about the end of the 16th century. Initially they settled at Beverley but in the reign of Charles I they began to acquire property in Ottringham and managed to secure a lease of the impropriate tithes which were worth some £200 a year over and above the rent. In 1647 they bought the former Crown manor for £1600.

Sir Francis Cobb (c.1580-1648) was one of the esquires of the body to James I and Charles I. In the Civil War he appears to have remained inactive but his son Francis served as a lieutenant colonel in the royal army and was appointed governor of Leicester.

Church St Wilfrid: Norman, Early English, Decorated and Perpendicular.

The minister was a perpetual curate.

(*East Riding Antiquarian Society Transactions*, iv (1896), 57. *Calendar, Committee for the Advance of Money*, 907, 911, 1089. *Calendar, Committee for Compounding*, 1551.)

OWTHORNE   Holderness

A coastal village to the east of Hedon. The parish of Owthorne included several hamlets. 1672: 28 households in Owthorne, 24 in Rimswell, 13 in South Frodingham and 7 in Waxholme. 1676: 150 persons aged 16 or more (parish).

Owthorne suffered badly from coastal erosion. At the beginning of the 18th century it was reported that the church was not above 200 paces from the German Ocean.

In 1615 the freeholders of Rimswell entered into an agreement for the enclosure of most of the common lands and two years later this was confirmed by a Chancery decree.

In 1634 Owthorne was struck by a fierce tempest which destroyed windmills and blew down houses.

In a Commonwealth survey of benefices the commissioners recommended that the inhabitants of South Frodingham and Rimswell, which were two miles from the parish church, should have a chapel built for them, 'they havinge formerly had one'. In the event nothing came of this proposal.

Church St Peter: Early English.

(*East Riding Antiquarian Society Transactions*, iv (1896), 58.)

PATRINGTON   Holderness

A large village situated on high ground in the southernmost part of the Holderness promontory. The parish of Patrington extended westwards as far as the Humber estuary where there was a small harbour in a creek known as Patrington Haven. There was no other village within the parish. 1672: 119 households (township of Patrington). 1676: 200 persons aged 16 or more (parish).

The inhabitants of Patrington 'do still boast of their antiquity and the former excellence of their Haven; nor do they less glory in the pleasantness of the place, having a very fine prospect, on this side as it looks toward the Ocean, and on that, as it surveys the Humber and the shores about it, together with the green skirts of Lincolnshire' (William Camden).

In 1310 Patrington had been granted the right to hold a weekly market and an annual fair. In the 17th century there was a Saturday market together with two fairs, one on 6 March and the other on 7 July.

The manor of Patrington belonged to the Crown. When a survey was carried out in 1657 it was noted that a considerable amount of land bordering the Humber estuary had been engulfed and that this process was continuing year by year.

Early in the reign of Charles II the open fields were divided and enclosed.

Of the 119 households of 1672 no fewer than 44 were exempted from payment of the hearth tax on grounds of poverty.

Sir Robert Hildyard (1612-1685), who was a gentleman of the Privy Chamber to both Charles I and Charles II, had a lease from the Crown of the demesnes of the manor of Patrington. In the Civil War he served as a colonel in the king's army and took part in the battle of Marston Moor. In 1680 he bought the Winestead estate from his nephew Henry Hildyard.

Church St Patrick: Early English, Decorated and Perpendicular.

In 1612 a new pulpit was installed and about the same time pews were introduced.

A church of exceptional beauty and size with a lofty spire which served as a landmark.

Schools There were schoolmasters at Patrington in the reign of Charles I and the 1650s. In 1655 one of these masters, Nicholas Sheeles, was included in a list of suspected royalists.

(G. Poulson, *The History and Antiquities of the Seigniory of Holderness* (1840-1), ii, 436-41, 443. A. G. Matthews, *Walker Revised* (1988), 398. W. J. Peacey, *St Patrick's Church, Patrington* (1923).)

PAULL   Holderness

A village on the Humber estuary to the south-east of Hull. The parish of Paull included the village of Thorngumbald which had a medieval chapel. 1672: 47 households in Paull and 26 in Thorngumbald. 1676: 250 persons aged 16 or more (parish).

The Holme family of Paull Holme had a long and impressive pedigree but a relatively modest estate. In the Civil War they came out in support of the king despite the threat presented by the parliamentary garrison at Hull. Christopher Holme (1591-1657) lived in the royalist garrison at York while his son Henry (1623-1678) appeared in arms.

In 1643 the royalists established a fort at Paull in furtherance of their aim of gaining control of Hull but this was destroyed by Parliament's warships.

In 1676 it was reported that there were 20 Quakers in the parish who consisted of tailors, shoemakers and weavers.

Church St Andrew and St Mary: Perpendicular.

In a Commonwealth survey of benefices the commissioners noted that the church had been 'burnt at the raising of Hull seidge, since which tyme the people have assembled in the minister's house'. Materials from the old church were used in the construction of a new church on a different site.

(*East Riding Antiquarian Society Transactions*, iv (1896), 57.)

POCKLINGTON   Harthill

A market town where quarter sessions were held. The parish of Pocklington included several hamlets. 1672: 168 households in Pocklington, 10 in Meltonby and 21 in Yapham.

By virtue of a charter of 1303 the town had a Saturday market and an annual fair. In the 17th century the fair was held on 25 July.

Church All Saints: Norman, Early English and Perpendicular.

The parish was subject to the peculiar jurisdiction of a Prebendary of York.

School A free grammar school founded in 1514 on the initiative of Dr John Dolman (or Dowman), Archdeacon of Suffolk. By a parliamentary act of 1552 it was placed under the control of the Master and fellows of St John's College, Cambridge.

The school attracted pupils from all parts of the county, many of them the sons of gentry. In the years 1650 to 1652 it admitted a total of 98 boys.

Principal family The Dolmans, who were a Catholic family, had long been connected with Pocklington where they owned considerable property. During the early 17th century they lived mainly in the West Riding but after selling the manor of Badsworth in 1653 they moved to Pocklington. In 1672 their house had 11 taxable hearths. (For a fuller account of the family see under Badsworth.)

(A. F. Leach, 'The Foundation and Re-foundation of Pocklington Grammar School', *East Riding Antiquarian Society Transactions*, v (1897). H. Lawrance, 'Pocklington School Admission Register, 1626-1717', *YAJ*, xxv (1920). P. C. Sands and C. M. Haworth, *A History of Pocklington School, East Riding 1514-1950* (1951).)

PRESTON   Holderness

A large village situated to the east of Hull and the north of Hedon. The parish of Preston included the town of Hedon and the hamlet of Lelley. In the 17th century the vicar of Preston usually put in a curate to officiate at the parochial chapel of St Augustine, Hedon. 1673: 127 households in Preston and 20 in Lelley.

Henry Hibbert, who was instituted as vicar of Preston in 1625, supported the king in the Civil War despite his Puritan sympathies. In 1643 he complained in a petition which he submitted to the Earl of Newcastle that he had been forced out of his living on account of his loyalty to the Crown and his conformity to the discipline of the Church.

Church All Saints: Norman in origin; Early English, Decorated and Perpendicular. The parish was subject to the peculiar jurisdiction of the Subdean of York.
(*YASRS*, lxi (1920), 155-6.)

REIGHTON   Dickering

A village situated between Bridlington and Filey. The parish of Reighton extended eastwards to the coast but contained no other village. 1672: 39 households (township of Reighton).
Church St Peter: Norman and Early English.

RICCALL   Ouse and Derwent

A village to the north of Selby. There was no other village within the parish. 1672: 126 households (township of Riccall).

On the east bank of the Ouse is Riccall 'where Harold Haardread arrived with a numerous fleet of the Danes' (William Camden).

In 1350 Riccall had been granted the right to hold a weekly market and an annual fair.

The Wormleys of Riccall were minor gentry who appear to have remained uncommitted during the Civil War.

Church St Mary: Norman, Early English and Perpendicular.

The parish was subject to the peculiar jurisdiction of a Prebendary of York. In 1636 the prebend was leased to Henry Wormley.

(YAS Library, MD 248 (h) (deeds of the Wormley family).)

RILLINGTON   Buckrose

A village to the north-east of Malton. The parish of Rillington included the village and chapelry of Scampston. 1672: 61 households in Rillington and 49 in Scampston. 1676: 150 persons aged 16 or more (parish).

Since 1253 Scampston had enjoyed the right to hold a weekly market and an annual fair.

In 1656 Philip Wheath, who was lord of the manor of Rillington, and the other freeholders entered into an agreement for the enclosure of the wastes and commons. Among other things, Wheath was allocated 70 acres out of the commons and Richard Etherington 49 acres. At the same time it was agreed that Etherington, who owned the impropriate rectory, should continue to enjoy all manner of tithes within the lordship.

In the reign of Charles II Sir Henry St Quintin, whose family had long been seated at Harpham, built himself a mansion at Scampston and settled there. (For the St Quintin family see the entry for Burton Agnes).
Church St Andrew: Norman and Decorated.
(N. A. Hudleston, *Rillington* (1954). C.5/45/80)

RISE   Holderness

A village to the east of Beverley. 1672: 30 households (township of Rise). 1676: 70 persons aged 16 or more (parish of Rise).
Church St Mary: 14th century.
Principal family Bethell of Rise Hall. Estate revenue: £1800 a year (1679).

Roger Bethell (c.1565-1627), who was a younger son of the Bethells of Ellerton, acquired a long lease of the Crown manor of Rise and took up residence there in the reign of James I.

In the Civil War the Bethells came out in support of Parliament, though Hugh Bethell (1589-1659) was much less actively involved than his son Sir Hugh (1615-1679). The latter, who attained the rank of colonel, fought at the battle of Marston Moor and was later made governor of Scarborough Castle. In 1652 he was appointed sheriff of Yorkshire and in 1654 he was named as one of the East Riding commissioners for the removal of scandalous ministers. In 1658 he was 'knighted' by Richard Cromwell but at the beginning of 1660 he took part in the Yorkshire rising in favour of a free Parliament and was given the command of a regiment of horse by General Monck.

Following the Restoration the king rewarded him for his services with a knighthood, an outright grant of the manor of Rise and the renewal of a Crown lease at a nominal rent. Sir Hugh also secured substantial amounts of property through his marriage to an heiress, Mary Michelburne, and a continuing programme of land purchases.

Some expenditure accounts which were kept on his behalf record details of commodities which were bought in, including meat and ale from Beverley, butter from Hornsea and clothes from Hull.

Sir Hugh had no surviving issue and in his will (1679) designated his nephew Hugh Bethell (1649-1717) as his heir and executor.

In 1686 the latter began legal proceedings against a number of persons who he claimed had kept large amounts of money belonging to his uncle. The defendants included Anne Crouch, a relative, who Sir Hugh had employed for several years before his death 'to take the oversight of his affaires and to Inspect the Mannagement thereof and to receive great summes of his money for his use'.

Rise Hall A gabled house of two storeys which was probably Jacobean.
In 1672 Sir Hugh Bethell was taxed on 13 hearths.

(East Riding of Yorkshire Archives Service, Bethell of Rise MSS. Barbara English, *The Great Landowners of East Yorkshire 1530-1910* (1990). BL, Harleian MSS 6288, fols. 88-90 and 94. C.10/270/6 and 272/13. C.38/223/23 February 1687/8).

ROOS   Holderness

A village situated between Hedon and the coast. The parish of Roos included a large part of the hamlet of Owstwick. 1672: 57 households in Roos and 17 in Owstwick. 1676: 200 persons aged 16 or more (parish).

In the 17th century the manor of Roos belonged to the Earls of Exeter who were also patrons of the living.

One of the most notable rectors of Roos was Anthony Stevenson, a Puritan divine who had been master of Hull Grammar School in the years 1633 to 1646. He had considerable medical expertise and when treating the poorer members of his congregation he declined to accept any payment. In 1662 he was ejected from the living on account of his nonconformity.

Churches All Saints: Early English, Decorated and Perpendicular.

In the reign of Charles II a Quaker meeting house was built in Owstwick and this became the main centre for the Holderness monthly meeting.

Schools There were schoolmasters at Roos in 1604 and 1654.

(A. G. Matthews, *Calamy Revised* (1934), 463.)

ROUTH   Holderness

A village to the north-east of Beverley. There was no other village within the parish. 1672: 45 households (township of Routh). 1676: 130 persons aged 16 or more (parish).

Church All Saints: Early English.

ROWLEY   Harthill

A decayed village to the north-west of Hull which was largely uninhabited. The parish of Rowley included the village of Little Weighton and several hamlets. 1672: 7 households in Bentley, 34 in Little Weighton and 6 in Risby. 1676: 155 persons aged 16 or more (parish of Rowley).

In 1638 Ezekiel Rogers, the Puritan rector of Rowley, departed for New England, taking some members of his congregation with him.

Church St Peter: Early English and Perpendicular.

Principal family Ellerker of Risby Hall. Estate revenue: £600 a year (1630); £700 a year (1654).

The Ellerkers were a Catholic family.

Sir Ralph Ellerker (c.1560-1641) had a recusant wife but for much of his life he took refuge in outward conformity.

In 1617 Sir William Acclom of Moreby alleged in a Star Chamber suit that Ellerker, a man of 'greate potencie' who owned the manor of Stillingfleet, had been responsible for stirring up opposition to his enclosing activities with the result that a full-scale riot had broken out.

Sir Ralph finally emerged as an open Catholic in 1630 when he was required to pay a composition rent of £50 a year. In 1637 he and his son Ralph and five other members of his family were presented as recusants.

Ralph Ellerker (1583-1654) took no part in the Civil War but two-thirds of his estate were sequestered for his recusancy. He had no issue and was succeeded by his nephew John Ellerker who claimed in a petition which he submitted in 1654 that he had been brought up as a Protestant, though in fact he had a Catholic father.

John Ellerker had no male issue and the estate eventually passed to Sir James Bradshaw, the son of a Chester alderman, who had married his daughter Dorothy.

At the time of the Monmouth Rebellion in 1685 the East Riding deputy lieutenants were instructed to arrest Bradshaw as a person who was disaffected.

Risby Hall In 1672 the house had 15 taxable hearths.

About 1684 Sir James Bradshaw built a new house on a different site.

The deer park at Risby Hall was first enclosed in the mid-16th century.

(A. Searle (ed.), *Barrington Family Letters, 1628-1632, Camden Fourth Series* (*Royal Historical Society*), vol. 28 (1983), 128-30, 167-8, 198-9, 225-6, 257-8. J. T. Cliffe, *The Puritan Gentry* (1984), 21-2, 44, 66, 71, 135-6, 159, 205. STAC 8/40/9.)

RUDSTON   Dickering

A Wolds village to the west of Bridlington with the distinguishing feature of a Bronze Age monolith in its churchyard. 'More inward into the Land is Rudston, where in the Church-yard is a kind of Pyramidal-stone of great height' (Edmund Gibson, 1695). The parish of Rudston included the depopulated villages of Caythorpe and Thorpe. 1672: 64 households (Rudston and Caythorpe).

The Constables of Caythorpe were a Catholic family but the manor and impropriate rectory of Rudston belonged to a major Puritan family, the Boyntons of Barmston.

Church All Saints: Norman, Early English and Decorated.

School For most of the 17th century Rudston had a school which was run by the parish clerk and funded by the community.

RUSTON PARVA Dickering

A village to the north-east of Great Driffield. There was no other village within the parish. 1672: 30 households (township of Ruston Parva).
Church St Nicholas: Norman in origin.
The minister was a perpetual curate.

SANCTON Harthill

A village to the south of Market Weighton. The parish of Sancton included Houghton and North Cliffe. 1672: 50 households in Sancton and Houghton and 22 in North Cliffe. 1676: 137 persons aged 16 or more (parish).
The manor of Sancton belonged to the Archbishop of York.
In the late 17th century the Langdales of Langthorpe, a leading Catholic family, moved to Houghton Hall which had formerly been a secondary house and took in a resident chaplain to meet their spiritual needs.
Church All Saints: Norman, Early English and Perpendicular.
School There had been a schoolmaster at Sancton in the reign of Elizabeth.
At the beginning of the 17th century Marmaduke Langdale had a schoolhouse built and in his will (1609) he founded a free grammar school for the instruction of boys from poor families in reading, writing and accounts. Provision was made for the payment of a stipend of £20 a year to the master who was to be an ordained minister and a preacher of God's Word.
In 1620 Simon Simpson was ordained and licensed to serve as vicar and schoolmaster of Sancton. A man of Puritan temperament, he was still there in 1650.
(J. G. Hall, *A History of South Cave and of Other Parishes in the East Riding of the County of York* (1892). W. K. Jordan, *The Charities of Rural England 1480-1660* (1961), 329-30.)

SCORBOROUGH Harthill

A small village to the north of Beverley. 1672: 19 households (township of Scorborough). 1676: 50 persons aged 16 or more (parish of Scorborough).
Church St Leonard: Norman in origin.
Principal family Hotham of Scorborough Hall (baronetcy 1622). Estate revenue: £2000 a year (1609); £2600 a year (1645); £2000 a year (1680).

Sir John Hotham (1589-1645) was a minor at his father's death in 1609 but since he was already married he managed to escape the attentions of the Court of Wards. In all, he married five times and this was a major factor in the growth of his personal fortune.

Clarendon wrote of him that he was 'by his nature and education a rough and a rude man; of great covetousness, of great pride, and great ambition; without any bowels of good nature, or the least sense or touch of generosity .... he was a man of craft, and more like to deceive than to be cozened'. According to Bulstrode Whitelocke he was highly unpopular on account of his rough carriage and 'very narrow living'.

In 1627 he was committed to prison for opposing the forced loan but when he was pricked as sheriff of Yorkshire in 1634 he willingly applied himself to the task of collecting ship money. In May 1635 he informed Wentworth that 'I have now executed the writs for the shipping businesse with all the industrie and dilligence that a man resolute and affectionate to his majesties service Could doe'.

In 1639 Wentworth observed that while Sir John was rather too self-willed 'he is very honest, faithful and hearty, which way soever he inclines' and that he felt certain that he could ensure his loyalty. The following year, however, he came out in opposition to ship money and as a result was stripped of all his offices and briefly imprisoned.

The decision of the Long Parliament to appoint him governor of Hull proved to be a momentous step. In April 1642 he refused to allow the king to enter the town and was immediately declared a traitor. Even so, he was a reluctant rebel who had no liking for Puritans or their aspirations. His eldest son John (1610-1645) was at first more deeply committed to the parliamentary cause. He embarked on military forays from the early stages of the war and rapidly attained the rank of lieutenant general. From December 1642 onwards, however, he was engaged in secret correspondence with a royalist general, William Earl of Newcastle, about the need for a peace treaty and told him that 'there is no man that hath any reasonable share in the Common Wealth can desire that either side shall be absolute conquerors ... I honour the King, and love the Parliament, but doe not desire to see either absolute conqueror'. In June 1643 the Hothams were arrested as suspected traitors to the cause and two years later they were both executed.

Sir Hugh Cholmley later wrote that the father 'was a man that loved libertie, which was an occation to make him ioyne att first with the puritan partie, to whome after he became neerer lincked meerely for his owne interest and security, for in more than concerned the civill libertie hee did not approve of their wayes'. Sir Henry Slingsby was of the same opinion, stressing that he was not at all in favour of changes in the ecclesiastical field.

At the time of his arrest Sir John had a large personal estate which was said to be worth at least £10,000. This included £4800 in ready money and stock in the East India Company. Shortly before his death he settled a substantial amount of landed property on his younger sons, apparently in the hope that it would escape sequestration.

Over a period of some years this property gradually reverted to the main branch of the family and Sir John Hotham (1632-1689) further increased his estate revenue by purchase and enclosure. He was a political radical who was strongly anti-Catholic. In 1663 he was imprisoned along with others for allegedly plotting a rebellion but was soon released. After a period of exile in James II's reign he accompanied the Prince of Orange on his journey to England in 1688.

His son Sir John (1655-1691) fell heavily into debt, mainly as a result of his improvidence. He also quarrelled with his wife who claimed in legal proceedings that the marriage had never been consummated on account of his impotence. In 1691 he went over to Holland where he died.

Since he had no issue the estate passed to his kinsman Sir Charles Hotham (1663-1723) who was a fellow of St John's College, Cambridge.

Scorborough Hall The Hothams, who had been seated at Scorborough since the 12th century, built a new two-storeyed house about the end of Elizabeth's reign.

The hall was damaged in the Civil War but was soon repaired. In 1672 Sir John Hotham was taxed on 24 hearths.

The house was completely destroyed by fire in 1705.

(Hull University Archives, Hotham MSS. P. Roebuck, *Yorkshire Baronets 1640-1760* (1980). P. Saltmarshe, *History and Chartulary of the Family of Hothams* (1914). W. D. Macray (ed.), *The History of the Rebellion and Civil Wars in England .... by Edward, Earl of Clarendon* (1888), ii, 261-3. Bulstrode Whitelocke, *Memorials of the English Affairs* (1853), i, 206. Sheffield Archives, Wentworth Woodhouse Collection, Strafford Letters, xv, Hotham to Wentworth, 5 May 1635. A. M. W. Stirling, *The Hothams* (1918). *YASRS*, cliii (2000), 131. D. Parsons (ed.), *The Diary of Sir Henry Slingsby* (1836), 92. C.6/191/20. C.10/463/49.)

SCRAYINGHAM   Buckrose

A village between York and Malton. The parish of Scrayingham included the villages of Howsham and Leppington. 1672: 27 households in Scrayingham, 29 in Howsham and 24 in Leppington. 1676: 227 persons aged 16 or more (parish of Scrayingham).

Church St Peter: Norman with later medieval features.

Principal family Bamburgh of Howsham Hall (baronetcy 1619). Estate revenue: £1300 a year (1631).

The family mainly owed their landed wealth to Thomas Bamburgh, a Suffolk man who for many years served the Earls of Rutland as the steward of their Yorkshire estates. In 1572 he bought the manor of Howsham from Edward Earl of Rutland and by the time of his death in 1593 had acquired several manors in the North Riding.

His son Sir William (1570-1623) purchased further property and built Howsham Hall. In his will (1623) he assigned one-third of the estate to his wife, Dame Mary, as her jointure and settled the remainder with the declared intention of facilitating negotiations with the Court of Wards over the wardship and marriage of the heir.

Any hopes of founding a dynasty were soon dashed with the deaths of his two sons Sir Thomas (1612-1624) and Sir John (1613-1631) while they were still wards of the Crown. In 1633 the Court of Wards ruled that the heirs were Sir William's only surviving daughter, Dame Katherine Hotham, and his grandchildren Thomas Wentworth of North Elmsall and William Robinson of Newby. At its direction a jury was assembled for the purpose of dividing the whole estate into three parts. In 1643, however, William Robinson died unmarried and two years later the Court of Wards reallocated his share to Thomas Wentworth and Sir Thomas Norcliffe of Langton who was Lady Hotham's eldest son by her first husband. Under the new arrangements for partitioning the estate the manor of Howsham was divided equally between the two heirs, though as previously agreed Wentworth was allowed to take over the hall.

In the event the Hothams kept hold of Norcliffe's share and it was not until 1652 that he was able to gain possession of the property.

Howsham Hall A two-storeyed Jacobean mansion built about 1612. Sir William Bamburgh is said to have used materials taken from Kirkham Priory.

In 1672 Dame Katherine Wentworth was taxed on 24 hearths.

The Bamburghs had a bowling green adjoining the house.

(BIHR, York Registry, will of Sir William Bamburgh, 25 January 1622/3. Wards 5/49. Wards 9/98/fols. 15, 16 and 250b. Wards 9/557/475. YAS Library, MD 237(c) and MS 721.)

SCULCOATES   Harthill

A hamlet situated near Hull. There was no other centre of population within the parish. 1672: 15 households (township of Sculcoates). In a Commonwealth survey of benefices the commissioners observed that 'there is in Sculcotts but eight or nine houses.'

The Carthusian priory of Sculcoates had been dissolved in 1539.

During the course of the 17th century much of the parish was enclosed.

The Alureds of Charterhouse, who were the main landed proprietors in Sculcoates, were reported to have an income of £400 to £500 a year. They were a Puritan family whose political views became increasingly radical. In 1626 Henry Alured (1581-1628) was hoping to secure a knighthood but the soundings made on his behalf failed to achieve the desired result. The following year the Privy Council was informed that he was unwilling to contribute to the forced loan. In 1638 his son John (1607-c.1654) was required to appear before the Council to answer an accusation that he had openly praised the Scottish rebels.

In the Civil War John Alured served as a colonel in the parliamentarian army and as a member of the East Riding committee. He also represented Hedon in the Long Parliament and in 1649 sat in judgement on the king and signed the death-warrant.

By his own early death he escaped the punishment meted out to the regicides but in 1668 his son John sold the Sculcoates estate to a Catholic landowner, John Dalton of Swine.

As patrons of the living of Sculcoates the Alureds displayed a marked preference for godly preaching ministers, among them John Spofford and Robert Luddington. In 1643 the latter sought refuge in Hull where he served as pastor of an Independent congregation until his death in 1663.

Church St Mary: possibly Early English.

(*East Riding Antiquarian Society Transactions*, ii (1894), 34. *HMC, Coke MSS*, i, 248. PRO, State Papers Domestic, Charles I, S.P.16/lxviii/51 and lxxi/64. *CSP Dom, 1637-8*, 558, 574. R. A. Marchant, *The Puritans and the Church Courts in the Diocese of York 1560-1642* (1960), 261, 280.)

SEATON ROSS   Harthill

A village to the west of Market Weighton. There was no other village within the parish. 1672: 77 households (township of Seaton Ross). 1676: 188 persons aged 16 or more (parish).

Church St Edmund: probably early medieval.

The minister was a perpetual curate.

SETTRINGTON   Buckrose

A village to the east of Malton. The parish of Settrington included the village of Scagglethorpe. 1672: 69 households in Settrington and 28 in Scagglethorpe. 1676: 290 persons aged 16 or more (parish)

The manor of Settrington belonged to the Crown until 1603. In 1600 a survey was undertaken which revealed that the unenclosed open fields covered an area of some 2700 acres, consisting of 1697 acres of arable land, 151 acres of meadow and 916 acres of pasture. The village then contained 78 houses and cottages.

In the Civil War the rector, John Carter, remained loyal to the Crown and was alleged to have provided the royalist forces with a man and a horse. As a result he was deprived of his living and imprisoned. In a petition which he submitted to the king after the

Restoration he stressed that another factor responsible for his vicissitudes was his acceptance of the doctrine and discipline of the Church.

In a Commonwealth survey of benefices the commissioners observed that 'We conceive it fitt that Scagglethorpe and Thorp Bassett be united into one parish, being but one mile apart and the way very good'. In the event the parochial arrangements remained unchanged.

In 1668 the owners of land in Settrington entered into an agreement for the enclosure of the greater part of the meadow and pasture grounds within the open fields. Two years later the agreement was formally endorsed by the Court of Chancery.

Church All Saints: Early English and Perpendicular.

School During the reign of Charles I Anthony Collinson kept a private school at Settrington.

(H. King and A. Harris (eds.). *A Survey of the Manor of Settrington*, YASRS, cxxvi (1962). *East Riding Antiquarian Society Transactions*, ii (1894), 63. A. G. Matthews, *Walker Revised* (1988), 391. *CSP Dom, 1660-1*, 219 and *CSP Dom, 1661-2*, 28.)

SHERBURN   Buckrose

A Wolds village on the road between Malton and Filey. There was no other village within the parish. 1672: 57 households (township of Sherburn). 1676: 140 persons aged 16 or more (parish).

The Constables of Sherburn were minor gentry who held long leases of the manor which belonged to the Crown. In 1629 Francis Constable, who was a gentleman usher in the queen's household, was granted a new lease for three lives. This was considered to be worth £160 a year over and above the rent of £36 a year.

In the Civil War his son Sidney took the royalist side.

Church St Hilda: Norman, Early English, Decorated and Perpendicular. There may possibly have been a Saxon church on the same site.

(BL, Harleian MSS 6288, fols. 61-5. Guildhall Library, London, Royal Contract Estates, Rentals, Box 7.11, Surveys, Yorkshire and Lincolnshire, 1639, p.19.)

SIGGLESTHORNE   Holderness

A small village to the west of Hornsea. The parish of Sigglesthorne included the hamlets of Catfoss, Little Hatfield, Seaton and Wassand and most of Great Hatfield. A chapel at Great Hatfield was destroyed by fire about the beginning of the 17th century and was never rebuilt. 1672: 27 households in Sigglesthorne, 9 in Catfoss, 29 in Great and Little Hatfield and 27 in Seaton and Wassand. 1676: 150 persons aged 16 or more (parish).

In 1314 Sigglesthorne had been granted the right to hold an annual fair.

In the early 17th century three gentry families with the surname of Constable were seated in the parish: the Constables of Catfoss, the Constables of Wassand and the Constables of Great Hatfield who died out in the male line in 1642. These were families of relatively modest estate with incomes of not more than £300 or £400 a year. In 1639 Christopher Constable of Great Hatfield began proceedings in the Court of Chivalry against his kinsman John Constable of Catfoss who he alleged had unlawfully assumed the style of esquire and as a result had 'taken place and used precedency' in both York and London. After a full investigation the Court ruled that both men were entitled to style themselves esquire.

Catfoss Hall and Wassand Hall were rebuilt in the early 17th century.

Church St Lawrence: mainly Early English. The chancel was rebuilt in brick during the reign of Elizabeth and the tower was restored in 1676.

One of the rectors, Dr Phineas Hodgson, was appointed Chancellor of York Minster in 1611; served as a member of the Council in the North; and established a charity for the relief of prisoners.

(G. D. Squibb, *The High Court of Chivalry* (1959), 56. W. K. Jordan, *The Charities of Rural England 1480-1660* (1961), 284-5.)

SKEFFLING   Holderness

A village situated in the southern tip of the Holderness promontory. The parish of Skeffling, which extended as far as the Humber estuary, contained no other centre of population. 1672: 36 households (township of Skeffling). 1676: 52 persons aged 16 or more (parish).

Burstall Priory, which was an establishment of Benedictine monks, may have been closed down as early as 1396.

Church St Helen: Perpendicular. The church had been consecrated in 1470. The minister was a perpetual curate with a meagre stipend.

SKERNE   Harthill

A hamlet to the south-east of Great Driffield. There was no other centre of population within the parish. 1672: 36 households (township of Skerne). 1676: 38 persons aged 16 or more (parish).

Church St Leonard: Norman, Early English, Decorated and Perpendicular.

The minister was a perpetual curate who was paid only £20 a year. In the Commonwealth period it was reported that the curate, Samuel Booth, preached after a fashion.

SKIPSEA   Holderness

A coastal village between Bridlington and Hornsea. The parish of Skipsea included the villages and hamlets of Bonwick, Dringhoe, Skipsea Brough and Upton and part of Ulrome. At Ulrome there was a medieval chapel. 1672: 69 households in Skipsea, 46 in Ulrome and 27 in Upton. 1676: 252 persons aged 16 or more, including 28 Protestant dissenters (parish).

A Norman fortress had been demolished in the 13th century and apparently never restored. By the 17th century most of the masonry had probably been removed.

In 1338 Skipsea had been granted the right to hold a weekly market and two annual fairs.

Two leading Quakers, George Fox and William Dewsbury, visited Skipsea and Ulrome and this probably accounts for the dissenters recorded in the census return of 1676.

About Skipsea 'they have a tradition of a town call'd Hide being devour'd by the Sea' (Edmund Gibson, 1695). Hyde or Hythe, a hamlet within the parish of Skipsea, had been completely engulfed before the end of the 14th century.

Church All Saints: Norman and Perpendicular.

SKIPWITH   Ouse and Derwent

A village to the north-east of Selby. The parish of Skipwith included the village of North Duffield. 1672: 48 households in Skipwith and 59 in North Duffield.

The Skipwiths of Skipwith were a declining gentry family. In the Civil War Willoughby Skipwith (1613-1658), who had been a ward of the Crown, fought on the royalist side and compounded for a sadly reduced estate.

Charters of 1294, 1313 and 1363 had conferred on North Duffield the right to hold a weekly market and an annual fair and this right was still being exercised in the 17th century.

In 1614 Sir William Constable of Flamborough sold the manor of North Duffield and for this purpose a particular of the estate was drawn up which gave the value as £580 a year and set the sale price at £9250. The property included a manor-house with orchards and extensive demesnes, a coney warren and a windmill. Much of the land, particularly within the demesnes, was divided into closes.

Church St Helen: Saxon, Norman, Decorated and Perpendicular.

The parish was subject to the peculiar jurisdiction of the Dean and Chapter of Durham.

(S.P.23/clxxxi/215, 221. YAS Library, MD59/19.)

SKIRPENBECK   Buckrose

A village to the north-east of York. There was no other village within the parish. 1672: 47 households (township of Skirpenbeck). 1676: 80 persons aged 16 or more (parish).

A neighbouring landowner, Sir Edward Payler of Thoralby, held various leases of property belonging to the Crown manor of Skirpenbeck. In 1629 he bought the manor. (See the entry for Bugthorpe.)

Church St Mary: Norman.

(BL, Harleian MSS 6288, fols. 74-7.)

SLEDMERE   Buckrose

A Wolds village situated between Malton and Bridlington. There was no other village within the parish. 1672: 52 households (township of Sledmere).

In 1303 Sledmere had been granted the right to hold a weekly market and an annual fair.

Church St Mary: Norman in origin.

In the Commonwealth period it was reported that the curate in charge was allowed only £10 a year by the impropriators.

SOUTH CAVE   Harthill

A village to the west of Hull. The parish of South Cave, which extended as far as the Humber estuary, included the village of Broomfleet (where there was a medieval chapel) and the hamlet of Faxfleet at the confluence of the Rivers Ouse and Trent. 1672: 112 households in South Cave, 36 in Broomfleet and 14 in Faxfleet.

Charters of 1291 and 1314 had conferred on South Cave the right to hold a weekly market and an annual fair and in 1301 Faxfleet had also been granted this right. In 1642 Henry Best of Elmswell wrote that 'On Trinity-munday ther is a Faire att South-Cave att which are many sheepe bought and sold. Horses allsoe goe well of there, and especially Mares'.

There were two manors in South Cave, East Hall and West Hall. In 1615 the wives of their respective owners, Thomas Danby and Nicholas Girlington, were presented for refusing to take communion and subsequently Margaret Danby emerged as a recusant. There were, however, relatively few Catholics in the parish.

By 1661 Francis Harrison had purchased both manors and as a result had become the main landed proprietor in South Cave.

In the Commonwealth period it was proposed that the chapelry of Broomfleet should be converted into a parish which would include Faxfleet. In the event no action was taken.

Church All Saints: Norman, Early English, Decorated and Perpendicular.

The parish was subject to the peculiar jurisdiction of the Dean and Chapter of York.

Schools During the first half of the 17th century the successive vicars of South Cave, Thomas Flint, Thomas Brabbs and John Seaman, all kept a private school there. In the Commonwealth period it was reported that Seaman preached on Lord's Days at South Cave.

(J. G. Hall, *A History of South Cave* (1892). D. Woodward (ed.), *The Farming and Memorandum Books of Henry Best of Elmswell, 1642* (1984), 118. Eleanor M. Reader, *Broomfleet and Faxfleet: Two Townships Through Two Thousand Years* (1972).)

SOUTH DALTON   Harthill

A village to the north-west of Market Weighton. There was no other village within the parish. 1672: 44 households (township of South Dalton). 1676: 100 persons aged 16 or more (parish).

In the reign of James I Richard Cholmley of Brandsby in the North Riding employed William Swale to carry out a survey of his manor of South Dalton. Swale reported that the manor contained 598 acres and that it was currently worth £148 a year. In the light of the survey Cholmley observed that if all the grounds lying in 'the Flatts' (which were then worth £76 6s 9d a year) 'were exchanged, layd together and inclosed, they would be better by a fourtht part then they be valued at here'.

Church St Mary: Perpendicular.

School Both before and after the restoration of the monarchy in 1660 the rector, Thomas Callis, kept a private school at South Dalton.

(*The Memorandum Book of Richard Cholmeley of Brandsby 1602-1623* (North Yorkshire County Record Office Publications No. 44) (1988), 13.)

SPROATLEY   Holderness

A small village situated to the north of Hedon. 1672: 37 households. 1676: 100 persons aged 16 or more.

The Constables of Burton Constable, whose park lay close to the village, owned property in Sproatley and were patrons of the living. Although they were a Catholic family the villagers were almost exclusively Protestant in religion.

Church St Swithin: Norman in origin.

STILLINGFLEET   Ouse and Derwent

A village to the south of York. The parish of Stillingfleet included the villages of Acaster Selby (in the West Riding), Kelfield and Moreby. 1672: 49 households in Stillingfleet (including Moreby) and 30 in Kelfield. 1676: 250 persons aged 16 or more (parish of Stillingfleet).

Church St Helen: Norman, Early English, Decorated and Perpendicular. The Moreby chapel was founded in 1336.

Principal families (1) Acclom of Moreby Hall. Estate revenue: £600 a year (1637).

Sir William Acclom (1582-1637) was involved in an acrimonious property dispute with Sir Ralph Ellerker, a Catholic squire who owned the manor of Stillingfleet. In a Star Chamber suit of 1617 he related that he had enclosed and ditched certain waste grounds called the Little Moor within his manor of Moreby 'for that therby a greater proffitt and comoditie would arise to your said subiect'. He had given Sir Ralph prior notice of his intentions and had been at pains to ensure that there was no adverse impact on customary rights of way. Sir Ralph, however, had urged the freeholders and tenantry of his manor of Stillingfleet to resist the enclosure and had proposed that £400 or £500 should be collected for the purpose of maintaining suits against him. Subsequently a crowd armed with assorted weapons had assembled in the vicinity of Moreby Hall and thrown down ditches and fences. In his response one of the defendants claimed that the inhabitants of Stillingfleet had rights of common in the Little Moor for the pasturing of all kinds of cattle.

When the forced loan scheme was launched in 1627 it was reported that Sir William had failed to respond when summoned to appear before the commissioners about his assessment.

Strains and tensions were also in evidence within the family. Sir William was embroiled in a financial dispute with his married sister, Margaret Durdent, which resulted in litigation in the Court of Chancery. Later on his wife, Dame Elizabeth, sought to persuade him to break an ancient entail in order to make it possible for his daughters to inherit the estate. Sir William, however, was unwilling to make any change.

While his daughter Isabel was staying with her grandfather, Sir Thomas Dawney, at Cowick Hall she secretly married one of his servants, John Nelson. This was regarded as so shocking that Sir William disowned her.

Following his father's death John Acclom (1618-1643) was made a ward of the Crown. His own premature demise was not apparently due to any involvement in the Civil War. He left an infant daughter, Elizabeth, whose maternal grandfather, Henry Wormley, assumed the guardianship. Wormley entered into possession of the estate and purchased her wardship from the Court of Wards.

On hearing of his brother's death Thomas Acclom, who considered himself to be the lawful heir, searched Moreby Hall for any relevant deeds but found that Wormley had forestalled him. In view of his support for the royalist cause the parliamentarians sequestered the estate on the assumption that it was his inheritance.

The estate eventually came into the possession of Sir Mark Milbanke of Halnaby in the North Riding who married Elizabeth Acclom in 1659.

(2) Stillington of Kelfield Hall. Estate revenue: £650 a year (1636).

William Stillington was a zealous Catholic who was frequently imprisoned. In 1604 he was described as 'the arch-recusant'.

In 1612 he was committed to York Castle after refusing to take the oath of allegiance. Following his conviction he automatically forfeited his estate to the Crown and in 1614 it was granted to a courtier, Henry Gibb. Shortly afterwards his nephew John Stillington (c.1594-1658) persuaded Gibb to surrender his interest in return for a payment of £600 but was then involved in litigation with the trustees to whom the manor of Kelfield had been conveyed.

By 1622 William Stillington was dead and, in accordance with his wishes, had been succeeded by his nephew who had a very different religious outlook.

In 1627 it was reported that John Stillington was refusing to contribute to the forced loan. During the Civil War he served as a member of the East Riding parliamentary committee and in 1654 he was named as one of the commissioners for the removal of scandalous ministers.

Moreby Hall The house, which was sometimes called Moreby Grange, appears to have been Tudor in origin. Since there is no reference to it in the hearth tax returns it seems likely that Sir Mark Milbanke ordered its demolition.

There was a park adjoining the house.

Kelfield Hall In 1672 Thomas Stillington was taxed on 10 hearths.

(STAC 8/40/9. Wards 5/49. C.22/759/6, 13 and 38. E.178/4864. C.3/380/3.)

SUTTON ON HULL   Holderness

A village on the northern outskirts of Hull. The parish of Sutton included the village of Stoneferry. 1672: 82 households in Sutton and 48 in Stoneferry. In 1676 it was reported that there were 42 Protestant dissenters in the parish.

'Sutton is about two miles from Hull and stands upon a hill of about a thousand acres' (Abraham de la Pryme, 1700).

In 1643 parliamentarian troops under the command of Sir Thomas Fairfax were quartered at Sutton and Stoneferry.

In an Exchequer case of 1653 it was said that in the early 17th century most of the inhabitants of Sutton were 'poor men of mean and small estate'.

The parish had a Quaker community from the 1650s onwards. In the late 17th century there was a Quaker burial ground at Stoneferry.

At Stoneferry there was a ferry which provided passage across the River Hull.
Church St James: Decorated and Perpendicular.
'The church is built of brick, but for such a little town is pretty larg, great and handsome' (Abraham de la Pryme, 1700).
The minister was a perpetual curate.
(T. Blashill, *Sutton-in-Holderness* (1900).)

SUTTON UPON DERWENT   Harthill

A village on the River Derwent to the east of York. 1672: 57 households (township of Sutton). 1676: 130 persons aged 16 or more (parish of Sutton).
Church St Michael: Norman and Perpendicular. In 1676 the church was said to be out of repair.
Principal family Vaughan of Sutton Hall (and Whitwell Hall, North Riding). Estate revenue: £1000 a year (1610); £400 a year (1657).
The Vaughans had moved from Wales to Yorkshire about the middle of the 16th century.
Sir Henry Vaughan (1581-c.1656) was made a ward of the Crown following the death of his father in 1597 while engaged in military operations in Ireland.
When his son John married Douglas Palmes in 1624 he allowed him to take over the manor of Sutton and moved to Whitwell Hall. During the reign of Charles I John Vaughan borrowed heavily from Humphrey Shalcrosse, a London scrivener, and mortgaged the manor as security.
In 1639 Sir Henry was involved in litigation over the manor of Whitwell which he had settled on the issue of his second marriage. Dismissing suggestions that it had already been entailed he confirmed that his son Thomas would inherit the manor after his death.
In the Civil War the Vaughans supported the royalist cause and John Vaughan and his sons Francis and Henry appeared in arms.
In 1647 Humphrey Shalcrosse began legal proceedings against John Vaughan who had defaulted on his interest payments. In his reply Vaughan claimed that he had offered to sell the manor of Sutton to him for £5000 over and above the sum of £7030 which he owed him.
Two years later the manor was bought by Thomas Lord Fairfax the parliamentarian general. Subsequently, in 1661, he sold it to George Monck, Duke of Albemarle.
Shortly after the Restoration the male line of the Vaughan family expired.
Sutton Hall The house was probably demolished after the sale of the estate in 1649. There was a park which had existed since the Middle Ages.
(E.178/6128. C.8/49/141.)

SWINE   Holderness

A village to the north-east of Hull. Within the extensive parish of Swine there were a number of hamlets, including Burton Constable and Langthorpe which are separately noticed. Bilton, Marton and South Skirlaugh had medieval chapels. 1672: 29 households in Swine, 17 in Benningholme, 26 in Bilton, 15 in Coniston, 26 in Ellerby, 12 in Ganstead, 14 in Marton, 42 in North Skirlaugh, Rowton and Arnold, 17 in South Skirlaugh, 10 in Thirtleby and 12 in Wyton. 1676: 400 persons aged 16 or more, including 47 recusants (parish).

Swine Priory was a Cistercian nunnery founded in the 12th century and dissolved in 1539. In the 17th century the site of the priory was in the possession of a Catholic family, the Daltons of Swine and Myton.

'The town has formerly been very larg and handsom, as the people report, before the times of the Reformation, tho' now 'tis very mean and inconsiderable, nobody inhabiting the same but a few country clowns'. The 'ruins of a famous old nunnery .... are scarce now visible' (Abraham de la Pryme, 1700).

Church St Mary: Norman, Decorated and Perpendicular. The church had belonged to Swine Priory.

It is 'a larg, capacious and indifferently magnificent church, which by the broken pillars and old arches, now walled up, seems to have been much larger and neater in former times' (Abraham de la Pryme, 1700).

School In his will (1609) Marmaduke Langdale made provision for the establishment of a school at South Skirlaugh (which he described as 'a bare and barren place') for the teaching of poor children of the chapelry.

Principal family Micklethwaite of Swine Hall. Estate revenue: £1200 a year (1660).

The manor of Swine was part of the jointure settled on Dame Elizabeth Darcy, the fourth and last wife of John Lord Darcy of Aston (c.1579-1635). In 1639 it was sold to Dr Joseph Micklethwaite (1594-1658), a physician resident in York. He added considerably to the estate which he inherited from his father.

In the Civil War he served as a parliamentarian captain, along with his brother Elias, and was also a member of the East Riding committee.

His son John (1628-1660), who was a barrister, took up residence at Swine and acted as a justice of the peace during the Interregnum. He was said to have left debts amounting to £4000 or more which had mainly been occasioned by his purchases of landed property.

During the minority of his son Joseph (1656-c.1712) the management of the estate was in the hands of agents employed by his mother's family, the Middletons of Stansted Mountfitchet in Essex. In a Chancery suit of 1669 his uncle Joseph Micklethwaite, acting on his behalf, claimed that one of these agents, Thomas Heath, had been guilty of gross negligence or worse. Two years later similar allegations were made against another agent,

George Cave, who in response presented detailed accounts of the rents which he had collected.

Despite this controversy Joseph Micklethwaite married his cousin Constance Middleton on his coming of age in 1677.

Swine Hall The house may have been rebuilt or enlarged during the 1650s.

In 1673 there were 13 taxable hearths.

(T. Thompson, *A History of the Church and Priory of Swine in Holderness* (1824). G. Poulson, *The History and Antiquities of the Seigniory of Holderness* (1840), 1841), ii, 266-7. C.6/201/57. C.10/159/105. C.33/226/fo.111.)

THORGANBY   Ouse and Derwent

A village situated to the north-east of Selby on the west bank of the River Derwent. The parish of Thorganby included the hamlet of West Cottingwith. 1672: 76 households in Thorganby with West Cottingwith. 1676: 123 persons aged 16 or more (parish).

Thicket Priory in West Cottingwith, which was an establishment of Benedictine nuns, had been founded in the 12th century and dissolved in 1539.

The manor of West Cottingwith had been sold by John Aske in 1596 to John Robinson, a London merchant. In 1622 Humphrey Robinson, a younger son, came into possession of one-half of the manor, including the site of Thicket Priory (the other half was acquired in 1659). The house known as Thicket Hall which became the family seat was described in 1606 as fair and large and it seems likely that it had been built by the Aske family.

Following the death of Humphrey Robinson in 1626 the estate descended to his son Richard who was declared a ward of the Crown. In the early stages of the Civil War he may have been reluctant to commit himself but in June 1645 he was included in the East Riding parliamentary committee. In 1656 a proposal to make him sheriff of Yorkshire led Colonel Robert Lilburne to plead with Cromwell to block the appointment:

> Mr Richard Robinson being pitched upon for sherriffe of this county, it gives distast….to many conscientous people; he being noted amongst them as one somewhat of a lose conversation, and one that is too much addicted to tippling, and that which is called good-fellowship, and was lately accus'd before the commissioners to be somewhat concerned in point of delinquency.

In the event the proposal was abandoned.

Church St Helen: Early English and Perpendicular. In 1690 the church was rebuilt in brick but the Perpendicular west tower was retained.

THORNTON   Harthill

A village to the south-west of Pocklington. The parish of Thornton included a number of villages, one of which, Allerthorpe, had a medieval chapel. 1672: 49 households in Thornton, 31 in Allerthorpe, 73 in Melbourne and Storwood and 13 in Waplington.

In 1616 piecemeal encroachments on the moors of Thornton had resulted in the enclosure of 33 acres. In 1652 the process was completed.

Church St Michael: Norman in origin; Decorated and Perpendicular.

The parish was subject to the peculiar jurisdiction of the Dean of York.

The minister was a perpetual curate who had a modest stipend.
(C.2/James I/A4/56. *Thurloe State Papers* (1742), iv, 397.)

THORPE BASSETT   Buckrose

A small village to the east of Malton. There was no other centre of population within the parish. 1672: 22 households.

John Philips, who served as rector in the years 1583 to 1605, was a Puritan whose preaching was highly regarded among the godly. In her diary Dame Margaret Hoby wrote that on Sunday 18 September 1603 her husband, her mother 'and my selfe, with our sarvants, went to Thorpbasitt wher we hard Mr phileps preach.' In the afternoon they heard him at Wintringham 'wher he Continewede his exercise until 5 a cloke att night'.

Church All Saints: Norman and Early English.

(Dorothy M. Meads (ed.), *Diary of Lady Margaret Hoby 1599-1605* (1930), 205.)

THWING   Dickering

A Wolds village situated to the west of Bridlington. The parish of Thwing included the hamlet of Octon. 1672: 40 households in Thwing and Octon. 1676: 135 persons aged 16 or more (parish).

In 1257 and again in 1292 Thwing was granted the right to hold a weekly market and an annual fair.

Thwing was the birthplace of Thomas Lamplugh (1615-1691) who was Archbishop of York from 1688 to 1691.

Church All Saints: Norman and Perpendicular.

School In 1682 there was an unlicensed schoolmaster at Thwing.

TUNSTALL   Holderness

A village to the east of Hull and a parish bordered by the German Ocean. The parish included the hamlet of Monkwith which, however, had vanished into the sea by the middle of the 17th century. 1673: 42 households (township of Tunstall).

Church All Saints: Norman, Decorated and Perpendicular.

The parish was subject to the peculiar jurisdiction of the Succentor of York Minster.

WALKINGTON   Howdenshire/Harthill

A village to the south-west of Beverley. There was no other village within the parish. 1672: 65 households (township of Walkington).

The patronage rights belonged to a leading Puritan family, the Barringtons of Hatfield Broad Oak in Essex. In the early 17th century two godly preaching ministers served the cure: Francis Nalton who was rector from 1570 to 1616 and William Chantrell who held the living from 1616 to 1643. Chantrell was in regular correspondence with the Barringtons to whom he offered spiritual advice and encouragement. In a letter addressed to Sir Francis Barrington in 1628 he expressed the hope that Parliament would be instrumental in 'the building up our English Zion.' With the country sliding into a civil war it was readily apparent that his sympathies lay entirely with Parliament. Writing to Sir Thomas Barrington he rejoiced in the fact that Sir John Hotham had retained control of Hull which he described as a place of singular importance and told him that he was putting pen to paper 'to stirre up those flames of pietie and holy zeale to god's cause which (I heare) hath not only warmed your frendes in the south but your well willers in this cold north.'

Church All Saints: Norman, Decorated and Perpendicular.

The parish was subject to the peculiar jurisdiction of the Dean and Chapter of Durham.

Schools In his will (1537) William Sherwood had settled some houses and lands for the relief of the poor, including the provision of schooling for their sons.

After his ejection from the living of Kirby Underdale in 1662 Peter Clark retired with his family to Walkington where he had inherited some property. Here he opened a private school and took in gentlemen's sons, some of whom were 'great ornaments and blessings to their country.'

(BL, Egerton MSS 2644, fols. 293, 295; 2645, fols. 23, 203, 226; and 2650, fols. 209, 211, 213-14. R. A. Marchant, *The Puritans and the Church Courts in the Diocese of York, 1560-1642* (1960), 238. A. G. Matthews, *Calamy Revised* (1934), 118.)

WARTER   Harthill

A village to the north-east of Pocklington. 1672: 82 households (township of Warter). 1676: 120 persons aged 16 or more (parish of Warter).

Warter Priory had been founded in 1132 for monks of the Augustinian order.

Church St James: possibly Norman in origin.

Principal family Stapleton of Warter Hall. Estate revenue: £500 a year (1640).

Sir Philip Stapleton (1603-1647), who was a younger son of Henry Stapleton of Wighill, bought the Warter estate in 1630. Clarendon wrote of him that he was 'a proper man, of a fair extraction' who 'spent his time in those delights which horses and dogs administer'.

His marriage in 1629 to a daughter of Sir John Hotham may have been one of the factors which helped to shape his political views.

In the Civil War he was a parliamentarian colonel who commanded troops at the battles of Edgehill and Newbury. He was also an active member of the Long Parliament. Initially regarded as a radical, he eventually emerged as one of the leaders of the Presbyterian party. When threatened with impeachment in 1647 he took ship for Calais where he died of the plague.

After his death he was described as 'a true and zealous Protestant, though not in any way new-fangled'. Roger Morrice, a nonconformist divine, subsequently wrote that 'He was a Brave Man who Espoused not the Professors of Religion as such, though he sheltered and laid out his Interest for them'.

His son John (c.1630-1697), who succeeded him, had daughters but no male issue. The eldest daughter, Isabel, was married to Sir William Pennington of Muncaster in Cumberland and in 1679 he entered into an agreement with his father-in-law for the purchase of the manor and rectory of Warter. In 1691 Sir William claimed in a Chancery suit that Stapleton was conspiring with others to break the agreement. In response Stapleton maintained that he had a life interest in the property but acknowledged that Pennington was entitled to enter into possession after his death.

Warter Hall In 1672 John Stapleton was taxed on 14 hearths.

Towards the end of his life he appears to have carried out major improvements. A two-storeyed house with gables and dormer windows.

(H. E. Chetwynd-Stapylton, *The Stapeltons of Yorkshire* (1897). W. D. Macray (ed.), *The History of the Rebellion and Civil Wars in England .... by Edward, Earl of Clarendon* (1888), i, 393. Dr Williams's Library, Morrice MSS, J, no pagination. C.10/72/136 and 342/14.)

WATTON   Harthill

A village situated between Beverley and Great Driffield. There was no other village within the parish. 1672: 64 households (township of Watton). 1676: 200 persons aged 16 or more (parish).

Watton Priory, which was an establishment of Gilbertine nuns and canons, had been founded in the 12th century and dissolved in 1540.

Church St Mary: Perpendicular. A brick church.

The minister was a perpetual curate who had only a modest stipend.

WAWNE   Holderness

A village near Beverley which was sometimes called Waghen in the 17th century. The parish of Wawne included the villages of Meaux and Sutton. 1672: 75 households (townships of Wawne and Meaux).

Meaux Abbey was a Cistercian monastery founded in 1150 and dissolved in 1539. After its dissolution it was rapidly demolished.

Church St Peter: Early English.

Principal families (1) Alford of Meaux Abbey (and Bilton Hall). Estate revenue: £1300 a year (1641).

The family moved from Wales to Yorkshire in the 16th century.

Sir Lancelot Alford (c.1550-1618) significantly advanced the fortunes of the family by marrying Anne Knowles, the only child of Sir William Knowles of Bilton.

His son Sir William (c.1571-1645), who was a man of considerable standing in the East Riding, was generally regarded as a supporter of the Crown in the disputes over Charles I's financial levies. In the summer of 1642 he was named as one of the king's commissioners of array but he took no part in the Civil War.

Sir William left no male issue and after his death the bulk of the estate came into the possession of his sons-in-law Sir Robert Strickland of Thornton Bridge and Thomas Grantham, a Lincolnshire squire.

(2) Grantham of Meaux Abbey (and Goltho Hall, Lincolnshire). Estate revenue: £1700 a year (1650).

Thomas Grantham (1612-c.1647) and his wife Dorothy received the Meaux property and the manor of Bilton as their share of the estate. Before long Meaux Abbey became the family's principal seat.

Although his father had a reputation for godliness Grantham earned the disapproval of Lucy Hutchinson who portrayed him as a young man steeped in 'sin and lewdnesse'. On the outbreak of the Civil War he threw in his lot with Parliament and in 1645 was nominated as a member of the East Riding parliamentary committee.

With the death of Vincent Grantham in 1674 the direct male line came to an end and eventually the estate was apportioned between his sisters Dorothy and Elizabeth.

Meaux Abbey The house known as Meaux Abbey was a Tudor mansion which was probably built by Sir Lancelot Alford. He acquired freehold possession of the site of the monastery in 1586.

In 1672 there were 16 taxable hearths.

(PRO, Exchequer, Parliamentary Surveys, E.317/35. Lucy Hutchinson, *Memoirs of the Life of Colonel Hutchinson* (ed. J. Sutherland) (1973), 23-4. C.33/233/fo.56. C.10/128/52.)

WEAVERTHORPE   Buckrose

A village to the east of Malton. The parish of Weaverthorpe included East and West Lutton (Luttons Ambo) where there was a dependent chapel. 1672: 38 households in Weaverthorpe and 36 in Luttons Ambo.

The manor of Weaverthorpe was of modest value. The Hebblethwaites of Norton bought it in 1607 for £400 and sold it in 1668 for £660.

Church St Andrew: Norman and Decorated.

The parish was subject to the peculiar jurisdiction of the Dean and Chapter of York.

(Hull University Archives, Sykes MSS, DDSY/70/4, 16.)

WELTON   Howdenshire

A village to the west of Hull. The parish of Welton included the village of Melton. 1672: 75 households in Welton and 21 in Melton.

In 1643 the vicar, John Norton, was alleged to have joined the rebels in Hull.

Church St Helen: Norman, Decorated and Perpendicular.

The parish was subject to the peculiar jurisdiction of the Dean and Chapter of Durham.

(J. G. Hall, *A History of South Cave and of Other Parishes in the East Riding of the County of York* (1892).)

WELWICK   Holderness

A village situated in the southernmost part of the Holderness promontory. The parish of Welwick included several hamlets. 1672: 56 households in Welwick, 12 in Ploughland Thorpe and 26 in Weeton. 1676: 100 persons aged 16 or more (parish).

Church St Mary: Early English and Decorated.

Principal family Wright of Ploughland Hall. Estate revenue: £800 a year (1630); £1200 a year (1640).

The Wrights were a Catholic family who managed to safeguard their financial interests by outwardly conforming.

William Wright (c.1550-1621), who was a Church Papist, added considerably to the estate during the reign of James I. His wife Anne was said to have been mentally afflicted for most of their married life. In 1604 it was reported that she 'hath long absented herself from the church, as is thought, in respect that she is lunatick'.

Wright's half-brothers John and Christopher participated in the Gunpowder Plot and were killed when resisting arrest.

His eldest son Robert died before him, leaving no male issue and the estate passed to the next son, William (c.1574-1648). He significantly increased the estate revenue by purchasing the manor and rectory of Welwick and acquiring several leases of church property.

In the Civil War he appears to have been anxious to avoid any commitment, though it was alleged in 1646 that he had supplied the king with a horse and armed rider.

In 1654, after a succession of deaths, the estate was in the hands of his nephew Francis Wright. The following year a North Riding gentleman, Thomas Crathorne, claimed in a Chancery suit that he had a better title by virtue of the fact that his mother had been the only surviving child of Robert Wright. The suit was unsuccessful but when Francis Wright died without issue in 1660 the male line expired and Crathorne was able to enter into possession of the estate. After this Ploughland Hall was sometimes occupied by a younger son of the Crathorne family and on occasion by a tenant.

Ploughland Hall In 1672 the Crathornes were taxed on 12 hearths.

(E. Peacock (ed.), *A List of the Roman Catholics in the County of York in 1604* (1872). C.5/21/27. North Yorkshire County Record Office, Crathorne MSS.)

WEST HESLERTON Buckrose

A village on the road between Malton and Filey. The parish of West Heslerton included the village of East Heslerton where there was a dependent chapel. 1672: 39 households in West Heslerton and 35 in East Heslerton. 1676: 240 persons aged 16 or more (parish).

In 1252 Heslerton had been granted the right to hold a weekly market and an annual fair.

In 1643 the Earl of Newcastle was informed that John Saltmarshe, the Puritan rector of West Heslerton, had removed to Hull 'where he hath uttered most seditious and rebellious doctrines.'

Church All Saints: Early English with later features.

(*YASRS*, lxi (1920), 155.)

WESTOW   Buckrose

A village to the south of Malton. The parish of Westow, which extended as far as the River Derwent, included a number of hamlets. 1672: 36 households in Westow, 32 in Eddlethorpe and Firby and 14 in Menethorpe. 1676: 200 persons aged 16 or more (parish).

George Mountaigne or Mountain (1569-1628) was by far the most prominent member of a minor gentry family, the Mountaignes of Westow. He was successively Bishop of Lincoln, Bishop of London, Bishop of Durham and Archbishop of York, though his tenure of this last appointment was very brief. To a large extent he owed this rapid advancement to his popularity at Court and his association with the Arminian wing of the Church.

Mountaigne left the bulk of his estate to his brother Isaac (d.1648) who erected a monument to him in Cawood church. In the Civil War he supported the royalist cause, as did his son George (1620-1669) who took up arms for the king.

Kirkham Priory, which was an establishment of Augustinian canons, had been founded in the 12th century and dissolved in 1539. In the 17th century the extensive ruins were an impressive reminder of Kirkham's monastic past.

Church St Mary: Norman in origin but with a Perpendicular tower.

The church had once belonged to Kirkham Priory but in the 17th century the Archbishop of York was the patron and owner of the impropriate rectory.

(*YASRS*, xviii (1895), 79.)

WETWANG   Buckrose

A Wolds village to the west of Great Driffield. The parish of Wetwang included the hamlet of Fimber which had a medieval chapel. 1672: 50 households in Wetwang and 16 in Fimber.

The parish was subject to the peculiar jurisdiction of a Prebendary of York. The descendants of Edwin Sandys, the Elizabethan Archbishop of York, had long leases of the rectory until 1699. In a Commonwealth survey it was valued at £140 a year.

The main proprietors of lands in Wetwang lived elsewhere and the majority of their tenants were copyholders. Farm produce consisted primarily of sheep and corn.

Thomas Wait, who became vicar of Wetwang in 1649, 'went by the name of a Burn Roast among his Parishioners because he commonly held them so long in his Preaching.' An ardent Puritan, he was deprived of his living in 1660.

Church St Nicholas: Norman, Early English and Perpendicular.

School After his ejection Thomas Wait decided to remain in Wetwang 'and his Wife taught Scholars, and he assisted her, and commonly heard them two Lessons a Day....

he continu'd preaching in his own House, and would have all his Scholars resort thither twice every Lord's Day'.

(E. Maule Cole, 'Notices of Wetwang', *East Riding Antiquarian Society Transactions*, ii (1894). A. G. Matthews, *Calamy Revised* (1934), 505.)

WHARRAM LE STREET   Buckrose

A Wolds village to the south-east of Malton. 1672: 25 households (nominally including Wharram Percy).

Church St Mary: Saxon and Norman with later medieval features.

The parish was subject to the peculiar jurisdiction of the Dean and Chapter of York.

WHARRAM PERCY   Buckrose

A deserted Wolds village lying to the south of Wharram le Street. The village had been depopulated in the early 16th century in order to make way for large-scale sheep farming. The parish of Wharram Percy included the hamlets of Raisthorpe, Thixendale and Towthorpe. Another hamlet, Burdale, had been depopulated at about the same time as Wharram Percy. 1672: 18 households in Raisthorpe and Thixendale and 11 in Towthorpe. 1676: 100 persons aged 16 or more (parish).

During the reign of James I the manor of Wharram Percy belonged to the Huttons of Marske, near Richmond, who valued it at £180 a year.

The only building in Wharram Percy which was still in use was the parish church which continued to serve the residents of the outlying hamlets. In a Commonwealth survey of benefices the commissioners reported that 'This church is above a mile from any town in the parish, it being about a mile distant from Wharram in the Streete. We conceive them fitt to be united'. This proposal, however, was not followed up.

Towards the end of the 17th century Raisthorpe and Towthorpe experienced the same fate as Wharram Percy and the congregation then consisted mainly of the people of Thixendale.

Church St Mary: Norman with some later medieval work. The chancel was remodelled in the course of the 17th century.

(M. W. Beresford and J. Hurst, *Wharram Percy. Deserted Medieval Village* (1991). North Yorkshire County Record Office, Hutton MSS, A485. *East Riding Antiquarian Society Transactions*, ii (1894), 60.)

WHELDRAKE   Ouse and Derwent

A village to the south-east of York. The parish of Wheldrake included the hamlet of Langwith. 1672: 115 households (township of Wheldrake). 1676: 280 persons aged 16 or more (parish).
    Church St Helen: Norman in origin but mainly Decorated and Perpendicular.
    Schools There were private schools at Wheldrake in 1623 and the late 1640s.
(*Wheldrake: Aspects of a Yorkshire Village* (Wheldrake Local History Society) (1971).)

WILBERFOSS   Harthill

A village to the east of York. The parish of Wilberfoss included the village of Newton upon Derwent which had a medieval chapel. 1672: 44 households in Wilberfoss and 36 in Newton upon Derwent. 1676: 182 persons aged 16 or more (parish).
    Wilberfoss Priory, which was an establishment of Benedictine nuns, had been founded in the 12th century and dissolved in 1539.
    Church St John Baptist: Perpendicular.
    The minister was a perpetual curate. In the Commonwealth period it was reported that the stipend amounted to £10 a year and that currently there was no minister.

WILLERBY   Dickering

A village on the northern edge of the Wolds near Filey. The parish of Willerby included the villages of Binnington and Staxton. 1672: 20 households in Willerby, 19 in Binnington and 27 in Staxton and Spittal. 1676: 200 persons aged 16 or more (parish of Willerby).
    Church St Peter: 13th century.
    In 1615 the church was reported to be in a poor state of repair.
    Principal family Coundon of Willerby Hall. Estate revenue: £600 a year (1646).
    The Coundons acquired the Crown manor of Willerby in 1602 and the manor of Binnington in 1636.
    Thomas Coundon (c.1580-1646) was a man of considerable wealth. The personal estate which he left at his death was said to be worth at least £6000.
    Neither he nor his son Thomas (1607-c.1661) appears to have played an active part in the Civil War. On succeeding to the estate the latter was almost immediately involved in a property dispute with his brother Philip.
    In the late 17th century the Coundons continued to buy property in Binnington and Willerby.

Willerby Hall The house may have been rebuilt after the purchase of the manor in 1602. In 1672 it had seven taxable hearths.
(C.6/15/23 and 24. C.8/106/126.)

WINESTEAD   Holderness

A village situated in the southern part of the Holderness promontory. 1672: 24 households (township of Winestead). 1676: 75 persons aged 16 or more (parish of Winestead).

Andrew Marvell, the father of the poet, was a Puritan divine who served as rector of Winestead during the years 1614 to 1624. After resigning the living he became master of the Charterhouse in Hull where he was also employed as a lecturer or preacher at Holy Trinity. In 1641 he was drowned while crossing the Humber.

His son Andrew (1621-1678) was born in the rectory at Winestead and received his schooling at Hull Grammar School.

Church St German: Perpendicular with a Jacobean chapel containing monuments of the Hildyard family.

Principal family Hildyard of Winestead Hall (baronetcy 1660). Estate revenue: £2300 a year (1640).

Sir Christopher Hildyard (1567-1634) inherited a large estate in Yorkshire and Lincolnshire after the death of his uncle and namesake in 1602. Eventually, through his marriage to an heiress, there was a further acquisition of property in Lincolnshire.

Hildyard served as sheriff of Yorkshire, as a deputy lieutenant and as a member of the Council in the North. When Thomas Lord Wentworth consulted Sir John Hotham about his choice of deputy lieutenants for the East Riding he was presented with an unflattering account of Hildyard's character:

> tis true he is somewhat lesse than nothinge yet he hath always made one as a Cypher to ad to the number and he wilbe sure to be of the safer side. He dwels nere the Sea Coast in the End of a Countrey, where is none Else neere him. Besides he hath beene longe one of your Councell and wilbe like hearbe John in the pot, noe good, small harme.

In November 1634, when he was on his deathbed, Sir Christopher made a nuncupative will in the presence of Francis Edgar, the rector of Winestead, and other witnesses. According to their testimony he 'blamed himselfe for neglecting the setting of his estate in order' and declared his intentions over the payment of portions and legacies.

The parish register records that he was buried 'under the blue marble stone next the Ile which he built at his owne charge'.

On succeeding to the estate his son Henry (1610-1675) appears to have been anxious to explore the possibility of increasing the revenue. In 1636 he employed George Osborne to carry out a survey of the manor of Winestead which was found to contain over 2000 acres.

In the Civil War he supported the king and signed the Yorkshire Engagement of February 1643 but his military involvement was short-lived. In contrast, his brother Robert (1612-1685) served as a royalist commander and distinguished himself at the battle of Marston Moor. After the Restoration he was rewarded for his loyalty with a baronetcy and a long lease of Crown property.

From the mid-1640s until his death Henry Hildyard resided at East Horsley in Surrey where he was on close terms with John Evelyn the diarist. For the day-to-day management of his northern estate he relied on a steward, Wilfrid Kemp.

In 1649 he sent two of his sons abroad with a tutor, Obadiah Walker of University College, Oxford. During their travels Walker, who was a 'concealed Papist', persuaded the eldest son, Henry, to adopt the Catholic faith. He later settled at Kelstern in Lincolnshire and in 1680 sold the Winestead estate to his uncle Sir Robert Hildyard for £6400.

Winestead Hall A castellated mansion built in 1579 on a site which was some distance from the previous moated house. In 1672 there were 17 taxable hearths.

The Hildyards rebuilt the house in the early years of the 18th century.

In 1636 there was a park of 154 acres together with the 'old park' which contained 42 acres. The parish register records the death in 1630 of Richard Kempe who had been the keeper of Winestead Park for many years.

(Hildyard MSS at Flintham Hall, Nottinghamshire. N. J. Miller, *Winestead and its Lords* (1933). *YPRS*, iv (1899, 1900). Sheffield Archives, Wentworth Woodhouse Collection, Strafford Letters, xii, letter of Sir John Hotham, 7 January 1628/9. BIHR, York Registry, will of Sir Christopher Hildyard, 22 November 1634.)

WINTRINGHAM   Buckrose

A Wolds village to the east of Malton. The parish of Wintringham included the village and chapelry of Knapton and several hamlets. 1672: 54 households in Wintringham and 52 in Knapton. 1676: 400 persons aged 16 or more (parish of Wintringham).

The manor of Wintringham belonged to the Stricklands of Boynton.

In 1655 the inhabitants of Wintringham sought some augmentation of their minister's income. They explained in their petition that although it was a large parish the vicar had never received more than £15 a year even in the best times and as a result the cure had generally been served by very weak and insufficient ministers.

Church St Peter, Wintringham: Norman, Decorated and Perpendicular with Jacobean pews and a nave roof of 1685.

Principal family Lister of Linton Grange. Estate revenue: £1500 a year (1640); £1000 a year (1650).

The Listers were a Puritan family.

Sir John Lister (1587-1641) was a Hull merchant and shipowner who served as mayor in 1618 and 1629. He bought a substantial amount of landed property, including the estate of Robert Dakins of Linton Grange which was acquired in 1620.

He left eight sons and four daughters. In his will (1640) he settled a considerable part of the estate on his younger sons and for his wife's jointure. At the same time he made provision for the establishment of a hospital or almshouses in Hull.

John Lister (1609-1651), who resided at Linton Grange, inherited an estate worth £700 a year from his father and also secured property worth £300 a year through his marriage to Jane Constable, the only child of Christopher Constable of Great Hatfield.

In the Civil War he took the side of Parliament but was not particularly active.

When his son John (1638-1715) succeeded him the estate was heavily encumbered with the jointures of his mother and grandmother. In 1673 he claimed in a Chancery suit that his stepfather, Sir Robert Hildyard, had taken the profits arising from the remainder of the estate.

Linton Grange The house was probably early Tudor in origin but Arthur Dakins had carried out improvements in the reign of Elizabeth.

In 1672 John Lister was taxed on 10 hearths.

(C.6/153/85. C.10/15/35 and 119/74. C.33/239/fo.370. YAS Library, DD99, B10.).

WITHERNWICK   Holderness

A village to the east of Beverley. The parish of Withernwick contained only part of the village; the remainder lay within the parish of Mappleton. 1672: 52 households (township of Withernwick). 1676: 200 persons aged 16 or more (parish).

Church St Alban: Norman in origin.

The parish was subject to the peculiar jurisdiction of a Prebendary of York.

WOLD NEWTON   Dickering

A Wolds village to the north-west of Bridlington. The parish of Wold Newton included the hamlet of Fordon. 1672: 36 households in Wold Newton with Fordon.

Church All Saints: Norman, Decorated and Perpendicular.

WRESSLE Howdenshire

A village to the north-west of Howden on the east bank of the River Derwent. The parish of Wressle included several hamlets. 1672: 28 households in Wressle and Loftsome and 27 in Newsham and Brind. 1676: 155 persons aged 16 or more (parish).

The Wressle estate, including the castle, belonged to the Earls of Northumberland.

Early on in the Civil War the castle was occupied by parliamentary troops. During the course of the war it came under siege but the garrison (which was commanded by Major Charles Fenwick) managed to hold out.

In 1646 Algernon Earl of Northumberland was informed by his agent that the damage caused by the garrison to the castle and its outbuildings together with the felling of trees in his woods and parks there amounted in financial terms to not less than £1000.

Church St John of Beverley: a medieval church which was demolished in the Civil War.

In a Commonwealth survey of benefices the commissioners observed that 'The church of Wressle was pulled downe in this tyme of warr, which, if it be rebuilt, we thinke it would stand well in Newsome Common being most convenient for all their ease'. In the event it was not until 1799 that a new church was built.

Castle Wressle Castle had been built about 1380 and modernised in the late 15th or early 16th century. When the Northumberland mansion at Leconfield was demolished in the reign of James I some of the materials were transported to Wressle for the repair of the castle.

In 1647 Parliament decreed that the castle should be made untenable. Demolition work was put in hand but eventually suspended. In 1650 a further order was issued for completion of the work; the Earl, however, obtained permission for this task to be entrusted to his own servants and part of the main building was kept intact for use as a manor-house.

(T. Allen, *A New and Complete History of the County of York* (1828, 1831), ii, 244-8. Barbara English, *The Great Landowners of East Yorkshire 1530-1910* (1990), 134. *East Riding Antiquarian Society Transactions*, ii (1894), 43-4.)

YEDINGHAM Buckrose

A remote hamlet situated between Malton and Scarborough. The parish of Yedingham included part of West Heslerton. 1672: 14 households (township of Yedingham). 1676: 53 persons aged 16 or more (parish).

A small Benedictine nunnery had been established at Yedingham in the 12th century and dissolved in 1540.

Church St John Baptist: Norman in origin.

The North Riding

DURING THE COURSE of the 17th century the North Riding justices of the peace held their quarter sessions (and occasionally special sessions) at a large number of places. The main locations were New Malton, Northallerton, Richmond and Thirsk though there were periods when such towns as Helmsley and Stokesley were also regularly included in the schedule.

The riding had three parliamentary boroughs in the early part of the 17th century: Richmond, Scarborough and Thirsk. From 1640 onwards New Malton and Northallerton also had the right to send two representatives to Westminster.

The region known as Richmondshire consisted of the wapentakes of Gilling East, Gilling West, Hang East, Hang West and Hallikeld. This was more of a geographical description than an administrative division.

ACKLAM   Langbaurgh

A small Cleveland village to the north of Stokesley. The parish of Acklam included the hamlet of Middlesborough, on the south bank of the River Tees, which had a medieval chapel. 1675: 19 households in Acklam and 15 in Middlesborough. 1676: 181 persons aged 16 or more (parish).

Church St Mary: Norman.

Principal family Hustler of Acklam Hall. Estate revenue: £2500 a year (1656).

Willam Hustler was a wealthy Bridlington draper who built up a substantial landed estate. (For his benefactions see under Bridlington, East Riding.)

In 1637 he bought the manor of Acklam together with some neighbouring property from Sir Matthew Boynton of Barmston.

During the Civil War he was imprisoned by both sides 'and enforced to pay severall greate sums of moneye to procure his libertye'. He also had domestic problems occasioned by his wife's 'ill carriage and demeanour unto him'.

Following his death in 1644 the family was heavily involved in litigation. Since his son William was still a minor the Court of Wards immediately stepped in but the financial negotiations had hardly been completed before it was abolished.

During the Interregnum there was a protracted legal dispute between Henry Simpson, the young man's uncle, and Sir John Savile of Lupset, a parliamentarian squire whom the Court of Chancery appointed as his guardian in 1651. Simpson alleged that Savile had been enriching himself while Hustler was travelling on the Continent; Savile, on the other hand, maintained that he had only been interested in recovering money which he had advanced to his ward and accused Simpson of forbidding the tenants to pay their rents to his agent. In 1654 Hustler married one of Savile's daughters.

Acklam Hall The house inherited by Sir William Hustler (c.1656-1730) had 11 taxable hearths in 1662 and nine in 1675. He subsequently built a new mansion of brick which was apparently completed in 1684.

(C.10/19/113; 56/220; and 100/169. C.33/208/fols. 607-8).

AINDERBY STEEPLE   Gilling East

A village to the south-west of Northallerton. The parish of Ainderby Steeple included a number of villages. 1675: 36 households in Ainderby Steeple, 37 in Morton cum Fairholme, 34 in Thrintoft and 29 in Warlaby cum Sowber.

In 1609 the North Riding magistrates were informed that at Morton upon Swale the king's 'high street' leading from Bedale to Northallerton was 'in great decaie'. It was therefore decided that the parish of Ainderby Steeple should be required to undertake the necessary remedial work but it was not until 1613 that the justices received confirmation that the road was 'now sufficiently repaired'.

In 1618 the magistrates approved a proposal that a stone bridge should be built at Morton upon Swale in place of the existing wooden bridge and agreed that the sum of £200 should be provided for this purpose by means of a general levy. Progress, however, was slow and expenditure ran out of control. By April 1627 the North Riding had contributed a total of £463 but further demands for cash continued to be made. The project was apparently completed in 1632 after the cost had risen to well over £500. Despite this major investment it was reported in 1640 that the new bridge was 'in decay' and as a result the sum of £60 was allocated for its repair.

In 1679 the inhabitants of Ainderby Steeple submitted a petition to the North Riding magistrates. It was their contention that they were 'overburthened and charged towards the maintenance of the poor ....and that the town of Warlaby ....hath few or none within it'. After considering the petition the justices decided that Warlaby should contribute to the relief of the poor.

Church St Helen: Decorated and Perpendicular.

School There was a school at Ainderby Steeple from 1622 onwards. A schoolmaster, Mr Lithe, who was teaching there in the reign of Charles I can probably be identified as Thomas Lyeth of Morton upon Swale, a clerk in holy orders, who was presented at the Thirsk quarter sessions in 1636. Along with two others he was charged with freeing a man from the stocks.

(*North Riding Records*, i (1884), 171; ii (1884), 35, 178, 249; iii (1885), 166, 291, 334, 342; iv (1886), 3, 63, 125, 177, 179; and vii (1889), 26.)

ALNE   Bulmer

A village to the south of Easingwold. The extensive parish of Alne included the villages and hamlets of Aldwark, Flawith, Tholthorpe, Tollerton and Youlton. 1675: 65 households in Alne, 29 in Aldwark, 41 in Linton cum Youlton, 57 in Tholthorpe cum Flawith and 87 in Tollerton. Linton was in the parish of Newton upon Ouse

The rectory manor of Alne and Tollerton belonged to the Bethell family of Ellerton in the East Riding (see under Ellerton).

In his poem *Drunken Barnaby's Four Journeys to the North of England* which was first published in 1638 Richard Braithwaite referred to the race meetings which were held at Tollerton:

> Thence to Towlerton where those Stagers
> Or Horse-coursers run for Wagers;
> Near to the Highwey the Course is,
> Where they ride and run their Horses.

Church St Mary: Norman, Decorated and Perpendicular.

Principal family Frankland of Aldwark Hall. Estate revenue: £500 a year (1623): £450 a year (1679). Lead mining in Aldwark.

The Franklands were new gentry who had settled at Aldwark in the reign of Elizabeth.

Sir Henry Frankland (c.1570-1623) had a particular interest in hawking. In 1609 his falconer, George Pearson, was granted permission by the magistrates to shoot crows, choughs, magpies, rooks, ring doves, jays and small birds 'for hawkes meat only'.

In 1616 Sir Henry and his son Anthony were granted a licence to travel abroad on the understanding that the latter would remain on the Continent for three years in order to complete his education. It was apparently during his sojourn on the Continent that

Anthony entered into a marriage contract with a Dutch woman 'of very lewd behaviour and a litle better then a whore'. In the event the marriage never took place.

In 1620 Thomas Watson, a labourer, was committed to prison for a year and fined £20 for assaulting Sir Henry who was one of the magistrates dealing with the case.

According to his second wife Sir Henry decided shortly before his death to settle the estate, or at least the bulk of it, on her own son Thomas because of his disapproval of Anthony's 'disobedient carriage'. When the dispute reached the Court of Wards, however, it was ruled that Anthony was entitled to the estate by right of entail.

In 1636 Anthony Frankland sold the manor of Aldwark to his uncle Thomas Frankland and moved to Ellerton Abbey where the remainder of his property was situated. On settling there he was immediately presented as a recusant.

From Thomas Frankland the manor of Aldwark descended to Sir Henry's sons by his second wife. The elder son, Thomas, died in 1644 while serving as a royalist officer and the property then passed to his brother Henry who was a London merchant. He settled at Aldwark Hall and sought to improve the estate revenue by mining lead ore within his grounds.

In 1680 his son Anthony sold the manor to Thomas Lord Fauconberg for £7550.

Alne Hall The house was medieval in origin. In 1675 the Bethells were taxed on 10 hearths.

Aldwark Hall A moated house of uncertain date. In 1675 it had 10 taxable hearths.

(Richard Braithwaite, *Drunken Barnaby's Four Journeys to the North of England*, 3rd edition (1723). Wards 9/95/fols. 31-7. C.10/119/21; 477/78; and 523/34. BL, Additional MSS 41,255, fo. 7.)

AMPLEFORTH   Ryedale/Birdforth

A village to the south-west of Helmsley which consisted of Ampleforth St Peter, Ampleforth Birdforth and Oswaldkirk Quarter. The parish of Ampleforth included only part of the village; the rest was in the parish of Oswaldkirk. 1675: 62 households in Ampleforth St Peter and Ampleforth Birdforth and 53 in Oswaldkirk cum Ampleforth.

In 1610 the North Riding magistrates were informed that there had been a riot at Ampleforth in which some 60 men had been involved.

In 1643 there was a report that 'the vicarage of Ampleforth is now left by the vicar, gone from hence and now residing in Beverley'.

Churches St Hilda: Norman.

The parish of Ampleforth was subject to the peculiar jurisdiction of a Prebendary of York.

In 1689 there was a Quaker meeting house near Ampleforth.

(*North Riding Records*, i (1884), 175 and vii (1889), 102. *YASRS*, lxi (1920), 151-2.)

APPLETON LE STREET   Ryedale

A village to the north-west of Malton. The parish of Appleton le Street contained several villages, including Amotherby which had a medieval chapel. 1675: 26 households in Appleton le Street, 38 in Amotherby and 43 in Swinton cum Broughton.

Hildenley, which was in this parish, consisted of little more than an Elizabethan mansion belonging to the Stricklands of Boynton in the East Riding. The Hildenley quarries were famous for their high quality freestone.

Churches All Saints: Norman, Early English, Decorated and Perpendicular.

In 1689 there were Quaker meeting houses at Appleton le Street and Broughton.

AYSGARTH   Hang West

A Wensleydale village to the west of Middleham. The parish of Aysgarth, which was the largest in the North Riding, contained a considerable number of villages and hamlets, including Askrigg and Hawes which had medieval chapels. 1675: 51 households in Aysgarth, 108 in Askrigg, 397 in Bainbridge constablery, 79 in West Burton cum Walden, 45 in Carperby cum Thoresby, 90 in Thoralby cum Newbiggin and 40 in Thornton Rust. Bainbridge constablery included Hawes, Gayle, Hardraw and other places in the western part of the parish.

In his poem *Drunken Barnaby's Four Journeys to the North of England* which was first published in 1638 Richard Braithwaite revealed his familiarity with the villages of Wensleydale:

> Thence to Carperby, very greedy,
> Consorts frequent, Victuals needy....
> Thence to Ayscarth, from a Mountain,
> Fruitful Valleys, pleasant Fountain;
> Woolly Flocks, Cliffs steep and snowy,
> Fields, Fenns, sedgy Rushes saw I....
> Thence to Bainbrig, where the River
> From its chanel seems to sever.....
> Thence to Askrig, Market noted.
> But no Handsomeness about it;
> Neither Magistrate nor Mayor
> Ever were elected there.
> Here poor People live by Knitting
> To their Trading, breeding fitting.
> Thence to Hardraw, where's hard Hunger.

> Barren Cliffs and Clints of Wonder....
> Inns are nasty, dusty, fusty
> With both Smoke and Rubbish musty.

Wensleydale had a mixed economy which mainly consisted of sheep and cattle farming, the mining of lead ore and the knitting of stockings and other items of clothing.

The most notable features of Aysgarth were the parish church of upper Wensleydale and the impressive series of waterfalls along the course of the River Ure (or Yore).

Since the reign of Elizabeth Askrigg had enjoyed the right to hold a weekly market and two annual fairs. In 1615 the churchwardens of Askrigg were indicted for 'suffering a markett to be kept in the Church-yearde there'.

After the Restoration there is some evidence of nonconformity in Askrigg which involved illegal gatherings or conventicles. In 1662 the North Riding magistrates dealt with a case in which 18 men and women were alleged to have engaged in 'a tumultuous and unlawful assembly or meeting under pretence or colour of religious worshipp' in the house of James Wetherill of Askrigg.

Bainbridge 'was formerly a Roman garrison, of which some remains are yet extant' (William Camden). In 1607 Yore Bridge, which spanned the River Ure at Bainbridge, was said to be 'in great ruyne and decaie'; and in 1632 it was described in similar terms in a petition which the inhabitants of Bainbridge forwarded to the North Riding magistrates. On both occasions it was decided that the repair work should be funded by means of a general levy.

A royal charter of 1305 had conferred on Carperby the right to hold a weekly market and two annual fairs. In 1700 Hawes finally acquired the same rights through the grant of a charter to Matthew Wetherald.

In 1688 the North Riding magistrates agreed that the sum of £140 should be paid to the inhabitants of West Burton for building a 'country bridge' there.

Churches St Andrew, Aysgarth: Early English and Perpendicular.

The patronage rights and tithes belonged to Trinity College, Cambridge.

In 1689 there were Quaker meeting houses at Bainbridge, Carperby, Countersett, Hawes and West Burton. George Fox had preached at Bainbridge and Carperby.

School In 1601 Anthony Besson, a London lawyer, established a free grammar school at Bainbridge which was called Yorebridge School. The intention was to provide a classical education for sons of the inhabitants of the chapelry of Askrigg.

In the late 17th century several of the pupils of this school went on to Cambridge University.

Principal family Metcalfe of Nappa Hall. Estate revenue: £1000 a year (1610); £600 a year (1661). Lead mining.

Nappa Hall, 'a house built with turrets, and the chief seat of the Metcalfs, which is counted the most numerous family this day in England' (William Camden).

Sir Thomas Metcalfe (1579-1655), who was known as the 'Black Knight of Nappa', was a man of strong character whose taste for litigation must have proved costly. He borrowed money freely, sold some of his property and mortgaged the rest. In 1617 he sought to recover the Raydale estate which was then in the hands of one of his creditors. With a force of 60 armed men he laid siege to Raydale House but after four days the authorities intervened and he was taken into custody. Two years later the Court of Star Chamber pronounced on the episode and as a result he was committed to prison and heavily fined. In 1622, however, he received a royal pardon and the fines were remitted.

Despite this reprieve his financial problems were so desperate that between 1617 and 1641 the Nappa estate was out of his possession. From 1625 onwards it was managed by trustees who had formally undertaken to employ the profits for the maintenance of Sir Thomas and his wife.

In the Civil War Scrope Metcalfe, a younger son, served as a major in the royal army but Sir Thomas and his other sons appear to have remained uncommitted.

When James Metcalfe (1604-1671), who was a barrister of Lincoln's Inn, inherited the Nappa estate from his father the family entered into a period of much greater stability.

Nappa Hall A fortified manor-house built in the 15th century. A wing was added in the reign of Charles I.

(Richard Braithwaite, *Drunken Barnaby's Four Journeys to the North of England*, 3rd edition (1723). *North Riding Records*, i (1884), 83; ii (1884), 103; iii (1885), 326, 331; and vi (1888), 61-2. C. Whaley, *History of Askrigg* (1890). Marie Hartley and Joan Ingilby, *Yorkshire Village* (1979) [Askrigg]. W. C. and G. Metcalfe (eds.), *Records of the Family of Metcalfe* (1891).)

BARNINGHAM   Gilling West

A village to the south-east of Barnard Castle. The parish of Barningham included the village of Scargill and part of the village of Newsham; the other part was in the parish of Kirkby Ravensworth. 1675: 56 households in Barningham, 32 in Scargill and 45 in Newsham.

The Tunstalls of Wycliffe, a Catholic family, owned the manors of Barningham and Scargill. During the early 17th century they enlarged their park at Barningham by taking in 60 acres from the commons.

In 1609 the inhabitants of Barningham and Newsham were indicted for refusing to name those responsible for throwing down an enclosure on Newsham Moor.

In 1682 a Scargill yeoman was presented at the Richmond quarter sessions for saying to a woman 'Thou art a known witch'.

Church St Michael: 14th century or earlier.

(*North Riding Records*, i (1884), 170, 210 and vii (1889), 55.)

BARTON LE STREET   Ryedale/Bulmer

A small village to the north-west of Malton. The parish of Barton le Street, which extended northwards as far as the River Rye, included several scattered hamlets. 1675: 23 households in Barton le Street, 16 in Butterwick cum Newsham and 18 in Coneysthorpe. 1676: 148 persons aged 16 or more (parish).

In 1246 Barton le Street had been granted the right to hold a weekly market and an annual fair.

In 1675 the inhabitants of Newsham were involved in a dispute over the provision of financial support for the poor of Amotherby in the neighbouring parish of Appleton le Street.

Church St Michael: Norman, Decorated and Perpendicular.

(*North Riding Records*, vi (1888), 235.)

BEDALE   Hang East/Hallikeld

Bedale 'is a pretty market town which has a handsome church. Here is a Free School… .also a hospital.' (Ralph Thoresby, 1682). The parish of Bedale included a number of villages and hamlets. 1675: 116 households in Bedale, 56 in Aiskew cum Leeming, 16 in Burrill cum Cowling, 56 in Great and Little Crakehall and 21 in Langthorne. Leeming was in the parish of Burneston.

A royal charter of 1328 had granted the right to hold a weekly market and two annual fairs.

There were two manors in Bedale: the Digby manor and the Stapleton manor. Sir Richard Theakston bought the Digby manor in 1594 and subsequently acquired a lease of the Stapleton manor from the Stapletons of Carlton in the West Riding. On his initiative, but with the agreement of the tenants and freeholders, the wastes and commons of Bedale were partitioned and enclosed with fences, dikes, hedges and trees.

In 1636 there was an outbreak of the plague in Bedale and the North Riding magistrates decided that the inhabitants of places within a radius of five miles of the town should contribute £10 weekly for the relief of the poor. It was noted that 240 persons in Bedale were in great need through 'their restrainte and want of tradeing and worke'.

Church St Gregory: Saxon, Early English, Decorated and Perpendicular.

Schools There had been a free grammar school at Bedale since the early 16th century. In 1628 Frances Countess of Warwick increased the endowment; and in 1674 a new schoolhouse was built in the churchyard.

In 1633 Bedale also had a Catholic school.

Almshouses A hospital for three poor widows was established in the reign of Charles II by two Catholic priests, Richard and Thomas Young, who were natives of Bedale.

In his will (1692) Peter Samwayes, the rector of Bedale, made provision for the building of almshouses for four poor aged men of the parish.

Firby Hospital, which was also known as Christ's Hospital, was founded in 1608 by John Chapman, a Chancery official. He settled a rent-charge of £30 a year to provide maintenance for a master and six brethren.

Principal family Peirse of Bedale Hall. Estate revenue: £700 a year (1641); £1200 a year (1675).

John Peirse (1593-1658), who was the son of a Bedale yeoman, grew rich as a London scrivener. In 1638 he secured a lease of the demesnes of the Stapleton manor at a modest rent and bought the Digby manor from Sir William Theakston who by that time was living at Flixton in Suffolk.

In 1648 the parliamentarians sequestered his estate on the grounds that he had provided support for the royalist forces. On his behalf two members of the North Riding committee testified that he had always been well affected to Parliament; that he had made a voluntary contribution of arms and horses to advance its interests; that he had been proclaimed a traitor by the Earl of Cumberland at York; and that early on in the war he had fled to Newcastle.

During the Interregnum the Peirse and Stapleton families were involved in a protracted legal battle over the ownership of the Stapleton manor. In the end the Stapletons managed to regain possession.

Richard Peirse (1641-1708) added considerably to the estate which he had inherited from his father by purchasing the manors of Hutton Bonville and Thimbleby.

Bedale Hall The house was destroyed in the Civil War and subsequently rebuilt.

Richard Peirse was taxed on 10 hearths in 1662. In 1675, however, he was living at Hutton Bonville.

(Hull University Archives, Beaumont of Carlton Towers MSS, DDCA/32/1 and 4. *North Riding Records*, iv (1886), 65. North Yorkshire County Record Office, Peirse of Bedale MSS. H. B. McCall, *The Early History of Bedale* (1907). Wards 9/573/238, 285. C.5/9/63. C.33/302/fo. 378. C.54/3215.)

BIRKBY   Allertonshire

A village near Northallerton. The parish of Birkby included the villages of Hutton Bonville and Little Smeaton. 1675: 28 households in Birkby, 30 in Hutton Bonville and 11 in Little Smeaton.

In 1614 there were 36 recusants within the parish.

In 1676 two Northallerton labourers were indicted for assaulting the rector of Birkby while he was conducting a service in the parish church.

Church St Peter: Norman.

The parish was subject to the peculiar jurisdiction of the Bishop of Durham.

School In 1604 it was reported that Christopher Newstead of Hutton Bonville, who was employed to teach the youth of the parish, 'cometh to the church but did not comunicate last Easter'.

Principal families (1) Conyers of Hutton Bonville Hall. Estate revenue: £500 a year (1627).

The Conyers family had acquired the manor of Hutton Bonville in 1397. They were ardent Catholics who declined to take refuge in outward conformity.

In 1637 Robert Conyers sold his estate to Richard Neile, the Archbishop of York, and his son Sir Paul. After this he was dependent on poor relief to support himself.

(2) Neile of Hutton Bonville Hall. Estate revenue: £1100 a year (1640).

In the Civil War Sir Paul Neile (1613-1686) supported the royalist cause and signed the Yorkshire Engagement of February 1643. He was at Oxford when it was surrendered to the parliamentarians.

In 1646 he was involved in litigation with his wife, Dame Elizabeth, over her claims on his estate.

After the Restoration he became an usher of the Privy Chamber and in 1663 was made a fellow of the Royal Society.

Sir Paul was said to have run through his estate. By 1670 he had sold the manor of Hutton Bonville to Richard Peirse of Bedale and had settled at White Waltham in Berkshire.

His son William (1637-1670) was a noted mathematician.

Hutton Bonville Hall A gabled building which was probably Elizabethan in origin.

In 1675 Richard Peirse was taxed on six hearths. He may subsequently have improved the house.

(*North Riding Records*, vi (1888), 248-9. E. Peacock (ed.), *A List of the Roman Catholics in the County of York in 1604* (1872), 93. *CRS*, liii (1961), 409. C.33/230/fo. 632.)

BOSSALL   Bulmer

A hamlet to the north-west of York. In 1662 it contained only five households but the township of Bossall cum Buttercrambe had a substantially larger population. The parish of Bossall contained several villages, including Buttercrambe which had a medieval chapel, and part of the village of Flaxton; the other part was in the parish of Foston. 1675: 56 households in Bossall cum Buttercrambe, 43 in Flaxton, 47 in Harton cum Claxton and 37 in Sand Hutton. 1676: 441 persons aged 16 or more (parish).

Royal charters of 1200, 1343 and 1353 had granted the right to hold a weekly market and an annual fair at Buttercrambe.

There were two bridges at Buttercrambe which spanned the River Derwent and connected the North and East Ridings. In 1656 it was reported that they were in great decay, apparently as a result of the wars, but the allocation of responsibility for the repair work proved to be a contentious issue. The North Riding magistrates initially took the view that the inhabitants of Buttercrambe, including the lord of the manor, should bear the cost; in the end, however, they concluded that it should be divided equally between the two ridings. In 1661 the sum of £200 was levied within the North Riding.

Church St Botolph, Bossall: Norman and Early English.

School The school which served the township of Bossall cum Buttercrambe was established in 1606.

Principal family Darley of Buttercrambe Hall. Estate revenue: £1000 a year (1627); £700 a year (1661).

The Darleys had bought the Buttercrambe estate in 1557. In the early 17th century they emerged as one of the leading Puritan families in Yorkshire.

Sir Richard Darley (1568–c.1653) had a succession of domestic chaplains, among them two nonconformist divines, Thomas Shepard and Francis Pecke. In 1631 Shepard was offered shelter at Buttercrambe Hall when he was in the process of being driven out of the Diocese of London. He had misgivings about travelling to 'so remote and strange a place' and was not impressed by the general ethos of the Darley household. On his arrival (he wrote) 'I found divers of them at dice and tables …. I was, I saw, in a profane house, not any sincerely good …. Yet the Lord did not leave me comfortless; for though the lady was churlish yet Sir Richard was ingenious'. He immediately set about the task of reformation and before his departure the whole family had been 'brought to external duties'.

Sir Richard's son Henry (1596–1671) was a political radical. In 1630 his initial reluctance to pay his knighthood composition led the Privy Council to issue a warrant for his arrest. Through his involvement in various Puritan colonising enterprises, in particular the Providence Island Company, he became closely associated with the leading political dissidents, including Lord Saye and Sele, Lord Brooke and John Pym. In September 1640 Strafford had him imprisoned in York Castle on hearing that he had been in contact with the Scottish Covenanters.

Although his father had settled an annuity of £350 on him he was in considerable financial difficulty on the eve of the Civil War and was contemplating the sale of the Essex property which he had acquired by marriage.

In the Civil War the Darleys were fully committed to the cause of Parliament. Sir Richard was a member of the North Riding committee and in 1646 was appointed sheriff of Yorkshire. Two years later Parliament awarded him the sum of £5000 as compensation for his losses in the war. His son Henry was MP for Northallerton and a North Riding committeeman. In June 1644 royalist troops made a surprise raid on Buttercrambe Hall and took him prisoner to Scarborough but he was soon released. During the Interregnum he served as a member of the Council of State.

After the Restoration he was suspected of plotting against the government. When he was arrested in 1665 a paper found in his pocket was branded as seditious but no charges were brought against him.

His son Richard (1631-1706) appears to have been anxious to avoid any political entanglement.

Buttercrambe Hall The hall was burnt down during the Civil War, probably in June 1644. A new two-storeyed house of modest size was built by Henry Darley, apparently on a different site. In 1662 he was taxed on nine hearths.

(*North Riding Records*, v (1887), 229, 230, 254 and vi (1888), 37. North Yorkshire County Record Office, Darley MSS. A. Young, *Chronicles of the First Planters of the Colony of Massachusetts Bay, 1623-1636* (1846), 522-6. C.10/466/6. C.54/3289 and 3290.)

BOWES Gilling West

A village to the south-west of Barnard Castle. The parish of Bowes included the villages of Boldron and Gilmonby. 1675: 130 households in Bowes (probably including Gilmonby) and 32 in Boldron.

Bowes was the site of a Roman fort and signal station. On the west side were the ruins of a Norman castle which had long been derelict. 'Bowes, at present a little village ....where, in former ages, the Earls of Richmond had a little castle' (William Camden).

In 1245 and 1310 Bowes had been granted the right to hold a weekly market and an annual fair.

In 1614 it was reported that the main road extending westwards from Bowes (which was Roman in origin) was 'in great decay and troblesome to passengers, arising by a sodaine inundation of waters by reason of a great snow there'.

In 1626 Bowes Bridge, over the River Greta, was said to be 'in great ruin and decay'.

In 1635 the North Riding magistrates received letters from the Earl Marshal and the Council in the North which requested them to ensure that the road to the west of Bowes was 'forthwith amended and made passable for cartes and coaches'. Accordingly they appointed four men to produce a cost estimate and act as surveyors.

Church St Giles: Norman and Perpendicular.

The minister was a perpetual curate.

School In his will (1693) William Hutchinson, a London lawyer, founded a grammar school at Bowes. Boys of the parish were to be taught free of charge.

(*North Riding Records*, ii (1884), 49; iii (1885), 256; and iv (1886), 39.)

BRAFFERTON
Bulmer

A village to the north of Boroughbridge. The parish of Brafferton included the village of Helperby and the hamlet of Thornton Bridge. 1675: 26 households in Brafferton and 88 in Helperby. 1676: 221 persons aged 16 or more (parish).

In his poem *Drunken Barnaby's Four Journeys to the North of England* which was first published in 1638 Richard Braithwaite referred to a fire at Helperby:

Thence to Helperby I turned,
Desolate and lately burned:
Not a Taphouse there but mourned,
Being all to Ashes turned.

In 1643 it was said that George Wilson the vicar of Brafferton 'hath for a long tyme absented himself and neglected his duty and is at this present at Kingston upon Hull'.

Church St Augustine: Perpendicular.

School A school had been established in 1564.

Principal families (1) Gerard of Brafferton Hall (and Fiskerton Hall, Lincolnshire) (baronetcy 1666). Estate revenue: £3900 a year (1687). Coalmining in County Durham.

The manor of Brafferton belonged to the Cholmleys of Brandsby until 1656 when Marmaduke Cholmley sold it to Ralph Rymer. Rymer was executed in 1664 after being found guilty of treason. In 1668 the manor was bought by John Cosin, the Bishop of Durham, and after his death in 1672 it descended to his daughter Mary who had married Sir Gilbert Gerard.

Sir Gilbert (c.1620-1687) was a former royalist officer and a courtier who eventually went over to the opposition and joined in the campaign for excluding James Duke of York from the succession to the throne. After the Restoration he became joint farmer of the northern excise revenue and it was apparently this lucrative undertaking which enabled him to build up a large estate in several counties.

In 1681 he was wounded in a duel which arose out of the exclusion controversy. Two years later, at the time of the Rye House Plot, the North Riding deputy lieutenants reported that they had been planning to search Brafferton Hall for arms but had been informed that Gerard had moved out of the county.

Sir Gilbert was killed when his coach overturned in York.

His son Sir Gilbert took the additional surname of Cosin.

(2) Strickland of Thornton Bridge Hall (and Sizergh Castle, Westmorland). Estate revenue: £800 a year (1640).

Sir Thomas Strickland (1563-1612) inherited a substantial estate but brought his family to the verge of ruin, mainly through his addiction to gaming. He sold some lands and granted a number of annuities for the purposes of raising money. In 1606 he encumbered the manor of Thornton Bridge with an annuity of £300 which was payable for three lives. At his death he left debts amounting to at least £10,000.

His second wife, Dame Margaret, was a zealous Catholic who had a dominant role in the religious upbringing of her children.

Sir Robert Strickland (1600-1671), who had been made a ward of the Crown after his father's death, managed to ensure that his family survived the financial crisis. Through his marriage to Margaret Alford he eventually secured a considerable amount of property in the East Riding.

Two of his brothers were sent to the English Catholic college at Douai but he conformed throughout his life.

In the Civil War he served as a royalist colonel and signed the Yorkshire Engagement of February 1643. His son Sir Thomas (1621-1694) also appeared in arms for the king and subsequently took part in the uprising of 1648.

Early on in Charles II's reign it was said that 'these Stricklands are in a declining condition occasioned by Sir Thomas living at Court'. In 1665 he was granted a 21-year lease of the salt tax revenue at a rent of £1800 a year but the yield proved to be far less than he had expected.

In 1674 Sir Thomas finally emerged as an open Catholic and three years later this cost him his seat in the House of Commons.

In 1680 he sold the manor of Thornton Bridge to his cousin Sir Roger Strickland for £7000.

When James II lost his throne Sir Thomas went into exile in France where he remained until his death.

Sir Roger Strickland (1640-1717) had the same religious convictions as his cousin. He was a distinguished naval commander who attained the rank of rear-admiral in the reign of James II. In 1689 he accompanied James when he went to Ireland and as a result he was attainted for high treason.

Brafferton Hall There are references in Richard Cholmley's memorandum book to the rebuilding of Brafferton Hall. In November 1611 he let a contract for the making of bricks there and by October 1612 some 320,000 had been produced. The actual building work was put in hand in 1621 and completed the following year. In December 1621 Cholmley noted that arrangements had been made for the glazing of 'my new howse'.

In 1675 Sir Gilbert Gerard was taxed on 16 hearths.

Thornton Bridge Hall The house was probably Tudor in origin. In 1675 there were 22 taxable hearths.

During the years 1692 to 1694 the steward, James Dibble, had extensive repairs carried out on the roof. This entailed the purchase of 9000 flat tiles.

In 1699 it was said that the park was so fully stocked with deer that it severely limited the scope for putting in cattle.

(Richard Braithwaite, *Drunken Barnaby's Four Journeys to the North of England*, 3rd edition (1723). *YASRS*, lxi (1920), 152. C.6/295/21. C.33/282/fols. 328-9. HMC, *Fifth Report*, Appendix (MSS of W. C. Strickland). H. Hornyold, *Genealo-gical Memoirs of the Family of Strickland of Sizergh* (1928). D. Scott, *The Stricklands of Sizergh Castle* (1908). Wards 9/94/fo. 553 and 215/ fols. 14-15. *The Memorandum Book of Richard Cholmley of Brandsby 1602-1623 (North Yorkshire County Record Office Publications* No. 44) (1988), 54, 57, 58, 61-2, 219, 221, 225, 231, 232, 234. E.134/11 William III/Michaelmas 9.)

BRANDSBY   Bulmer

A village near Easingwold. The parish of Brandsby included the hamlet of Stearsby. 1675: 50 households (township of Brandsby cum Stearsby). 1676: 157 persons aged 16 or more, including 60 recusants (parish of Brandsby).

The number of recusants within the parish tended to increase in the course of the 17th century, primarily through the influence of the Cholmleys of Brandsby Hall.

Church All Saints: Perpendicular.

Principal family Cholmley of Brandsby Hall. Estate revenue: £860 a year (1609); £470 a year (1636); £520 a year (1653); £610 a year (1660). Number of servants : 25 (1618).

The Cholmleys, who were a cadet branch of the Cholmley family of Whitby, had settled at Brandsby in the early years of Elizabeth's reign. During the 17th century successive heads of the family were indicted as recusants.

Richard Cholmley (1571-1623) inherited the estate at a time when the persecution of Catholics was at its height. He was imprisoned in 1605 and again in 1606 and was subjected to continuing harassment by the Northern High Commission. In 1609 he and his wife Mary were granted a royal pardon for relieving seminary priests, though this was apparently procured only after the payment of a substantial sum. In his memorandum book he noted that in 1606 he was forced to dismiss all his Catholic servants but later on his domestic establishment usually contained a number of recusants.

In 1616 he was fined for entertaining and supplying food to seven 'players of Enterludes, vagabundes and sturdy beggars'.

Following an approach to the Privy Council in 1621 he was given a licence to travel to London, Westminster, Bath and Oxford to enable him to engage in litigation over his estate and to seek a remedy for his ill health.

Cholmley was an efficient landowner who managed his estate on a tight rein. As he recorded in his memorandum book, some of his tenants considered him to be a very harsh landlord.

His nephew Marmaduke Cholmley (1603-c.1674), who succeeded to the estate in 1631, was said to have been married by a 'popishe preist in the feildes in Lincolnshier'.

In 1632 he compounded for his recusancy and was required to pay a rent of £50 a year. At this time William Clitherow, a seminary priest, was serving as his chaplain.

In the Civil War Cholmley revealed his royalist sympathies by signing the Yorkshire Engagement of February 1643, though he does not appear to have been particularly active. His estate was sequestered by the parliamentary authorities both for his recusancy and his support for the king.

His son Thomas (1628-1690) was one of a number of recusant squires who were appointed as justices of the peace in the reign of James II.

Brandsby Hall The house was probably built in the reign of Elizabeth. There were 12 taxable hearths in 1675.

(North Yorkshire County Record Office, Cholmeley MSS. *The Memorandum Book of Richard Cholmeley of Brandsby 1602-1623* (*North Yorkshire County Record Office Publications* No 44) (1988). BIHR, High Commission Act Books, RVII/AB9, fols. 79, 252, 323 and AB12, fols. 77, 355.)

BRIGNALL   Gilling West

A village to the south of Barnard Castle. There was no other village within the parish. 1675: 33 households (township of Brignall).

In 1265 Brignall had been granted the right to hold a weekly market and an annual fair.

The hamlet of Greta Bridge, which was partly in the parish of Brignall, was on the site of a Roman fort.

Church St Mary: Early English.

School Ralph Johnson, who was vicar of Brignall from 1662 to 1695, kept a private school for much of that time. This appears to have enjoyed a considerable reputation. A number of Johnson's pupils, including his son Francis, completed their education at Cambridge University.

BROMPTON   Pickering Lythe

A village on the road between Pickering and Scarborough. The parish of Brompton included part of the village of Snainton which had a medieval chapel. The other part of Snainton was in the parish of Ebberston. 1675: 134 households in Brompton, Sawdon and Troutsdale and 76 in Snainton. 1676: 400 persons aged 16 or more (parish).

Church All Saints: Norman in origin; Decorated and Perpendicular.

Principal family Cayley of Brompton Hall (baronetcy 1661). Estate revenue: £700 a year (1640).

Edward Cayley (c.1580-1642) settled at Brompton where he steadily built up his estate. His son Sir William (1610-1681), who was knighted in 1641, served as one of the king's commissioners of array in the summer of 1642. In February 1643 he signed the Yorkshire Engagement in which money was pledged for the royalist cause. He subsequently claimed, however, that he had been forced to sign as a prisoner of the royalists and as a result the parliamentary authorities decided to free his estate from sequestration. His brother Arthur served as a captain of horse in the king's army.

Brompton Hall In 1675 Sir William Cayley was taxed on eight hearths and his son William on 12.

(C.8/143/21. S.P.19/cxx/63. *Calendar, Committee for the Advance of Money,* 850, 907, 913. *Calendar, Committee for Compounding,* 953.)

BROUGH   Hang East

A hamlet within the parish of Catterick. 1675: 4 households.

Principal family Lawson of Brough Hall (baronetcy 1665). Estate revenue: £800 a year (1640). Coalmining in Durham and Northumberland.

The Lawsons were a Catholic family who had migrated from Northumberland where they still owned property.

Sir Ralph Lawson (c.1548-1623), who was a lawyer, had acquired the Brough estate after the death of his father-in-law Roger Burgh in 1574. Following his imprisonment for recusancy in 1580 he avoided further trouble by outwardly conforming for the rest of his life. Lawson was an enterprising landowner who mined coal on an extensive scale. His son James, who acted as his steward, was badly wounded in a riot occasioned by the ploughing up of some pasture grounds at Scremerston in the Palatine of Durham. Sir Ralph fell heavily into debt and was forced to sell some of his outlying property.

His eldest son Roger (1571-1614), who was also a lawyer, shared his preference for outward conformity but married an ardent Catholic, Dorothy Constable, who had a decisive impact on the religious outlook of the family. According to her chaplain, William Palmes, she ensured that their children were all brought up as Catholics and 'solidly instructed in Christian doctrine' and subsequently sent most of them to Continental colleges and religious houses.

Their eldest son Henry (1601-1636) compounded for his recusancy in 1629 and was required to pay a rent of £50 a year. His sons Roger (1622-1637) and Henry (1623-1644) succeeded in turn and were made wards of the Crown. The Court of Wards demanded a wardship fine of £1000 and a rent of £100 a year and was informed that Sir Thomas Riddell felt unable to assume the role of guardian on the grounds that the estate was incapable of bearing such charges.

In the Civil War Henry Lawson took up arms for the king and was slain at Melton Mowbray. He was succeeded by his brother John who was a royalist captain. The estate was put up for sale by the Treason Trustees but he managed to recover it.

Sir John Lawson (1627-1698) may have owed his baronetcy to the loyalty he had displayed during the Civil War. A staunch recusant, he was imprisoned in 1679 for refusing to take the oaths of allegiance and supremacy. James II, however, appointed him as a deputy lieutenant shortly before the political upheaval which cost him his throne.

Brough Hall A gabled Elizabethan house of two storeys. Sir John Lawson added two wings in the late 17th century.

In 1675 there were 17 taxable hearths.

(William Palmes, *Life of Mrs Dorothy Lawson of St Anthony's, near Newcastle-upon-Tyne* (ed. G. B. Richardson) (1851). STAC 8/24/21. Wards 9/572/133.)

BULMER   Bulmer

A village to the south-west of Malton. 1675: 36 households in Bulmer, 32 in Henderskelfe and 27 in Welburn. 1676: 144 persons aged 16 or more (parish of Bulmer).

Henderskelfe Castle dated from the 14th century. It was rebuilt by Charles Earl of Carlisle in 1683 but ten years later the house was destroyed by fire. In 1699 his grandson Charles the third Earl commissioned John Vanbrugh to design a new house on a grand scale and Nicholas Hawksmoor was also brought in, apparently to act as clerk of works. The following year work began on what was to be called Castle Howard.

Church St Martin: Saxon, Norman and Perpendicular.

BURNESTON   Hallikeld

A village to the south-east of Bedale. The extensive parish of Burneston included a number of villages. 1675: 48 households in Burneston, 40 in Carthorpe, 70 in Exelby, Leeming and Newton, 11 in Gatenby and 24 in Theakston.

The Theakstons of Bedale, who owned the manor of Burneston during the years 1591 to 1639, appear to have been primarily responsible for the enclosing activities which went on in the early 17th century. When Sir William Theakston mortgaged some of his property there in 1630 it was described in the deed of conveyance as consisting of 16 oxgangs of arable, meadow and pasture which were severally divided and enclosed.

In 1624 some 200 acres of the 'great common' of Burneston were enclosed and divided among the freeholders. Two years later 15 men were charged with entering the enclosure and throwing down the fences.

Leeming had been granted the right to hold a weekly market and an annual fair in a royal charter of 1300. It was situated on a former Roman road which was still called Watling Street and would later be known as the Great North Road. In 1612 it was reported that the bridge at Leeming, 'being the passage of the country and the usuall way from London to Barwicke, Carlell, Newcastell, and other places, and lying betwixt the parishes of Bedall and Burneston in Watling Street, is in great decaie'. In 1633 the inhabitants of Burneston were indicted for failing to repair Leeming Lane which was a section of the major trunk road.

Early in the reign of Charles I Leeming suffered badly from an outbreak of the plague. This lasted from August 1625 to February 1626.

In 1669 the inhabitants of Burneston informed the North Riding magistrates that they were 'over-charged with poor' and suggested that Carthorpe, Theakston and Gatenby should be required to contribute to the relief of a poor widow who had five children. In the event their proposal was accepted.

Church St Lambert: Perpendicular.

In 1627 Thomas Robinson of Allerthorpe Hall gave £50 for the provision of pews.

One of the most notable vicars of Burneston was Matthew Robinson who held the living from 1651 to 1691. He had studied medicine at university and he continued to practice as a physician during his incumbency. He was also a fellow of St John's College, Cambridge.

Schools In 1680 Matthew Robinson founded a free grammar school at Burneston for children of the parish. The master, who was paid a salary of £16 a year, was required to teach Latin and Greek. The school hours were 6.30 am to 5.30 pm in summer and 7.30 am to 4.30 pm in winter.

Robinson also established a petty school for the younger children.

Almshouses At the same time Robinson founded almshouses for the poor of the parish; and for this purpose he erected a two-storeyed building of brick which also housed the schools.

At Burneston Dr Robinson 'has built, and amply endowed, a very curious hospital for six poor persons, who have each £4 10s per annum' (Ralph Thoresby, 1694).

(C.54/2834. *North Riding Records*, i (1884), 253; ii (1884), 34; iii (1885), 269, 281, 349; and vi (1888), 131-2. H. B. McCall, 'Burneston Hospital and Free School', *YAJ*, xix (1907).)

CATTERICK Hang East/Hang West/Gilling East

A village to the south-east of Richmond which had grown up near the site of a Roman camp. The extensive parish of Catterick contained a considerable number of villages and hamlets, including Bolton upon Swale, Hipswell and Hudswell (partly in the parish of

Easby) which had dependent chapels. Brough, Kiplin and Scorton are separately noticed. 1675: 45 households in Catterick cum Killerby, 17 in Appletons Ambo (East and West Appleton), 28 in Colburn, 68 in Ellerton, Bolton and Whitwell, 34 in Hipswell, 67 in Hudswell and 47 in Tunstall.

Catterick is 'a very small village …. yet remarkable for its situation by a Roman highway which crosses the river here, and for those heaps of rubbish up and down, which carry some colour of antiquity' (William Camden).

Catterick Bridge, which spanned the River Swale, was on the main road between York and Carlisle. A stone structure built in the 15th century, it was often reported to be in decay and during the course of the 17th century large sums of money were levied for its repair.

At Killerby there were the remains of a medieval castle.

In 1624 the North Riding magistrates were informed that Ellen Batty of Catterick was responsible for the handling of ordinary mail and that she 'provideth drinke for all such as ride post'.

Henry Jenkins, who was buried at Bolton upon Swale in 1670, was said to have been born in 1500.

Church St Anne: Perpendicular. A contract was let for the rebuilding of the church in 1412 and chapels were added in 1491 and 1505.

In 1658 the chancel was said to be out of repair.

Schools In his will (1658) Michael Syddall, the vicar of Catterick, made provision for the establishment of a free grammar school which was eventually built in 1688.

There was a school at Hipswell from 1635 onwards. This was probably founded by Christopher Wandesford of Kirklington who was lord of the manor.

Almshouses Syddall was also the founder of a hospital for six poor widows of the parish. This was built in 1688 on a site adjoining the school.

Principal family Braithwaite of Catterick Hall (and Burneside Hall, Westmorland). Estate revenue: £480 a year (1640); £600 a year (1660); £800 a year (1683).

Richard Braithwaite (1588-1673), who was the second son of a Westmorland landowner, acquired the manor of Catterick by marriage in 1639 and decided to settle there. In the Civil War he took up arms for the king and was forced to compound for his estate.

Braithwaite was the author of many poetical works, including *Drunken Barnaby's Journeys*, which earned him considerable popularity. Anthony Wood wrote of him that he was 'a noted wit and poet' and that he left behind him 'the character of a well bread Gentleman and a good Neighbour'.

Although he was himself a Protestant his younger son Sir Stafford Braithwaite and other members of the family were presented for recusancy.

Catterick Hall In 1675 the manor-house had seven taxable hearths.
(*North Riding Records*, iii (1885), 193, 314, 323, 331, 342. Anthony Wood, *Athenae Oxonienses* (1691), ii, columns 378-9. M. W. Black, *Richard Braithwait* (1928). C.33/265/fo.37.)

COVERHAM   Hang West

A small village to the south-west of Middleham. The parish of Coverham included a number of villages and hamlets. 1675: 23 households in Coverham cum Agglethorpe, 37 in Caldbergh, 82 in Carlton Dale, 39 in Carlton township, 33 in Melmerby and 23 in West Scrafton.

Ranulph Fitz Ralph 'built a small Monastery for Canons at Coverham (now contractedly called Corham) in Coverdale' (William Camden). Coverham Abbey, belonging to the Premonstratensian canons, had been established in the 13th century and dissolved in 1536.

From time to time Coverham Bridge, near the abbey ruins, was reported to be in great decay. On these occasions the North Riding magistrates met the cost of repairs by means of a general levy.

The Tophams of Agglethorpe Hall were one of the dominant families in the parish. Among other property they owned the manors of Agglethorpe and Melmerby. During the early 17th century they were a predominantly Catholic family: Edward Topham (c.1575-1628) emerged as a recusant in 1626 and his son Francis (c.1600-1643) compounded for his recusancy in 1632. After the Restoration, however, the Tophams no longer had any Catholic affiliations.

In the Civil War Francis Topham and his brother Henry came out in support of the king. Henry served as a lieutenant colonel in a regiment of horse and died at the battle of Marston Moor in 1644.

Churches Holy Trinity: Early English, Decorated and Perpendicular.

The minister was a perpetual curate.

In 1689 there was a Quaker meeting house at Carlton.

School During the reign of Charles II there was a private school at Melmerby.

(*North Riding Records*, i (1884), 179; iv (1886), 125; and vi (1888), 19. H. Aveling, *Northern Catholics. The Catholic Recusants of the North Riding of Yorkshire 1558-1790* (1966), 175, 262, 308, 354.)

COWESBY   Birdforth

A small village to the south-east of Northallerton. The parish of Cowesby included part of the village of Kepwick; the other part was in the parish of Leake. 1675: 20 households in Cowesby and 35 in Kepwick.

The Leptons of Kepwick, who had an estate worth £330 a year, sold out to Thomas Lord Fauconberg in 1631 and disappeared from the ranks of the landed gentry.

In 1657 a Cowesby man was presented at the Northallerton quarter sessions for locking the door of the parish church and preventing the minister and his congregation from entering.

Church St Michael: Saxon in origin.

The parish was subject to the peculiar jurisdiction of the Bishop of Durham.

School In the reign of Charles II Richard Forster, who had graduated from Queen's College, Oxford in 1664, kept a private school at Cowesby. He was a son of Christopher Forster, vicar and schoolmaster of Leake.

Almshouses The 17th century hospital at Cowesby provided accommodation for four poor tenants of the lord of the manor. Its foundation has traditionally been attributed to Nathaniel Lord Crewe, Bishop of Durham, who bought the estate towards the end of the century.

(C.3/425/7. *North Riding Records*, v (1887), 236.)

COXWOLD   Birdforth

A village to the south-east of Thirsk. The parish of Coxwold contained a number of villages and hamlets, including Birdforth which had a dependent chapel. 1675: 32 households in Coxwold, 10 in Birdforth, 68 in Byland cum membris, 37 in Oulston, 13 in Thornton cum Baxby and 36 in Yearsley. 1676: 320 persons aged 16 or more (parish).

Byland Abbey, which was an establishment of Cistercian monks, had been founded in the 12th century and dissolved in 1538.

A royal charter of 1304 had granted the right to hold a weekly market and an annual fair. By the 17th century only the fair may have survived.

Church St Michael: Perpendicular.

School In 1604 Sir John Harte, a London merchant, founded a grammar school for children of the parish. He had been born at Kilburn to the north of Coxwold.

Almshouses In his will (1653) Thomas Viscount Fauconberg set up trusteeship arrangements for the hospital which he had built some years before. This provided accommodation for ten poor widows.

His grandson Thomas Earl Fauconberg built a hospital for ten poor men. In 1696 he endowed it with a rent-charge of £59 a year.

Principal family Belasyse (or Bellasis) of Newburgh Hall (baronetcy 1611; peerage as Baron Fauconberg 1627, then as Viscount 1643 and Earl Fauconberg 1689). Estate revenue: £3000 a year (1640); £4000 a year (1680). Number of servants: 51 (1609).

Newburgh Priory had been an establishment of Augustinian canons before its dissolution in 1538. Two years later the house and site, together with the manor of Newburgh, had been granted to Anthony Belasyse and following his death in 1552 they had descended to his nephew Sir William Belasyse.

Sir Henry Belasyse (1555-1624) was an efficient landowner who farmed on a considerable scale. He bought a substantial amount of property: in 1608 alone he spent over £8000 on land purchases. With his great wealth he was able to maintain a large establishment of servants and dispense lavish hospitality.

His son Thomas Lord Fauconberg (1577-1653) was an enclosing landlord whose activities sometimes aroused opposition. According to a fellow squire he was prepared 'to rend awaye the inheritances of poore men'. He also added to the estate.

Fauconberg was a leading opponent of Thomas Lord Wentworth and with the help of fabricated evidence sought to have him removed from his office of Lord President of the Council in the North. The attempt failed and in 1631 he spent several months in the Fleet prison. His son Henry (1604-1647) was also committed to prison after publicly insulting the Lord President.

In the Civil War Fauconberg threw in his lot with the Crown and took part in the battle of Marston Moor. After the battle he fled abroad but returned in 1649. His sons Henry and John also joined the royalist army and the latter's exploits earned him the rank of lieutenant general and the title of Lord Belasyse of Worlaby.

Towards the end of his life Fauconberg emerged as a recusant. On the other hand, the parliamentary authorities were informed that his grandson Thomas the second Viscount (1628-1700) was a Protestant who attended church, received communion, kept a chaplain in his house and 'uses prayers twice every day according to the protestant religion'.

In 1657 he married Mary Cromwell, one of Oliver Cromwell's daughters, and received with her a portion of £15,000. According to Gilbert Burnet she was 'a wise and worthy woman' who would have been more likely to maintain the Protectorate regime than either of her brothers.

By supporting the restoration of the monarchy Fauconberg ensured that his Cromwellian connections were overlooked. During the years 1660 to 1687 and 1689 to 1692 he served as Lord Lieutenant of the North Riding. Politically, he was a Whig.

In 1680 he compiled a list of all his purchases of property. These included residences in London and Chiswick and manors and lands in Yorkshire worth over £800 a year.

Newburgh Hall Sir William Belasyse (c.1525-1604) built a large gabled mansion on the site of Newburgh Priory after inheriting the estate in 1552. Parts of the priory were incorporated into the new building. Further building work was carried out in the early 17th century.

Among the rooms listed in a schedule of 1622 were the hall, the great parlour, the dining chamber, the gallery, the great chamber and the study. There was also a chapel.

In 1675 Thomas Lord Fauconberg was taxed on 36 hearths. Five years later he wrote that he had spent about £4000 on building work at Newburgh.

The deer park, which dated from the 14th century, contained 450 acres.

(North Yorkshire County Record Office, Newburgh Priory MSS. HMC, *Various Collections*, ii (MSS of Sir George Wombwell). C.3/364/41 and 425/7. J. T. Cliffe, *The Yorkshire Gentry* (1969), 297-8, 302. Gilbert Burnet, *History of His Own Time* (1724), 83. BL, Additional Charter 30,952 and Additional MSS 41,255, fols. 7,10.)

CRAMBE   Bulmer

A village situated between York and Malton. The parish of Crambe was bordered on the east by the River Derwent. 1675: 32 households in Crambe, 34 in Barton le Willows and 20 in Whitwell on the Hill. 1676: 400 persons aged 16 or more (parish).

The manor of Whitwell was one of the seats of the Vaughan family. See the entry for Sutton upon Derwent in the East Riding.

Churches St Michael: Norman, Early English and Perpendicular.

The Archbishop of York had the patronage rights.

In 1689 there were Quaker meeting houses at Crambe and Barton le Willows.

CRATHORNE   Langbaurgh

A Cleveland village on the River Leven to the south of Yarm. 1675: 28 households (township). 1676: 140 persons aged 16 or more, including 61 recusants (parish).

Church All Saints: Norman with later medieval features. The church had formerly belonged to Guisborough Priory.

Principal family Crathorne of Crathorne Hall. Estate revenue: £800 a year (1630); £1600 a year (1660).

The Crathornes had been seated at Crathorne since the beginning of the 14th century. They were a Catholic family who sometimes had a resident chaplain.

Thomas Crathorne (1582-1639) had been made a ward of the Crown after the death of his father in 1592. He and his wife Katherine, together with five servants, were presented as recusants in 1604 but for many years he chose to conform.

By 1624 he had ceased to attend services at Crathorne church. In 1629 he compounded for his recusancy and shortly afterwards his son Ralph followed suit. In all, they were required to pay £90 a year to the Crown.

Thomas Crathorne's brother John was a Jesuit missioner who died while serving in Yorkshire and another brother, Francis, became a Benedictine monk.

Ralph Crathorne played little part in the Civil War. Although he pledged support for the king by signing the Yorkshire Engagement of February 1643 he claimed that he had been forced to do so when threatened by royalist officers. During the Interregnum two-thirds of the estate were sequestered for his recusancy.

In 1660 the Crathornes inherited a large estate in the East Riding when Francis Wright of Ploughland Hall died without issue.

In 1688 James II appointed Thomas Crathorne as a deputy lieutenant in the East Riding.

Crathorne Hall The house appears to have been rebuilt in the late 17th century. A two-storeyed building with dormer windows.

In 1675 Ralph Crathorne was taxed on 16 hearths.

The Crathornes had a park of 100 acres. In 1615 three men were indicted for breaking into the park and hunting deer with greyhounds.

(North Yorkshire County Record Office, Crathorne MSS. C.5/21/27.)

CROFT   Gilling East

A village on the River Tees to the south of Darlington. The parish of Croft included the village of Dalton upon Tees and the hamlets of Halnaby, Jolby and Walmire. 1675: 41 households in Croft and 20 in Dalton upon Tees.

A royal charter of 1299 had conferred the right to hold a weekly market and an annual fair.

The discovery of sulphurous springs at Croft in the reign of Charles II eventually led to the development of a spa where visitors could drink or bathe in the medicinal waters.

The 15th century bridge which spanned the River Tees was often in need of repair. In 1673 there was a meeting of North Riding and Durham magistrates about the division of cost and it was agreed that the middle of the third pillar should be regarded as the boundary mark. On this occasion the North Riding's share of the expenditure amounted to £110.

Croft was the birthplace of Thomas Burnet (c.1635-1715) who became master of the Charterhouse in London and was the author of several treatises. He provoked a spirited debate by propounding a theory about the way in which the physical features of the world had been formed.

Church St Peter: Norman, Decorated and Perpendicular.

Principal families (1) Chaytor of Croft Hall (baronetcy 1671). Estate revenue: £800 a year (1625); £1000 a year (1666).

The Chaytors had inherited the Croft estate from the Clervaux family in the latter part of the 16th century.

Sir William Chaytor (1592-1640) was made a ward of the Crown following his father's death in 1612 but the financial demands of the Court of Wards were relatively modest. The Court of Wards again intervened in 1641 when his grandson John Chaytor (1635-1659) was left fatherless.

In the Civil War Sir William's second son Henry (1617-1664) served as a royalist colonel and was made governor of Bolton Castle in Wensleydale. In 1660 he managed to gain possession of the manor of Croft by negotiating a financial deal with the widow of his nephew John who had a life interest in the property.

Henry Chaytor had no legitimate issue. He was nevertheless anxious 'to uphold and contineu his name and familie in the house of Croft' and in his will (1664) settled the estate on William Chaytor, the son and heir of Nicholas Chaytor of Butterby in Durham. The settlement was challenged by Sir Francis Liddell and his wife Dame Agnes who as Henry Chaytor's sister claimed that she was the rightful heir. They questioned the legality of the will and sought to prevent the grant of probate. William Chaytor evicted Lady Liddell from Croft Hall but her husband took possession of the house by force.

Sir William Chaytor (1639-1721) settled at Croft after the Court of Chancery ruled in his favour. In 1675 he finally decided to marry. His bride was Peregrina Cradock whom he described as 'young, handsome and of an excellent good charracter'. They had eight sons and five daughters, all of whom died before their father.

Chaytor experienced severe financial problems as a result of such factors as the cost of litigation and his own lack of business acumen. In 1701 he was arrested for debt and committed to the Fleet prison. For the rest of his life he was forced to live as an exile in London.

(2) Milbanke of Halnaby Hall (and Dalden Tower, Durham) (baronetcy 1661). Estate revenue: £3400 a year (1690).

Mark Milbanke was a wealthy Newcastle merchant who built up a large estate in Durham, Northumberland and Yorkshire. About 1650 he purchased the manor of Halnaby from Sir Francis Boynton of Barmston.

His son Sir Mark (c.1630-1680), who was the first baronet, settled at Halnaby and married an heiress, Elizabeth Acclom. On the death of his father in 1677 he inherited his extensive landed possessions and a personal estate which was said to be worth over £100,000.

He was succeeded by his son Sir Mark (c.1659-1698) who took a keen interest in horse-racing. In 1684 Sir William Chaytor was informed that he 'has had great fortune this year with his horses'.

Croft Hall The house was probably a Tudor building. In 1675 Sir William Chaytor was taxed on eight hearths.

In 1641 there were two parks: the Winter Park and the Summer Park.

Halnaby Hall The hall was described as 'a good Howse' in 1637 but the Milbankes decided to replace it. Not long after their purchase of the manor they built a three-storeyed house of brick.

Sir Mark Milbanke the first baronet was taxed on 15 hearths in 1662 and 17 in 1675.

'I passed by a house of Sir Mark Milborn on a hill, a brick building severall towers on the top, good gardens and severall rows of trees up to the house' (Celia Fiennes, 1698).

In a Chancery case of 1705 Halnaby Hall was said to be 'a large Mansion house furnished with all sorts of rich furniture'.

(Durham County Record Office, Chaytor MSS. *The Papers of Sir William Chaytor of Croft (1639-1721) (North Yorkshire County Record Office Publications* No. 33) (1984). Wards 9/102A/fo. 162. C.5/311/13. C.10/97/33 and 103/96. C.33/274/fo. 655 and 308/fo. 560.)

CUNDALL   Hallikeld/Birdforth

A small village to the north-east of Boroughbridge. The parish of Cundall included the hamlets of Leckby and Norton le Clay and part of the hamlet of Fawdington; the other part was in the parish of Brafferton. 1675: 32 households in Cundall, Thornton and Leckby and 19 in Norton le Clay. The hamlet of Thornton Bridge was situated in the parish of Brafferton.

The Walters family of Cundall Hall were new entrants to the landed gentry. Sir Robert Walters, a York merchant, had bought the manor of Cundall in 1597 and having no issue settled it on his brother William who was also engaged in commerce. In the Civil War Robert Walters served as an officer in the parliamentarian army and a member of the North Riding committee.

Church St Mary and All Saints: Saxon in origin.

DALBY   Bulmer

A village situated between Easingwold and Malton. 1675: 29 households in Dalby and Skewsby. 1676: 78 persons aged 16 or more, including 16 recusants (parish of Dalby).

Church St Mary: Norman and Perpendicular.

Principal family Ayscough of Skewsby Hall. Estate revenue: £600 a year (1640).

Christopher Ayscough was a Richmond merchant who built up a sizeable estate in Yorkshire and Durham. His son Allen (1596-1673), who succeeded him in 1626, eventually settled at Skewsby. In 1632 he compounded for his recusancy and was required to pay a rent of £8 a year which was later increased to £30 a year.

In the Civil War he and his eldest son James had their estates sequestered as Catholic royalists. Another son, Francis, served as a lieutenant of horse in the king's army.

After the Restoration the family remained steadfastly loyal to the Catholic faith.

Skewsby Hall In 1675 Francis Ayscough was taxed on seven hearths.

(*CRS*, liii (1961), 345, 425. *Calendar, Committee for Compounding*, 2718.)

DANBY   Langbaurgh

A moorland village situated between Stokesley and Whitby. The extensive parish of Danby contained the villages of Castleton and Glaisdale, which had a medieval chapel, and several hamlets. 1675: 147 households in Danby (probably including Castleton) and 120 in Glaisdale. 1676: 516 persons aged 16 or more, including 8 recusants and 36 Protestant dissenters (Danby cum Glaisdale).

Danby Castle had been built in the 14th century. At Castleton there were the ruins of a Norman castle.

In 1631 Samuel Rabanke settled a rent-charge of £18 10s a year for charitable purposes and in his will he stipulated that the bequest should mainly be used for the relief of nine poor persons of Danby. Rabanke, who died in 1635, had been steward to Henry Earl of Danby, the owner of the manor. A monumental inscription in Danby church testified that 'His life was an academy of virtues; his conversation a precedent for piety; his estate a storehouse for charity'.

Churches St Hilda: Norman, Early English and Perpendicular.

The minister was a perpetual curate.

In 1689 there were Quaker meeting houses at Danby and Glaisdale.

(J. W. Ord, *The History and Antiquities of Cleveland* (1846), 329-44.)

DANBY WISKE   Gilling East

A village to the north-west of Northallerton. The parish of Danby Wiske also included the village of Yafforth which had a medieval chapel. 1675: 50 households in Danby Wiske and 26 in Yafforth.

At Yafforth there were the remains of a Norman castle.

Church [Patron saint unknown]: Norman, Early English, Decorated and Perpendicular.

School Thomas Smelt, who was rector of Danby Wiske, kept a private school there during the Civil War period. According to one of his former pupils 'he taught about three score boys, the greater part of which were gentlemen's sons, or sons of the more substantial yeomanry of that part of Yorkshire or the south parts of the bishopric of Durham'.

In 1652 he became master of the free grammar school at Northallerton.

(*YASRS*, xxxiii (1903), introduction, lxvii-lxviii.)

DOWNHOLME   Hang West

A Swaledale village to the south-west of Richmond. The parish of Downholme included several hamlets. 1675: 38 households in Downholme cum Walburn and 24 in Stainton cum Ellerton.

Ellerton Priory, which was an establishment of Cistercian nuns, was founded in the 12th century and dissolved in 1536.

In 1618 the Walburn estate was bought by the Beckwiths of Aldburgh Hall, near Masham. Walburn Hall, which became a secondary seat, was a fortified house built in the early 16th century and enlarged in the reign of Elizabeth. In 1675 it had 15 taxable hearths.

Church St Michael: Norman, Early English and Decorated.

The minister was a perpetual curate.

EASBY   Gilling West/Gilling East

A Swaledale hamlet on the eastern approaches to Richmond. The parish of Easby included two villages together with the hamlet of Aske. 1675: 16 households in Easby, 8 in Aske, 63 in Brompton on Swale and 25 in Skeeby.

Easby Abbey, which was an establishment of Premonstratensian canons, had been founded in the 12th century and dissolved in 1537.

Sir Thomas Wharton, the father of Philip Lord Wharton, bought the manor of Aske from the Bowes family in 1610 and eventually took up residence there.

Skeeby Bridge was often reported to be in a ruinous condition. In 1635 and again in 1663 the sum of £30 was allocated for its repair.

In 1682 the North Riding magistrates were informed that 'by the late violent floods' the bridge at Brompton on Swale had fallen down; that the inhabitants were too poor to meet the cost of restoring it; and that the building of a new bridge 'for cart and carriage' would require an outlay of £60. After due consideration they decided that £30 should be raised by means of a general levy. In the event it was not until 1691 that the building work was completed.

Church St Agatha: Norman, Early English and Perpendicular.

(*North Riding Records*, iv (1886), 43, 45: vi (1888), 65; and vii (1889), 59.)

EASINGTON   Langbaurgh

A Cleveland village situated to the east of Loftus. The parish of Easington included the village of Liverton which had a medieval chapel and the coastal hamlet of Boulby. 1675: 49 households in Easington and 57 in Liverton. 1676: 253 persons aged 16 or more, including 23 Protestant dissenters (parish of Easington).

Churches All Saints: Norman.

In 1689 there was a Quaker meeting house at Liverton.

School Richard Smelt, who became rector of Easington in 1640, kept a private school there. Among his pupils were Timothy Mauleverer of Ingleby Arncliffe and Thomas Rokeby of Mortham.

Principal family Conyers of Boulby Hall. Estate revenue: £600 a year (1640); £1400 a year (1685). Alum mining in Boulby.

The Conyers family owned the manors of Easington and Boulby.

Robert Conyers (1601-1640) married a Catholic, Anne Conyers, but this had no lasting effect on the family's religious loyalties.

When his son Nicholas (1629-1686) succeeded to the estate he was made a ward of the Crown. Because of his extreme youth he took no part in the Civil War but two of his uncles, Leonard and Edward Conyers, died while in arms for the king. Captain Nicholas Conyers, a parliamentarian, was probably another of his uncles.

In a Chancery suit of 1648 Sir Francis Boynton, the ward's Puritan guardian, claimed on his behalf that Anne Conyers and her associates had taken possession of the whole estate without just cause; that they were denying the young man any allowance for his maintenance; and that they had been felling timber trees on the estate for their own personal gain.

At Boulby there was an alum mine which Nicholas Conyers asserted in a Chancery suit of 1655 was potentially worth £1000 a year. During his minority, however, he had been persuaded to grant a long lease of the close in which it was situated at the modest rent of £24 a year.

In the reign of Charles II he worked the mine himself but in 1685 he agreed to stop production following an approach from John Earl of Mulgrave and Sir Hugh Cholmley who were seeking to establish an alum monopoly. In recompense he was paid a rent of £450 a year.

Through his third wife, Margaret Freville, he acquired considerable property in Durham and as a result he sometimes resided at South Biddick in that county. In 1675 he was appointed sheriff of Durham.

After his death the manors of Easington and Boulby (apart from the alum mine) passed to his sister Catherine Middleton.

Boulby Hall The house was probably Elizabethan in origin.

(C.3/439/11. E.134/1653/Easter 9. C.10/41/29. C.33/269/ fo. 666.)

EASINGWOLD
Bulmer

A small market town on the edge of the Forest of Galtres. The parish of Easingwold included the village of Raskelf which had a medieval chapel. 1675: 155 households in Easingwold and 87 in Raskelf. 1676: 562 persons aged 16 or more (parish of Easingwold).

A royal charter of 1291 had conferred the right to hold an annual fair. The market rights, however, were prescriptive.

In 1606 there was a major fire in Raskelf.

In 1619 the inhabitants of Easingwold came out in opposition to the enclosure of 300 acres in the Forest of Galtres which they claimed had serious implications for their rights of common. In response to their petition the authorities decided that they should be allocated 205 acres of land as compensation. In September 1620, however, the Lord President of the Council in the North complained to the Privy Council that the enclosure had caused a great deal of suffering among the poor of Easingwold.

In 1639 Charles I granted to George Hall and his heirs the right to hold a market every Friday, a fortnightly cattle market and two annual fairs. Seven years later the inhabitants of Easingwold allowed Hall to take over part of the market place, subject to certain conditions.

Church All Saints: Early English, Decorated and Perpendicular.

School A grammar school had been established in 1564.

Almshouses In his will (1599) Ralph Stringer, the vicar of Easingwold, bequeathed Fossbridge House as a residence for two poor persons.

In 1676 Frances Driffield founded almshouses for four poor single women.

(*North Riding Records*, i (1884), 53 and v (1887), 41-2 and 93. G. C. Cowling, *The History of Easingwold and the Forest of Galtres* (undated).)

EAST COWTON
Gilling East

A village near Northallerton which was also known as Long Cowton. 1675: 51 households (township of East Cowton).

Church St Mary: Perpendicular.

School A public grammar school which had been founded by the Dakins family in 1556.

Principal family Anderson of East Cowton Hall. Estate revenue: £1300 a year (1640).

Sir Henry Anderson (c.1583-1659) was a Newcastle businessman who owned considerable property in the neighbouring county of Durham. In 1621 he bought the manor of East Cowton from Sir Arthur Dakins, a declining landowner, for £5000. The following year he began legal proceedings against Dakins, claiming that the manor was heavily encumbered and that the rent yield was less than he had been led to believe. Because of this disagreement he delayed payment of part of the purchase money.

Between 1621 and 1640 his income from the manor increased from £258 to £1000 a year. This was due partly to the expiration of leases and partly to his enclosing activities which were carried on with little regard for the interests of others.

In 1628 he told Sir John Coke, one of the Secretaries of State, that on account of his ill health and the need to discharge his debts he had turned over most of his estate to his children and was living in a retired fashion in Yorkshire. During the 1630s he was involved in a bitter dispute with a neighbour who had a lease of the rectory of East Cowton which he was anxious to secure for himself.

In 1637 Thomas Lord Wentworth was informed that Sir Henry had managed to obtain an audience with the king and had urged him to abandon ship money and call a parliament. In response the king had sharply rebuked him for his effrontery.

On the eve of the Civil War he was in serious financial difficulties. Most of his Durham property had been sold and he had conveyed the East Cowton estate to trustees with the proviso that they should pay him £400 a year for his subsistence.

Sir Henry represented Newcastle in the Long Parliament. On the outbreak of the Civil War he initially embraced the cause of Parliament, perhaps because of his Puritan sympathies, but from the outset he favoured a negotiated settlement. Early on in the war he was captured by the royalists and for 14 weeks was held prisoner in York Castle. As a relative of the Hothams he immediately fell under suspicion when they were arrested by the parliamentarians. In September 1643, when he was living in the royalist garrison at Oxford, the Commons expelled him on the grounds that he had joined the king's party. About this time he drew up some peace propositions in which he suggested that both armies should be disbanded, that papists should be disarmed and confined to their houses and that the government of the Church should be determined by learned divines.

In December 1643 Parliament committed him to the Tower of London. As a result of the Civil War his financial problems grew even more acute: his goods and chattels were plundered by both sides and his estate was sequestered. During the last decade of his life he was detained in a debtor's prison.

His son Henry was a parliamentarian captain and a member of the North Riding committee. In 1662 he sold the East Cowton estate to Thomas Earl of Elgin.

East Cowton Hall In 1675 the house had 11 taxable hearths.

(C.2/James I/A1/13. C.6/155/2. C.8/43/48. C.10/476/18. C.33/207/fo. 236 and 217/fo. 740. C.54/2452. HMC, *Coke MSS*, ii, 372. W. Knowler (ed.), *The Earl of Strafforde's Letters and Dispatches* (1739), ii, 56. HMC, *Fifth Report*, Appendix, 134.)

EAST HARLSEY
Birdforth

A village to the north-east of Northallerton. 1675: 53 households (township of East Harlsey).

Within the parish there were the remains of a medieval castle and a Carthusian monastery. Mount Grace Priory had been founded in 1398 and dissolved in 1539. Much of it still survived and in 1654 the guest house was converted into a private residence.

In 1634 the North Riding magistrates were informed of a dispute between the inhabitants of East Harlsey and those of a hamlet described as Mount Grace over the provision of poor relief. It had been the practice for each community to look after its own poor but the justices took the view that the poor rates should be assessed for the parish as a whole.

Churches St Oswald: Norman in origin.

The minister was a perpetual curate.

In 1689 there was a Quaker meeting house near Harlsey Castle.

(*North Riding Records*, iii (1885), 353 and vii (1889), 103.)

EAST WITTON
Hang West

A Wensleydale village to the south-east of Middleham. There was no other village within the parish. 1675: 112 households (township of East Witton).

Jervaulx Abbey, which was an establishment of Cistercian monks, had been founded in the 12th century and dissolved in 1538.

Royal charters of 1307 and 1400 had conferred on East Witton the right to hold a weekly market and two annual fairs.

Church St Martin: Norman.

School In 1625 there was a Catholic school at East Witton.

EBBERSTON
Pickering Lythe

A village to the east of Pickering. The parish of Ebberston included the village of Allerston where there was a dependent chapel. 1675: 84 households in Ebberston and 72 in Allerston.

Church St Mary: Norman and Early English with later features.

The parish was subject to the peculiar jurisdiction of the Dean of York.

Schools In 1606 the North Riding magistrates decided to compensate Stephen Smith, a schoolmaster of Allerston, for the losses which he had sustained in a fire.

During the reign of Charles II there was a private school at Ebberston.

Principal families (1) Egerton of Allerston Hall. Estate revenue: £2400 a year (1630); £400 a year (1663).

Shortly before his death in 1627 Sir Richard Egerton of Ridley in Cheshire settled the bulk of his substantial estate on trustees for the purpose of raising marriage portions for his daughters. His son Richard (1603-1663) managed to gain possession of all the property in Cheshire and Staffordshire before the trustees had fully discharged their responsibilities. As a result of his extravagance he was soon heavily in debt and within a few years he had disposed of his whole patrimony except for Allerston.

In the Civil War he took up arms for the king and as a consequence his estate was sequestered. In 1661 he secured permission from the overlord of his manor to enclose a tract of waste land and build seven houses on it.

In 1686 his nephew Ralph Egerton sold the Allerston estate.

(2) Etherington of Ebberston Hall. Estate revenue: £600 a year (1628).

The Etheringtons had owned the manor of Ebberston since 1566.

In 1606 Sir Richard Etherington was appointed to the Duchy of Lancaster offices of steward and receiver of Pickering Lythe and constable of Pickering Castle.

In 1620 the Lord President of the Council in the North complained to the Privy Council about his enclosing activities in the Forest of Galtres. These were causing great distress among the poor of Easingwold and Kirby who were being deprived of their rights of common.

By this time Sir Richard was in serious financial difficulties. In 1623 he was described as insolvent and outlawed for debt and the sheriff of Yorkshire seized his estate on behalf of the creditors. Finally, in 1629, he and his son Thomas sold the manor of Ebberston to Henry Earl of Danby.

After the loss of Ebberston the family settled at Rillington in the East Riding where they owned the impropriate rectory.

Allerston Hall In 1675 Thomas Egerton was taxed on 10 hearths.

Ebberston Hall This was probably an Elizabethan house.

(*North Riding Records*, i (1884), 53. C.5/420/101. C.10/32/10, 39/10 and 476/100. *CSP Dom*, 1619-23, 7, 102, 181. PRO, Exchequer, King's Remembrancer, Bills and Answers, E.112/142/1694. E.134/8 Charles I/Michaelmas 12.)

ELLENTHORPE   Hallikeld

A hamlet on the north bank of the River Ure which was situated within the parish of Aldborough in the West Riding. In the 17th century it was often called Ellingthorpe. 1675: 5 households.

Church In 1689 the Brookes family of Ellenthorpe Hall established a nonconformist chapel. This was initially served by visiting preachers, in particular Cornelius Todd and

Noah Ward. In her will (1691) Priscilla Brookes gave direction that the sum of £500 should be invested for the purpose of supporting a nonconformist preacher at Ellenthorpe chapel.

Principal families (1) Aldburgh of Ellenthorpe Hall. Estate revenue: £1000 a year (1641).

The Aldburghs were an old gentry family who had owned property at Ellenthorpe since the 15th century.

Arthur Aldburgh purchased the Crown manor of Aldborough in 1629. The following year he was arrested on the orders of the Privy Council after displaying some initial reluctance to pay his knighthood composition. As a result he appears to have fallen into line.

In 1636 he settled some property on his son Richard with the proviso that he should pay his debts which then amounted to £1500. In the event they remained unpaid.

Richard Aldburgh (1607-1649) was elected to the Long Parliament as MP for Aldborough but in September 1642 was expelled after a considerable period of absence. In June he had been appointed a commissioner of array by the king and subsequently he signed the Yorkshire Engagement of February 1643. When his father, who was also a royalist, compounded for their sequestered estate in 1649 he declared that he was £3000 in debt.

Financial ruin came swiftly despite the extent of the family's landed possessions. By 1653 the whole estate had been sold and the family sank into oblivion.

(2) Brookes of Ellenthorpe Hall (baronetcy 1676). Estate revenue: £1200 a year (1660).

The Brookes family were Presbyterians in religion.

James Brookes, a York merchant, built up a large estate. He bought the Ellenthorpe property from the Aldburghs in 1653 and made it his country seat.

Under the terms of Charles II's Declaration of Indulgence of 1672 Ellenthorpe Hall was licensed for Presbyterian worship.

Sir John Brookes (c. 1635-1691), who succeeded his father in 1675, received part of his education from a Puritan divine, Peter Williams of York. He was one of the earliest fellows of the Royal Society.

In 1682 Sir John Reresby described him as a member of the 'factious' group in York and added that he was 'one of little judgment and lesse courage, but the only Churchman amongst them'. The following year, after the discovery of the Rye House Plot, his house in York was searched for arms.

According to Abraham de la Pryme his son Sir James (c.1675-1742) was a melancholy man who once tried to shoot himself but only fired at his reflection in a looking-glass.

Ellenthorpe Hall In 1675 there were 16 taxable hearths.

(C.10/35/204. C.33/210/fols.261-2; 313/fols.438-40; and 317/fo.435. *Memoirs of Sir John Reresby* (ed. A. Browning and others) (1991), 580.)

ELLERBURN   Pickering Lythe

Ellerburn, situated to the east of Pickering, consisted of little more than the parish church. The parish contained two villages, Farmanby and Wilton which had a dependent chapel. 1675: 52 households in Farmanby and 27 in Wilton.

The manor of Farmanby belonged to the Dean and Canons of Windsor who let it out to tenants.

Church St Hilda: Norman and Perpendicular.

The parish was subject to the peculiar jurisdiction of the Dean of York.

School Robert Rogerson, who was a convicted recusant, kept a private school at Farmanby. In 1658 the authorities finally caught up with him.

(*North Riding Records*, vi (1888), 8. R. W. Jeffery, *Thornton-le-Dale* (1931).)

FELIXKIRK   Birdforth

A small village to the north-east of Thirsk. The parish of Felixkirk contained several villages, including Boltby which had a medieval chapel. 1675: 20 households in Felixkirk, 42 in Boltby, 48 in Sutton under Whitestone Cliffe and 31 in Thirlby. 1676: 300 persons aged 16 or more (parish).

In 1654 Robert Bradley, who was the minister at Boltby, was imprisoned for scandalising and abusing two gentlemen. He was described as a common swearer, a drunkard and a prophaner of the Sabbath.

Church St Felix: Norman and Perpendicular.

School In 1633 William Tankard, a convicted recusant, was keeping a school at Felixkirk.

(*North Riding Records*, v (1887), 168. H. Aveling, *Northern Catholics. The Catholic Recusants of the North Riding of Yorkshire 1558-1790* (1966), 296.)

FINGHALL   Hang West

A village to the east of Leyburn. The parish of Finghall included the villages of Akebar, Constable Burton and Hutton Hang. 1675: 39 households in Finghall and 35 in Constable Burton.

A royal charter of 1321 had granted the right to hold a weekly market and an annual fair at Constable Burton.

In 1611 it was reported that the high street which passed through the lordship of Constable Burton to the coal-pits was 'in great ruyne'.

Church St Andrew: Early English and Decorated.

Principal family Wyvill of Constable Burton Hall (baronetcy 1611). Estate revenue: £1000 a year (1640).

The Wyvills were a family of considerable antiquity who had acquired the Constable Burton estate by marriage in the mid-16th century. During the early 17th century they were mainly Catholic in religion, though successive heads of the family preferred to conform.

Sir Marmaduke Wyvill (1540-1618), who was the first baronet of the family, had been pardoned for taking part in the Northern Rebellion of 1569 and had subsequently held office in Queen Elizabeth's household.

As a landowner he had his problems. In a Star Chamber bill of 1608 he complained that a moorland enclosure of his at Newton le Willows had twice been destroyed by men armed with a variety of weapons.

His grandson Sir Marmaduke (c.1595-1648) married an heiress, Isabel Gascoigne, and through her secured the Sedbury estate. His wife was convicted of recusancy and for this reason he was included in a list compiled by the House of Commons in 1626 of local officials who were regarded as suspect in religion. Despite this he retained all his offices and in 1633 was pricked as sheriff of Yorkshire. In 1638 Sir Edward Osborne, the Vice-President of the Council in the North, suggested to Lord Deputy Wentworth that he should be appointed as a deputy lieutenant: there was no gentleman in the western part of the riding, he wrote, who was 'soe capeable of the place as Sr Marmaduke Wivell if his wive's Recusancye be noe impediment'.

In the summer of 1642 Sir Marmaduke acted as one of the king's commissioners of array and after the outbreak of hostilities he continued to support the royalist cause, though he later claimed that he had never been in arms.

His son Sir Christopher (1614-1681) took a contrary path and was named in 1645 as a member of the North Riding parliamentary committee. He was the first head of the family to marry a Protestant and to make a complete break with the Church of Rome.

During the Interregnum Sir Christopher regularly attended the sermons which Edward Bowles, a Presbyterian minister, delivered in York Minster. In 1660 his wife, Dame Ursula, was the dedicatee of a published sermon which a Puritan divine had preached at the funeral of her sister Margaret Marwood. In dedicating it to her George Ewbank described her as a 'most Noble and vertuous Saint'.

Sir Christopher revealed his Protestant convictions in two small books which he published in the reign of Charles II: *The Pretensions of the Triple Crown Examined* and *A Discourse Prepared for the Ears of Some Romanists*. In the latter work he dismissed the concept of the papal supremacy as absurd.

Constable Burton Hall In the early 17th century the Wyvills built a new house of two storeys. In 1675 it had 18 taxable hearths.

The deer park was medieval in origin. In 1693 a Grinton man was found guilty of stealing a deer from the park.

(STAC 8/309/2. Sheffield Archives, Wentworth Woodhouse Collection, Strafford Letters, xviii, Sir Edward Osborne to Wentworth, 5 December 1638. George Ewbank, *The Pilgrim's Port* (1660).)

FOSTON   Bulmer

A village to the north-east of York. 1675: 24 households in Foston and 22 in Thornton le Clay. 1676: 140 persons aged 16 or more (parish of Foston).

In 1619 Pethuel Otby was succeeded as rector of Foston by his son Tristram who was a man with Puritan leanings. From 1637 onwards he was a pluralist when he also served as rector of the neighbouring parish of Bulmer. In the Civil War period, however, he was deprived of both livings by the parliamentary authorities and Andrew Perry, a Scotsman, became minister of Foston. After the Restoration Otby regained the living of Foston and continued there until his death in 1666.

On the eve of the Civil War the common fields of Foston were enclosed on the initiative of Sir John Hotham who held the manor in right of his wife. Tristram Otby initially opposed the scheme but finally consented when Sir John undertook to add 90 acres to the rectory lands.

Churches All Saints: Norman.

In 1689 there was a Quaker meeting house at Thornton le Clay.

School Pethuel Otby kept a private school at Foston during his incumbency. Sir Henry Slingsby refers in his diary to 'Phatuell Otby with whom I was brought up at School from the age of six until I was 15 years old'. Although Foston was only about twelve miles from the Slingsby mansion at Moor Monkton he and his brother Thomas apparently lived at the parsonage: in August 1613, for example, their father sent Otby £5 'towardes the buyinge of Mr Henry Slingesbie and Mr Thomas Slingesbie some clothes and other nessissaries', together with a further sum of £8 for their 'dyet and learninge' over a period of six months.

(R. A. Marchant, *The Puritans and the Church Courts in the Diocese of York 1560-1642* (1960), 267. E. 134/1657/Michaelmas 9. D. Parsons (ed.), *The Diary of Sir Henry Slingsby of Scriven, Bart.* (1836), 3, 275.)

GATE HELMSLEY   Bulmer

A small village to the east of York. There was no other village within the parish. 1675: 23 households (township of Gate Helmsley).

Church St Mary: Norman and Perpendicular.

The parish was subject to the peculiar jurisdiction of a Prebendary of York.

GILLING

Gilling West/Gilling East

A village to the north of Richmond. The extensive parish of Gilling included a considerable number of villages of which Barton, Eryholme, Forcett and South Cowton had dependent chapels. 1675: 125 households in Gilling cum Hartforth, 25 in Barforth, 68 in Barton, 30 in Eppleby, 29 in Eryholme, 58 in Forcett, 28 in Hutton Magna, 54 in North Cowton, 18 in Ovington and 23 in South Cowton.

'The village [of] Gilling was rather holy upon the account of Religion than strong in respect of its fortifications; ever since Oswius K[ing] of Northumberland….was slain in this place which is called by Bede Gethling. To expiate whose murder a Monastery was built here' (William Camden). The monastery had been destroyed by the Danes in 897.

In 1678 the lands in Barton were valued for fiscal purposes at £900 a year and those in Eryholme at £600 a year.

Church St Agatha: Norman and Decorated.

Schools In the reign of Charles I there was a private school at Gilling. The master may be identified as Lancelot Langhorn who had been educated at Queens' College, Cambridge and ordained priest in 1622.

In 1678 Sir Thomas Wharton, a younger brother of Philip Lord Wharton, founded a free grammar school at Hartforth. The master was to teach 30 poor scholars from Hartforth, Gilling and other villages in the area.

We travelled 'to Hartforth, where kindly entertained at worthy Mr Smith's….. a feoffee of Sir Thomas Wharton's benefaction, viz. a very delicate school-house (which on the Lord's-day they use as a meeting-house) and a very fine convenient house for the master, which he endowed with £40 per annum, viz. £20 per annum to the master, and the rest for repairs, and putting forth poor boys apprentices to trades' (Ralph Thoresby, 1694).

Principal families (1) Wharton of Gillingwood Hall. Estate revenue: £1000 a year (1683). Lead mining.

By the time of his death in 1635 Humphrey Wharton had built up a sizeable estate in the North Riding and Westmorland. Among other things, he purchased the manor of Gilling in 1609 and the manor of Hartforth in 1612. He mined lead at Hartforth and in 1628 he took a lease of the Crown's lead mines in the parish of Grinton.

His son Thomas held the office of receiver of the king's revenue in Northumberland, Durham and Richmond. Following his death in 1641 it was found that he owed the Crown £4138 and steps were taken to recover this sum from his estate by means of annual instalments.

Although his son Humphrey (1626-1694) was made a ward of the Crown the Court of Wards was unusually restrained in its financial demands, perhaps on account of the debt recovery arrangements. In the Civil War his political sympathies remained conveniently hidden but his uncle Anthony Wharton served with some distinction as a royalist officer.

A man of parts, Humphrey Wharton was both a barrister and, in his own words, 'a great trader'. A lease which he secured of lead mines belonging to the Bishop of Durham proved to be highly profitable and he also increased his income through the purchase of land. As a Whig of the more radical sort he fell under suspicion in 1683 after the discovery of the Rye House Plot and the authorities carried out a search of Gillingwood Hall.

(2) Calverley of Eryholme Hall. Estate revenue: £1000 a year (1660).

The Calverleys had acquired the Eryholme estate in 1580.

John Calverley (1618-1660) appears to have taken no part in the Civil War but his brother Timothy was in arms for the king. His younger son Sir Henry (c.1641-1684), who inherited the estate in 1668, was a barrister of the Middle Temple. In 1683 he was suspected of being involved in the Rye House Plot and as a result Eryholme Hall was searched for arms. In the circumstances he considered it prudent to go into exile on the Continent where he was drawn into other Whig plots. With his death the male line expired.

Gillingwood Hall A gabled house of three storeys which was built by Humphrey Wharton following his purchase of the manor of Gilling in 1609. In 1675 it had 13 hearths.

Eryholme Hall The house may have been Elizabethan in origin. In 1675 Sir Henry Calverley was taxed on 12 hearths.

(*North Riding Records*, vii (1889), 9. *CSP Dom, 1641-3*, 173-4, 318. Wards 9/220/64. *CSP Dom, 1683-4*, 39, 62. HMC, *Various*, ii, 174.)

GILLING EAST   Ryedale

A village to the south of Helmsley. 1675: 32 households in Gilling East, 21 in Cawton and 5 in Grimston. 1676: 184 persons aged 16 or more (parish of Gilling East).

Church Holy Cross: Norman and Decorated with an Elizabethan west tower.

School In his will (1570) Sir Nicholas Fairfax gave direction to his eldest son that he should build and maintain a free school within the parish for poor scholars who were to be brought up in good manners, erudition and learning. The school was established in 1590.

Principal family Fairfax of Gilling Castle (and Walton Hall, in the Ainsty of York) (peerage as Viscount Fairfax of Emley, 1629). Estate revenue: £3000 a year (1642).

The Fairfaxes had inherited the Gilling estate towards the end of the 15th century.

Sir Thomas Fairfax (1575-1636), who became the first Viscount, was a major figure in the North Riding. He served as sheriff of Yorkshire, as a deputy lieutenant and justice of the peace and as a member of the Council in the North. Although his first wife,

Katherine, was a recusant this was not regarded as a serious obstacle to his employment, particularly since the authorities were satisfied that he was not himself a Catholic.

Sir Thomas was on close terms with his kinsman Thomas Wentworth the future Earl of Strafford. After his death Wentworth wrote that he had always been 'esteemed and beloved in my family … as one of the Noblest kinsmen and freinds wee had'.

Fairfax was an efficient landowner who improved his estate and engaged in sheep farming on a considerable scale. His social ambitions led him to purchase an Irish viscountcy which was said to have cost him £1300.

As a Protestant he was anxious to stem the growth of Catholicism in his family which was largely due to the influence of his first wife. Sir John Hotham recalled in a letter to Wentworth that he 'lamented that the misfortune of Popish Recusancie should fall into his house by whiche he hath said with passion to me that he plainlie forsawe the diminution of his house would follow both in State and otherwise'. He was therefore dismayed when his eldest son Thomas returned from a Continental tour with his Catholic beliefs reinforced and as a result refused to let him take up residence at Walton Hall.

In a codicil to his will (1634) he nominated Wentworth and his own second son, Henry, as guardians of his grandson William Fairfax on the clear understanding that he would be brought up in the Protestant religion.

Thomas the second Viscount (c.1599-1641) compounded for his recusancy and that of his wife, Alathea, in 1637 and was required to pay a rent of £251 a year. In defiance of his father's wishes he refused to hand over his son William and took steps to ensure that he was schooled in the Catholic faith.

When William Fairfax (1630-1648) succeeded as third Viscount the Court of Wards stepped in and demanded a wardship fine of £3000 and a rent of £1000 a year. The Court was so concerned about his religious upbringing that it assigned the wardship to a number of Protestant landowners, including Ferdinando Lord Fairfax. The latter quickly despatched him to Felsted School in Essex which had a Puritan master.

The third Viscount had one surviving son, Thomas, who died shortly after his father. The estate and title then passed to the boy's uncle, Charles Fairfax, who was soon involved in litigation with his brother's widow, Elizabeth Viscountess Fairfax. She had been awarded possession of lands worth £700 a year by right of dower but in a Chancery suit of 1651 she claimed that he and his associates were preventing her from receiving her rents.

Charles the fifth Viscount (c.1632-1711) was a recusant who had Benedictine chaplains. In 1683 he was described by Sir John Reresby as 'a great leader of the popish party'. Four years later James II appointed him Lord Lieutenant of the North Riding but he was soon replaced. In the last decade of the century he was marked down as a suspected Jacobite.

Gilling Castle A 14th century house which had been substantially improved by Sir William Fairfax in the reign of Elizabeth. The magnificent great chamber was completed in 1585. Other rooms mentioned in a series of inventories include the hall, the dining parlour, the gallery and the schoolhouse.

In 1645 William Lord Fairfax was informed by the steward that 'the leads of Gilling Castle are quite decayed, so that it raineth into the house at above forty places which rotteth the Timber'.

In 1675 Charles Lord Fairfax was taxed on 21 hearths.

The deer park was medieval in origin. In 1374 a licence had been obtained for the imparking of 1000 acres of woodland.

(J. Bilson, 'Gilling Castle', *YAJ*, xix (1907). H. Aveling, 'The Catholic Recusancy of the Yorkshire Fairfaxes', *CRS, Biographical Studies*, iii (1955-6) and *Recusant History*, iv (1957-8). *CRS*, liii (1961), 412-15, 426-7. S.P.16/ccvii/34. Wards 9/220/fo. 55. C.9/13/47. C.10/43/215. BL, Additional MSS 18,979, fo. 198.)

GREAT AYTON   Langbaurgh

A village to the south-west of Guisborough. The parish of Great Ayton included the hamlets of Little Ayton and Nunthorpe which had a medieval chapel. 1675: 70 households in Great Ayton, 17 in Little Ayton and 17 in Nunthorpe.

In 1253 Great Ayton had been granted the right to hold a weekly market and an annual fair.

In 1694 a Great Ayton yeoman was indicted on the grounds that he had uttered the seditious comment that 'This King William has ruined us all'.

Church All Saints: Norman.

The minister was a perpetual curate.

(*North Riding Records*, vii (1889), 142.)

GREAT EDSTONE   Ryedale

A small village to the south-east of Kirkby Moorside. 1675: 22 households in Edstones Ambo (including Little Edstone which was in the parish of Sinnington) and 2 in North Holme. 1676: 62 persons aged 16 or more (parish of Great Edstone).

Church St Michael: Early English.

GREAT LANGTON   Gilling East

A village on the River Swale between Richmond and Northallerton. 1675: 25 households in Great Langton and 17 in Little Langton.

In 1622 it was reported that a wooden bridge over the River Swale known as Langton Bridge was in decay. Since it carried only a minor road the view was taken that it should be repaired by the inhabitants of Great Langton.

Church St Wilfrid, Great Langton: Norman and Decorated.

(*North Riding Records*, iii (1885), 144.)

GREAT SMEATON   Gilling East/Allertonshire/Langbaurgh

A village to the south-east of Darlington. It was situated partly in the parish of Great Smeaton and partly in the parish of Croft. The parish of Great Smeaton included the villages of Appleton Wiske, which had a dependent chapel, and Hornby. 1675: 46 households in Great Smeaton, 44 in Appleton Wiske (including 9 in Hornby) and 25 in Hornby (Allertonshire return).

In 1615 Marmaduke Vincent, who was the squire of Great Smeaton, was presented at the Richmond quarter sessions for admitting into his house certain 'players of enterludes', some of whom were recusants from Egton.

In 1666 an inhabitant of Great Smeaton was indicted for saying that he 'doth not value his Majesty nor his officers'.

In 1678 the lands in Great Smeaton were valued for fiscal purposes at £620 a year.

Towards the end of Charles II's reign a new bridge was built at Appleton Wiske. The North Riding magistrates had allocated the sum of £20 for the project but in 1682 they heard that the surveyors had negotiated a contract price of £16 and had not yet paid the workmen the full amount that was due to them.

For some time the office of constable of Great Smeaton was jointly exercised by a woman, Anne Sigsworth, and her son. In 1695, when they relinquished the office, the magistrates gave direction that the inhabitants of the village should reimburse Mrs Sigsworth for the expenditure which she had incurred on their behalf.

Church St Eloy: Perpendicular.

This was the only church in England which was dedicated to St Eloy.

(*North Riding Records*, ii (1884), 110-11; vi (1888), 107; and vii (1889), 9, 58-9, 153.)

GRINTON
Hang West/Gilling West

A Swaledale village to the west of Richmond. The extensive parish of Grinton included two large townships: Muker, which had an Elizabethan chapel, and Reeth. 1675: 79 households in Grinton, 179 in Muker (including Angram, Keld and Thwaite) and 191 in Reeth (including Fremington and Healaugh).

The area was rich in lead ore. The Crown had lead mines in Grinton, Fremington and other places within the parish.

Philip Lord Wharton (1613-1696) owned the manors of Healaugh, Muker and Reeth. At Healaugh he mined lead on a major scale. In a Chancery suit of 1677 he complained that his Swaledale tenants had been enclosing parcels of the wastes without securing licences from him or paying any fine or rent.

Grinton was a parish in which Catholic influences still remained comparatively strong. In 1604 there were 38 recusants and 23 noncommunicants. As late as 1690 a total of 36 recusants was recorded.

The bridges at Grinton and Reeth were often reported to be in a dilapidated condition. The cost of repairs was invariably met by means of a general levy: in 1659, for example, the North Riding magistrates approved an allocation of £40 for each of these bridges.

In 1607 Henry Simpson the vicar of Grinton testified before the justices at Richmond that he had reason to believe that Henry Simpson of Reeth and two of his associates intended to kill him or burn down his house. Accordingly it was decided that these men should be taken into custody.

In 1661 a yeoman of Keld was indicted for saying to another man 'Thou had best be quiet for those that thou buildest upon I hope they will not last long....I lived as well when there was no King and I hope to do so again'.

In 1691 the inhabitants of Reeth complained that they had been 'much imposed upon' by the inhabitants of Muker in all their assessments since the constablery embracing both townships had been split into two about 1667. They therefore proposed that the new constableries should be reunited but the magistrates decided to take no action until the villagers of Muker had been given an opportunity to express their views on the matter.

In 1695 Philip Lord Wharton procured letters patent which authorised the establishment at Reeth of a weekly market and four annual fairs.

Churches St Andrew, Grinton: Norman, Decorated and Perpendicular.

In 1689 there were four Quaker meeting houses within the parish of Grinton.

Schools James Hutchinson, a York merchant, built a school at Fremington and in his will (1643) provided an endowment. It was specified that the school should be open to all qualified students within the parish of Grinton and that children from poor families should be educated free of charge. Fremington was Hutchinson's birthplace.

In his will (1678) Anthony Metcalfe founded a school at Muker. The master was required to teach eight poor scholars reading, writing, accounts and the Church catechism.

(C.10/130/114. H. Aveling, *Northern Catholics. The Catholic Recusants of the North Riding of Yorkshire 1558-1790* (1966), 429. *North Riding Records*, i (1884), 67; vi (1888), 19, 42; and vii (1889), 118. *CSP Dom, 1694-5*, 13, 60. W. K. Jordan, *The Charities of Rural England 1480-1660* (1961), 342.)

GUISBOROUGH   Langbaurgh

A small Cleveland market town. The parish of Guisborough included the village of Upleatham, which had a medieval chapel, and several hamlets. 1675: 214 households in Guisborough, 14 in Hutton Lowcross, 14 in Pinchingthorpe and 31 in Upleatham.

Guisborough Priory was a large Augustinian monastery founded in the 12th century and dissolved in 1538.

A royal charter which the priory had been granted in 1263 conferred the right to hold a weekly market and an annual fair. In 1696 William Chaloner secured a licence for two additional fairs.

Towards the end of the 16th century Sir Thomas Chaloner discovered alum deposits near Guisborough and began to engage in mining activities. This marked the birth of the Yorkshire alum industry.

In January 1643 a parliamentarian force under the command of Sir Hugh Cholmley and Sir Matthew Boynton routed a detachment of royalist troops on the outskirts of Guisborough.

In 1669 it was reported that there were 30 Quakers in the parish.

Guisborough 'stands upon a rising ground; at present a small town …. The place is really fine …. the soil is fruitful, and produces grass and fine flowers a great part of the year; it richly abounds with veins of metal and Alum-earth …. from which they now begin to extract the best sort of Alum and Copperas in great plenty' (William Camden).

'The Abbey-Church of Gisburgh seems by the ruins to have been comparable to the best Cathedrals in England. The Inhabitants of this place are observ'd by Travellers to be very civil and well bred, cleanly in dressing their diet, and very decent and neat in their houses' (Edmund Gibson, 1696).

Churches St Nicholas: Perpendicular.

In 1689 the town had a Quaker meeting house.

School A free grammar school founded by Robert Pursglove, the last prior of Guisborough, in 1561.

Almshouses Pursglove also established a hospital for six poor men and six poor women.

Principal family Chaloner of Guisborough Hall (and Steeple Claydon House, Buckinghamshire) (baronetcy 1620). Estate revenue: £1500 a year (1615); £1600 a year (1665). Alum mining.

The Chaloners had purchased the site of Guisborough Priory in 1550 and the manor and township in 1558.

Sir Thomas Chaloner (1561-1615) was a courtier who served as governor or tutor to Prince Henry, the elder son of James I.

When the king took over the alum monopoly in 1609 it was agreed that during the years 1617 to 1638 the Chaloners would be paid £1000 a year as compensation. In the event the Crown soon went back on its undertaking.

At the time of his death Sir Thomas was heavily in debt. He had already pawned his plate and jewels and in his will (1615) he gave direction that some of his landed property should be sold.

His son Sir William (1588-1641), who never married, spent much of his time abroad and died in Turkey. With his death the baronetcy became extinct.

The heir was his nephew Edward Chaloner (1625-1680) who was knighted in 1672. He took no part in the Civil War but his uncles Thomas and James Chaloner were zealous parliamentarians while their half-brother Henry fought for the king. Thomas Chaloner signed the king's death warrant in 1649 and fled abroad at the Restoration.

In 1663 Edward Chaloner secured a private act for the purpose of making a new settlement of his estate. According to this act he had 'layd out and expended by building and other wayes all the moneys raised by the sale of his said wife's Lands in and upon the said Manor of Gisborne alias Gisborough for the improving thereof and hath thereby improved the same to the value of two hundred and fifty pounds per annum at the least'.

Guisborough Hall Sir Thomas Chaloner (1521-1565) probably built the original house which was a gabled building of three storeys.

Sir Edward Chaloner apparently made some improvements. He was taxed on 14 hearths in 1662 and 17 in 1675.

His son William (1655-1716) was responsible for a major addition around the end of the 17th century.

(North Yorkshire County Record Office, MSS of Lord Gisborough. PRO, Wills, PROB11/126/95. C.2/James I/F11/44. C.8/55/123. C.10/477/57. House of Lords, Private Act, 15 Charles II, no. 33. B. J. D. Harrison and G. Dixon (eds.), *Guisborough Before 1900* (1981). R. B. Turton, *The Alum Farm* (1938).)

HACKNESS   Whitby Strand

A village to the west of Scarborough. The parish of Hackness included the hamlets of Broxa, Harwood Dale, Silpho and Suffield cum Everley. 1675: 39 households in

Hackness and a total of 100 in the outlying hamlets. 1676: 280 persons aged 16 or more, including 16 recusants and 24 Protestant dissenters (parish of Hackness).

Hackness is 'a very litle small towne and no market towne and not fitting to lodge or enterteyne any gentlemen of quality, there being but two small Alehouses in the towne' (Court of Wards deposition, 1638).

In 1691 the inhabitants of the constablery of Hackness complained in a petition that they were 'already much burthened with poor'.

Churches St Peter, Hackness: Saxon, Norman, Early English and Perpendicular. The spire had been added in 1450.

In 1634 Sir Thomas Hoby built a public chapel at Harwood Dale and this was consecrated two years later.

Principal family Hoby of Hackness Hall. Estate revenue: £1500 a year (1633). Number of servants: 14 (1600).

Sir Thomas Posthumous Hoby (1566-1640) was a younger son of the Hoby family of Bisham Abbey in Berkshire. He acquired the Hackness estate through his marriage to Margaret Sidney, the only child of Arthur Dakins, who had twice been widowed.

Hoby and his wife were strict Puritans who had a succession of domestic chaplains and provided support and encouragement for godly preachers. In 1626 they were described as 'patternes of Piety' and 'Patrons of pious and godly men, and of their labours'. Lady Hoby's diary, which covers the years 1599-1605, graphically conveys the Puritan atmosphere of Hackness Hall.

Sir Thomas displayed great diligence in performing his duties as an MP, deputy lieutenant and magistrate. A fellow Puritan, Sir William Brereton, considered him to be 'the most understanding, able and industrious justice of peace in this kingdome'. He was, however, a deeply unpopular figure in the North Riding, particularly on account of his unremitting campaign against Catholics.

In his memoirs Sir Hugh Cholmley refers to Hoby's bitter feud with his father, Sir Richard, which was carried on in the Star Chamber and Exchequer Courts. Sir Thomas, he writes, 'haveing a full purse, noe children and as it was thought not able to get one, delighted to spend his mony and tyme in sutes'.

During their later years the Hobys lived from time to time in Middlesex, first at Twickenham and then at Isleworth where they had a house built.

Since he had no children Sir Thomas settled the estate on his relatives the Sydenhams of Brympton in Somerset and did his best to ensure that they continued the Puritan tradition at Hackness. The Sydenhams, however, remained seated in Somerset and Hackness Hall appears to have been used only as a dower house.

Hackness Hall A timbered Elizabethan house. In 1675 Dame Anne Sydenham was taxed on 21 hearths.

(Wards 9/573/204. Dorothy M. Meads (ed.), *The Diary of Lady Margaret Hoby 1599-1605* (1930). Nicholas Byfield, *The Rule of Faith* (1626). *Surtees Society*, cxxiv (1914), 6.

J. Binns (ed.), *The Memoirs and Memorials of Sir Hugh Cholmley of Whitby 1600-1657*, YASRS, cliii (2000), 72.)

HAUXWELL   Hang West

A village situated between Middleham and Richmond which was also known as East and West Hauxwell. The parish of Hauxwell included the village of Barden. 1675: 39 households in Hauxwell and 21 in Barden.

Church St Oswald: Norman and Early English.
Principal family Dalton of Hauxwell Hall. Estate revenue: £700 a year (1650).

Sir William Dalton (c.1570-1650) was a younger son of an East Riding Catholic family, the Daltons of Swine. He became a lawyer and served as the King's Attorney in the North and a legal member of the Council in the North. Through the profits of office he was able to build up a considerable estate. In 1631 he bought the manor of West Hauxwell together with property in East Hauxwell. The purchase price amounted to some £3000 but as late as 1649 it was alleged that he had not yet paid the whole sum. While he continued to live in York his son John (1603-1645) took up residence at Hauxwell.

In the Civil War the Daltons supported the royalist cause. Sir William and his son signed the Yorkshire Engagement of February 1643 in which the king was promised financial assistance. John Dalton also served as an officer in the royal army and died in Newark Castle of wounds received in an engagement at Burton on Trent.

Although the Daltons appear to have been a largely Protestant family one of John Dalton's younger sons, Marmaduke, was a seminary priest who acted as chaplain to the Tunstalls of Wycliffe.

The orderly descent of the estate was seriously disrupted as a result of the premature death by drowning of Sir Marmaduke Dalton (1655-1680) who left only daughters. Eventually, however, his brother Sir Charles gained possession of the Hauxwell property.

Hauxwell Hall The manor-house in West Hauxwell which became the Dalton family seat had been built by the previous owners, the Jobsons, in the reign of James I. In 1675 it had 14 taxable hearths.

(C.5/381/74. S.P.19/cxx/99, 104, 107. G. Anstruther, *The Seminary Priests. III. 1660-1715* (1976), 45.)

HAWNBY   Birdforth

A village to the north-west of Helmsley. The extensive moorland parish of Hawnby contained a number of villages and hamlets. 1675: 40 households in Hawnby, 28 in

Arden cum Ardenside, 52 in Bilsdale cum Snilesworth and 8 in Dale Town. 1676: 251 persons aged 16 or more (parish).

Arden Nunnery had been founded in the 12th century and dissolved in 1537. The Tankards of Arden Hall were a cadet branch of modest estate. In the Civil War Charles Tankard supported the king and as a result his house and grounds were plundered.

Church All Saints: Norman.

Principal family Meynell of Hawnby Hall. Estate revenue: £700 a year (1615).

In the early 17th century the Meynells were a family with divided religious loyalties. The situation was described by Robert Meynell, a younger son, on his admission to the English College at Rome in 1635. According to this account his father Edmund Meynell (c.1570-1615) had lived and died a Protestant (or 'heretic' as he called him). His three children by his first wife, including Charles his son and heir, were also Protestants but the seven children who were the issue of his second marriage were all Catholics. These Catholic children owed their religious orientation primarily to the influence of their mother, Elizabeth Meynell, who (it had been reported in 1616) had 'persisted contemptuous in her Recusancy'. Robert Meynell, for his part, was ordained priest and two years later he left for England.

Charles Meynell was heavily involved in horse-racing and his growing financial difficulties may have been due at least in part to his gambling instincts. In 1624 he sold the manor of Hawnby to James Morley, a Chancery official, who also acquired his other manors. Morley agreed to pay him an annuity of £20 which was apparently his only means of subsistence. In 1650 he was acting as Charles II's agent in Rome.

Hawnby Hall In 1675 the house had 11 hearths.

(*CRS*, lv (1963), 447-8. *North Riding Records*, ii (1884), 113. PRO, State Papers Supplementary, S.P.46/cvii/fo.93. C.6/2/99.)

HELMSLEY   Ryedale

A market town on the River Rye. The extensive parish of Helmsley contained a number of villages, including Bilsdale, Harome and Pockley which had dependent chapels. 1675: 162 households in Helmsley, 54 in Bilsdale and Kirkham, 43 in Harome, 48 in Nawton cum Beadlam, 29 in Pockley, 45 in Rievaulx and 31 in Sproxton. Nawton was in the parish of Kirkdale. 1676: 1149 persons aged 16 or more (parish of Helmsley and chapelry of Bilsdale).

Rievaulx Abbey, which was a Cistercian monastery, had been founded in the 12th century and dissolved in 1538.

The ancient market rights appear to have been prescriptive. In 1670 there was a formal grant of the right to hold a weekly market and three annual fairs.

The manor and castle belonged to the Earls of Rutland until the reign of Charles I when they were inherited by George Villiers, second Duke of Buckingham. As a royalist he had his estate confiscated and in 1650 the manor of Helmsley was granted to Thomas Lord Fairfax. Eventually, however, he managed to regain possession of the manor through his marriage to Mary Fairfax who was Lord Fairfax's only child. In 1695 his trustees sold the manor, together with other property, to Sir Charles Duncombe, a London banker, for some £85,000. As a result of this transaction Duncombe became the owner of a North Riding estate worth £4771 a year.

In January 1607 it was reported that there had been a great fire at Helmsley which had resulted in the destruction of a number of houses.

In 1615 the North Riding magistrates were informed that Helmsley was 'overcharged with poore people so as they ar not able to releive them'.

According to a petition which the magistrates received in 1625 there had been a fire at Rievaulx which had resulted in the destruction of ten dwellings together with barns and other buildings.

During the early part of the Civil War the castle was garrisoned by royalist troops under the command of Sir Jordan Crosland. In 1644 Sir Thomas Fairfax mounted a siege and the garrison eventually surrendered.

Churches All Saints: Norman and Early English.

In 1648 the church was said to be 'in great decay and likely to come to ruin if speedy course be not taken for repair'.

In 1689 there was a Quaker meeting house in Helmsley.

Castle Helmsley Castle had originally been built in the 12th century and subsequently improved and enlarged in the 13th, 14th and 15th centuries. In the reign of Elizabeth further additions had been made by Edward Manners, Earl of Rutland.

In 1647 Parliament decided that the castle should be rendered untenable.

During the reign of Charles II it was partly restored by George Duke of Buckingham who took up residence there. After his death in 1687, however, it was allowed to decay.

School There had been a school at Helmsley as early as the 13th century.

In 1625 the vicar of Helmsley informed the Northern High Commission that the schoolmaster, Roger Conyers, had been taking in Catholic pupils. Significantly, Conyers made no attempt to deny the allegation.

(*North Riding Records*, i (1884), 64; ii (1884), 84; iii (1885), 226; and v (1887), 6. C.33/319/fo.591. C.38/251/20 May 1695. BIHR, High Commission Act Book, RVII/AB9/fo.362. J. McDonnell (ed.), *A History of Helmsley, Rievaulx and District* (1963). W. M. I'Anson, 'Helmsley Castle', *YAJ*, xxiv (1917).)

HINDERWELL   Langbaurgh

A village situated in a coastal area to the north-west of Whitby. The parish of Hinderwell included the village of Roxby which had a medieval chapel and the fishing hamlets of Runswick and Staithes. 1675: 50 households in the township of Hinderwell and 55 in Roxby. 1676: 496 persons aged 16 or more, including 5 recusants and 36 Protestant dissenters (parish).

In 1603 a merchant ship which ran aground brought the plague to Hinderwell. In all, 49 of the inhabitants died as a result of this bizarre incident.

The manor of Roxby belonged to the Boyntons of Barmston in the East Riding who founded the chapel there in the 15th century. They sometimes resided at Roxby. About 1637 Roxby House was described as 'laitlie built' by Sir Matthew Boynton.

George Fox the Quaker leader noted in his journal that in 1651 he visited Staithes 'wher I mett with many professors and ranters: and great meetinges I had amongst them'.

'…within a few miles of Whitby we passed not far from Runswick, the place where, near by the sea-side, stood a little village of six or ten houses the last spring, of which I find from credible persons, the report we had of its being swallowed up of the earth, too true, though blessed be God, all the inhabitants were saved' (Ralph Thoresby, 1682).

Churches St Hilda: Saxon or Norman in origin.

In 1689 there were Quaker meeting houses at Hinderwell and Roxby.

(J. W. Ord, *The History and Antiquities of Cleveland* (1846), 296. N. Penney (ed.), *The Journal of George Fox* (1911), i, 22. J. Howard, *Staithes. Chapters from the history of a seafaring town* (2000).)

HOLTBY   Bulmer

A village to the east of York which was partly in the parish of Holtby and partly in the parish of Warthill. Conversely, the parish of Holtby included some of the houses in the village of Warthill. 1675: 25 households in Holtby and 26 in Warthill.

Church Holy Trinity: early medieval.

The parish was subject to the peculiar jurisdiction of the Dean and Chapter of Durham.

HORNBY   Hang East

A hamlet near Bedale. The parish of Hornby contained several other hamlets. 1675: 11 households in Hornby, 2 in Ainderby cum Holtby and 22 in Hackforth. Ainderby Mires appears to have been a depopulated village.

Church St Mary: Norman, Decorated and Perpendicular. The church was a peculiar which was subject to the jurisdiction of the Dean and Chapter of York.

Principal family Darcy of Hornby Castle (peerage as Baron Darcy and Conyers 1641, then as Earl of Holderness 1682). Estate revenue: £3300 a year (1640).

The Darcys mainly acquired their extensive landed estates by marriage and inheritance.

Thames Darcy married one of the daughters and coheirs of John Lord Conyers of Hornby Castle. He was a Catholic who partially conformed for a time. In 1605 two of his servants were found guilty of high treason and executed.

His son Sir Conyers (1570-1654), who succeeded him in 1605, was a firm Protestant who was described by his half-brother Thomas as a Puritan.

In 1630 he was summoned before the Council in the North, severely reprimanded and fined for abusing his authority as a justice of the peace. Later that year he was drawn into an abortive plot devised by his brother-in-law Thomas Lord Fauconberg who was attempting to secure the removal of Wentworth from his office of Lord President of the Council in the North.

In the Civil War he managed to remain uncommitted but his son Conyers was a royalist who served as a commissioner of array and signed the Yorkshire Engagement of February 1643. When Parliament established the Northern Association in 1645 the latter was named as a member of the Yorkshire committee; even so he was forced to compound as a delinquent.

The family inherited a large estate in the West Riding after the death of their kinsman John Lord Darcy of Aston in 1635 but twenty years later Conyers Lord Darcy (1599-1689) disposed of a substantial part of this property for the sum of £15,000.

In 1680 he came into possession of further lands which had belonged to John Lord Darcy. This property included Aston Hall which he appears to have found more agreeable than Hornby Castle.

Hornby Castle The castle had been built in the 14th century and significantly improved in the late 15th century.

In 1675 there were 26 taxable hearths.

(BL, Egerton MSS 3402. C.10/465/195. C.22/822/56.)

HOVINGHAM   Ryedale

A village situated between Helmsley and Malton. The parish of Hovingham included a number of hamlets. 1675: 68 households in Hovingham, 1 in Airyholme, 18 in Coulton, 30 in East and West Ness, 4 in Fryton, 11 in South Holme and 1 in Wath. West Ness was in the parish of Stonegrave. 1676: 430 persons aged 16 or more, including 53 recusants (parish of Hovingham).

A royal charter of 1252 had conferred the right to hold a weekly market and an annual fair.

Churches All Saints: Saxon and Norman.

In 1689 there was a Quaker meeting house in the parish.

Principal family Worsley of Hovingham Hall. Estate revenue: £600 a year (1664).

The Worsleys, who had long been seated in Lancashire, had bought the manor of Hovingham in 1563 but do not appear to have settled there until the reign of James I.

In the early 17th century there was a certain ambivalence about their religious loyalties. Thomas Worsley (c.1580-1659) was the son of a staunch Protestant but in 1619 he was presented as a recusant along with his wife Katherine and his daughter Elizabeth. Shortly afterwards Ingram Lister, the minister of Stonegrave, informed the North Riding magistrates that they 'are no Recusantes but go orderlie to Church, as some of the Bench knowe'. Subsequently an informer, Richard Heaton, began to take a close interest and in 1629, on the basis of his evidence, Worsley was required to pay a composition rent of £40 a year on account of his recusancy. In 1631 the Bishop of Chester issued a certificate of conformity after he had attended a service in his chapel but in 1633 he was described as a relapsed recusant.

In 1625 Worsley began legal proceedings against Sir John Wood whose daughter Elizabeth had married Thomas his son and heir. His basic allegation was that Wood had failed to provide the portion specified in the marriage settlement but he also claimed that he had been seeking to gain possession of his estate by striking a deal with one of his creditors.

His grandson Thomas Worsley (1624-1664) was made a ward of the Crown following the death of his father in 1627.

In a petition submitted to Parliament in 1648 Thomas Worsley the elder, his wife and two of his children related that although they had always detested popery they had been great sufferers under the prelates on account of their nonconformity to the Book of Common Prayer and had been indicted and convicted as recusants. They also stressed that they had demonstrated their loyalty to Parliament in many ways and not least through their willingness to make financial contributions.

During the Interregnum the grandson sought to defend his property rights by bringing legal actions against his grandfather and his uncle John Worsley.

In 1667 there was a further bout of litigation. Thomas Worsley (1649-1715) complained that his stepmother and her new husband, Benjamin Norcliffe, had taken possession of the whole estate and were committing great waste. In particular, they were felling timber, pulling down houses, destroying hedges and fences and granting leases at uneconomic rents.

Hovingham Hall A modest house which was probably Jacobean. In 1675 there were six taxable hearths.

(C.3/390/10. C.10/51/209 and 489/163. C.22/834/25 and 944/31. C.33/244/fo.136. HMC, *Seventh Report*, Appendix, 59-60.)

HUNTINGTON   Bulmer

A village on the River Foss to the north of York. The parish of Huntington included the hamlet of Earswick and part of the hamlet of Towthorpe; the other part was in the parish of Strensall. 1675: 57 households (township of Huntington). 1676: 96 persons aged 16 or more (parish).

In 1606 the inhabitants of Huntington were presented at the Thirsk quarter sessions for neglecting to repair the king's highway leading to York. In spite of continuing pressure from the authorities they were slow to take any action, as were their neighbours in Earswick, but in 1608 the magistrates were informed that the road had now been paved to a satisfactory standard.

Huntington was within the bounds of the royal Forest of Galtres. Sir Arthur Ingram, who bought the manor of Huntington in 1612, engaged in enclosing activities there as the first step in a project for the extensive development of lands within the forest for agricultural purposes.

Church All Saints: Norman, Early English and Perpendicular.

School In 1604 it was reported that Luce Scaife, the recusant wife of Thomas Scaife, 'teacheth children'.

(*North Riding Records*, i (1884), 34, 63, 134. A. F. Upton, *Sir Arthur Ingram c.1565-1642* (1961), 196-9. E. Peacock (ed.), *A List of the Roman Catholics in the County of York in 1604* (1872), 118.)

HUSTHWAITE   Birdforth

A village to the north of Easingwold. The parish of Husthwaite included the village of Carlton Husthwaite which had a dependent chapel. 1675: 75 households in Husthwaite and 33 in Carlton Husthwaite.

In 1651 George Robson of Husthwaite was indicted for publicly reading the Book of Common Prayer.

The chapel at Carlton Husthwaite (St Mary) was built in the 17th century.

Church St Nicholas: Norman and Perpendicular.

The parish was subject to the peculiar jurisdiction of a Prebendary of York.

The minister was a perpetual curate.

(*North Riding Records*, v (1887), 85.)

HUTTON BUSCEL   Pickering Lythe

A village to the south-west of Scarborough. The parish of Hutton Buscel included the village of West Ayton. 1675: 78 households in Hutton Buscel and 43 in West Ayton. 1676: 264 persons aged 16 or more (parish).

In West Ayton there were the ruins of a fortified mansion (Ayton Castle) which had been built in the 14th century.

In 1626 there was an outbreak of the plague at Hutton Buscel and Aytons Ambo (West Ayton and East Ayton in the parish of Seamer).

In 1664 17 men of Hutton Buscel were indicted 'for riotous and illegal assembly, and for assault'.

In 1669 it was reported that there were 200 Quakers in Hutton Buscel and the neighbouring village of Wykeham.

Ayton or West Ayton Bridge carried the Pickering-Scarborough road across the River Derwent. In the reign of Charles II it required major restoration work. In 1674 and 1675 the North Riding magistrates allocated a total of £140 for this purpose.

Church St Matthew: Norman, Early English and Perpendicular.

(*North Riding Records,* iii (1885), 264 and vi (1888), 78, 213, 224. G. Lyon Turner (ed.), *Original Records of Early Nonconformity under Persecution and Indulgence* (1911-14), i, 161.)

HUTTON CONYERS   Allertonshire

A small village to the north-east of Ripon. Although it was deemed to be outside the parish system it had no church of its own. 1675: 29 households (township of Hutton Conyers).

In the early 17th century the Hutton Conyers estate with its Elizabethan manor-house belonged to the Mallory family of Studley in the West Riding who treated it as a secondary seat.

In 1646 the North Riding magistrates decreed that 'whereas Hutton Conyers hath been visited with the Plague and did releive themselves, they shalbe discharged of their assessment for the releife of Richmond during the time the towne was visited'.

In 1669 the magistrates received a petition from the inhabitants of Hutton Conyers and Nunwick in which they related that 'the bridge called the King's Bridge' (which spanned the River Ure) was 'in great decay....and that the same is a very necesssary bridge for the use of the country'. They considered it appropriate that the cost of the repair work should be met from general funds and this argument met with a favourable reception.

(*North Riding Records*, iv (1886), 250 and vi (1888), 142.)

HUTTONS AMBO   Bulmer

Twin villages (High and Low Hutton) situated to the south-west of Malton. The parish of Huttons Ambo extended as far as the west bank of the River Derwent. 1675: 68 households (townships of Huttons Ambo). 1676: 140 persons aged 16 or more (parish).

Hugh Lenge, who took over as perpetual curate of Huttons Ambo in 1626, was a man with Puritan leanings. At the ecclesiastical visitation of 1632 he absented himself when faced with a charge of neglecting to wear the surplice. In 1651 he was presented at the Thirsk sessions for openly reading the Book of Common Prayer. Subsequently, in 1654, he was again in trouble with the authorities for performing a marriage ceremony which was contrary to the law. As a result he was deprived of his office of parish registrar.

Church St Margaret, High Hutton: possibly Norman in origin.

The parish was subject to the peculiar jurisdiction of the Dean and Chapter of York.

(R. A. Marchant, *The Puritans and the Church Courts in the Diocese of York 1560-1642* (1960), 259. *North Riding Records*, v (1887), 83, 161-2.)

INGLEBY ARNCLIFFE   Langbaurgh

A village between Northallerton and Stokesley. 1675: 35 households (township). 1676: 55 persons aged 16 or more (parish).

Church All Saints: Norman and Perpendicular.

Principal family Mauleverer of Arncliffe Hall. Estate revenue: £800 a year (1632).

The family had been seated at Ingleby Arncliffe since the 15th century.

William Mauleverer (1557-1618) was described in 1616 as 'an ancient and renowned Justice of Peace' when his fellow magistrates ordered the arrest of a man who was said to have uttered 'many raling and opprobrious speaches' against him.

His son James (1591-1664) was one of the leading opponents of the knighthood composition scheme which was launched in 1630 with the aim of extracting money from the landed gentry. At a meeting of the North Riding gentry in July 1632 Sir David Foulis reportedly praised him as 'a brave spirit, and a true Yorkshireman'. In contrast, Thomas Lord Wentworth called him a most peevish refuser and a silly wilful fool.

Mauleverer sought to challenge the legality of the proceedings in the Exchequer Court but the judges rejected his arguments. As a result of the severe financial penalties which were exacted he fell heavily into debt. In 1639 he borrowed £6000 from Robert Earl of Kingston and undertook to pay interest at the rate of £480 a year out of his mortgaged estate.

In the Civil War he served as a parliamentarian colonel. The dislocation caused by the war may well have been a contributory factor in his failure to continue the interest payments. By 1648 Henry Earl of Kingston was in possession of lands with a rent yield of some £580 a year and Arncliffe Hall was occupied by a tenant. Mauleverer was declared bankrupt in 1651 and died in York Castle where he had long been imprisoned for debt.

His son Timothy (1627-1687) took on responsibility for his financial affairs after the bankruptcy proceedings. He eventually managed to regain possession of the manor of Ingleby Arncliffe, though many years were to elapse before it was freed from the mortgage. During the 1650s he was involved in protracted litigation with Christopher Beckwith who had acted as his father's steward in the years 1641 to 1643.

Arncliffe Hall A gabled mansion built by William Mauleverer towards the end of the 16th century. It cost him £2000.

In 1675 the house had 11 taxable hearths.

The park adjoining the hall dated from the 14th century.

(*North Riding Records*, ii (1884), 135. Sheffield Archives, Wentworth Woodhouse Collection, Strafford Letters, xxi (b), Lord Wentworth to Francis Lord Cottington, 11 August 1632. C.3/453/99. C.7/201/70. BL, Egerton MSS 3562, 3563 and 3568. C.22/674/56. C.33/200/fo. 610. W. Brown, *Ingleby Arncliffe and its Owners* (1901). 'Ingleby Arncliffe', *YAJ*, xvi (1902).)

INGLEBY GREENHOW   Langbaurgh

A village in the Cleveland Hills near Stokesley. 1675: 38 households in Ingleby Greenhow, 18 in Battersby and 29 in Greenhow. 1676: 232 persons aged 16 or more (parish).

Church St Andrew: Norman.

School A school was established in 1618.

Principal family Foulis of Ingleby Manor (baronetcy 1620). Estate revenue: £1400 a year (1632); £1200 a year (1655).

Sir David Foulis (c.1580-1642) was a Scottish courtier who accompanied James I on his journey into England and served as cofferer or treasurer to Prince Henry and Prince Charles. In 1617 he sold this office to Sir Henry Vane. Within a few years of James I's accession he had built up a large estate in the North Riding, partly through a grant of Crown lands and partly by purchase. In 1625 he was appointed a member of the Council in the North and the following year he was made *custos rotulorum* for the North Riding.

Foulis was an enclosing landlord. In 1625 the North Riding magistrates were informed that he had enclosed some 30 acres of land in Ingleby Greenhow and Great Ayton 'with a view to statuteable improvement'; that 'certain evil intentioned people' had thrown down part of the enclosure; and that the local inhabitants were refusing to name those responsible.

Despite his Court connections Foulis emerged as one of the leading opponents of the knighthood composition scheme which was launched in 1630. At a public meeting held in July 1632 he urged the gentry to refuse payment and was reported to have said that the Yorkshire gentry 'had been in time past accounted and held stout-spirited men, and would have stood for their rights and liberties .... but now in these days Yorkshiremen were become degenerate, more dastardly and more cowardly than the men of other countries [counties]'. Wentworth attributed his conduct to the fact that his activities as cofferer had recently come under scrutiny. In August 1632 the auditors who had been examining his books concluded that there was £5000 owing to the Crown.

In November 1633 Sir David and his son Henry were tried in the Court of Star Chamber and found guilty on various charges relating to the knighthood composition scheme. The Court decided that Sir David should be imprisoned, stripped of all his offices and required to pay a fine of £5000 to the Crown and £3000 in damages to Wentworth. His son was also imprisoned (though only for a brief period) and fined £500.

Sir David spent seven years in the Fleet prison and died shortly before the Civil War. According to Roger Morrice, a nonconformist divine, he 'was never accounted inclined to the Puritans as such, but a lover of them as Englishmen, and very kind and helpfull to them in their troubles'.

On the outbreak of the Civil War Sir Henry Foulis (1608-1643) took up arms and served as a lieutenant-colonel under Sir Thomas Fairfax. In a Chancery suit of 1648 he was said to have died intestate without settling any of the debts he had contracted before the war.

His son Sir David (1633-1695) was a justice of the peace during the Interregnum. The only member of his family to serve as an MP, he represented Northallerton in the Parliament of 1685 where he sat as a Tory.

His brother Henry (1638-1669) was the author of a popular work entitled *The History of the Wicked Plots and Conspiracies of Our Pretended Saints*. In this he attacked both the Presbyterians and the Jesuits.

Ingleby Manor A two-storeyed Elizabethan mansion with pinnacles. In 1675 there were 17 taxable hearths.

When Sir David Foulis bought the manor of Ingleby Greenhow in 1608 there were two parks, a fallow deer park and a red deer park.

(*Calendar of the De L'Isle (Foulis) MSS. North Riding Records,* iii (1885), 234. J. T. Cliffe, *The Yorkshire Gentry* (1969), 138, 300-1, 303. Dr Williams's Library, Morrice MSS, J, no pagination. C.3/453/99. C.5/41/56.)

KILBURN   Birdforth

A village to the south-east of Thirsk. The parish of Kilburn had formerly been a chapelry in the parish of Coxwold. It contained the village of Over Silton, which had a medieval chapel, and a number of hamlets. 1675: 77 households in Kilburn and 29 in Over Silton. 1676: 326 persons aged 16 or more (parish).

The Archbishop of York owned the manor of Kilburn and the patronage rights.

Church St Mary: Norman and Perpendicular.

The minister was a perpetual curate.

KILDALE   Langbaurgh

A village to the south of Guisborough. There was no other village within the parish. 1675: 38 households (township of Kildale).

In 1253 Kildale had been granted the right to hold a weekly market and an annual fair.

Near the church were the remains of a castle which, as William Camden noted, belonged to the Earls of Northumberland. They had owned the manor of Kildale since the 12th century.

In 1623 Francis Mason carried out a survey of the manor on behalf of Henry Earl of Northumberland. The estate remained in the possession of the Percys until 1662 when it was bought by John Turner of Kirkleatham.

Church St Cuthbert: Norman or Early English.

(North Yorkshire County Record Office, Turner of Kirleatham MSS.)

KIPLIN   Hang East

A hamlet within the parish of Catterick. 1675: 8 households.

Kiplin was the birthplace of Sir George Calvert, Lord Baltimore (c.1579-1632) who served as one of James I's Secretaries of State during the years 1619 to 1625. He was the son of a Catholic gentleman of modest means. In 1616 he received a grant of the manor of Danby Wiske from the Crown and three years later he purchased the manor of Kiplin.

Calvert finally revealed that he was a Catholic in 1625 and immediately surrendered his office of Secretary of State. He was allowed to sell the office to his successor and was raised to the peerage as Lord Baltimore.

Partly for religious reasons he sought to colonise a province of Newfoundland which he named Avalon and he and his family lived there for a time. Subsequently he began to take an interest in the New England territory of Maryland and shortly after his death it was granted to his son Cecil Lord Baltimore (1606-1675).

Kiplin Hall In 1622 Roger Dodsworth noted in his journal that Sir George Calvert was building 'a faire hous' at Kiplin. In June of that year Sir Thomas Wentworth, the future Earl of Strafford, told his kinsman Christopher Danby that Calvert 'hath a buildinge in hand' and asked him to provide 30 trees as he was in need of timber.

The outcome of this building activity was an oblong house of brick with gables and projecting towers.

In 1675 there were 12 taxable hearths.

(*Camden Fourth Series*, 12 (1973), 172-3.)

KIRBY HILL   Hallikeld

A village to the north of Boroughbridge. The parish of Kirby Hill (or Kirby on the Moor) included the village of Langthorpe.

1675: 46 households (township of Kirby cum Langthorpe).

Church All Saints: Saxon, Norman and Perpendicular.

School A grammar school had been established in 1555.

Principal family Tankard (or Tancred) of Brampton Hall (baronetcy 1662). Estate revenue: £750 a year (1651); £800 a year (1662).

The seclusion of Brampton Hall, on the north bank of the River Ure, must have had special appeal for the Tankards as a major Catholic family.

Thomas Tankard (c.1580-1627) had a recusant wife but in 1607 he was said to have conformed and he was never subsequently convicted.

His son Thomas (1603-1663) was sent to the English College at Douai in 1621 and studied there for two years. He married an heiress, Frances Maltby, but they sold the property which she had inherited.

In 1630 Tankard compounded for his recusancy. The rent payable was initially £66 13s 4d a year but this was to rise periodically, on the expiry of rent-charges and annuities, until it reached a maximum of £192 a year. In 1637 he petitioned the king in an attempt to secure a reduction in his composition rent. His debts, he claimed, were daily increasing and he had been forced to give over housekeeping and to sell a great part of the lands for which he had compounded. Along with his petition he enclosed a certificate signed by a number of Protestant gentry and ministers in which they testified that he had always conducted himself like a loving and dutiful subject (his recusancy excepted) and that he had ever been esteemed as an honest neighbour and a good housekeeper who was completely free from any disorder or factious disposition.

When Brampton Hall was searched by a pursuivant in 1638 a collection of popish books was found and Tankard was faced with the allegation that he had been harbouring a seminary priest.

In 1641 he conveyed his estate to trustees for the purpose of discharging his debts and reserved only £100 a year for his own use. At the end of the year he and his family were reported to be living in York.

In the Civil War he supported the royalist cause and signed the Yorkshire Engagement of February 1643. As a result his estate was sequestered. Probably it was in recognition of the financial consequences of his loyalty that he was granted a baronetcy shortly before his death.

His son Sir William (c.1630-1703) was also a convicted recusant. He had at least two Catholic chaplains, John Young who died in 1672 and William Pearson who succeeded him and was still serving at Brampton Hall in 1692.

Brampton Hall A gabled house which appears to have been part-Tudor and part-Jacobean.

In 1675 Sir William Tankard was taxed on 13 hearths.

(BL, Lansdowne MSS 153, fo. 264. S.P.16/ccclxviii/66. Sir Thomas Lawson-Tancred, *The Tancreds of Brampton* (1921).)

KIRBY KNOWLE   Birdforth

A village to the north-east of Thirsk. The parish of Kirby Knowle included the village of Bagby which had a dependent chapel. 1675: 26 households in Kirby Knowle, 46 in Bagby cum Fawdington and 13 in Balks Ambo. Fawdington was situated in the parishes of Brafferton and Cundall. 1676: 325 persons aged 16 or more (parish).

During the early 17th century the parish had a sizeable Catholic community. There were 21 recusants in 1600, 29 in 1611, 33 in 1623 and 36 in 1632. In the latter part of the century, however, the number of Catholics declined sharply.

The Constables of Kirby Knowle were a Catholic family who played a key role in the sheltering of priests. In the Civil War they supported the king, though John Constable claimed that he had done no more than seek refuge in the royalist garrison at Helmsley.

The medieval castle at Kirby Knowle was accidentally burnt down in 1568. Sir John Constable decided to replace it with a mansion which was more contemporary in design but the work was unfinished at the time of his death. In 1654 John Constable's daughters sold the manor of Kirby Knowle to James Danby who repaired and added to the house which was already called the New Building.

Church St Wilfrid: Norman and Early English.

(H. Aveling, *Northern Catholics. The Catholic Recusants of the North Riding of Yorkshire 1558-1790* (1966), 274, 311, 415-16. S.P.23/ccxxiv/621.)

KIRBY MISPERTON   Pickering Lythe

A village to the south of Pickering. The parish of Kirby Misperton included a number of villages. 1675: 32 households in Kirby Misperton, 29 in Barughs Ambo, 23 in Habtons Ambo and 43 in Ryton. 1676: 350 persons aged 16 or more (parish).

Thomas Phelippes, who had bought the manor of Kirby Misperton in 1594, was a collector of customs in the Port of London. In 1606 the manor was the subject of an official inquiry which led to the imposition of an annual charge for the purpose of recovering money owing to the Crown. In this situation Phelippes was forced to borrow heavily and the estate eventually came into the possession of his principal creditor, George Shiers of Slyfield Manor in Surrey.

In the early 17th century there were frequent reports that Kirby Misperton Bridge, which spanned the River Costa, was in a ruinous condition and money was periodically levied for its repair.

On the River Rye 'stands Riton, the old estate of an ancient family the Percehaies, commonly called Percyes' (William Camden). The Percehays had been seated at Ryton since the 13th century. In the early part of the 17th century they were still a predominantly Catholic family. When William Percehay, the son and heir of Thomas Percehay (c.1569-1626), was admitted to the English College at Rome in 1618 he related that his father, stepmother and half-brother Christopher were 'schismatics' or conforming Catholics but thought that his mother might have been a Protestant. Of his sisters, he observed, two were Catholics, two were Protestants and the other one was a 'schismatic'. His intention was to become a priest but in 1620 he died before completing his studies.

By 1624 Thomas Percehay had emerged as a recusant. After his death the estate descended to his son Christopher (1604-1669) who promptly married one of the daughters of a leading Puritan squire, Walter Strickland of Boynton in the East Riding. In the Civil War he threw in his lot with Parliament and served as a member of the North Riding committee.

The estate of Christopher Percehay was not particularly large but an improvement in the family fortunes appeared to be in prospect when his son Walter married an heiress, Barbara Staveley. In 1660, however, Walter died while still comparatively young; his widow soon remarried; and the Percehays were involved in litigation over her jointure.

Christopher Percehay (1654-c.1710) sold the Ryton estate in 1685 and settled at Malton.

Church St Laurence: Perpendicular.

School In his will (1637) William Smithson, a local landowner, made provision for the establishment of an elementary school at Kirby Misperton. At this school children of the parish were to be taught free of charge until they could read and write perfectly and were ready to move on to a public grammar school in the neighbourhood.

Among his other bequests Smithson settled an annuity of £5 for a weekly distribution of bread to the poor.

(E.178/4797. *CSP Dom, 1611-18*, 124. *CSP Dom, 1619-23*, 146-7. *CSP Dom, 1623-5 and Addenda*, 543. *CRS*, liv (1962), 320. C.7/380/45 and 50. C.10/491/137. W. K. Jordan, *The Charities of Rural England 1480-1660* (1961), 242, 298, 337.)

KIRBY SIGSTON   Allertonshire

A hamlet to the east of Northallerton. The parish of Kirby Sigston also included some other hamlets. 1675: 17 households in Kirby Sigston, 10 in Sowerby under Cotcliffe and 15 in Winton.

Near Winton there were the remains of Sigston Castle which had been built in the 14th century but had probably been abandoned at the beginning of the 16th century.

In 1608 Francis Lascelles bought the manor of Winton Stank together with its Elizabethan manor-house, Stank Hall. Following his death in 1628 he was succeeded by his grandson Francis (1612-1667) who became a ward of the Crown. In the Civil War he served as a colonel in the parliamentarian army and a member of the North Riding committee. Subsequently he was elected as a recruiter MP to the Long Parliament and in 1654 was made a commissioner for the removal of scandalous ministers. His brothers Peregrine and Thomas also took up arms for Parliament.

In 1679 the inhabitants of Kirby Sigston submitted a petition to the North Riding magistrates. They complained that they were 'sore charged with poor people, and that the Constableries of Winton, Sowerby, and the hamlet of Foxton, all within the parish of Kirby Sigston, have few or no poor within them'. In the light of this petition it was decided that the constableries should contribute to the cost of relieving the poor of Kirby Sigston.

Churches St Lawrence: Norman, with a chantry chapel built in 1343.

In 1689 Winton had a Quaker meeting house.

School In the early years of Charles II's reign there was a schoolmaster at Kirby Sigston. He may be identified as Luke Smelt who graduated from Christ's College, Cambridge in 1664 and became rector of Easingwold in 1668.

(*North Riding Records*, vii (1889), 28, 103.)

KIRBY WISKE   Gilling East

A village on the River Wiske to the west of Thirsk. The parish of Kirby Wiske included several villages and hamlets. 1675: 33 households in Kirby Wiske, 37 in Maunby and 43 in Newby Wiske.

Kirby Wiske was the birthplace of Roger Ascham (1515-1568) who was tutor to Queen Elizabeth and the author of *The Scholemaster* (1570).

In 1607 it was reported that Maunby had been 'inclosed and pittifully depopulated' by William Middleton, the lord of the manor, about sixteen years since. Breckenbrough, a hamlet in this parish, also appears to have been depopulated.

In 1646 there was an outbreak of the plague at Newby Wiske.

In 1685 the North Riding magistrates decided to pay Edward Saltmarsh of Newby Wiske a gratuity of £100 for building a stone bridge there. This was on condition that the inhabitants of the parish of Kirby Wiske would meet any additional cost and would also maintain the bridge at their own charge.

Church St John Baptist: Norman, Decorated and Perpendicular.

Principal family Lascelles of Breckenbrough Hall. Estate revenue: £500 a year (1616).

While his family was mainly Catholic Sir Thomas Lascelles (c.1554-1619) fully conformed in matters of religion. He was said to have inherited an estate worth £1500 a year but his extravagance and mismanagement led inexorably to financial ruin.

His son William (1575-c.1614) came under pressure from the Northern High Commission as a suspected recusant but in 1613 it was noted that he had conformed. On the other hand, his wife and some of their children, including the heir, were indicted for recusancy in 1614 and four of his younger sons became Catholic priests.

When Sir Thomas died in 1619 there was only one remaining property, the manor of Breckenbrough, which was heavily burdened with debt. In 1623 his grandson William sold the manor to Sir Arthur Ingram for £3500 and the family sank into oblivion.

Breckenbrough Hall In the reign of Henry VIII John Leland had referred to the Lascelles mansion as newly built.

In 1618 Lord Cavendish was supplied with a detailed description of the house by his agent:

> The house is fayre and very substantiall, consisting of two strong large bricke towers of three stories high, well leaded over, th'one sutable to th'other in proportion and uniformity. Betwene them is onely the hall, which is faire and large, high roofed, well lighted, and a large and good chimney. From each of those towers goes out a wing towards the gate, which makes a handsome four-square courte, wherein is a fayre well, which serveth the house with verie clere and good water. In th'one of those wings there be two kitchins, bakehouse, brewe house, and other houses of office, with lodging chambers over. In th'other wing there be lodgings and other roomes.

There was a park adjoining the house.
(*North Riding Records*, i (1884), 78; iv (1886), 250; and vii (1889), 73. C.2/James

I/L3/51. W. Greenwell (ed.), 'Some Lascelles Deeds and Evidences', *YAJ*, ii (1873). *Surtees Society*, liii (1868), 269-70.)

KIRKBY   Langbaurgh

A village to the south of Stokesley. The parish of Kirkby included Great and Little Broughton (Broughtons Ambo). 1675: 33 households in Kirkby and 65 in Broughtons Ambo. 1676: 481 persons aged 16 or more (parish).

In 1605 the inhabitants of Great Broughton were indicted for digging up the highway leading from Ingleby Greenhow to Stokesley. In the reign of Charles II they came forward with a proposal for building a bridge. In 1677 the North Riding magistrates decided to allocate the sum of £5 for this purpose but with the proviso that it should be 'a sufficient stone bridge'.

Church St Augustine: Norman in origin.
(*North Riding Records*, i (1884), 12 and vi (1888), 273.)

KIRKBY FLEETHAM   Hang East

A village to the north-east of Bedale. The parish of Kirkby Fleetham included the hamlets of Great and Little Fencote (Fencotes Ambo). 1675: 28 households in Kirkby Fleetham and 28 in Fencotes Ambo.

At Kirkby Fleetham there were the remains of a medieval castle.

The Smelts were rising gentry who bought the manor of Kirkby Fleetham in 1600 and the manor of Great Fencote in 1634. Matthew Smelt (c.1590-1652) sided with Parliament in the Civil War and served as a member of the North Riding committee.

Church St Mary: Norman, Early English, Decorated and Perpendicular.
School In the reign of Charles I there was a private school at Kirkby Fleetham.

KIRKBY MOORSIDE   Ryedale

A small market town situated at the northern end of the Vale of Pickering. The parish of Kirkby Moorside included several villages. 1675: 133 households in Kirkby Moorside, 65 in Gillamoor and Fadmoor and 103 in Farndale cum East Side Bransdale. 1676: 660 persons aged 16 or more (parish of Kirkby Moorside).

A royal charter of 1254 had conferred the right to hold a weekly market and an annual fair.

Keldholme Priory, which was an establishment of Cistercian nuns, had been founded in the 12th century and dissolved in 1538.

William Denton, who had been instituted as vicar of Kirkby Moorside in 1595, appears to have been a man of forceful character and strong opinions. In 1605 a warrant was issued for his arrest along with other members of his family. Subsequently, in 1618, he was again in trouble with the authorities for allegedly making scandalous speeches about the king and the North Riding magistrates.

In 1616 James I granted the manor of Kirkby Moorside to his favourite George Villiers, later Duke of Buckingham. His son George the second Duke died at Kirkby Moorside in 1687 after sustaining an injury while hunting. In 1695 the manor was purchased by Sir Charles Duncombe.

Churches All Saints: Norman, Early English and Perpendicular.

In 1652 it was reported that 'the quire or chancell of the parish church of Kirkbymoorside is in great decay and like to fall, by which means the inhabitants of that parish, resorting to that church, may be in danger'. This was considered to be due to the negligence of the impropriators of the living.

In 1689 there were Quaker meeting houses at Kirkby Moorside, Fadmoor and Farndale.

School There was a school at Kirkby Moorside in the early years of the 17th century.

(*North Riding Records*, i (1884), 19; ii (1884), 173, 182; v (1887), 119, 124-5; and vii (1889), 103.)

KIRKBY RAVENSWORTH (KIRBY HILL)   Gilling West

A small village to the north-west of Richmond. The parish of Kirkby Ravensworth contained several villages. It also included part of the village of Newsham; the other part was in the parish of Barningham. 1675: 20 households in Kirby Hill, 54 in Dalton cum Gayles, 45 in Newsham and 75 in Ravensworth cum Whashton.

At Ravensworth there were the ruins of a medieval castle which, along with the surrounding estate, belonged to the Crown during the years 1571 to 1629. In 1607 the property was the subject of a formal inquiry. This revealed, among other things, that ten loads of stone had recently been removed by Sir Francis Boynton's workmen and that within the last sixteen years many trees had been felled and taken away.

The inhabitants of the parish included a considerable number of Catholic families. There were 25 recusants in 1623, 43 in 1641, 90 in 1665 and 73 in 1690.

In 1609 there was a major incident on Newsham Moor where Thomas Earl of Exeter, who was lord of the manor, had recently enclosed a substantial tract of land. Under cover of darkness a number of men assembled on the moor and pulled down large sections of the walls and fences. Since the inhabitants of Newsham and the neighbouring villages refused to identify those responsible they were indicted at the Richmond quarter sessions.

In 1647 it was reported that there had recently been some enclosing activity on the commons of Whashton.

Church St Peter and St Felix: Norman, Early English, Decorated and Perpendicular.

Schools and almshouses Shortly before his death in 1547 William Knight, who was Bishop of Bath and Wells, made provision for the establishment of a school and almshouses at Kirkby Ravensworth. The task of implementing these plans was left to his executor, John Dakin, who was then rector of Kirkby Ravensworth and in 1556 he secured letters patent which set up the charity on a formal basis.

It was originally the intention that the hospital should accommodate five poor persons but in 1557 a generous donation by William Walker, a London lawyer who was a native of the district, made possible a significant increase in its capacity.

The school, which was located within the hospital building, provided boys of the parish with free instruction in grammar, rhetoric and verse.

In the reign of Charles II there was also a private school at Kirkby Ravensworth. Among its pupils was Mark Milbanke, the son and heir of Sir Mark Milbanke of Halnaby Hall.

(E.178/4798. H. Aveling, *Northern Catholics. The Catholic Recusants of the North Riding of Yorkshire 1558-1790* (1966), 438. *North Riding Records*, i (1884), 170, 210 and iv (1886), 266. W. K. Jordan, *The Charities of Rural England 1480-1660* (1961), 258, 314-15.)

KIRKDALE   Ryedale

As a place Kirkdale consisted only of a church which was situated in a secluded valley to the south-west of Kirkby Moorside. In contrast, the parish of Kirkdale covered an extensive area and included several villages. 1675: 82 households in Bilsdale and Skiplam, 30 in East and West Ness cum Muscoates, 48 in Nawton cum Beadlam, 30 in Welburn and 40 in Wombleton. (Beadlam, Bilsdale and East and West Ness were in other parishes). 1676: 284 persons aged 16 or more (parish of Kirkdale).

In 1675 the North Riding magistrates received a complaint from the inhabitants of Wombleton who informed them that they were 'overcharged with poor'. Shortly afterwards the inhabitants of Muscoates and Sunley Coates submitted a petition in which they expressed their concern about the heavy burden of poor relief and suggested that Skiplam and other hamlets which in their estimation had no poor should be required to contribute. Their request, however, was rejected.

Churches St Gregory: Saxon and Norman with some later features.

In 1689 there was a Quaker meeting house at Welburn.

Principal family Gibson of Welburn Hall. Estate revenue: £500 a year (1626).

Sir John Gibson (c.1540-1613) was a lawyer who was employed by the ecclesiastical authorities at York and was also a member of the Council in the North. In 1597 he bought the manor of Welburn.

His son Sir John (1576-1639) took part in military operations in the Low Countries and Ireland. He was a friend and ally of Thomas Lord Wentworth who drew him into his alum undertaking and made him one of his deputy lieutenants in the North Riding. In 1630 he was pricked as sheriff of Yorkshire.

He was succeeded by his son Sir John (1606-1665) who had been knighted by Wentworth, in his capacity as Lord Deputy of Ireland, in 1636. In the Civil War he served as a captain of horse in the king's army. In 1655 he wrote of his vicissitudes in some autobiographical verse:

Welburne my carefull time had all
Ioyn'd with a troubled life,
When uncivill civill warres withall
Did bloudshed bringe and strife....
The Decimation of my 'state
'Tis not worth valuation.
I feare 'twill prove a common fate
To all of this same Nation.

Welburn Hall A house built by the first Sir John Gibson about 1603. It replaced a medieval timber house.

In 1675 John Gibson was taxed on 19 hearths.

(*North Riding Records*, vii (1889), 103. BL, Additional MSS 37,719. *Surtees Society*, cxxiv (1915), 52-3. T. Parker, 'Welburn Hall', *YAJ*, ix (1886).)

KIRKLEATHAM   Langbaurgh

A village between Guisborough and the coast. The parish of Kirkleatham included the villages of Coatham and Wilton. 1675: 68 households in Kirkleatham and 69 in Wilton cum membris. 1676: 305 persons aged 16 or more (parish of Kirkleatham).

Church St Cuthbert: Decorated and Perpendicular.

School Sir William Turner gave £1000 for building a free school, £2000 for a master and £1000 for an usher. Letters patent for the establishment of the school were obtained in 1679 but it was not actually built until 1709.

Almshouses Turner's Hospital was built and endowed by Sir William Turner in 1676. The original intention was to accommodate 10 poor aged men and 10 poor aged women.

In addition, the hospital was to be responsible for the relief and upbringing of 10 poor boys and 10 girls.

Principal family Turner of Kirkleatham Hall. Estate revenue: £750 a year (1640); £1200 a year (1676).

John Turner, who came from Herefordshire, was manager of the Guisborough alum works. He was said to be a harsh employer who preferred to pay his workmen in corn rather than in money.

In 1623 he bought the manors of Kirkleatham and Coatham and in 1634 acquired the manor of Yearby for £3600.

The Turners appear to have played no part in the Civil War. John Turner died in 1643 and was succeeded by his son John.

John Turner (1613-1688) was a serjeant at law and recorder of York. The profits of his legal work enabled him to purchase several manors and when his son Charles married in 1676 he received a portion of £6700 under the terms of the settlement.

His brother Sir William (1615-1693) was a wealthy London woollen draper and one of the leading philanthropists of the late 17th century. In his will (1690) he left a substantial landed estate to the senior branch of the family.

Kirkleatham Hall John Turner the elder built a house following his purchase of the Kirkleatham estate. His son John either rebuilt or considerably enlarged the hall in the reign of Charles II. He was taxed on seven hearths in 1662 and 18 in 1675.

An H-shaped house of two storeys with Dutch gables.

(North Yorkshire County Record Office, Kirkleatham MSS. C.33/313/fo.267.)

KIRK LEAVINGTON Langbaurgh

A village to the south-east of Yarm. The parish of Kirk Leavington included the market town of Yarm, which had a medieval chapel, and several hamlets. Yarm is separately noticed. 1675: 55 households in Kirk Leavington, 12 in Castle Leavington, 15 in Low Worsall and 18 in Picton. 1676: 316 persons aged 16 or more (parish of Kirk Leavington, excluding the chapelry of Yarm).

At Castle Leavington there were the remains of a Norman castle.

In 1682 the North Riding magistrates gave direction that the inhabitants of Kirk Leavington, Castle Leavington and Picton should contribute to the relief of the poor of Low Worsall. This ruling was apparently occasioned by the fact that the residents of Low Worsall had been 'at great charge' over the maintenance of the four children of Thomas Simpson who had died there.

Church St Martin: Norman and Early English.

The minister was a perpetual curate.

(*North Riding Records*, vi (1888), 61, 76.)

KIRKLINGTON   Hallikeld

A village to the east of Masham. The parish of Kirklington included several hamlets. 1675: 46 households in Kirklington cum Upsland, 2 in East Tanfield and 19 in Sutton Howgrave. East Tanfield had been depopulated in the early Tudor period.

Church St Michael: Early English, Decorated and Perpendicular.

Principal family Wandesford of Kirklington Hall (baronetcy 1662). Estate revenue: £560 a year (1612); £3000 a year (1640); £3200 a year (1660).

The Wandesfords had been seated at Kirklington since the 14th century.

Sir George Wandesford (1572-1612) was a negligent landowner who granted leases at uneconomic or even nominal rents and left a heavily burdened estate.

His son Christopher (1592-1640) was made a ward of the Crown shortly before attaining his majority. He paid all his father's debts, put the estate on a much sounder footing, engaged in demesne farming for the provisioning of his household and adopted a policy of 'frugal hospitality'. By the time of his death the rent-roll had been increased from £560 to £1040 a year.

He was a benevolent as well as an efficient landlord. Besides operating a general welfare scheme he sent poor children who showed promise to good free schools and then to university. A devout Protestant, he had household prayers three times a day and usually kept a chaplain.

Wandesford was a close friend and political ally of Thomas Lord Wentworth. In 1633 he was appointed Master of the Rolls in Ireland and in 1640, shortly before his death, he succeeded Wentworth as Lord Deputy. During his time in Ireland he purchased the Castlecomer estate which was worth £2000 a year.

In a reference to his period of service in Ireland his daughter Alice Thornton wrote that 'such was the sweete affability and prudence of his carriage in general that none which went from England gained soe much upon affections of that nation …. His life was given for a publicke good to that kingdome'.

In a book of instructions which he left Wandesford laid down certain rules of conduct for the benefit of his son George: 'To govern your Family with Prudence, your Estate with Providence; to be easie and familiar with your Neighbours, hospitable to Strangers, moderate in your Expences; without Scandall to converse with all Sorts of People, are the principall Duties you are to observe'.

George Wandesford (1623-1651) also became a ward of the Crown. In April 1642 he was granted a licence to travel abroad with a tutor, George Anderson. He returned to England the following year but despite his royalist sympathies he decided to avoid any commitment. According to his sister Alice Thornton 'he saw it was in vaine to strive against that impetuous streame and involve himselfe in utter ruine willfully when noe good could possibly be don by his service to the king otherwaise then by our praiers and teares for him'.

In 1651 he was drowned in the River Swale and his brother Christopher succeeded to the estate.

Sir Christopher Wandesford (1628-1714) was involved in a bitter dispute with his sister Alice over the personal estate left by their mother. The rift between them was further widened when a disagreement over the Irish property led him to start legal proceedings against her husband.

Kirklington Hall A gabled Elizabethan house. In 1675 there were 15 taxable hearths.

Christopher Wandesford (1592-1640) built new stables and a dairy, enclosed the gardens and orchards with brick walls and improved the water supply by means of a system of lead pipes.

(YAS Library, Duke of Leeds MSS. Thomas Comber, *Memoirs of the Life and Death of the Right Honourable the Lord Deputy Wandesforde* (1778). Thomas Comber (ed.), *A Book of Instructions, written by .... Christopher Wandesforde* (1777). Surtees Society, lxii (1873), 20, 26, 40, 119-20, 182-3, 185. H. B. McCall, *Story of the Family of Wandesforde of Kirklington and Castlecomer* (1904). C.10/57/276.)

LASTINGHAM   Ryedale

A village to the north-east of Kirkby Moorside. The parish of Lastingham included several villages. 1675: 26 households in Lastingham, 103 in Farndale East Side, 28 in Hutton le Hole, 22 in Rosedale West Side, 23 in Spaunton and 45 in Wood Appleton (Appleton le Moor). 1676: 556 persons aged 16 or more, including 40 Protestant dissenters (parish).

Leonard Conyers, who became vicar of Lastingham in 1637, managed to hold on to his living in the Civil War period but was eventually forced out. In 1657 he was charged at the Northallerton quarter sessions with assaulting his successor, Philip Peckett, and preventing him from taking over the vicarage. After the Restoration Peckett was himself ejected.

Early on in Charles II's reign Marmaduke Rawdon with some friends visited 'a poor towne', Lastingham, 'where they lodgd in a poore ale howse.... Here in this towne is a very antient fashiond church, and in the churchyard tombe stones of much antiquitie' (Life of Marmaduke Rawdon, entry for 1664).

Churches St Mary: Saxon in origin; Norman, Early English and Perpendicular.

The church was built on the same site as a monastery established in 1078 and abandoned a few years later. It incorporated a crypt and other architectural features of the monastic building.

In 1689 there was a Quaker meeting house at Hutton le Hole.

(*North Riding Records*, v (1887), 236-7. F. H. Weston, *History of the Ancient Parish of Lastingham* (1914). R. H. Hayes and J. Hurst, *The History of Hutton le Hole* (1976).)

LEAKE   Allertonshire/Birdforth

A hamlet to the south-east of Northallerton. The parish of Leake contained a number of villages and hamlets, including Nether Silton which had a medieval chapel. 1675: 6 households in Leake cum Kepwick, 54 in Borrowby, 14 in Gueldable, 72 in Knayton, 10 in Landmoth cum Catto and 36 in Nether Silton. Kepwick was partly in the parish of Cowesby.

In 1605 Robert Metcalf of Borrowby was indicted at the Richmond quarter sessions for giving shelter to five men and boys who were described as gypsies 'to the great terror' of his neighbours.

The inhabitants of the parish included a considerable number of Catholic families of which the most notable were the Danbys of Leake, the Greenes of Landmoth and the Jacksons of Knayton. In 1674 there were 50 recusants.

In the Civil War the Danbys were fervent royalists. John Danby served as a major in the king's army and his brother Thomas was killed in an engagement at Newark.

Churches St Mary: Norman, Decorated and Perpendicular.

The parish was subject to the peculiar jurisdiction of the Bishop of Durham.

In 1689 there was a Quaker meeting house at Borrowby.

Schools During the reign of Charles I two recusant schoolmasters were presented for teaching without a licence: Thomas Wood of Leake and Emmanuel Dawson of Landmoth. In the same period there was a school at Knayton which may also have had links with the Catholic community.

During the Interregnum Christopher Forster, the minister of Leake, kept a private school.

(*North Riding Records*, i (1884), 21 and vii (1889), 103. H. Aveling, *Northern Catholics. The Catholic Recusants of the North Riding of Yorkshire 1558-1790* (1966), 244, 246, 257, 293, 308-9, 315, 418-19.)

LEVISHAM   Pickering Lythe

A village to the north-east of Pickering. There was no other village within the parish. 1675: 30 households (township). 1676: 70 persons aged 16 or more (parish).**Church** St Mary: Saxon in origin.

School There was a private school at Levisham in the middle years of the 17th century. The master may be identified as Mathias Boyce.

LOFTUS   Langbaurgh

A Cleveland village to the north-east of Guisborough. The parish of Loftus (or Lofthouse) included the hamlet of Wapley. 1675: 70 households (township of Loftus). 1676: 179 persons aged 16 or more (parish).

Handale Priory, which was an establishment of Cistercian nuns, had been founded in the 12th century and dissolved in 1540. The Beckwiths, who had acquired the site of the priory in 1544, had a house near the ruins which they called Handale Abbey.

In 1615 a number of farmers joined together to buy the manor of North Loftus and embarked on the enclosure and division of the common fields.

The manor was subsequently purchased by the Steward family. In 1657 Zachary Steward leased all the alum rock within the manor to Thomas Lechmere and other London businessmen on the basis that he would have a share of the profits from their undertaking. The syndicate spent over £3000 on the development of alum mines at Lingbury Hill, near the coast, and the construction of a pier and staithes. In the event the amount of alum produced was well below the planned output, apparently because there were insufficient stocks of kelp, wood and coal. About 1662 the syndicate suspended operations and discharged the workmen. Agents acting on behalf of the Crown offered to pay £300 a year for a lease of the mines but Lechmere and Steward insisted on a rent of £400 a year and the negotiations fell through. In 1673 it was said that the works were in a state of decay and that much of the pier was 'broke downe by the violence of the sea'. This was not, however, the end of alum manufacture in the parish of Loftus.

Church St Leonard: Norman in origin.
(E.134/23 Charles II/Easter 41 and 25 Charles II/Easter 23.)

LYTHE   Langbaurgh

A village to the north west of Whitby. The parish of Lythe, which extended to the coast, contained a number of villages and hamlets, including Egton which had a medieval chapel. 1675: 83 households in Lythe, 53 in Barnby, 9 in Borrowby, 181 in Egton, 18 in Ellerby, 29 in Hutton Mulgrave, 39 in Mickleby, 21 in Newton Mulgrave and 45 in Ugthorpe.

A charter of 1254 had conferred the right to hold a weekly market and an annual fair in Lythe.

In the course of the 17th century the bridges at Egton and Grosmont were frequently reported to be in a dilapidated condition. In 1631 the North Riding magistrates decided that the sum of £90 should be levied for 'the new building' of Grosmont Bridge with stone but in 1690 they found it necessary to allocate £200 for its repair.

Catholicism was still a potent force in the parish of Lythe and particularly within the chapelry of Egton.

In 1626 there was an outbreak of the plague in the hamlet of Egton Bridge.

Churches St Oswald: Perpendicular.

In 1689 there was a Quaker meeting house at Mickleby.

Principal family Sheffield, Lords Sheffield of Mulgrave Castle (and Normanby Hall, Lincolnshire) (Earl of Mulgrave 1626 and Marquess of Normanby 1694). Estate revenue: £4000 a year (1640); £6000 a year (1660). Alum mining at Mulgrave, Kettleness and Sandsend.

Edmund Lord Sheffield, later Earl of Mulgrave (1565-1646) had served as a naval captain during the Armada crisis and in 1592 had been granted the Mulgrave estate as a reward. He was Lord President of the Council in the North and Lord Lieutenant of Yorkshire between 1603 and 1619 and in addition held the appointment of Vice Admiral of Yorkshire.

His estate was rich in alum deposits and in 1607 he secured a royal patent in which he and his associates were granted manufacturing and marketing rights. Two years later the Crown took over the industry on the basis that the patentees and their families would be compensated with annuities. During the reign of Charles I Mulgrave received £1640 a year as his share.

In 1614 three of his sons, including the heir, were drowned while crossing the Humber. Two other sons also met with violent deaths.

In the Civil War Mulgrave sided with Parliament and his sons James and Thomas served as parliamentarian officers.

His grandson Edmund the second Earl (c.1611-1658) succeeded him as Vice Admiral of Yorkshire. In 1649 he was elected to the Council of State and from 1654 onwards was a member of the Protector's Council, though he was never a political radical.

In 1648 he was involved in a dispute with the Dowager Countess of Mulgrave over the family's alum works. After the matter was settled in his favour he was put to great expense in restoring the works but by 1660 the profits were averaging over £3600 a year.

His son John the third Earl (1648-1721) took part in maritime operations against the Dutch while still a minor and in 1673 was made a naval captain.

During his minority he quarrelled with Sir John Monson who was managing the estate on his behalf and in a Chancery suit of 1667 argued that he was capable of performing this role himself. In 1685 he entered into an agreement with Sir Hugh Cholmley which had as its aim the establishment of an alum monopoly. Under the terms of the agreement he was to receive two-thirds and Cholmley one-third of the clear profits. In 1698, when the agreement was about to expire, it was said to have been 'beneficiall to both partyes'.

Mulgrave was a prominent courtier and politician in the reigns of Charles II, James II, William III and Queen Anne. At the local level he held the appointments of Lord

Lieutenant of the East Riding and Vice Admiral of Yorkshire. In 1685 James II made him Lord Chamberlain and a Privy Councillor. According to Gilbert Burnet 'he went with the King to Mass, and kneeled at it' yet he was 'looked on as indifferent to all religions'.

Mulgrave Castle A Norman castle with a keep built about 1300 and some late 16th century improvements. Edmund Lord Sheffield probably commissioned some work after acquiring the estate in 1592.

During the Civil War the castle was garrisoned by royalist troops and in 1650 the Council of State ordered that it should be made untenable. As a result the outer walls and several 'stately' rooms were demolished. In 1654 it was decided that the Earl of Mulgrave should be paid £1000 as compensation.

In 1662 it was reported that the castle had many rooms but they were all unoccupied; and that 'Mr Richard Shipton lives in part of the outhousing'.

It was not until the early 18th century that a new house was built.

Mulgrave Castle stood in a large park.

(*North Riding Records*, iii (1885), 264, 314, 342 and vii (1889), 103, 108. W. J. Sheils, 'Catholics and Their Neighbours in a Rural Community: Egton Chapelry, 1590-1780', *Northern History*, xxxiv (1998). R. B. Turton, *The Alum Farm* (1938). HMC, *Seventh Report*, Appendix, 24, 27, 30, 32. *CSP Dom, 1660-1*, 378. C.10/84/67. C.33/210/fo. 224; 215/fo. 730; 229/fo. 21; and 260/fo. 590. C.38/200/4 May 1678 and 260/13 July 1698. Gilbert Burnet, *History of His Own Time* (1724), 683.)

MALTON   Ryedale

An important market town consisting of Old and New Malton. The parish of St Mary, Old Malton included the chapelries of St Leonard and St Michael, New Malton. 1675: 105 households in Old Malton and 194 in New Malton. In the 17th century the main streets were Castlegate, Greengate, Old Maltongate, Wheelgate, Yorkersgate and Newbiggin. 1676: 1147 persons aged 16 or more (Old and New Malton).

New Malton had long enjoyed borough status and until the reign of Charles II was governed by burgesses.

Quarter sessions were regularly held at Malton. In December 1640 the Long Parliament decided that it should have the right to send two representatives to Westminster. By 1661 it had a postmaster and a deputy postmaster.

Markets and fairs had been held by prescription since the 13th century or earlier.

The wooden bridge over the River Derwent was often in need of repair and considerable sums were levied for the restoration work.

In the 17th century there were comparatively few Catholics in Malton. In 1669 it was reported that the Quakers were very numerous and that from time to time there were as many as 300 in the town.

Malton is 'a market-town, famous for its vent of corn, horses, fish and Country-utensils' (William Camden).

At New Malton 'ther is a markett of great resort and of as great fame for sale of corne, fish, foule, husbandry ware, horse, beasts and sheep, as any market in Yorkshire' (Roger Dodsworth).

'Thence we went to Maulton which is a pretty large town built of stone, but poor, there is a large market place and severall great houses of Gentlemens round the town' (Celia Fiennes, 1697).

In 1624 an attempt was made to secure a charter of incorporation but this proved unsuccessful. In the petition which was submitted it was said that there were 300 families living in the town.

In 1625 William Lord Eure, as owner of the manor of Old Malton, entered into an agreement with the freeholders, tenants and other inhabitants over the division and enclosure of the lands belonging to the manor.

In 1626 there was an outbreak of the plague.

At the beginning of the Civil War Malton House, the seat of Lord Eure, was garrisoned by the royalists. In January 1643, however, Sir Hugh Cholmley took Malton for Parliament and left a garrison there.

In the reign of Charles II the town was involved in a dispute over its legal status which ended with a judgement in favour of the Crown. As a result the burgesses were made subordinate to a borough bailiff who was appointed by the owner of the manorial rights.

Churches St Mary, Old Malton: Early English and Perpendicular.

After the dissolution of the Gilbertine priory in 1539 its church had been converted for use as the parish church.

In 1636 the central tower was pulled down after it had been judged unsafe.

The church was badly damaged in the Civil War and in 1672 some restoration work was carried out with funds raised by public subscription.

St Leonard, New Malton: Norman and Perpendicular.

St Michael, New Malton: Norman and Perpendicular.

In 1689 New Malton had two Quaker meeting houses.

School A public grammar school which had been founded and endowed in 1547 on the initiative of Robert Holgate, Archbishop of York.

Almshouses At the beginning of the 17th century there were hospitals in both Old and New Malton. In 1619, however, the North Riding magistrates decided that the latter should be 'utterlie dissolved and disallowed' and that the five inmates should be paid £2 a year each for life.

Principal family Eure of Malton House, Lords Eure. Estate revenue: £3000 a year (1640). Coalmining in County Durham.

The Eures were an ancient family who owned, among other things, the manors of Old and New Malton.

William Lord Eure (c.1579-1646), who succeeded his father in 1617, sold a considerable amount of property but remained heavily indebted.

He and other members of his family were Catholics. He was first presented for recusancy in 1618 but managed to avoid any financial penalties.

With the aim of discharging his debts Eure settled his estate on trustees. This became the subject of litigation and in 1632 the Court of Chancery issued an injunction which required him to put the trustees in possession of Malton House. Eure, however, refused to comply and attempts to execute the writ were met with force. In the end the sheriff of Yorkshire broke the deadlock by resorting to the use of cannon. Two servants were arrested and Eure himself spent some time in the Tower of London.

In 1635 Eure complained in a petition to the king that the trustees had failed to pay many of his debts. At the same time he stressed his willingness to accept any propositions for clearing the debts provided he was allowed to keep Malton House and the park.

In 1641 he was accused of harbouring popish priests in his house.

In the Civil War he supported the king and signed the Yorkshire Engagement of February 1643. His younger son Sir William served as a royalist colonel and was killed at the battle of Marston Moor. Sir William left two daughters, Margaret and Mary, who eventually inherited the estate after the death of their cousin William Lord Eure in 1652.

Margaret Eure married Thomas Danby of Thorpe Perrow while her sister became the wife of William Palmes whose family had formerly been seated at Lindley in the West Riding.

In 1666 the two families came to an agreement over the division of the estate but they were very soon at loggerheads.

Finally, in 1675, the issue was resolved by a writ of partition.

Malton House A large mansion in Old Malton which was built by Ralph Lord Eure about the beginning of the 17th century. In his diary Sir Henry Slingsby cited Malton House as an example when referring to 'an emulation in the structure of our houses'.

In 1662 the house had 31 taxable hearths. The dispute between the Danby and Palmes families led to its demolition (except for the gatehouse) in 1674.

Mrs Mary Palmes 'now makes use of the roomes off the out buildings and gate house for weaving and linneing cloth, haveing set up a manuffactory for Linnen which does employ many poor people' (Celia Fiennes, 1697).

(N. A. Hudleston, *History of Malton and Norton* (1962). BL, Additional MSS 24,453, fo. 16. *CSP Dom, 1631-3*, 425, 436, 441 and *1635*, 28, 284. C.5/420/6. C.10/217/61. C.33/317/fo. 177.)

MANFIELD   Gilling East

A village to the west of Darlington. The parish of Manfield included the hamlet of Cliffe which was situated on the south bank of the River Tees. 1675: 54 households in Manfield and 5 in Cliffe.

The parish had 24 recusants in 1616, 28 in 1641 and 101 in 1690.

Church All Saints: Early English and Decorated.

Principal family Witham of Cliffe Hall. Estate revenue: £1600 a year (1660).

The Withams were one of the richest Catholic families in the North Riding. Besides their Yorkshire estate they owned a substantial amount of property in the adjoining county of Durham.

John Witham (1581-1656) was described as a recusant and noncommunicant in 1604 but for many years he conformed sufficiently to avoid any financial impositions. In 1629 he and his son William (c.1612-1642) compounded for their recusancy and were required to pay a rent of £100 a year.

In the Civil War John Witham appears to have been anxious to avoid any commitment. Although he provided the royalists with a trained band horse he later claimed he had been forced to do so by the Earl of Cumberland. The parliamentary authorities accepted this explanation but sequestered two-thirds of the estate on account of his recusancy. During the latter part of his life he had a resident chaplain, William Meynell.

His grandson John Witham supported the royalist cause in 1648 and was killed at the battle of Preston. In 1656 the estate descended to his brother George (c.1629-1703) who subsequently purchased further property. He and his wife Grace were staunch recusants and a number of their children became Catholic priests and nuns. One of their sons served as Northern Vicar General while another was President of the English College at Douai.

A list of Catholic provenance which was compiled in 1692 refers to two of George Witham's chaplains, Francis Hodgson and his son Christopher Witham. Of the latter it was noted that 'he is but young and been about 7 or 8 years in the mission. He halts a little but very pious and regular and preaches often. He resides at Cliffe with his father and mother and is a help to many poor people that come thither'.

Cliffe Hall A gabled Elizabethan or Jacobean house of two storeys. In 1675 George Witham was taxed on 17 hearths.

There had been a park adjoining Cliffe Hall since the 13th century.

(W. J. Stavert (ed.), *The Parish Register of Manfield 1594-1812* (1895). PRO, State Papers Domestic, Commonwealth Exchequer Papers, S.P.28/209A. *CRS*, ix (1911), 111.)

MARRICK   Gilling West

A Swaledale village to the west of Richmond. 1675: 52 households (township of Marrick).

Lead had been mined on Hurst Moor during the period of the Roman occupation.

Marrick Priory, which was a Benedictine nunnery, had been founded in the 12th century and dissolved in 1539. The priory church had also served as the parish church and after the dissolution it continued to fulfil this role. During the years 1592 to 1630 the site of the priory belonged to the Huttons of Marske Hall.

In 1659 Robert Myles of Marrick was indicted at the Richmond quarter sessions for declaring that Oliver Cromwell was burning in hell 'for taking so many honest gentlemen's lives away'.

Church St Andrew: Early English, Decorated and Perpendicular.

Principal family Bulmer of Marrick Hall. Estate revenue: £1200 a year (1640). Lead mining at Marrick.

William Bulmer (1601-1682) was the son of a Durham landowner who dissipated his estate. He acquired the manor of Marrick through his marriage to an heiress, Dorothy Sayer, who was a niece of John Sayer of Great Worsall. In 1634 he purchased the tithes of lead from the owner of the rectory for £750.

At their peak the profits of his lead mines amounted to around £1000 a year. During the 1630s, however, he had growing financial problems and by 1636 his debts had risen to £4938. This situation may have been due partly to the effects of his father's improvidence and partly to the development costs associated with his mining operations.

Bulmer and his wife were both Catholics. In 1637 he compounded for his recusancy and was required to pay a rent of £78 6s 8d a year.

During the Civil War he supported the king and in 1644 his estate was sequestered on account of his delinquency and recusancy.

In 1671 the Marrick estate was sold to Charles Powlett, Lord St John of Basing and subsequently Marquess of Winchester. By then it was heavily encumbered.

Marrick Hall In 1662 William Bulmer was taxed on four hearths.

There was a park adjoining the house.

(*North Riding Records*, vi (1888), 18. W. D. Hoyle, *Historical Notes of the Baronial House of Bulmer and its Descendants* (1896). PRO, Palmer's Index 17,349, fo. 17 and State Papers Domestic, Commonwealth Exchequer Papers, S.P.28/215/order book, 1651-2, fo.102. C.10/492 /107.)

MARSKE   Gilling West

A Swaledale village to the west of Richmond. 1675: 86 households (township of Marske).

Church St Edmund: Norman, Early English and Perpendicular. The church was restored in 1683.

School In his will (1659) Dr John Bathurst founded a school for reading and writing.

Principal family Hutton of Marske Hall. Estate revenue: £1400 a year (1616); £1000 a year (1625); £230 a year (1640); £500 a year (1660).

The Huttons were new gentry who mainly owed their advancement to Matthew Hutton, Archbishop of York (1529-1606). He and his son Sir Timothy (1569-1629) purchased a substantial amount of property, including the manor of Marske which was acquired in 1597. In addition, the family had valuable church leases which Sir Timothy described in 1617 as 'a greate part of the portion which my deare father left unto my selfe and manye of my lyttle selves'.

In 1608 Sir Timothy was characterised as 'a man made up of divine wisedome, honour, humanitie, charitie and one in whose rank it is rare to find the like for true humilitie'.

He was a patron of such Puritan ministers as John Jackson and Daniel Sherrard. In his will (1629) he stipulated that his son Matthew should always have a resident chaplain and expressed the wish that this practice should be followed 'soe longe as it should please God to continue the poore posterity of this poore house which it hath pleased God soe lately to rayse out of the duste'.

Matthew Hutton (1597-1666) was a spendthrift who had already fallen heavily into debt while his father was still alive. In 1626 he and his father secured a private act enabling them to sell his wife's jointure lands at Wharram Percy. By the time of the Civil War he had sold most of the estate and the manor of Marske was in the possession of his father-in-law Sir Conyers Darcy.

During the Civil War he served in the royalist army and signed the Yorkshire Engagement of February 1643. In 1645 he was a prisoner at York.

His son John (1625-1664) was able to recover the manor of Marske which had been sequestered by the parliamentarians. The Darcy family surrendered their interest and received certain lands and leases in return.

The Huttons were no longer one of the leading families in the riding but in 1680 their financial prospects began to improve when John Hutton (1659-1731) married an heiress.

In 1685 he built a stone bridge over the River Swale between Marske and Downholme. This bridge, which was designed 'for cart and carriages', cost him over £200. The North Riding magistrates decided to contribute £100 from public funds on the grounds that it would be of great benefit to the whole county.

Marske Hall The house was probably rebuilt by Sir Timothy Hutton after his father conveyed the manor to him in 1601.

An inventory of 1629 refers to the hall, the great chamber, the parlour, the study and Mr Jackson's chamber.

Matthew Hutton commissioned some work in the 1630s.

There were 14 taxable hearths in 1662 and 16 in 1675.

(North Yorkshire County Record Office, Hutton MSS. J. Raine (ed.), *The Correspondence of Dr Matthew Hutton, Archbishop of York, Surtees Society*, xvii (1843). J. Raine, 'Marske', *Archaeologia Aeliana*, New Series, v (1861). *North Riding Records*, vii (1889), 72, 75-6.)

MARSKE   Langbaurgh

A Cleveland village on the northern coast of the county. The parish of Marske included the fishing village of Redcar. 1675: 85 households in Marske and 39 in Redcar.

In 1676 the North Riding magistrates decided to allocate the sum of £20 as compensation for several persons in Redcar who had suffered great losses 'by a suddaine and lamentable fire'.

Church St Germain: Norman.

Principal families (1) Pennyman of Marske Hall (baronetcy 1628). Estate revenue: £950 a year (1628); £1800 a year (1640). Alum mining in Skelton.

William Pennyman (1564-1628), who was illegitimate, grew rich as a barrister and one of the Six Clerks in Chancery. He built up a large estate in the North Riding, including a manor in Marske, and also bought some property in Hertfordshire.

His enclosing activities in Marske aroused opposition. In 1628 it was reported that some men had destroyed an enclosure he had made on an adjoining moor and had put in their own sheep.

At his death he left debts amounting to over £8000.

His son William (1609-1643) was granted a baronetcy and made a ward of the Crown in the same year. Through his marriage to an heiress, Anne Atherton, he acquired a substantial amount of property in Marske, Skelton and Eston. At Skelton there were alum mines which were potentially valuable. Eventually they were leased to Sir Paul Pindar the alum farmer in return for a rent of £600 a year.

Sir William was a close friend and ally of Thomas Lord Wentworth who appointed him as one of his deputy lieutenants and a member of the Council in the North. In 1635 he was made sheriff of Yorkshire and proceeded to collect the whole amount of ship money which was charged on the county.

In 1637 Wentworth recommended him for the important office of *custos rotulorum* for the North Riding. Among other things, he laid stress on his integrity and his good affection to the king's service.

During the 1630s Sir William was becoming heavily indebted and in 1637 he mortgaged his lands in Skelton and Eston.

In 1638 he informed Wentworth that he had bought an office in the Star Chamber and intended to perform the duties in person. In recent years (he told him) the average profits had amounted to nearly £2000 a year but in the event the office proved to be less lucrative than he had expected.

During the summer of 1642 he served as one of the king's commissioners of array and raised a troop of horse. As a royalist colonel he took part in the battle of Edgehill and was subsequently appointed governor of Oxford. He died at Oxford after succumbing to the fever which was then raging. Clarendon wrote of him that he had carried out the duties of governor 'to the great satisfaction of all men, being a very brave and generous person, and who performed all manner of civilities to all sorts of people, as having had a very good education, and well understanding the manners of the Court'.

Sir William had no issue and following the death of his widow the estate was divided between Conyers Lord Darcy and James Pennyman of Ormesby. The debts which he left were said to be of the order of £20,000.

(2) Lowther of Marske Hall (baronetcy 1697). Estate revenue: £900 a year (1660); £1200 a year (1680).

In 1649 James Pennyman sold the Marske estate and adjoining property to Sir John Lowther and his brother Robert, who was a London draper, for £13,000. Three years later Robert Lowther purchased his brother's interest.

His grandson William (c.1670-1705) was the first baronet of the family. He added to his estate by marrying a Lancashire heiress, Catherine Preston.

Marske Hall A two-storeyed house with three projecting turrets which was built in 1625.

In 1675 Anthony Lowther was taxed on 18 hearths.

(*North Riding Records*, vi (1888), 247. North Yorkshire County Record Office, Zetland (Dundas) MSS. J. W. Pennyman (ed.), *Records of the Family of Pennyman of Ormesby* (1904). Wards 5/49. Wards 9/567/fols. 149, 184, 372. W. Knowler (ed.), *The Earl of Strafforde's Letters and Dispatches* (1739), ii, 70, 258. W. D. Macray (ed.), *The History of the Rebellion and Civil Wars in England ... by Edward, Earl of Clarendon* (1888), iii, 406. Surtees Society, cxci (1976, 1977), 64, 68, 86.)

MARTON   Langbaurgh

A village to the west of Guisborough. The parish of Marton included the hamlets of Newham and Tollesby. 1675: 79 households (township of Marton). 1676: 225 persons aged 16 or more (parish).
   Church St Cuthbert: Norman and Early English.
   The Archbishop of York was the patron of the living.

MARTON IN THE FOREST   Bulmer

A village to the east of Easingwold within the bounds of the Forest of Galtres. The parish of Marton included the hamlet of Moxby. 1675: 30 households (township of Marton). 1676: 75 persons aged 16 or more (parish).
   Marton Priory, which was an establishment of Augustinian canons, had been founded in the 12th century and dissolved in 1536. At Moxby there had been an Augustinian nunnery which had been converted into a house.
   Church St Mary: Norman in origin but mainly Perpendicular.
   The minister was a perpetual curate.

MASHAM   Hang East

A small market town situated near the River Ure. The parish of Masham included a number of villages and hamlets. 1675: 91 households in Masham, 10 in Burton upon Ure, 27 in Ellingstring, 52 in Ellington, 34 in Fearby, 49 in Healey cum Sutton, 38 in Ilton cum Pott and 34 in Swinton cum Warthermarske. The whole area with the sole exception of Burton upon Ure was known as Mashamshire.
   A royal charter of 1251 had granted the right to hold a weekly market and an annual fair. In 1328 authority for an additional fair had been obtained.
   From time to time there were reports that Masham Bridge which spanned the River Ure was in need of repair. In 1665 the North Riding magistrates decided that the sum of £400 should be levied for this purpose.
   Churches St Mary: Norman and Perpendicular.
   The church was subject to the peculiar jurisdiction of the Dean and Chapter of York.
   In 1689 there was a Quaker meeting house in Masham.
   Principal families (1) The manor of Masham and most of the land within the parish belonged to the Danby family who resided for much of the 17th century at either Thorpe Perrow (see under Well) or Farnley near Leeds. About 1689 they settled at Swinton.

(2) **Beckwith of Aldburgh Hall (and Walburn Hall)** (baronetcy 1681). Estate revenue: £1300 a year (1630); £1500 a year (1690).

The family had settled at Aldburgh, within the township of Burton upon Ure, as recently as 1597.

Roger Beckwith (c.1550-1635) steadily built up a large estate and was the first member of the family to occupy Aldburgh Hall.

In 1630 he was hauled before the Privy Council after displaying some initial reluctance to pay his knighthood composition.

He apparently found it difficult to come to terms with the recusancy of his eldest son Thomas who had to be satisfied with a modest patrimony. The bulk of the estate descended to his half-brother Arthur who, ironically, married a Catholic, Mary Wyvill.

In the Civil War Arthur Beckwith (1615-1642) and his brother Matthew served as captains in the parliamentary army. Early on in the conflict Arthur was killed in action and left a widow and several young children.

In 1647 the Commons belatedly decided that the guardianship of the children should be vested in their grandmother Susanna Beckwith and two Protestant uncles. Mary Beckwith, however, managed to retain custody and in 1650 the Council of State intervened in an attempt to insulate them from Catholic influences. Matthew Beckwith and others were instructed to remove them from their mother's house and hand them over to the designated guardians.

Sir Roger Beckwith (c.1640-1700), who succeeded to the estate after the death of his elder brother, was presented for recusancy in 1664 but probably conformed immediately. His first wife, Elizabeth Clapham, died not long after their marriage, leaving a newly born son, Arthur. In 1674 her father, Sir Christopher, began legal proceedings against Beckwith over his failure to make a settlement of the estate.

In 1700 Arthur Beckwith died while travelling on the Continent and shortly afterwards Sir Roger committed suicide by shooting himself with a pistol.

Swinton Hall After selling his Thorpe Perrow estate in 1688 Sir Abstrupus Danby built himself a house at Swinton.

Aldburgh Hall Roger Beckwith must have begun to build a new house shortly after his purchase of the estate in 1597. A gabled mansion of two storeys.

(*North Riding Records*, vi (1888), 87. C.5/225/34. C.8/52/15. C.33/243/fo. 223. *CJ*, v, 281. *CSP Dom, 1650*, 3-4. J. Fisher, *The History and Antiquities of Masham and Mashamshire* (1865).)

MELSONBY
Gilling West

A village to the north-east of Richmond. The parish of Melsonby included part of the village of East Layton; the other part was in the parish of Stanwick. 1675: 70 households in Melsonby and 49 in Laytons Ambo (East and West Layton).

East Layton Hall, which was rebuilt in 1623, belonged to the Laytons of Sexhow.

To the south of Melsonby was Gatherley Moor where the local gentry raced their horses. In 1621 Thomas Meynell noted in his journal that the family had once won the first prize, a gold bell, at a meeting held there.

Church St James: Saxon in origin; Early English.

The parish was subject to the peculiar jurisdiction of the Dean of York.

(*CRS*, lvi (1964), 35.)

MIDDLEHAM
Hang West

A small market town in Wensleydale. 1675: 107 households.

A royal charter of 1389 had conferred the right to hold a weekly market and an annual fair.

In 1604 the Crown granted Middleham Castle to Sir Henry Lindley and in 1628 sold the manor of Middleham to the City of London. In 1661 the manor passed into private hands.

At the beginning of the Civil War the castle was garrisoned on behalf of Parliament.

Church St Mary and St Alkelda: Decorated and Perpendicular.

The church was a royal peculiar and the minister had the title of dean.

Castle The great Norman keep was built in the 12th century and additions were made in the 13th and 14th centuries.

In 1647 Parliament decided that the castle should be rendered untenable.

MIDDLETON
Pickering Lythe

A village to the north-west of Pickering. The parish of Middleton contained a number of villages, including Cropton, Lockton and Rosedale East Side which had dependent chapels. Rosedale West Side was in the parish of Lastingham. 1675: 37 households in Middleton, 25 in Aislaby, 38 in Cropton cum Cawthorn, 22 in Hartoft, 60 in Lockton, 41 in Rosedale East Side and 34 in Wrelton. 1676: 318 persons aged 16 or more in the parish of Middleton (excluding Lockton) and 120 in the chapelry of Lockton.

Rosedale Priory, which was an establishment of Cistercian nuns, had been founded in the 12th century and dissolved in 1538.

In 1606 Richard Greenecall of Aislaby, a parish clerk, was accused of attacking Ralph Chapman the vicar of Middleton. According to the indictment the incident took place immediately after a service in the parish church. In 1612 it was alleged that Margery Chapman the vicar's wife had assaulted James Brewster the village constable who had been attempting to execute a warrant for their arrest.

Churches St Andrew: Saxon, Norman, Early English, Decorated and Perpendicular. In 1689 there were Quaker meeting houses at Rosedale and Wrelton.

School Lawrence Hardwick, who was vicar of Middleton in the years 1632 to 1652, kept a private school there.

(*North Riding Records*, i (1884), 32, 116; ii (1884), 2; and vii (1889), 103.)

MIDDLETON TYAS   Gilling East

A village to the north-east of Richmond. The parish of Middleton Tyas included the village of Moulton and the hamlet of Kneeton. 1675: 61 households in Middleton Tyas and 30 in Moulton.

During the early 17th century the inhabitants of the parish included a considerable number of Catholics. There were 30 recusants in 1611 and 40 in 1641. By the end of the century, however, there had been a marked decline in the amount of recusancy.

In 1607 John Hutchinson of Middleton Tyas, who was described as a yeoman, was accused of uttering words which displayed contempt for the Crown. He was alleged to have declared that 'The Kinges Majestie hath no Lawes whereby to grant commission to take Recusantes goodes; neither can make any lawes so to doe'; and that 'Seminarie priests were messengers sent from God'.

The Frankes of Kneeton Hall were one of the leading Catholic families in the parish. In the Civil War Marmaduke Franke (1597-1666) supported the royalist cause. Even before this he was in serious financial difficulties: his Kneeton estate, worth £150 a year, had been mortgaged and charged with an interest payment of £120 a year. In 1661 the North Riding magistrates were informed that he was threatening 'to put his tenants forth of the possession of their lands which they enjoy in Kneaton'. As a result of this official interest he undertook to suspend action for a limited period.

In the middle years of the 17th century the Smithsons of Moulton were busily engaged in building operations. Moulton Manor was substantially improved and a completely new mansion, Moulton Hall, was erected.

George Smithson had served as a major in the parliamentarian army. In 1690 it was agreed that the house of Thomas Smithson at Moulton could be used for divine worship by Protestant dissenters.

Church St Michael: Norman, Early English and Decorated.

(H. Aveling, *Northern Catholics. The Catholic Recusants of the North Riding of Yorkshire 1558-1790* (1966), 436. *North Riding Records*, i (1884), 90; vi (1888), 41; and vii (1889), 109. S.P.23/lxxxi/139-40, 146-7.)

MYTON   Bulmer

A village on the River Swale near Boroughbridge. 1675: 27 households (township of Myton). 1676: 100 persons aged 16 or more (parish of Myton).

There was a ferry at Myton.

Church St Mary: Early English.

Principal family Stapleton of Myton Hall (baronetcy 1660). Estate revenue: £1000 a year (1655).

The Stapletons were a cadet branch of the Stapleton family of Wighill in the Ainsty.

Brian Stapleton (1589-1658) bought the manor of Myton about 1610. He was receiver general of the Crown revenue in northern England.

When the knighthood composition scheme was launched in 1630 he was slow to pay his assessment and in 1633 he refused to allow the Yorkshire muster master to receive his fee. Following the latter incident Thomas Lord Wentworth observed that he was 'a factious ill affected person' who 'doth nothing but brabble and tyrannise over his poor neighbours'; and that he was 'as arrant a saucy Magna Charta man as in all the Country'.

Stapleton assured the Privy Council that he was ready to conform for the future but eventually it was decided that he should be removed from the commission of the peace.

During the 1630s he was involved in a property dispute with Thomas Graver of Myton which was fought out in the courts at York and Westminster. The quarrel was resumed in 1653 when he complained in a Chancery suit that the Gravers had stopped up a highway in Myton.

In the Civil War he and his son Henry (c.1617-1679) served as members of the North Riding parliamentary committee. In 1647 the latter was elected to the Long Parliament as MP for Boroughbridge but was secluded the following year in Pride's Purge. The grant of a baronetcy in 1660 suggests that he may have been an active participant in the events which led to the restoration of the monarchy.

His son Sir Brian (c.1657-1727) emerged as a Tory politician in the last decade of the century.

Myton Hall In 1623 Brian Stapleton let a contract for the building of 'a new house of Bricke together with a Court to be walled about'. The project did not go smoothly. In a Chancery suit of 1626 he related that although he had ordered 100,000 bricks half of them had still to be delivered and that he had found 'many doores, Chimneys, windowes, and ovens in the saide new house misplaced, false wrought and wrong sett upp'.

In 1675 Sir Henry Stapleton was taxed on 15 hearths.

Among the rooms listed in an inventory of 1679 were the hall, the great dining parlour, the green parlour, the wainscot chamber and the study.

The house was rebuilt or remodelled by Sir Brian Stapleton towards the end of the 17th century. A brick-built mansion of two storeys.

(North Yorkshire County Record Office, Stapylton of Myton MSS. Sheffield Archives, Wentworth Woodhouse Collection, Strafford Letters, v, Thomas Lord Wentworth to Sir John Coke, 23 December 1633. C.3/415/67. C.5/381/186. PRO, Probate Inventories, PROB 4/11,442.)

NEWTON UPON OUSE   Bulmer

A village to the north-west of York. The parish of Newton included the village of Linton upon Ouse and the hamlet of Beningbrough. 1675: 65 households in Newton cum Beningbrough and 41 in Linton cum Youlton. 1676: 250 persons aged 16 or more (parish of Newton).

A royal charter of 1282 had conferred the right to hold a weekly market and an annual fair.

In 1607 the North Riding magistrates decided that Linton Bridge should be repaired at the expense of the inhabitants of the parish.

In 1697 it was reported that the inhabitants of Newton had spent about £120 on the construction of a stone bridge across the River Ouse between Newton and Linton.

Church All Saints: Norman.

Principal families (1) Bourchier of Beningbrough Grange. Estate revenue: £1000 a year (1620); £1200 a year (1658); £2000 a year (1672).

Following the death of his father in 1598 William Bourchier (1559-1626) had been formally declared a lunatic. He remained in that condition until his death and outlived both his wife and his eldest son Robert. In 1623 the Court of Wards granted custody of the lunatic and his lands to Sir John Bourchier (c.1593-1660) who by that time had become the heir apparent.

Sir John was a zealous Puritan who probably owed his religious fervour to the influence of his mother, a member of the Barrington family of Essex. Roger Morrice, a nonconformist divine, wrote that he was 'a serious person, an open professor of Religion, and gave Encouragement and Protection to those that did so'.

When the forced loan scheme was introduced in 1627 he sent word to the commissioners that he was unwilling to contribute. Subsequently he opposed the creation of a new park within the royal forest of Galtres on the grounds that it seriously affected his rights of common and in May 1633 some parts of the fencing were destroyed on his direct orders. As a result he was imprisoned for nearly a year 'with much hardshipp' and was fined £1000. Wentworth commented that 'This Gentleman generally observed to inherit a frenzy Constitution from his parent And to be more than halfe madd allready'.

In the Civil War he took up arms on behalf of Parliament and was a member of the North Riding committee.

In 1647 he entreated Ferdinando Lord Fairfax to 'take into consideracion the greate wante of mayntenance for preaching ministers in this poore blynde Countrye' and stressed the need to bring the Gospel to 'an ignorant and sottishe people'.

Sir John was one of the judges at the trial of the king and signed the death-warrant. Subsequently he served as a member of the republican Council of State.

After the Restoration he was taken into custody but died before he could be put on trial. On his deathbed he refused to express any regret for the execution of the king: 'I tell you it was a just act, and God and good men will owne it'.

His son Barrington (1627-1680), who had also embraced the cause of Parliament, assisted in the process of restoring the monarchy. As a result he was allowed to retain possession of the estate which he had inherited.

During the years 1659 to 1668 he bought a substantial amount of landed property.

(2) Appleby of Linton Hall, Linton upon Ouse. Estate revenue: £550 a year (1653).

Ambrose Appleby (c.1585-1649) was a Catholic lawyer who was employed for a time as clerk and solicitor to Sir John Mallory of Studley. In 1625 he bought the manor of Linton upon Ouse and settled there. Following the purchase he brought in Thomas Cowling to carry out a survey of the manor and instructed him to report not only on the acreage but on the nature of the soil.

His wife Mary was presented for recusancy in 1626 but he was not convicted until shortly before the Civil War. During the war he appears to have been an inactive royalist.

His son Thomas (1618-1689) remained politically neutral but in 1653 two-thirds of his estate were sequestered on account of his recusancy. For some years he had a resident chaplain.

In 1678 Appleby was involved in litigation with Henry Hunt who had been serving as his steward. He complained that Hunt had refused to give him any account of his activities or to pay rent for a farm which had been leased to him but these allegations were strongly contested.

In 1701 the male line of the family expired.

Beningbrough Grange An Elizabethan house which had been built by Sir Ralph Bourchier. In 1675 Barrington Bourchier was taxed on 11 hearths.

Among the rooms listed in an inventory of 1695 were the hall, the dining room and the drawing room.

There was a park belonging to the manor.

Linton Hall The house was probably built in the reign of Charles I. It contained a chapel.

In 1675 there were nine taxable hearths.

The park had originally been enclosed towards the end of the 14th century.

(*North Riding Records*, i (1884), 41, 82, 88, 104, and vii (1889), 161. Wards 9/93/fols. 43-4, 62, 222-3; 94/fols. 473-4, 650; and 95/fo. 61. Dr Williams's Library, Morrice MSS, J, no pagination. Sheffield Archives, Wentworth Woodhouse Collection, Strafford Letters, xvii, Lord Wentworth to Sir John Coke, 13 May 1634. BL, Additional MSS 18,979, fo. 232. *Camden Fourth Series*, 21 (1978), 183. Pat Taylor, 'The Restoration Bourchiers of Beningbrough Grange', *YAJ*, lx (1988). Wards 9/567/333. C.10/130/3.)

NORMANBY   Ryedale

A small village to the south-west of Pickering. 1675: 23 households in Normanby and 3 in Thornton Riseborough. 1676: 70 persons aged 16 or more (parish).

In 1615 it was reported that the bridge at Normanby, spanning the River Seven, was 'in decay and ruinated now more than it was att anie time before or since the building thereof, by force of this last flood'. On this and subsequent occasions the cost of the repair work was met through a general levy. The authorities, however, were insistent that local responsibilities should be properly discharged. In 1651 three Normanby men were required to explain why they had neglected to remove sand beds from the Seven 'by reason whereof Normanby Bridge is brought into great decay'; and in 1663 the inhabitants of the village were indicted 'for not scouring of the river of Seaven'.

In 1632 Thomas Lord Wentworth sold the manor of Thornton Riseborough to Sir Arthur Robinson of Deighton in the East Riding. According to a particular which had been drawn up two years earlier the rental value had fallen from £256 to £207 a year and the sale price was £3828. Sir Arthur settled the property on his elder son Luke and it was probably about this time that a new house was built.

In the Civil War Luke Robinson (1610-c.1669) was strongly committed to the parliamentary cause yet in 1643 he secured a pass to go abroad. Eventually he became a member of the Long Parliament and after the establishment of a republic he was appointed to the Council of State.

In June 1660 he wrote in a letter to one of his associates
itt is well knowne I have had noe Respect to my
owne Advantadge in what I did, that I have beene A greate
Looser by the tymes, have waisted my estate and have contracted
debts upon itt, have suffered much from others and have had
noe Repayration though my habitation were distroyed and
A damadge fallen upon mee which I shall never Recover, have
not added one peny to my estate by any man's dammadge..

Church St Andrew: Norman, Early English and Perpendicular.

School In her will (1700) Judith Boynton made provision for the establishment of a free school at Normanby for the teaching of reading, writing, arithmetic and the Church catechism.

(*North Riding Records*, ii (1884), 88, 92, 101, 237; iii (1885), 330, 331; iv (1886), 74; v (1887), 137; and vi (1888), 66. Sheffield Archives, Wentworth Woodhouse Collection, Strafford Letters, vol. 20 (a). *CJ*, iii, 161. BL, Additional MSS 21,425, fols.221-2.)

NORTHALLERTON   Allertonshire

One of the most important market towns in the North Riding. The parish of Northallerton included a number of villages. 1675: 186 households in Northallerton, 51 in Brompton, 36 in Deighton, 17 in High Worsall and 38 in Romanby.

Royal charters of 1555 and 1611 conferred the right to hold a weekly market on Wednesdays. There were several annual fairs of which the earliest derived from a charter of 1200. The fair for oxen, cows and sheep was considered to be the greatest in England.

Northallerton was not a corporate town and in the 17th century there appears to have been no formal kind of municipal government. On the other hand, it was a town where quarter sessions were held, generally on a regular basis; and in December 1640 the Long Parliament decided to restore its ancient right to send elected representatives to Westminster. Because of its position on a major trunk road it was designated as a post town.

The manor of Northallerton belonged to the Bishops of Durham.

Northallerton 'is nothing but a long street, yet the most throng Beast-fair upon St Bartholomew's day that ever I saw' (William Camden).

'This towne affords most excelent ale and beere, and very good entertainement' (Life of Marmaduke Rawdon, entry for 1664).

Northallerton ale was also highly praised by Giles Mornington in a poem published in 1697:

Northallen, in Yorkshire, does excel
All England, nay all Europe, for strong ale.

Church All Saints: Norman, Early English, Decorated and Perpendicular.
Three new bells were hung in 1656 and another one in 1692.
The parish was subject to the peculiar jurisdiction of the Dean and Chapter of Durham.

Episcopal palace The Norman castle had been demolished in the late 12th century and materials had apparently been taken from it for the building of a palace or fortified manor-house for the Bishops of Durham. In the 17th century the palace was in ruins.

School A free grammar school dating from the 14th century or earlier.

The most notable of the masters who taught there in the 17th century was Thomas Smelt who was described as 'an excellent grammarian, both of Latin and Greek, diligent in his office and vigilant in his care and observation of the boys'. He usually had around 80 scholars yet he had no assistant.

Almshouses The Maison Dieu, which had been founded in 1476, provided accommodation for four poor women.

Principal family Sayer of High Worsall Hall. Estate revenue: £1500 a year (1630); £800 a year (1660). Lead mining at Marrick.

The Sayers, who were a leading Catholic family, were the most substantial landowners resident in the parish.

John Sayer (c.1560-1635) was described in 1604 as a recusant of long standing. In 1607 he was granted a licence to travel outside a five-mile compass of his principal residence in order to engage in the sports of hunting and hawking and to visit his other houses at Colburn and Marrick.

In 1629 he compounded for his recusancy and was required to pay a rent of £260 a year which was the same as the annual fine he had been paying for many years.

As he had no children the estate was split up after his death: the manor of High Worsall passed, along with other property, to his nephew Lawrence Sayer while the manor of Marrick descended to his niece Dorothy and her husband, William Bulmer.

Lawrence Sayer (1598-1658), who settled at High Worsall, was also convicted of recusancy. Even before the Civil War he was having to raise money by granting rent-charges and annuities out of his landed property. When hostilities began he took up arms for the king and signed the Yorkshire Engagement of 1643. As a result his estate was first sequestered and then sold by the Treason Trustees.

The estate was eventually recovered but this entailed heavy borrowing and his son Lawrence proved incapable of overcoming the financial crisis in which he was involved. In 1671 he sold the manor of High Worsall and by 1673 he had disposed of virtually his whole patrimony. In 1684 he was living in Ireland.

High Worsall Hall There is no reference to the hall in the hearth tax return of 1662. In the last years of his life Lawrence Sayer the elder was living at Yarm.

(C. G. D. Ingledew, *The History and Antiquities of North Allerton* (1858). J. L. Saywell, *The History and Annals of Northallerton* (1885). YASRS, xxxiii (1903). *CSP Dom, 1603-11*, 352. C.7/179/117. C.9/9/34. C.10/476/65.)

NORTH OTTERINGTON Allertonshire/Birdforth

A hamlet to the south of Northallerton. The parish of North Otterington included the village of Thornton le Moor and part of the village of Thornton le Beans; the other part was in the parish of Northallerton. 1675: 9 households in North Otterington, 52 in Thornton le Beans and 51 in Thornton le Moor.

The wastes of Thornton le Moor were enclosed in 1652.

Church St Michael: Norman.

The parish was subject to the peculiar jurisdiction of the Bishop of Durham.

NUNNINGTON Ryedale

A village to the south-east of Helmsley. Only part of the village was situated in the parish of Nunnington: other parts were in the parishes of Helmsley and Stonegrave. 1675: 45 households (township of Nunnington). 1676: 92 persons aged 16 or more (parish of Nunnington).

The bridge at Nunnington spanned the River Rye. In 1665 it was reported that 'Nunnington Bridge is very much in decay, which hath been occasioned by the late unhappy differences, and the inhabitants allege that they are not well able to repair the same as formerly they have been'. The North Riding magistrates took the view that it was the responsibility of the local community to keep the bridge in good repair. In 1671, however, they decided that the North Riding as a whole should provide the sum of £120 'towards the building of a stone bridge at Nunnington for cart and carriage with two arches, sufficient battlements and causways'. This was subject to the proviso that the inhabitants of Nunnington should meet the residue of the expenditure and that in future they should be solely responsible for any repair work.

The manor of Nunnington belonged to the Crown until 1630. For many years the Norcliffes of Langton in the East Riding held Nunnington Hall and its demesnes on long leases and frequently resided there. Towards the end of the 16th century they undertook a substantial amount of building work. During the Civil War the house was occupied for a time by parliamentarian troops who left it in a dilapidated condition.

In 1655 Ranald Graham, a London woollen draper, bought the estate for £9500. Five years later he was involved in litigation with Sir Thomas Norcliffe who he alleged had committed great waste within the manor and had allowed the house to fall into ruin. In fact Sir Thomas had taken many of the fittings and a large quantity of lead to Langton where he had been building a new mansion.

After the death of Ranald Graham in 1685 the Nunnington estate descended to his great nephew Sir Richard Graham (1648-1695) who had been made Viscount Preston four years earlier. In the reign of James II he was appointed Secretary of State (North) and a member of the Privy Council. When the king went into exile he remained one of his most loyal supporters and in 1691 he was arrested and condemned to death. Eventually, however, he secured a pardon and was able to recover his estate. During the last years of his life he carried out considerable improvements to Nunnington Hall which he had made his principal residence.

Church All Saints and St James: late 13th century.

In 1672 Ranald Graham rebuilt the west tower and it was at this time that the church acquired the dedication to St James.

School and almshouses During the 1670s Ranald Graham founded a school and a hospital at Nunnington. For this purpose he erected a single-storeyed building which contained six rooms for the occupants of the hospital and two for the school and the schoolmaster.

(*North Riding Records*, vi (1888), 95, 161. C.10/58/48. *CSP Dom, 1690-1*, 65, 219, 228-9, 349, 359, 388.)

OLD BYLAND   Birdforth

A village to the north-west of Helmsley. There was no other village within the parish. 1675: 33 households (township of Old Byland).

Church All Saints: Norman.

The minister was a perpetual curate.

ORMESBY   Langbaurgh

A Cleveland village to the west of Guisborough. The parish of Ormesby contained several villages and hamlets, including Eston which had a medieval chapel. 1675: 51 households in Ormesby, 49 in Eston, 9 in Morton and 22 in Normanby.

Church St Cuthbert: Norman.

During the Interregnum it was reported that the chancel was in great decay.

Principal families (1) Pennyman of Ormesby Hall (baronetcy 1664). Estate revenue: £600 a year (1630); £1000 a year (1661).

The Pennymans bought the manor of Ormesby in 1600 and resided there until 1961.

In the Civil War James Pennyman (1579-1655) helped to muster troops for the king and his son Sir James (1608-1679) served as a royalist colonel.

Following the death of their kinsman Sir William Pennyman of Marske in 1643 the family inherited a substantial amount of property but this was sold in 1649 for £13,000.

The main factors responsible for the sale were Sir William's legacy of unpaid debts and the fines imposed by Parliament. By the time of the Restoration, however, the Pennymans had significantly increased their estate revenue.

Sir Thomas Pennyman (1642-1708), who succeeded his father in 1679, held the office of Lord Privy Seal in the reign of William III.

(2) Morley of Normanby. Estate revenue: £3500 a year (1642). Coalmining at Harraton in Durham.

The Morleys had lived at Normanby for generations but they never owned the manor. At the beginning of the 17th century they were a minor gentry family with few pretensions.

James Morley (1576-1642) was a barrister who made a fortune as one of the Six Clerks in Chancery. He rapidly built up a great estate in the North Riding and also secured valuable leases. His lease of the Harraton colliery, which he acquired in 1638, was said to be worth £800 a year over and above the rent.

In pushing ahead with his programme of land purchases he overstrained his resources and had to resort to heavy borrowing. In 1641 his debts amounted to over £10,000.

In the Civil War his son Cuthbert (c.1610-1669) supported the royalist cause and as a result his estate was sequestered. In 1651 Jeremy Elwes, who was the principal creditor, managed to gain possession of lands worth some £1500 a year which had been mortgaged to his father. After the Restoration Morley sought to recover this property but failed. He left an only child, Anne, who along with her husband Bernard Grenville continued the legal battle with the Elwes family. The Grenvilles were eventually successful but in the 1680s they disposed of most of the estate which they had inherited.

Ormesby Hall A modest Jacobean house which was built shortly after the Pennymans bought the manor. In 1675 Sir James Pennyman was taxed on 10 hearths.

(J.W. Pennyman (ed.), *Records of the Family of Pennyman of Ormesby* (1904). *Surtees Society*, cxci (1976, 1977), 64, 168. C.10/475/105. C.33/218/fo. 37; 222/fols. 229-30; and 233/fols. 535-6. C.38/175/22 June 1671.)

OSBALDWICK   Bulmer

A small village to the east of York. The parish of Osbaldwick included the village of Murton which had a medieval chapel. 1675: 23 households in Osbaldwick and 21 in Murton.

Church St Thomas: Norman.

The parish was subject to the peculiar jurisdiction of a Prebendary of York.

OSMOTHERLEY Allertonshire

A village to the north-east of Northallerton. The parish of Osmotherley included several villages. 1675: 63 households in Osmotherley, 26 in Ellerbeck, 35 in Thimbleby and 25 in West Harlsey.

In 1621 the inhabitants of Osmotherley were indicted 'for diverting the ancient course of the Wiske, in not cleaning and scouring the ditches behind Osmotherley and so through Clacke unto Mount Grace Abbey, whereby the inhabitants of West Rounckton and divers other townes adjoyninge the said river are molested in sommer-time for lacke of water for their cattle'.

In 1674 the residents of Osmotherley complained in a petition which they forwarded to the North Riding magistrates about the cost of poor relief within their constablery and suggested that Thimbleby, West Harlsey and Ellerbeck should make a greater contribution. A year later the magistrates noted that the lands in Osmotherley were valued at £250 a year and those in Thimbleby, West Harlsey and Ellerbeck at £950 a year and upwards.

Churches St Peter: Saxon in origin; Norman, Decorated and Perpendicular.

The parish was subject to the peculiar jurisdiction of the Bishop of Durham.

In 1689 there were Quaker meeting houses in all four villages.

School There was a school at Osmotherley in the early 17th century.

(*North Riding Records*, iii (1885), 111 and vi (1888), 221, 236, 239. *CRS*, lv (1963), 447. O. Thompson, *Osmotherley* (1938).)

OSWALDKIRK Ryedale

A village to the south of Helmsley. There was no other village within the parish. 1675: 53 households in Oswaldkirk cum Ampleforth. 1676: 54 persons aged 16 or more (parish).

Roger Dodsworth the antiquary (1585-1654) was born at West Newton Grange in this parish.

West Newton Grange subsequently became the seat of Sir Henry Cholmley (1609-1666), a younger brother of Sir Hugh Cholmley of Whitby. In the Civil War he served as a colonel in the parliamentary army and (unlike his brother) remained loyal to the cause. Sir Hugh described him as 'a kind well natured man and loving trew friend, valliant and ingenious, and a good solliscitor in law businesses and diligent in all his affayres'.

Church St Oswald: Norman and Early English.

School There was a school at Oswaldkirk in the early years of the 17th century.

(J. Binns (ed.), *The Memoirs and Memorials of Sir Hugh Cholmley of Whitby 1600-1657, YASRS*, cliii (2000), 77.)

OVERTON
Bulmer

A hamlet to the north of York. The parish of Overton included the village of Shipton. 1675: 57 households (township of Shipton cum Overton). 1676: 140 persons aged 16 or more (parish of Overton).

Church St Cuthbert: Norman.

School In her will (1655) Ann Middleton, a merchant's widow, bequeathed £1000 for the building and endowment of a free grammar school at Shipton.

The master was paid a salary of £40 a year.

Principal family Scudamore of Overton Hall. Estate revenue: £500 a year (1621); £700 a year (1660).

Thomas Scudamore (c.1560-1621) was receiver general of the Crown revenue in Yorkshire. He took a lease of the Crown manor of Overton in 1595 and received a grant of the estate in 1605.

His son William (1591-1661) purchased the manor of Shipton shortly after entering into his patrimony. Probably as a means of funding this transaction he sold some outlying property and borrowed money on a considerable scale. Sensing an opportunity for a profitable investment Sir Thomas Wentworth (the future Earl of Strafford) paid off the principal creditors and in 1624 had the manor of Overton extended for debt. From 1626 until his death he received all the rents which amounted to about £5000.

In a petition which he submitted to the House of Lords in 1641 Scudamore related that he had been 'divers times arrested and imprisoned for debts occasioned by the said Extents'. In the event Parliament declined to intervene on his behalf. In 1650 he took legal action against Strafford's surviving trustee and was eventually able to regain possession of the manor of Overton. His financial problems, however, continued and in 1659 his debts amounted to some £3600, of which £2500 was owing to his brother-in-law Sir John Bourchier.

In the early years of Charles II's reign his son Thomas (1616-1673) sold the manors of Overton and Shipton to Barrington Bourchier.

Overton Hall The house had been built in 1406. In the Chancery case of 1650 it was said that the hall had been in a ruinous condition when Wentworth had taken possession of the manor and that he had been put to great expense in repairing it and making it fit for a tenant to live in.

In 1662 Overton Hall had only five taxable hearths.

(Sheffield Archives, Wentworth Woodhouse Collection, Strafford Letters xxi (a), Wentworth to Richard Marris, 4 November 1627. House of Lords MSS, petition of William Scudamore, 19 January 1640/1. C.9/5/189. C.10/129/10. C.33/254/fo. 277. C.38/207/4 February 1680/1.)

PATRICK BROMPTON   Hang East/Hang West

A village to the north-west of Bedale. Part of the village was situated in the parish of Patrick Brompton while the other part was in the parish of Bedale. The parish of Patrick Brompton included the village of Hunton, which had a dependent chapel, and parts of Newton le Willows and Scotton. 1675: 34 households in Patrick Brompton, 70 in Hunton, 54 in Newton le Willows cum Ruswick and 18 in Scotton.

Church St Patrick: Norman and Decorated.

The Bishop of Chester had the patronage rights.

PICKERING   Pickering Lythe

Pickering was described in 1656 as an ancient market town containing 300 families. The parish of Pickering embraced several villages and hamlets, including Goathland which had a medieval chapel. 1675: 238 households in Pickering town and Pickering Marishes, 43 in Goathland and 12 in Kingthorpe.

The honour, manor and castle of Pickering belonged to the Duchy of Lancaster which employed a number of local officials. The town had long had borough status.

A royal charter of 1291 had granted the right to hold two fairs a year. On the other hand, the ancient market rights appear to have been prescriptive.

Pickering is 'a pretty large town belonging to the Dutchy of Lancaster, seated upon a hill, and fortified with an old Castle' (William Camden).

During the course of the Civil War the castle was besieged and taken by parliamentarian troops.

Churches St Peter and St Paul: Norman, Early English, Decorated and Perpendicular.

The parish was subject to the peculiar jurisdiction of the Dean of York.

In 1689 there was a Quaker meeting house in Pickering.

Castle The castle had originally been built in the 12th century and further work had been carried out in the 13th, 14th and 15th centuries.

Schools There was a school at Pickering in the early years of the 17th century.

Subsequently a grammar school was built there in accordance with the provisions of a charitable trust which was set up by Elizabeth Viscountess Lumley in 1657.

House of correction In 1652 the North Riding magistrates went ahead with their plan for locating a house of correction at Pickering 'to punish and cause to work persons wandering idle'. This was in addition to the existing establishment at Richmond. Arrangements were made for the inmates to undertake such types of work as spinning and knitting.

(*CSP Dom, 1656-7*, 182. W. K. Jordan, *The Charities of Rural England 1480-1660* (1961), 344-5. *North Riding Records*, v (1887), 106-8. R. B. Turton (ed.), *The Honor and Forest of Pickering, North Riding Record Society*, New Series, i (1894).)

PICKHILL   Hallikeld/Allertonshire

A village to the west of Thirsk. The parish of Pickhill included a number of villages and hamlets. Some of the hamlets may have suffered from depopulating enclosures, perhaps in the early 16th century. 1675: 58 households in Pickhill cum Roxby, 7 in Ainderby Quernhow, 3 in Howe, 24 in Sinderby and 10 in Swainby cum Allerthorpe.

In 1307 Pickhill had been granted the right to hold a weekly market and an annual fair.

Church All Saints: Norman, Early English and Perpendicular.

School In the reign of Charles I there was a private school at Pickhill.

Principal family Harrison of Allerthorpe Hall. Estate revenue: £1000 a year (1642). The Harrisons acquired the manors of Allerthorpe and Swainby in 1626.

Sir Thomas Harrison (c.1590-1664), who was a lawyer resident in York, bought a large estate at Copgrove in the West Riding shortly before the Civil War. During the war he appears to have been sympathetically inclined towards the royalist cause but without displaying any significant degree of commitment. In contrast, his son Thomas (1627-1687) was a zealous parliamentarian who served as sheriff of Yorkshire in the years 1656 to 1658. It is probably an indication of his religious outlook that in 1654 he was selected as a commissioner for the removal of scandalous ministers.

Allerthorpe Hall A house built in 1608 by the Robinson family. In 1675 Thomas Harrison was taxed on 12 hearths.

(PRO, Exchequer, Lay Subsidy Rolls, E.179/209/364. *YASRS*, cxviii (1951), 12, 13.)

RICHMOND   Gilling West

An important market town on the River Swale. 1675: 328 households. As recorded in the hearth tax return of 1675 there were three wards or districts: Bailey, Bargate and Frenchgate.

The town had enjoyed borough status since the Norman period. Under the provisions of a royal charter of 1577 it was governed by a corporation which consisted primarily of an alderman and 12 capital burgesses. In a further charter of 1668, however, these were replaced by a mayor and 12 aldermen. The first mayor was William Wetwang who had held the office of alderman under the previous arrangements.

Richmond had been made a parliamentary borough in the charter of 1577 and it was also one of the main quarter sessions towns in the riding.

The right to hold markets and fairs had been granted and confirmed in a series of medieval and Tudor charters. The town's principal industry was the manufacture of hand-knitted stockings.

In the 17th century the parish of Richmond had comparatively few Catholics. In 1669 it was reported that there were 40 or 50 Quakers.

A number of gentry families had residences in the town, among them the Huttons of Marske Hall and the Yorkes of Gouthwaite Hall in the West Riding.

Richmond had a long association with horse-racing. Race meetings had been held on the neighbouring moors since the early part of the 16th century. In his commonplace book Thomas Meynell noted that in April 1623 'ther was seaven horses which did rune at Richemond for a bowl worth £12 and a salte worth six'.

Richmond, 'the chief city' of Richmondshire, is 'enclos'd with walls of no great compass; yet by the suburbs which shoot out in length to the three gates it is pretty populous' (William Camden).

Richmond 'stands on a hill …. its buildings are all stone …. there is a very large space for the Markets which are divided for the fish market, flesh market and corn; there is a large Market Crosse a square space walled in with severall steps up …. there is by it a large Church and the ruines of a Castle …. it looks like a sad shatter'd town and fallen much to decay and like a disregarded place' (Celia Fiennes, 1698).

The town escaped the ravages of the Civil War but in 1646 there was an outbreak of the plague.

Churches St Mary: Norman, Early English and Perpendicular.

Holy Trinity chapel: originally Norman but rebuilt in the 14th century.

The north aisle of the chapel was used for the transaction of municipal business.

Castle The building of Richmond Castle had begun shortly after the Norman Conquest. The keep was erected in the 12th century and further work was carried out in the 14th century.

School There had been a grammar school at Richmond in 1392.

In 1567 the town obtained a royal charter for the founding of a free grammar school and this was built in St Mary's churchyard. One of its most celebrated masters was Dr John Bathurst who held the appointment from about 1620 until 1631. He later became Oliver Cromwell's physician and in 1659 died a rich man.

Almshouses The medieval hospital of St Nicholas had been dissolved in the reign of Henry VIII.

The Bowes Hospital, which housed three poor widows, was founded by Eleanor Bowes in 1607. In her will (1618) she endowed it with a rent-charge of £10 a year.

At the end of the 17th century George Pinkney, an alderman, made provision for the establishment of almshouses for three poor women aged 60 or more.

House of correction In 1611 the North Riding magistrates decided that Richmond should have a house of correction which would serve the needs of the entire riding but it was not until 1620 that the plan was fully realised.

There was also a town prison which was under the control of the corporation.

(C.8/430/70. *CRS*, lvi (1964), 36. *North Riding Records*, i (1884), 225, 249, 254, 257; ii (1884), 229-30; and iv (1886), 251, 253. W. K. Jordan, *The Charities of Rural England 1480-1660* (1961), 271, 317-18. C. Clarkson, *The History and Anti-quities of Richmond* (1821). R. Fieldhouse and B. Jennings, *A History of Richmond and Swaledale* (1978). Jane Hatcher, *The History of Richmond* (2000).)

ROKEBY   Gilling West

A village to the south-west of Barnard Castle. The parish of Rokeby extended as far as the River Tees. 1675: 42 households in Rokeby cum Egglestone.

Egglestone Abbey, which was an establishment of Premonstratensian canons, had been founded in the 12th century and dissolved in 1540. About the middle of the 16th century part of the abbey was converted into a house.

The Rokebys were an ancient family which had long been seated at Mortham. Their residence, Mortham Tower, had been built in the 14th century and enlarged towards the end of the 15th century.

Although the Rokebys were still attached to the Catholic faith in the early years of the 17th century it had virtually ceased to exert any influence over them by the time of the Civil War. Sir Thomas Rokeby (c.1570-1633) was presented as a recusant in 1628 but as a general rule he preferred outward conformity. Despite this caution, however, he was a man with serious financial problems. In 1610 he sold 700 acres in Rokeby and Mortham to William Robinson, a London merchant; and in February 1621 he was a prisoner in York Castle, probably on account of an unpaid debt.

In 1691 Thomas Rokeby (1639-1722) sold the Mortham estate.

William Robinson settled his family at Rokeby and built a new house there. In the Civil War he and his elder son Thomas, who was a barrister, supported the cause of Parliament. The latter took up arms and in 1643 was killed in an engagement near Leeds. In contrast, the Rokebys appear to have played no part in the war.

Church St Mary: Norman in origin.

(E. Peacock (ed.), *A List of the Roman Catholics in the County of York in 1604* (1872), 78-9. *North Riding Records*, iii (1885), 302. C. 33/139/fo. 606.)

ROMALDKIRK   Gilling West

A village situated to the north-west of Barnard Castle in one of the most remote parts of the North Riding. The extensive parish of Romaldkirk was bordered by the counties of Durham and Westmorland and contained large tracts of moorland as well as a considerable number of scattered villages and hamlets. 1675: 237 households in Mickleton with Romaldkirk, 127 in Cotherstone, 56 in Hunderthwaite and 52 in Lartington.

At Cotherstone there were the ruins of a medieval castle.

Romaldkirk Bridge, which spanned the River Tees, was partly in the North Riding and partly in Durham and this division was reflected in the arrangements for the funding of repair work. Lune Bridge, near Mickleton, was of considerable local importance as it carried the road linking Romaldkirk with the other villages in the parish. In the reign of Charles I it was reported to be in a ruinous condition.

By the end of Elizabeth's reign there was hardly any residual trace of Catholicism within the whole parish. The Applebys, who bought the manor of Lartington in 1639, were a recusant family but they appear to have had little influence on the religious loyalties of their tenantry. In the Civil War Francis Appleby supported the royalist cause.

Churches St Romald: Norman, Early English, Decorated and Perpendicular.

In 1689 there were Quaker meeting houses at Cotherstone and Lartington.

Schools A school had been established at Romaldkirk in 1548 and the village had a schoolmaster in the middle years of the 17th century. In 1686 Charles Parkin, a clergyman, founded a free school there with an endowment of £300.

There was a schoolmaster at Lartington in the reign of Charles I. In the late 17th century John Parkin and Francis Appleby contributed a total of £100 for the endowment of a free school and other members of the local community built a schoolhouse. This was probably the school which is mentioned in the hearth tax roll of 1675.

Almshouses In 1674 William Hutchinson, a London lawyer, built a hospital at Romaldkirk for six poor people and in his will (1693) made a settlement of property for its support.

(*North Riding Records*, iii (1885), 329, 347, 352; vi (1888), 233; and vii (1889), 75, 102. H. Aveling, *Northern Catholics. The Catholic Recusants of the North Riding of Yorkshire 1558-1790* (1966), 439. K. Shallcross Dickinson, *History of the Church and Parish of Romaldkirk* (1936). E. W. Crossley, 'The Manor of Cotherston with Hunderthwaite', *YAJ*, xxxv (1943).)

RUDBY   Langbaurgh

A Cleveland village on the River Leven to the south-west of Stokesley. The extensive parish of Rudby included a considerable number of villages, some of which (marked *) had dependent chapels. 1675: 26 households in Rudby, 32 in Carlton, 19 in *East Rounton, 41 in *Faceby, 25 in *Hilton, 62 in Hutton Rudby, 27 in *Middleton upon Leven, 28 in Newby, 23 in *Newton, 43 in Potto, 59 in *Seamer, 1 in Skutterskelfe and 103 in *Whorlton. 1676: 1071 persons aged 16 or more, including 64 recusants (parish).

The most prominent physical feature in the parish was Roseberry Topping which towered over the village of Newton. Roseberry Topping, 'a steep mountain and all over green, riseth so high that it appears at a great distance; and it is the land-mark that directs sailers, and a prognostick to the neighbours hereabouts. For when its top begins to be darken'd with clouds rain generally follows' (William Camden).

At Whorlton there were the ruins of a medieval castle which had long since been abandoned. By virtue of royal charters of 1269 and 1307 Whorlton enjoyed the right to hold a weekly market and an annual fair.

At Hutton Rudby a new stone bridge across the River Leven was built between 1621 and 1625. In 1635, however, it was reported to be in a ruinous condition.

Church All Saints: Decorated and Perpendicular.

The church had formerly belonged to Guisborough Priory.

Schools Christopher Coulson, a London dyer who had bought the manor of Great Ayton, built a schoolhouse at Newby (in the chapelry of Seamer) where he had been born. In his will (1640) he made financial provision for the teaching of poor children of Newby and Seamer.

There was a Catholic school at Hutton Rudby on the eve of the Civil War. In 1670 Oliver Nicholson of Hutton Rudby was indicted for teaching boys without a licence.

Principal family Layton of Sexhow Hall. Estate revenue: £1000 a year (1612); £1500 a year (1634).

Charles Layton was an enclosing landlord. In 1606 he was involved in a dispute with some of his tenants over a projected enclosure of certain pasture grounds. At his death in 1617 he left a large and flourishing estate.

His son Sir Thomas (1597-1650) was appointed sheriff of Yorkshire in 1631 at a time when the controversy over the knighthood composition scheme was at its height. He incurred the displeasure of Thomas Lord Wentworth by levying fines on a number of men who had already paid their assessments. In July 1632 he made his house available for a meeting of North Riding gentry which had been called to discuss the knighthood composition scheme. At this meeting his relative Sir David Foulis spoke in favour of outright opposition.

In 1633 Sir Thomas found himself in the Court of Star Chamber along with Sir David and his son Henry but was discharged through lack of evidence. In Wentworth's opinion he was a fool and a coxcomb who had been led by the nose.

Sir Thomas does not appear to have played an active part in the Civil War but in 1649 he had his estate sequestered as an alleged royalist.

Towards the end of his life he was in serious financial difficulties which were partly occasioned by the fact that he had acted as surety when his son-in-law Sir Henry Foulis was negotiating a loan. At his death the estate was heavily burdened with debt and in the reign of Charles II several manors were sold.

His grandson Charles Layton (1640-1675) left no issue and after his death a substantial amount of property passed to his sister Bridget who took it out of the family. The manor of Sexhow, on the other hand, came into the possession of his uncle Sir Robert Layton.

Sexhow Hall A gabled house which was mainly two storeys in height. It probably dated back to the early 16th century.

(*North Riding Records*, i (1884), 42-3; iii (1885), 115, 139, 233; iv (1886), 44; and vi (1888), 147. W. K. Jordan, *The Charities of Rural England 1480-1660* (1961), 338. Sheffield Archives, Wentworth Woodhouse Collection, Strafford Letters, xxi (b), Wentworth to Lord Cottington, 11 August 1632. C.3/451/74. C.33/234/fo.968 and 236/fo. 620.)

SALTON   Ryedale

A village to the south of Kirkby Moorside. The parish of Salton included the hamlet of Brawby. 1675: 39 households in Salton cum Brawby.

In 1607 the North Riding magistrates were informed that Salton had been depopulated by William Lord Eure about 24 years ago.

Richard Miller, the Puritan vicar of Salton, found himself in trouble with the ecclesiastical authorities at the visitation of 1632. He was admonished and reminded of the need for strict observance of the Book of Common Prayer.

Church St John of Beverley: Norman.

(*North Riding Records*, i (1884), 79. R.A. Marchant, *The Puritans and the Church Courts in the Diocese of York 1560-1642* (1960), 263.)

SCALBY   Pickering Lythe

A village to the north-west of Scarborough. The parish of Scalby, which extended as far as the coast, contained several villages, including Cloughton which had a dependent chapel. 1675: 90 households in Scalby cum Newby, 48 in Burniston, 72 in Cloughton cum Staintondale and 13 in Throxenby.

The manor of Scalby and other property in the parish belonged to the Duchy of Lancaster.

Churches St Lawrence: Norman and Early English. The west tower was built, or rebuilt, in 1683.

In 1689 there was a Quaker meeting house at Staintondale.

Almshouses In the reign of Charles I Christopher Keld founded a hospital at Scalby for four poor widows or widowers.

SCARBOROUGH   Pickering Lythe

A market town and a major port. 1675: 536 households.

The hearth tax returns of 1662 and 1675 refer to five quarters or districts: Aldborough, Falsgrave, Newborough, St Mary's and Undercliffe.

The town had enjoyed borough status since the 12th century. Although it had a mayor in the 1650s and 1680s it was usually governed by a senior and a junior bailiff.

In 1603 Charles Earl of Nottingham, the Lord High Admiral, described Scarborough as 'a place of good importaunce and worthy to be cherissed, beinge a great succor to all vessels that trade to the Northerne partes'.

Royal charters issued in the 12th and 13th centuries had granted the right to hold markets and fairs. In 1661 there were markets on Thursdays and Saturdays and three annual fairs. Besides the fishing industry, which was the most important source of employment, there was also a growing shipbuilding industry.

The population of the town included very few Catholics but there were other forms of religious dissent in the late 17th century. In 1697 Celia Fiennes noted that there was an 'abundance of Quakers'.

Scarborough's spa well was first discovered about 1620 and in the latter part of the 17th century it was attracting many visitors from the upper levels of society. Alice Thornton of East Newton wrote that in 1659 she and her husband spent a month at Scarborough and that 'upon drinking of the waters I did by the blessing of God recover my strength'.

Scarborough was the birthplace of Sir John Lawson (d.1665), a distinguished naval commander who served as an admiral under both Cromwell and Charles II.

Scarborough 'haith a reasonable good port for shipping and a large castle in which is a garison of soldiers .... Att the bottome of the towne .... is a spaw, very medicinable and much frequented by ladies that have a desire to be gott with child' (Life of Marmaduke Rawdon, entry for 1664).

Scarborough 'drives a great trade with fish taken in the Sea thereabout, wherewith they supply the City of York, tho' thirty miles distant. Besides Herings .... they have

Ling, Cod-fish, Haddock, Hake, Whiting, Makrel, with several other sorts, in great plenty' (Edmund Gibson, 1695).

'Scarborough is a very pretty Sea-port town built on the side of a high hill, the Church stands in the most eminent place above all the town ... the ruines of a large Castle remaines .... the sand is so smooth and firme .... on this sand by the Sea shore is the Spaw Well which people frequent' (Celia Fiennes, 1697).

In 1613 the great pier was destroyed in a violent storm. This led the Privy Council to impose a permanent tax on all colliers travelling along the east coast in order to finance the reconstruction and maintenance of the pier.

In 1624 it was reported that the town was 'sore grieved with sicknes and infection of the plague' but by January 1625 this had abated.

In the Civil War Scarborough was regarded as a town of considerable strategic importance on account of its harbour facilities. Early on in the war Sir Hugh Cholmley took control of the town on behalf of Parliament but in March 1643 he declared for the king. After a brief period in which the castle was held by parliamentarian troops it became a royalist stronghold with Cholmley as its governor. In February 1645 a parliamentarian force took possession of the town and proceeded to lay siege to the castle. The royalist garrison put up a spirited resistance but in July Cholmley finally surrendered. About the same time there was an outbreak of the plague in Scarborough.

In 1648 Matthew Boynton, the governor of Scarborough, went over to the royalist side. After a further siege the parliamentarians regained possession of the castle.

Scarborough suffered badly in the wars. Many buildings were destroyed or damaged; the town and harbour were plundered by both sides; and the quartering of soldiers added to the general misery. After the severe disruption of trade the economic recovery was slow to materialise.

In 1661 it was said that the town was populous but factious and that there was a need for a garrison to maintain security.

Churches St Mary: Norman, Early English, Decorated and Perpendicular.

The church was badly damaged in the fighting. The central tower collapsed in 1659 and was replaced with a new tower in 1669.

St Thomas's chapel was destroyed during the Civil War.

In 1676 there was a Quaker meeting house in Scarborough.

Castle The castle had been built in the 12th century and improved in the 13th and 14th centuries.

During the siege of 1645 the Norman keep was bombarded and partly reduced to rubble.

In 1651 the Council of State gave order for the demolition of the castle but shortly afterwards suspended the decision for security reasons.

School The grammar school may have been founded in the reign of Edward VI.

The schoolhouse was destroyed during one of the sieges. In 1648 the municipal authorities decided to relocate the school within the parish church of St Mary.

Almshouses St Thomas's Hospital, which dated from the 13th century, provided accommodation for 12 poor men and women.

Trinity House was established in 1602 for the care of poor seamen's widows.

Other almshouses were founded in 1628 (Farrer's Hospital) and 1697 (Trott's Hospital).

(T. Hinderwell, *The History and Antiquities of Scarborough*, 3rd edn. (1832). A. Rowntree (ed.), *The History of Scarborough* (1931). J. Buckley, *The Outport of Scarborough, 1602-1853 – A Maritime History* (1951). *North Riding Records*, iii (1885), 214. Sir Hugh Cholmley, 'Memorialls tuching Scarborough', *YASRS*, cliii (2000). J. Binns, '*A Place of Great Importance*': Scarborough in the Civil Wars (1996). *CSP Dom, 1661-2*, 21.)

SCAWTON   Ryedale

A village to the west of Helmsley. There was no other village within the parish. 1675: 32 households (township of Scawton). 1676: 79 persons aged 16 or more (parish).

Church St Mary: Norman.

SCORTON   Hang East

A village within the parish of Catterick. 1675: 65 households.

Principal family Wastell of Scorton Hall. Estate revenue: £200 a year (1630); £600 a year (1659).

The Wastells were a new gentry family with Puritan leanings. The manor of Scorton was purchased about 1616.

John Wastell (1594-1659) inherited a modest estate from his father in 1629. He was a barrister who was recorder of both Ripon and Richmond. In April 1642 he significantly advanced his legal career by securing appointment as one of the Masters in Chancery.

In the Civil War he was a colonel in the parliamentary army and a member of the North Riding committee.

Partly as a result of his marriage to an heiress, Anne Robinson, he added considerably to his estate. She was described as 'a prudent and ffrugall person' who engaged in moneylending during her widowhood.

After the Restoration the family ceased to be politically active.

Scorton Hall The house was probably Jacobean. In 1675 it had 12 taxable hearths. (C.10/56/223; 69/150; and 118/88 and 95.)

SCRUTON   Hang East

A village to the west of Northallerton. There was no other village within the parish. 1675: 63 households (township of Scruton).
   Church St Radegund: Norman, Early English and Perpendicular.
   School In the reign of Charles I Thomas Lith kept a private school at Scruton.

SEAMER   Pickering Lythe

A village to the south-west of Scarborough. The parish of Seamer, which extended as far as the coast, contained several villages, including Cayton and East Ayton which had medieval chapels. 1675: 94 households in Seamer, 76 in Cayton cum Osgodby, 50 in East Ayton and 24 in Irton.

A royal charter of 1382 had conferred on Seamer the right to hold a weekly market and an annual fair. The existence of a market there was a matter of concern to the burgesses of Scarborough who regarded it as a serious rival to their own market. In 1609, however, James I renewed the charter of 1382 on the understanding that this would not be to the detriment of markets and fairs in other places.

At the beginning of the 17th century the manor of Seamer belonged to the Gate family. Edward Gate (1547-1622) had inherited an estate worth £1000 a year but he was already in serious financial difficulties. In a desperate attempt to raise money he had been granting long leases of property in Seamer in return for immediate cash payments and eventually he sold the manor. In 1631 it was purchased by the Napier family of Luton Hoo in Bedfordshire who entrusted it to the care of a steward. By the reign of Charles II the revenue from their Yorkshire estate (which included virtually all the land in the parish of Seamer) amounted to £1700 a year.

In 1612 a number of houses in Seamer were destroyed or damaged in a fire. On hearing of this the North Riding magistrates decided to provide compensation.

In 1641 some troopers from the king's northern army went on a rampage in Seamer and caused the inhabitants to fear for their lives. For over two hours they went up and down the main street brandishing their swords, hurling stones and hitting out with sticks and cudgels. In the course of this episode several men were wounded, including a justice of the peace.

   Church St Martin: Norman with some later features.
   (C.2/James I/13/11. C.33/322/fo.506. *North Riding Records*, i (1884), 262. *CSP Dom, 1640-1*, 473-5.)

SESSAY
Allertonshire

A village to the south of Northallerton. The parish of Sessay included the village of Hutton Sessay. 1675: 62 households in Sessay and Hutton Sessay. 1676: 120 persons aged 16 or more (parish).

Sessay was one of the seats of the Dawney family of Cowick in the West Riding who had a deer park there. In 1675 Sir John Dawney was taxed on 14 hearths.

William Wakefield, who was rector of Sessay from 1632 to 1665, was a man of Puritan inclinations, though he managed to retain his living at the Restoration. In 1632 he was presented for neglecting to comply with the Book of Common Prayer. Although the ecclesiastical authorities were informed that he had since fallen into line they decided to suspend him for a time when he failed to certify his conformity.

Church St Cuthbert: Norman in origin.

(R. A. Marchant, *The Puritans and the Church Courts in the Diocese of York 1560-1642* (1960), 288-9.)

SHERIFF HUTTON
Bulmer

A village to the north of York. The parish of Sheriff Hutton included the village of Farlington, which had a medieval chapel, and several hamlets. 1675: 192 households in Sheriff Hutton cum membris (including 9 in Cornbrough and 23 in East and West Lilling) and 33 in Farlington. 1676: 487 persons aged 16 or more (parish).

A royal charter of 1378 had granted the right to hold a weekly market and an annual fair.

Sheriff Hutton Park contained some 700 acres. In the reign of James I it was leased by the Crown to Sir Arthur Ingram who was required to keep 300 deer there for the king's use. Sir Arthur built a substantial hunting lodge which was completed by 1621. In 1628 the lease was granted to him in perpetuity.

East Lilling appears to have been depopulated in the 15th century. In a Crown survey of 1625 it was noted that it 'retaineth the name of East Lilling township, though at this day there do remain but only one house wherein.... Mistress Hall now dwelleth, a competent house for a gentleman'.

Stittenham had been depopulated in the early 16th century. There were two houses in 1662 and only one, Stittenham Hall, in 1675. In 1676 the inhabitants of Sheriff Hutton complained that they were 'overcharged' with poor people and added that in contrast Stittenham had no poor. The North Riding magistrates therefore decided that Stittenham should contribute towards the cost of poor relief.

In 1680 Stittenham was rated at £585 a year for fiscal purposes and Cornbrough at £415 a year.

Churches St Helen, Sheriff Hutton:Norman, Early English, Decorated and Perpendicular.

In 1689 there were Quaker meeting houses at Stittenham and Foss House within the parish.

Castle Sheriff Hutton Castle dated from the 14th and early 15th centuries. For many years it had belonged to the Crown and in the reign of Elizabeth it had been used as a prison. By 1618 it was in ruins.

School In the reign of Charles I Ralph Troy kept a private school at Sheriff Hutton.

Almshouses James Westroppe of Cornbrough had founded almshouses at Sheriff Hutton in the reign of Elizabeth.

Principal families (1) Gower of Stittenham Hall (baronetcy 1620). Estate revenue: £1000 a year (1640).

The Gowers had been seated at Stittenham since the 12th century or earlier.

Sir Thomas Gower (1584-1651) had been made a ward of the Crown following the death of his father in 1592.

In 1626 the Court of Wards was informed that he had agreed to take a young ward into his household for his better education and upbringing but had abused his trust by marrying him to a poor kinswoman at Stittenham Hall.

In 1631 the North Riding magistrates dealt with the case of a man who was said to have declared that Gower 'was an unjust Justice, and one that would sooner write his letters and mainteine whores and knaves then honester people'. As a punishment he was required to make a humble submission in the parish churches of Sheriff Hutton and Crambe.

In November 1632 Sir Thomas was arrested in London by officers of the Council in the North. In a letter to the Privy Council Wentworth and his legal associates explained that they had received information that Gower had 'in an open Quarter Sessions of the Peace, upon the Bench, after his frequent and lavish manner, spoken publiqly very scandalous words against his Majesties Attorney here; and indeed thorow him fixed a great imputation upon us all'. After promising to answer the charge he had gone into hiding and could not be brought in even though the serjeant-at-arms had searched his house on several occasions. Gower, they went on, had taken up residence in Holborn, 'closse by others of the like affections; where it seemes they, their children and followers soe demeane and declare themselves against the government, as we heare they are there wantonly termed the Rebels of the North'. In the event Gower was kept a prisoner for several months.

During the Civil War the Gowers supported the king. Sir Thomas was named as a commissioner of array in June 1642; contributed a loan of £1500 in August; and signed the Yorkshire Engagement of February 1643. His son Sir Thomas was serving as sheriff of Yorkshire during the growing political crisis. He was also included in the commission of array and on 5 August 1642 informed his uncle Sir Richard Leveson that he had been assigned the task of raising a force of 1000 dragoons. In 1645 his involvement in the Civil War was brought to an end when he was taken prisoner at Rowton Heath. During the course of the war Stittenham Hall was plundered by parliamentarian troops.

Sir Thomas the second baronet (c.1605-1672) fell under suspicion in 1657 and two of his brothers were imprisoned at York. At the end of 1659 he joined Thomas Lord Fairfax when he came out in favour of a free Parliament. From 1663 until his death he was governor of York.

When Ralph Thoresby visited Stittenham Hall in 1680 he was impressed by the contents of the library which he had left to his heir. It was, he wrote, 'the best furnished with ancient fathers and commentators, both Popish and Protestant, upon the Scriptures, of any that I have seen; the rest were mostly on Medicine, for which Sir Thomas was justly famous'.

His younger son William (c.1647-1691) inherited an estate worth £3000 a year from his great uncle Sir Richard Leveson and assumed the name of Leveson Gower. When the main line of the Gower family expired in 1689 the Leveson Gowers also came into possession of the Stittenham estate.

(2) Westroppe of Cornbrough Hall. Estate revenue: £700 a year (1620); £400 a year (1640).

Thomas Westroppe was made a ward of the Crown after inheriting the estate of his elder brother in 1618. In 1621 he obtained a licence to travel abroad but this was later suspended by the Privy Council on hearing that he was engaged in litigation with his wife Joan. In 1624 the Privy Council was informed that he had deserted his wife some years earlier and had left her without any maintenance. Accordingly he was ordered to provide her with an allowance of £60 a year.

Westroppe was a wastrel who was found guilty in the Court of Star Chamber of cheating with false dice. He began to sell property almost immediately and in 1642 disposed of his Cornbrough estate.

Sheriff Hutton Hall A house built by Sir Arthur Ingram between 1617 and 1621. In 1624 it was described as 'a very fayre new lodge of brick'.

Stittenham Hall The hall was rebuilt or considerably enlarged in the reign of Charles II. There were 18 hearths in 1662 and 26 in 1675.

Cornbrough Hall The house was probably Elizabethan.

(A. F. Upton, *Sir Arthur Ingram c.1565-1642* (1961), 150-1, 197. BL, Harleian MSS 6288, fols. 1-2, 26-8. M. W. Beresford, 'The Lost Villages of Yorkshire', *YAJ*, xxxviii (1955), 284, 306. *North Riding Records*, vi (1888), 253 and vii (1889), 34. Wards 9/95/fols. 461-2. J. T. Cliffe, *The Yorkshire Gentry* (1969), 301-2. C.8/75/29 and 463/13. C.33/248/fols. 595-6. Wards 9/92/fo. 800. *Acts of the Privy Council, 1621-3*, 46, 252, 259 and *1623-5*, 383. HMC, *Fourth Report*, Appendix, 34.)

SINNINGTON   Pickering Lythe/Ryedale

A village situated between Kirkby Moorside and Pickering. The parish of Sinnington included the hamlets of Little Edstone and Marton (but not Great Edstone which was a parish in its own right). 1675: 33 households in Sinnington, 22 in Edstones Ambo and 18 in Marton. 1676: 157 persons aged 16 or more (parish).

In 1303 Sinnington had been granted the right to hold a market and an annual fair.

At Sinnington there were two bridges spanning the River Seven: one of them carried the Kirkby Moorside-Pickering road while the other was primarily for the convenience of residents of the parish. The periodic repair work which became necessary was funded by means of a general levy on the North Riding. In 1646 the inhabitants of Sinnington submitted a petition to the parliamentarian magistrates about the state of their bridges which may have sustained damage in the course of the Civil War. As a result one of the justices was asked to carry out an investigation in order to establish 'whether one bridge will serve, yea or noe' and 'what the decayes are'. In the end it was agreed that the sum of £13 should be levied for the repair of the main bridge.

In 1669 there was a report of a Quaker conventicle at Sinnington.

Church All Saints: Norman.

The minister was a perpetual curate.

School An elementary school was established at Sinnington with money provided from a charitable trust set up by Elizabeth Viscountess Lumley in 1657. She usually resided at Sinnington where she owned the manor.

(*North Riding Records*, iv (1886), 254, 262. W. K. Jordan, *The Charities of Rural England 1480-1660* (1961), 279, 345. R. W. Jeffery, *Thornton-le-Dale* (1931).)

SKELTON   Bulmer

A village to the north-west of York. It was in two parishes: Skelton and Overton. 1675: 63 households in Skelton cum Rawcliffe. The hamlet of Rawcliffe was in the parishes of St Olave and St Michael le Belfry, York.

The Lovells of Skelton, who owned the manor, sided with the king in the Civil War. In 1675 Thomas Lovell was taxed on ten hearths.

Church All Saints: Early English.

SKELTON   Langbaurgh

A village near Guisborough. The parish of Skelton contained several villages, including Brotton which had a dependent chapel. 1675: 91 households in Skelton, 74 in Brotton cum Skinningrove, 33 in Kilton and 70 in Moorsholm. 1676: 650 persons aged 16 or more (parish).

By virtue of a royal charter of 1310 Skelton had the right to hold a weekly market and an annual fair. From the 1630s onwards alum was mined there.

'Upon the shore, Skengrave [Skinningrove], a small village, flourishes by the great variety of fish it takes' (William Camden).

Church All Saints: Norman and Decorated.

School In the reign of Charles II there was a school at Kilton.

Principal families (1) Trotter of Skelton Castle. Estate revenue: £800 a year (1664); £1300 a year (1685). Alum mining in Skelton.

The Trotters were new entrants to the landed gentry. At the beginning of the century they had residual Catholic sympathies but there was a comparatively rapid transition from outward conformity to fully-fledged Protestantism.

Following the death of Sir Henry Trotter in 1623 his son George (1609-1647) was made a ward of the Crown. In February 1642 he signed a Cleveland petition which expressed the hope that 'we may be secured, a happy Reformacion afforded, And the lawes of God and the King without favour or delay iustly putt in execution against Papists'. During the Civil War he served as a member of the North Riding parliamentary committee.

In his will (1647) he stipulated that his funeral should be without 'all pompe and unnecessarie and superflous expence of monies'. He also committed his son Henry to the tuition and care of two fellow parliamentarians, Sir William Strickland and Sir Henry Cholmley.

During the 1650s the Trotters substantially increased their Skelton estate, partly by purchase and partly through an exchange of property.

In 1669 Edward Trotter (1637-1709) and his father-in-law Sir John Lowther decided to embark on a joint venture for the mining of alum in Skelton. To assist them they brought in Matthew Shipton as a partner, apparently on the basis that he would provide the necessary professional expertise. Shortly before this Trotter had been involved in a legal dispute over the application of manorial rights to the gathering of seaweed or tangle kelp which was used as a fuel in the manufacturing process.

In furtherance of their objective of creating an alum monopoly John Earl of Mulgrave and Sir Hugh Cholmley agreed in 1685 that they would pay Trotter a rent of £400 a year in return for an undertaking that he would abandon his mining activities.

(2) Thweng of Kilton Hall (and Heworth Hall, near York). Estate revenue: £450 a year (1640); £700 a year (1677).

The Thwengs (or Thwings) were a Catholic family.

When Robert Thweng was admitted to the English College at Rome in 1624 he related that his parents were 'schismatics' or Church Papists while his brothers and sisters were all openly Catholic. He became a Jesuit missioner and served in the Midlands.

His brother George, who succeeded to the estate, was convicted of recusancy in 1632. Some time before the Civil War he bought the manor of Kilton which had once belonged to his medieval ancestors.

On the outbreak of the war he took up arms for the king and in 1648 was heavily fined. Three years later the authorities sequestered two-thirds of his estate on account of his recusancy.

His grandson Thomas Thweng (c.1650-1677) appears to have travelled abroad after his marriage in 1670. In 1678 his widow, Jane, was involved in litigation with other members of the family over her jointure lands. In the course of these proceedings she thought it expedient to make the point that she was a true Protestant while the defendants were all popish recusants.

Thomas Thweng had a daughter, Ann, who eventually inherited the manor of Kilton.

Skelton Castle The castle, which was Norman in origin, had been described in 1490 as ruinous. During the reign of James I Sir Henry Trotter repaired the walls and tower and built a square hall and a dining room on the site of the chapel.

In 1675 Edward Trotter was taxed on 17 hearths.

There was a park adjoining the castle.

Kilton Hall A gabled house of two storeys which may have been built before George Thweng purchased the manor. In 1675 it had only five taxable hearths.

The Norman castle belonged to the manor of Kilton but it had been in a ruinous condition since the 14th century.

Thomas Thweng had two parks in Kilton which were known as the Old and New Parks.

(Wards 5/49. *Surtees Society*, cxci (1976, 1977), 155, 157, 177-8, 188, 189, 247, 250. BIHR, York Registry, will of George Trotter, 5 March 1646/7. C.10/104/87. C.33/269/fo. 666. C.38/260/13 July 1698. *CRS*, lv (1963), 377. C.5/288/63. C.10/132/126 and 127. C.33/261/fo. 745.)

SLINGSBY Ryedale

A village to the north-west of Malton. There was no other village within the parish. 1675: 65 households (township). 1676: 170 persons aged 16 or more (parish).

'Slyngsby is watered with a sweete rivulet called Wath Beck....Ther is the walls of a fine chappell nere as bigg as the church within the castle walls, wher they had service in tyme of warres within themselves' (Roger Dodsworth, 1619). The castle which Dodsworth saw was a medieval fortress which had formerly belonged to the Hastings family.

In the 1620s Sir Charles Cavendish, a younger brother of William Earl of Newcastle, demolished most of the old castle and built a large and handsome mansion which was situated in parkland. The architect was probably John Smythson who had undertaken other work for the family. Although the new house was called Slingsby Castle its role was purely domestic.

After Sir Charles's death in 1654 the house passed to the main line of the family. By 1749 it was in ruins.

In 1655 the Cavendishes entered into an agreement with the freeholders for 'a general enclosure and improvement' of 354 acres of land within the manor.

Church All Saints: Norman, Early English and Perpendicular.

(A. St Clair Brooke, *Slingsby and Slingsby Castle* (1904). M. Girouard, *Robert Smythson and the Architecture of the Elizabethan Era* (1966), 142-3, 190-2.)

SNEATON Whitby Strand

A village to the south of Whitby. There was no other village within the parish. 1675: 43 households (township). 1676: 130 persons aged 16 or more (parish).

Church St Hilda: Norman in origin.

School During the 1650s there was a private school at Sneaton.

SOUTH KILVINGTON Birdforth

A village to the north of Thirsk. The parish of South Kilvington contained the hamlets of Thornborough and Upsall. 1675: 37 households in South Kilvington, 10 in Thornborough and 17 in Upsall. 1676: 190 persons aged 16 or more (parish).

There was a sizeable minority of Catholics in the parish throughout the 17th century. In the latter part of Elizabeth's reign the authorities discovered that Upsall Castle, a medieval building with a maze of vaults, was a place where mission priests were given shelter. Seminary priests were captured there in 1593 and 1609; and later on it was used by the Jesuits.

The Constables of Kirby Knowle, who were the owners of Upsall Castle, died out in the male line in the middle of the 17th century and after that it appears to have been abandoned and allowed to decay.

Church St Wilfrid: Norman and Decorated.

(H. Aveling, *Northern Catholics. The Catholic Recusants of the North Riding of Yorkshire 1558-1790* (1966), 141-2, 161, 238, 247, 415.)

SOUTH OTTERINGTON   Birdforth

A village to the south of Northallerton. There was no other village within the parish. 1675: 31 households (township). 1676: 31 persons aged 16 or more (parish).

Church St Andrew: Norman. There was apparently some rebuilding work in the course of the 17th century.

School In the reign of Charles I Thomas Harwood kept a private school at South Otterington.

SPENNITHORNE   Hang West

A village to the north-east of Middleham. The parish of Spennithorne included two other villages. 1675: 25 households in Spennithorne, 45 in Bellerby and 21 in Harmby.

The Scropes of Danby, a Catholic family, owned the Spennithorne estate and had a secondary house there.

In the Civil War Thomas Metcalfe of Bellerby appeared in arms for the king and was forced to compound for his estate. Adrian his son and heir was a physician who lived at Lincoln. He left property in Yorkshire and elsewhere worth £500 a year.

Church St Michael: Norman, Early English, Decorated and Perpendicular. The north chapel was added about 1620.

(S.P.23/cxci/383, 388. C.8/148/66. D. S. Hall, *Bellerby, a Dalesend Village* (1989).)

STAINTON   Langbaurgh

A village to the north-west of Stokesley. The parish of Stainton contained a number of villages and hamlets, including Thornaby which had a medieval chapel. 1675: 41 households in Thornton, Stainton and Stainsby, 7 in Hemlington, 25 in Ingleby Barwick, 22 in Maltby and 36 in Thornaby. 1676: 405 persons aged 16 or more (parish).

Although the Gowers of Stainsby Hall, a Catholic family, were only minor gentry they appear to have been intensely proud of their social status. When John Gower was summoned for jury service in 1619 he refused to attend on the grounds that it would not be fitting for him to 'come and .....serve amongst such a sorte of flatcapps, he being an Esquier'.

Church St Peter and St Paul: Early English and Perpendicular.

(*North Riding Records*, ii (1884), 206.)

STANWICK
Gilling West/Gilling East

A hamlet to the north of Richmond. The parish of Stanwick contained several villages, including Cleasby which had a dependent chapel. 1675: 9 households in Stanwick cum Carlton, 39 in Aldbrough, 37 in Caldwell and 39 in Cleasby.

In the reign of Henry VIII John Leland had been impressed by the Celtic fortifications within the parish.

Stanwick was one of the most Catholic parishes in the North Riding, mainly through the influence of the Catterick family. In 1669 it was reported that there were about 100 papists in the parish.

In 1638 there was an outbreak of the plague at Aldbrough.

In 1640 the North Riding magistrates endorsed a proposal by the overseers of Cleasby that Christopher Fletcher, 'a poore Minister there, should be settled in the house-ende of one house in which Mark Bell of Cleasby now dwells in the one ende thereof'.

Church St John Baptist: mainly Early English.

Principal family Smithson of Stanwick Hall (baronetcy 1660). Estate revenue: £1800 a year (1670).

Sir Hugh Smithson (c.1598-1670), who had been born at Newsham in the North Riding, made a fortune as a haberdasher in London. In 1638 he bought the manor of Stanwick from Anthony Catterick and went on to build up a substantial estate in the North and West Ridings. Following the sale of Stanwick the Cattericks moved to Carlton Hall in the same neighbourhood.

In the 1650s Smithson helped to keep the exiled Charles II well supplied with money and was rewarded with a baronetcy at the Restoration.

Both his parents were recusants but he took shelter in outward conformity.

In his will (1670) Sir Hugh settled a large jointure on his wife, Dame Dorothy. In Chancery proceedings the following year their son Sir Jerome (c. 1630-1684) formally acknowledged that the will was valid.

Sir Jerome, who was also a Church Papist, appears to have possessed an unruly temperament. In 1665 he was indicted for saying to Sir Joseph Cradock 'Thou art a base fellow. You thinke yourself impowered by being in the commission of the peace'. As a result he was bound over to keep the peace.

His son Sir Hugh (1657-1733) was presented as a recusant in 1690 but conformed in 1711. Three of his daughters became nuns.

The Smithsons eventually inherited the vast estates of the Dukes of Northumberland and adopted the surname of Percy.

Stanwick Hall In 1662 the Smithsons either rebuilt or improved the Tudor manor-house of the Catterick family. There were only six taxable hearths in 1662 and 1675 but the house seems to have been considerably enlarged before the major building programme carried out in 1740.

(*North Riding Records*, iv (1886), 90, 94, 185. C.3/398/59. C.10/119/112. *Surtees Society*, xl (1861), 131.)

STARTFORTH Gilling West

A village on the other side of the River Tees from Barnard Castle. The parish of Startforth included the village of Arkengarthdale which had a dependent chapel. 1675: 63 households in Startforth and 62 in Arkengarthdale. The village of Boldron, which had ties with Startforth parish church, is included in the entry for Bowes.

Startforth Bridge, linking the counties of Yorkshire and Durham, had been built in 1569.

Church Holy Trinity: 13th century or earlier.

School In his will (1659) Dr John Bathurst, who had been Cromwell's physician, endowed a grammar school at Arkengarthdale.

(W. K. Jordan, *The Charities of Rural England 1480-1660* (1961), 346.)

STILLINGTON Bulmer

A village to the south-east of Easingwold. There was no other village within the parish. 1675: 98 households (township of Stillington).

The prebendal manor of Stillington belonged to the Archbishop of York until the time of the Civil War when it was seized by Parliament and eventually sold to Sir Christopher Croft, a York merchant, who already held it on a long lease. After the Restoration the Crofts were able to keep possession of the estate, no doubt through the negotiation of a financial settlement with the Dean and Chapter.

Churches St Nicholas: Perpendicular.

The parish was subject to the peculiar jurisdiction of a Prebendary of York.

In 1689 there was a Quaker meeting house at Stillington.

STOCKTON ON THE FOREST Bulmer

A village to the north-east of York which was within the bounds of the Forest of Galtres. There was no other village in the parish. 1675: 42 households (township of Stockton).

Church Holy Trinity: 13th century or earlier.

The parish was subject to the peculiar jurisdiction of a Prebendary of York.

The minister was a perpetual curate.

STOKESLEY   Langbaurgh

A small Cleveland market town on the River Leven. The parish of Stokesley included the village of Westerdale and several hamlets. 1675: 121 households in Stokesley, 16 in Easby, 37 in Great and Little Busby and 46 in Westerdale. 1676: 826 persons aged 16 or more, including 105 recusants and 97 Protestant dissenters (parish of Stokesley).

The town's market rights were apparently prescriptive. A royal charter of 1224 had granted the right to hold an annual fair.

In the parish of Stokesley there were various kinds of religious nonconformity. In 1669 it was reported that there were 30 or 40 Quakers and 30 or 40 Anabaptists.

During the years 1623 to 1661 the manor of Stokesley belonged to Sir Richard Forster, a Catholic courtier who served as treasurer to Charles II during his exile in France.

In 1675 the lands within the township of Stokesley were valued at £800 a year for fiscal purposes.

Churches St Peter and St Paul: Perpendicular.

In 1689 there were Quaker meeting houses at Stokesley and Westerdale.

Principal family Marwood of Busby Hall, Little Busby (baronetcy 1660). Estate revenue: £1000 a year (1660).

The Marwoods had bought the Little Busby estate in 1587. They were a Puritan family.

Henry Marwood (c.1580-1639) inherited the estate following the death of his elder brother in 1620. It was, however, heavily encumbered and his first priority was to satisfy his brother's creditors.

His son George (1601-1680) took a lease of the manor of Nun Monkton in the West Riding from the Archbishop of York and he was living there on the eve of the Civil War. In August 1642 royalist troops plundered Nun Monkton Hall while he was away and seized his money and plate. During this episode they insulted his wife, calling her Protestant whore and Puritan whore.

In the Civil War Marwood was a parliamentarian who served as a local committeeman and in 1651 he was appointed sheriff of Yorkshire. At the beginning of 1660, however, he signed the Yorkshire petition which called for a free Parliament and it was presumably this change of stance which led to the grant of a baronetcy later that year.

In 1660 George Ewbank his Puritan chaplain published a sermon which he had preached at the funeral of his daughter-in-law Margaret Marwood. In this sermon he testified that she was 'eminently pious …. The vanities of this life did not affect her … her Garb was rather comely then costly … She was not at all given to foolish talking, unseemly jesting … but grave and sober'.

Sir Henry Marwood (c.1635-1725) may have inherited some of his father's radical instincts. In 1680 he was removed from the commission of the peace on the grounds that he was 'a traducer of petitioning, by setting his hand to a paper for that purpose'.

Towards the end of James II's reign he declared himself in favour of some degree of toleration for nonconformists.

Busby Hall The house was probably Elizabethan in origin. In a survey of the Little Busby estate which was carried out in 1606 it was described as a 'good Mannor house'.

Some building work appears to have been undertaken in the early years of Charles II's reign. The family was taxed on 10 hearths in 1662 and 12 in 1675.

(*North Riding Records*, vi (1888), 223 and vii (1889), 103. North Yorkshire County Record Office, Marwood MSS. C.2/James I/A1/40. C.10/523/70. C.33/284/ fo.83. W. Cobbett, *Cobbett's Parliamentary History of England* (1806-20), ii, columns 1450-1. George Ewbank, *The Pilgrim's Port* (1660).)

STONEGRAVE   Ryedale

A village near Hovingham. The parish of Stonegrave included the village of West Ness and parts of East Newton, Laysthorpe and Nunnington. 1675: 19 households in Stonegrave, 30 in East and West Ness and 4 in East Newton and Laysthorpe. East Ness was in the parish of Hovingham. 1676: 138 persons aged 16 or more (parish of Stonegrave).

The right to hold a weekly market and an annual fair had been granted in a charter of 1257.

Church Holy Trinity: Norman and Perpendicular.

School There was a school at East Newton in the latter part of the 17th century. The master may be identified as John Denton who had been ejected from the living of Oswaldkirk in 1662 and given shelter by his brother-in-law William Thornton of East Newton.

Principal family Thornton of East Newton Hall. Estate revenue: £600 a year (1655).

The Thorntons had been seated at East Newton since the 14th century. The autobiography of Mrs Alice Thornton (1626-1707), who was a daughter of Christopher Wandesford of Kirklington, provides an illuminating account of the family.

In the early years of the 17th century the family was still largely Catholic, though neither William Thornton (d.1617) nor his son Robert (d. 1637) was ever indicted for recusancy.

Robert Thornton's first wife, Dorothy, was a recusant and their three daughters all married Catholic gentlemen. In accordance with their mother's dying wish they were given substantial portions which were funded by the felling of 'great and beautifull woods' at East Newton.

His second wife, Elizabeth, was the eldest daughter of a Puritan squire, Sir Richard Darley of Buttercrambe. She was 'a very good and vertuous woman'. Their issue consisted of four sons and two daughters who were all 'brought up in the way of strict presbiterians'.

The eldest son, William (1624-1668), was the first-born of twins. Because of his upbringing he preferred extemporised prayers to the formality of the Book of Common Prayer. He was 'much addicted to a melancolicke humour which had seized on him by fitts for severall yeares before he was twenty yeares old'.

Following his father's death in 1637 he was made a ward of the Crown. In the negotiations over the wardship it was claimed that he had inherited debts amounting to £800 and that no provision had been made for his brothers and sisters.

Thornton took no part in the Civil War. After spending some time at Emmanuel College, Cambridge he was admitted in 1645 to Gray's Inn. In 1652 he was named as one of the Yorkshire commissioners for the monthly assessment.

He married Alice Wandesford in 1651 but only after some hesitation on her part. She was strongly attached to 'the true protestant church of England' and feared that there were major differences of view in matters of religion which would make for an unhappy marriage. She was reassured, however, when he told her that he was in favour of 'a moderated episcopacy and kingly government'.

In the latter part of his life he was heavily involved in litigation and found himself in serious financial difficulties. His funeral was very well attended and his wife wrote that he was 'most generally beloved of his countrey; a man of great pietie, peace and honesty. There was a great lamentation for him'.

He left only one son, Robert (1663-1692), who took holy orders and became a parish priest in 1691. With his death the male line expired and the estate was divided between his two sisters.

Dr Thomas Comber, Dean of Durham, married one of these sisters and through her acquired the East Newton estate. In his autobiography he wrote that William Thornton his father-in-law was 'a Person of good learning, great sobriety, and courteous temper, who though he was educated amongst the Presbyterians, yet I had fully reconciled him to the Church of England long before his death'.

East Newton Hall The house was apparently in a poor condition in 1651 and a major building programme was put in hand almost immediately. During the years 1660 to 1662 the Thorntons lived at Oswaldkirk until the hall was ready for occupation.

In 1675 East Newton Hall had 19 taxable hearths.

Roger Dodsworth noted in 1619 that Robert Thornton had a park at East Newton. The following year Thornton secured formal confirmation from the Crown of his rights of free warren. In 1624 he began proceedings in the Court of Star Chamber over a spate of deer poaching and related that with the help of neighbouring landowners he had stocked the park with 80 fallow deer which was the maximum number so 'little a ground would well keepe and maintaine'.

(*The Autobiography of Mrs Alice Thornton of East Newton, Co. York* (ed. C. Jackson), *Surtees Society*, lxii (1875). Wards 5/49. Wards 9/100/fo. 248. *Surtees Society*, clvi (1946), 5-6. STAC 8/281/21.)

STRENSALL   Bulmer

A village to the north of York. The parish of Strensall included the village of Haxby which had a medieval chapel. 1675: 62 households in Strensall and 55 in Haxby.

Strensall Bridge carried a minor road across the River Foss. In 1672 the North Riding magistrates agreed that the sum of £30 should be levied for the repair of the bridge but with the proviso that the inhabitants of Strensall should contribute £40. Later that year it was decided to allocate a further £10 to enable the work to be completed.

Churches St Mary: 14th century or earlier.

The parish was subject to the peculiar jurisdiction of a Prebendary of York.

In 1689 there was a Quaker meeting house at Strensall.

(*North Riding Records*, vi (1888), 169, 178 and vii (1889), 103.)

SUTTON ON THE FOREST   Bulmer

A village to the north of York which was also called Sutton in Galtres. 1675: 95 households in Sutton and 65 in Huby. 1676: 400 persons aged 16 or more, including 40 Protestant dissenters (parish).

The manor of Sutton belonged to the Crown. In the reign of Charles I the process of disafforestation which was officially sanctioned had serious implications for the tenants of the manor, particularly with regard to their grazing rights. As compensation they were assigned 1500 acres of land.

In New Park there was a royal hunting lodge. A survey of the park which was carried out in 1649 revealed that it then contained 270 deer.

Churches All Saints: Norman, Decorated and Perpendicular.

The Archbishop of York was the patron of the living.

In 1649 Dame Anne Hutton, the impropriator of the rectory of Sutton, was presented at the Thirsk quarter sessions 'for not repairing the quire or chancell'.

In 1689 there were Quaker meeting houses at Sutton and Huby.

(*North Riding Records*, v (1887), 38-9 and vii (1889), 102.)

TERRINGTON   Bulmer

A village to the west of Malton. 1675: 69 households in Terrington and 20 in Ganthorpe. 1676: 230 persons aged 16 or more (parish of Terrington).
   Church All Saints: Norman and Perpendicular.
   School Elias Micklethwaite, who became rector of Terrington in 1682, built a schoolhouse there towards the end of the century.

THIRKLEBY   Birdforth

A village near Thirsk. The parish of Thirkleby included the hamlet of Osgoodby. 1675: 50 households (Great and Little Thirkleby).
   Church All Saints: Norman.
   The church had once belonged to Newburgh Priory.
   Principal families (1) Frankland of Thirkleby Hall (baronetcy 1660). Estate revenue: £800 a year (1632).
   In the main the Franklands owed their wealth to William Frankland, a London cloth merchant who built up a large estate in Hertfordshire and Yorkshire. His acquisitions included the manor of Great Thirkleby which he purchased in 1576.
   Following the death of Hugh Frankland in 1607 the Hertfordshire estate descended to his nephew William Frankland (1572-1640). He bought the manors of Great Thirkleby and Islebeck from his cousin Richard Frankland in 1609 and subsequently disposed of the Hertfordshire property.
   His son Henry (1609-1672) went over to Dublin in 1636 and was knighted by Lord Deputy Wentworth. In the Civil War he sided with Parliament but appears to have been largely inactive.
   He was succeeded by his son Sir William (c.1639-1697) who was the first baronet of the family. As an MP he voted in favour of excluding the Catholic Duke of York from the succession to the throne.
   His memorial in Thirkleby church records that he was 'A true lover of his country, a constant assertor of its liberties, a promoter of its welfare and a defender of its laws in all capacities, as a representative in Parliament, a public magistrate, a friendly, courteous and charitable neighbour, a prudent and indulgent father'.
   (2) Ayscough of Osgoodby Grange. Estate revenue: £600 a year (1630); £780 a year (1695).
   The Ayscoughs were a Puritan family who held long leases of the Osgoodby estate and the rectory of Thirsk from the church authorities.
   William Ayscough (1598-1635) was made a ward of the Crown in 1601 following the death of his father. His son William also succeeded to the estate while still a minor

and his wardship was granted to several persons, including John Pym the future political leader.

In the Civil War William Ayscough (1620-1695) served as a parliamentarian captain of horse and was also a member of the North Riding committee. In 1645 he was elected as MP for Thirsk but was secluded three years later in Pride's Purge. A zealous Presbyterian, he was named in 1654 as one of the North Riding commissioners who were assigned the task of ejecting scandalous ministers and schoolmasters.

Although he was knighted in 1660 there were rumours that he might be involved in plots against the government. In 1661 George Duke of Buckingham, who was then Lord Lieutenant of the West Riding, instructed the postmaster at Boroughbridge to examine all letters addressed to him. After the discovery of the Rye House Plot in 1683 his house was searched for arms.

Sir William had a succession of domestic chaplains, among them the Presbyterian divines John Denton and Thomas Coulton. In his will (1691) he left the sum of £200 for the relief of poor Protestant ministers and also gave direction that £150 a year should be employed on educating 'hopeful young men' in order to fit them for the preaching of the Gospel in accordance with the Articles of the Church of England.

At his death he had no surviving male issue and the estate was divided between his two granddaughters.

Thirkleby Hall A gabled house built by William Frankland about 1612.

In 1662 and 1675 the Franklands were taxed on 14 hearths.

In 1704 an estimate was obtained for a projected rebuilding of Thirkleby Hall.

Osgoodby Grange A Jacobean house with some late 17th century features.

In 1662 there were 13 taxable hearths.

(North Yorkshire County Record Office, Frankland MSS. YAS Library, Frankland (Thirkleby Magna) MSS and Payne-Gallwey MSS. PRO, Chancery Masters' Exhibits, C.113/226, Frankland deeds. Bodleian Library, MS Fairfax 31, fols. 21, 49. C.33/293/fols. 515-6 and 299/fols. 423-4. C.38/275/29 August 1702. T. Frankland, *The Franklands of Thirkleby* (2004).)

THIRSK   Birdforth

The parish of Thirsk contained the villages of Sand Hutton and Sowerby and part of Carlton Miniott, all of which had dependent chapels. The other part of Carlton Miniott was in the parish of Kirby Knowle. 1675: 230 households in Thirsk, 37 in Carlton Miniott, 44 in Sand Hutton and 64 in Sowerby.

The town enjoyed the status of a borough by prescription. In the 17th century its principal officials were two constables. Quarter sessions were regularly held there and it also had two parliamentary seats.

The fair and market rights were prescriptive. There had been a weekly market since the 12th century.

The manor of Thirsk belonged to the Earls of Derby.

During the early 17th century the inhabitants of Thirsk were beginning to acquire a reputation for unruly behaviour. In 1614 the North Riding magistrates dealt with a case in which 16 persons from Thirsk, both male and female, were indicted as 'hedge breakers and filchers of rayles, trees and topps of trees'. They decided that these 'verie evill disposed' miscreants should be publicly whipped on a market day in Thirsk unless they were able to make restitution for the damage which they had caused. Shortly after the death of James I a crowd of about sixty residents of Thirsk assembled on a neighbouring moor and cut down and took away a large quantity of wood. Some of them, it was reported, had been shouting that the king was dead and there was no law in force.

In 1652 the republican magistrates issued a warrant for the apprehension of Edward Manwaring the minister of Sowerby who was alleged to have conducted marriage services in private and according to the proscribed Book of Common Prayer.

In 1666 there was a fire at Thirsk which resulted in losses estimated at £700 or more.

During the 17th century there are references to horse-racing at Thirsk.

Churches St Mary: Perpendicular.

The church had once belonged to Newburgh Priory.

In 1689 there was a Quaker meeting house at Thirsk.

School Thirsk School appears to have owed its existence to a chantry in the parish church. John Wildman was master in the years 1671 to 1679.

House of correction The North Riding magistrates periodically discussed the possibility of establishing a house of correction at Thirsk. In 1659 they took the view that Thirsk would be the ideal location since it was in the centre of the riding. The project finally came to fruition in 1667 when the Chantry House of St Anne was converted for this purpose.

(*North Riding Records*, ii (1884), 43; iii (1885), 232-4; vi (1888), 24-5, 115-16; and vii (1889), 103. J. B. Jefferson, *The History of Thirsk* (1821).)

THORMANBY   Bulmer

A village between Thirsk and Easingwold. There was no other village within the parish. 1675: 35 households (township of Thormanby). 1676: 93 persons aged 16 or more (parish).

Church St Mary: Norman.

THORNTON DALE   Pickering Lythe

A village to the east of Pickering. 1675: 101 households (township of Thornton Dale). 1676: 400 persons aged 16 or more (parish).

A royal charter of 1281 had conferred on Thornton the right to hold a weekly market and an annual fair.

In 1638 there was an outbreak of the plague in Thornton. The parish register records that on 16 May Roger Sawer was buried 'whose house was the first house that was suspeckted to have the plague in it after a child died in the house'.

In the Civil War some of the inhabitants came out in support of Parliament, among them Robert Hunter who owned one of the manors in Thornton. The rector, John Robinson, was deprived of his living but managed to regain it in 1653.

In 1669 it was reported that there was a Quaker conventicle in Thornton.

Roxby Castle, to the west of Thornton, was one of the seats of the Cholmleys of Whitby. The manor, however, was sold by Sir Richard Cholmley (1580-1631) and by the middle of the 17th century the castle was in a dilapidated condition.

Thornton was the birthplace of John Leng (1665-1727), a distinguished Latin scholar who received his early education at the school there. In 1723 he became Bishop of Durham.

Church All Saints: Norman in origin; Decorated.

School In 1657 Elizabeth Viscountess Lumley made a settlement of landed property for the purpose of establishing and maintaining a school and almshouses. In the event it was not until 1670 that the building programme was finally completed.

During the latter part of the 17th century the free grammar school of Thornton had a succession of masters: Nicholas Grey, Thomas Wilson, Henry Hunter and John Garnett.

Almshouses The almshouses, which cost £150 to build, provided accommodation for 12 poor men and women of Thornton, Sinnington and the neighbourhood.

(R. W. Jeffery, *Thornton-le-Dale* (1931). *North Riding Records*, iv (1886), 99, 110. W. K. Jordan, *The Charities of Rural England 1480-1660* (1961), 279, 345.)

THORNTON LE STREET   Allertonshire

A small village near Thirsk. The parish of Thornton le Street, which included the hamlet of North Kilvington, was subject to the peculiar jurisdiction of the Bishops of Durham. 1675: 16 households in Thornton le Street and 10 in North Kilvington.

In 1607 North Kilvington was described as a township which had been enclosed and pitifully depopulated by the Meynells.

Within the parish of Thornton le Street there were 64 recusants in 1641 and 56 in 1671.

Church St Leonard: Norman.

Principal families (1) Meynell of Kilvington Hall. Estate revenue: £500 a year (1630); £600 a year (1660). Number of servants: 11 or more (1636).

The Meynells had bought the manor of North Kilvington in 1544. They were a zealous Catholic family who had resident chaplains and sent some of their children to Continental establishments.

Thomas Meynell (1565-1653) wrote in one of his notebooks that 'I dare boldly say no family of England can more exactly fetch and derive them selves even from the Conquest'. In his genealogical account of the family he paid tribute to the virtuous qualities and housekeeping skills of both his wives.

Meynell never wavered in his loyalty to the Catholic faith. He was imprisoned for a time at the end of Elizabeth's reign and subjected to frequent harassment by the Northern High Commission in the early years of James I's reign. In 1608 he confessed that he had been a recusant all his life.

In 1624 Kilvington Hall was searched in the hope of finding missionary priests or evidence of Catholic practices.

Recusancy fines were a regular feature of Meynell's expenditure. In 1629 he and his son Anthony (1591-1669) were required to pay a composition rent of £100 a year.

Neither of them played any part in the Civil War but Anthony Meynell's eldest son Thomas was a royalist captain who died while in arms.

The recusancy of the Meynells led to the sequestration of two-thirds of their estate. Anthony Meynell became heavily indebted but managed to avoid any significant sale of land.

Roger Meynell (c.1640-1683), who succeeded his grandfather in 1669, was an obdurate recusant like his predecessors. In 1679 he was imprisoned in York Castle for refusing to take the oaths of allegiance and supremacy.

(2) Talbot of Thornton Hall. Estate revenue: £300 a year (1640).

The Talbots were a Protestant family who had Catholic relations. John Talbot (1599-1659), who was a justice of the peace, allowed his daughter Isabel to marry Richard Meynell.

In the summer of 1642 Talbot acted as one of the king's commissioners of array. During the Civil War he served as a royalist colonel and was appointed deputy governor of Helmsley Castle. His son Roger (1620-1680) also took up arms on behalf of the king.

Kilvington Hall The house was medieval in origin but had been improved during the course of the 16th century. Thomas Meynell (1565-1653) made some additions and built new stables.

Among the rooms listed in an inventory of 1653 were the hall, the great parlour and the great chamber.

In 1675 Roger Meynell was taxed on 17 hearths.

Thornton Hall A moated house near the old Roman road which went northwards from York.

In 1675 there were 10 taxable hearths.

(H. Aveling (ed.), 'Recusancy Papers of the Meynell Family', *CRS*, lvi (1964). BIHR, High Commission Act Book, RVII/AB 12, fols. 5, 19, 29, 43, 70, 89, 139.)

THORNTON STEWARD   Hang West

A village to the east of Middleham. There was no other village within the parish. 1675: 36 households (township of Thornton Steward).

Throughout the 17th century the parish had a sizeable Catholic community. In 1669 it was reported that its inhabitants included 100 or 120 papists. There were 17 recusants in 1630, 26 in 1679 and 24 in 1690.

Ulshaw Bridge, which spanned the River Ure, was often said to be in decay. In 1625 the North Riding magistrates decided that the sum of £40 should be levied for its repair and the following year they allocated a further sum of £120 for the same purpose.

The triumph of Parliament in the Civil War was probably regarded as an unmitigated disaster by the majority of people in the parish. In 1653 Reynold Parnaby of Thornton Steward was indicted 'for speaking scandallous words against the present Government'.

The most important Catholic family in the parish was the Scropes of Danby Hall whose house stood in parkland to the west of Thornton Steward. Francis Scrope (c.1560-1626) took refuge in outward conformity but his wife Dorothy (who left him early in their married life) was a thoroughgoing recusant.

During the early 17th century successive heads of the family preferred to conform but Simon Scrope (1615-1691), who inherited the estate in the course of the Civil War, was an open Catholic for much of his life. Although he contrived to remain neutral during the war two-thirds of the estate were sequestered on account of his recusancy. In his later years he sought to advance his fortunes by mining lead but this proved to be a costly undertaking.

In 1692 a Catholic chaplain, Thomas Cornforth, was living at Danby Hall.

Church St Oswald: Saxon in origin; Norman and Early English.

School In the reign of James I Francis Roberts had a private school in Thornton Steward.

(H. Aveling, *Northern Catholics. The Catholic Recusants of the North Riding of Yorkshire 1558-1790* (1966), 175, 194-5, 211-12, 262-3, 294, 318-19, 326, 354, 430. *North Riding Records*, iii (1885), 252, 268 and v (1887), 131. *CRS*, ix (1911), 111.)

THORNTON WATLASS   Hang East

A small village to the south-west of Bedale. 1675: 21 households in Thornton Watlass and 39 in Rookwith and Clifton.

In the reign of Elizabeth the wastes and commons of Thornton Watlass and Thirn (a neighbouring hamlet) had been divided and enclosed. One of the main beneficiaries was John Dodsworth (c.1540-1609) whose family had owned the manor of Thornton Watlass since the early 15th century.

In 1611 the North Riding magistrates were informed that the high street within the parish of Thornton Watlass was 'in great ruine and decay' and that it was the responsibility of the inhabitants of the parish to carry out the necessary repair work.

On the outbreak of the Civil War John Dodsworth (1596-1670) threw in his lot with Parliament but was almost immediately taken prisoner by royalist troops. During his captivity he signed the Yorkshire Engagement of February 1643 in which many landowners pledged financial support for the king. When the parliamentary authorities heard of this they suspected that he had changed sides and promptly took possession of his estate. He maintained, however, that he had only signed under duress and in 1650 it was decided that as there was no proof of any delinquency the sequestration should be discharged.

Church St Mary: Decorated.

(E.178/2681. *North Riding Records*, i (1884), 215. S.P.19/cxx/120-28. PRO, State Papers Supplementary, S.P.46/cvii/fo.15.)

TOPCLIFFE   Birdforth/Hallikeld

A village on the River Swale between Thirsk and Boroughbridge. The extensive parish of Topcliffe contained a number of villages and hamlets, including Dishforth and Marton le Moor which had dependent chapels. 1675: 98 households in Topcliffe, 36 in Asenby, 40 in Baldersby, 28 in Catton, 40 in Dalton, 52 in Dishforth, 9 in Eldmire cum Crakehill, 33 in Marton le Moor, 54 in Rainton cum Newby and 23 in Skipton on Swale. 1676: 1590 persons aged 16 or more (parish of Topcliffe).

To the south of Topcliffe were the ruins of a Norman castle which had belonged to the Earls of Northumberland.

By virtue of a royal charter of 1327 Topcliffe enjoyed the right to hold a weekly market and an annual fair.

In 1605 there was an outbreak of the plague at Topcliffe.

During the 17th century the condition of the bridges at Topcliffe and Skipton on Swale necessitated heavy expenditure which was met by means of general levies. In 1610 it was reported that Skipton Bridge, which was then a wooden structure, 'is likely to be in a short time in great decay ..... by the severall carriages of milnestones, coales and other carriages of great burden'. The North Riding magistrates therefore decided that the bridge should be kept under lock and key with the object of diverting the heavier traffic to a ford across the Swale. Subsequently the sum of £300 was allocated for the building of a new bridge of stone and by the beginning of 1625 the project was completed. In 1631, however, the magistrates were informed that a major crack had appeared in the bridge.

Church St Columba: Norman in origin.

The parish was subject to the peculiar jurisdiction of the Dean and Chapter of York.

School A free grammar school founded in 1548. In the course of the 17th century the endowment was significantly increased by private benefactions.

Principal family Robinson of Newby Hall (and Roecliffe Hall, near York) (baronetcy 1660 and 1690). Estate revenue: £1000 a year (1640).

The Robinsons had bought the Newby estate in 1586. They were a merchant family based in York who became major landowners and secured a coat of arms in 1616.

William Robinson (1575-1626) was an alderman of York who in 1619 served as lord mayor. His son Sir William (1601-1658) received his knighthood in 1633 at the coronation of Charles I in Scotland. For a time he was engaged in commercial activities but eventually he assumed the role of a country squire. In 1639 he found himself pricked as sheriff of Yorkshire and was required to levy ship money.

In the Civil War he took up arms for the king and signed the Yorkshire Engagement of February 1643. When compounding for his estate he claimed that he had suffered considerable loss through the activities of the Earl of Newcastle's royalist army. Houses and other buildings had been demolished, timber felled and fences destroyed.

Since his eldest son William had died in Paris in 1643 the estate descended to his second son Metcalfe Robinson (1629-1689) who was granted a baronetcy at the Restoration.

In 1660 George Batty, the keeper of his park at Newby, was fatally wounded when attempting to prevent the poaching of deer. Sir Metcalfe offered a reward of £10 per head for the capture of the three assailants but they managed to flee abroad. Eventually, however, two of them were arrested and executed.

As an MP Sir Metcalfe generally supported the Crown and was not in favour of excluding James Duke of York from the throne.

Since he left no issue the baronetcy expired at his death. The estate passed to his nephew William Robinson (c.1654-1736) who secured a new baronetcy.

Newby Hall A gabled house of two storeys which was probably built towards the end of Elizabeth's reign or in the reign of James I.

In 1634 some travellers noted that on the outskirts of Topcliffe there was 'a fayre and neat Building, a Knight's House, most sweetly situated on the River Swale'.

Sir Metcalfe Robinson appears to have carried out some building work in the reign of Charles II. He was taxed on 16 hearths in 1662 and 20 in 1675.

In 1635 Sir William Robinson was granted a licence to establish a deer park of 150 acres within his manor of Newby.

(*North Riding Records*, i (1884), 12, 204-5 and iii (1885), 118, 193, 202, 227, 312, 329. W. K. Jordan, *The Charities of Rural England 1480-1660* (1961), 312. York City Library, Robinson MSS. *Surtees Society*, xl (1861), 164.)

UPPER HELMSLEY   Bulmer

A hamlet to the north-east of York. There was no other centre of population within the parish. 1675: 8 households (township). 1676: 30 persons aged 16 or more (parish).

Church St Peter: Norman in origin.

WARTHILL   Bulmer

A village to the north-east of York which was partly in the parish of Warthill and partly in the adjoining parish of Holtby. The parish of Warthill included some of the houses in the village of Holtby. 1675: 26 households in Warthill and 25 in Holtby.

Church St Mary: 14th century or earlier.

The parish was subject to the peculiar jurisdiction of a Prebendary of York.

WATH   Hallikeld/Allertonshire

A village to the north of Ripon. The parish of Wath included the village of Melmerby and two hamlets. 1675: 38 households in Wath, 32 in Melmerby, 16 in Middleton Quernhow and 11 in Norton Conyers.

In 1606 Thomas Atkinson of Melmerby, a licensed innkeeper, was presented at the Richmond quarter sessions 'for allowing vaine and disordered persons to drink and remaine in his house'.

Church St Mary: Decorated and Perpendicular. Some further work was carried out in 1629.

School A grammar school built by Peter Samwayes, the rector of Wath, in 1684.

Almshouses Samwayes also founded almshouses for two poor parishioners.

Principal families (1) Musgrave of Norton Conyers. Estate revenue: £700 a year (1623).

Sir Thomas Musgrave succeeded his father in 1617. Four years later Sir Robert Monson, his wife's stepfather, informed the Master of the Court of Wards that he was a lunatic and unfit to manage his estate. When a formal inquiry was held some of his servants testified that he had been acting strangely and threatening violence. In 1623 he claimed in a Star Chamber suit that he was the victim of a conspiracy and that Monson was seeking to deprive him of his estate. It was alleged, however, that Lady Musgrave had been forced to take flight and was afraid to return to her husband who was 'soe outragiouslie bent against her'.

(2) Graham (or Grahme) of Norton Conyers (and Netherby Hall, Cumberland) (baronetcies 1629 and 1662). Estate revenue: £1490 a year (1640); (Norton Conyers line) £960 a year (1660); £1500 a year (1690). Number of servants: 24 (1640).

Sir Richard Graham (1583-1654), who was gentleman of the horse to the first Duke of Buckingham, built up a large estate in Yorkshire and Cumberland. In 1624 he married Sir Thomas Musgrave's daughter Catharine and bought the manor of Norton Conyers from his father-in-law.

On the outbreak of the Civil War he immediately joined the royalist army. He was wounded early on at the battle of Edgehill and taken prisoner in 1645. During the course of the war his house was plundered by parliamentarian troops.

After his death there was a division of the estate: the Cumberland property descended to his elder son Sir George (c.1624-1658) who settled at Netherby and the Yorkshire property to his second son Richard (1636-1711) who resided at Norton Conyers.

Richard Graham was granted a baronetcy by Charles II in recognition of his father's services.

In 1681 Sir John Reresby described him as 'my perticular friend, one that I had been intimate with both in France and Italy'.

Norton Conyers An early Tudor house of brick which was remodelled in the course of the 17th century. The shaped gables were probably added in the reign of Charles I.

Sir Richard Graham was taxed on 18 hearths in 1662 and 16 in 1675.

There was a large deer park at Norton Conyers. In 1570 it was said to have been a mile and a half in compass.

(*North Riding Records*, i (1884), 147. STAC 8/209/23. HMC, *Sixth Report*, Appendix (MSS of Sir Reginald Graham). C.10/193/34 and 475/109. R. T. Spence, 'The First Sir Richard Graham of Norton Conyers and Netherby', *Northern History*, xvi (1980).)

WELBURY   Birdforth

A village to the north-east of Northallerton. There was no other village within the parish. 1675: 41 households (township). 1676: 88 persons aged 16 or more (parish).

Church St Leonard: Norman in origin.

WELL   Hang East

A village near Masham. The parish of Well included the village of Snape. 1675: 73 households (Snape constablery, including Well).

The manors of Well and Snape belonged to the Cecils, Earls of Exeter.

Churches St Michael: Early English, Decorated and Perpendicular.

In 1689 there was a Quaker meeting house at Snape.

Schools The free grammar school of Well had been founded by John Lord Latimer in 1543.

Thomas Wentworth, Earl of Strafford; Henry Clifford, Earl of Cumberland; Sir Thomas Wharton; and Christopher Wandesford of Kirklington had been contemporaries at the school.

In 1605 Thomas Earl of Exeter and his wife Lady Dorothy established a school for the purpose of instructing 12 poor girls in sewing, knitting, spinning and religious knowledge.

Almshouses The Hospital of St Michael had been founded in 1342 and re-endowed by the Cecil family in the mid-16th century. It provided accommodation for eight poor men and eight poor women.

Principal family Danby of Thorpe Perrow (and Farnley Hall, near Leeds). Estate revenue: £2000 a year (1624); £2500 a year (1660); £2200 a year (1680); £1600 a year (1690). Coalmining on Colsterdale Moor, near Masham, and at Farnley. Number of servants: 16 (1649).

The family had been seated at Thorpe Perrow since the mid-15th century.

Christopher Danby (1582-1624) was for many years a ward of the Crown. His mother, a devout Catholic, and his wife were both convicted of recusancy but he conformed for most of his life.

Danby experienced severe financial difficulties, partly through the self-serving activities of a corrupt steward and partly through his own mismanagement. He also had marital problems: he and his wife often lived apart and they were both accused of infidelity.

His son Sir Thomas (1610-1660) was the first Protestant head of the family. In 1626 his wardship was assigned to Christopher Wandesford who proceeded to improve the estate and pay all his father's debts.

When Sir Thomas was appointed sheriff of Yorkshire in 1637 he was faced with the need to collect ship money which proved to be a difficult task. In 1638 he borrowed the sum of £5000 and mortgaged his Mashamshire estate.

In the Civil War he served as a colonel in the royalist army. In January 1643 he was taken prisoner but eventually managed to escape. In 1644, however, he surrendered to the parliamentarian forces.

In his will (1659) he gave direction that the manor of Thorpe Perrow and other lands worth altogether £450 a year should be sold in order to pay his debts and provide portions for his many children.

His son Thomas (c.1632-1667), who was the first mayor of Leeds, secured property worth £500 a year through his marriage to an heiress, Margaret Eure. He assured the trustees appointed by his father that he could overcome the financial problems which he had inherited without resorting to the sale of land. When, however, he sought to raise the rents of his tenants many of them surrendered their leases and some men even set fire to their houses.

When Danby was killed in a tavern brawl in London the financial crisis was still unresolved. To make matters worse the family was involved in protracted litigation over such issues as the ownership of the Mashamshire estate and the widow's right of dower. In 1680 the family's debts amounted to some £20,000.

Christopher Danby, who succeeded to the estate in 1683, was finally able to clear the Mashamshire property of the long-standing mortgage.

In 1688 his son Sir Abstrupus (c.1662-1727) sold the manor of Thorpe Perrow and other lands for £12,000 and following these transactions moved to Swinton, near Masham.

Snape Castle The castle had been built in the 15th century and substantially improved by the Cecils in the reign of Elizabeth. It remained habitable until the end of the 17th century.

In 1675 John Earl of Exeter was taxed on 30 hearths.

Thorpe Perrow The house had probably been rebuilt in the 16th century. In 1675 there were 17 taxable hearths.

The park was already in existence at the beginning of the 17th century.

(W. K. Jordan, *The Charities of Rural England 1480-1660* (1961), 286, 311, 355. North Yorkshire County Record Office, Cunliffe-Lister (Swinton) MSS. STAC 8/120/2. C.5/186/98. C.8/52/15. C.10/125/35. C.33/253/fo. 261; 255/fo. 80; 265/fols. 338-41; 296/fols. 362-5; and 307/fols. 139-42. PRO, Chancery Masters' Exhibits, C.104/110, part 3, Danby papers. C. Whone, 'Christopher Danby of Masham and Farnley', *Thoresby Society*, xxxvii (1936-42).)

WENSLEY Hang West

A village on the River Ure. The parish of Wensley contained several villages and there were medieval chapels at Castle Bolton and Redmire. 1675: 71 households in Wensley, 37 in East and West Bolton, 61 in Leyburn, 57 in Preston under Scar and 76 in Redmire.

Royal charters of 1307 and 1318 had granted the right to hold a weekly market and an annual fair at Wensley.

In 1684 Charles Marquess of Winchester obtained a market charter for Leyburn. He played a major part in the development of Leyburn which in due course outstripped Wensley as a trading centre.

Coal and lead were worked at Wensley in the 16th and 17th centuries.

The bridge at Wensley dated from the 15th century. In 1637 the North Riding magistrates agreed that the sum of £100 should be levied for its repair.

In 1645 Bolton Castle was besieged and taken by parliamentarian troops.

Church Holy Trinity: Early English, Decorated and Perpendicular.

Castle The contract for the building of Bolton Castle was let in 1378 and a licence to crenellate was granted the following year.

In 1647 the House of Commons decided that it should be made untenable.

Principal family Scrope of Bolton Castle, Lords Scrope (Earl of Sunderland 1627). Estate revenue: £5300 a year (1630). Coalmining in County Durham.

Emanuel Lord Scrope (1584-1630) served as Lord President of the Council in the North and Lord Lieutenant of Yorkshire in the years 1619 to 1628. In the House of Commons he was regarded as suspect in religion. In a petition submitted to the king in 1626 it was said that he neglected to take communion, went riding with his hawks on fast days and showed too much favour to Catholics. In 1628 he told Sir Thomas Wentworth that 'I am to bee given up for a non-communicate' but stressed that he was confident that when the informers had done their worst 'they shall neither in this particulare, nor anye other, be able to touch mee'.

His addiction to gambling was apparently a matter of common knowledge. In 1620 it was alleged that William Clough, the Puritan vicar of Bramham, had declared that he was a fool who was only fit for gaming.

Scrope left no legitimate issue but had four children by Martha Jones, a servant of lowly birth. Under a settlement of 1629 his son John Scrope alias Jones inherited a substantial amount of property, including the manor and castle of Bolton.

In the Civil War John Scrope took up arms for the king and was serving as governor of Bolton Castle when it came under siege in 1645. The following year he died in London of the plague.

Since he had no children the Scrope estates were divided among his three sisters, subject to the jointures of the Countess of Sunderland and Martha Jones. Mary the eldest sister eventually came into possession of the Bolton estate and her second husband, Charles Marquess of Winchester, made it his principal seat. In 1689 he was created Duke of Bolton.

Bolton Hall A late 17th century house near Wensley which superseded Bolton Castle as a residence. It was built or substantially enlarged in 1678 by the Marquess of Winchester.

The park existed in 1630.

(*North Riding Records*, iv (1886), 74. *Camden Fourth Series*, 12 (1973), 292. *CSP Dom, 1619-23*, 71, 187.)

WEST ROUNTON   Allertonshire

A small village to the north-east of Northallerton. There was no other village within the parish. 1675: 24 households (township of West Rounton).
Church St James: Norman.
The parish was subject to the peculiar jurisdiction of the Dean and Chapter of Durham.

WEST TANFIELD   Hallikeld

A village to the south-east of Masham on the north bank of the River Ure. The parish of West Tanfield contained several hamlets, including Thornbrough with its prehistoric earthworks. 1675: 100 households (township of West Tanfield).
Close to the church were the ruins of Tanfield Castle which had been built by the Marmions in the 14th century.
In 1611 the North Riding magistrates allocated the sum of £30 for the 'erecting and building' of a new bridge at West Tanfield where the Ripon-Masham road crossed the River Ure.
Church St Nicholas: Norman, Decorated and Perpendicular.
School In the reign of Charles I there was a private school at West Tanfield.
(*North Riding Records*, i (1884), 210 and ii (1884), 29.)

WEST WITTON   Hang West

A Wensleydale village to the west of Middleham. There was no other village within the parish. 1675: 57 households (township of West Witton).
Church St Bartholomew: Norman.

WHENBY   Bulmer

A hamlet to the west of Malton. There was no other centre of population within the parish. 1675: 18 households (township). 1676: 62 persons aged 16 or more, including 22 recusants (parish).

Catholic influences remained comparatively strong throughout the 17th century.

Church St Martin: Perpendicular.

Principal family Barton of Whenby Hall. Estate revenue: £600 a year (1626 and 1641).

The Bartons, who were a Catholic family, had owned the Whenby estate since the early 15th century.

Thomas Barton, who succeeded his father in 1610, had a recusant wife but was himself a Church Papist until 1626. In 1615 the Northern High Commission decided to place him in the custody of one of their pursuivants for making what were termed disgraceful speeches. The following year he was indicted at the Thirsk quarter sessions for entertaining and supplying food to seven 'players of Enterludes, vagabundes and sturdy beggars' who may have staged a Catholic play.

In 1629 he compounded for his recusancy and that of his wife and was required to pay a rent of £80 a year.

In his will (1642) he left bequests to a number of persons, among them Thomas Robinson the vicar of Whenby. Following the death of his widow, Alice Barton, the estate descended to his only child, Elizabeth, who had married a Catholic squire, Sir Edward Radcliffe of Dilston in Northumberland.

Whenby Hall A relatively modest house which had six hearths in 1675.

(H. Aveling, *Northern Catholics. The Catholic Recusants of the North Riding of Yorkshire 1558-1790* (1966), 414. BIHR, High Commission Act Book, RVII/AB9/fols. 5, 54. *North Riding Records*, ii (1884), 59, 122 and iii (1885), 272. *CRS*, liii (1961), 310. *YASRS*, ix (1890), 69-70.)

WHITBY Whitby Strand/Langbaurgh

A market town and port which had formerly been under the dominance of its Benedictine abbey. The extensive parish of Whitby contained a number of villages and hamlets, including Robin Hood's Bay and Ugglebarnby which had dependent chapels. 1675: 341 households in Whitby (181 on the west and 160 on the east side), 19 in Aislaby, 41 in Eskdaleside (including Sleights), 186 in Fylingdales (including the village of Robin Hood's Bay), 56 in Hawsker cum Stainsacre, 62 in Newholm cum Dunsley, 25 in Ruswarp and 41 in Ugglebarnby. 1676: 1640 persons aged 16 or more, including 24 recusants and 97 Protestant dissenters (parish of Whitby).

Whitby had enjoyed borough status since the 12th century. Government of the town and port was effectively in the hands of the Cholmley family as owners of the liberty of Whitby Strand.

Whitby Abbey had been granted market rights shortly after the Norman Conquest. Following the dissolution of the abbey in 1539 these rights were vested in the liberty of Whitby Strand.

The main sources of employment were fishing, shipbuilding, maritime trade and, from 1649 onwards, alum mining. Whitby was the principal port for the shipment of alum mined at Mulgrave and other places in the North Riding.

In this period jet, which was plentiful around Whitby, was fashioned into rings, bracelets, beads and more prosaic items.

Throughout the 17th century there was a small but steadfast Catholic minority within the town and parish. In the latter part of the century the religious spectrum included Presbyterians and Quakers.

The bridge across the River Esk linked the east and west parts of the town. This was a kind of drawbridge which was raised by a bridgemaster to allow vessels to pass through. During the course of the 17th century the bridge was frequently in need of repair. In 1661 it was said that extensive damage had been caused by the practice of tying ships by their cables to the bridge while in 1684 it was reported to be 'much ruinated' as the result of the winter storms and 'land floods'.

At Whitby 'is a reasonable good port and harbour for shippinge, and a place of prettie good trade. Uppon the top of the hill adjoyninge to this towne was a famous abbey .... a good part of which church is yet standinge' (Life of Marmaduke Rawdon, entry for 1664).

'Whitby has a secure harbour for vessels, which by a drawbridge, after the Dutch manner, are let into the town, which is of good esteem for trade' (Ralph Thoresby, 1682).

Whitby 'hath a very fair and commodious Haven. There are about sixty Ships of 80 Tuns or more belonging to the Town' (Edmund Gibson, 1695).

In 1603 there was an outbreak of the plague.

In 1630 the inhabitants of Whitby sought corporate status for the town in a petition to the king. They failed, however, to secure approval as their request was opposed by Sir Hugh Cholmley who was anxious to protect his seignorial rights.

In 1632 Cholmley obtained the king's agreement to a nation-wide appeal for contributions towards the cost of building a new west pier. The response was mixed but work was eventually put in hand.

During the early stages of the Civil War royalist troops took possession of Whitby. In June 1644, however, a parliamentarian force captured the town and put a garrison in Sir Hugh Cholmley's mansion house.

In 1665 the Great Plague of London caused alarm even in the more remote parts of England. The North Riding magistrates were disturbed to hear that 'several ships, fisher boats, cobles and other vessels come loaden from the city of London and other places infected with the contagious sickness of the plague to the town of Whitby and other places adjacent'. In view of the potential danger they decided to introduce quarantine arrangements which applied not only to the vessels and their crews but also to the freight which they were carrying.

In 1675 Sir Hugh Cholmley, the fourth baronet, was granted permission by the Crown to develop a new port in Saltwick Bay, within the manor of Whitby, in order to facilitate the shipment of alum from his mines there.

Churches St Mary: Norman and Early English.

The minister was a perpetual curate.

In 1676 the Quakers opened a meeting house in Whitby.

Almshouses In 1654 Luke Bagwith established almshouses for two poor widows.

The Seamen's Hospital was founded in 1676. Its function was the relief of seamen and their widows and children.

House of correction In 1636 the North Riding magistrates decided that there was a need for a house of correction for the parishes of Whitby, Lythe, Sneaton and Hinderwell 'by reason that the trade of fishing doth in those partes increase a multytude of poore who, in wynter tyme, when the said trade faileth, are either driven to begg or wander, or else cast upon the chardges of the severall parishes'. This was established at Whitby in 1637 but it appears to have been short-lived.

Principal family Cholmley of Whitby House (baronetcy 1641). Estate revenue: £1500 a year (1626); £3700 a year (1683). Alum mining at Saltwick. Number of servants: 30 or more (1636).

The Cholmleys had purchased the liberty of Whitby Strand and the manor of Whitby in 1555.

In his memoirs Sir Hugh Cholmley (1600-1657) included a detailed account of his immediate predecessors.

Sir Henry Cholmley (c.1556-1616) was for many years a Church Papist while his wife was a convicted recusant but after some kind of conversion they 'lived and dyed very zealous Protestants'. He fell heavily into debt as a result of his extravagant style of living, his addiction to 'fleet hounds and horses' and, above all, his lax estate management. In this situation he resorted to the sale of land.

His son Sir Richard (1580-1631) was 'a little too imperious over his servants and tennants' but was 'charitable to the poore, liberall and compassionate to those in distresse'.

Like his father he had growing financial problems which were attributable to such factors as his protracted litigation with Sir Thomas Hoby of Hackness, the expenditure which he incurred as sheriff of Yorkshire and the high rate of interest which he had to pay on loans. In 1626 he made over the estate to his son Hugh, reserving to himself an allowance of £400 a year, and saddled him with the task of clearing his debts which then exceeded £11,000.

Sir Hugh (1600-1657) managed to avoid financial ruin but only with great difficulty. Some land was sold and long leases were granted in return for substantial entry fines.

In 1640 he came out in opposition to ship money. During the early months of the Civil War he achieved some success as a parliamentarian colonel but he was always in favour of a negotiated settlement. In January 1643 he wrote in a letter to the Speaker of the House of Commons that 'it grieves my heart to see how these calamities increase and how I am forced to draw my sword not onely against my countrymen but many near friends and allies'.

In March 1643 he changed sides and took on a new role as royalist governor of Scarborough. After a lengthy siege he finally surrendered the castle in July 1645 and went into exile.

His brother Sir Henry Cholmley remained faithful to the cause of Parliament while his half-brother Sir Richard died in the service of the king.

On his return to England in 1649 Sir Hugh entered into an agreement with a London businessman, Sir Nicholas Crispe, for the development of alum mines at Saltwick, near Whitby.

In 1665 his second son Hugh inherited the estate and title. Sir Hugh (1632-1689) was responsible for the construction of a harbour mole at Tangier which was part of Queen Catherine's dowry. At home he derived handsome profits from the alum undertaking. In 1688 these were valued at £1500 a year though he considered that the potential yield was much more. Despite his great wealth, however, he was in serious financial difficulties in the latter part of his life, perhaps as a result of his building activities.

In 1685 a Whitby publican was presented at the Thirsk sessions for allegedly saying that 'Sir Hugh Cholmley is a thick, idle, sapheaded, sleepy drone'.

Sir Hugh's only child, Mary, was married in 1683 to Nathaniel Cholmley, a London merchant who was apparently a distant kinsman. He took over management of the alum mines and in 1685 bought a substantial amount of landed property from his father-in-law at a cost of some £26,000. The remainder of the estate was inherited by his son Hugh and the Cholmley name was preserved.

Whitby House The house in its original form had been built by Francis Cholmley in the 1580s. In the years 1633 to 1636 Sir Hugh Cholmley encased the timber walls in stone and carried out other improvements, including the installation of lead water pipes. His wife, Dame Elizabeth, did much to beautify the interior of the house.

During the reign of Charles II his son Sir Hugh was responsible for major additions. According to the hearth tax returns there were 19 hearths in 1662 and 39 in 1675.

'Adjoining to the Abbey Sir Hugh Cholmley has a most delicate and stately hall, supposed to be exceeded by few in England for the bigness of it. The hall is of freestone, with large courts and walks ... and ... a delicate bowling-green' (Ralph Thoresby, 1682).

(*North Riding Records*, v (1887), 78; vi (1888), 47, 95-6; and vii (1889), 67, 75. J. Binns (ed.), *Memoirs and Memorials of Sir Hugh Cholmley 1600-1657*, YASRS, cliii (2000). *CSP Dom, 1629-31*, 177, 181, 213, 251 and *1673*, 274, 327. HMC, *Thirteenth*

Report, Appendix, 90. C.6/41/151. C.33/229/fols. 292-3; 269/fols. 663-6, 1156; and 273/fo. 153. C.38/230/20 July and 20 November 1688 and 260/13 July 1698. G. Young, *A History of Whitby* (1817). A. White, *A History of Whitby* (2nd edition, 2004). J. Binns, *Sir Hugh Cholmley of Whitby 1600-1657* (2008).

WIGGINTON   Bulmer

A village to the north of York which was within the bounds of the Forest of Galtres. There was no other village within the parish. 1675: 41 households (township of Wigginton).

Church St Nicholas: Perpendicular.

In 1652 William Wright, the long-serving rector of Wigginton, was presented at the Thirsk quarter sessions 'for suffering the chancell of the parish church to be in decay'.

The parish was subject to the peculiar jurisdiction of the Treasurer of York Minster. (*North Rding Records*, v (1887), 117.)

WYCLIFFE   Gilling West

A hamlet to the east of Barnard Castle on the south bank of the River Tees. The parish of Wycliffe was sparsely populated. 1675: 7 households (township of Wycliffe, including Girlington Hall and Thorpe Hall).

In 1669 it was reported that there were 30 or more papists in the parish.

Church St Mary: Decorated.

Principal family Tunstall of Wycliffe Hall (and Barningham Hall). Estate revenue: £1100 a year (1640). Coalmining in Scargill. Number of servants: 12 or more (1604).

The Tunstalls had moved from Lancashire to Yorkshire after purchasing the manor of Barningham in 1565. They remained attached to the Catholic faith throughout the 17th century.

Francis Tunstall (c.1570-1641) lived at Barningham Hall. In 1602 he was brought before the Northern High Commission and instructed to do his best to persuade his wife to conform; to provide them with a list of his household servants; and to discharge any servants who were recusants. Two years later he was presented as a recusant along with his wife, a private tutor and twelve servants.

In 1629 he compounded for his recusancy and was required to pay a rent of £55 a year for property worth some £500 a year. The rest of the estate was in the possession of his son Marmaduke who had a recusant wife but was himself a Church Papist.

Marmaduke Tunstall (c.1590-1657) acquired half the manor of Wycliffe through his marriage to an heiress, Katherine Wycliffe, and in 1633 bought the other half for £3155.

He took up residence at Wycliffe Hall which became the family's principal seat.

In the Civil War he joined the royalist garrison in Newark Castle and was captured in 1645 and held prisoner until 1647.

In the latter part of the century the head of the family, Francis Tunstall, was a persistent recusant. In 1679 he was imprisoned for a time in York Castle after refusing to take the oaths of allegiance and supremacy; and in 1688 he allowed the Catholic bishop James Smith and one of his chaplains, Edward Parkinson, to use Wycliffe Hall as a base for their activities.

Wycliffe Hall A gabled Elizabethan house which was approached through a gatehouse.

In 1675 Francis Tunstall was taxed on 18 hearths.

(East Riding of Yorkshire Archives Service, Burton Constable MSS. BIHR, High Commission Act Book, RVII/AB 19, fo. 248.)

WYKEHAM   Pickering Lythe

A village between Pickering and Scarborough. The parish of Wykeham included the hamlet of Ruston. 1675: 95 households (township of Wykeham cum Ruston). 1676: 177 persons aged 16 or more (parish of Wykeham).

The Priory of St Mary the Virgin at Wykeham had been founded in the 12th century. It was a Cistercian nunnery.

In 1626 there was an outbreak of the plague at Wykeham.

Church All Saints: Decorated.

The church had formerly belonged to Wykeham Priory.

Principal family Hutchinson of Wykeham Abbey. Estate revenue: £500 a year (1630 and 1641).

The Hutchinsons had bought the Wykeham estate in 1544, shortly after the dissolution of the priory.

Stephen Hutchinson (1573-1648) sided with Parliament during the Civil War but his son Edward (c.1616-1653) served first as a commissioner of array and then as a colonel of horse in the royalist army. In his will (1646) the father disinherited the son on the grounds that he had been 'disaffected to the state, and thereby hath incurred my displeasure'. The estate was settled on trustees for the benefit of his grandson Edward Hutchinson who was then a minor.

Towards the end of the 17th century the Hutchinsons had a resident schoolmaster who not only taught the children of the family but took in pupils from as far away as Bridlington and Hunmanby.

Wykeham Abbey The house had been built either by Richard Hutchinson who had bought the estate in 1544 or his son Edward. It was situated near the priory buildings which were probably used as a source of materials.

In 1675 Edward Hutchinson was taxed on 14 hearths.

In the 17th century the house was usually called Wykeham Abbey.

(*North Riding Records*, iii (1885), 264. *YAJ*, xviii (1905), 238-9.)

YARM   Langbaurgh

An ancient market town on the River Tees and a chapelry within the parish of Kirk Leavington. 1675: 130 households. 1676: 375 persons aged 16 or more, including 15 Catholics and 15 Protestant dissenters.

Yarm had formerly been the main port on the Tees and in the 17th century was still engaged in the export of agricultural produce.

The town had enjoyed borough status since at least the 13th century and was governed by two bailiffs. Markets and fairs were also medieval in origin. In 1674 Thomas Lord Fauconberg, who owned the manor of Yarm, was granted the right to hold an annual market in May and two fairs each year.

Because of its low-lying situation the town was subject to periodic flooding. There are references to severe floods in 1624 and 1684.

The stone bridge across the Tees had originally been built by Bishop Skirlaw of Durham about the beginning of the 15th century. In the early 17th century the inhabitants of Yorkshire and Durham were at loggerheads over the funding of repairs to the bridge.

In the Civil War the town was initially garrisoned for Parliament but in February 1643 a royalist force defeated the parliamentarians in a fierce battle at Yarm Bridge. In 1645 an outbreak of the plague caused further suffering.

Church St Mary Magdalene: Norman in origin with some later work.

The patron of the church (technically a chapel) was the Archbishop of York.

School A free grammar school which had been established by letters patent of 1590 and endowed by Thomas Conyers. In 1669 there was a legal dispute over the ownership of property which Conyers had charged with the sum of £7 a year for the master's stipend.

(*North Riding Records*, i (1884), 7, 19, 36, 48, 51; iii (1885), 51-9, 215; and iv (1886), 77, 85, 107, 180. J.W. Wardell, *A History of Yarm* (1957). C5/623/109.)

The West Riding

THE WEST RIDING justices of the peace held their quarter sessions at Barnsley, Doncaster, Halifax, Knaresborough, Pontefract, Rotherham, Skipton, Wakefield and Wetherby.

There were five parliamentary boroughs: Aldborough, Boroughbridge, Knaresborough, Pontefract and Ripon.

The Ainsty was under the jurisdiction of the city of York but, as contemporary maps make clear, it was regarded as belonging physically to the West Riding.

ABERFORD   Barkston Ash/Skyrack

A village between Leeds and Tadcaster which was situated on what the postal authorities called 'the northern road'. 'Aberford, a little town…..famous for its art of pin-making, those here made being in particular request among the Ladies…..there is the foundation of an old Castle……still visible' (William Camden). The parish of Aberford included the hamlet of Parlington. 1674: 47 households in Aberford and 16 in Parlington. 1676: 110 persons aged 16 or more, including 15 recusants (parish).

Aberford featured in Richard Braithwaite's poem about the journeys of 'Drunken Barnaby' which was first published in 1638:

> Thence to Aberford, whose Beginning
> Came from buying Drink with Pinning:
> Poor they are, and very needy,
> Yet of Liquor very greedy:
> Had they never so much Plenty
> Belly'd make their Purses empty.

By virtue of royal charters of 1251, 1307 and 1335 Aberford had the right to hold a weekly market and an annual fair. It continued to exercise this right throughout the 17th century.

According to a survey carried out in the reign of Charles I the parish of Aberford contained 1789 acres, including 354 acres of meadow, 539 acres of arable land and 668 acres of pasture.

The manors of Aberford and Parlington belonged to the Gascoignes of Barnbow Hall, a major Catholic family (see the entry for Barwick in Elmet). In 1642 the manor of Parlington with its enclosed demesnes was valued at £386 a year. Parlington Hall was rebuilt or remodelled in the early 17th century, probably by Sir John Gascoigne. In 1674 it had 12 hearths.

Church St Ricarius: Norman and Decorated.

School A school had been established in 1580.

(Richard Braithwaite, *Drunken Barnaby's Four Journeys to the North of England* (3rd edition, 1723). WYAS, Leeds, Gascoigne of Barnbow MSS, GC/E2/2 and E12/2/2.)

ACASTER MALBIS   Ainsty/Ouse and Derwent

A village to the south of York which was situated on the River Ouse. The parish of Acaster Malbis included part of the East Riding village of Naburn; the other part was in the parish of St George, York. Naburn is separately noticed. 1665: 53 households (township of Acaster Malbis). 1676: 205 persons aged 16 or more (parish, excluding the chapelry of Naburn).

Church Holy Trinity: Decorated.

In 1627 the chancel was reported to be in 'very greate decay'.

School In his will (1603) John Knowles, a yeoman, left the sum of £100 for the support of a schoolmaster at Acaster Malbis who was to provide free elementary education.

In 1614 Tobias Thomlinson was licensed to teach at Acaster Malbis.

(*YAJ*, xv (1900), 225. W. K. Jordan, *The Charities of Rural England 1480-1660* (1961), 328.)

ACASTER SELBY   Ainsty

A village to the east of Tadcaster which was situated on the west bank of the River Ouse. It was in the East Riding parish of Stillingfleet. 1665: 34 households (township of Acaster Selby).

The manor of Acaster Selby belonged to the Harrison family who were new gentry. It contained 600 acres and on the eve of the Civil War was worth £180 a year.

Robert Harrison was a merchant and alderman of York. Following his death in 1630 he was succeeded by his grandson Cuthbert who was already a ward of the Crown. Shortly before this the Court of Wards had been informed that the hall was much decayed through lack of proper maintenance.

In the Civil War Cuthbert Harrison (1618-1699) served as a captain of foot in the royalist army.

School In the 15th century Robert Stillington, who was the Bishop of Bath and Wells, had founded a free grammar school at Acaster Selby. This was still flourishing in the 17th century.

(S.P.23/cxc/739,753. Wards 5/49. Wards 9/566/116. W. K. Jordan, *The Charities of Rural England 1480-1660* (1961), 305.)

ACKWORTH   Osgoldcross

A village consisting of High and Low Ackworth to the south-west of Pontefract. There was no other village within the parish. 1674: 122 households (township of Ackworth). 1676: 200 persons aged 16 or more (parish).

In 1638 Rosamund Wright of Ackworth was indicted for committing two acts of burglary, both at dead of night. From the house of Alice Howett of Ackworth, a widow, she stole various items of clothing, three pairs of linen sheets and some money.

In 1641 the West Riding magistrates ordered the inhabitants of the parish to repair 'the king's highway within the town of Ackworth'.

During the Civil War Samuel Carter, the Puritan rector of Ackworth, was reported to have abandoned his cure of souls and to have joined up with the parliamentarians.

In 1645 there was an outbreak of the plague in Ackworth.

Church St Cuthbert: Perpendicular.

Almshouses In 1666 cottages were built as accommodation for two elderly widows.

(*YASRS*, liv (1915), 72-3, 277. R. A. Marchant, *The Puritans and the Church Courts in the Diocese of York 1560-1642* (1960), 238. J. L. Saywell, *Parochial History of Ackworth* (1894). W. A. Green, *Historical Antiquities of Ackworth* (1910).)

ACOMB   Ainsty

A village to the west of York. The parish of Acomb included parts of Dringhouses and Knapton. 1665: 54 households in Acomb, 29 in Dringhouses and 19 in Knapton.

At the beginning of the 17th century the manor of Acomb belonged to the Crown but in 1623 it was conveyed to the Archbishop of York in exchange for certain property in London.

In 1612 the Newarks of Acomb acquired a 40-year lease of the manor from the Crown. They were a minor gentry family who were sometimes vehemently at odds over property matters. In a Chancery suit of 1624 Thomas Newark claimed that his cousin Henry Newark of Askham Bryan had deprived him of his estate but this was strenuously denied. In responding to the allegation the latter described himself as an aged man who had been a servant for almost all his life.

During the Civil War the Newarks appear to have remained resolutely neutral.

At an ecclesiastical visitation in 1633 Robert Ray was presented for 'bringing his dogg continually to the church, which disturbeth the congregation'.

Church St Stephen: Norman in origin.

The parish was subject to the peculiar jurisdiction of the Dean and Chapter of York.

School In 1637 Thomas Stillington was teaching children at Acomb without a licence.

(C.2/James I/N5/64. C.3/410/25. C.10/99/145. *YAJ*, xv (1900), 225. BIHR, High Commission Act Books, RVI/A24/fo.18. H. G.Richardson (ed.), *Court Rolls of the Manor of Acomb*, YASRS, cxxxi (1969). H. G. Richardson, *A History of Acomb* (1963).)

ADDINGHAM   Staincliffe and Ewecross/Claro

A village situated between Skipton and Ilkley. The parish of Addingham included part of the village of Beamsley; the other part was in the parish of Skipton. 1674: 92 households in Addingham and 66 in Beamsley.

The manor of Addingham belonged to a leading Catholic family, the Vavasours of Hazlewood Castle, but they appear to have had little or no influence on the religious loyalties of their tenants.

In 1615 it was reported that Beamsley Bridge, which spanned a tributary of the Wharfe known as Kex Beck, 'is fallen into great ruin and decay for want of repair, so that many of his Majesties subjects are put in great danger of theire lives in passing the same att every flood of water'. Since the bridge was not on a main road the West Riding magistrates took the view that it should be repaired at the expense of the inhabitants of Beamsley.

The River Wharfe flows through Beamsley, 'the seat of the famous family of Claphams' (William Camden).

The Claphams had lived at Beamsley since the early 15th century. Christopher Clapham (c.1608-1686), who succeeded his father in 1629, inherited a relatively modest estate. In 1640 he let his property in Beamsley, including the manor-house, to George

Slinger for a term of seven years and apparently went to live in London. Five years later Slinger was unable to pay the rent, which had been set at £170 a year, on account of the losses which he had sustained in the course of the Civil War. When the matter was referred to arbitration it was decided that, taking into account the quartering of troops, the rent should be reduced by £30 a year. On regaining possession of the estate Clapham alleged that, among other things, Slinger had allowed Beamsley Hall 'to goe and fall much to decay for want of repaire'.

During the Civil War Clapham was careful to avoid any commitment but three of his younger brothers took up arms for the king.

Clapham was an ambitious man who clearly regarded the world of a minor squire in Wharfedale as unduly restrictive. For a time he served as steward of the Clifford estates in Westmorland but his growing prosperity was mainly due to financially advantageous marriages. In seeking to build up his income he secured a lease of the rectory of Aysgarth and bought the manor of Wakefield. During the Interregnum he settled at Uffington in Lincolnshire, leaving his son Sheffield to look after his Yorkshire property. In 1660 he was elected MP for Appleby and granted a knighthood; and in 1682 he was appointed sheriff of Lincolnshire.

His grandson Christopher Clapham (1657-1748) borrowed heavily and mortgaged his estate in Yorkshire and Lincolnshire. In 1703 he sold the manor of Beamsley.

Church St Peter: Perpendicular.

Almshouses In 1593 Margaret Clifford, Countess of Cumberland, founded a hospital at Beamsley which she intended should accommodate 13 poor women. For this purpose a suitable site was made available by George Clapham of Beamsley Hall. When the Countess died in 1616 the building work was still in progress and it was left to her daughter Lady Anne Clifford to complete the project.

(*YASRS*, liv (1915), 21. C.8/22/27 and 47/148. E.134/23 Charles II/Easter 25. C.38/248/29 December 1694 and 2 March 1694/5. R. T. Spence, *Lady Anne Clifford* (1997), 9-10, 19, 38, 85, 98-9.)

ADEL   Skyrack

A village to the north of Leeds. The parish of Adel included the villages of Arthington and Eccup. 1674: 75 households in the township of Adel cum Eccup and 50 in Arthington. 1676: 436 persons aged 16 or more (parish of Adel).

During the Civil War period Robert Hitch the rector of Adel had his living sequestered by the parliamentary authorities. In a petition which he submitted to Cromwell in 1657 he claimed that he had suffered much at the hands of the royalist party on account of his loyalty to Parliament.

In the late 17th century the remains of a Roman camp aroused considerable interest in antiquarian circles.

Church St John Baptist: Norman with Decorated and Perpendicular features.

In the Commonwealth period there was a proposal that the church should be rebuilt in a more central position but nothing came of this.

Principal family Arthington of Arthington Hall. Estate revenue: £700 a year (1610); £560 a year (1623).

At the beginning of the 17th century the Arthingtons were still inclined towards Catholicism though with less commitment than they had once shown. William Arthington (c.1588-1622) had a recusant wife but he preferred to conform.

His son Henry (1615-1671), who became a ward of the Crown, had a Protestant upbringing under the guardianship of his stepfather Francis Nevile. In 1638 he married Mary Fairfax, a daughter of Sir Ferdinando Fairfax the future parliamentarian general. The marriage may both have reflected and helped to strengthen his Puritan beliefs.

In the Civil War he took the side of Parliament and served as a member of the West Riding committee.

Mary Arthington had bouts of religious melancholia. Her sister Dorothy Hutton urged her to 'beleeve that the hungring after grace is a speciall sign of grace, and know that the sence of the want of humility is humility'. In 1671 Oliver Heywood the nonconformist divine hastened to Arthington Hall to comfort her over the death of her husband.

Following the death of their son Henry (1655-1682) without any issue the estate passed by a prior settlement to his kinsman Cyril Arthington (c.1666-1720). The new squire was a man of a scholarly disposition who immersed himself in a range of scientific and antiquarian pursuits. In 1701 he was made a fellow of the Royal Society.

Arthington Hall The old house was probably Tudor in origin. In 1664 and 1674 the Arthingtons were taxed on 19 hearths.

About the end of the 17th century a new house was built. Ralph Thoresby wrote that Cyril Arthington 'has lately erected a noble Hall at Arthington and furnish'd it with Water convey'd in Pipes of Lead from an Engine he has contrived at his Mill upon the River Wharf'.

(A. G. Matthews, *Walker Revised* (1988), 394. *CSP Dom, 1656-7*, 298. Wards 5/49. Bodleian Library, Add A119 (letter-book of Mary Arthington). C.10/510/4. H. T. Simpson, *Archaeologia Adelensis: a History of the Parish of Adel in the West Riding of Yorkshire* (1879). W. H. Draper, *Adel and its Norman Church* (1909).)

ADLINGFLEET   Osgoldcross

A village near the River Trent in the eastern extremity of the riding. The parish of Adlingfleet included the villages of Eastoft and Haldenby and the hamlet of Fockerby.

1674: 43 households in Adlingfleet, 16 in Fockerby and 44 in Haldenby cum Eastoft.
1676: 374 persons aged 16 or more (parish of Adlingfleet).

Adlingfleet enjoyed market rights by virtue of a royal charter of 1260.

Church All Saints: 13th century and Perpendicular.

School A grammar school founded in 1589.

Principal families (1) Eastoft of Eastoft Hall. Estate revenue: £650 a year (1653).

John Eastoft (c.1565-1639) was named as a recusant in 1597 but he quickly conformed. In 1617 he was accused in the Court of Star Chamber of poaching deer belonging to the Crown within Hatfield Chase and of abusing his powers as a magistrate.

A Crown survey of Eastoft in 1637 revealed that he had enclosed 88 acres out of the common and that this had left about 200 acres for the use of the inhabitants of the village.

From 1623 onwards the Eastofts were involved in protracted litigation with the Moysers over their title to the estate of Robert Stockdale of Lockington.

Thomas Eastoft (1604-1658) does not appear to have taken an active part in the Civil War but in 1645 he was included in the West Riding parliamentary committee for the monthly assessment.

(2) Haldenby of Haldenby Hall. Estate revenue: £600 a year (1655).

During the early 17th century the family was twice subjected to the financial exactions of the Court of Wards as the result of successive minorities. After the death of Francis Haldenby (1583-1621) the estate descended to his son Robert (1600-1629) who was described in a submission made to the Court of Wards as 'Infirme and lame from the knees downewards soe as he goeth altogether upon Crutches, not having any use of knees, legs or feet'.

In the same submission the Court was informed that the manor of Haldenby and other lands belonging to the family were 'compassed about with the mayne Rivers of Owse, Trent and other great waters, wherby they are drowned almost every winter season and oftentimes in sommer when the bancks burst out by reason of the greate tydes and swellings of the saide waters'.

John Haldenby, who succeeded his father in 1629, died while still a minor. His brother Robert, who was a royalist, fell heavily into debt and was said to be 'destitute of money to supply his domesticke occasions'.

After the Restoration the family sank into obscurity.

Eastoft Hall In April 1620 the house and its contents were destroyed by a fire 'casually happening'. John Eastoft, who put his losses at £2000, began to rebuild more or less immediately. In 1658 the main rooms consisted of the hall, the great and little parlours and the great chamber.

Some building work was undertaken in the reign of Charles II. John Eastoft was taxed on six hearths in 1664 and nine in 1674.

Haldenby Hall The house was probably a modest structure. There is no reference to it in the hearth tax returns of 1664 and 1674.

(East Riding of Yorkshire Archives Service, Eastoft of Eastoft MSS. STAC8/27/5. E.178/5805. Wards 5/49. C.5/29/20.)

ADWICK LE STREET   Strafford and Tickhill

A village near Doncaster. The parish of Adwick included the hamlet of Hampole. 1674: 47 households in Adwick and 4 in Hampole cum Stubbs. 1676: 116 persons aged 16 or more (parish of Adwick).

Hampole Priory, which was an establishment of Cistercian nuns, had been founded in the 12th century and dissolved in 1540.

Church St Laurence: Norman with later medieval features.

School A grammar school founded in 1564.

Principal family Washington of Adwick Hall. Estate revenue: £330 a year (1653); £600 a year (1668).

The Washingtons owned the manors of Adwick and Hampole.

In the Civil War Darcy Washington (1590-1658) was an ardent royalist. Two of his sons died while in arms for the king.

Adwick Hall In 1653 Adwick Hall was described as 'consistinge of one large Hall, two parlours, one Dyninge Roome, one Kitchin, one Buttery with other necessary Low Roomes, seaven Chambers with lofts over them'.

Richard Washington (c.1638-1678) rebuilt the house in 1673. In 1674 he was taxed on 16 hearths, as compared with 14 in 1664.

(C.7/381/62. S.P.23/lviii/fo.67.)

ADWICK UPON DEARNE   Strafford and Tickhill

A small village on the River Dearne between Barnsley and Doncaster. There was no other village within the parish. 1674: 21 households (township of Adwick upon Dearne). 1676: 120 persons aged 16 or more (parish).

In 1655 Michael Noble the vicar of Adwick was ejected from his living by the West Riding commissioners for the removal of scandalous ministers.

Church St John: Norman and Early English.

(A. G. Matthews, *Walker Revised* (1988), 396.)

ALDBOROUGH Claro/Hallikeld

A village to the south-east of Boroughbridge. The parish of Aldborough, which straddled the border between the West and North Ridings, included the market town of Boroughbridge (which had a medieval chapel), several villages and parts of Dunsforth (which also had a chapel), Humberton and Milby. Boroughbridge and Ellenthorpe are separately noticed. 1674: 77 households in Aldborough, 32 in Dunsforth, 6 in Humberton cum Milby, 40 in Minskip and 39 in Roecliffe.

The village had its origins in a Roman military fort. Near Boroughbridge 'is Aldburrow, confirm'd to be the Isurium of the Ancients from several Roman Coyns and chequer'd Pavements digg'd up there.... Here are some fragments of Aquiducts cut in great stones, and cover'd with Roman tyle' (Edmund Gibson, 1695).

In 1628 the freeholders of Aldborough came to an agreement among themselves over the enclosure of some 420 acres of arable land in the common fields. Generally, each individual was assigned a single block of land in place of a number of scattered strips and the boundary of his new holding was marked by hedges.

That same year the Crown conveyed the manor of Aldborough to the City of London and in 1629 it was purchased by Arthur Aldburgh of Ellenthorpe Hall for the sum of £1473. Before long he was involved in a boundary dispute with Thomas Tankard of Brampton who had property in Aldborough. In 1654 Aldburgh, who by then was heavily in debt, sold the manor to his son-in-law John Wentworth of Woolley. In the reign of Charles II it was valued at £316 a year.

Aldborough was a parliamentary borough which sent two representatives to Westminster. For many years the electorate consisted merely of nine burgage tenants. In 1679, however, it was decided that all men who paid municipal taxes known as 'scot and lot' should be eligible to vote and as a result Aldborough acquired some fifty new electors.

The widening of the franchise enabled the lord of the manor to exert greater influence at election time. Between 1685 and 1695 Sir Michael Wentworth (the son of John Wentworth) was returned as MP for Aldborough on no fewer than four occasions.

Church St Andrew: Perpendicular.

The parish was subject to the peculiar jurisdiction of the Dean and Chapter of York.

Schools There was a school at Aldborough from 1608 onwards.

In 1604 it was reported that Francis Barwick of Minskip 'being a poore man doth teach children to write and rede'.

(Sir Thomas Lawson-Tancred, *Records of a Yorkshire Manor* (1937). C.33/210/fols.261-2. E. Peacock (ed.), *A List of the Roman Catholics in the County of York in 1604* (1872), 51. T. S. Turner, *History of Aldborough and Boroughbridge* (1853). Lady M. E. Lawson-Tancred, *Guide Book to the Antiquities of Aldborough and Boroughbridge* (1927).)

ALDFIELD
Claro

A small village and chapelry within the parish of Ripon. 1674: 28 households (including Studley Royal).

Church St Laurence: Decorated.

Principal families (1) Mallory of Studley Hall. Estate revenue: £1500 a year (1656).

In the reign of James I Sir John Mallory (c.1557-1620) was involved in a long-running feud with his neighbour Sir Stephen Proctor of Fountains Hall. In the course of litigation it was alleged that he was 'backwarde in religion' and that as a magistrate he had done little or nothing to apprehend seminary priests or other dangerous papists. In fact he was a Protestant though with Catholic connections.

In 1607 he commissioned Solomon Swale to carry out a survey of the manor of Studley. No doubt he was seeking to increase his revenue as a response to his growing financial difficulties.

His son William (c.1579-1646) frequently represented Ripon in Parliament and in 1622 spent six months in the Tower of London as a punishment for his outspoken defence of the public liberties. In the Civil War he supported the king, though he was never apparently in arms.

In his will (1646) he left an annuity to his household chaplain, Thomas Jackson.

His son Sir John (1610-1656) was a royalist colonel who was appointed governor of Skipton Castle. He sold some property after the Civil War but was still £11,000 in debt at the time of his death.

One of his daughters, Elizabeth, was said to have become possessed of an evil spirit through the machinations of a witch but she was eventually cured.

(2) Aislabie of Studley Hall. Estate revenue: £1300 a year (1675).

When the male line of the Mallorys expired in 1667 the bulk of the estate passed to George Aislabie (1618-1675), the registrar of the Consistory Court at York, who had married the eldest surviving daughter of Sir John Mallory. In January 1675 he was mortally wounded in a duel.

His son John (c.1671-1742) was responsible for the landscaping of the grounds between Studley Hall and Fountains Abbey which was carried out from 1720 onwards.

Studley Hall A 15th century mansion which appears to have been enlarged by George Aislabie. The hearth tax returns record 10 hearths in 1664 and 15 in 1674.

The house was destroyed by fire in 1716.

(WYAS, Leeds, Vyner MSS. J. R. Walbran, 'A Genealogical and Biographical Memoir of the Lords of Studley, in Yorkshire', *Surtees Society*, lxvii (1876). C.10/477/4. C.33/269/fo.1252. S. V. Mallory Smith, *A History of the Mallory Family* (1985).)

ALDWARK　　　　　　　　　　　　　　　　　　　　　Strafford and Tickhill

Aldwark was situated within the parish of Rawmarsh, near Rotherham, though it also had links with the parish of Ecclesfield. According to the hearth tax returns there were two houses in 1664 but only one, Aldwark Hall, in 1674.

Principal family Foljambe of Aldwark Hall (baronetcy 1622). Estate revenue: £3000 a year (1614); £1000 a year (1640). Coalmines and ironstone deposits at Walton in Derbyshire.

Sir Francis Foljambe (c.1590-1640) was born a younger son but inherited a large estate following the death of his elder brother without issue. He was described as a person 'of small understandinge by reason of his education to manage so great an estate' and also had a reputation for extravagance and excessive hospitality. These and other factors such as expensive litigation led to the sale of land on a major scale.

In 1631 the Court of Star Chamber found him guilty of forgery and fined him £1000.

In his will he studiously avoided any reference to his wife, Dame Elizabeth, who emerged as a recusant in 1641.

Sir Francis left no male issue and the Aldwark estate was eventually inherited by a distant kinsman, Francis Foljambe (1643-1707).

Aldwark Hall An early Tudor house with later features. It was a two-storeyed building with a long range of straight gables. There were 11 taxable hearths in 1664 and 17 in 1674.

Francis Foljambe, who was in possession by 1674, replaced the old hall with a three-storeyed house in a plain classical style.

(Nathaniel Johnston, 'History of the Family of Foljambe', *Collectanea Topographica et Genealogica*, ii (1835). C.3/425/20. BIHR, York Registry, will of Sir Francis Foljambe, 31 August 1640.)

ALLERTON MAULEVERER　　　　　　　　　　　　　　　　　　　Claro

A village to the east of Knaresborough which was only partly in the parish of Allerton Mauleverer; the other part was in the parish of Whixley. 1674: 26 households in Allerton cum Flaxby and 8 in Hopperton. Flaxby was in the parish of Goldsborough.

There were probably few remaining traces of Allerton Priory, a 12th century Benedictine foundation.

Church St Martin: 14th century and Perpendicular but possibly with earlier features.

Principal family Mauleverer of Allerton Hall (baronetcy 1641). Estate revenue: £1500 a year (1640).

The antiquity of the Mauleverer family aroused the interest of William Camden who wrote that Allerton Mauleverer was 'the Seat of a truly ancient and famous family the Mallivers'.

Sir Thomas Mauleverer (1599-1655) was for many years a ward of the Crown.

Despite the grant of a baronetcy he took up arms for Parliament on the outbreak of the Civil War and raised two regiments of horse and one of foot. During the course of the war he acquired a reputation for exceptional brutality. In 1649 he acted as one of the king's judges and signed the death-warrant.

Sir Thomas claimed that he had spent some £15,000 in the service of Parliament. In the last few years of his life he was paying £400 a year in mortgage interest.

In contrast, his son Sir Richard (c.1623-1675) was a zealous royalist who fought for the king in both the first and second Civil Wars. In 1655 he took part in Lord Wilmot's rising and was captured but managed to escape.

After the Restoration he was in danger of having his estate confiscated on account of his father's involvement in the act of regicide but it was decided not to proceed in view of his own loyalty. In 1660 he was appointed a gentleman of the Privy Chamber.

During the late 17th century the Mauleverers often sojourned in London and this may have been a factor in their growing indebtedness.

Sir Thomas Mauleverer (c.1643-1687) was described by Sir John Reresby as a suspected papist but there is no specific evidence of any Catholic affiliations. In 1678 he killed a man while acting as Sir Henry Goodricke's second in a duel. He and his wife Dame Katherine had serious marital problems and he left no legitimate issue.

Although Sir Thomas sold the lands which his wife had brought him he still had debts amounting to £5500 at the time of his death.

His brother Sir Richard succeeded to the estate but died in 1689. He settled an annuity of £290 on Dame Katherine and in his will (1688) made financial provision for Sir Thomas's natural son, Thomas Newsham alias Mauleverer.

Allerton Hall A large mansion which in 1674 had 24 taxable hearths.

There was a deer park adjoining the house.

(Nottingham University Library, Galway of Serlby MSS. PRO, Wills, PROB 11/384/107 and 394/42.)

ALMONDBURY   Agbrigg and Morley

A village to the south of Huddersfield which was heavily involved in the production and sale of cloth. The extensive parish of Almondbury contained a number of villages and hamlets, including Honley which had a dependent chapel and Meltham where a chapel was built in 1651. The village of Marsden, which also had a public chapel, was partly in the parish of Almondbury and partly in the parish of Huddersfield. 1674: 124 households in Almondbury, 70 in Austonley cum membris, 70 in Crosland Half (South Crosland), 39 in Farnley Tyas, 71 in Honley, 36 in Marsden and 69 in Meltham Half. 1676: 2000 persons aged 16 or more (parish).

Almondbury had been entitled to hold a weekly market on Thursdays ever since 1294. This was the only cloth market in the Colne valley until Huddersfield received a market charter in 1671.

Church All Hallows: Early English and Perpendicular.

Schools The Kayes of Woodsome Hall had founded a school at Almondbury in the mid-16th century.

In 1608 James I's free grammar school of Almondbury was formally established by letters patent.

In his will (1672) Godfrey Beaumont, a yeoman, left a rent-charge of £3 a year for the support of a schoolmaster at South Crosland.

Almshouses In 1614 Robert Nettleton settled property on trustees for the purpose of building almshouses at Almondbury.

Principal families (1) Ramsden of Longley or Nether Longley Hall (and of Byram Hall) (baronetcy 1689). Estate revenue: £2000 a year (1679). Coalmines, iron works, fulling mills.

William Ramsden (1558-1623) was an enterprising landowner who added considerably to the estate. His son Sir John (1594-1646) inherited his business acumen and continued the process of land acquisition. In 1634 he took as his second wife Anne Poole, the widow of a London merchant, who brought him a portion of £12,000 and lands in Essex. In return he agreed to settle a jointure of £1000 a year on her.

In the Civil War he raised a regiment for the king and served as a troop commander with the rank of colonel. In April 1644 he was taken prisoner when the Fairfaxes captured Selby but was soon exchanged. He died in Newark Castle while it was under siege.

During the Commonwealth period his son William (1625-1679) was involved in litigation with his stepmother who had remarried. In 1651 he alleged that Dame Anne and her new husband were felling timber trees on the estate, pulling down many of the buildings and allowing others 'to fall into great ruyne and decaie'. Subsequently, in 1657, he claimed that he had been obliged to pay all his father's debts which had amounted to £10,000.

After the Restoration the Ramsdens lived mainly at Byram Hall (see under Brotherton).

(2) Kaye of Woodsome Hall (and Denby Grange) (baronetcy 1642). Estate revenue: £1000 a year (1651 and 1664). Coalmines, fulling mills. Number of servants: 19 (1648).

The Kayes were efficient landowners who steadily accumulated property. John Kaye (1578-1641) searched for coal on his estate and dug pits in various places, though this was primarily to meet his own domestic needs.

In the Civil War Sir John Kaye (1616-1662) took up arms for the king and was in Sheffield Castle when it was surrendered in August 1644.

Oliver Heywood the nonconformist minister relates that Sir John Kaye (c.1641-1706) showed great antagonism towards dissenters. When Sir John summoned him to

Woodsome Hall in January 1673 he found that 'many waiting-men were playing at cards at the table' and was even more disturbed by the spectacle of a large assembly of gentlemen engaged in feasting, dancing and revelling. A few years later Kaye was employing an Anglican chaplain, Thomas Hepworth, to attend to the spiritual needs of his household.

James Rimmington, who was Sir John's steward, is said to have haunted Woodsome Hall after his death in 1697.

Longley Hall Longley where 'Ramsden haith planted a house for a seat for himself and his posterity' (Roger Dodsworth). A two-storeyed house with gables built in the reign of Elizabeth. In 1584 it was called 'New Hall'.

William Ramsden was taxed on 24 hearths in 1664 and 25 in 1674.

Woodsome Hall Arthur Kaye (d.1571) began the rebuilding of Woodsome Hall in the early years of Elizabeth's reign but his grandson Robert (1547-1620) was responsible for much of the stonework. Further building work was carried out by John Kaye (1578-1641) and his son Sir John (1616-1662).

There were 17 taxable hearths in 1664 and 22 in 1674. In 1664 it was noted that the house was empty, presumably because the family was then living at Denby Grange (see under Kirkheaton).

According to the family journal John Kaye (1578-1641) enclosed part of the park at Woodsome Hall.

(W. B. Crump and Gertrude Ghorbal, *History of the Huddersfield Woollen Industry* (Tolson Memorial Museum Publications, Handbook IX) (1935). W. K. Jordan, *The Charities of Rural England 1480-1660* (1961), 272, 318-19. WYAS, Leeds, Ramsden Collection. C.3/334/6. C.8/634/4. C.10/32/121. C.33/208/fo.1027; 210/fo.752; and 279/fo.818. YAS Library, MS 178 (Kaye family journal). BL, Additional MSS 24,467, fo.250. C. A. Hulbert, *Annals of the Church and Parish of Almondbury* (1882). T. Dyson, *Almondbury and its Ancient School* (1926). K. M. Cocker and H. Taylor (eds.), *Historic Almondbury: the Village on the Hill* (1975).)

ARKSEY Strafford and Tickhill

A village to the north of Doncaster. The parish of Arksey included the village of Bentley. 1674: 121 households in Bentley cum Arksey. 1676: 200 persons aged 16 or more (parish).

Brian Cooke of Doncaster, and later of Wheatley, bought the manor of Bentley in 1654. He already owned the impropriate rectory of Arksey.

Church All Saints: Norman, Early English, Decorated and Perpendicular.

School Brian Cooke, who died in 1661, left the sum of £800 for the establishment of a grammar school at Arksey. His intention was that the master should be paid a salary of £40 a year.

In 1683 his brother Sir George bequeathed a further sum of £200 for the erection of a more suitable building to house the school.

Among the early masters were Roger Kirchivall, who died in 1670, and John Leigh.

Almshouses Brian Cooke also made provision through a trust arrangement for the building of a hospital at a cost of £60. This was to accommodate twelve poor persons who were to have £5 a year each for maintenance.

(W. K. Jordan, *The Charities of Rural England 1480-1660* (1961), 280, 346-7. YAS, *Parish Register Series*, clxvi (2001), 157, 196.)

ARMLEY   Agbrigg and Morley

A clothing village within the parish of Leeds. 1674: 67 households.

There was an outbreak of the plague in 1645.

Church In the reign of Charles I Ralph Hopton of Armley Hall made land available for the building of a parochial chapel. Because of the Civil War the work was not completed until the 1650s.

Principal family Hopton of Armley Hall. Estate revenue: £1000 a year (1640). Fulling mills.

At the beginning of the 17th century the family still had residual Catholic sympathies but these do not appear to have survived the death of John Hopton in 1615.

In the Civil War Sir Ingram Hopton (1614-1643) took up arms for the king and was killed in an engagement at Winceby in Lincolnshire. After his death most of the estate, including the Armley property, descended to Mary his only child who married Miles Stapleton of Wighill.

Armley Hall A large mansion which may have been Tudor in origin. After it ceased to be a family seat it was drastically reduced in size and converted into a farmhouse. According to Ralph Thoresby this involved the demolition of 26 rooms.

(C.10/40/217.)

ARMTHORPE   Strafford and Tickhill

A village to the north-east of Doncaster. There was no other village within the parish. 1674: 87 households (township of Armthorpe). 1676: 96 persons aged 16 or more (parish).

Church St Mary: Norman.

ARNCLIFFE   Staincliffe and Ewecross

A small village on the River Skirfare in Littondale. The parish of Arncliffe contained the village of Buckden and several hamlets, including Halton Gill and Hubberholme which had dependent chapels. 1674: 25 households in Arncliffe, 67 in Buckden and 19 in Hawkswick.

In 1640 the West Riding magistrates received a report about 'the great ruyne and decay of Hubbram bridge, situate over the river of Wharfe…..the said bridge beinge the high roade way leadinge betweene the market towne of Lancaster…..and the markett towne of Newcastle upon Tyne and other places in the countie of Northumberland'. In the light of this report it was decided that two of the justices should carry out an inspection of the bridge.

Church St Oswald: Norman and Perpendicular.

School In his will (1619) Henry Fawcett left an annuity of £10 as a stipend for the curate of the chapel at Halton Gill on the basis that he would provide free elementary education for poor men's children. He was a native of Halton Gill who had grown rich as a wool merchant in Norwich.

In 1626 his brother William, who was a London merchant, rebuilt the chapel and also erected a modest building which was to serve both as the curate's dwelling and as a schoolhouse.

In his will (1630) he settled rents amounting to £13 6s 8d a year as an augmentation of the curate's stipend.

In the latter part of the 17th century John Hargreaves and Francis Bryer served as both curates and schoolmasters.

(A. Raistrick, *Old Yorkshire Dales* (1971), 155-7. W. Boyd and W. A. Shuffrey, *Littondale: Past and Present* (1893).)

ASKHAM BRYAN   Ainsty

A village to the south-west of York. There was no other village within the parish. 1665: 36 households (township of Askham Bryan). 1676: 70 persons aged 16 or more (parish).

Church St Nicholas: Norman.

ASKHAM RICHARD   Ainsty

A village to the south-west of York. There was no other village within the parish. 1665: 25 households (township of Askham Richard). 1676: 160 persons aged 16 or more (parish).

In 1633 George Flint the vicar of Askham Richard was in trouble with the ecclesiastical authorities 'for reading divine service without a surplisse.....for singinge psalmes immediately after the lessons' and for preaching without a licence. At the same time the churchwardens were admonished for not presenting him. Flint was not slow to conform and he continued to hold the living until his death in 1669.

Church St Mary: Norman.

(*YAJ*, xv (1900), 226. R. A. Marchant, *The Puritans and the Church Courts in the Diocese of York 1560-1642* (1960), 247.)

ASTON   Strafford and Tickhill

A village to the east of Sheffield. The parish of Aston included the village of Aughton. 1674: 56 households (township of Aston cum Aughton). 1676: 200 persons aged 16 or more (parish of Aston).

Church All Saints: 12th and 14th century.

Principal family Darcy of Aston Hall, Lords Darcy. Estate revenue: £4000 a year (1635).

John Lord Darcy of Aston (c.1579-1635) was known as 'the good Lord Darcy'. He married four times but left no issue. His second wife, Isabel, provided generous support for Puritan ministers. In some verse she was praised for her virtue, piety, munificence and hospitality.

The fourth wife, Elizabeth, who had a jointure of £1500 a year settled on her, survived her husband and in 1636 married Sir Francis Fane. After their marriage they lived at Aston Hall.

The bulk of the estate, in possession and reversion, was settled on another branch of the family, the Darcys of Hornby Castle in the North Riding, and eventually they began to use Aston Hall as a secondary seat.

Aston Hall A castellated house which had apparently been built in the early 16th century. In 1664 and 1674 there were 27 taxable hearths.

There was a deer park adjoining the house.

(C.22/822/56. BL, Egerton MSS 3402, fols.49, 53.)

AUSTERFIELD   Strafford and Tickhill

A village to the south-east of Doncaster which was close to the border with Nottinghamshire. It was also a chapelry within the Nottinghamshire parish of Blyth. 1674: 34 households (township of Austerfield).

In 1641 John Wright of Austerfield, who styled himself 'gentleman', was indicted for assaulting Robert Whittacre the constable.

Church St Helen: Norman and Early English.

(*YASRS*, liv (1915), 332.)

BADSWORTH   Osgoldcross

A village between Wakefield and Doncaster. The parish of Badsworth included the villages of Thorpe Audlin and Upton. 1674: 21 households in Badsworth, 44 in Thorpe Audlin and 19 in Upton.

In 1639 the West Riding magistrates received a petition from the overseers of the poor of Thorpe Audlin. The petitioners related that their village was 'overcharged wth a great number of poore people' and that Badsworth and Upton, 'haveinge fewe or noe poore', were refusing to provide any financial assistance. In response the justices ruled that Badsworth and Upton should contribute as they had formerly done.

Church St Mary: Norman, Decorated and Perpendicular.

Principal families (1) Dolman of Badsworth Hall (and Gunby Hall and Pocklington, East Riding). Estate revenue: £700 a year (1652).

The Dolmans were a zealous Catholic family who sent some of their children to Continental establishments.

Sir Robert Dolman (c.1560-1628) usually resided at Gunby Hall when he was in Yorkshire, though in 1615 it was reported that 'he lived altogether' at London. His son Thomas (1582-1639) was the first head of the family to settle at Badsworth which had been acquired by marriage in the reign of Elizabeth. In 1629 he compounded for his recusancy and was required to pay a rent of £110 a year. In 1633 he commissioned a survey of the manor of Badsworth which was found to contain 1400 acres and this may have provided the stimulus for his enclosing activities on the common.

His son Robert (1625-1695) was made a ward of the Crown. He fought for the king in both Civil Wars and was heavily mulcted for his loyalty. As a result he was forced to sell the Badsworth estate and move to Pocklington.

(2) Bright of Badsworth Hall (and Carbrook Hall) (baronetcy 1660). Estate revenue: £1600 a year (1660); £3200 a year (1687). Coalmining at Handsworth.

The Brights were a Puritan family whose growing prosperity was largely due to their business expertise. They had been granted a coat of arms as recently as 1641.

Sir John Bright (1619-1688) bought the Badsworth estate in 1653 for £8600 and made it his principal seat. In the two Civil Wars he had served with great distinction as a parliamentarian colonel and had commanded troops at the battles of Marston Moor and Preston.

He was a highly efficient landlord who engaged in commercial farming and coalmining and lent money on a considerable scale. By the time of his death he was one of the most substantial landowners in the county.

Sir John's domestic chaplains were generally Puritans, men such as William Bagshaw, Matthew Sylvester and Jeremy Wheat.

Oliver Heywood wrote of him that he was a 'mighty man of wealth' and that he was 'in torturing pain' for two years before his death.

Since Sir John had no surviving male issue he settled the bulk of his estate on John Liddell, the second son of his daughter Dame Catherine Liddell, who in accordance with his wishes assumed the name Liddell-Bright.

Badsworth Hall Immediately after purchasing the estate Bright let contracts for the building of new stables and the heightening of the garden wall. At some stage he appears to have rebuilt the house, though there is no clear evidence.

The hearth tax returns show that he was taxed on 25 hearths in 1664 and 20 in 1674 but no explanation is given for the variation.

(*YASRS*, liv (1915), 117-118. STAC8/175/4. Sheffield Archives, Wentworth Woodhouse Collection, Bright MSS. P. Roebuck, *Yorkshire Baronets 1640-1760* (1980).)

BARDSEY   Skyrack

A village to the north-east of Leeds. The parish of Bardsey included part of the hamlet of Wike; the other part was in the parish of Harewood. 1674: 38 households in Bardsey cum Rigton, 11 in Wike and 1 in Wothersome. 1676: 186 persons aged 16 or more (parish).

Bardsey was the birthplace of William Congreve (1670-1729) the dramatist and poet.

Wothersome, which may have been depopulated, belonged to the Mauleverer family of Ingleby Arncliffe in the North Riding. It included a park which was sometimes let to a tenant.

Church All Hallows: Saxon, Norman, Decorated and Perpendicular.

BARNBROUGH   Strafford and Tickhill

A village to the west of Doncaster. The parish of Barnbrough included part of the hamlet of Bilham; the other part was in the parish of Hooton Pagnell. 1674: 42 households in Barnbrough and 13 in Bilham. 1676: 124 persons aged 16 or more (parish).

In 1639 the West Riding magistrates received a complaint from the inhabitants of Barnbrough about the way in which local taxes were levied within the parish. Individual charges were based on the number of cattle which each parishioner put into the commons in the course of a year. As a result, it was pointed out, 'many of the richer sort haveinge enclosed grounds to putt theire cattell to are thereby freed and the poorer sort oppressed'. The justices clearly regarded this method as both irrational and inequitable and decided that in future the assessment should be made 'according to the quantitie and quallitie of acres everye one occupieth and enjoyeth'.

The manor of Barnbrough and its Elizabethan hall belonged to the descendants of Sir Thomas More, though for much of the 17th century they were absentee landlords. Basil More, however, sold his Hertfordshire estate and by 1680 had taken up residence at Barnbrough Hall with the result that a solidly Protestant parish now had a Catholic squire.

In contrast, the Vincents of Barnbrough Grange had Puritan leanings. Thomas Vincent (1598-1667) played no part in the Civil War and seems to have been guided mainly by self-interest. In 1644 he claimed that his loyalty to Parliament had cost him £1500 through the depredations of Newcastle's troops, though at the same time there were suspicions that he had royalist sympathies. In 1648 his estate was sequestered but the parliamentary authorities eventually concluded that he was no delinquent.

His son John (1625-1676) was a more committed parliamentarian. In 1654 he was appointed as one of the West Riding commissioners for the ejection of scandalous ministers.

Church St Peter: Norman, Decorated and Perpendicular.

(*YASRS*, liv (1915), 130. Nottinghamshire Record Office, Nevile of Thorney MSS, 221/7. *Calendar, Committee for the Advance of Money*, 849, 851.)

BARNBY DUN   Strafford and Tickhill

A village to the north-east of Doncaster which was situated on the River Don. The parish of Barnby Dun included the hamlet of Thorpe in Balne and parts of Burghwallis and Stainforth (see the entries for Burghwallis and Hatfield). 1674: 66 households (township of Barnby Dun).

There was a man-made ford at Barnby Dun which enabled the inhabitants to cross the river on stepping-stones at most times of the year.

Church St Peter and St Paul: 14th century and Perpendicular.

School A public grammar school founded in 1564.

Principal families (1) Gregory of Barnby Dun. Estate revenue: £600 a year (1630).

William Gregory (c.1570-1633), who was granted a coat of arms in 1601, owned one of the manors in Barnby Dun, the rectory of Barnby and property in Lincolnshire and Nottinghamshire.

His son Gilbert (1600-1644) appears to have taken no part in the Civil War.

(2) Portington of Barnby Dun. Estate revenue: £640 a year (1640).

The Portingtons were a much older gentry family who had been seated at Barnby Dun since the 15th century.

Sir Roger Portington (1544-1605) was said to have had an estate worth £1600 a year. He had no issue and some part of the estate passed to a cousin, Robert Portington of Tudworth, who settled at Barnby Dun. He was steward of the manor of Hatfield and deputy master of the game in Hatfield Chase. In 1628 the Privy Council ordered his arrest following allegations by Sir Cornelius Vermuyden about his involvement in the rioting provoked by his drainage project.

In 1631 Robert Portington was succeeded by his grandson Roger (1609-1683) who proved to be a zealous royalist. In the Civil War he spent some £9000 in raising and maintaining a troop of horse for the king. He again took up arms in 1648 and was heavily fined on compounding for his estate. The financial consequences of his loyalty were serious but not disastrous.

Houses The seat of the Gregory family was on the south side of Barnby Dun. In the reign of Charles II, or perhaps earlier, Francis Gregory carried out some building work: according to a hearth tax return of 1671 the number of hearths had been increased from 11 to 13.

The house of the Portingtons, which was more to the north, was much smaller: in 1664 and 1674 Roger Portington was taxed on five hearths.

(C.7/439/51. C.9/20/54. C.10/35/193.)

BARNOLDSWICK   Staincliffe and Ewecross

A village to the south-west of Skipton. The parish of Barnoldswick included several hamlets. 1674: 111 households (township of Barnoldswick). 1676: 405 persons aged 16 or more (parish).

During the early 17th century Barnoldswick had two Puritan ministers, John Eastwood and Francis Peel. In 1627 and 1632 Peel found himself in trouble with the ecclesiastical authorities for performing clandestine marriages.

In 1630 the City of London sold the manor of Barnoldswick (which had formerly belonged to the Crown) to Lawrence Halstead of Sonning in Berkshire. In the Civil War Halstead supported the royalist cause and when compounding for his estate valued the manor at £500 a year.

In the Commonwealth period it was said that the inhabitants of the parish had suffered considerably for their loyalty to Parliament.

In 1696 the tenants of the manor of Barnoldswick claimed in an Exchequer suit that their lands had formerly been monastic property and were therefore exempt from the payment of tithes. A Cistercian abbey had been founded at Barnoldswick in 1147 but five years later the monks had moved to Kirkstall, near Leeds.

Church St Mary, Coates: Perpendicular.

The minister was a perpetual curate.

(R. A. Marchant, *The Puritans and the Church Courts in the Diocese of York 1560-1642* (1960), 245, 268. S.P.23/ccxii/521. C.7/180/68. E.134/7 William III/ Easter 2. J. H. Warner, *History of Barnoldswick* (1934).)

BARNSLEY   Staincross

A market town and chapelry within the parish of Silkstone. 1674: 129 households (town of Barnsley). 1676: 638 persons aged 16 or more (chapelry).

By virtue of a royal charter of 1249 the town enjoyed the right to hold a weekly market and an annual fair.

For most of the 17th century the manor of Barnsley belonged to the Crown. In the reign of William III it was granted to William Bentinck, Earl of Portland.

Barnsley had long been noted for its wire manufacture. In the early 17th century William Bower was one of the leading figures in the industry.

At the beginning of the Civil War the town was garrisoned by royalist troops.

In his will (1646) Edmund Rogers made provision for the income from 62 acres of land to be used for the relief of the poor of Barnsley.

At a special sessions held at Barnsley in 1675 'divers and sundry persons made complaint that they were oppressed by the poore.....whereof great numbers wandered begging, whereupon the principal inhabitants of the town.....being present did likewise complain that the number of the poore was so many that of themselves they were not able to maintain, relieve or raise a stock for to employ the poore without the assistance of the hundred [wapentake]'. In the light of these representations the magistrates decided that the wapentake of Staincross should make a monthly contribution of £10 towards the relief of the poor of Barnsley and this arrangement continued for four years.

In 1679 a local squire, John Wentworth of Woolley, gave the sum of £50 'for the raising and advancing of the stock to employ the poore of Barnsley'.

Church St Mary: a public chapel which was probably Perpendicular.

School A free grammar school founded in 1660 by Thomas Keresforth for children born in Barnsley, Dodworth and Keresforth Hill. In 1665 he built a schoolhouse and endowed it with £20 a year.

Almshouses In 1493 Edmund Brookhouse had founded almshouses for three poor and impotent men. At the time of the Reformation this property had come into the possession of the Wentworths of West Bretton and as a result had fallen into disuse. In 1616, following an inquiry, the Lord Chancellor ruled that they should be reinstated in accordance with the terms of Brookhouse's bequest and the following year Matthew

Wentworth conveyed the premises to the churchwardens and overseers of the poor of Barnsley.

(W. K. Jordan, *The Charities of Rural England 1480-1660* (1961), 347. YAS Library, Bretton Hall MSS, Bundle 59. R. Jackson, *The History of the Town and Township of Barnsley* (1858). B. Elliott, *The Making of Barnsley* (2004).)

BARWICK IN ELMET   Skyrack

Barwick in Elmet 'which is said to have been the royal seat of the Kings of Northumberland' (William Camden). A village to the north-east of Leeds. The parish of Barwick in Elmet contained a number of hamlets, including Barnbow, Kiddal and Roundhay. 1674: 162 households in the township of Barwick and 20 in Roundhay. 1676: 750 persons aged 16 or more (parish).

Church All Saints: Perpendicular.

School Nathaniel Jackson, who was rector of Barwick in Elmet between 1647 and 1660, kept a private school there. He was a Puritan who was deprived of his living at the Restoration.

Principal families (1) Gascoigne of Barnbow Hall (and Parlington Hall) (baronetcy 1635). Estate revenue: £1000 a year (1629); £1600 a year (1642). Coalmines at Barnbow, Garforth, Parlington and Scholes.

The Gascoignes were a leading Catholic family who often had a resident chaplain. Except in the middle years of the 17th century the financial consequences of their recusancy were relatively modest.

Sir John Gascoigne (1554-1637) and his son Sir Thomas (c.1593-1686) were business-minded landowners who enclosed and developed waste land and exploited mineral resources. On occasion they employed a surveyor, Solomon Swale, to undertake work on their behalf. In 1642 Sir Thomas wrote that within the wastes and commons of Barwick, Scholes, Bramham and Clifford 'there is good possibilitie of improvement by Inclosure, planting of Connye Warrens, and by the Quarries of stone and lymestone thereof'.

In the 1630s the Gascoignes added considerably to their estate.

During the Civil War Sir Thomas strove to remain neutral but had two-thirds of his estate sequestered for his recusancy.

In 1669 it was reported that his house was frequented by Catholics, including 'nigh 20 families' from Barwick. A decade later he was arrested as the result of allegations made by two former employees of his who had been dismissed. They claimed that he had been holding meetings at Barnbow Hall for the purpose of drawing up plans for an uprising. In 1680 he was tried for treason but acquitted. Shortly afterwards he retired to the monastery of Lambspring in Germany where his brother John was the abbot. An English consul who visited him related that he was 'a very good, harmless gentleman'.

Sir Thomas Gascoigne (c.1659-1718) was faced with a major domestic crisis which led to protracted litigation. In 1686 his wife Magdalen left Barnbow Hall at dead of night and never returned. There were suggestions that he had denied her any financial support but his steward, Robert Carre, described him as 'A very kind and obliegeing gentleman and Courteous to all persons'.

(2) Ellis of Kiddal Hall (and Roall Hall, Kellington). Estate revenue: £500 a year (1640).

In the early 17th century the Ellis family held the same religious beliefs as the Gascoignes.

In the Civil War John Ellis (1583-c.1644) and his sons William, Henry and Charles all lost their lives while in arms for the king. With the death of William Ellis in 1647 the estate descended to his son William (c.1643-1726) who appears to have been brought up as a Protestant. In 1670 he was involved in a property dispute with Sir Thomas Gascoigne.

Barnbow Hall In his will (1635) Sir John Gascoigne referred to the repair work which he had carried out on his 'severall houses, outhouses and Mills, all left unto me ruynous and in greate decay'. When Ralph Thoresby visited Barnbow Hall in 1709 he concluded that it was Jacobean.

The rooms listed in an inventory of 1661 include the hall, the gallery, the dining room, the great and little parlours, the chapel and the vestry.

There were 17 taxable hearths in 1664 and 19 in 1674.

Kiddal Hall A medieval house which had been enlarged by Thomas Ellis about the beginning of the 16th century.

In 1671 it was reported that the number of hearths had been reduced from 11 to 9.

(F. S. Colman, *History of Barwick-in-Elmet*, Thoresby Society, xvii (1908). WYAS, Leeds, Gascoigne of Barnbow MSS. G. D. Lumb (ed.), *Wills, Registers and Monumental Inscriptions of the Parish of Barwick-in-Elmet* (1908). C.5/402/106. C.8/428/3 and 452/13. C.10/193/31 and 426/37. C.22/81/23. C.33/205/fo.1180 and 206/fols.445-6. C.38/167/21 February 1669/70.)

BASHALL (BASHALL EAVES)   Staincliffe and Ewecross

A village in Craven which was situated in the parish of Mitton. 1674: 47 households.

Principal families (1) Talbot of Bashall Hall. Estate revenue: £500 a year (1620).

The Talbots died out in the male line in 1620. There were two joint heirs, Elizabeth and Margery Talbot, who were then aged 6 and 5 respectively. Suitors began to appear as early as 1627 and they were both married off at a tender age while they were still wards of the Crown.

(2) White of Bashall Hall. Estate revenue: £640 a year (1642).

Margery Talbot was married to William White (1606-1661), a man of modest social origin who was a Court of Wards official. He acquired half the estate by this means and purchased the other half for £3800. Both marriages led to protracted litigation.

During the 1630s White borrowed heavily and sold a considerable amount of land in Bashall to Sir John Preston who leased it back to him at a rent of £140 a year.

Early in the Civil War he was appointed a member of the West Riding parliamentary committee and much later on he was accorded the rank of colonel. When the royalists gained control of most of the county he moved to London where he acted as agent to Ferdinando Lord Fairfax in his capacity as a parliamentary general.

In 1644 Sir John Preston sought to take over his estate and Prince Rupert's troops seized goods of his to the value of £800 and imprisoned his servants at York.

In 1649 he took as his second wife Frances Barkham, a daughter of Sir Edward Barkham, and settled on her a jointure which included Bashall Hall and lands within Bashall Moor which he had recently enclosed.

White left no issue and in his will (1660) nominated his nephew John Ferrers, a lawyer of Clifford's Inn, as his heir and executor. In 1666 Ferrers was involved in litigation with Frances White and her father who he claimed had been seeking to deprive him of his inheritance. In reply they denied the allegation and acknowledged that he was the rightful heir.

Bashall Hall Although the house was medieval or early Tudor in origin it appears to have been largely rebuilt by William White. In 1674 John Ferrers was taxed on 14 hearths.

There were deer in Bashall Park in 1586 but William White preferred to grant leases for the grazing of cattle.

(Wards 9/98/fols.42-3 and 575/120. BL, Additional Charter 19,546. C.5/47/25.)

BATLEY   Agbrigg and Morley

A clothing village to the north of Dewsbury. The parish of Batley contained several villages, including Gildersome and Morley which had dependent chapels. Morley is separately noticed. 1674: 91 households in Batley, 31 in Churwell and 45 in Gildersome. 1676: 683 persons aged 16 or more, including 80 Protestant dissenters (parish). These dissenters were probably concentrated in the chapelry of Morley.

Joseph Howard, who was vicar of Batley in the years 1602 to 1635, was a suspected Puritan. At the visitation of 1632 it was alleged that he had substituted psalms in place of canticles but no action was taken against him. His successor, Roger Audesley, was ejected in 1655 by the West Riding commissioners for the removal of scandalous ministers. In 1660 he was reinstated.

Church All Saints: Decorated and Perpendicular.

Schools There had been a school at Batley in the reign of Elizabeth. About the beginning of James I's reign a fee-paying school was established there.

In 1612 William Lee, a Cambridgeshire clergyman with local ties, founded a free grammar school at Batley for the children of inhabitants of the whole parish. As an endowment he settled lands for the support of a master who was to teach English, Greek and Latin. The first governors of the school included Sir John Savile of Howley Hall in Morley and Edward Copley of Batley Hall.

Principal family Copley of Batley Hall. Estate revenue: £500 a year (1630).

The Copleys were a family of ancient lineage who owned the manor and impropriate rectory of Batley.

Alvery Copley (c.1590-1631), who succeeded his father in 1616, enhanced his social status by marrying a daughter of Sir John Savile (later Lord Savile) of Howley Hall. He also bought the estate of a neighbouring landowner, William Eland of Carlinghow Hall, whose family had lived there for nearly 300 years.

His son John (1618-1643) was made a ward of the Crown. The financial exactions of the Court of Wards were not unduly heavy but in 1640 he was forced to sell some of his outlying property. He died of wounds which he received while fighting for the king.

The heir to the estate was his brother Edward (1622-1676) who served as a royalist captain in both Civil Wars. Oliver Heywood relates that after the Restoration he was a violent persecutor of nonconformists and that he was involved in a scandal over the collection of hearth tax money which cost him 'thousands of pounds'.

His son Edward (1666-1716) was the last member of the family to live at Batley Hall.

Batley Hall A Tudor mansion with medieval features. It contained a private chapel.

Among the rooms listed in an inventory of 1644 were the hall, the great chamber, the great parlour and the chapel parlour.

(R. A. Marchant, *The Puritans and the Church Courts in the Diocese of York 1560-1642* (1960), 255. A. G. Matthews, *Walker Revised* (1988), 389. W. K. Jordan, *The Charities of Rural England 1480-1660* (1961), 331. Wards 9/98/fo.134 and 126/fols.404-5. Oliver Heywood, *His Autobiography, Diaries, Anecdote and Event Books* (ed. J. Horsfall Turner) (1882-5), i, 362. YASRS, xv (1893), 183-4. M. Sheard, *Records of the Parish of Batley* (1894).)

BAWTRY   Strafford and Tickhill

A village to the south-east of Doncaster which was close to the border with Nottinghamshire. It was also a chapelry within the Nottinghamshire parish of Blyth. 1674: 53 households (township of Bawtry).

In view of its position on 'the northern road' Bawtry was for most travellers coming from the Midlands or southern England the main point of entry into Yorkshire and for some it was a convenient place for an overnight stop. In 1686 its inns had 57 'guest beds' and stabling for 69 horses.

It also benefited economically from its situation on the River Idle which was used by commercial traffic as a means of access to the River Trent and ultimately to the port of Hull. Such commodities as hardware from Sheffield and lead from Derbyshire were taken to a riverside depot at Bawtry where they were loaded on to barges and other flat-bottomed boats. In addition, the depot handled imported goods, including wine. The tolls which were levied formed part of the revenue of the manor of Bawtry which in the reign of James I belonged to the Crown.

In his will (1640) Sir John Lister, a Hull merchant, left the manor of Bawtry to one of his younger sons, Thomas, who settled there. In 1674 his house had 22 hearths.

Church St Nicholas: Norman, Early English, Decorated and Perpendicular.

Almshouses Morton's Hospital, which had a chapel associated with it, had apparently been founded in the 13th century. In the 17th century it housed two poor widows.

(PRO, W.O.30/48, fo.205. E.134/21 James I/Easter 12.)

BEESTON   Agbrigg and Morley

A village within the parish of Leeds which produced bone lace and straw hats and also had rich coal deposits. In the Commonwealth period there were said to be 150 communicants. 1674: 80 households.

Church St Mary: a public chapel which was Norman in origin.

Principal families (1) Wood of Beeston Hall. Estate revenue: £650 a year (1620). Coalmining in Beeston.

In 1608 Ralph Beeston sold the manor of Beeston and later that year it was bought by Sir John Wood who settled there after disposing of his Cambridgeshire estate.

In the 1630s the family experienced a major financial crisis which entailed heavy borrowing and the rapid break-up of the estate. In 1642 the manor of Beeston, or what was left of it, was sold by trustees acting on their behalf.

Thomas Wood, who was Sir John's only surviving son, had been granted a life annuity of £120 out of the manor for his maintenance. During the Civil War he took up arms for the king. At his death in 1649 he left a daughter Isabel who was one of a number of persons with claims on the manor.

(2) Hodgson of Newhall in Beeston Park. Estate revenue: £700 a year (1654).

Christopher Hodgson, who was a legal officer of the Council in the North, was the first member of the family to take up residence in Beeston. Following his death in 1616 his son John was made a ward of the Crown.

John Hodgson (1601-1654) served as an alderman of Leeds after it acquired its new status as a corporate town. In 1642 he added to his estate by purchasing the manor of Beeston. During the Civil War he supported the king but was never in arms. He was succeeded by his son Christopher (c.1631-1660) who in 1655 sold the manor of Beeston to Leonard Scurr, the assistant minister at Beeston chapel, for £600. Scurr, who later married Thomas Wood's daughter, was ejected in 1662 on account of his nonconformity and took up a new occupation as a colliery manager at Beeston. In 1680 he was killed in a fierce struggle with thieves who had broken into his house. They then murdered his mother and their maid.

Shortly after the death of Christopher Hodgson, who left an infant son, the Newhall property was sold to Gervase Nevile.

Beeston Hall According to John Hodgson one of his mansion houses was burnt down by Scottish troops in the Civil War. This was probably Beeston Hall since Newhall was the only major building in Beeston to feature in the hearth tax returns of Charles II's reign.

Newhall A house built by Christopher Hodgson towards the end of the 16th century. In 1664 and 1674 Gervase Nevile was taxed on 17 hearths.

(C.10/49/143; 409/11; and 477/114. G. E. Kirk, *Beeston, Leeds: its ancient parochial chapelry, chapel and present St Mary the Virgin* (1936).)

BENTHAM   Staincliffe and Ewecross

A large village consisting of High and Lower Bentham in the north-west corner of the riding. The parish of Bentham included the village of Ingleton which had a medieval chapel. 1674: 137 households in Bentham, 72 in Ingleton and 37 in Ingleton Fell.

In 1602 it was said that the commons of Bentham and Ingleton covered an area of 6000 acres, of which 2000 had been 'improved'.

During the reign of Elizabeth the Cholmleys of Whitby had been involved in a long-running dispute with the copyhold tenants of their manors of Bentham and Ingleton who had resorted to litigation in defence of their interests. The main point at issue had been the size of the fines which were a more important source of revenue for the landlord than the copyhold rents payable.

Sir Gerrard Lowther was related to the Cholmleys and as a lawyer had been of considerable assistance to them in their legal battle with the tenants. At the beginning of the 17th century he acquired the manors of Bentham and Ingleton and continued to maintain that the copyholders were merely tenants at will.

Following his death the manor of Ingleton passed to his brother William who took up residence there. He was succeeded by his son Richard who was a barrister of Gray's Inn.

In 1642 Richard Lowther mortgaged the manor of Ingleton which by then contained a small colliery. When the Civil War broke out he and his son Gerrard threw in their lot with the king and as a result the estate was sequestered. After the Restoration the manor came into the possession of Anthony Bouch who was a major creditor.

George Fox the Quaker leader noted in his journal that when he and his captors arrived at Bentham in 1665 they were met by 'many troopers and a marshall; and many of ye gentry of ye country was come in and aboundans of people to stare at mee'.

Church St John, Lower Bentham: Perpendicular.

Schools William Walker, who was master of Giggleswick School in the years 1648 to 1656, taught for a time at Bentham.

A school had been established at Ingleton in 1571. Probably this was the school which was in existence there in the reign of Charles II.

(J. T. Cliffe, *The Yorkshire Gentry* (1969), 41-2. C.2/Elizabeth/I3/72. C.54/3289. C.10/93/86. N. Penney (ed.), *The Journal of George Fox* (1911), ii, 93.)

BILBROUGH   Ainsty

A small village to the north-east of Tadcaster. There was no other village within the parish. 1665: 27 households (township of Bilbrough). 1676: 60 persons aged 16 or more (parish).

The manor of Bilbrough and the patronage rights belonged to the Fairfaxes of Denton.

In his poem on Bilbrough hill, which was dedicated to Thomas Lord Fairfax the parliamentarian general, Andrew Marvell wrote

> See how the arched Earth does here
> Rise in a perfect Hemisphere!
> The stiffest Compass could not strike
> A Line more circular and like;
> Nor softest Pensel draw a Brow
> So equal as this Hill does Bow.
> It seems as for a Model laid,
> And that the World by it was made.

In 1671 Fairfax was buried in the church.

Church St James: Perpendicular.

The minister was a perpetual curate.

(Andrew Marvell, *Upon the Hill and Grove at Bill-borow*.)

BILTON   Ainsty

A village on the road between York and Wetherby. The parish of Bilton included the villages of Bickerton and Tockwith. 1665: 40 households in Bilton, 23 in Bickerton and 48 in Tockwith.

Christopher Nodding, who served as vicar of Bilton between 1631 and 1657, was a Puritan who appears to have remained conformable before the time of the Civil War. In 1640 he also became vicar of Wighill. Significantly, the Stapletons of Wighill Hall had a lease of the prebend of Bilton.

The Snawsells of Bilton Hall were a gentry family of moderate income. In 1645 Hugh Snawsell (1582-1661) was named as a commissioner for taking accounts on behalf of Parliament in the city of York and the Ainsty.

In the early 17th century the manor of Bickerton belonged to the Yaxleys of Yaxley in Suffolk who were a predominantly Catholic family. In 1653 Charles Yaxley related in a Chancery suit that the manor was worth £400 a year.

Church St Helen: Norman and Perpendicular.

The parish was subject to the peculiar jurisdiction of a Prebendary of York.

(R. A. Marchant, *The Puritans and the Church Courts in the Diocese of York 1560-1642* (1960), 265. C.5/24/140.)

BINGLEY   Skyrack

A clothing town on the River Aire to the north of Bradford. The parish of Bingley included the village of Morton. According to a Commonwealth survey there were 1000 communicants in the parish in the early 1650s. 1674: 228 households in Bingley and 57 in Morton.

A charter of 1212 had conferred the right to hold a weekly market but it is unclear whether this right was exercised in the 17th century.

In the Civil War the inhabitants of Bingley embraced the cause of Parliament. In 1642 and 1643 reinforcements were sent from Bradford to assist in the defence of the town against royalist attacks.

In 1686 the West Riding magistrates gave order that Bingley Bridge should be rebuilt at a cost of £270. This apparently involved the replacement of the old wooden bridge with one constructed of stone.

Churches All Saints: Perpendicular.

In 1695 a Presbyterian chapel was founded and in 1698 there were also five licensed meeting places for other Protestant dissenters.

School A free grammar school founded in 1529. During the 16th and 17th centuries there were a number of voluntary contributions for the purpose of endowing the school.

One of the major benefactors was William Wooler, a York merchant who was a native of Bingley.

In 1604 a schoolhouse was bought.

A Chancery decree of 1622 established a committee of 'governors and feoffees for the school and poor of Bingley'.

In 1637 a start was made on the building of a new schoolhouse in a corner of the churchyard and this work continued during the Civil War.

(J. Horsfall Turner, *Ancient Bingley* (1897). E. E. Dodd, *A History of Bingley Grammar School 1529-1929* (1929). E. E. Dodd, *Bingley* (1958).)

BIRKIN   Barkston Ash

A small village between Pontefract and Selby. The parish of Birkin contained several villages, including Chapel Haddlesey which had a dependent chapel. 1674: 22 households in Birkin, 18 in Chapel Haddlesey, 23 in Hirst Courtney, 18 in Temple Hirst and 26 in West Haddlesey.

Church St Mary: Norman with some later features.

Principal family Cressy of Birkin Hall. Estate revenue: £1000 a year (1625).

Everingham Cressy (c.1580-1644) was a recusant in the early years of the 17th century but he soon conformed. In 1631 he mortgaged considerable property in Birkin as security for a loan of £2500. After he defaulted on his interest payments there was a legal dispute over the ownership of the premises. Neither he nor his son Everingham appears to have played any part in the Civil War despite the amount of military activity in the area.

The Cressys owned the impropriate rectory of Birkin and Everingham Cressy (1612-1671) served for some years as the minister. In 1663, however, it was reported that he had ceased to perform his duties and no longer came to church. His son Everingham (1641-1679) was faced with serious financial problems which may have been inherited. He was beginning to sell land as early as 1672 and in 1678 he mortgaged the estate. His brother Gervase, who succeeded him, was imprisoned for debt in York Castle and died there in 1682. Four years later the manor of Birkin was put up for sale.

Birkin Hall Among the rooms listed in an inventory of 1679 were the hall, the great chamber, the best parlour, the withdrawing room and the chaplain's chamber. There is also a reference to 40,000 bricks which suggests that some major building work may have been planned.

(C.10/141/79 and 143/111. C.7/382/71. C.8/8/33 and 42/103. C.33/264/ fo.418. C.38/225/7 May and 30 June 1686. J. N. Worsfold, *History of Haddlesey: Its Past and Present* (1894).)

BIRSTALL   Agbrigg and Morley

A clothing village in the township of Gomersal which was situated to the north of Dewsbury. The parish of Birstall, which was one of the largest in the West Riding, contained a number of villages, including Cleckheaton and Tong which had medieval chapels. Tong is separately noticed. 1674: 184 households in Gomersal (including Birstall), 64 in Cleckheaton, 55 in Drighlington and Adwalton, 51 in Heckmondwike, 31 in Hunsworth, 110 in Liversedge and 54 in Wyke. 1676: 3000 persons aged 16 or more, including 300 Protestant dissenters (parish).

In the early years of the 17th century some landowners and their tenants were beginning to make inroads into the wastes and commons of Birstall, Gomersal and Heckmondwike and their enclosing activities led to boundary disputes. In 1607 two gentlemen who were involved in a quarrel over their respective property rights agreed that the matter should be settled by arbitration.

For a time fairs were held at Adwalton but it was alleged in Exchequer suits in Charles I's reign that unfair competition from Bradford was putting their future in doubt.

Liversedge was a coalmining area. In 1639 the inhabitants were ordered to fill up the coal pits on Liversedge Common.

In 1641 it was reported that a bridge near Birstall parish church which was known as the church bridge was 'ruinous and in great decay'. The West Riding magistrates decided that the cost of repairing it should be met by the inhabitants of the parish. In January 1642, however, they received information that four men were contemptuously refusing to contribute.

Dr Richard Marsh, who became vicar of Birstall in 1614, was a member of the Northern High Commission and a close ally of Richard Neile the Laudian Archbishop of York. Early on in the Civil War he was taken prisoner by the parliamentarians and deprived of his livings of Birstall and Halifax. At Birstall he was replaced by his curate, Edward Harrison, whose Puritan outlook appears to have been more in accord with the religious aspirations of his parishioners.

In June 1643 a royalist force routed the Fairfaxes on Adwalton Moor and went on to capture Bradford.

John Batt of Oakwell Hall served as a royalist captain in the Civil War but surrendered to Ferdinando Lord Fairfax in 1644. Five years later he settled wth most of his family in Virginia, though his eldest son was residing at Oakwell Hall after the Restoration.

In 1646 the parliamentary authorities received a petition from some of the inhabitants of the parish on behalf of their minister, Edward Harrison. They related that following the royalist victory on Adwalton Moor his house had been plundered and he had been forced to flee with his wife and family into Cheshire. They also claimed that the parish had sustained losses amounting to £3000 as a result of the activities of the royalist troops and the charges arising from the presence of the Scottish army. In a similar petition which was forwarded from Cleckheaton it was stressed that the inhabitants of the chapelry had always been loyal to Parliament.

In 1669 the ecclesiastical authorities were informed that at Cleckheaton the dissenters were as numerous as those who attended church. Here Joseph Dawson, an ejected minister, conducted Presbyterian services in his own house. In contrast, there was an Independent congregation at Heckmondwike which in 1674 elected Josias Holdsworth as its minister.

Church St Peter: Norman, Decorated and Perpendicular.

Schools William Ermystead, who was vicar of Birstall in the years 1537 to 1558, was primarily responsible for the establishment of a grammar school there. In 1556 he settled land for the support of a master and also assigned the sum of £100 for the building of a schoolhouse. Among the masters in the 17th century were William Musgrave (who was the curate of Tong chapel), John Castley and Richard Atkinson.

During the years 1670 to 1672 John Baskerville kept a private school at Drighlington while serving as curate of Rastrick chapel. In 1672 he was appointed master of Wakefield Grammar School.

Not long afterwards James Margetson the Archbishop of Armagh founded a free grammar school at Drighlington where he had been born. He built a schoolhouse together with a house for the master and in his will (1678) he provided an endowment of £60 a year. The first master was John Dyson who died in 1701.

(YAS Library, Bretton Hall MSS, Bundle 15. E.134/5 Charles I/Michaelmas 22 and 6 Charles I/Michaelmas 7. *YASRS*, liv (1915), 107, 327, 349, 352. *Calendar, Committee for the Advance of Money*, 911. *Calendar, Committee for Compounding*, 945-6. YAS, *Parish Register Series*, cxlvi (1983), 34, 239. H. C. Cradock, *A History of the Ancient Parish of Birstall, Yorkshire* (1933). H. Ashwell Cadman, *Gomersal Past and Present* (1930). J. Sprittles, *History of Oakwell Hall and Manor* (1947).)

BISHOPTHORPE Ainsty

A village to the south of York which was situated on the west bank of the River Ouse. The parish of Bishopthorpe included part of Dringhouses. 1665: 42 households in Bishopthorpe and 29 in Dringhouses. 1676: 88 persons aged 16 or more (parish).

The Ouse 'marches by Bishops-Thorp, that is, the Bishop's Village' (William Camden). The Archbishop of York's palace had been built in the 13th century and enlarged in the late 15th century. Immediately after the Restoration the Archbishop, Accepted Frewen, commissioned a major rebuilding programme. In 1665 there were 27 taxable hearths.

Church St Andrew: a medieval church dating from the 13th century or earlier.

In 1619 the churchwardens reported that 'Their church-yard and church are all ruinous and like utterly to be ruinated by reason of the undacion of the water'. They were ordered to carry out necessary repairs.

School There was a schoolmaster at Bishopthorpe in 1693.

(*YAJ*, xv (1900), 229.)

BOLTON BY BOWLAND   Staincliffe and Ewecross

A village in Ribblesdale near the border with Lancashire. There were no other villages within the parish of Bolton. 1674: 87 households (township of Bolton). 1676: 340 persons aged 16 or more (parish of Bolton).

In 1657 Ambrose Pudsay, the squire of Bolton, John Shaw the minister and other inhabitants agreed that they would make bequests to the common stock for the relief of the poor within the parish.

Church St Peter and St Paul: 13th century and Perpendicular. The Pudsays had a family chapel on the south side of the choir.

School A school existed in 1617.

Principal family Pudsay of Bolton Hall (and Barforth Hall, North Riding). Estate revenue: £1000 a year (1627); £1300 a year (1659). Mining of lead and coal at Rimington.

William Pudsay (c.1560-1629) was the recusant head of what in his day was a largely Catholic family. According to a local tradition he mined silver ore at Rimington and minted coins called Pudsay shillings.

The quarrel which he had with his eldest son Ambrose (1595-1629) may have been occasioned at least in part by differences over religion. In 1616 Ambrose married Rosamund Ramsden who was the daughter of a Protestant squire, William Ramsden of Longley Hall. In legal proceedings begun in 1622 William Pudsay alleged that through Ramsden's influence his son had behaved in a disobedient and unnatural way towards his parents and had been very prodigal and careless in his financial affairs.

After the death of William Pudsay the family abandoned the Catholic faith. His grandson Ambrose (1629-1674) was for many years a ward of the Crown. As a supporter of the royalist cause he joined in Sir George Booth's rising in 1659. During the early years of Charles II's reign he sold the manors of Barforth and Rimington and mortgaged the Bolton estate. In 1673 it was alleged in a Chancery suit that he had been attempting to defraud his creditors by making secret and fraudulent conveyances of his property. As a final resort he went over to Ireland where he served for a time as a regular army officer.

His son Ambrose (1655-1716) managed to keep possession of the remainder of the estate, mainly no doubt through the benevolence of his father-in-law Henry Marsden who was a major creditor.

Bolton Hall 'Bolton Hall standeth very pleasantly amongst sweet woods and fruit tr[ees]' (Roger Dodsworth). A three-storeyed medieval house with Tudor additions. There was a domestic chapel of Catholic provenance.

In 1674 Ambrose Pudsay was taxed on eight hearths.

(*The Pudsay Deeds*, YASRS, lvi (1916). *YPRS*, xix (1904). C.2/James I/P27/541. C10/124/53. C.33/252/fo.603.)

BOLTON PERCY   Ainsty

A village near Tadcaster. The parish of Bolton Percy included the villages of Appleton Roebuck and Colton and the hamlet of Steeton. The latter had been depopulated in the 15th century. 1665: 32 households in Bolton Percy, 61 in Appleton Roebuck and 27 in Colton. 1676: 412 persons aged 16 or more (parish of Bolton Percy).

Church All Saints: consecrated in 1424. The burial place of Ferdinando Lord Fairfax (for his family see under Denton).

School A school was established at Bolton Percy in 1617.

Principal families (1) Fairfax of Steeton Hall. Estate revenue: £1400 a year (1607); £650 a year (1628).

Sir Philip Fairfax (1587-1613) was made a ward of the Crown following his father's death in 1603. As a courtier he acquired extravagant tastes which led to heavy borrowing. He also neglected his estate which was left in the hands of a steward, Ralph Baltrus, whose primary concern was self-enrichment. An exchange of manors with his kinsman Sir Thomas Fairfax of Denton, who was a major creditor, resulted in a significant reduction in the size of his estate.

His son Edmund (1609-1628) also became a ward of the Crown. He left no issue and was succeeded by his brother Sir William (1610-1644) who served for some years as a professional soldier and only settled at Steeton in 1641.

On the outbreak of the Civil War Sir William took up arms for Parliament and raised a regiment of foot amongst his tenantry. As a colonel under the Earl of Essex he fought at the battle of Edgehill and subsequently commanded troops at the battle of Marston Moor. In September 1644 he died of wounds which he received while engaged in the relief of Montgomery Castle.

Robert Fairfax, who succeeded to the estate in 1694 on the death of his brother William, served as a naval commander and eventually attained the rank of Vice Admiral. He moved the family seat from Steeton to Newton Kyme.

(2) Moyser of North Hall, Appleton. Estate revenue: £750 a year (1640).

Thomas Moyser (1580-1643) was one of the leading opponents of the knighthood composition scheme launched in 1630 but finally submitted in 1635. He and his eldest son were involved in protracted litigation with the Eastoft family over the descent of an East Riding estate.

In the early stages of the Civil War he was in London where he was preoccupied with his legal affairs. Shortly before his death he heard that his mansion houses in Yorkshire had been plundered, his rents seized and stables, barns and tenements set on fire.

As a minor his son James (1629-1695) was subjected to the financial exactions of the Court of Wards. In 1650 he married Dame Frances Reresby, a widow who brought with her a jointure of £450 a year. His stepson Sir John Reresby described him as a 'very hansome gentleman' and observed that he was 'kind and just' to his wife and her children.

He lived mainly at Beverley where he had built a large house for himself.

Steeton Hall A moated 14th century mansion which was enlarged and partly rebuilt by Sir William Fairfax during the years 1594 to 1597. The Fairfaxes had a domestic chapel where their children were usually baptised.

In the early 17th century there are references to a park known as the New Park.

North Hall, Appleton In 1665, when the house was occupied by a relative, there were only five taxable hearths.

Nun Appleton Hall When Thomas Lord Fairfax (1612-1671) retired from public life in 1650 he settled at Nun Appleton Hall. Andrew Marvell composed his poem *Upon Appleton House* while employed as tutor to Fairfax's daughter Mary in the early 1650s when the plans for a new house had still to be realised. A few years later Sir Thomas Widdrington was writing that Fairfax (to whom he was related) 'hath of late built a very goodly and fair house'; and Fairfax himself recorded the event in some verse. The new house consisted of a central block surmounted by a cupola and two projecting wings.

In 1665 Fairfax was taxed on no fewer than 33 hearths.

Ralph Thoresby wrote in 1711 that the house had been 'a noble palace' but added that it had been 'abundantly too large'.

Fairfax had a domestic chapel where his household chaplain, Richard Stretton, conducted nonconformist services which were frequented by many neighbouring families.

Adjoining the house was a large park which was stocked with 300 head of deer.

(M. W. Beresford, 'The Lost Villages of Yorkshire', *YAJ*, xxxviii (1955), 225, 227. G. W. Johnson (ed.), *The Fairfax Correspondence*, vol.i (1848). C.54/ 2113 and 2129. Wards 5/49. Wards 13/130, no pagination. HMC, *Fifth Report*, Appendix, 76, 87. Sir Thomas Widdrington, *Analecta Eboracensia* (ed. C. Caine). (1897), 136. Marjorie J. Harrison, *Four Ainsty Townships: The History of Bolton Percy, Appleton Roebuck, Colton and Steeton 1066-1875* (2000).)

BOLTON UPON DEARNE Strafford and Tickhill

A village on the River Dearne between Barnsley and Doncaster. The parish of Bolton upon Dearne included the hamlet of Goldthorpe. 1674: 65 households (township of Bolton). 1676: 200 persons aged 16 or more (parish).

For most of the 17th century the manor and impropriate rectory of Bolton and the manor of Goldthorpe belonged to the Jackson family of Hickleton. They had a colliery in Goldthorpe: between 12 November 1681 and 3 February 1683 the gross profits amounted to £646 and the expenditure to £395.

Shortly before the Restoration Nathan Denton was ordained as a Presbyterian minister and assigned the living of Bolton. After his ejection in 1662 he was able to preach in Hickleton church for about a year through the patronage of Dame Catherine Jackson. In 1689 he was granted permission to use his house in Bolton for nonconformist worship.

Church St Andrew: Norman, Decorated and Perpendicular.

(C.38/217/12 December 1684. A. G. Matthews, *Calamy Revised* (1934), 163.)

BOROUGHBRIDGE Claro

A market town on the River Ure, a major road junction and a chapelry within the parish of Aldborough. Because of its position it was designated as a post town and had its own postmaster. 1674: 49 households.

Boroughbridge is 'a little town so call'd from the bridge there which is made of stone' (William Camden). In 1639 the bridge, which spanned the River Ure, was reported to be in 'great decay and ruyne'.

The river at Boroughbridge 'affords very good fish, salmon and codffish and plenty of crawffish' (Celia Fiennes, 1697).

A charter of 1310 had conferred the right to hold three fairs every year and a weekly market on Saturdays. In the 17th century Boroughbridge still had its Saturday market.

In a petition which they submitted to the Commons in 1673 the burgesses and boroughmen of Boroughbridge related that the town was 'an ancient Borough by prescription and not by Charter, wherein there is no Established Government, or any Mayor or Bailif'.

Boroughbridge was a parliamentary borough which sent two members to Parliament. The electorate consisted of around sixty burgage holders.

In 1604 the town suffered badly from an outbreak of the plague. The vicar of Aldborough noted in his register that it had resulted in the deaths of at least eighty persons.

The prehistoric monoliths near Boroughbridge attracted considerable interest. In 1695 Edmund Gibson referred to them as the Pyramids or Devil's Arrows while in 1703 Ralph Thoresby described them as 'the celebrated Roman Obelisks, commonly called the Devil's arrows'.

Church St James: a public chapel rebuilt in the 13th century but retaining Norman features.

School A public grammar school which was medieval in origin. In 1548 it was reported that the school was housed in the chapel.

(*YASRS*, liv (1915), 157-8. Sir Thomas Lawson-Tancred, *Records of a Yorkshire Manor* (1937), 122, 204. T. S. Turner, *History of Aldborough and Boroughbridge* (1853). Sir Thomas Lawson-Tancred, 'Parliamentary History of Aldborough and Boroughbridge', *YAJ*, xxvii (1924). Lady M. E. Lawson-Tancred, *Guide Book to the Antiquities of Aldborough and Boroughbridge* (1927).)

BOWLAND FOREST   Staincliffe and Ewecross

A sparsely populated region adjoining the border with Lancashire. For fiscal purposes it was treated as a single administrative area. 1674: 101 households.

Principal family Parker of Browsholme Hall. Estate revenue: £500 a year (1630).

The Parkers held the office of bowbearer of the Forest of Bowland and were responsible for the management and protection of the royal deer.

Thomas Parker (c.1555-1635) added to the estate and carried out improvements to his ancestral mansion. At his death he left a substantial personal estate which was said to have been worth at least £5000.

His son Edward (1602-1667) may have hoped that the rural seclusion of Browsholme Hall would enable him to remain aloof from the Civil War but he was marked down as a man who had royalist sympathies. In May 1643 he was apprehended by parliamentarian troops and taken to Bradford where he was forced to buy his freedom.

In 1650 he was involved in litigation with his sister Jennett Caryer who claimed that he owed her money.

Browsholme Hall An early Tudor building which was re-fronted in 1603 with red sandstone. For the design of this façade Thomas Parker employed the York architect Thomas Holt. A three-storeyed house with gables.

In 1674 Thomas Parker (1631-1695) was taxed on nine hearths.

(*Description of Browsholme Hall, in the West Riding of the County of York* (1815). C.8/123/33.)

## BOWLING	Agbrigg and Morley

A village within the parish of Bradford. 1674: 72 households. There was an outbreak of the plague in 1645.

Principal family Tempest of Bolling Hall (and Bracewell Hall in Craven). Estate revenue: £1000 a year (1601); £1400 a year (1639); £700 a year (1651). Coalmines in Bowling and Allerton.

The Tempests had owned the Bolling Hall estate since 1497.

Sir Richard Tempest (1575-1639) inherited a large estate and considerably increased his income by acquiring a long lease of the rectory of Bradford. According to his wife, Dame Elizabeth, he disapproved of the marriages of both their daughters on the grounds that the husbands failed to satisfy his financial and social criteria.

When his son Richard (1621-1657) married Frances Clifton in 1636 it was agreed that she should have an allowance of £135 a year during his lifetime and a jointure of £600 a year after his death. By marrying so early he was able to escape the attentions of the Court of Wards when he succeeded to the estate.

During the Civil War Richard Tempest served as a royalist colonel but in the summer of 1644 he surrendered to Ferdinando Lord Fairfax. He was heavily fined in 1646 and again in 1649 after he had once more taken up arms. Partly for this reason and partly on account of his extravagance and gambling he found himself in severe financial difficulties. In 1649 he sold the manor of Bowling, together with corn mills in Bradford, for £7180.

After quarrelling with his wife and daughter he went over to France where according to his own testimony he lived in a sad condition. On returning to England in 1657 he was arrested for debt in London and shortly afterwards he died in prison. He was the last of the male line.

Henry Savile, who bought the manor of Bowling in 1649, sold it to Francis Lindley in 1668. The Lindleys lived mainly in Manchester and in the late 17th century Bolling Hall was usually occupied by their steward.

Bolling Hall A 15th century house which was extended and improved by Sir Richard Tempest in the early 17th century. In 1674 there were 19 taxable hearths.

The Tempests had two parks, Bowling Park and Denholme Park where they kept deer.

(BL, Additional MSS 40,670. Mrs E. B. Tempest, 'The Tempest family at Bowling Hall'. *Bradford Antiquary*, New Series, i (1900). C.2/Charles I/WW 60/44. W. Cudworth, *Histories of Bolton and Bowling* (1891).)

## BRACEWELL	Staincliffe and Ewecross

A village to the south-west of Skipton. There was no other village within the parish. 1674: 29 households (township of Bracewell). 1676: 120 persons aged 16 or more (parish).

The manor of Bracewell belonged to the Tempests of Bolling Hall, near Bradford, until the middle of the 17th century. When Richard Tempest compounded for his estate with the parliamentary authorities he put the value of the manor at £173 a year which included demesne lands worth £148 a year. The Tempests sometimes resided at Bracewell Hall but by the early 18th century the house was in ruins.

Church St Michael: Norman and Perpendicular.

(S.P.23/ccxi/755, 759.)

BRADFORD   Agbrigg and Morley

A market town whose main source of employment was the manufacture of textile goods. The extensive parish of Bradford contained a considerable number of villages, many of them heavily populated, which were engaged in the same type of economic activity. These included Haworth, Thornton and Wibsey which had dependent chapels. The chapel at Wibsey, which owed its existence to the efforts of the local community, was consecrated in 1636. The village of Bowling is separately noticed. 1674: 222 households in Bradford, 90 in Allerton cum Wilsden, 84 in Clayton, 53 in Eccleshill, 183 in Haworth, 59 in Heaton cum Clayton, 132 in Hortons Ambo (Great and Little Horton), 65 in Manningham, 124 in North Bierley, 31 in Shipley and 106 in Thornton. The main streets of Bradford included Kirkgate and Westgate. 1676: 4414 persons aged 16 or more (parish).

Bradford is 'a towne that makes great store of Turkey cushions and carpetts' (John Aston, 1639).

Bradford is 'a great towne and wealthy, they havinge a greate trade of makinge Turkieworke stooles, chaires, and carpitts' (Life of Marmaduke Rawdon, entry for 1664).

The parish of Bradford was a strongly Protestant area. In the early 17th century the parish church had several Puritan ministers: John Okell who served as vicar during the years 1615 to 1639; David Ellison who was one of the curates; and Jeremiah Collier who was employed as a lecturer. In March 1642 twelve men and women were charged with assaulting Nathan Bentley, who was described as a preacher of God's Word, while a service was in progress. The cause of this disturbance remains obscure but it was presumably fuelled by religious fervour.

On the eve of the Civil War there was an outbreak of the plague.

When the war began Bradford was under parliamentarian control. 'In this war Bradford was deeply engaged; the generality of the town and parish, and the towns about, stood up for the Parliament, and it was made a little garrison … and the inhabitants were firm to the cause, and to one another' (Joseph Lister of Bradford). In December 1642 royalist troops besieged and bombarded the town but withdrew when Sir Thomas Fairfax arrived with a relief force. About this time Francis Corker the vicar of Bradford fled to Pontefract where he acted as one of the chaplains who preached to the royalist troops there. As a result his parsonage house was pillaged and his living was sequestered. In July 1643 the Earl of Newcastle marched on Bradford which was again bombarded. His troops seized and plundered the town and set fire to some of the houses. Sir Thomas Fairfax, who had been appointed governor, managed to escape.

By the end of 1644 Bradford was again in the hands of the parliamentarians. In 1645 there was a further outbreak of the plague which resulted in many deaths.

As a consequence of the Civil War Bradford entered into a long period of economic decline.

In 1669 it was reported that in the parish of Bradford there were many conventicles of Quakers, Anabaptists, Independents and Presbyterians and that the participants were mainly 'the middle sort of people'.

Abraham Sharp (1653-1742), the celebrated mathematician and scientific instrument maker, was born at Horton Hall in Little Horton. His father, John Sharp, had served as financial secretary to Sir Thomas Fairfax. John Sharp (c.1645-1714), who was a native of Bradford, was Archbishop of York from 1691 until his death. The two families may have been distantly related.

Church St Peter: mainly Perpendicular with a chapel built in 1615.

The patronage rights belonged to the Crown.

During the Civil War some of the parliamentarian soldiers were stationed in the church and on the steeple which was hung with wool packs. Despite the royalist bombardments the church appears to have escaped serious damage.

Schools The grammar school at Bradford had been founded in 1548. In 1662 a royal charter was granted in which it was formally designated as 'The Free Grammar School of King Charles the Second at Bradford'. During the 17th century the masters included William Hastead, William Wilcocke, Gervase Worrall, Jeremiah Crossley, Anthony Coates, John Sturdy and Thomas Wood.

Following the death of William Wilcocke in 1635 Archbishop Neile of York put in his own nominee, Gervase Worrall, without consulting the parishioners. This eventually led to the submission of a petition to the Long Parliament.

In 1637 Christopher Scott, a Yorkshireman who was rector of Chastleton in Oxfordshire, founded a free grammar school at Haworth. The master, who was allowed a stipend of £18 a year, was required to teach Greek and Latin.

During the reign of Charles II schools were established at Thornton and Wilsden; and in the same period there are references to schoolmasters at Horton and Wibsey.

(R. A. Marchant, *The Puritans and the Church Courts in the Diocese of York 1560-1642* (1960), 112-13, 239, 245, 266. YASRS, liv (1915), 367. *Autobiography of Joseph Lister of Bradford, 1627-1709* (ed. T. Wright) (1842). A. G. Matthews, *Walker Revised* (1988), 391. YASRS, lxi (1920), 151. W. K. Jordan, *The Charities of Rural England 1480-1660* (1961), 337. J. James, *The History and Topography of Bradford* (1841) and

Continuation and Additions to the History of Bradford, and the Parish (1866). W. Claridge, *Origin and History of the Bradford Grammar School* (1882). H. Hird, *Bradford in History* (1968). J. Horsfall Turner, *Haworth Past and Present* (1879).)

BRAITHWELL   Strafford and Tickhill

A village to the north-west of Tickhill. The parish of Braithwell included the village of Bramley. 1674: 55 households in Braithwell and 24 in Bramley. 1676: 210 persons aged 16 or more (parish).

Since 1289 Braithwell had enjoyed the right to hold a weekly market and an annual fair.

During the early 17th century Braithwell had two Puritan-minded ministers, Richard Clark and Thomas Bosvile. The latter, who served as vicar from 1638 until his death in 1674, was the head of a minor gentry family which had property in Braithwell. His son Thomas succeeded him as minister.

Church St James: Norman, Early English, Decorated and Perpendicular.

School John Gleadall, who died in 1688, left a modest sum for the teaching of four poor children.

In 1693 a school was founded at Braithwell by John Bosvile, a younger brother of Thomas Bosvile who was instituted as vicar in 1638.

(R. A. Marchant, *The Puritans and the Church Courts in the Diocese of York 1560-1642* (1960), 231, 239.)

BRAMHAM   Barkston Ash

A village to the west of Tadcaster which was situated on the main northern road. The parish of Bramham included the hamlet of Oglethorpe and part of the village of Clifford; the other part was in the parish of Collingham. 1674: 70 households in Bramham (including Oglethorpe) and 39 in Clifford.

In 1614 the West Riding magistrates ruled that Clifford 'shall beare a third with Bramham in all assessments to church and Kinge, and no more'.

In 1620 William Clough, the Puritan vicar of Bramham, was imprisoned by the Council in the North following allegations that he had condemned in seditious language the king's ordinances on the Sabbath, attacked the Church's ceremonial requirements and verbally abused his parishioners.

Richard Gascoigne the antiquary (1570-c.1661) lived for some years at Bramham Biggin.

Church All Saints: Norman, Early English and Perpendicular.

The parish was subject to the peculiar jurisdiction of the Dean and Chapter of York.

Principal family Oglethorpe of Oglethorpe Hall. Estate revenue: £600 a year (1627).

The financial ruin of the Oglethorpe family was comparatively rapid. In 1627 they borrowed £1000 from Robert Viscount Newark (later Earl of Kingston) and mortgaged their estate as security. Three years later William Oglethorpe, who was then in prison for debt, failed to pay the half-year interest of £40 which was due and the Earl entered into the estate. After Oglethorpe's death his son Sutton attempted to regain possession of the manors of Bramham and Clifford but the Earl refused to come to terms with him and about 1635 sold them to Sir Thomas Gascoigne of Barnbow Hall.

Some years later Sutton Oglethorpe was forced to part with the manor of Oglethorpe which was the last remnant of his estate. The purchaser was Henry Fairfax the rector of Bolton Percy.

Oglethorpe Hall In 1674 the house had 10 taxable hearths.

(*YASRS*, liv (1915), 21. *CSP Dom, 1619-23*, 128-9, 187-8, 241. C.5/402/106. WYAS, Leeds, Gascoigne of Barnbow MSS, GC/E12/1. BL, Additional Charter 1801. C.10/34/149.)

BRAMHOPE   Skyrack

A village within the parish of Otley. 1674: 43 households.

Church A public chapel built during the Commonwealth period. In 1649 Robert Dyneley and other freeholders vested in trustees some 130 acres within the common of Bramhope for the purpose of erecting a chapel and maintaining an able and godly minister. It was the intention that the right to appoint a minister should be wholly in the hands of the trustees and four of the most godly inhabitants but after the Restoration the chapel was brought within the jurisdiction of the Church.

Principal family Dyneley of Bramhope Hall. Estate revenue: £800 a year (1617). A fulling mill in Pool.

Sir Robert Dyneley (1578-1617) was heavily involved in litigation. In 1616 he accused William Arthington of Arthington Hall of undermining his property rights by enclosing a great part of the common of Bramhope. In a Chancery bill of 1619 his widow, Dame Olive, described him as 'a playne and simple gentleman, ignorant and without any experience what belonged to suits in lawe' and alleged that his solicitor, William Slater, had been guilty of 'deepe and Covetous extorcion'. Sir Robert, she related, had left debts amounting to £1000 and for a time she had been forced to give up housekeeping and live with her sister-in-law.

Their son John (1606-1628) was made a ward of the Crown. In his will (1628) he settled considerable property (in particular the East Riding manor of Duggleby) on his only child, Olive, but his brother Robert (1607-1689) argued that he was entitled to all or most of the estate by right of entail. In the end the Court of Wards ruled in favour of Olive Dyneley who eventually married Thomas Croft.

Robert Dyneley was left with a modest estate which mainly consisted of the manor of Bramhope. He was a zealous Puritan who served as a parliamentarian captain in the Civil War. In 1654 he was appointed as one of the West Riding commissioners for the ejection of scandalous ministers. After the Restoration his house was 'a common receptacle' for nonconformist ministers, among them Oliver Heywood who regularly preached there.

Bramhope Hall A small manor-house which was Tudor in origin. In 1628 it was alleged that during John Dyneley's minority his mother had allowed the house to decay.

In 1674 Robert Dyneley was taxed on eight hearths.

(C.3/306/92 and 96. C.8/14/30; 106/127; and 107/58. C.22/775/16. Wards 9/567/fo.181. Wards 13/130, no pagination.)

BRAYTON   Barkston Ash

A village to the south of Selby. The parish of Brayton contained several villages, including Barlow and Gateforth which had dependent chapels. In the 17th century Barlow was usually spelt 'Barley'. 1674: 45 households in Brayton, 38 in Barlow, 29 in Burn, 45 in Gateforth, 77 in Hambleton and 23 in Thorpe Willoughby.

Church St Wilfrid: Norman, Decorated and Perpendicular.

The parish was subject to the peculiar jurisdiction of the Dean and Chapter of York.

Principal families (1) Twisleton of Barlow Hall (baronetcy 1629). Estate revenue: £500 a year (1626); £800 a year (1635).

Sir George Twisleton (1603-1635) purchased a baronetcy when the price had fallen significantly; even so, he was forced to pay £50 for his knighthood composition.

He left no issue and the manor of Barlow eventually passed to his cousin John Twisleton of Dartford in Kent (1614-1682), a parliamentarian officer who was created a baronet by Cromwell in 1657. The new owner occasionally visited Barlow but he never took up residence there. Responsibility for managing the Barlow estate and looking after the house and grounds was entrusted to a steward and bailiff.

(2) Yonge of Burn Hall. Estate revenue: £540 a year (1653).

The Yonges were a Catholic family.

Sir Andrew Yonge (c.1585-c.1657) acquired property in Northumberland and Durham through his marriage to Mary Fenwick. In 1629 he compounded for his recusancy.

Early in the Civil War he pledged financial support for the king but later denied that he had been a royalist. Two-thirds of his estate were sequestered for his recusancy.

Sir Andrew, who died in France, left no issue and the estate descended to his three surviving sisters. John Assheton, a Lancashire gentleman, bought the manor of Burn and settled there.

Barlow Hall A Tudor house with some medieval features.

Burn Hall Sir Andrew Yonge appears to have been engaged in rebuilding or enlarging the house when the Civil War broke out. In a parliamentary survey of 1653 it was noted that Burn Hall was 'builded with bricke and covered with Tile ... consisting of a Hall, a Buttery, a Kitchin, a dyninge roome wainscoted, two Chambers and three seeled Garretts over them with some other roomes thereunto adioyning ... There is some part of the said building that was never finished and the other part much defaced and broken in the time of the late Warre'.

During the reign of Charles II John Assheton undertook some building work. In 1671 it was reported that the number of hearths had been increased from six to eight.

(C.54/3049. E.134/2JamesII/Michaelmas 36. S.P.23/lviii/fo.40. C.10/468 /8.)

BRODSWORTH   Strafford and Tickhill

A village to the north-west of Doncaster. There was no other village within the parish. 1674: 51 households (township of Brodsworth). 1676: 170 persons aged 16 or more (parish).

Darcy Wentworth of Brodsworth Hall (1592-1667) was a younger brother of Sir Thomas Wentworth of North Elmsall. When Thomas Lord Wentworth ruled Ireland as Lord Deputy he served as gentleman usher of the black rod in his household. In the Civil War he sided with Parliament but does not appear to have performed any military function.

Scawsby, in the south-east corner of the parish, may have been depopulated at some stage. In 1674 there was only one house, Scawsby Hall, which was occupied by Dame Mary Adams, the widow of Sir William Adams of Owston. In 1679 the manor of Scawsby was said to be worth £300 a year.

Church St Michael: Norman and Early English.

The patronage rights belonged to the Archbishop of York.

(C.33/253/fo.86.)

BROTHERTON   Barkston Ash

A village on the River Aire near Castleford. The parish of Brotherton included the hamlets of Byram cum Poole and Sutton. 1674: 54 households in Brotherton, 10 in Byram cum Poole and 20 in Sutton.

In 1645 there was an outbreak of the plague in Brotherton.
Church St Edward: Norman in origin.
The parish was subject to the peculiar jurisdiction of the Dean and Chapter of York.
School A free grammar school founded in 1640.
Principal families (1) Tindall of Brotherton Hall. Estate revenue £800 a year (1632); £630 a year (1640); £470 a year (1687). Coalmining in Castleford and Houghton.

In the early 17th century the Tindalls were a predominantly Catholic family. The head of the family, Francis Tindall (1584-1657) was presented for recusancy in 1615 but soon conformed. He was already in financial difficulties before the Civil War and had to sell some property.

In the Civil War Francis Tindall, his sons and his brother William all threw in their lot with the king.

By the time of the Restoration the family had abandoned the Catholic faith.

Bradwardine Tindall (1640-1686), the grandson and heir of Francis Tindall, also fell heavily into debt. In 1690 his creditors began legal proceedings against his executors and his steward, Richard Goldsbrough.

(2) Ramsden of Byram Hall (and Longley Hall, Almondbury) (see under Almondbury).

Brotherton Hall An Elizabethan house but apparently with some additional features introduced in the reign of Charles II.

Bradwardine Tindall was taxed on 15 hearths in 1664 and 19 in 1674.

Byram Hall Sir John Ramsden (1594-1646) bought the manor of Byram in 1630 and built a large mansion there (26 hearths in 1674). This became the family's principal residence.

In 1642 Sir John moved many of the contents of Byram Hall to Pontefract Castle and York for safe custody. When the parliamentarians took possession of the house in 1644 they searched for hidden money and other items of value. In the process they destroyed or damaged ceilings, panelling and windows and left 'but baire walles'.

(BL, Egerton MSS 3568. C.10/412/11. C.10/32/121.)

BROUGHTON   Staincliffe and Ewecross

A village near Skipton. The parish of Broughton included the hamlet of Elslack. 1674: 68 households (Broughton cum Elslack).

Church All Saints: originally Norman but mainly Perpendicular.

Principal family Tempest of Broughton Hall. Estate revenue: £700 a year (1674). Number of servants: 13 (1691).

The Tempests were a Catholic family who had a succession of resident chaplains. Sir Stephen Tempest (c.1553-1625) was a Church Papist but his descendants were unwilling to conform.

Stephen Tempest (1593-1651) was an enterprising landowner who was heavily engaged in the production of lime on his Roundhay estate. In 1625 he killed his opponent in a duel but managed to obtain a royal pardon while in 1632 he was cleared of an assault charge after pleading that he had acted in self-defence.

In the Civil War Stephen Tempest and his brothers came out in support of the king and Robert Tempest was killed in a skirmish near Broughton.

Sir Stephen Tempest (1617-1672), who was the next head of the family, served as a royalist captain and was taken prisoner at the battle of Naseby.

The Tempests were related to the Gascoignes of Barnbow Hall and Stephen Tempest (1654-1742) was accused of being involved in the so-called Barnbow Plot. In 1682, after a period of imprisonment, he was put on trial for treason but acquitted.

Broughton Hall An Elizabethan house completed in 1597. It was a gabled mansion of three storeys with attic chambers on top.

The hall was badly damaged in the Civil War and required extensive repairs.

In 1674 the Tempests were taxed on 19 hearths. Their steward, John Yorke, had two taxable hearths.

(BL, Additional MSS 40,670. Mrs E. B. Tempest, 'Broughton Hall and its Associations', *Bradford Antiquary*, New Series, iv (1921). C.10/480/172.)

BURGHWALLIS   Osgoldcross/Strafford and Tickhill

A small village to the north-east of Doncaster. It was situated partly in the parish of Burghwallis and partly in two other parishes, Barnby Dun and Owston. 1674: 24 households (township of Burghwallis). 1676: 80 persons aged 16 or more, including 20 recusants (parish of Burghwallis).

The manor of Burghwallis belonged to the Annes of Frickley Hall, a leading Catholic family, who had acquired it by marriage at the beginning of the 17th century. Burghwallis Hall was used as a secondary house. (For the Anne family see the entry for Hooton Pagnell.)

Church St Helen, Burghwallis: mainly Norman.

BURNSALL   Staincliffe and Ewecross

A Wharfedale village to the north-east of Skipton. The extensive parish of Burnsall contained a number of villages and hamlets, including Bordley, Conistone and Rylstone which had dependent chapels. 1674: 53 households in Burnsall, 49 in Appletreewick, 30 in Conistone (including Kilnsey), 20 in Cracoe, 36 in Harlington, 50 in Hetton cum Bordley and 44 in Rylstone. 1676: 440 persons aged 16 or more (parish of Burnsall but excluding the chapelry of Conistone) and 195 in Conistone chapelry.

The manors of Burnsall and Thorpe belonged to the Tempests of Broughton, a leading Catholic family, but the parish was largely Protestant.

In the early years of the 17th century the parish benefited in various ways from the philanthropic instincts of Sir William Craven who had been born at Appletreewick and had made a fortune as a London merchant. He built four bridges within the parish, including (in Roger Dodsworth's words) 'a very faire one' at Burnsall.

The River Wharfe 'runs down by Kilnesey-Cragge (the highest and the deepest that ever I saw) to Burnsall, where Sir William Craven.....is now building a stone bridge' (William Camden).

In 1673 Burnsall Bridge was badly damaged by flood waters and had to be rebuilt.

Richard Tennant, who was rector of Burnsall during the years 1619 to 1653, had pronounced Puritan sympathies. In 1627 he was required to appear before the Northern High Commission and admitted that he had held conventicles. As a result he was forbidden to preach outside the parish. Despite his religious outlook he supported the royalist cause in the Civil War.

By virtue of a charter of 1310 Appletreewick had the right to hold an annual fair and this right continued to be exercised during the 17th century and beyond. The Yorkes of Gouthwaite Hall, who owned the manor of Appletreewick, had lead mines there.

Church St Wilfrid: mainly Perpendicular.

Sir William Craven had the church refurbished at a cost of some £200. Among other things, it was provided with 'stalles and seates of waynscote'.

Schools A free grammar school was founded at Burnsall in 1602 by Sir William Craven. In 1605 he settled it on trustees, including John Topham the rector of Burnsall, and in 1615 he made provision for the payment of a salary of £20 a year to the master.

One of the first masters was Robert Mason: in the reign of Charles I a number of his pupils were admitted to St John's College, Cambridge.

During the 1650s there was a school at Conistone.

(*YASRS*, xxxiv (1904), 238-9. R. A. Marchant, *The Puritans and the Church Courts in the Diocese of York 1560-1642* (1960), 41, 45-7, 283.)

BURTON LEONARD   Claro

A village to the north-west of Knaresborough. There was no other village within the parish. 1674: 45 households (township of Burton Leonard).

When Roger Dodsworth visited Burton Leonard he noted in his journal that Sir William Wentworth (the father of Strafford) had sold the manor to the tenants.

Church St Helen: Norman in origin.

The parish was subject to the peculiar jurisdiction of the Dean and Chapter of York.

(*YASRS*, xxxiv (1904), 186.)

CALVERLEY　　　　　　　　　　　　　　　　　　Agbrigg and Morley

A clothing village to the north-east of Bradford. The parish of Calverley contained several villages, including Idle and Pudsey which had dependent chapels. 1674: 87 households in Calverley cum Farsley, 18 in Bolton, 126 in Idle and 116 in Pudsey. 1676: 894 persons aged 16 or more (parish).

In 1645 there was an outbreak of the plague at Pudsey.

Church St Wilfred: Norman, Decorated and Perpendicular.

School In the reign of James I there was a school at Calverley which was run on a fee-paying basis. The master may be identified as James Smith who was vicar of Calverley in the years 1612 to 1626. In his will (1658) Joseph Hillary, a Leeds clothier who was a native of Calverley, provided the school with an endowment in order to put it on a more permanent footing. In 1674 it was described as a free school.

Principal family Calverley of Calverley Hall (and Esholt Hall). Estate revenue: £350 a year (1613); £530 a year (1634); £620 a year (1650); £1100 a year (1665). A fulling mill in Calverley.

Walter Calverley (c.1580-1605) was executed at York for murdering two of his infant sons. According to Roger Dodsworth he had fallen into 'a desperat humour after he had greatly entangled and consumed his estate by his riotous courses'. The episode featured in the play *A Yorkshire Tragedy* which was performed at the Globe theatre.

Henry Calverley (1604-1652), who was the only surviving son, was for many years a ward of the Crown and during his minority the estate was managed by his stepfather Sir Thomas Burton. In 1625 Calverley was advised to draw up a true and perfect rental of his lands and 'To vewe the decayes of your howses, mylnes etc, woodes and underwoods'. In proceedings in the Court of Wards he claimed that Sir Thomas had abused his position as guardian.

In the Civil War he helped to raise money for the royalist cause and as a result was heavily fined.

His son Walter (1629-1691), who was a barrister of Gray's Inn, advanced the fortunes of his family by marrying an heiress who was the only child of Henry Thomson of Esholt. Following Thomson's death in 1665 the Calverleys entered into possession of the Esholt estate and other property.

Calverley Hall Mainly of the 15th century (including a domestic chapel of that period) but with some 17th century work. Among the rooms listed in an inventory of 1652 were the hall, the great chamber and the great parlour.

Walter Calverley was taxed on 14 hearths in 1664 but only 10 in 1674. He often resided at Esholt Hall.

A settlement made by Henry Calverley in 1626 refers to a close of pasture and wooded ground 'walled, paled and fenced about called or knowne by the name of the Parke in Calverley'. This contained 110 acres and a lodge which was described as newly built.

(W. K. Jordan, *The Charities of Rural England 1480-1660* (1961), 345. BL, Additional MSS 27,410 and 27,411 and Additional Charter 17,116 (Calverley MSS). YAS Library, MS 427. BL,Harleian MSS 797, fo.15. S. Rayner, *The History and Antiquities of Pudsey* (1887). Ruth Strong, *The Making of a West Riding Clothing Village: Pudsey to 1780* (1999).)

CAMPSALL   Osgoldcross

A village situated between Doncaster and Pontefract. The extensive parish of Campsall included several villages. 1674: 43 households in Campsall, 25 in Fenwick, 44 in Moss, 51 in Norton and 33 in Sutton cum Askern. 1676: 500 persons aged 16 or more (parish).

Since 1284 Campsall had enjoyed the right to hold a weekly market and an annual fair.

During the years 1638 to 1642 the West Riding magistrates received complaints from the inhabitants of Campsall, Norton and Askern about the assessments for the relief of the poor. In 1638 the justices drew a distinction between the enclosed lands and the open and unenclosed lands in Campsall when determining the rates to be applied. This, however, was not the end of the matter and in 1639 they felt obliged to order a detailed survey in view of the fact that there were major differences in 'the yearely valliditie and profittes of the landes in that parish'. In 1640 the inhabitants of Norton claimed that Fenwick (which was in the same constablery) was not contributing its fair share while in 1642 it was alleged in a petition from Askern that a number of gentlemen and other landowners with property there were refusing to pay 'theire proporconable rates'. In both cases the magistrates responded sympathetically.

In 1645 there was an outbreak of the plague at Campsall. Between September and December no fewer than 60 persons died, among them the vicar and his three sons.

The Franks of Campsall were rising gentry who owed their landed wealth to the profits of commercial enterprise. John Frank (c.1570-1624) was a Pontefract merchant who was twice mayor of the town. His son Richard (1593-1662) took up residence at Campsall Hall which was an Elizabethan or Jacobean mansion. In the Civil War he appears to have avoided any commitment to either side. Having outlived his sons he settled the estate on his infant grandson Edward Ashton with the request that he should adopt the surname of Frank. From litigation which Ashton's father began in 1665 it is clear that this request was already being honoured.

In 1626 Edmund Yarburgh of Balne Hall in Snaith bought the Campsall estate of Thomas Fletcher and this became the seat of a cadet branch of the family.

Church St Mary Magdalene: Norman, Decorated and Perpendicular.

(*YASRS*, liv (1915), 99, 127, 142, 204, 385. Sheffield Archives, Bacon Frank MSS, Box 17. C.10/81/1.)

CANTLEY   Strafford and Tickhill

A village to the east of Doncaster. The parish of Cantley included the village of Brampton. 1674: 50 households in Cantley and 21 in Brampton. 1676: 56 persons aged 16 or more (parish).

John Slack, who served as vicar of Cantley during the years 1593 to 1643, was a Puritan who was suspended for a time in 1632. He was also master of the hospital at Bawtry. In 1640 his wife Bridget was one of a number of residents of Cantley who were indicted for tracking and killing hares at Hatfield.

In 1641 the West Riding magistrates were informed that John Scales of Brampton and William Chester of Cantley kept 'very disordered alehowses and tiplinghowses' and allowed 'men's servantes to tiple and game att cardes and other unlawfull games'. It was therefore decided to prohibit them from brewing or selling ale or beer for a period of three years.

In 1642 some of the inhabitants of the parish complained to the magistrates that 'there is a great inequalitie there in the rateing and assessing their assessmentes for the poore'.

Church St Wilfrid: Norman, Early English, Decorated and Perpendicular.

(R. A. Marchant, *The Puritans and the Church Courts in the Diocese of York 1560-1642* (1960), 279. *YASRS*, liv (1915), 189, 191, 335, 360.)

CARLETON   Staincliffe and Ewecross

A village to the south-west of Skipton. There was no other village within the parish. 1674: 91 households (township of Carleton). 1676: 200 persons aged 16 or more (parish).

The Ferrands of Carleton owed their emergence as country gentry to William Ferrand who had been chief steward to the Cliffords, Earls of Cumberland. He had built Carleton Hall in 1584 and had secured a coat of arms in 1587. His son Thomas, who died in 1627, also served the Cliffords.

In the next generation there was a sharp reversal of fortune. Although Edmund Ferrand appears to have remained uncommitted in the Civil War he found himself in serious financial difficulties. When offered the sum of £4500 for his house and lands in Carleton he declined to sell with the comment that he hoped to pay his debts and save the estate. His expectations, however, proved to be ill-founded. In a Chancery suit of 1655 Thomas Parkinson complained that although he had paid some £2000 with a view to purchasing the property Ferrand was refusing to accept that he was now the rightful owner. In the end the Court ruled in Parkinson's favour.

Church St Mary: Norman in origin but mainly Perpendicular.

Almshouses In 1698 Ferrand Spence founded a hospital at Carleton for 12 poor widows.

(C.10/31/152. C.22/783/42.)

CARLTON   Barkston Ash

A village and chapelry within the parish of Snaith. 1674: 89 households.

There was a ferry service on the River Aire which provided a vital link between Carlton and Snaith. Its upkeep was the responsibility of the lord of the manor of Carlton.

Church St Mary: parochial chapel which was rebuilt in 1688.

School At an ecclesiastical visitation in 1637 Robert Palm was presented for teaching children without a licence.

Almshouses Stapleton's almshouses, for four poor widows, were established towards the end of the 17th century. The first occupants were Ann Ryley, Catherine Bawn, Mary Briggs and Mary Silverwood.

Principal family Stapleton of Carlton Hall or House (baronetcy 1662). Estate revenue: £1200 a year (1660).

The Stapletons were a Catholic family who had resident chaplains. The register of Carlton chapel records that Gilbert Stapleton, the recusant head of the family, was buried on 18 April 1636, 'by home I know not'.

His eldest son Richard (1621-1670) was a lunatic from 1642 and his second son Gregory became a Benedictine monk. The estate therefore descended to his third son Miles who was the first and last baronet of the family.

As a Catholic Sir Miles (1626-1707) was no stranger to adversity. In 1681, amid rumours of a popish conspiracy, he was indicted for high treason but acquitted by a jury at York. On 16 December 1688 an anti-Catholic mob burst into his house and for a time he was held captive.

Carlton Hall A large Elizabethan mansion built by Brian Stapleton (c.1535-1606) at a cost of £4000 or £5000.

In 1638 there was a debate in the Court of Wards about the condition of the house. On the one hand, it was alleged that through the negligence of Elizabeth Stapleton, who had possession of it as part of her jointure, it was 'in great decay' and that many of the rooms had been damaged by rainwater. On the other hand, Robert Johnson her steward testified that at her direction he had arranged for the roof to be well covered with lead and that he had heard her say that during her widowhood she had spent £500 on repair work.

In 1668 Sir Miles Stapleton converted part of the gallery into a chapel and in 1676 had the roof re-leaded.

The park belonging to Carlton Hall had apparently been divided up into closes.

(BIHR, High Commission Act Books, RVI/A24/fo.133. Hull University Archives, Beaumont of Carlton Towers MSS. *YPRS*, xcvi (1934). Wards 9/96/fols.263-5 and 573/fols.238,256. *The Ancestor*, ii and iii (1902).)

CASTLEFORD Osgoldcross

A village to the north-west of Pontefract. The parish of Castleford included the village of Houghton. 1674: 36 households in Castleford and 36 in Houghton. 1676: 220 persons aged 16 or more (parish).

Near the union of the Calder and Aire 'stands the little village Castleford'. Its Roman past 'is confirmed by those great numbers of Coins (called by the common people Sarasins-heads) dug up here in Beanfeild, a place near the Church.....not to mention its situation by a Roman way' (William Camden).

The manors of Castleford and Houghton belonged to the Bland family of Kippax Park who mined coal there.

In 1611 and 1638 the West Riding magistrates received reports about the poor condition of Castleford Bridge. On the latter occasion they decided, on the advice of Sir Thomas Bland their fellow justice, that the sum of £40 should be levied on the riding as a whole to enable the repair work to be completed.

During the Civil War Dr Thomas Bradley the rector of Castleford joined the royalist garrison at Pontefract and acted as one of the military chaplains there.

In 1645 there was an outbreak of the plague at Castleford.

Besides the coalmines around Castleford there was a glass foundry at Houghton. From Aberford 'we went to Castleton Bridge [Houghton].....where was a Glass house; we saw them blowing white glass and neale [anneal] it in a large oven by the heate of the furnace' (Celia Fiennes, 1697). The village was eventually re-named Glass Houghton.

Church All Saints: Norman in origin.

(E.134/3 and 4 Charles I/Hilary 2. *YASRS*, liv (1915), 4, 69-70. A. G. Matthews, *Walker Revised* (1988), 389-90.)

CHEVET Staincross

Chevet was situated in the parish of Royston, near Wakefield. It had been depopulated in the early years of the 16th century. In the reign of Charles II it consisted only of a mansion house with its outbuildings and a deer park.

Principal family Nevile of Chevet Hall. Estate revenue: £1400 a year (1640); £1200 a year (1673).

Francis Nevile (1592-1665) lent money on a considerable scale. In the Civil War he was an ardent royalist who garrisoned Pontefract Castle and his own castle of Sandal. His brother Gervase also took up arms for the king.

After succeeding his father Sandford Nevile (1621-1673) fell heavily into debt, mortgaged the manor of Chevet and other property and sold his Northumberland estate. In 1677 his son Francis (1649-1707) claimed in a Chancery suit that Robert Benson, a lawyer who had been employed by the family, had been seeking to deprive him of his whole estate. By this time, however, Benson was dead and the fortunes of the family eventually took a turn for the better.

Chevet Hall A large mansion built by Sir John Nevile in 1529. He also enclosed the park and made fish ponds.

In 1674 Francis Nevile was taxed on 33 hearths.
(C.10/130/51 and 273/71. C.33/252/fo.103.)

CHURCH FENTON   Barkston Ash

A village to the south-east of Tadcaster which was also known as Kirk Fenton. The parish of Church Fenton included the hamlets of Biggin and Little Fenton. 1674: 47 households in Church Fenton and 36 in Little Fenton cum Biggin.

Church St Mary: Early English, Decorated and Perpendicular.

The parish was subject to the peculiar jurisdiction of a Prebendary of York.
(G. E. Kirk, *The Church of St Mary, Kirk Fenton* (1938).)

CLAPHAM   Staincliffe and Ewecross

A village near Settle in the north-west part of the riding. The parish of Clapham also included the village of Austwick. 1674: 77 households in Clapham, 185 in Austwick and 48 in Newby cum Clapham.

Church St Michael: 13th century or earlier with a Perpendicular tower.

School In 1611 Thomas Remington of Clapham, a husbandman, left some land for a schoolhouse there.

There was a schoolmaster at Clapham in the reign of Charles II.

Principal family Ingleby of Lawkland Hall. Estate revenue: £1100 a year (1628); £500 a year (1640).

The Inglebys were a Catholic family who appear to have been in close contact with a Benedictine missioner, Richard Huddleston (1583-1655). Despite the financial exactions arising from their recusancy the estate was still basically intact when John

Ingleby (c.1600-1648) succeeded his father in 1622 but he was faced with a growing burden of debt.

In 1627 he confirmed the customs of the manor of Clapham and in return for a payment of £500 authorised the tenants to enclose and improve the commons belonging to the manor. The following year William Mason was commissioned to carry out a survey of the rectory manor of Hutton Rudby in the North Riding which was the subject of a complicated series of trusteeship arrangements. By 1633 the manor had been sold with the result that the family suffered a severe loss of income.

Ingleby took no part in the Civil War but two-thirds of his estate were sequestered for his recusancy. In 1650 it was reported that his widow, Mary Ingleby, had conformed in religion.

Mary Ingleby kept possession of Lawkland Hall till her death in 1667 and claimed a life interest in the whole estate. Her stepson Arthur Ingleby (1632-1701) challenged this claim in a Chancery suit which he brought in 1650 but was obliged to live for some years in modest circumstances at Clapdale Hall in Clapham. In the course of this litigation he complained that she had chosen persons of mean quality and evil conversation as his tutors.

In 1662 his half-brother Columbus shot and killed Brian Redman of Ingleton but was acquitted when put on trial.

Another younger brother was Sir Charles Ingleby (1644-1719), a Catholic lawyer who was appointed a Baron of the Exchequer Court in 1688.

Lawkland Hall An Elizabethan house which was enlarged in the early 17th century.

(W. K. Jordan, *The Charities of Rural England 1480-1660* (1961), 340. C.10/43/121 and 128/15.)

COLLINGHAM   Skyrack/Barkston Ash

A village near Tadcaster. The village of Clifford was in two parishes: Collingham and Bramham. 1674: 26 households in Collingham and 39 in Clifford. 1676: 132 persons aged 16 or more (parish of Collingham).

Church St Oswald: Perpendicular with much older features.

School A free grammar school established in 1638.

Principal family Beilby of Micklethwaite Grange (and Killerby Hall, Cayton, North Riding). Estate revenue: £500 a year (1626); £870 a year (1661).

In the 17th century the Beilby family's main seat was Micklethwaite Grange which they had acquired by marriage in the reign of Elizabeth.

For several decades they had a tenuous attachment to the Catholic religion. Thomas Beilby was married to a Catholic, Thomasine Thweng, but he was either a Protestant or a Church Papist. His son William (1591-1663), who had a Protestant wife, was convicted of recusancy in 1626, compounded for his lands and goods in 1629 and conformed in 1636. Following his father's death in 1637 he was found to be a lunatic who was incapable of managing his estate and the Court of Wards granted custody of his person and property to his wife Susan and other relatives. In 1650 he related in a Chancery suit that his deeds had been plundered during the Civil War and that his nephew Langdale Sunderland had taken advantage of the situation to claim title to his estate. In reply Sunderland strongly denied the allegation; offered the opinion that Beilby was still 'a lunatique person'; and suggested that the suit had actually been initiated by Susan Beilby and 'some of her adherents' in order to secure possession of deeds relating to the estate and thereby 'to use meanes' to disinherit Beilby's elder son.

William Beilby was survived by his second son John (c.1635-1702) whose succession marked the final break from Catholicism.

Micklethwaite Grange The house was rebuilt or substantially improved in 1660. In 1674 John Beilby was taxed on 12 hearths.

(Wards 9/572/635. C.6/108/18.)

CONISBROUGH   Strafford and Tickhill

A village to the south-west of Doncaster. The parish of Conisbrough included the hamlets of Clifton and Firsby. 1674: 85 households (township of Conisbrough). 1676: 200 persons aged 16 or more (parish).

Conisbrough has 'an old Castle......situated upon a rock' (William Camden).

'The Castle here hath been a large strong built Pile, whereof the out-walls are standing, situate on a pleasant ascent from the river, but much over-topp'd by a high hill on which the town stands. Before the gate is an agger, by tradition said to be the burying place of Hengist' (Edmund Gibson, 1695).

The Norman castle, together with its demesne lands, had been granted by Queen Elizabeth to Henry Lord Hunsdon and it remained in the possession of his family until the death without male issue of John Earl of Dover in 1677. At the beginning of the 17th century the castle was already in a ruinous state and no garrison was put in during the Civil War.

In 1623 Henry Viscount Rochford, the grandson of Henry Lord Hunsdon, began proceedings in the Court of Exchequer against Sir John Hewett and others who he alleged had been enclosing land out of the commons of Firsby without legal authority. Hewitt, who had recently secured a baronetcy, was the tenant of Firsby Hall.

Henry Saxton, who served as vicar of Conisbrough from 1615 until 1665, was a Puritan with a flair for self-preservation. At a visitation in 1632 he was accused of engaging in acts of nonconformity but the ecclesiastical authorities merely suspended him for a short period. The churchwardens, for their part, were admonished for not presenting him.

In 1645 there was an outbreak of the plague in Conisbrough.

Church St Peter: Saxon, Norman, Decorated and Perpendicular.

School There was a school at Conisbrough from 1619 onwards. The first master was Andrew Taxter who does not appear to have been a graduate.

In his will (1694) Henry Saxton settled a rent-charge of £2 a year as an addition to the schoolmaster's salary. He was the grandson of Henry Saxton the former vicar.

(E.134/21 James I/Easter 4. R. A. Marchant, *The Puritans and the Church Courts in the Diocese of York 1560-1642* (1960), 275.)

COPGROVE Claro

A hamlet to the south-west of Boroughbridge. There was no other centre of population within the parish. 1674: 17 households (township of Copgrove).

The Withes family had acquired the manor of Copgrove in the mid-16th century but before the outbreak of the Civil War they had sold most of their landed property. In 1641 the subsidy commissioners noted that virtually the whole manor had recently been purchased by Sir Thomas Harrison of York.

In the late 17th century Copgrove was becoming a popular health resort on account of a cold spring known as St Mungo's well. In 1693 Ralph Thoresby bathed in the well after drinking from 'the sulphur Spa' at Harrogate. Four years later Celia Fiennes wrote in her journal that from Harrogate to Copgrove

> is 6 mile, where is a Spring of an exceeding cold water called St Mongers Well…..I cannot but think it is a very good Spring, being remarkably cold, and just at the head of the Spring so it's fresh which must needs be very strengthning, it shutts up the pores of the body immediately so fortifyes from cold, you cannot bear the coldness of it above 2 or 3 minutes…..some of the Papists I saw there had so much Zeale as to continue a quarter of an hour on their knees at their prayers in the Well, but none else could well endure it so long at a tyme.

Church St Michael: Norman.

School John Wyncope, who served as rector of Copgrove in the years 1583 to 1637, also kept a private school there and took in many boarders from the ranks of the gentry. (PRO, Exchequer, Lay Subsidy Rolls, E.179/209/364. J. Hunter (ed.), *The Diary of*

Ralph Thoresby, FRS (1830), i, 234. C. Morris (ed.), *The Journeys of Celia Fiennes* (1949), 81-2. H. D. A. Major, *Memorials of Copgrove* (1922).)

COPMANTHORPE   Ainsty

A small village to the south-west of York. The chapelry of Copmanthorpe formed part of the parish of St Mary Bishophill Junior, York. 1665: 24 households (township of Copmanthorpe).

The manor of Copmanthorpe or Temple Copmanthorpe belonged to the Sprignell family of Highgate in Middlesex who bought it from Sir Francis Hildesley in 1611. When Sir Richard Sprignell made a settlement of his estate in 1652 the manor was valued at £324 a year.

Church St Giles: Norman in origin.

The chapelry was subject to the peculiar jurisdiction of the Dean and Chapter of York.

(*YASRS*, liii (1915), 103, 144. Wards 5/14. C.7/327/4.)

COWICK   Osgoldcross

Cowick 'the pleasant Seat of the ancient family of the Dawneys' (Edmund Gibson, 1695). A village within the parish of Snaith. 1674: 94 households.

School There was a school at Cowick in the reign of Charles II.

Principal family Dawney of Cowick Hall (and Sessay, North Riding) (baronetcy 1642, peerage 1681 as Viscount Downe). Estate revenue: £3000 a year (1642).

Sir Thomas Dawney (1563-1642) was described in 1639 as 'a man given to licentiousnesse and excesse of drinking'. His son and heir John died in 1630 and his grandson Thomas in 1639. The latter, who was a ward of the Crown, was fatally injured in a riding accident. The estate descended in turn to his brothers Sir Christopher, a royalist who died in 1644, and Sir John (1625-1695) who was subsequently ennobled as Viscount Downe.

Cowick Hall Sir John Dawney built a new mansion designed on classical lines in the reign of Charles II. The hearth tax returns reflect both the demolition of the old house and the building of its replacement: there were four taxable hearths in 1664 and 26 in 1674.

(C.10/7/114. *Surtees Society*, cxviii (1910), 6-7.)

COWTHORPE   Claro

A hamlet to the north-east of Wetherby. There was no other centre of population within the parish. 1674: 16 households (township of Cowthorpe). 1676: 66 persons aged 16 or more (parish of Cowthorpe).

In 1645 there was an outbreak of the plague in Cowthorpe.

Church St Michael: Perpendicular.

School Henry Flint, who was rector of Cowthorpe in the years 1638 to 1671, kept a school there.

CROFTON   Agbrigg and Morley

A village to the south-east of Wakefield. There was no other village within the parish. 1674: 45 households (township of Crofton).

In 1641 there was a dispute among the inhabitants of Crofton about the method of apportionment to be followed in the levying of local taxes. Some men, it was reported, 'doe alleadge and stand upon an auncient custome to laye their assessementes according to their oxegange lands'. The West Riding magistrates considered that this would result in an unfair burden on the poorer members of the community and ruled that in future the assessments should be made 'according to the quantitye and qualitye of acres everye one occupieth and enjoyeth'. The following year, however, they decided to revert to the customary method after hearing that two farmers were obstinately refusing to pay the arrears which were due from them.

Church All Saints: Perpendicular.

Principal family Ireland of Crofton Hall. Estate revenue: £600 a year (1654). Coalmining in Crofton and elsewhere.

The Irelands were a Catholic family who settled at Crofton after selling the Nostell Priory estate in 1629. The financial problems which they were experiencing at this time were due partly to the fact that they had been buying land with the help of borrowed money and partly to the exactions of the Court of Wards. During the early 17th century they sustained two minorities and Sir Francis Ireland (1600-1634) and his son William were both made wards of the Crown.

Sir Francis had a Catholic chaplain, John Wilks, who also acted as tutor to his children. Following the death of his father William was brought up in the household of his grandfather, William Lord Eure, at Malton and it was there in 1638 that he was first presented as a recusant.

In the Civil War two-thirds of the estate were sequestered on account of his mother's recusancy and he himself was suspected of being a royalist. During the early 1650s he was mining coal in various places but in 1655 he entered into an agreement with a neighbouring colliery owner in return for a complete suspension of his industrial activities. (See also the entry for Warmfield).

In 1657 Ireland borrowed £1000 and mortgaged his estate as security. He managed nevertheless to avoid financial ruin and the family was still seated at Crofton in the 18th century.

Crofton Hall Sir Francis Ireland may have rebuilt or enlarged the house when he moved to Crofton. Before that it had been let to tenants.

(*YASRS*, liv (1915), 283, 350-1, 383. Wards 5/49. *Surtees Society*, xl (1861), 47-8. C.7/457/73. C.10/40/19. Nottingham University Library, Galway of Serlby MSS, 9310, 9763, 9765. *YPRS*, lxii (1918), 34, 36, 59, 86.)

CUDWORTH   Staincross

A village near Barnsley which was situated within the parish of Royston. 1674: 42 households.

Principal family Jobson of Cudworth Hall (baronetcy 1635). Estate revenue: £800 a year (1662). Coalmining in Cudworth.

Thomas Jobson (1606-1653) was born after his father's death. His mother, who re-married in 1611, had social aspirations: in 1635 she secured a baronetcy for herself and the heirs male of her body and thereafter styled herself Dame Mary Bolles, baroness.

Her son sought to remain disengaged in the Civil War. In 1644 and again in 1648 it was alleged that he was a royalist but no proof was forthcoming. On the first occasion he made a contribution to the pay of the forces under Ferdinando Lord Fairfax. In the Commonwealth period he served as a justice of the peace.

He was succeeded by his son Thomas (c.1634-1661) who subsequently borrowed £4000 from Lady Bolles and mortgaged much of his landed property as security. He died unmarried and the estate passed to his brother William (1636-1666). Following the death of Lady Bolles in 1662 William inherited the baronetcy together with further property, including Heath Hall and a lease of the rectory of Royston.

Sir William had no male issue and the Cudworth estate descended to his daughter Lucy who married Robert Earl of Londonderry.

Cudworth Hall The house had probably been built in the reign of Elizabeth when the Jobsons settled at Cudworth.

Sir William Jobson moved to Heath Hall after his grandmother's death in 1664 and there is no reference to Cudworth Hall in the 1674 hearth tax return. It may therefore have been demolished.

(Sheffield Archives, Bankes Muniments. BL, Additional Charter 5151.)

DARFIELD
Strafford and Tickhill/Staincross

A village to the east of Barnsley. The extensive parish of Darfield contained a number of villages, including Wombwell and Worsborough which had medieval chapels. Great Houghton, Wombwell and Worsborough are separately noticed. 1674: 43 households in Darfield, 38 in Ardsley, 21 in Billingley and 19 in Little Houghton. 1676: 600 persons aged 16 or more (parish).

The parish church of Darfield consisted of two medieties, one held by a rector and the other by a vicar. The second mediety was in the gift of Trinity College, Cambridge which also owned half the tithes.

Dr Walter Stonehouse, who became rector of Darfield in 1631, was a student of natural history and a collector of coins and medals. He was ejected by the parliamentarians.

In 1669 it was reported that there were considerable numbers of Presbyterians, Independents and Quakers within the parish who met in private houses.

Church All Saints: Norman, Decorated and Perpendicular.

DARRINGTON
Osgoldcross

A village near Pontefract. The parish of Darrington included Stapleton and part of Cridling Stubbs; the other part was in the parish of Womersley. 1674: 39 households in Darrington, 11 in Cridling Stubbs and 11 in Stapleton. 1676: 180 persons aged 16 or more (parish).

In the early 17th century the manor of Darrington belonged to the Savile family of Thornhill. It was worth £127 a year in 1623 and £200 a year on the eve of the Civil War. In 1641 Sir William Savile sold the manor to Thomas Lord Savile for £4160.

In 1645 there was an outbreak of the plague in Darrington.

Church St Luke and All Saints: Norman, Early English, Decorated and Perpendicular.

(Nottinghamshire Record Office, Savile of Rufford MSS, 28/5. *Camden Society*, New Series, xxxi (1883), 32.)

DARTON
Staincross

A village on the River Dearne near Barnsley. The parish of Darton included several villages and hamlets. 1674: 69 households in Darton, 37 in Barugh and 34 in Kexbrough. 1676: 600 persons aged 16 or more (parish of Darton).

In 1622 there was a dispute between the Huttons of Nether Poppleton and Michael Wentworth of Woolley who was alleged to have dug for coal within their manor of Darton. In 1634 the Wentworths bought the manor and continued to mine coal there.

Church All Saints: Perpendicular. The building work was completed in 1517.

School A school had been established at Darton in 1564.

In 1668 George Beaumont, a York merchant, settled property for the support of a good schoolmaster who was to teach the children of Darton free of charge.

Principal family Burdett of Birthwaite Hall, Kexbrough (baronetcy 1665). Estate revenue: £800 a year (1637).

Francis Burdett (1578-1637) added considerably to the estate but after his death there were two minorities in succession which exposed the family to the financial exactions of the Court of Wards.

The wardship of his son Francis (1617-1644) cost the family £500. For some years the estate was managed by his uncle Robert Rockley who was alleged to have abused his position as guardian. In 1643 Burdett pledged financial support for the royalist cause by signing the Yorkshire Engagement but this appears to have been the extent of his involvement.

In spite of the war the Court of Wards intervened once more when Francis Burdett (1641-c.1719) succeeded his father. In 1645 his mother married Sir John Kaye of Woodsome Hall who took on responsibility for his upbringing. Later, in 1647, Francis Rockley was awarded possession of the bulk of the estate by virtue of a lease which his late father had held for trusteeship purposes. In the course of protracted litigation Kaye alleged that Rockley had been managing the estate for his own personal gain and had granted leases to his friends and agents at little or no rent.

Sir Francis Burdett, as he became in 1665, was a profligate who fathered a number of illegitimate children. Through his extravagance he began to borrow heavily and before his death had disposed of the whole estate.

Birthwaite Hall A gabled Tudor building. An inventory of 1637 refers to a quantity of ashlar stone which had been prepared for new building work. The house was of moderate size: in 1674 Sir Francis Burdett was taxed on eight hearths.

(C.5/32/96. C.10/28/14 and 464/84. C.38/139/4 September 1660. BL. Additional MSS 24,467, fols.247-8.)

DENTON   Claro

A small village within the parish of Otley. 1674: 26 households.

Principal family Fairfax of Denton Hall (and Nun Appleton Hall) (enobled 1628 with the title Baron Fairfax of Cameron). Estate revenue: £3000 a year (1628); £1000 a year (1696).

The Fairfaxes were one of the leading Puritan families in Yorkshire.

Sir Thomas Fairfax (1560-1640) became Lord Fairfax of Cameron on payment of £1500. In 1630 he told his friend Thomas Lord Wentworth that he had served the Crown for nearly 50 years and in the process had spent many thousands of pounds out of his own patrimony. The author of a treatise on horsemanship, he took a keen interest in the breeding of horses and established a stud at Denton which was continued by his son Ferdinando.

Before the outbreak of the Civil War there was nothing to suggest that the Fairfaxes would take up arms against the king, though their relations with Wentworth were not always harmonious. In 1638 Sir Edward Osborne the Vice-President of the Council in the North informed Wentworth that

> Sr Ferdinando Fairefax (a Gentleman I have ever found my freind, and one that uppon all occasions since I had ye honour to serve his Majestie under your Lordship hath shewed all due respect and observance both to my place and authority) comminge to visite me att Kiveton.....acquainted me with your Lordship's displeasure conceaved against him, which he confidently beleeves was att first begunn and since fomented by some bad freinds of his, for he protests before God his innocencye of giveinge any witting or willinge offence to your Lordship.

Ferdinando Lord Fairfax (1584-1648) was appointed general of Parliament's northern forces in November 1642. As a military commander he experienced mixed fortunes. His son Sir Thomas, the third Lord Fairfax (1612-1671) was described by Clarendon as 'a perfect Presbyterian in judgment'. He took part as a cavalry commander in the battle of Marston Moor. In January 1645 he was made commander-in-chief of the parliamentary army and shortly afterwards he defeated the king at the battle of Naseby. After the purge of the Long Parliament he became increasingly disillusioned with the trend of events and in 1660 he helped to bring about the restoration of the monarchy.

In the latter part of his life he lived in retirement at Nun Appleton Hall where he engaged in major building operations. A patron of Roger Dodsworth and Andrew Marvell, he was the author of a number of poems and translations and two autobiographical works relating to the Civil War.

After his death Richard Stretton his Presbyterian chaplain wrote that 'the losse of so worthy a person cannot but affect all that knew him'. A substantial part of the estate descended to his only child Mary who had married George Villiers, Duke of Buckingham while the residue, including Denton Hall, passed to his cousin Henry Fairfax of Oglethorpe (1631-1688) who became the fourth Lord Fairfax.

Henry Lord Fairfax was regarded as the head of the Presbyterian party in Yorkshire.

In June 1684 Ralph Thoresby visited Denton Hall and noted in his diary that on the Sabbath Thomas Clapham the chaplain 'preached exceedingly well ... Was much pleased with the good order observed in my Lord's religious family, all which was called in'. He also attended Lord Fairfax's funeral at which (he wrote) 'was the greatest appearance of the nobility and gentry that ever I had seen; the poor wept abundantly – a good evidence of his charity'.

Denton Hall A gabled building erected in 1612. Ferdinando Lord Fairfax garrisoned the house early on in the Civil War but in June 1643 it was seized by royalist troops.

The Fairfaxes were taxed on 22 hearths in 1664 but only 19 in 1674. In 1702 Ralph Thoresby described the house as 'a strong and stately building'.

There was a deer park adjoining the hall.

(BL, Additional MSS 11,325, 18,979 and 20,778 and Additional Charters 1790-1 and 1797-8 (Fairfax MSS). BL, Additional MSS 70,011, fo.260. Sheffield Archives, Wentworth Woodhouse Collection, Strafford Letters, xviii, Sir Edward Osborne to Lord Wentworth, 5 December 1638. J. Hunter (ed.), *The Diary of Ralph Thoresby* (1830), i, 176, 187 and ii, 432. *Short Memorials of Thomas Lord Fairfax* (1699). G. W. Johnson (ed.), *The Fairfax Correspondence. Memoirs of the Reign of Charles the First* (1848). R. Bell (ed.), *Memorials of the Civil War* (1849). A. J. Hopper, *'Black Tom': Sir Thomas Fairfax and the English Revolution* (2007).)

DEWSBURY   Agbrigg and Morley

A small town in the Calder valley where woollen goods were produced. In the reign of James I Roger Dodsworth described it as a market town. The parish of Dewsbury included several villages. 1674: 104 households in Dewsbury, 116 in Ossett and 74 in Soothill.

In 1638 the West Riding magistrates were informed that the king's highway at a place near Dewsbury mills 'is now ruinous and in great decay for lack of repair'.

In January 1641 it was reported that the plague at Dewsbury had so impaired the trade and commerce of the town that some 270 persons were now dependent on poor relief. The West Riding magistrates therefore decided that the sum of £200 should be levied in order to alleviate 'the distressed estate of the inhabitantes'.

Samuel Pearson, a Puritan divine, was vicar of Dewsbury from 1642 until his death in 1655. He had previously served as curate there and in 1632 had been admonished for neglecting to wear the surplice when preaching.

Dewsbury appears to have escaped lightly in the Civil War but in 1645 there was a further outbreak of the plague.

Church All Saints: Saxon in origin.

The living was in the gift of the Crown.

School A free grammar school founded in 1563.

(*YASRS*, liv (1915), 93, 260-1, 286-7. R. A. Marchant, *The Puritans and the Church Courts in the Diocese of York 1560-1642* (1960), 267-8. J. B. Greenwood, *The Early Ecclesiastical History of Dewsbury* (1859). S. J. Chadwick, 'Notes on Dewsbury Church and Some of its Rectors and Vicars', *YAJ*, xix (1907).)

DINNINGTON   Strafford and Tickhill

A small village to the south-east of Rotherham. One part of the village was in the parish of Dinnington and the other part in the parish of Laughton en le Morthen. 1674: 26 households (township of Dinnington). 1676: 30 persons aged 16 or more (parish of Dinnington).

Church St Nicholas: Norman in origin.

DONCASTER   Strafford and Tickhill

A market town on the River Don. The parish of Doncaster included several villages and hamlets. The township of Wheatley cum Long Sandall is separately noticed. 1674: 422 households in Doncaster, 36 in Hexthorpe cum Balby and 25 in Loversall. The main streets consisted of Barton Gate, Baxter Gate, Fisher Gate, French Gate, Hall Gate, Marsh Gate and St Sepulchre's Gate, together with the High Street. 1676: 3000 persons aged 16 or more (parish of Doncaster).

Doncaster was a major trading centre and a manufacturing town which was particularly noted for its knitted goods. Because of its position on the main road from London to York it was designated as a post town and it was also a convenient stopping place for travellers.

In 1660 Cuthbert Gibson was appointed postmaster. Some thirty years later Elizabeth Marshall was employed as deputy postmistress.

Royal charters of 1467 and 1664 provided a legal basis for the government of the town which had a mayor and 12 aldermen.

By 1600 horse-racing was already well established at Doncaster: in 1595 there were two racecourses on the Town Moor.

'Doncaster, a faire towne and antient, beinge a collonie in the time of the Romans; itt is famous for knitting of stockings, wascots, and weomen's pettiecoates' (Life of Marmaduke Rawdon, entry for 1664).

Doncaster is 'a great town of trade .... hath one fair church in it, and the market is on Saturday. Here they make excellent stockings for horsemen of very fine yarn and variety of colours' (Thomas Baskerville, 1675).

Doncaster 'is and always has been a town of good note, trade, and buildings. It has had a strong castle in it, the ruins of which is visible in the walls of some houses' (Abraham de la Pryme, 1694).

'Doncaster is a pretty large town of Stone Buildings, the streetes are good; there is a handsome Market Cross …. the Church is neate and pretty large' (Celia Fiennes, 1697).

There were outbreaks of the plague in 1604, 1606 and 1645.

In 1637 it was decided that the town hall, which was situated in a disused churchyard, should be refurbished.

When the Civil War began Doncaster was occupied by parliamentarian troops but it was soon in royalist hands. The Earl of Newcastle appointed Sir Francis Fane as governor and then replaced him with Sir Charles Lucas who was ordered to fortify the town. In July 1644 the Earl of Manchester arrived in Doncaster with a large parliamentarian force and declared his intention to remain there until he received further instructions.

The town appears to have suffered little physical or economic damage as a result of the Civil War.

In 1694 the corporation approved a project for conveying water from the River Don to various parts of the town.

Churches St George: Decorated and Perpendicular.

'A very spacious faire church, but few monuments or matters remarkeable in it' (John Aston, 1639).

There was little nonconformity in Doncaster but in the 1690s a meeting house was built for a small Presbyterian congregation.

School There are references to a grammar school in 1351 and 1528.

In the early years of Elizabeth's reign two aldermen, Thomas Symkinson and Thomas Ellis, settled property for the endowment of the school and in 1575 the corporation provided a new schoolhouse.

In the 17th century the masters of the grammar school included John Lister, George Holme, Anthony Ashton and Francis Meare.

Almshouses The Hospital of St Thomas, which was founded by Thomas Ellis in 1557, had accommodation for six poor men and women.

Inns There were many inns, including the White Hart, the Three Cranes and the Angel.

In 1675 Thomas Baskerville and his companions decided to stay at the Three Cranes but since the ale was not to their liking they moved elsewhere.

(*A Calendar to the Records of the Borough of Doncaster*, vol. i (1899). PRO, State Papers Domestic, Charles II, S.P.29/v/124. E.178/5 William and Mary/Trinity 9 and 13. E. Miller, *The History and Antiquities of Doncaster and its Vicinity* (1804). C. W. Hadfield, *Historical Notices of Doncaster* (1866). J. Tomlinson, *Doncaster from the Roman Occupation to the Present Time* (1887).)

DRAX
Barkston Ash

A village to the north-east of Snaith. The parish of Drax included several villages and hamlets. 1674: 100 households in Drax cum Birland (probably including Long Drax and Newland) and 33 in Camblesforth.

'Drax, a little village, formerly famous for a Monastery, where Philip de Tollevilla......had a castle strongly situated in the midst of rivers, woods, and marshes' (William Camden).

The Augustinian priory at Drax had been founded in the 12th century and dissolved in 1536.

In 1640 Joseph Inchbald was found guilty of 'enclosing and obstructing with hedges and ditches a common horse way between the town of Armine and the market town of Selbye.....so that the King's lieges could not travel by that way as of old accustomed'.

In 1681 the Court of Exchequer was asked to determine whether certain farms in the parish were part of the possessions of the former priory and therefore (as 'abbey land') exempt from the payment of tithes.

Church St Peter and St Paul: Norman, Early English, Decorated and Perpendicular.

School Charles Read, a judge who was a native of Drax, built a schoolhouse there and in his will (1669) provided a substantial endowment. His declared intention was that children of the parish should receive free instruction in reading, writing and accounts and (as required) in Latin, Greek or Hebrew.

Almshouses Read also left money for the building of a hospital for six poor people.

(*YASRS*, liv (1915), 188, 230. E.134/33 Charles II/Easter 7.)

EAST ARDSLEY
Agbrigg and Morley

A village to the north-west of Wakefield. There was no other village within the parish. 1674: 46 households (township of East Ardsley). 1676: 150 persons aged 16 or more (parish).

The Fields of East Ardsley were a minor gentry family. John Field, who died in 1587, had acquired a considerable reputation as a mathematician with a particular interest in astronomy.

In 1641 Robert Hall of East Ardsley was indicted at the Wakefield quarter sessions for keeping 'a very disordered alehowse, to the great disquiett and disturbance of his neighboures'. He was found guilty and banned from brewing and selling ale or beer for a period of three years.

Church St Michael: Norman and Perpendicular.

The minister was a perpetual curate.

(O. Field, 'John Field of East Ardsley', *YAJ*, xiv (1898). *YASRS*, liv (1915), 328-9.)

ECCLESFIELD

Strafford and Tickhill

A village to the north of Sheffield. Besides extensive tracts of moorland the parish of Ecclesfield contained a large number of villages and hamlets, including Bolsterstone, Bradfield and Midhope which had dependent chapels. 1674: 306 households in Ecclesfield and 403 in Bradfield (townships, including outlying settlements). 1676: 3267 persons aged 16 or more (parish).

There were several minor gentry with houses in the township of Ecclesfield: in particular, the Greenes of Thundercliffe Grange, the Scotts of Barnes Hall and the Shiercliffes of Ecclesfield Hall. In the Civil War Robert Greene and William Shiercliffe joined the royalists at York and as a result were forced to compound for their estates. On the other hand, some men from the township of Bradfield took up arms for Parliament.

Sir Richard Scott of Barnes Hall, who was a man of considerable ability, served as comptroller of Wentworth's household in Ireland and was appointed a member of the Privy Council there. At his death in 1638 he had no surviving issue.

In 1637 Henry Page of Bolsterstone, 'a common brewster', was indicted for having a drinking session in his house on the Sabbath day.

In 1641 Richard Watts, a clergyman, and others were indicted for entering Barnes Hall and ejecting the occupant, Samuel Vanpanie. Watts had inherited the hall from his half-brother Sir Richard Scott.

Church St John Baptist: mainly Perpendicular.

'This church is called (and that deservedly) by the vulger the Mynster of the Moores, being the fairest church for stone, wood, glass and neat keeping that ever I came in of contry church' (Roger Dodsworth, 1620).

Schools A school had been established at Ecclesfield in 1529 but its subsequent history remains obscure.

In 1622 Ralph Ellis of York endowed a school at Bolsterstone for the free education of children of the village. One of the first masters was Henry Hodgkinson who taught there for many years.

In his will (1653) Richard Spoone, a yeoman, made provision for the support of a schoolmaster at Stannington within the parish. He was to be responsible for teaching poor children of the neighbourhood. Spoone had already built a chapel at Stannington.

Almshouses Sir Richard Scott founded a hospital at Ecclesfield for six poor men. This was built in 1639 and had an endowment of £30 a year.

In 1693 Edward Sylvester provided Ecclesfield with another hospital. It contained accommodation for seven poor men or women who were to receive £3 a year each. Preference was to be given to persons from the north side of the parish.

(*YASRS*, liv (1915), 41, 330-1. W. K. Jordan, *The Charities of Rural England 1480-1660* (1961), 273, 334-5, 343-4. J. Eastwood, *History of the Parish of Ecclesfield* (1862). R. Gatty, *Guide to Ecclesfield Church* (1917).)

EDLINGTON

Strafford and Tickhill

A village near Doncaster. There were no other villages in the parish of Edlington. In a Commonwealth survey it was described as a small parish containing 24 families. 1674: 21 households. 1676: 83 persons aged 16 or more.

Peter Saxton, who was rector of Edlington between 1614 and 1640, was an ardent Puritan who was said to have described the surplice as a 'whore's smock'. In 1636 he was suspended for a time but he managed to retain his living. It has been conjectured that he might have been a son of Christopher Saxton the cartographer.

Church St Peter: Norman, 13th century and Perpendicular.

School A grammar school established in 1621.

Principal families (1) Stanhope of Edlington Hall (and Grimston Hall, Kirkby Wharfe). Estate revenue: £1000 a year (1626).

The Stanhopes owed their landed wealth to the professional ability of Sir Edward Stanhope (c.1540-1604), a lawyer who was Surveyor General of the Duchy of Lancaster and a legal member of the Council in the North.

His son Sir Edward (c.1570-1646) was a friend and ally of Strafford who called him 'cousin'. Perhaps as a result of improvidence he fell heavily into debt and between 1622 and 1639 disposed of most of his estate. On the eve of the Civil War the only remaining property was the manor of Grimston.

The manor of Edlington was sold in 1631 to a neighbouring landowner, Thomas Bosvile of Warmsworth. In 1662 it was bought by Sir Thomas Wharton, a brother of Philip Lord Wharton.

(2) Wharton of Edlington. Estate revenue: £2500 a year (1684).

Sir Thomas Wharton (c.1614-1684) had a reputation for great piety. In 1661 he was granted the reversion of the office of Warden of the Mint for himself and his son Philip. At his death he left a personal estate valued at over £8000 which included East India Company stock.

Philip Wharton (c.1652-1685) eventually became Warden of the Mint and shared the profits (amounting to between £400 and £500 a year) with his father. His first wife was Elizabeth Hutton, the only child of Richard Hutton of Goldsborough, and following her father's death in 1683 he inherited his large estate. His second wife, Angelica Magdalena, who was a Frenchwoman, brought him a portion of £6000. In the course of litigation in 1694 it was said that he 'was always reputed a ffrugall man and Litle or nothing indebted and free from any extravagant Expenses'.

In 1690 Mary Wharton his daughter and sole heir was abducted by Captain James Campbell and forced to marry him against her will. This was regarded as so shocking that a nation-wide hunt was launched. By 1693 she was lawfully married to a kinsman, Robert Byerley.

Edlington Hall A three-storeyed Elizabethan house built by Sir Edward Stanhope the elder. In 1674 Sir Thomas Wharton was taxed on 21 hearths.

(R. A. Marchant, *The Puritans and the Church Courts in the Diocese of York 1560-1642* (1960), 275-6. *Catalogue of the Lumley MSS.* C.10/218/92; 273/113; and 346/14.)

ELLAND   Agbrigg and Morley

A clothing village to the south of Halifax which was situated on the River Calder. It was also a chapelry within the parish of Halifax. 1674: 148 households (township of Elland cum Greetland).

Since 1317 Elland had enjoyed the right to hold a weekly market and two annual fairs.

The manor of Elland, which included a park, belonged to the Savile family of Thornhill and later of Rufford in Nottinghamshire. It was worth £108 a year in 1623 and £203 a year in 1651. In 1668 Sir George Savile (the future Marquess of Halifax) was ennobled as Baron Savile of Eland and Viscount Halifax. His son and heir was known as Lord Eland. The choice of this subsidiary title was a reflection of the family's long association with Elland. They had acquired the manor in the 14th century through the marriage of Sir John Savile and Isabel de Eland and for a time they had been seated there.

One of the more prominent residents of Elland in the early 17th century was Jasper Blythman (1558-1633) who was for some years the tenant of Elland Hall. He was the second husband of Margaret Wentworth, the sister of Sir William Wentworth of Wentworth Woodhouse, and through this alliance he was also related to the Saviles of Thornhill. Sir William does not appear to have approved of the marriage. In 1607 he wrote of his brother-in-law that he was 'a pore gentleman.....sometime servant to my father' and subsequently to his sister's first husband. Blythman, however, managed by one means or another to build up an estate which was considered to be sufficiently large to justify his appointment as a West Riding magistrate.

In 1637 the inhabitants of Elland were ordered to repair the road descending from Elland Bank into the centre of their village.

Church St Mary: mainly Perpendicular.

(Nottinghamshire Record Office, Savile of Rufford MSS, 28/5. *Wentworth Papers 1597-1628* (ed. J. P. Cooper), *Camden Fourth Series*, 12 (1973), 31-2. *YASRS*, liv (1915), 32. J. Watson, *The History and Antiquities of the Parish of Halifax* (1775).)

EMLEY   Agbrigg and Morley

A village between Huddersfield and Barnsley which was situated in moorland. The parish of Emley included the hamlet of Kirkby and part of Cumberworth Half (the modern

Skelmanthorpe); the other part was in the parish of Kirkburton. 1674: 72 households in Emley and 31 in Cumberworth. 1676: 360 persons aged 16 or more (parish).

By a royal charter of 1253 Emley had the right to hold a weekly market and an annual fair.

The manor of Emley belonged to the Saviles of Thornhill and later of Rufford in Nottinghamshire who had a deer park there. The annual revenue from the property rose from £189 in 1623 to £524 in 1651. Coal was mined in Emley but this appears to have been conducted on a modest scale.

In the early 17th century Emley had two Puritan rectors, Robert Kay and Laurence Farrington. At a visitation in 1632 Farrington was accused of substituting psalms for canticles and was suspended for a time.

In 1637 Edith Castlehouse of Flockton was indicted for assaulting Thomas Roods at Emley and 'beating, wounding, and maltreating him so that his life was despaired of'.

The Asshetons of Kirkby Hall were a cadet branch of the Asshetons of Middleton in Lancashire. In the reign of James I Sir Richard Assheton built a house for his son Ralph at Kirkby. Ralph Assheton (c.1590-1645) had an estate there and elsewhere in the West Riding which produced an income of some £300 a year. In his commonplace book he recorded a number of developments, mainly of local significance, in the months preceding and immediately following the outbreak of the Civil War. On 23 September 1642 the high constable, acting on the directions of Sir William Savile and other royalists, summoned all the West Riding trained bands to assemble at Wakefield but, Assheton noted, most of them failed to appear. Within a matter of days the inhabitants of Emley received a message from the Yorkshire parliamentarians which called upon the trained bands to rendezvous at Leeds where they were to be inspected by Ferdinando Lord Fairfax and Sir John Savile of Lupset. The following day Sir John was captured by royalist troops.

On 13 December 1642 Sir William Savile issued a warrant to the constable of Emley which ordered the trained bands to appear at Wakefield. In response to this warrant Assheton sent his servant John Wilkinson with some weapons and a letter requesting Sir William to take the horse which he had lent him in lieu of the sum of £3 which he was demanding. At the end of the year a parliamentarian force under Sir Henry Foulis descended on Emley and took away rich hangings, carpets and other goods belonging to Sir William Savile to the value of £1000.

On 21 January 1643 parliamentarian troops again arrived in Emley and Assheton was taken prisoner to Halifax. Sir Thomas Fairfax, however, ordered his release. In the course of this operation many of the deer in Emley Park were killed.

On 9 July 1643 the Earl of Newcastle, who was then in control of the West Riding, gave Assheton a pass authorising him to travel to and from Middleton in Lancashire without hindrance.

Church St Michael: Norman and Perpendicular.

School William Wigglesworth founded a school at Emley in the reign of Charles II. A schoolhouse was built in 1673.

(Nottinghamshire Record Office, Savile of Rufford MSS, 28/5. R. A. Marchant, *The Puritans and the Church Courts in the Diocese of York 1560-1642* (1960), 246, 258. *YASRS*, liv (1915), 30. C.10/17/3 and 474/3. BI., Additional MSS 24,475 (papers of Ralph Assheton of Kirkby.))

FARNHAM   Claro

A small village to the north of Knaresborough. The parish of Farnham included the village of Scotton and parts of Arkendale and Ferrensby; the other parts were in the parish of Knaresborough. 1674: 25 households in Farnham, 52 in Arkendale, 17 in Ferrensby and 37 in Scotton.

At the beginning of the 17th century there were two minor gentry families residing in Scotton: the Percys of Percy Hall and the Pulleynes of Scotton Hall. Both families had Catholic affiliations. John Percy (1588-c.1670) moved to Walden Stubbs, near Pontefract, before the time of the Civil War while John Pulleyne (1559-1618) is said to have been the last member of his family to die at Scotton Hall.

In 1670 a Quaker burial ground was established at Scotton.

Church St Oswald: Norman, Decorated and Perpendicular.

(Catherine Pullein, *The Pulleyns of Yorkshire* (1915).)

FARNLEY   Agbrigg and Morley

A village and chapelry within the parish of Leeds. 1674: 39 households.

Farnley was one of the seats of the Danby family (see under Well, North Riding). They mined coal in the wastes.

In 1663 the authorities arrested a number of men involved in the so-called Farnley Wood Plot. It was alleged that a group of Presbyterians and Anabaptists had been preparing to take part in a general uprising. Following this episode 24 men were convicted and executed.

Church St Michael: a public chapel which had originally been established in the early 15th century as a chantry chapel.

Farnley Hall A gabled Elizabethan house which was completed by Sir Thomas Danby in 1586. In 1664 and 1674 there were 19 taxable hearths.

In a particular of the Danby estate drawn up in 1624 the rents and profits of Farnley Park and the colliery were valued at £60 a year.

(North Yorkshire County Record Office, Cunliffe-Lister (Swinton) MSS. A. Hopper, 'The Farnley Wood Plot and the Memory of the Civil Wars in Yorkshire', *The Historical Journal*, 45 (2002).)

FEATHERSTONE   Osgoldcross/Agbrigg and Morley

A village to the west of Pontefract. The parish of Featherstone included several villages. 1674: 43 households in Featherstone, 21 in Ackton, 58 in Purston Jaglin and 24 in Whitwood. 1676: 338 persons aged 16 or more (parish).

In 1640 the West Riding magistrates were informed that 'the King's highway leading between the market towns of Wakefeild and Pontefract.....within the Township of Purston Jacklin.....is now in great decay for lack of repair'.

The following year sixteen inhabitants of the parish of Featherstone were indicted for recusancy. The survival of Catholicism in the parish owed much to the influence of the Hamertons of Purston Jaglin, a gentry family of ancient lineage. The head of the family was usually a convicted recusant who was prepared to accept the financial consequences of his religious beliefs.

In the Civil War Matthew Hamerton (1574-1644) supported the royalist cause and his sons Philip (1602-1651) and Edward both took up arms for the king.

Another Catholic family, the Beckwiths of Ackton, managed to remain neutral during the war. In 1650 Thomas Beckwith sold the manor of Ackton and lands in Featherstone to Langdale Sunderland for £4400. Sunderland disposed of his estate in the parish of Halifax and settled at Ackton. In 1671 he told his sons that if the coalmines on Featherstone Moor were properly managed, with 'a true banksman' in charge, they would produce a clear profit of nearly £200 a year.

Church All Saints: Norman in origin.

Almshouses In 1568 John Hamerton endowed a small hospital which he had built at Featherstone. This provided accommodation for four poor women of the parish.

(*YASRS*, liv (1915), 187, 297. *CRS*, liii (1961), 309-10. S.P.23/cxx/831. F.H. Sunderland, *Marmaduke Lord Langdale* (1926), 215. W. K. Jordan, *The Charities of Rural England 1480-1660* (1961), 262.)

FELKIRK   Staincross

Felkirk, situated to the north of Barnsley, consisted of little more than a church. The parish of Felkirk included several villages and hamlets. 1674: 39 households in Brierley, 9 in Havercroft, 23 in Shafton and 36 in South Hiendley. 1676: 200 persons aged 16 or more (parish of Felkirk).

Church St Peter: Norman in origin but mainly Perpendicular.

School In her will (1637) Mrs Prudence Berrie left £100 to provide support for a schoolmaster for the parish of Felkirk. A school was duly established at Havercroft.

Principal family Berrie of Hodroyd Hall, South Hiendley. Estate revenue: £1500 a year (1651). Coalmines in Havercroft and South Hiendley.

Dr Richard Berrie (c.1586-1651) was a physician with a lucrative practice in London who became a major Yorkshire squire. Between 1623 and 1640 he bought a number of manors, some of them belonging to Sir Richard Gargrave. In 1637 he acquired further property through his marriage to Sir Richard's niece Prudence Gargrave of Hodroyd. Shortly afterwards she was presented for recusancy while in 1648 it was alleged that he and most of his servants were suspected papists.

Berrie managed his estate in a businesslike way and went in for agricultural experiment. He also engaged in moneylending on an extensive scale.

During the Civil War he lent £400 for the service of Parliament but it was later alleged that he had supported the royalist cause. In 1649 he wrote that 'I was always well affected to the parliament, and never spoke nor did any thing for the king's partie but by compulsion and for feare'. He was exonerated shortly before his death.

Since he had no legitimate issue he gave direction in his will (1651) that the bulk of his estate should descend to his natural daughter Mary. She married Marmaduke Monckton (c.1623-1688) who in compliance with her father's wishes assumed the name of Berrie. According to a contemporary he was 'a gentleman of great worth and ingenuity, to whom for some contrivances in mechanical motions many are indebted'.

Following the death of Mary Berrie in 1691 without issue the estate was divided between the heirs.

Hodroyd Hall Dr Berrie rebuilt or substantially improved the house.

(BL, Additional MSS 24,470 and 24,475. Nottingham University Library, Galway of Serlby MSS, 9308, 9468, 9486, 12,804. C.6/311/7.)

FERRY FRYSTON   Osgoldcross

A village to the north-east of Pontefract. Some houses were in the parish of Ferry Fryston and the rest in the parish of Pontefact. The neighbouring village of Ferrybridge (which was described in 1641 as a hamlet) appears to have been wholly within the parish of Pontefract but it is included here on account of its close links with Ferry Fryston. 1674: 61 households in Ferrybridge and Ferry Fryston.

At Ferrybridge 'the northern road' crossed the River Aire. From Wentbridge 'we ascended a very steepe hill and so to Ferry-bridge 3 mile, where we pass'd the fine River called the Aire, large for Barges' (Celia Fiennes, 1697).

Because of its geographical position Ferrybridge had an importance out of all proportion to its size. Not only did it have a postmaster (in common with such towns as York and Doncaster) but it provided services for travellers journeying up and down the king's highway. In 1686 its inns had 34 'guest beds' and stabling for 95 horses.

In 1638 the West Riding magistrates received a report about 'the great ruyne and decay of Ferry bridge, the same being the high roade way betweene the cittye of London and the cittye of Yorke for all passengers, both foote and horse'. They decided that the sum of £20 should be levied on the riding as a whole to meet the cost of the repair work.

In 1641 the magistrates were informed that it had been the practice to have a deputy constable in Ferrybridge 'when the constable is chosen in Ferryfriston because of the highroade through.....Ferrybriggs and multitudes of people that doe usually resort thither'. In the light of this submission it was agreed that the custom should continue to be followed and that the present constable of Ferry Fryston should appoint a deputy.

At the same quarter sessions there was a complaint by some of the inhabitants of Ferry Fryston that they were 'sore overchardged in their constable layes' and that 'the meanest and poorest sort of people, which are relieved by the parish, are lyable to as great a proporcon as the ablest and richest persons'. The magistrates responded sympathetically and ruled that every assessment, whether on behalf of the Church or the Crown, should be based on the number of acres which each man occupied.

During the Civil War there were many comings and goings through Ferrybridge. In March 1645 a parliamentarian force fared badly there at the hands of Sir Marmaduke Langdale's troops.

In 1667 Captain John Mason, who was being taken under guard to York, was freed by an armed gang which mounted an ambush at Ferrybridge. This was considered to be 'the most insolent act against the King and the Government that had hapned of a long time'.

Church St Andrew: Norman and Perpendicular.

(*YASRS*, liv (1915), 69, 282, 284. PRO, W.O. 30/48, fo.207. *Memoirs of Sir John Reresby* (ed. A Browning and others) (1991), 69-70.)

FEWSTON Claro

A village to the north of Otley which was situated on the River Washburn. Besides extensive moorland the parish of Fewston contained several villages, including Thruscross which had a dependent chapel. 1674: 80 households in Timble cum Fewston, 20 in Blubberhouses, 72 in Norwood cum Clifton and 82 in Thruscross.

In 1640 the West Riding magistrates received a report about 'the great ruyne and decay of Fewston Bridge, leadinge betweene the markett townes of Knaresbrough and Skipton'. They asked two of their number, Ferdinando Lord Fairfax and Ingram Hopton, to view the bridge and assess the cost of the necessary repair work; and they ruled that it should be funded by a levy on the whole wapentake. Subsequently they were informed that the cost would amount to £45.

Church St Lawrence: Perpendicular, but largely rebuilt in 1697.

(*YASRS*, liv (1915), 213, 343-4, 378-9, 400.)

FISHLAKE   Strafford and Tickhill

A village to the north-east of Doncaster which was situated on the River Don. The parish of Fishlake included the village of Sykehouse which had a dependent chapel. 1674: 118 households in Fishlake and 95 in Sykehouse. 1676: 564 persons aged 16 or more, including 136 Protestant dissenters (parish).

At a visitation in 1632 Thomas Petty the vicar of Fishlake was accused of neglecting to wear a surplice and of substituting psalms for canticles. He had held the living since 1589.

In December 1697 there was a heavy snowfall which was followed by severe flooding. A flood 'came roeing all of a suddain, about eleven a clock at night, unto Bramwith, Fishlake, Thorn and other towns…..the loss is vastly great. The people of Sikehouse, and many in Fishlake, being drownded up to the very eves, so that they reckon no less than 3000 pound damage to be done by the same in the parish of Fishlake' (Abraham de la Pryme).

Church St Cuthbert: Norman, Early English, Decorated and Perpendicular.

School In 1641 Richard Rands, who was the rector of Hartfield in Sussex, left £300 for the establishment and support of a free grammar school at Fishlake where he had been born.

(R. A. Marchant, *The Puritans and the Church Courts in the Diocese of York 1560-1642* (1960), 268-9. W. K. Jordan, *The Charities of Rural England 1480-1660* (1961), 341.)

FOUNTAINS   Claro

Fountains Abbey was 'formerly a stately Abbey, as appears by the very ruins, now full of trees within the very body of it; and a stately modern hall' (Ralph Thoresby, 1682).

The Fountains Abbey estate, which was situated within the parish of Ripon, contained few houses. 1674: 9 households.

The abbey, which was an establishment of Cistercian monks, had been founded in the 12th century and dissolved in 1539.

Principal families (1) Proctor of Fountains Hall. Estate revenue: £600 a year (1618). Lead mining in Bewerley.

Sir Stephen Proctor bought the house and site of the dissolved monastery of Fountains in 1598 and the manor of Fountains and Fountains Park in 1604.

An arch-enemy of Catholics, he was involved in protracted litigation with such families as the Inglebys of Ripley and the Mallorys of Studley who not only regarded him as a self-seeking upstart but took strong exception to his activities as a magistrate and Collector and Receiver of Fines on Penal Statutes. In 1611 it was said of him that 'hee hath ben by the evell affected reputed too officious and malliced'. He himself complained in a Star Chamber suit that Sir William Ingleby out of his 'great hatred and mallice' had sought to make him spend £3000 or £4000 in legal proceedings. In 1614 he was found guilty of slander but acquitted on appeal.

At the time of his death (c.1619) he was in severe financial difficulties. He left four daughters but no son.

In 1622 his widow, Dame Honor, and others of the family sold the Fountains estate.

(2) Messenger of Fountains Hall. Estate revenue: £300 a year (1641).

In 1627 Richard Ewens bought the Fountains estate for £4000. Shortly afterwards it was in the possession of his son-in-law John Messenger who had contributed £2700 of the purchase money.

Ironically, the Messengers were a zealous Catholic family who sometimes had a resident chaplain.

In the Civil War John Messenger served as a royalist captain and Fountains Hall was plundered on several occasions by parliamentarian troops.

Fountains Hall Sir Stephen Proctor built the hall using stone from the abbey ruins. It was completed in 1611 at a cost of £3000 and this probably explains why he sold a grange in Fountains Park and other property for £2800 at about the same time.

In 1674 William Messenger was taxed on 11 hearths.

(WYAS, Leeds, Vyner MSS. *Surtees Society*, lxvii (1878). C.33/212/fo.408. STAC8/227/1, 3, 4, 6, 7, 35, 36.)

GARFORTH Skyrack

A village to the east of Leeds. The parish of Garforth included part of the hamlet of Austhorpe; the other part was in the parish of Whitkirk. 1674: 44 households in Garforth and 17 in Austhorpe. 1676: 120 persons aged 16 or more (parish).

The manor of Garforth belonged to the Gascoignes of Barnbow Hall who mined coal there. In 1638 the West Riding magistrates ordered Sir Thomas Gascoigne to 'fill upp the fences or hedges about the coal pitts on the waste commonly called Garforth more'.

The manor was worth £150 a year in 1642 and £134 a year in 1661.
Church St Mary: Saxon or Norman in origin.
(WYAS, Leeds, Gascoigne of Barnbow MSS, E12/2/2 and EG/11. *YASRS*, liv (1915), 61.)

GARGRAVE   Staincliffe and Ewecross

A village to the north-west of Skipton. The parish of Gargrave included several villages. 1674: 69 households in Gargrave, 22 in Bank Newton, 35 in Coniston Cold, 29 in Eshton and 42 in Flasby cum Winterburn. 1676: 583 persons aged 16 or more (parish).

Gargrave is 'a pretty village' (Roger Dodsworth).

In 1638 the West Riding magistrates were informed that Gargrave Bridge, which was a wooden structure, was in 'great ruyne and decay' and that the sum of £300 would need to be spent on replacing it with a stone bridge, 'which must of necessitie be soe, because there is noe tymber in that parte of the countrye fitt for that worke, and the said bridge being soe usefull and commodious for the whole countrye, being the high roade way betweene the city of London and the countyes of Westmorland and Cumberland'. After debating the question of financial responsibility the justices decided that £200 should be levied on the wapentakes of Staincliffe, Ewecross and Claro and that the remainder should be treated as a charge on the West Riding as a whole. In July 1639 it was reported that the work was now half-finished but that so far only £160 had been collected; accordingly the magistrates gave order that the financial process should be speeded up.

In July 1643 the royalist committee for the West Riding received information that John Waite the vicar of Gargrave 'hath absented himself from his said cure and joined himself to his majesty's enemies'.

Church St Andrew: Perpendicular.
School In 1686 Henry Coulthurst, a local landowner, founded a free school at Gargrave for the sons of residents of the parish.
(*YASRS*, liv (1915), 70-1, 125, 137 and lxi (1920), 153-4.)

GIGGLESWICK   Staincliffe and Ewecross

A village in Ribblesdale. The parish of Giggleswick included the market town of Settle and several villages. 1674: 89 households in Giggleswick, 30 in Langcliffe, 49 in Rathmell, 101 in Settle and 48 in Stainforth. 1676: 716 persons aged 16 or more (parish of Giggleswick).

Giggleswick appears briefly in Richard Braithwaite's poem about the journeys of 'Drunken Barnaby' which was first published in 1638:

Thence to Giggleswick most steril,
Hemm'd with Rocks and Shelves of Peril.

'....to Giggleswick, where viewed the noted well.....that ebbs and flows daily, though far from sea; where likewise is a pretty church, and noted school, founded by Mr Bridges, and endowed with about £50 per annum' (Ralph Thoresby, 1681).

Christopher Shute, who served as vicar of Giggleswick in the years 1576 to 1626, was the leading Puritan clergyman in Craven. Anthony Lister, who was presented to the living in 1641, held similar views but was willing to conform at the Restoration and remained as vicar until his death in 1686.

In July 1643 the royalist committee for the West Riding was informed that Lister had 'late absented himself from his cure and joined with his majesty's enemies'.

The right to hold a market and a fair at Settle had been granted by a charter of 1249. The primary function of the weekly market was the sale of livestock.

In 1670 Richard Frankland (1630-1698), a Presbyterian divine, opened an academy at Rathmell, where he had been born, and this shortly assumed the role of a training establishment for nonconformist ministers.

Churches St Alkelda, Giggleswick: Norman in origin but basically Perpendicular.

In 1689 a licence was obtained for a Quaker meeting place in Settle.

School There was a school at Giggleswick in the early years of the 16th century and in 1512 a schoolhouse was built.

Giggleswick Grammar School was refounded by letters patent in 1553 when provision was made for the appointment of governors. Christopher Shute was master of the school in the years 1616 to 1619. Among his successors were Robert Dockray (who was also vicar between 1632 and 1641), William Walker, William Briggs and John Armitstead.

(Richard Braithwaite, *Drunken Barnaby's Four Journeys to the North of England* (3rd edition, 1723). R. A. Marchant, *The Puritans and the Church Courts in the Diocese of York 1560-1642* (1960), 22, 24, 31, 260, 278. E. A. Bell, *A History of Giggleswick School from its foundation, 1499-1912* (1912). H. L. Mullins (ed.), *The Giggleswick School Register 1499-1913* (1913). T. Brayshaw and R. M. Robinson, *A History of the Ancient Parish of Giggleswick* (1932).)

GISBURN   Staincliffe and Ewecross

A township in Ribblesdale. The extensive parish of Gisburn included a number of villages and hamlets. 1674: 40 households in Gisburn, 16 in Horton, 13 in Middop, 9 in Nappa, 13 in Newsholme, 36 in Paythorne, 69 in Rimington and 13 in Swinden. 1676: 950 persons aged 16 or more (parish of Gisburn).

A royal charter of 1260 had granted the right to hold a weekly market on Mondays and an annual fair.

At Rimington there were lead and coal workings.

Early on in the Civil War Thomas Bullingham the royalist vicar of Gisburn was apprehended by parliamentarian troops and imprisoned for eight weeks at Manchester.

Church St Mary: Norman tower but mainly Perpendicular.

School A free grammar school had been established at Gisburn in 1580. In the 17th century the masters included Richard Tennant, John Oddie and Nicholas Robinson.

Principal families (1) Lister of Lower Hall, Westby and Arnolds Biggin, Rimington. Estate revenue: £1100 a year (1660).

Following the death of Thomas Lister in 1619 his son Thomas was made a ward of the Crown. In negotiations with the Court of Wards his grandfather Thomas Heber claimed that the deceased had been heavily in debt. Some of his property in Gisburn had been leased to tenants for 4000 years.

Thomas Lister (1615-1642) was killed early on in the Civil War while serving as a parliamentarian captain. His son Thomas (1635-1660) also became a ward of the Crown, though by this time the Court of Wards was coming under the control of Parliament. He left only an infant daughter, Katherine, and his brother John (1642-1674) entered into possession of the estate. In 1681 Katherine and her husband Thomas Yorke began legal proceedings in which they claimed that she was entitled to the bulk of her father's landed property. In the event the Court of Chancery found in favour of Thomas Lister (1665-1706) who also inherited an estate from a distant relative.

(2) Marsden of Gisburn Hall (and Wennington Hall, Malling, Lancashire). Estate revenue: £1200 a year (1688).

Henry Marsden (c.1625-1688) was a man of modest social origin who grew rich as an attorney and moneylender and built up a large estate.

Arnolds Biggin A Jacobean house near Gisburn but within the township of Rimington. In his will (1619) Thomas Lister referred to the completion of his new house at Arnolds Biggin. In the mid-17th century it superseded Lower Hall, Westby as the family's principal residence.

In 1674 John Lister was taxed on 16 hearths.

Gisburn Hall There were 11 taxable hearths in 1664 and 1674.

(*YASRS*, lxi (1920), 157. Wards 5/49. C.10/483/325. C.10/438/21.)

GOLDSBOROUGH   Claro

A village near Knaresborough. The parish of Goldsborough included the hamlets of Coneythorpe and Flaxby. 1674: 30 households in Goldsborough, 26 in Allerton cum Flaxby and 17 in Coneythorpe. Allerton Mauleverer was a separate parish.

Church St Mary: Norman, Early English, Decorated and Perpendicular.

Principal family Hutton of Goldsborough Hall (and Hooton Pagnell Hall). Estate revenue: £1000 a year (1641 and 1660).

Sir Richard Hutton (1561-1638) bought the Goldsborough estate in 1601. An eminent lawyer, he eventually became a judge of the Court of Common Pleas. In 1637 he was one of the judges who found in favour of John Hampden in the famous ship money case.

His son Sir Richard (c.1594-1645) was a brother-in-law of Strafford. In the Civil War he served as a royalist colonel of foot and was fatally wounded at the battle of Sherburn. An elegy in his honour was published by Sir Francis Wortley in 1646.

Richard Hutton (c.1626-1683) inherited a heavily encumbered estate which was charged with two jointures. He left only a daughter, Elizabeth, who had married Philip Wharton of Edlington (see under Edlington).

Goldsborough Hall The house of the Goldesborough family was largely demolished towards the end of Elizabeth's reign, though some part of 'the old howse' was being used for storage purposes in the late 17th century.

Sir Richard Hutton (1561-1638) built a new mansion during the reign of James I. A large gabled house of brick.

Richard Hutton was taxed on 26 hearths in 1664 and 29 in 1674.

Among the rooms listed in an inventory of 1684 were the great hall, the little hall, the great and little parlours, the great dining room, the gallery and the study. The inventory also refers to the great staircase where four large pictures and 30 smaller ones were displayed.

There was a deer park belonging to the hall.

(C.10/228/46 and 273/66 and 113.)

GREAT HOUGHTON   Strafford and Tickhill

A small village within the parish of Darfield, near Barnsley. 1674: 25 households.

In 1645 there was an outbreak of the plague.

Principal family Rodes of Houghton Hall. Estate revenue: £600 a year (1637). Coalmining.

Sir Edward Rodes (1601-1667), who succeeded his father in 1634, was a man with strong Puritan convictions. Although he was a brother-in-law of Strafford he immediately took up arms for Parliament on the outbreak of the Civil War and eventually became a member of Cromwell's Council of State. In September 1642 a royalist force attacked and plundered Houghton Hall and destroyed the outbuildings. One of his servants was killed and others wounded.

In 1650 Sir Edward built a Presbyterian chapel in the grounds of Houghton Hall for the use of his household and tenantry. After the Restoration the ecclesiastical authorities appear to have taken the view that it was a domestic chapel. In 1669 they were informed that it was used for conventicles which were attended by some 60 Presbyterians and Independents.

At the time of his death Sir Edward was heavily in debt. In his will (1664) he referred to the fact that much of his property in Great Houghton (including part of his wife's jointure) had been mortgaged to Sir John Bright of Badsworth.

Following the Declaration of Indulgence in 1672 his widow, Dame Mary, secured a licence for Jeremiah Milner, a Presbyterian divine, to serve as minister at Great Houghton and he was employed for some years as household chaplain. Many nonconformist ministers were invited to preach in the chapel. In his diary Oliver Heywood records that in May 1679 he rode over to Houghton Hall and 'conversed with that sweet ingenious family' and that on his next visit in July he 'prayed and preached 4 or 5 houres, a full assembly'.

In April 1681 Lady Rodes and her son Godfrey died within a few days of each other and this drew forth some elegiac verse which contained the exhortation

Let Houghton Hall their memory revive
keep up Religion ye that do survive.

In 1689 William Rodes (1639-1696) had the house and chapel licensed for the purposes of nonconformist worship.

Houghton Hall An H-shaped Elizabethan mansion built by Francis Rodes. In 1664 there were 19 taxable hearths.

When Ralph Thoresby visited Houghton Hall in 1686 he wrote that there were portraits of some eminent statesmen of Queen Elizabeth's reign and 'family pieces' of the Earl of Strafford and Sir Edward Rodes.

(Sheffield Archives, Crewe MSS. J. T. Cliffe, *The Puritan Gentry Besieged 1650-1700* (1993), 112-15, 120-1, 193, 195, 223-4.)

GREAT MITTON   Staincliffe and Ewecross

A Craven village on the exteme western edge of the riding. The parish of Mitton contained several Yorkshire villages, including Grindleton and Waddington which had dependent chapels, and also extended into Lancashire. The village of Bashall is separately noticed. 1674: 34 households in Great Mitton, 77 in Grindleton, 60 in Waddington and 41 in West Bradford. 1676: 1139 persons aged 16 or more (parish, including the Lancashire section).

Within the parish there were a considerable number of Catholics who enjoyed the patronage of a wealthy gentry family, the Sherburnes of Stonyhurst in the Lancashire part of the parish.

During the reign of James I Roger Brearley, a radical Puritan, was curate of Grindleton chapel. At a visitation in 1615 he was charged, among other things, with neglecting to use the Book of Common Prayer and two years later his nonconformity led to proceedings before the Northern High Commission. Brearley's theological opinions had a pronounced mystical character and the novelty of his preaching aroused great interest among the inhabitants of the district. In 1619 the ecclesiastical authorities were informed that 'many goe to Grindleton and neglect their owne parish church'. Brearley's followers came to be known as Grindletonians.

Church St Michael: Early English and Perpendicular.

In 1594 a chapel was added to serve as a burial place for the Sherburne family.

(R. A. Marchant, *The Puritans and the Church Courts in the Diocese of York 1560-1642* (1960), 40, 231. F. G. Ackerley, *A History of the Parish of Mitton* (1947).)

GREAT OUSEBURN Claro

A village to the south-east of Boroughbridge. The parish of Great Ouseburn included part of Upper Dunsforth; the other part was in the parish of Aldborough. 1674: 56 households in Great Ouseburn and 32 in Dunsforth.

Church St Mary: Norman, Early English and Perpendicular.

GUISELEY Skyrack

A village near Otley. The parish of Guiseley contained several villages, including Horsforth and Rawdon which had dependent chapels. (For Rawdon chapel see below). 1674: 33 households in Guiseley, 116 in Horsforth, 56 in Rawdon and 64 in Yeadon.

Robert Moore, who was rector of Guiseley in the years 1581 to 1644, was a Puritan who declared in his will that while he had strong reservations about 'needles Ceremonyes' he had considered it 'fitt and convenient to submitt my selfe to a wise and discreete Tolleratinge and usinge of them till the tyme of reformacion'. At the same time he took the opportunity to launch an attack on the lay ownership of rectories and tithes and the prevalence of 'ignorant reading Ministers' within the Church.

His successor, Robert Hitch, was also rector of Adel. In the Civil War period the parliamentarians deprived him of his living of Adel but allowed him to retain his living of Guiseley. In 1657 he claimed that he had always been loyal to Parliament.

Church St Oswald: Norman, Early English and Perpendicular.

The rectory was built in 1601.

School In his will (1642) Robert Moore the rector settled property for the maintenance of a schoolmaster. The master was to be appointed by the rector of Guiseley.

Principal family Layton of East Hall, Rawdon. Estate revenue: £370 a year (1640); £600 a year (1669).

Francis Layton (1578-1661) was an official of the Jewel House in London. In 1614 he bought the manors of Rawdon and Yeadon and one-fifth of the manor of Horsforth but did not take up residence at East Hall until some years later.

In the Civil War he was branded as a royalist for refusing to assist the parliamentary forces at Bradford. In 1645 he was said to be £3550 in debt.

Layton had been planning to build a public chapel for the inhabitants of Rawdon during the reign of Charles I and in 1631 had obtained the consent of Robert Moore, the rector of Guiseley. Since, however, Archbishop Neile of York refused to grant him the right of presentation he decided to shelve the project and it was not until the late 1640s that he put work in hand. In 1652 he made arrangements for continuing this work by settling an annuity of £40 on trustees. In his will (1653) he stipulated that the minister should be paid £20 a year and that the Layton family should have the right of presentation.

His son Henry (1622-1705) completed the building work and the chapel was consecrated in 1684. He was described by Ralph Thoresby as 'a good historian and accomplished gentleman'. His literary works included a book on English coins (1697) and a series of anonymous pamphlets published between 1692 and 1704 in which he questioned the concept of the immortality of the soul.

East Hall A gabled Elizabethan house built of millstone grit. In 1674 Henry Layton was taxed on nine hearths.

(R. A. Marchant, *The Puritans and the Church Courts in the Diocese of York 1560-1642* (1960), 20-1, 25-6, 212-14, 263-4. A. G. Matthews, *Walker Revised* (1988), 394. *CSP Dom, 1656-7*, 298. W. Cudworth, 'The Layton Family of Rawdon', *Bradford Antiquary*, New Series, ii (1905). W. Robertshaw, 'A Rawdon Cavalier', *Bradford Antiquary*, New Series, viii (1962). BL, Additional MSS 10,039, fo.26. P. Slater, *History of the Ancient Parish of Guiseley* (1880).)

HALIFAX Agbrigg and Morley

A market town and one of the major centres of the clothing industry in the West Riding. The parish of Halifax was believed to be as large as, if not larger than, the county of Rutland. It contained a large number of villages and no fewer than twelve public chapels, including parochial chapels at Elland and Heptonstall. Elland, Midgley, Northowram, Rastrick (with Fixby) and Skircoat are separately noticed. 1674: 464 households in

Halifax, 97 in Barkisland, 74 in Erringden, 99 in Heptonstall, 140 in Hipperholme cum Brighouse, 60 in Langfield, 53 in Norland, 196 in Ovenden, 72 in Rishworth, 63 in Shelf, 116 in Southowram, 340 in Sowerby, 89 in Stainland, 184 in Stansfield, 147 in Wadsworth and 188 in Warley. 1676: 14,000 persons aged 16 or more, including 150 Protestant dissenters (parish of Halifax but excluding Rastrick chapelry).

The town had the right to hold a market by prescription rather than by charter.

The clothing trade was carried on not only in Halifax but in all the surrounding villages. In the reign of Charles I there were said to be 12,000 textile workers within the parish.

The term 'Halifax law' referred to the practice of summarily executing anyone who was caught stealing cloth. The 'engine' used for this purpose was an apparatus similar to a guillotine which continued in use until at least 1650. This method of justice was primarily responsible for the Yorkshire saying

From Hell, Hull and Halifax
Good Lord deliver us.

Coal was mined in Hipperholme, Sowerby and elsewhere within the parish.

The parish was a strongly Protestant area. In 1637 it was claimed that there was not a single popish recusant. During the early 17th century the parish church had a succession of Puritan incumbents and lecturers or preachers. The most celebrated of these ministers was John Favour who served as vicar from 1593 until his death in 1623 and was also an author and physician. Although he was a member of the Northern High Commission he was presented in 1619 for neglecting to wear a surplice. In 1669 it was reported that within the parish there were 20 or 30 Independents and 100 Quakers.

Nothing 'is so admirable in this town as the industry of the inhabitants who .... have so flourish'd by the Cloath trade .... that they are both very rich, and have gain'd a reputation for it above their neighbours' (William Camden).

In 1635 it was said that Halifax was much impoverished because of the great multitude of poor people who were daily increasing and the heavy burden of assessments for their relief which was forcing many persons of substance to move elsewhere.

There were outbreaks of the plague shortly before the Civil War and in 1645.

At the beginning of the Civil War Halifax was garrisoned for Parliament. In July 1643 royalist troops took over the town after the garrison had fled but a year later the parliamentarians regained possession. During the war Dr Richard Marsh the royalist vicar of Halifax was apprehended by parliamentarian troops and deprived of his livings.

In 1645 it was reported that in Halifax and Northowram there were some 1600 poor people who were living on charity.

John Tillotson (1630-1694), who became Archbishop of Canterbury in 1691, was born in Sowerby.

Churches St John Baptist: Norman, Decorated and Perpendicular. In 1628 the steeple was damaged by lightning.

After the passage of the Act of Toleration in 1689 a number of nonconformist meeting houses were established.

School Heath Grammar School or the Free School of Queen Elizabeth had been founded in 1585 (see the entry for Skircoat).

There had been a school at Heptonstall in 1564. In 1638 Abraham Wall, a London glazier who was a native of Heptonstall, left the sum of £4 a year for the support of a schoolmaster who was to teach poor children free of charge. Shortly afterwards Charles Greenwood built a schoolhouse there and in 1642 made provision for a more substantial endowment.

In his will (1651) Matthew Broadley, a London jeweller, left the sum of £40 for the building of a schoolhouse at Hipperholme where he had been born. The free grammar school which he founded was generously endowed by his nephew and executor.

In 1658 Sarah Gledhill, who was the daughter of a local squire, bequeathed the sum of £200 for the founding of a school at Barkisland.

Workhouse In letters patent issued in 1635 Nathaniel Waterhouse, a Halifax businessman, was appointed as the first master of a workhouse which he was planning to establish. In his will (1642) he indicated that he was already building a house for this purpose and left some landed property for its support.

The object of this charity was to provide accommodation and maintenance for 20 orphans, boys and girls, and to set them to work. Waterhouse stipulated that they should wear blue coats and the institution therefore became known as the Blue Coat Hospital or School.

Almshouses The first almshouses in Halifax were built in 1610 at the expense of Ellen Hopkinson and Jane Crowther. The stated purpose was to accommodate 18 poor widows.

In his will Nathaniel Waterhouse referred to the almshouses he had recently founded for 12 aged or impotent poor persons and left the sum of £24 a year for their support.

Inns There were numerous inns in Halifax, including the Cross, the Crown, the Swan, the Talbot and the Turk's Head. The Cross Inn was described by a visitor as 'one of the fairest innes in England' (John Aston, 1639).

(R. A. Marchant, *The Puritans and the Church Courts in the Diocese of York 1560-1642* (1960), 29-30, 43, 246. W. K. Jordan, *The Charities of Rural England 1480-1660* (1961), 276, 290, 338, 344-6. J. Watson, *The History and Antiquities of the Parish of Halifax* (1775). J. Crabtree, *A Concise History of the Parish and Vicarage of Halifax, in the County of York* (1836). T. W. Hanson, *The Story of Old Halifax* (1920). H. Heaton, *The Yorkshire Woollen and Worsted Industries* (1920). Martha Ellis François, 'The Social and Economic Development of Halifax 1558-1640', *Proceedings of the Leeds Philosophical and Literary Society, Literary and Historical Section*, xi (1966). J. Smail, *The Origins of*

Middle-class Culture. Halifax, Yorkshire 1660-1780 (1994). J. A. Hargreaves, *Halifax* (1999). R. Mitchell, *Brighouse* (1953).)

HAMPSTHWAITE   Claro

A village on the River Nidd to the west of Knaresborough. The parish of Hampsthwaite contained a number of villages and hamlets. 1674: 37 households in Hampsthwaite, 56 in Birstwith and 72 in Menwith cum Darley. 1676: 566 persons aged 16 or more, including 6 recusants and 60 Protestant dissenters.

In 1640 it was reported that Hampsthwaite Bridge was in a ruinous condition and that it 'will not be new builte of stone there under the summe of fower hundreth poundes, and the scarcitye of wood there is such that itt is not possible to provyde wood to rebuild the same'. In view of the potential cost the West Riding magistrates opted for a relatively modest repair programme and it was not until 1658 that a decision was taken to build a new bridge.

In 1655 Laurence Favill the vicar of Hampsthwaite was deprived of his living by the West Riding commissioners for the removal of scandalous ministers.

Church St Thomas of Canterbury: Perpendicular.

(*YASRS*, liv (1915), 200, 281-2, 343, 401. A. G. Matthews, *Walker Revised* (1988), 393. H. Speight, *Nidderdale from Nun-Monkton to Whernside* (1906). B. Jennings (ed.), *A History of Nidderdale* (1983).)

HANDSWORTH   Strafford and Tickhill

A village to the south-east of Sheffield. There was no other village within the parish. 1674: 106 households (township of Handsworth).

In the early years of the 17th century the manor of Handsworth belonged to the Earls of Shrewsbury. It contained an extensive park and a small mansion built in 1580 where they sometimes resided. In addition, there were coalmines which were usually worked by leaseholders.

The Talbots died out in the male line in 1618 and the estates descended to the three daughters of Gilbert Earl of Shrewsbury and their husbands.

In the mid-17th century Thomas Earl of Arundel and Surrey (a grandson of Earl Gilbert) owned two-thirds of the manor while the remainder was in the possession of the Saviles of Rufford in Nottinghamshire. In 1659 Sir George Savile offered to sell his part of the manor to Colonel John Bright for the sum of £2559 which included £600 for one-third of the coalmines. In the event nothing came of this proposal.

At that time Bright was already mining coal in Handsworth in the lands of Thomas Earl of Arundel and Surrey. After acquiring a lease in 1650 from the parliamentary authorities he had spent £320 on the initial development but the net profits of his mine were disappointingly modest.

William Carte, who served as vicar of Handsworth from 1628 until his death in 1644, was a Puritan of the more moderate sort. Although he had reservations about wearing a surplice he conformed when admonished for this offence. He was succeeded by his son John who was ejected from the living in 1662.

Church St Mary: Norman, Early English and Perpendicular. The church is said to have been rebuilt in 1472.

The parish was subject to the peculiar jurisdiction of the Chancellor of York.

School After his ejection John Carte, who was described as an 'eminent scholar', kept a private school at Handsworth.

(*Calendar, Committee for Compounding*, 2474, 2478. BL, Additional MSS 27,534. Nottinghamshire Record Office, Savile of Rufford MSS, 28/5. Sheffield Archives, Wentworth Woodhouse Collection, Bright MSS, 52. P. Roebuck, *Yorkshire Baronets 1640-1760* (1980), 206, 208-9, 217. R. A. Marchant, *The Puritans and the Church Courts in the Diocese of York 1560-1642* (1960), 298. A. G. Matthews, *Calamy Revised* (1934), 102.)

HAREWOOD Skyrack/Claro

A village to the north of Leeds. The parish of Harewood included a number of villages and hamlets. 1674: 60 households in Harewood, 17 in Alwoodley, 24 in Dunkeswick, 36 in East Keswick, 26 in Weardley, 42 in Weeton cum Newby and 14 in Wigton. 1676: 688 persons aged 16 or more (parish).

The River Wharfe 'flows in a chanel, bank'd on both sides with Limestone, by Harewood, where stands a neat and strong Castle, which has always chang'd its master as the times turn'd' (William Camden).

The Gawthorpe estate in Harewood belonged to the Wentworths of Wentworth Woodhouse who had acquired it through marriage to a Gascoigne heiress. They sometimes resided at Gawthorpe Hall and in the early 17th century they had a standing arrangement for the weekly relief of the poor of Gawthorpe.

Towards the end of Elizabeth's reign Sir William Wentworth bought the manor of Harewood from Robert Ryther for £11,000.

In 1636 the Gawthorpe property was valued at £476 a year and the manor of Harewood at £1369 a year.

In the Commonwealth period William Earl of Strafford sold the Harewood estate to Sir John Cutler, a London businessman.

Church All Saints: Perpendicular.

In 1681 Ralph Thoresby wrote in his diary that he spent some time 'viewing the monuments in Harwood church, which are indeed extraordinary, especially that for the famous Judge Gascoyne'.

Castle Harewood Castle had been rebuilt in the 14th century. It was still habitable in the early 17th century but it appears to have suffered considerable damage during the course of the Civil War.

'And upon the Warf is Harewood-castle, reduc'd to a skeleton in the late Civil-wars' (Edmund Gibson, 1695).

(*Wentworth Papers 1597-1628* (ed. J. P. Cooper), *Camden Fourth Series*, 12 (1973), 29-31, 33-5, 275. Sheffield Archives, Wentworth Woodhouse Collection, Strafford Letters, xxix. J. Jones, *History of Harewood* (1859).)

HARTHILL   Strafford and Tickhill

A village near the border with Derbyshire. The parish of Harthill included the hamlets of Kiveton and Woodhall. 1674: 79 households (township of Harthill and Woodhall).

Church All Hallows: 13th century, Decorated and Perpendicular.

School There was a school at Harthill in the mid-17th century. The master was James Buller.

Principal family Osborne of Kiveton Hall (baronetcy 1620; peerage initially as Viscount Latimer 1673). Estate revenue: £1000 a year (1640); £1200 a year (1665). Coalmining in Wales Wood.

Sir Edward Osborne (1596-1647) was made a ward of the Crown following the death of his father. He bought considerable property in Yorkshire and settled at Kiveton. He became a close friend and ally of Strafford who in 1633 appointed him as Vice-President of the Council in the North. Shortly after he took on this responsibility Sir John Coke, one of the Secretaries of State, wrote that he was a young man of good understanding who was 'very forward' to promote the king's service. It was an office of major importance in view of Strafford's absence in Ireland but he had to contend with growing opposition.

In the Civil War he was heavily involved in the task of raising men and money for the royalist cause.

According to his niece Alice Thornton he was 'a very good, wise and prudent man ... a most excelent good Christian, true and orthodox to the church of England, a faithfull loyall subject to the king, and of a sweete and affable disposition to all'.

His son Sir Thomas (1632-1712) had a chequered career as a statesman. He served as Lord High Treasurer (in effect, the king's chief minister), 1673-1679, and Lord Lieutenant of the West Riding, 1674-1679. He was impeached in 1678 and again in 1679 on various charges and imprisoned in the Tower from 1679 to 1684.

He was one of the leading figures in the northern revolt of 1688 against James II and the political moves which led to the accession of William and Mary. In 1689 he was appointed President of the Council.

His public career was marked by an impressive accumulation of wealth and titles. He was made Viscount Latimer in 1673, Earl of Danby in 1674, Marquess of Carmarthen in 1689 and Duke of Leeds in 1694.

He acquired substantial amounts of landed property in Yorkshire and elsewhere, in some cases through royal favour. By the end of the century the Yorkshire estate alone was producing an income of nearly £1900 a year.

At his death he left landed property in England and Wales worth some £8000 a year and a personal estate worth £50,000.

Kiveton Hall Sir Edward Osborne may have built the hall on settling at Kiveton. There were 26 taxable hearths in 1664 and 1674.

During the years 1694 to 1704 the Duke of Leeds built a new house in the classical style.

The Osbornes had parks at Kiveton and Todwick.

(YAS Library, Duke of Leeds MSS. *The Autobiography of Mrs Alice Thornton*, Surtees Society, lxii (1873), 54-5. BL, Additional MSS 28,088, fo.126. C.33/326, part 2/fo.433.)

HARTSHEAD   Agbrigg and Morley

A chapelry within the parish of Dewsbury. The hilltop villages of Hartshead and Clifton were usually linked together for both ecclesiastical and fiscal purposes. 1674: 86 households in Hartshead cum Clifton. 1676: 300 persons aged 16 or more (chapelry of Hartshead).

In 1641 it was reported that the inhabitants of Clifton, Hipperholme cum Brighouse and Shelf had been 'infected and visited with the contagious disease of the plauge' and that a number of persons had died.

Church Parochial chapel of St Peter: Norman. The minister was a perpetual curate.

Principal family Armitage or Armytage of Kirklees Hall (baronetcy 1641). Estate revenue: £2500 a year (1677). Coalmines and stone quarries in Clifton.

In the course of the 17th century 'Armytage' became the usual spelling.

John Armitage (1573-1650), who was the grandson of a clothier, was described at his death as 'a man pious, prudent, hospitable and in every virtue most exemplary'. He took no part in the Civil War and in 1644 was complaining about the expense to which he had been put for the maintenance of the parliamentarian forces. His son Sir Francis, who had a Catholic wife, and his brother Gregory were both royalists. The death of Sir Francis, who was buried in York Minister in June 1644, occurred while he was involved in the defence of the city.

In 1683 Sir Thomas Armytage (1652-1693) began legal proceedings against Walter Curwen, his father's steward, claiming that he had been enriching himself at the family's expense.

Kirklees Hall Following their purchase of the Kirklees Priory estate in 1565 the Armitages erected a mansion overlooking the River Calder. The main front was built by John Armitage (1573-1650) in the reign of James I. An E-shaped house of two storeys.

In 1674 there were 24 taxable hearths.

In the grounds was 'Robin Hood's Tomb, who was a generous robber, and very famous' (William Camden).

(*YASRS*, liv (1915), 328. *A Catalogue of the Muniments at Kirklees* (1900). C.9/15/145. C.33/259/fo.648.)

HATFIELD   Strafford and Tickhill

A village to the north-east of Doncaster. The parish of Hatfield included the village of Thorne which had a medieval chapel and part of the village of Stainforth; the other part was in the parish of Barnby Dun. Stainforth also had a medieval chapel. 1674: 134 households in Hatfield, 80 in Hatfield Woodhouse, 63 in Stainforth cum Bramwith and 255 in Thorne. 1676: 642 persons aged 16 or more (parish but probably excluding the chapelries).

Since 1348 Stainforth had enjoyed the right to hold a weekly market and an annual fair. Thorne was granted a market charter in 1661.

There was a ferry at Stainforth which was situated on the River Don.

In Hatfield Chase 'there is special good Deer-hunting' (William Camden). The chase, which covered an area of 180,000 acres, had been a royal hunting ground since the 14th century. At the beginning of the 17th century the lands bordering Hatfield Level contained large numbers of deer: in 1607, for example, it was estimated that there were about a thousand red deer. Administrative responsibility for the chase was vested in a master of the game who had under him a sizeable contingent of keepers. In practice it was difficult to police such an extensive area and deer poaching, fishing and fowling were valuable sources of food and income for the poorer inhabitants of the district.

The Level of Hatfield Chase consisted of some 70,000 acres of fen country. In 1626 the Crown entered into an agreement with Cornelius Vermuyden for the drainage of the Level. Progress was rapid and within a few years the work had been largely completed. There was, however, strong opposition from those who saw the project as a threat to their interests. This resulted in frequent riots in which some of the Flemish workmen were killed or wounded and appeals to the Privy Council which led to concessions.

In 1629 Vermuyden was knighted and allowed to purchase the manor of Hatfield. During the 1630s the manor changed hands several times. By 1637 it was in the possession of Sir Edward Osborne, the Vice-President of the Council in the North. According to some notes he made it was then worth £848 a year and he had paid £12,278 for it, partly with borrowed money. Shortly afterwards Sir Arthur Ingram bought the manor and before long was involved in litigation with the tenants. In the 1650s the property was worth £1000 a year.

In 1641 the West Riding magistrates were informed of 'the great ruine and decay' of Thorne Bridge, which spanned the River Don, 'being the high roade betweene the markett townes of Leedes, Wakefeild, and other westerne partes, unto the port towne of Kingston upon Hull'. They decided that the sum of £10 should be levied on the riding to meet the cost of the repair work.

Between the outbreak of the Civil War and the Restoration the drainage system in Hatfield Level suffered badly, partly through lack of maintenance and partly as a result of military action.

Towards the end of 1687 'there happened a great inundation in the Levels by means of the much rains that fell, and the high tides, which increased the waters so that they broke the banks and drownded the country for a vast many miles about' (Abraham de la Pryme).

Church St Lawrence: Norman, Early English, Decorated and Perpendicular.

Schools Around the end of the 16th century a schoolhouse was built at Hatfield with money donated by the local community. In his will (1619) John Spivey, a yeoman, left the sum of £40 for the support of a schoolmaster.

In 1628 Thomas Wormley, a gentleman who had close associations with Hatfield, made a settlement of lands worth £200 for the purpose of augmenting the schoolmaster's salary. His declared intention was that the master of the grammar school should be an able graduate who would provide free instruction for boys of the parish.

Thomas Tomkinson, who was the minister of Hatfield in the years 1639 to 1669, kept a private school there to supplement his income. Late on in Charles II's reign there was another private school in the village.

During the years 1680 to 1702 William Eratt served as both minister and schoolmaster at Hatfield. One of his pupils was Abraham de la Pryme.

(*CSP Dom, 1660-1*, 555. BL, Landsowne MSS 879 (Abraham de la Pryme's manuscript history of Hatfield). J. Hunter, *South Yorkshire*, i (1828), 150-197. YAS Library, Duke of Leeds MSS, Box 13. A. F. Upton, *Sir Arthur Ingram c.1565-1642* (1961), 199. WYAS, Leeds, Temple Newsam MSS, TN/EA/12/17. *YASRS*, liv (1915), 339. W. K. Jordan, *The Charities of Rural England 1480-1660* (1961), 333.)

HAWKSWORTH   Skyrack

A village within the parish of Otley. For fiscal purposes it was linked with the village of Esholt. 1674: 53 households (Hawksworth and Esholt).

Principal families (1) Hawksworth of Hawksworth Hall (baronetcy 1678). Estate revenue: £1100 a year (1634 and 1641); £1200 a year (1650). Coalmining in Baildon. Number of servants: 24 (1658).

Walter Hawksworth (1558-1620) was a benevolent landlord who granted leases for three lives. In his will (1619) he urged his son Richard to be good to his tenants and refrain from increasing their rents.

Sir Richard Hawksworth (1594-1658) was an arrogant and quarrelsome individual with a taste for litigation. In 1627 he was fined for committing adultery and his wife, Dame Mary, left him, taking with her their infant son. This precipitated a long-running dispute over custody of the child and the provision of financial support. The matter engaged the attention of the Privy Council and the Archbishop of York who came down in favour of Lady Hawksworth. In 1632 it was said that the dispute had cost Sir Richard £500 in legal expenses.

In 1638 he was presented at the West Riding quarter sessions for insulting William Taylor, burning a petition which he had brought and saying publicly that 'he cared not for anie Justice of Peace in Yorkshire'.

In October 1642 his royalist brother-in-law Sir John Goodricke sent a troop of horse to Hawksworth Hall to apprehend him and he was kept a prisoner at York until July 1644. After his release he served as a member of the West Riding parliamentary committee.

Sir Richard was anxious to overturn his father's leasing policy and on seeking legal advice was assured that the leases for lives could be terminated. In his will (1652) he instructed his son Walter to treat the tenants well 'and suffer them to continue upon their ould rents, I haveing raysed them myselfe'.

After the death of Walter Hawksworth (1625-1677) Oliver Heywood the nonconformist divine wrote that he 'hath lived a very private life and gathered vast treasures, some say ten thousand pounds in money and £80,000 in bonds'.

Heywood also recorded two untoward events which occurred at Hawksworth Hall in 1680 when the owner was Sir Walter Hawksworth (c.1657-1684). While Sir Walter was playing at tennis his steward was accidentally struck on the head and fell down dead. A few weeks later, when several gentlemen were drinking and ranting, one of them challenged his uncle to a fight and was killed.

(2) Thomson of Esholt Hall. Estate revenue: £500 a year (1638). Fulling mills in Esholt, Guiseley and Yeadon.

The Thomsons were a Catholic family. Henry Thomson (1602-1667), who succeeded his father in 1620, was convicted of recusancy but eventually conformed. In the reign of

Charles I he fell heavily into debt and mortgaged part of the estate to his father-in-law, Walter Stanhope.

Despite his Catholic background he served as a parliamentarian captain in the Civil War.

Thomson left no male issue and the estate descended to his daughter Frances who had married Walter Calverley of Calverley (see under Calverley).

Hawksworth Hall In the early years of the 17th century Walter Hawksworth pulled down the old hall and built a new house which was completed in 1611. Among the rooms listed in an inventory of 1658 were the hall, the dining parlour, the gallery, the great chamber and the chapel chamber. An extension was built in 1664.

A long two-storeyed building with gables. In 1674 there were 17 taxable hearths.

Esholt Hall A Tudor house incorporating part of Esholt Priory. Some building work was apparently carried out in the reign of Charles II: according to the hearth tax returns there were 10 hearths in 1664 and 14 in 1674.

The rooms listed in an inventory of 1691 included the hall, the dining room, the chapel parlour and the gallery chamber.

The house was rebuilt by Sir Walter Calverley between 1706 and 1710.

(Sheffield Archives, Wentworth Woodhouse Collection, Bright MSS. J. T. Cliffe, *The Yorkshire Gentry* (1969). C.22/638/39 and 848/14. *YASRS*, liv (1915), 64. BL, Additional MSS 4460, fo.23. WYAS, Bradford, Spencer Stanhope MSS. H. Speight, 'Hawksworth Hall and Its Associations', *Bradford Antiquary*, New Series, ii (1905).)

HEALAUGH   Ainsty

A village north of Tadcaster. There was no other village in the parish of Healaugh. During the Commonwealth period it was proposed that the parish should incorporate the neighbouring village of Catterton, then in the parish of Tadcaster, but this came to nothing. 1665: 58 households (township of Healaugh). 1676: 183 persons aged 16 or more (parish of Healaugh).

The remains of Healaugh Priory, an Augustinian foundation, had been drawn on as a source of building material in the 16th century.

In 1636 the open fields and other common lands were enclosed by agreement.

Church St John Baptist: Norman.

Principal family Wharton of Healaugh Hall (and Wharton Hall, Westmorland and Wooburn House, Buckinghamshire) (noble family). Estate revenue: £2100 a year (1605); £5000 a year (1673). Coalmines in Cumberland and coal and lead mines in Yorkshire.

Philip Lord Wharton (1555-1625) had estates in Cumberland, Durham and Westmorland as well as in Yorkshire.

He and his second wife Dorothy lived apart for many years. His two sons died before him and he was succeeded by his grandson Philip Lord Wharton (1613-1696). He lived mainly at Healaugh before the outbreak of the Civil War. Through his marriage to Jane Goodwin, the only daughter and heir of Arthur Goodwin, he acquired a large estate in Buckinghamshire. He eventually settled at Wooburn, near Beaconsfield, which became his principal seat but he sometimes resided at Healaugh.

A zealous Puritan, he was one of the most politically influential of the noblemen who supported the parliamentary cause in the Civil War and for some years a close associate of Cromwell.

After the Restoration he emerged as a great patron of nonconformist ministers, employing a number of them as chaplains and tutors and providing financial assistance for others. One of these ministers, John Gunter, resided at Healaugh and acted as steward of his northern estates.

In the reign of Charles II Wharton was involved in a dispute with some of his Swaledale tenants over their enclosing activities.

Ralph Thoresby records in his journal that in September 1692 he went to Healaugh to wait upon 'that excellent pattern of true nobility and piety', Philip Lord Wharton, 'who received me with abundant respects and kindness'. Thoresby was a willing assistant when Lord Wharton launched his charity scheme for the distribution of bibles. In October 1691 Wharton told him that he was sending him 80 bibles and catechisms and asked him to supply the names of such children as would be worthy recipients.

Healaugh Manor The house was built by Thomas Lord Wharton (c.1495-1568) following his acquisition of the Healaugh Priory estate in 1540.

A deed of 1640 refers to the 'Old Manor' and the 'New Manor'.

In 1665 Philip Lord Wharton was taxed on 25 hearths.

A survey map of 1636 shows the house in the middle of a park.

(PRO, Chancery Masters' Exhibits, C.104/110, part 1. K. J. Allison, 'Enclosure by Agreement at Healaugh (W.R.)', *YAJ*, xl (1961).)

HEMSWORTH   Staincross

A village to the north-east of Barnsley. The parish of Hemsworth included the hamlet of Kinsley. 1674: 65 households (township of Hemsworth). 1676: 235 persons aged 16 or more (parish).

At the beginning of the 17th century the manors of Hemsworth and Kinsley belonged to Sir Richard Gargrave of Nostell Priory. In 1603 he obtained a grant of free warren for Kinsley (where he had another mansion house) and proceeded to create a deer park of 1000 acres. According to Roger Dodsworth this resulted in the depopulation of Kinsley.

In the reign of James I coal was being mined in the wastes of Hemsworth.

Stephen Charman, a Puritan divine, served as rector of Hemsworth during the years 1637 to 1662 when he was ejected. In 1643 he was said to have abandoned his cure and joined the parliamentarians.

'Thence to Hemsworth.....where we could meet with no lodging, only little ale-houses to give one a pot of beer' (Celia Fiennes, 1697).

Church St Helen: Norman and Decorated.

School In 1547 Robert Holgate, Archbishop of York, secured permission from the Crown to found a grammar school at Hemsworth and the following year made provision for its endowment.

In the 17th century the masters included John Battison, Gervase Worrall, William Horncastle and James Wood.

Almshouses in his will (1556) Archbishop Holgate settled lands for the establishment and support of almshouses at Hemsworth. Holgate's Hospital, which was built near the church, had accommodation for 20 men and women who were known as brothers and sisters.

In the parish registers of Hemsworth there are many references to the deaths of inmates of the hospital.

(C.2/James I/S14/43. R. A. Marchant, *The Puritans and the Church Courts in the Diocese of York 1560-1642* (1960), 231, 238. A. G. Matthews, *Calamy Revised* (1934), 111. W. K. Jordan, *The Charities of Rural England 1480-1660* (1961), 258-9, 311-12. YPRS, lxxix (1926).)

HICKLETON   Strafford and Tickhill

A small village situated between Barnsley and Doncaster. There was no other village within the parish. 1674: 19 households (township of Hickleton). 1676: 55 persons aged 16 or more (parish).

In 1669 it was reported that as many as 60 or 80 persons attended Presbyterian conventicles at the house of William Smyth in Hickleton and that such meetings had formerly taken place at Hickleton Hall.

Church St Wilfrid: Norman in origin but largely Perpendicular.

Principal family Jackson of Hickleton Hall (baronetcy 1660). Estate revenue: £1300 a year (1680). Coalmining at Goldthorpe.

Sir John Jackson (d.1623), a wealthy lawyer, built up a large estate which was dissipated by his descendants before the end of the century.

Sir John Jackson (d.1637) was 'very studious, a good scholar, as also a good poet for Latin'. His second wife, Dame Fiennes, who was a sister of Sir William Waller, also wrote poems.

Sir John Jackson (1631-1670), who was for some years a ward of the Crown, was too young to play an active part in the Civil War. After the Restoration he employed Hugh Everard, a nonconformist minister, as his chaplain.

Sir John Jackson (1653-1680) fell heavily into debt as a result of his extravagance. After his death there was a family dispute over the descent of the estate. In 1682 the trustees sold the manor of Hickleton to John Wentworth of Woolley and then proceeded to dispose of the remaining property.

Hickleton Hall Built by Francis Rodes in the reign of Elizabeth. It was a large mansion (32 hearths in 1674).

(C.5/505/9. C.33/259/fo.565. C.38/217/12 December 1684 and 229/7 May 1687. A. G. Matthews, *Calamy Revised* (1934), 186.)

HIGH HOYLAND   Staincross

A village to the north-west of Barnsley. The parish of High Hoyland included the village of Clayton West and part of Cumberworth which had a medieval chapel; the other part was in the parish of Silkstone. 1674: 26 households in High Hoyland, 26 in Clayton (West) and 33 in Cumberworth.

The rectory of High Hoyland consisted of two medieties, each with its own minister. In the 17th century the first mediety was under the patronage of the Wentworths of West Bretton while the other was in the gift of the Saviles of Methley. William Wilkinson, a man of Puritan temperament, was rector of the first mediety in the years 1604 to 1623.

In 1640 the West Riding magistrates were informed of a disagreement between the inhabitants of High Hoyland and Clayton over the assessments for the relief of the poor.

In 1642 some of the residents of the parish complained that Andrew Higholme of Clayton was keeping 'a disordered alehowse, to the great disquiett and vexacon of all his neighboures'. The justices decided to impose a three-year ban on his activities as an alehouse keeper.

Church All Hallows: Norman in origin. A west tower was built in 1679.

School Robert Inman, who was rector of the first mediety, was ejected in 1662 and afterwards kept a private school at Clayton West.

(R. A. Marchant, *The Puritans and the Church Courts in the Diocese of York 1560-1642* (1960), 292. *YASRS*, liv (1915), 182, 351. A. G. Matthews, *Calamy Revised* (1934), 289.)

HIGH MELTON   Strafford and Tickhill

A small village to the west of Doncaster which was sometimes called Melton on the Hill. There was no other village within the parish. 1674: 26 households (township of High Melton). 1676: 50 persons aged 16 or more (parish).

Dr John Levitt, a lawyer, bought the manor of High Melton in 1634 but he appears to have overstretched his resources in the process and was soon heavily in debt. In 1641 Sir Arthur Ingram was given a particular of the manor, perhaps as a potential buyer. According to this valuation the total revenue amounted to £628 a year. In 1649 Levitt sold the manor to his principal creditor, Dr Richard Berrie of Hodroyd Hall.

By 1667 the estate was in the possession of John Fountayne who had married Elizabeth Monckton, a great niece of Dr Berrie. Although he had substantial landed property in various counties he chose to make High Melton his family seat. In 1674 he was taxed on 13 hearths.

Church St James: Norman, Decorated and Perpendicular.

(C.3/454/29. C.9/5/144. WYAS, Leeds, Temple Newsam MSS, TN/EA16. BL, Additional MSS 24,470, fols.82,84.)

HOOTON PAGNELL   Strafford and Tickhill

A small village to the north-west of Doncaster. The parish of Hooton Pagnell included the township of Clayton cum Frickley. The hamlet of Bilham was situated in two parishes: Hooton Pagnell and Barnbrough. There were dependent chapels at both Clayton and Frickley. The medieval chapel at Frickley, which may once have been a domestic chapel, was sometimes described as a parish church but without any adequate justification. 1674: 39 households in Hooton Pagnell, 13 in Bilham and 33 in Clayton cum Frickley. 1676: 184 persons aged 16 or more (parish).

Church All Saints: Norman with some later features.

Principal families (1) Hutton of Hooton Pagnell Hall (and Goldsborough Hall) (see under Goldsborough).

Sir Richard Hutton purchased the manor in 1605. After the death of Richard Hutton in 1683 it passed by inheritance to the Whartons of Edlington.

(2) Anne of Frickley Hall (and Burghwallis Hall). Estate revenue: £800 a year (1620).

When John Anne was admitted to the English College at Rome in 1623 he related that his parents and his brothers and sisters were all Catholic. Successive heads of the family disdained to take refuge in outward conformity. This necessarily had financial consequences for them, though Philip Anne (1591-1647) was only required to pay £20 a year when he compounded for his recusancy.

In 1626 he appears to have had strong reservations about the Crown's compulsory loan scheme. At Frickley Hall the collector's agent met with a hostile reception: two of Anne's servants 'threw the privy Seale out of the dores after him'.

In the Civil War Philip Anne and his son Michael took up arms for the king and were involved in the defence of Pontefract Castle.

Hooton Pagnell Hall A medieval and Tudor mansion with a 14th century gatehouse. In 1674 Lady Hutton was taxed on 23 hearths.

Frickley Hall A house of moderate size (10 hearths in 1674) which may have been medieval in origin. Dr Nathaniel Johnston the 17th century historian described it as 'standing in a clay bottom, moated around, part stone, part stud and mortar'.

Stables dated 1572.

(C.5/19/3. *CRS*, lv (1963), 374-5. PRO, SP Dom, Charles I, S.P.16/xxvi/32. A. G. Ruston and D. Witney, *Hooton Pagnell: The agricultural revolution of a Yorkshire village* (1934).)

HOOTON ROBERTS Strafford and Tickhill

A small village to the north-east of Rotherham. There was no other village within the parish. 1674: 24 households (township of Hooton Roberts). 1676: 80 persons aged 16 or more (parish).

Richard Northropp, who served as rector of Hooton Roberts between 1620 and 1639, was a man of Puritan temperament. At a visitation in 1636 he was reprimanded over his reluctance to wear a surplice.

The manor of Hooton Roberts belonged to the Wentworths of Wentworth Woodhouse. According to a survey of 1636 it was then worth £123 a year. After Strafford's execution in 1641 his widow, Elizabeth Countess of Strafford, took up residence at Hooton Roberts Hall. This was an Elizabethan or Jacobean mansion which in 1674 had 14 hearths.

In 1663 the Dowager Countess let her coalmines in Hooton Roberts to James Moyser for 21 years at a rent of £20 a year. Moyser spent some £600 on developing them and then assigned his interest in the lease to his stepson Sir John Reresby of Thrybergh who already owned property there. According to his own testimony Sir John invested a further £1000 in the undertaking.

Church St John Baptist: Norman.

(R. A. Marchant, *The Puritans and the Church Courts in the Diocese of York 1560-1642* (1960), 265. Sheffield Archives, Wentworth Woodhouse Collection, Strafford Letters, xxix. C.33/244/fo.226.)

HORBURY   Agbrigg and Morley

A clothing village within the parish of Wakefield. 1674: 79 households.

Church St Leonard: a public chapel which was Norman in origin. In the late 17th century two new lofts were built in order to provide additional seating for the growing population of Horbury.

School A school was established in 1628.

Principal families (1) Savile of Lupset Hall. Estate revenue: £650 a year (1641).

Sir John Savile (c.1600-1660), a younger son of the Savile family of Thornhill, had a considerable estate settled on him, including the rectory manor of Wakefield. In her will (1625) his mother, Dame Elizabeth, recorded her conviction that she was 'one of the number of the faithfull and elect children of God'.

In the Civil War he took up arms for Parliament and served as a member of the parliamentary committee for the West Riding.

His son Thomas (c.1648-1677), who never married, left the whole estate to his sister Anne and her husband John Harris of the Inner Temple. In a Chancery case of 1677 his brother John (1651-c.1704) claimed that they had conspired to rob him of his inheritance. Thomas, he related, 'was always from his childhood of very weake capacity and utterly unable to … manage his owne affairs' and had been easily led by fair speeches or threats. For some years Harris and his wife had been seeking to persuade him that John had evil designs against him and 'by debaucherys and continuall drunkenness to render him more incapable and less apt to understand his affaires and duty'.

In the event John Savile failed to convince the Court that his brother's will was invalid but in 1700 he had the good fortune to inherit the large estates belonging to the senior branch of the family.

(2) Harris of Lupset Hall. Estate revenue: £1198 a year (1692).

Following the death of Anne Harris in 1681 Oliver Heywood the nonconformist divine wrote that she had 'lived a most debaucht, vicious and voluptuous life, drunk all the men she met with, and drank to death several men, openly professed to her husband she would take her liberty to lye with whom she pleased and he might take the like, he living in London, she at Lupsit. She had a child in his absence'.

In 1695 the Harris family sold the Yorkshire estate to Richard Witton for £13,500.

Lupset Hall The house was probably Tudor in origin. In 1674 Thomas Savile was taxed on 18 hearths.

The mansion depicted in a drawing by Samuel Buck was built in 1716.

(T. Taylor, *History of Wakefield: the Rectory Manor* (1886). C.10/205/54. C.38/258/2 July 1697.)

HORTON IN RIBBLESDALE   Staincliffe and Ewecross

A village on the River Ribble in the north-west corner of the riding. There was no other village within the parish. 1674: 109 households (township of Horton).

The most notable feature of the extensive fell country surrounding the village was the mass of Penyghent.

Church St Oswald: Norman and Perpendicular.

HOYLAND   Strafford and Tickhill

The villages of Upper and Nether Hoyland were situated within the extensive parish of Wath upon Dearne. 1674: 54 households.

Principal family Rokeby of Skiers Hall (baronetcy 1661). Estate revenue: £580 a year (1651); £1000 a year (1666). Coalmining in Upper Hoyland.

The most prominent member of the family was Sir William Rokeby (1601-c.1676) who considerably increased the estate and acquired a baronetcy. In 1651 he wrote that his coalmine required a new sough to drain off the water but he believed that it would hold out for several generations.

In the Yorkshire Engagement of February 1643 he undertook to contribute money for the royalist cause while in June he was one of the recipients of a letter from the Earl of Newcastle about the supply of provisions for his army. He appears, however, to have been reluctant to commit himself too openly, though in 1660 it was said that he had been sequestered for his loyalty to the Crown.

In 1678 Sir William's family abruptly died out in the male line.

Skiers Hall Sir William Rokeby either rebuilt or improved the house.

In 1664 and 1674 he was taxed on 16 hearths.

(East Riding of Yorkshire Archives Service, Legard of Anlaby MSS. C10/143/6.)

HUDDERSFIELD   Agbrigg and Morley

One of the major clothing towns of the West Riding, Huddersfield specialised in the manufacture of kerseys. The parish of Huddersfield contained a number of villages, including Scammonden and Slaithwaite which had dependent chapels. Marsden, which also had a public chapel, was situated in two parishes: Huddersfield and Almondbury. 1674: 139 households in Huddersfield, 69 in Golcar, 50 in Lindley, 52 in Longwood, 36 in Marsden, 63 in North Crosland, 37 in Scammonden and 103 in Slaithwaite. 1676: 1787 persons aged 16 or more (parish of Huddersfield).

Edward Hill, who was vicar of Huddersfield in the years 1619 to 1646, was a man with strong Puritan sympathies but before the time of the Civil War he conformed sufficiently to avoid antagonising the ecclesiastical authorities. In 1662 he was ejected from the living of Crofton.

John Crosse, who served for a time as curate of Scammonden, was a thoroughgoing nonconformist who publicly condemned the wearing of surplices and the use of the cross in baptism. In 1617 his controversial preaching, which attracted large crowds, led George Crosland the vicar of Almondbury to proceed against him in the Court of Chancery.

In 1640 the West Riding magistrates received a petition from the inhabitants of Huddersfield in which they complained that there was a great inequality 'in the rateinge and assessinge [of] their layes and assessmentes for his Majesties service'. They laid the blame entirely on the assessors and in response to the petition the justices gave order that new assessors should be appointed.

In 1642 it was reported that Huddersfield Bridge, 'being a very usefull and necessary bridge for the countrye [county], is through the violence of the water decayed and quite taken away'. For the funding of the necessary repair work the magistrates decided that the sum of £30 should be levied on the riding as a whole.

In the Civil War the neighbouring gentry favoured the royalist cause but the town itself played little part in the conflict.

The Ramsdens of Longley Hall bought half the manor of Huddersfield in 1599 and the other half in 1631. They owned Huddersfield mills (a corn mill and a fulling mill), worked coal seams within the boundaries of the township and presented ministers to the living of Huddersfield. In 1671 they secured cloth market rights for the town and as a result it emerged as the main trading centre of the Colne valley.

Church St Peter: originally Norman but rebuilt at the beginning of the 16th century and consecrated in 1503.

Schools There was a school at Huddersfield from at least 1563.

In the reign of Charles I John Taylor kept a private school at Slaithwaite. Towards the end of the 17th century Slaithwaite had another school.

(R. A. Marchant, *The Puritans and the Church Courts in the Diocese of York 1560-1642* (1960), 35-8, 44, 242, 254. *YASRS*, liv (1915), 232, 381. WYAS, Leeds, Ramsden Collection. D. F. E. Sykes, *The History of Huddersfield and Its Vicinity* (1898). T. Dyson, *The History of Huddersfield and District* (1932). W. B. Crump and Gertrude Ghorbal, *History of the Huddersfield Woollen Industry* (Tolson Memorial Museum Publications, Handbook IX) (1935). R. Brook, *The Story of Huddersfield* (1968). C. Stephenson, *The Ramsdens and their estate in Huddersfield* (1972). G. Redmonds, *Huddersfield and District under the Stuarts* (1985).)

HUNSINGORE   Claro

A village to the north-east of Wetherby. The parish of Hunsingore included the village of Cattal and several hamlets. 1674: 37 households in Hunsingore, 34 in Great Cattal, 1 in Little Cattal and 14 in Walshford cum Great Ribston.

Church St John Baptist: medieval in origin.

Principal family Goodricke of Ribston Hall (baronetcy 1641). Estate revenue: £1000 a year (1640).

Sir John Goodricke (1617-1670) was educated at the University of Aberdeen because his father considered that the discipline there was more strict than at the English universities; and he afterwards travelled in France with a Scotsman as his governor. In March 1639, when the king was assembling an expeditionary force, he was interrogated in London about his Scottish connections.

In the Civil War he sided with the king and commanded a troop of horse. He was wounded when taking part in the siege of Bradford in December 1642 and spent most of the war as a prisoner, first in Manchester and then in the Tower of London.

His son Sir Henry (1642-1705) was described by his friend Sir John Reresby as 'a gentleman of fine parts naturally, and thos improoved by great reading and travell'. He served as ambassador to the Court of Spain and in the reign of William III was appointed Lieutenant General of the Ordnance and a Privy Councillor.

Ribston Hall Sir John Goodricke thought of rebuilding the hall but died before the project could be put in hand. The demolition of the old house (which was probably a mid-Tudor building) is reflected in the hearth tax returns. In 1671 it was noted that the number of hearths had been reduced from 28 to 15 while in 1674 there were only nine taxable hearths. Sir Henry Goodricke completed the building of the new hall (a two-storey house of brick) in 1674.

The medieval family chapel (St Andrew) did not figure in this rebuilding programme. However, a tablet records that Sir Henry repaired and embellished it in 1700.

The Goodrickes kept deer in their park at Ribston Hall. In 1637 three men were imprisoned for forcibly entering the park and hunting a buck with greyhounds.

The famous apple known as the Ribston pippin is said to have been introduced from Normandy about 1707.

(C. A. Goodricke, *History of the Goodricke Family* (1897) and *Ribston* (1902). YASRS, liv (1915), 33.)

ILKLEY   Skyrack/Claro

The Wharfe passes by Ilkley 'which I imagine to be Olicana in Ptolemy . It is, without question, an ancient town ... it was rebuilt in Severus's time' (William Camden). A small market town on the site of a Roman fort. The parish of Ilkley included the village of Nesfield. 1674: 61 households in Ilkley, and 36 in Nesfield. 1676: 360 persons aged 16 or more (parish of Ilkley).

A royal charter of 1253 had granted the right to hold a weekly market and an annual fair.

In 1638 the West Riding magistrates were informed that the bridge which was under construction at Ilkley had been 'sodainely taken away by the violence of a flood'. Following an inquiry it was concluded that this was not due to any negligence on the part of the workmen but was 'onely the act of God'. The bridge was again destroyed by flooding in January 1659. It was decided that the cost of replacing it should be met by the riding as a whole and a contract was let for the building of a bridge of hewn stone which was to consist of one pillar and two arches. The contract price was £400.

Church All Saints: Early English and Perpendicular.

School About the end of the 16th century George Marshall left £100 for godly and charitable purposes. It was decided that this should be used to found a grammar school and that the vicar of Ilkley should serve as master if he was judged competent. In 1636 the inhabitants of the town agreed to a voluntary rate to enable a schoolhouse to be built and the work was completed the following year. The endowment was augmented in 1696 in the will of Reginald Heber, a lawyer whose family owned land in the parish.

(*YAJ*, v (1879), 374. C.6/47/37. W. K. Jordan, *The Charities of Rural England 1480-1660* (1961), 321. R. Collyer and J. H. Turner, *Ilkley* (1885). M. Dixon, *Ilkley: History and Guide* (2002).)

KEIGHLEY   Staincliffe and Ewecross

A clothing town in the Aire valley. The extensive parish of Keighley included a number of hamlets, among them Eastwood, Ingrow and Oakworth, in a largely moorland area. 1674: 262 households (township of Keighley). 1676: 600 persons aged 16 or more (parish of Keighley).

Keighley is 'a pretty marcat towne' (Roger Dodsworth). By a charter of 1305 it enjoyed the right to hold a weekly market and an annual fair.

In his poem on the travels of 'Drunken Barnaby', which was first published in 1638, Richard Braithwaite wrote

> Thence to Kighley, where are Mountains
> Steepy-threatning, lively Fountains;
> Rising Hills, and barren Vallies.

The town was famous for a particular kind of cloth known as Keighley kerseys or whites.

In 1645 there was an outbreak of the plague.

Church St Peter: Norman in origin.

School It was not until the early 18th century that Keighley acquired an endowed grammar school but some kind of school existed before that time. In 1638 John Holmes, a blacksmith, was indicted for assaulting John Greene of Keighley, schoolmaster. At the same time Greene was accused of stealing pieces of timber and boards belonging to the churchwardens.

Principal family Murgatroyd of East Riddlesden Hall (in the parish of Bingley but closer to Keighley). Estate revenue: £500 a year (1662). Coalmining.

Oliver Heywood the nonconformist divine regarded the Murgatroyd family with contempt: 'that family is the most dreadful instance in the country; all that know tell strange passages of them'. In the reign of Charles I several members of the family were fined and excommunicated following their 'horrible profanation' of the public chapel at Luddenden, near Halifax.

James Murgatroyd, a wealthy clothier, bought the East Riddlesden estate in 1638 and proceeded to rebuild the house. During the Civil War he and his sons appear to have been reluctant to come out in support of either side.

In 1653 he was succeeded by his son John who was said to have been 'a profane debauched man'. He borrowed large sums of money and at his death in 1662 the estate was heavily encumbered.

His eldest son James had been disinherited after a quarrel and was involved in a dispute with his brother John over the descent of the estate. The matter was referred to arbitration and in 1663 John Murgatroyd was put in possession. He died without issue in 1667 when the estate passed to his brother William who had been apprenticed to Nathaniel Spencer, a Leeds merchant.

Spencer was a major creditor of the Murgatroyds and in 1668 secured the arrest of William and his brothers Henry and Thomas. In 1673 Oliver Heywood noted in his journal that Thomas Murgatroyd had been imprisoned in York Castle for several years and that after attempting to escape he had been shackled with leg-irons.

Eventually the East Riddlesden estate came into the possession of Edmund Starkie, a grandson of James Murgatroyd the original purchaser.

East Riddlesden Hall A gabled house begun in 1642 and completed in 1648.

In 1692 Edmund Starkie added a new range in a more classical style.

(Richard Braithwaite, *Drunken Barnaby's Four Journeys to the North of England* (3rd edition, 1723). *YASRS*, liv (1915), 64-5, 77. C.6/191/89. C.10/99/137.)

KELLINGTON Osgoldcross

A village to the north-east of Pontefract. The parish of Kellington included several villages. 1674: 40 households in Kellington, 54 in Beal, 33 in Eggboroughs Ambo (High and Low Eggborough) and 37 in Whitley.

In 1639 the constable of Kellington was instructed to distrain the goods of John Ellis of Roall Hall on account of his refusal to pay local taxes. His main residence was Kiddal Hall in the parish of Barwick in Elmet.

William Hall, who had been serving as vicar of Kellington since 1633, was deprived of his living in 1655 by the West Riding commissioners for the removal of scandalous ministers.

Church St Edmund: Norman, Early English and Perpendicular.

(*YASRS*, liv (1915), 131. A. G. Matthews, *Walker Revised* (1988), 393.)

KETTLEWELL Staincliffe and Ewecross

A Wharfedale village to the north of Skipton. The parish of Kettlewell included the hamlet of Starbotton. 1674: 77 households (township of Kettlewell). 1676: 435 persons aged 16 or more (parish).

Kettlewell had enjoyed market rights since the 13th century and in a survey of 1605 was described as a market town.

In 1628 the Crown conveyed the manor of Kettlewell with its lead mines to the City of London as part of a general financial transaction. In 1656 the City sold the manor to Matthew Hewitt the rector of Linton and seven other men who were acting as trustees on behalf of the freeholders. They embarked on the piecemeal sale of houses and land to the tenants but retained possession of the royalties of the manor, including the lead mines. Before long a formal trust was established and management responsibility was vested in men known as the Trust Lords of Kettlewell who were elected by the freeholders. In 1669 they granted a lease of the lead mines to two Quaker businessmen, Francis Smithson and Philip Swale.

Richard Tennant, who served as vicar of Kettlewell during the years 1632 to 1653, was also the rector of one of the medieties of Burnsall. Although he was a Puritan he supported the king in the Civil War. (See the entry for Burnsall).

Henry Motley, who held the living of Kettlewell in the years 1670 to 1699, was the son of a previous incumbent. For many years he was also the master of Threshfield School. (See the entry for Linton).

In 1686 there was a violent storm which resulted in extensive flooding. According to one account the inhabitants of Kettlewell and Starbotton 'were almost all drowned' but this was probably an inflated estimate of the death toll. Starbotton was particularly badly hit: many houses and cottages were destroyed and a major rebuilding programme had to be undertaken.

Church St Mary: Norman.

School In the reign of Charles II Sir Solomon Swale built a schoolhouse on the waste of Kettlewell for the education of children of the village.

(A. Raistrick, *Old Yorkshire Dales* (1971), 43-5, 47-8, 161. R. A. Marchant, *The Puritans and the Church Courts in the Diocese of York 1560-1642* (1960), 283.)

KILDWICK Staincliffe and Ewecross

An Airedale village to the south of Skipton. The extensive parish of Kildwick included a number of villages but there appears to have been no chapel of ease until Silsden chapel was consecrated in 1712. 1674: 27 households in Kildwick, 49 in Bradley (High and Low Bradley), 90 in Cowling Head, 57 in Farnhill cum Cononley, 47 in Glusburn, 145 in Silsden, 47 in Steeton (including Eastburn), 32 in Stirton and 51 in Sutton. 1676: 1544 persons aged 16 or more (parish).

Kildwick Bridge, which had originally been built in the 14th century, was described by Roger Dodsworth as 'a faire stone bridge'. To the south of Kildwick there was a bridge at Eastburn which spanned a tributary of the River Aire. In 1642 it was reported that Eastburn Bridge 'in the high streete or roade way betwixt London and Kendall, for all passengers and travellers, who continually doe travaile that way with packes and other carriages.....by reason of excessive floodes.....is nowe wholly ruinated and decayed'.

During the early 17th century Kildwick had a succession of Puritan ministers. Roger Brearley, who had previously been the curate of Grindleton in the parish of Mitton, was the leader of a sect known as the Grindletonians who favoured a mystical form of religion. When he appeared before the Northern High Commission in 1627 he admitted that he had been holding conventicles. One of his successors, John Webster, threw in his lot with the Grindletonians.

The Currers of Kildwick had owned the manor since the beginning of Elizabeth's reign. In the early 17th century they built a new house of three storeys. On the outbreak of the Civil War Henry Currer, a younger son, took up arms for Parliament and attained the rank of lieutenant colonel. In 1654 he bought the manor of Farnhill (which had formerly belonged to the Eltoft family) for £3100.

Church St Andrew: Norman, Decorated and Perpendicular.

Schools There had been a school at Kildwick since 1563 and this was still functioning in the mid-17th century.

In 1612 William Laycock made provision for the establishment of a free school for the education of five poor boys from Silsden and Steeton.

In the Commonwealth period there was a private school at Silsden.

In 1665 Hugh Smith founded a school at Cowling for the teaching of poor boys and girls.

(*YASRS*, liv (1915), 377. R. A. Marchant, *The Puritans and the Church Courts in the Diocese of York 1560-1642* (1960), 20, 40, 127-8, 233-4, 247, 290. BL, Egerton MSS 3568. W. K. Jordan, *The Charities of Rural England 1480-1660* (1961), 340. E. W. Brereton, *History of the Ancient and Historic Church of S. Andrews, Kildwick-in-Craven* (1909).)

KIPPAX   Skyrack

A village to the east of Leeds where coal was mined extensively. In the church registers there are many references to men employed in the mines. The parish of Kippax included several villages and hamlets. Ledston was situated in two parishes: Kippax and Ledsham. 1674: 77 households in Kippax, 21 in Allerton Bywater and 29 in Ledston. 1676: 568 persons aged 16 or more (parish).

Church St Mary: Norman with later additions.

School A free school founded by the Rev. George Goldsmith in 1544. In the 17th century the masters included John Lambart, John Freeman, William Freeman and Thomas Atkinson.

Almshouses In his will (1612) Sir Thomas Bland made provision for the establishment of almshouses for four 'oulde poore men' who were of 'honest and vertuous disposicion'.

Principal families (1) Baildon, then Slingsby of Kippax Hall. Estate revenue (Slingsby): £1000 a year (1668); £800 a year (1695). Coalmining and lime manufacture.

When Sir William Slingsby bought out the Baildons in the late 1620s he seems to have been interested primarily in extending the coalmining activities in which he was already engaged in Kippax.

His son Henry (c.1620-1688) was described as a Catholic in 1639 but in 1645 he was named as a member of the West Riding parliamentary committee. In 1668 he inherited a considerable estate in Cambridgeshire from his father-in-law. During the reign of Charles II he spent much of his time in London as Master of the Mint. In contrast, his son Henry, who died in 1695, was content to remain at Kippax where he lived 'in greate creditt and Esteem amongst his Neighbours'. With the death of his brother Anthony in 1697 the male line expired.

(2) Bland of Kippax Park (baronetcy 1642). Estate revenue: £1000 a year (1639). Coalmining.

Sir Thomas Bland (d.1612) built up a substantial estate, including the manor of Kippax Park which he bought in 1595. According to Sir William Wentworth he owed his wealth to the way in which he exercised his responsibilities as under-sheriff of Yorkshire.

His son Sir Thomas (c.1592-1653) was made a ward of the Crown. He fell heavily into debt and had to sell some outlying property. For many years before his death he was incapacitated in some way and his son Thomas took on the management of the estate.

Sir Thomas Bland (1617-1657), who was the first baronet of the family, took up arms for the king in 1642 but was captured at Wakefield the following year. In 1654 he was involved in litigation with his mother, Dame Katherine, over her jointure. According to his heir he died 'much indebted'.

In a Chancery suit of 1699 it was alleged that Sir John Bland (1663-1715) had sabotaged the Slingsby colliery (worth £200 a year) in order to increase the profitability of his own colliery. In response Sir John denied the accusation and also argued that he had a right of way across the lands belonging to Kippax Hall for his coach, carts and carriages.

Kippax Hall A house of modest size which in 1674 had seven taxable hearths. The Slingsbys never sought to emulate the Blands in the matter of housebuilding, though in the 1690s Henry Slingsby the younger carried out some renovation work.

Kippax Park. A three-storeyed house built by the first Sir Thomas Bland towards the end of the 16th century. In 1660 it was described as 'a rich and goodly structure'.

In 1674 the house had 15 taxable hearths.

The Blands had a deer park of 230 acres which in 1611 contained many fallow deer.

(*YPRS*, x (1901). WYAS, Leeds, Temple Newsam MSS, TN/EA16. C.5/633/44. C.6/102/75 and 107/30. C.8/568/59 and 70. C.22/540/18. BIHR, York Registry, will of Sir Thomas Bland, 11 October 1612. C.5/30/3. C.7/47/127 and 422/10. C.33/215 /fo.208. BL, Additional MS 38,599, fo.95.)

KIRK BRAMWITH   **Osgoldcross/Strafford and Tickhill**

A village to the north-east of Doncaster which was situated on the north bank of the River Don. The parish of Kirk Bramwith also included the hamlet of Bramwith or South Bramwith on the other side of the river. 1674: 35 households in Kirk Bramwith. 1676: 48 persons aged 16 or more (parish).

The existence of a ferry suggests that there was no bridge across the Don at this point.

Church St Mary: Norman, Early English, Decorated and Perpendicular.

Principal family Hodgson of Bramwith Hall. Estate revenue: £1000 a year (1682).

Sir Thomas Hodgson settled at Bramwith in the reign of Charles II. In 1682 his Yorkshire estate consisted of the manors of Bramwith, South Bramwith and Barnby Dun, together with Bramwith Hall. In addition, he had property in Nottinghamshire, Lincolnshire, Northamptonshire and Huntingdonshire.

(C.33/305/fo.436. PRO, Chancery Masters' Exhibits, C.112/207.)

KIRKBURTON   Agbrigg and Morley

A clothing village to the south-east of Huddersfield. The extensive parish of Kirkburton contained a number of villages, including Holmfirth which had a dependent chapel. 1674: 68 households in Kirkburton, 324 in Holmfirth, 46 in Shelley, 36 in Shepley and 43 in Thurstonland. The figure for Holmfirth probably covers Cartworth, Fulstone, Hepworth and Wooldale which were within the chapelry. 1676: 1600 persons aged 16 or more, including 60 Protestant dissenters (parish).

In 1641 the West Riding magistrates received a petition from the inhabitants of the parish. In the first place, they complained that their vicar, Gamaliel Whitaker, 'hath not for many yeares last past, nor doth now…..pay any assessment for the releife of the poore' although his living was worth £160 a year. Secondly, they alleged that the churchwardens (who were no fewer than eight in number) charged them 'with many unjust and unreasonable disbursements' and in particular inflated the cost of the bread and wine. In response to this petition the magistrates decided that Whitaker should be assessed in the same way as his parishioners and that the churchwardens should present detailed accounts of their receipts and disbursements to two neighbouring justices.

In the early stages of the Civil War Whitaker's royalist sympathies resulted in the sequestration of his living and at the request of some of the parishioners the House of Commons put in a Puritan minister, Daniel Clark.

In 1645 there was an outbreak of the plague at Shelley.

Church St John Baptist: Norman and Perpendicular.

Schools A school was established at Kirkburton in 1619.

In his will (1642) Richard Charlesworth settled lands for the support of a free school at Hepworth.

(*YASRS*, liv (1915), 258, 262-3. A. G. Matthews, *Walker Revised* (1988), 400. H. J. Morehouse, *The History and Topography of the Parish of Kirkburton* (1861).)

KIRKBY MALHAM   Staincliffe and Ewecross

A small Craven village in a remote area between Ribblesdale and Wharfedale. The parish of Kirkby Malhamdale included a number of villages and hamlets. 1674: 27 households in Kirkby Malham, 32 in Airton, 17 in Calton, 21 in Hanlith, 46 in Malham town, 32 on Malham Moor, 17 in Otterburn and 19 in Scosthrop. 1676: 440 persons aged 16 or more, including 39 Protestant dissenters (parish of Kirkby Malhamdale).

Church St Michael: Perpendicular.

In 1617, following a dispute over pew rights, the churchwardens decided that Josias Lambert and other well-to-do inhabitants of the parish should take on responsibility for the allocation of seats among the parishioners 'accordinge to their degrees and estates'.

In 1622 a three-storeyed vicarage was built.

School In his will (1598) Benjamin Lambert settled certain property for the establishment and support of a school for boys of the parish. The will was declared invalid but his friend John Topham, who was joint owner of the property, was anxious to ensure that his wishes were fulfilled and in a deed of 1606 made financial provision for a free grammar school which duly came into being.

The Puritan Nicholas Walton, who was presented to the living of Kirkby Malhamdale in 1623, also acted as schoolmaster.

Principal family Lambert of Calton Hall. Estate revenue: £500 a year (1627).

Josias Lambert (1554-1632) succeeded his half-brother Benjamin in 1598 and was soon involved in a property dispute with his widow, Mary Lambert, and her daughter Elizabeth. He owned the manors of Airton, Calton, Hanlith, Kirkby and East Malham and half the manor of West Malham. In the latter part of his life he was in serious financial difficulties and granted long leases, some of them for 6000 years, in return for large entry fines.

Following his father's death John Lambert (1619-1684) was made a ward of the Crown. The estate was then heavily encumbered and the Court of Wards feodary reported that it was only worth £300 a year.

On the outbreak of the Civil War Lambert took up arms for Parliament and subsequently commanded troops at the battles of Marston Moor, Preston, Dunbar and Worcester. His military prowess earned him rapid promotion and in 1647 he was advanced to the rank of major-general. During the Interregnum he emerged as a leading political radical with extensive support within the army and was mainly responsible for the Instrument of Government which defined the constitution of the Protectorate. In 1659 he declared in a parliamentary speech that those who had opposed the king in the Civil War were 'an honest, sober, grave people that groaned under oppression, thirsted after grace, the reformed party of the nation'.

After the Restoration he was taken into custody and remained a prisoner on the island of Guernsey until his death. His estate was forfeited but in 1665 the family managed to recover it at a price.

Lambert's son John (d.1702) inherited from him a love of painting. Ralph Thoresby described him as an ingenious painter, an excellent scholar and a man of much reading; and he also extolled the skills which he displayed in such sports as bowling and shooting.

Calton Hall A Tudor house with some medieval features. In 1674 it had nine taxable hearths.

During the Civil War Calton Hall was sacked by royalist troops. Some years later General Lambert wrote that it was uninhabitable, 'beinge quit puld downe and ruinated'. It was also damaged by fire in the late 17th century but was once again repaired.

(Wards 5/49. J. W. Morkill, *The Parish of Kirkby Malhamdale* (1933). J. T. Rutt (ed.), *Diary of Thomas Burton* (1828), iii, 187-8. BL, Additional MSS 21,426, fo.185. W. H. Dawson, *Cromwell's Understudy: The Life and Times of General John Lambert* (1938).)

KIRKBY MALZEARD   Claro

A village to the south of Masham. The parish of Kirkby Malzeard extended westwards into Nidderdale and encompassed large tracts of moorland and a considerable number of villages and hamlets, including Middlesmoor which had a medieval chapel. It also covered part of the village of Azerley; the other part was in the parish of Ripon. Stonebeck Down is separately noticed. 1674: 69 households in Kirkby Malzeard, 76 in Azerley, 41 in Fountains Earth, 90 in Grewelthorpe, 67 in Hartwith, 73 in Laverton and 77 in Stonebeck Up (including Middlesmoor).

At Kirkby Malzeard there were the remains of the Norman castle of the Mowbrays.

Since 1307 Kirkby Malzeard had enjoyed the right to hold a weekly market and two annual fairs.

At the beginning of the 17th century Catholic influences were still relatively strong in this part of the county. In 1604 it was reported that there were 24 recusants and 83 noncommunicants in the parish. Significantly, no information had been forthcoming from Stonebeck Down and Stonebeck Up where the Yorkes of Gouthwaite Hall acted as patrons of their fellow Catholics.

Kirkby Malzeard was a village of modest cottages. In 1674 the largest house was the rectory.

In the Civil War James Earl of Derby, who owned the manor of Kirkby Malzeard, raised troops there on behalf of the king. In 1647 it was reported that the village had been fortified by the royalists.

Church St Andrew: Norman, Early English, Decorated and Perpendicular.

The parish was subject to the peculiar jurisdiction of a Prebendary of York.

School In his will (1640) Gilbert Horseman settled a rent-charge of £5 a year for the support of five poor scholars at a school in Kirkby Malzeard.

(E. Peacock (ed.), *A List of the Roman Catholics in the County of York in 1604* (1872), 34-9. *Calendar, Committee for Compounding*, 33, 1100, 1576. H. Speight, *Nidderdale and the Garden of the Nidd* (1894) and *Nidderdale from Nun-Monkton to Whernside* (1906). B. Jennings (ed.), *A History of Nidderdale* (1983).)

KIRKBY OVERBLOW   Claro

A village situated on high ground between Knaresborough and Leeds. The extensive parish of Kirkby Overblow contained a number of villages and hamlets, including Stainburn which had a medieval chapel. 1674: 43 households in Kirkby Overblow, 30 in Kearby cum Netherby, 53 in Rigton, 41 in Sicklinghall and 34 in Stainburn. 1676: 395 persons aged 16 or more (parish).

Thomas Jaggard, who became rector of Kirkby Overblow in 1639, appears to have been a man of Puritan outlook. In 1643 it was reported that he had abandoned his cure and joined the parliamentarians. Dr William Bethell, who served as rector from 1647 until his death in 1685, was a younger son of Puritan gentry, the Bethells of Ellerton in the East Riding. He married a daughter of Sir John Bourchier the regicide.

In 1645 there was an outbreak of the plague at Rigton.

Church All Saints: Decorated.

School In 1575 Robert Vavasour, a London merchant, left the sum of £10 for the support of poor children in a school at Kirkby Overblow.

Francis Rogers, who was rector in the years 1686 to 1712, was involved in a scheme for the building of a proper schoolhouse.

(R. A. Marchant, *The Puritans and the Church Courts in the Diocese of York 1560-1642* (1960), 257. W. K. Jordan, *The Charities of Rural England 1480-1660* (1961), 327. H. Speight, *Kirkby Overblow and District* (1903).)

KIRKBY WHARFE   Barkston Ash

A village near Tadcaster. The parish of Kirkby Wharfe included the village of Ulleskelf. 1674: 17 households in Kirkby Wharfe (possibly including North Milford), 15 in Grimston and 51 in Ulleskelf.

In 1645 there was an outbreak of the plague at Grimston.

Church St John Baptist: Norman, Decorated and Perpendicular.

The parish was subject to the peculiar jurisdiction of a Prebendary of York.

Schools In 1604 Richard Lilburne, a recusant, was described as 'late scolemaster of Kirkby Wharf'.

In the mid-17th century there was a schoolmaster at Ulleskelf.

Principal families (1) Leeds of North Milford Hall. Estate revenue: £1200 a year (1657).

When Sir John Leeds of Wappingthorn, Sussex died without issue in 1657 his estate, which included the manor of North Milford, passed to his kinsman Englebert Leeds (1638-1703) who took up residence at North Milford Hall. This apparently put an end to the family's Catholic affiliations.

In a Chancery case of 1698 John Leeds, who was the squire's son and heir, alleged that through the malign influence of his stepmother he had been forced to enlist in the French army and that an attempt was being made to disinherit him.

(2) Stanhope of Grimston Hall. Estate revenue: £500 a year (1659).

By the time of the Civil War Sir Edward Stanhope (c.1570-1646) and his son Edward (d.1659) had sold all their landed property except for the manor of Grimston (see under Edlington). In 1641 they secured a royal protection which granted them temporary immunity from the attentions of their creditors.

In the Civil War they were alleged to have supported the royalist cause and the Grimston estate was sequestered. In 1645, however, Sir Edward claimed that he had never taken up arms or performed any service for the king.

After the Restoration the Stanhopes entered upon a period of greater financial stability, though they were no longer a major county family.

North Milford Hall A brick house built by Englebert Leeds in the late 17th century. This presumably replaced the house which had seven taxable hearths in 1674.

Grimston Hall A gabled Tudor house of considerable size. In 1674 John Stanhope was taxed on 24 hearths.

(E. Peacock (ed.), *A List of the Roman Catholics in the County of York in 1604* (1872), 26. C.10/373/30. C.33/253/fols.809-10.)

KIRK DEIGHTON   Claro

A village to the north of Wetherby. The parish of Kirk Deighton included the village of North Deighton, the hamlet of Ingmanthorpe and part of the hamlet of Stockeld. The other part of Stockeld was in the parish of Spofforth. 1674: 27 households in Kirk Deighton and 20 in North Deighton. 1676: 150 persons aged 16 or more (parish).

The manor of North Deighton belonged to the Inglebys of Ripley who had a secondary house there. An inventory drawn up in 1618 refers to the hall, the great chamber, a number of parlours, the study and the chapel.

Church All Saints: Norman, Decorated and Perpendicular.

(*YAJ*, xxxiv (1929), 198-201.)

KIRK HAMMERTON   Claro/Ainsty

A village situated between Knaresborough and York. 1674: 43 households (township of Kirk Hammerton).

On the other side of the River Nidd, and within the Ainsty, the parish of Kirk Hammerton encompassed the battlefield of Marston Moor and the hamlet of Wilstrop which had been depopulated in the late 15th century. In 1665 there were 11 households in Wilstrop.

Church St John: Saxon and Norman.

(M. W. Beresford, 'The Lost Villages of Yorkshire', *YAJ*, xxxviii (1955), 223-4.)

KIRKHEATON   Agbrigg and Morley

A village near Huddersfield which was involved in the manufacture of woollen goods. The parish of Kirkheaton included several villages. 1674: 79 households in Kirkheaton, 68 in Dalton, 86 in Lepton and 71 in Whitley. 1676: 600 persons aged 16 or more (parish of Kirkheaton).

Early on in the Civil War Richard Sykes the rector of Kirkheaton fled to Pontefract where he acted as one of the chaplains who preached to the royalist troops there. As a result the parliamentarians deprived him of his living, which was worth £300 a year, and he was required to pay a fine of £1350 when compounding for his estate.

Church St John Baptist: 13th century and later. In 1663-4 an addition was made on the north side of the church at the expense of a number of subscribers who included Sir John Kaye and Sir Thomas Beaumont. Beaumont family chapel, formerly a chantry chapel, of the 14th century.

School A free grammar school which was of two storeys in height was built about the end of the 16th or beginning of the 17th century and a number of donations were made for its maintenance. In 1685 William Lyley left a rent-charge of £5 a year for educating 10 poor boys at the school.

Principal families (1) Beaumont of Whitley Hall or Whitley Beaumont (baronetcy 1628). Estate revenue: £1000 a year (1620); £800 a year (1653); £1300 a year (1699). Coalmining at Whitley.

'Whitley, the Seat of the ancient and famous family of the Beaumonts' (William Camden).

Sir Richard Beaumont (1574-1631), who was known as 'Black Dick', was reputed to be a gambler, a philanderer and even a highwayman. His sporting activities included hunting and cockfighting. Perhaps because of his bad reputation he failed in his attempts to secure a wife and at his death left only an illegitimate daughter. The baronetcy then became extinct while the bulk of his estate passed to a distant kinsman, Thomas Beaumont of Kexbrough (1605-1668).

In the Civil War Thomas Beaumont took up arms for the king and served as governor of Sheffield Castle until its surrender in July 1644. In 1660 he was knighted for his loyalty.

As a child his grandson Richard (1654-1692) injured his back through the negligence of his nurse and as a result he acquired the nickname 'Crook-back'd Dick'.

(2) Kaye of Denby Grange (and Woodsome Hall, Almondbury). (See under Almondbury).

Whitley Hall The house was built by Sir Richard Beaumont about the end of Elizabeth's reign and enlarged in 1704. An inventory of 1644 refers, among other things, to the hall, the dining room, the new parlour and the gatehouse chamber.

When Sir Thomas died in 1668 his personal estate included materials prepared for building work.

The Beaumonts had a deer park at Whitley.

Denby Grange In 1636 John Kaye (1578-1641) largely rebuilt Denby Grange. The principal rooms of the new house consisted of the hall, the parlour, the dining chamber and the gallery. In addition, he built a new stable and a coach-house and 'brought water in …. troughs to the Brew-house, and in lead to the kitchen'.

(*Calendar, Committee for Compounding*, 977. A. G. Matthews, *Walker Revised* (1988), 399. L. Tolson, *History of the Church of St John the Baptist, Kirkheaton, Yorkshire and Annals of the Parish* (1929). WYAS, Kirklees, Whitley Beaumont MSS. P.Roebuck, *Yorkshire Baronets 1640-1760* (1980). W. D. Macray (ed.), *Beaumont Papers* (1884).)

KIRK SANDALL (or SANDALL PARVA)   Strafford and Tickhill

A small village on the River Don to the north of Doncaster. The parish of Kirk Sandall included the hamlet of Streetthorpe. 1674: 24 households. 1676: 100 persons aged 16 or more (parish of Kirk Sandall).

Church St Oswald: Norman, Early English and Perpendicular.

School In his will (1626) Robert Wood, the rector of Kirk Sandall, settled property for the support of a schoolmaster who was to take on responsibility for a free grammar school in the parish.

Principal family Swyft of Streetthorpe Hall (peerage as Viscount Carlingford 1628). Estate revenue: £2200 a year (1635).

Sir Robert Swyft (1551-1625) was the grandson of a mercer who had been primarily responsible for advancing the fortunes of the family. He was an expert swordsman and, according to Abraham de la Pryme, a witty and merry gentleman. Unusually he served twice as sheriff of Yorkshire.

His son Barnham Viscount Carlingford (1606-1635) appears to have had extravagant tastes: according to his wife he spent at least £2000 on clothes within a period of two years. He died shortly after arriving in France, leaving only a daughter, Mary, who was made a ward of the Crown. After his death the bulk of the estate passed by entail to his sister Dame Mary Anstruther, the wife of Sir Robert Anstruther (see under Wheatley).

Mary Swyft (1634-1682) inherited lands worth some £800 a year. She married Robert Fielding, a courtier, who sold off all her property.

Streetthorpe Hall The house was built by Sir Robert Swyft and completed in 1606. (Wards 5/32. C.9/2/61. C.22/743/34.)

KIRK SMEATON   Osgoldcross

A village to the south-east of Pontefract which was situated on the River Went. There was no other village within the parish. 1674: 37 households (township of Kirk Smeaton).

John Noble, a Puritan divine, served as minister of Kirk Smeaton from 1646 until his ejection in 1662. He had previously been vicar of Whitgift. He was said to have been strongly opposed to the factions of the times and to have engaged in lively disputations with the Quakers.

Church St Peter: Norman, Early English, Decorated and Perpendicular.

(A. G. Matthews, *Calamy Revised* (1934), 366-7.)

KNARESBOROUGH   Claro

A market town situated on a sandstone cliff overlooking the River Nidd. The parish of Knaresborough included a number of villages and hamlets. 1674: 219 households in Knaresborough, 52 in Arkendale, 22 in Brearton, 73 in Harrogate cum Bilton and 20 in Scriven.

Knaresborough was both a sessions town and a parliamentary borough. Its market rights dated from 1310.

Features noted by visitors included the fields of liquorice, the chapel of St Robert and the dropping or petrifying well. 'The town is a pretty stone building, in it a large Market place .... there is a little Chapple cut out of the Rock .... it's called St Robert Chapple' (Celia Fiennes, 1697).

At the beginning of the Civil War Sir Richard Hutton of Goldsborough garrisoned Knaresborough Castle for the king. The garrison finally surrendered in December 1644.

During the course of the 17th century Harrogate became increasingly popular as a health resort. Its medicinal waters included a sweet spring discovered about 1620 and a stinking or sulphur spring. A Yorkshire parson referred in a letter to 'our new Spaw .... the tast is truly inkish, as the Spaw in Germany. The vertues greate, as the cures shew' (Ezekiel Rogers, 1626). Harrogate is 'a village made good by reason of the resort of people to the wells, it stands in a delicate place for pleasure in the summer time' (Thomas Baskerville, 1675). I spent 8 and 9 June 'at the Spaws, in drinking the waters at the usual times; and in company, wherewith better furnished than ordinary, with Sir Ralph Jennyson of Newcastle.....and that accomplished gentleman, Charles Scrimshaw, Esq. of Staffordshire' (Ralph Thoresby, 1681).

Scriven Hall was the ancient seat of the Slingsbys who often represented Knaresborough in the Commons (see under Moor Monkton).

Thomas Stockdale (1593-1653) bought the Bilton Park estate in 1630 and mined coal there. He was a radical Puritan and parliamentarian and a close associate of the Fairfaxes. In his will (1651) he put his net losses in the Civil War at £4016

Church St John Baptist: Norman, Early English, Decorated and Perpendicular. Monuments to members of the Slingsby family.

Castle A royal castle dating mainly from the 14th century. In 1647 the Commons decided that it should be made untenable.

'There are the ruinated walls of the Castle remaines but of no use, but some part is made a prison and some vaults made Cellars' (Celia Fiennes, 1697).

School In 1616 Robert Chaloner, who was rector of Amersham in Buckinghamshire, founded and endowed a grammar school at Knaresborough. The intention was that boys from Knaresborough and Goldsborough should be taught free of charge but that the school should also be open to boys from other parishes. Particular importance was attached to providing the students with a grounding in the Greek and Latin authors.

One of the early masters was Thomas Bateson who was also a physician.

In 1641 it was reported that there were many children of recusants at the school.

(BL. Egerton MSS 2644, fo.240. WYAS, Leeds, Bilton Park MSS. G. W. Johnson (ed.), *The Fairfax Correspondence* (1848), ii, 104, 107, 215, 288. W. Grainge, *The History and Topography of Harrogate, and the Forest of Knaresborough* (1871). W. Wheater, *Knaresborough and its Rulers* (1907). E. S. Wood, *The Ancient Buildings of the Harrogate District* (1946). B. Jennings, *A History of Harrogate and Knaresborough* (1970). A. Kellett, *The Knaresborough Story* (1990). M. G. Neesam, *Harrogate Great Chronicle, 1332-1841* (2005).)

LAUGHTON EN LE MORTHEN   Strafford and Tickhill

A village to the south-east of Rotherham. The extensive parish of Laughton en le Morthen contained a number of villages and hamlets, including Firbeck, Letwell, North and South Anston, Thorpe Salvin, Throapham and Wales which had dependent chapels. 1674: 101 households in Laughton, 70 in Anston cum membris, 22 in Firbeck, 19 in Letwell, 31 in Thorpe Salvin, 23 in Woodsetts cum Gildingwells and 42 in Wales. In Wales Wood the Osbornes of Kiveton had a major colliery.

In 1604 the ministers and churchwardens of the parish refused to attend the Archbishop's visitation on the grounds that it was exempt from such scrutiny by virtue of its privileged status as a peculiar. The ecclesiastical authorities, however, were not prepared to accept this argument.

Robert Giffard succeeded his father as vicar of Laughton in 1603 and held the living until his death in 1649. A Puritan like his father, he was reprimanded on a number of occasions for such acts of nonconformity as neglecting to wear a surplice and failing to use the sign of the cross in baptism. At the visitation of 1632 the churchwardens were criticised for not presenting him.

In 1641 Thomas Spencer was indicted at the Doncaster quarter sessions for saying to Anthony Stacie, the constable of Laughton, 'Thou art a bankrupt, roaguish and knavishe constable'.

A number of gentry families were seated in the parish at one time or another, in particular the Eyres and Hatfields of Laughton, the Wests of Firbeck, the Mauleverers of Letwell and the Knights of Langold. The Wests died out in the male line in 1659.

In the Civil War Sir Gervase Eyre took up arms for the king and was slain at the siege of Newark in 1644.

John Mauleverer (1610-1650) was one of the first of the Yorkshire gentry to declare for Parliament. He was commissioned as a colonel and eventually became governor of Hull. At the time of his death he was heavily indebted. In 1662 the manor of Letwell was sold to Sir Ralph Knight, a former parliamentarian officer who was a Presbyterian in religion. At Langold he substantially enlarged the house which he had acquired.

In 1636 Sir Edward Osborne of Kiveton bought the Thorpe Salvin estate with its Elizabethan mansion which became a secondary seat. In 1674 Thomas Earl of Danby, who was then Lord Treasurer, was taxed on 20 hearths.

Church All Saints: Saxon, Norman, Early English, Decorated and Perpendicular.

The main distinguishing feature of the church was the tall and elegant spire which was visible many miles away.

The parish was subject to the peculiar jurisdiction of the Chancellor of York.

Schools In 1605 a two-storeyed schoolhouse was built at Laughton and in the course of the century a number of the pupils were sent to Cambridge University. The master of the grammar school in the reign of Charles II may be identified as John Broomhead.

In 1619 Edmund Laughton and Anthony Eyre made a settlement of property for the purpose of founding an elementary school for poor children of the parish.

During the reign of Charles I Robert Seton kept a private school at Laughton.

(*Acts of the Privy Council, 1598-9*, 657. R. A. Marchant, *The Puritans and the Church Courts in the Diocese of York 1560-1642* (1960), 248-9. *YASRS*, liv (1915), 332. C.8/73/17. C.9/14/79. C.10/47/111. W. K. Jordan, *The Charities of Rural England 1480-1660* (1961), 333.)

LEATHLEY   Claro

A village to the north-east of Otley. The parish of Leathley included the hamlet of Castley which was situated on the River Wharfe. 1674: 56 households in Leathley and 18 in Castley. 1676: 215 persons aged 16 or more (parish).

In a Commonwealth survey of benefices it was noted that Castley was a mile and a half from the parish church and that the road or path between them was, for the most part, impassable in winter.

Church St Oswald: Norman and Perpendicular.

Principal family Lindley of Leathley Hall. Estate revenue: £750 a year (1630).

In 1604 the Lindleys bought Middleham Castle and some of the demesne lands from the Crown.

Arthur Lindley (c.1583-1636), who succeeded his father in 1613, served as a justice of the peace but appears to have avoided any involvement with the political factions of the day. Following his death the estate was divided between his two daughters. Jane Lindley, who inherited the Middleham Castle property, married Sir Edward Loftus. Her sister Ellen, who had the manor of Leathley as her share, married twice. Her first husband was Sir Ingram Hopton of Armley who died in 1643 while fighting for the king. She then became the wife of another royalist officer, Robert Brandling, who took up residence at Leathley. At his death in 1669 he left an estate in Yorkshire, Northumberland and Durham worth £900 a year.

Brandling had no male issue and his daughter Alathea carried the manor of Leathley into the Hitch family.

Leathley Hall A gabled Elizabethan or Jacobean mansion. In 1674 it had 11 taxable hearths.

(*YASRS*, civ (1940), 82-3, 87, 111. C.5/446/32.)

LEDSHAM   Barkston Ash

A village to the north of Castleford. The parish of Ledsham included the village of Fairburn and part of the village of Ledston; the other part was in the parish of Kippax. 1674: 25 households in Ledsham, 40 in Fairburn and 29 in Ledston. 1676: 200 persons aged 16 or more (parish of Ledsham).

Church All Saints: Saxon, Norman and Perpendicular.

Almshouses In his will (1670) Sir John Lewis made provision for the establishment of a hospital or almshouses for ten poor people, half of them men and half women, who were to be drawn from the inhabitants of Ledston or Ledsham or, failing that, of his other manors (see below). This eventually led to the building of St John's Hospital, a two-storeyed range of almshouses, at a cost of £400.

Principal families (1) Witham of Ledston Hall. Estate revenue: £600 a year (1606).

The Withams were a family which rose and fell within the compass of three generations.

Henry Witham (1581-c.1629) was the son of William Witham whose death in 1593 had been attributed to witchcraft. For some years he was a ward of the Crown. In 1607 he began to sell land and before long he had disposed of his whole estate.

The most valuable part of the estate was the manor of Ledston which in 1616 was surveyed by Robert Saxton. The following year Witham sold it to Sir Thomas Wentworth the future Earl of Strafford (see under Wentworth).

(2) Lewis of Ledston Hall (baronetcy 1660). Estate revenue: £3000 a year (1671).

In 1655 William Earl of Strafford sold the manor of Ledston to Sir John Lewis (1615-1671), a merchant who had made a large fortune in India and Persia. He had strong Yorkshire connections as a nephew of Thomas Lewis of Marr whose landed property eventually came into his possession.

After his death the substantial estate which he had built up was divided between his two surviving daughters, Elizabeth who married Theophilus Earl of Huntingdon and Mary who became the wife of Robert Lord Deincourt.

Sir John left a rent-charge of £60 a year for the support of the occupants of his almshouses and the maintenance of the fabric. This included an allowance for clothes: gowns 'grey faced and Edged in the Seames with black stuff suteable to my Livery', hose and shoes, and hats for the men and kerchiefs for the women. In addition, he asked his executors to buy them silver badges with his crest or coat of arms which were to be worn on the sleeves of their gowns.

In 1678 the vicar of Ledsham and the churchwardens and overseers for the poor alleged in a Chancery suit that the executors, the Earl and Countess of Huntingdon and Lord and Lady Deincourt, had been seeking to frustrate Sir John's declared intentions. In response the defendants claimed that there was a technical defect in this part of the will but emphasised their willingness to promote and support such a charitable and pious objective.

Ledston Hall The Withams had largely rebuilt the house in Elizabeth's reign.

An entry for 1622 in a commonplace book of the Shann family records that 'This yere was builded the newe hall at Ledstone by Sir Thomas Wintworth …. There was before A verie pretie stone house but much of it pulled downe when they builded the new worke, to contrive the new worke for their purpose'. Wentworth carried out major extensions to the south but some part of the Witham house was left intact.

Sir John Lewis built an east range with Dutch gables and undertook other work. In 1671 it was reported that the number of hearths had been reduced from 26 to 25.

(WYAS, Leeds, Ledston MSS. C.10/132/2. BL, Additional MSS 38,599, fo.55.)

LEEDS

Skyrack/Agbrigg and Morley

A market town on the River Aire and a major centre of the West Riding woollen industry. The extensive parish of Leeds contained a large number of villages, including Armley, Beeston, Bramley, Chapel Allerton, Farnley, Headingley, Holbeck and Hunslet which had dependent chapels. The chapels at Armley, Headingley and Hunslet were built in the early 17th century. Armley, Beeston and Farnley are separately noticed. 1674: 1135 households in Leeds, 66 in Bramley, 78 in Chapel Allerton, 53 in Headingley cum Burley, 144 in Holbeck, 134 in Hunslet, 24 in Potter Newton and 63 in Wortley. The main streets in Leeds included Briggate, Kirkgate, Millhill and Boar Lane which was the most fashionable part of the town. 1676: 12,000 persons aged 16 or more, including 150 Protestant dissenters (parish of Leeds).

The town is one of the most populous in England, 'it hath in it above 12,000 people' (John Taylor the Water Poet, 1640).

'Leeds is a large town, severall large streetes cleane and well pitch'd and good houses all built of stone .... this is esteemed the wealthyest town of its bigness in the Country .... they have provision soe plentifull that they may live with very little expense and get much variety' (Celia Fiennes, 1698).

In 1639 it was said that cloth to the value of £200,000 a year was made within the borough of Leeds. The town was a finishing centre for cloth produced in the surrounding villages and an extremely busy emporium. There were two weekly markets, on Tuesdays and Saturdays. For many years the cloth market was located on Leeds Bridge but in 1648 it was moved to Briggate where there was opportunity for expansion.

There were outbreaks of the plague in 1610, 1617, 1623, 1635, 1637, 1640 and 1645.

In 1626 a royal charter was obtained for the incorporation of Leeds as a borough with a chief alderman, 9 burgesses and 20 assistants. The first person to be nominated as chief alderman was Sir John Savile of Howley Hall who was a patron of the West Riding clothiers.

In 1639 the corporation sought parliamentary representation for the borough but the petition failed in its purpose.

In the early months of the Civil War Leeds was held by royalist troops under the command of Sir William Savile. In January 1643 Sir Thomas Fairfax captured the town for Parliament but in July it was once more in royalist hands. In April 1644 however, Fairfax regained possession. The Civil War highlighted existing tensions within the community: some wealthy cloth merchants supported the king but the townspeople as a whole favoured the cause of Parliament.

During the course of the conflict Leeds was bombarded on several occasions and many buildings were destroyed or badly damaged. The social and economic problems arising from the war were exacerbated by the plague of 1645 which resulted in a death-toll of 1325.

In 1656 Cromwell received a Leeds petition which complained that the charter of 1626 had been procured without the general consent of the clothiers and the populace at large and called for changes in the structure of the corporation. Eventually, in 1661, a new charter was issued which established a corporation consisting of a mayor, 12 aldermen and 24 assistants.

In the last decade of the 17th century George Sorocold carried out a project for conveying river water by lead pipes to various parts of the town. I was 'several times with Mr Sorocold's workmen, who this day began in Kirk Gate to lay the lead pipes to convey the water to each family' (Ralph Thoresby, 22 August 1694).

Among the most notable inhabitants of Leeds were the cloth merchant John Harrison (1579-1656) who was a great benefactor of the town and the antiquarian Ralph Thoresby (1658-1725) who had a museum containing ancient coins, prints and manuscripts. Besides his charitable works Harrison 'built a wholle street with faire howses on booth sides' (Life of Marmaduke Rawdon, entry for 1664). This was known as New Street or New Kirkgate.

Within the township of Headingley there were the substantial remains of Kirkstall Abbey, an establishment of Cistercian monks which had been founded in the 12th century and dissolved in 1539. In the 17th century the Kirkstall estate belonged to the Saviles of Howley Hall and their successors who had iron mills there.

In 1611 the West Riding magistrates were informed that the stone bridge known as Kirkstall Bridge which had recently been erected was 'altogether ruinate and taken away with ye water'. They therefore decided that a new stone bridge should be built at the expense of the whole riding.

Churches Parish church of St Peter: Norman, Decorated and Perpendicular.

As the population grew in size it became clear that St Peter was not large enough to accommodate all the townspeople. In 1632, therefore, John Harrison began to build a new church, St John's, at his own expense. This was consecrated by Archbishop Neile in September 1634 and the first minister was Robert Todd, a Puritan whose preaching gained him a considerable following.

A Presbyterian chapel was built in Leeds following the Declaration of Indulgence of 1672.

Schools A free grammar school was founded in 1552. Lawrence Rawson settled property for its support in 1597 and 1602. John Harrison built a new schoolhouse on his own grounds; and Godfrey Lawson, who was mayor in 1669, added an apartment and donated books to the library.

In 1656 John Garnet, the master of Leeds Grammar School, caused a stir by circulating a pamphlet entitled 'Cautions for Choice'. He was required to appear before the Council of State but after being cross-examined he was allowed to return home.

There were other schools in Leeds. Ralph Thoresby was educated at a private grammar school while in 1698 Celia Fiennes noted that there was 'a good school for young Gentlewomen'.

In his will (1676) Samuel Sunderland made a settlement of property for the maintenance of a schoolmaster who was to teach the children of Wortley free of charge. The following year William Farrer, who owned the manor of Wortley, provided a schoolhouse.

Almshouses Harrison's Hospital was built by John Harrison in 1639. An entry in the parish register records that there were '20 Hospital houses for 40 poore people'.

In his will (1643) Josiah Jenkinson settled on trustees the almshouses which he had recently erected. According to Thoresby they provided accommodation for 16 poor people.

Workhouse In 1638 Alderman Richard Sykes and others built a workhouse for the purpose of setting poor people to work. Some men called it a house of correction.

(John Taylor, *Part of this Summer's Travels* (1640), 22. *CSP Dom, 1625-6*, 371. *CSP Dom, 1639-40*, 251-2. *CSP Dom, 1656-7*, 114, 159, 181, 214, 241. *CSP Dom, 1660-1*, 460, 475, 503. *CSP Dom, 1661-2*, 67, 69. *YASRS*, liv (1915), 4. *The First and Second Decree of the Committee of Pious-Uses in Leedes* (1926). W. K. Jordan, *The Charities of Rural England 1480-1660* (1961), 275, 277, 286, 314. E. Parsons, *History of Leeds* (1834). A. C. Price, *A History of the Leeds Grammar School* (1919). M. W. Beresford and G. R. J Jones, *Leeds and its Region* (1967). S. Burt and K. Grady, *The Illustrated History of Leeds* (1994).)

LINTON
Staincliffe and Ewecross

A Wharfedale village to the north of Skipton. The parish of Linton included several villages. 1674: 48 households in Linton, 49 in Grassington, 36 in Hebden and 38 in Threshfield. 1676: 400 persons aged 16 or more (parish).

The church living of Linton consisted of two medieties, each with a rector who officiated in turn. Henry Hoyle, who served as one of the rectors in the years 1615 to 1636, was also vicar of Gisburn. He was a Puritan who found himself in trouble with the ecclesiastical authorities in 1619 and 1632. On the latter occasion he was suspended for a time but managed to retain his livings.

Since 1281 Grassington had enjoyed the right to hold a weekly market and an annual fair. To the north, on Grassington Moor, there were lead mines which belonged to the Earls of Cumberland and their successors. These were an important source of employment for the inhabitants of the parish.

In 1661 the medieval bridge which spanned the River Wharfe between Grassington and Linton was in a dilapidated condition and a major repair programme was put in hand.

Church St Oswald: Norman, Decorated and Perpendicular.

School In his will (1674) Matthew Hewitt, who was rector of Linton and a considerable landowner, made provision for the building of a grammar school at Threshfield. From the property which he settled for this purpose the master was to be paid £20 a year and the usher £10 a year. In addition, he endowed four scholarships at St John's College, Cambridge.

Latin and English grammar were taught free of charge but a fee was payable for tuition in writing and accounts.

During the last two decades of the 17th century the master of Threshfield School was Henry Motley who also served as vicar of Kettlewell. He sent no fewer than nine of his pupils, including his son Thomas, to St John's College where he had himself been educated.

(R. A. Marchant, *The Puritans and the Church Courts in the Diocese of York 1560-1642* (1960), 256. R. T. Spence, 'Mining and Smelting in Yorkshire by the Cliffords, Earls of Cumberland, in the Tudor and early Stuart Period', *YAJ*, 64 (1992). A. Raistrick, *Old Yorkshire Dales* (1971), 164-5. Susan D. Brooks, *A History of Grassington* (1979). D. Joy, *Hebden, The History of a Dales Township* (2002).)

LITTLE OUSEBURN   Claro

A village to the north-east of Knaresborough. The parish of Little Ouseburn included several hamlets. 1674: 29 households (township of Little Ouseburn).

Church Holy Trinity: Norman and Perpendicular.

The parish was subject to the peculiar jurisdiction of the Precentor of York Minster.

LONG MARSTON   Ainsty

A village to the west of York. The parish of Long Marston included the hamlets of Angram and Hutton Wandesley. 1665: 50 households in Long Marston and 37 in Angram and Hutton Wandesley. 1676: 220 persons aged 16 or more (parish).

The Thwaites family of Marston Hall were ardent Catholics who sent their sons to the English College at Douai for their education. In 1630 John Thwaites compounded for his own recusancy and for that of his wife, his father and his grandmother and was required to pay the relatively modest rent of £26 6s 8d a year.

In the Civil War John Thwaites remained neutral but two-thirds of the estate were sequestered on account of his recusancy.

During the late 17th century there were two major families residing in the parish: the Roundells of Hutton Wandesley and the Thompsons of Long Marston.

William Roundell (1646-1693) appears to have owed his wealth to one factor in particular: his marriage in 1665 to Hannah Elwyck, the only child of a York merchant. By the time of his death he had built up an estate worth £1300 a year.

Sir Henry Thompson (c.1625-1683), who was a York wine merchant, bought the manor of Long Marston from the Thwaites family and also acquired a large estate at Escrick in the East Riding. He was a close friend of Andrew Marvell and held similar political views. Sir John Reresby described him as one of the factious party in the city of York and expressed the opinion that he and his brother Edward were 'both very antimonarchicall persons'.

Church All Saints: mainly Perpendicular.

In the early 15th century a new church had been built on a different site with materials brought from the old church.

School In 1627 George Reiner was presented for teaching children at Long Marston without a licence.

(*CRS*, liii (1961), 321. C.7/286/40 and 296/190. *Memoirs of Sir John Reresby* (ed. A. Browning and others) (1991), 57, 303. *YAJ*, xv (1900), 234.)

LONG PRESTON   Staincliffe and Ewecross

A Ribblesdale village to the north-west of Skipton. The parish of Long Preston included several villages and hamlets. 1674: 94 households in Long Preston, 35 in Hellifield, 30 in West Halton and 69 in Wigglesworth. 1676: 900 persons aged 16 or more (parish).

In 1604 there were a number of Catholics in the parish, though these mainly consisted of noncommunicants.

In 1639 the West Riding magistrates were informed that 'a bridge, commonly called Cow Bridge, within the parish of Long Preston, and leading between the market town of Skipton and that of Preston in Amundernesse in Lancashire, is now in great decay for lack of repair'. It was therefore decided to levy the sum of £30 on the wapentake of Staincliffe and Ewecross but in the event this proved insufficient.

Hellifield Peel, a fortified manor-house, was the seat of an ancient gentry family, the Hamertons, who had obtained a licence to crenellate it in 1440. They still had an attachment to the Catholic faith but successive heads of the family tended to conform. In the Civil War they appear to have avoided any commitment.

Church St Mary: Decorated.

Almshouses In his will (1615) James Knowles, a London cloth merchant with his roots in the parish, founded a hospital at Long Preston.

'....Long Preston, a pretty country town, where is a hospital for twelve poor widows, who have each 40s per annum, by James Knowles, who left the remainder of the interest of £800 to the use of the church' (Ralph Thoresby, 1681).

Workhouse Knowles also bequeathed £200 for the setting up of a workhouse which would provide employment for the needy poor.

(E. Peacock (ed.), *A List of the Roman Catholics in the County of York in 1604* (1872), 19. *YASRS*, liv (1915), 135, 213. W. K. Jordan, *The Charities of Rural England 1480-1660* (1961), 268-9, 286. P. Ryder and J. Birch, 'Hellifield Peel – a North Yorkshire Tower-House', *YAJ*, 55 (1983).)

MALTBY   Strafford and Tickhill

A village to the east of Rotherham. The parish of Maltby included the hamlet of Hooton Levitt and the Sandbeck estate. 1674: 63 households (township of Maltby). 1676: 200 persons aged 16 or more (parish of Maltby).

Near Sandbeck Hall were the ruins of Roche Abbey, a Cistercian monastery founded in the 12th century.

Church St Bartholomew: Norman with some Perpendicular features.

Principal family Saunderson of Sandbeck Hall (and Saxby, Lincolnshire) (baronetcy, 1611; peerage as Viscount Castleton, 1627). Estate revenue: £10,000 a year (1675).

The Saundersons were one of the wealthiest landed families in England. In 1641 their Yorkshire possessions included the manors of Maltby, Roche Abbey and Sandbeck. Their main power base, however, was in Lincolnshire.

Sir Nicholas Saunderson the first Viscount (c.1561-1630) added substantially to the estate which he had inherited in 1582.

Because of a series of deaths in the male line the Saundersons took no part in the Civil War. In 1650 George Saunderson (1631-1714), who was a younger son, succeeded to the estate and title as the fifth Viscount. During the Commonwealth period he was involved in royalist plots and in 1659 was imprisoned in the Tower.

He had property in Yorkshire, Lincolnshire, Lancashire and Ireland.

Sandbeck Hall Sir Nicholas the first Viscount built the house and often resided there. Some building work was carried out in the reign of Charles II. George Viscount Castleton had 25 taxable hearths in 1664 and 30 in 1674.

There was a park adjoining the house.

(*Catalogue of the Lumley MSS*. C.33/328, part 1/fo.461. T. W. Beastall, *A North Country Estate. The Lumleys and Saundersons as Landowners, 1600-1900* (1975).)

MARR   Strafford and Tickhill

A small village to the north-west of Doncaster. There was no other village in the parish. 1674: 25 households (township of Marr). 1676: 70 persons aged 16 or more (parish).

Thomas Lewis (1578-1663) bought the manor of Marr in 1605 and built a new house there. In the reign of Charles I, however, he experienced a major change of fortune: he was forced to sell his property at High Melton and his only son (who had married an heiress) died without issue.

Although he apparently took no part in the Civil War his financial problems continued to worsen and his creditors began to close in. In 1659 he sold the manor of Marr, which was worth some £300 a year, to his nephew Sir John Lewis who almost immediately complained in a Chancery suit that the estate was heavily encumbered.

Church St Helen: Norman, Early English, Decorated and Perpendicular.
(C.6/42/81. C.8/265/115. C.9/5/144. C.33/257/fo.757.)

MARTON   Claro

A village to the south of Boroughbridge. The parish of Marton included the village of Grafton. 1674: 56 households in Marton cum Grafton.

Church Christ Church: Norman.

MARTON IN CRAVEN   Staincliffe and Ewecross

A small parish, consisting mainly of the villages of East and West Marton. 1674: 47 households (township of Marton). 1676: 80 persons aged 16 or more (parish).

Church St Peter, East Marton: Norman and later.

Principal family Heber of Marton Hall, West Marton. Estate revenue: £600 a year (1640).

Although the Hebers were related to General John Lambert and may have held similar political views they do not appear to have been actively engaged on behalf of Parliament before 1649. However, Thomas Heber (c.1621-1679) proved to be a loyal servant of the Commonwealth.

Oliver Heywood relates that in 1681 a nonconformist minister told Thomas Heber (c.1647-1683) that his father had been a traitor and that Heber responded by striking him on the head.

Marton Hall An E-shaped building with mullioned windows. This was apparently a Tudor house which had a new wing added in the early 17th century. In 1674 there were 11 taxable hearths.

The Hebers also had a secondary house at Stainton.
(Wards 9/575/210.)

METHLEY   Agbrigg and Morley

A clothing village near Leeds. 1674: 121 households (township of Methley). 1676: 246 persons aged 16 or more (parish of Methley).

Besides the lords of the manor there were a number of minor gentry resident in Methley, including the Flowers of Hessle House and the Yonges of West House.

During the years 1605 to 1609 Methley suffered badly from the plague: in the last three months of 1605 it caused the death of 37 persons.

In 1610 the West Riding magistrates agreed that £250 should be levied to enable Methley Bridge to be rebuilt in stone; but in 1638 they found it necessary to authorise further expenditure.

Church St Oswald: Decorated and Perpendicular.

Inn In 1642 there was an inn called the Rose and Crown.

Principal family Savile of Methley Hall (baronetcy 1611). Estate revenue: £850 a year (1607); £2500 a year (1632); £3000 a year (1659); £4000 a year (1693). Fulling mills. Number of servants: 17 (1632).

Sir John Savile (1546-1607), who bought the Methley estate in 1588, was a successful lawyer who was eventually appointed a Baron of the Exchequer and a Justice of Assize on the Northern Circuit.

His son Sir Henry (1579-1632) added considerably to the estate. He was involved in a bitter dispute with the copyholders of Methley over the assessment of copyhold fines. In Chancery proceedings which he began in 1612 the defendants described him as a harsh landlord whose excessive demands were likely to ruin them. Writing to his friend Thomas Lord Wentworth in 1629 he stressed the importance of the clothing industry which was 'of the Essence and indeede the very Subsistence of our neighbourhood'.

At his death Sir Henry had no surviving issue and the baronetcy expired. The bulk of his estate passed to his half-brother John (1588-1659) whom he had once conjectured might become 'a ploddinge common lawyer'.

In the Civil War John Savile supported the cause of Parliament. It was alleged that in April 1643 Roger Hollings of Methley had told him that he was a traitor and that he hoped to see him hanged. In his will (1658) he gave direction that he should be buried 'without pompe or ostentation' and asked his executors to ensure that his children were carefully and religiously educated and brought up in the fear of God. The personal estate which he left included £10,632 in ready cash.

During the latter part of the 17th century the Saviles continued to prosper. Under the terms of a marriage settlement of 1693 John Savile undertook to purchase further lands worth £1000 a year.

Methley Hall Originally built in the 15th century, the house was no more than a shell when Sir John Savile bought the estate. He 'began to repair the same, and brought yt to A fayre house Againe'. The rooms listed in an inventory of 1607 include the hall, the great chamber, the gallery, the study and the chapel.

Sir Henry Savile 'pulled down the roofe of the house, and builded up the Stone woorke therof higher then ever it was before, and mayd it A flatt roofe and covered it over with Leade'. This was the situation in 1611 but his building operations were not finally completed until 1622.

One of the largest mansions in Yorkshire (43 hearths in 1674). A two-storeyed house with three towers which was surrounded by a moat.

In 1592 the park contained 132 acres. In 1627 Sir Henry Savile 'began to take in his new parke' and diverted a road which ran through it. The following year he 'finnished the pails and put deare into his parke'.

(H. S. Darbyshire and G. D. Lumb, *The History of Methley*, Thoresby Society, xxxv (1934). *YASRS*, liv (1915), 69. WYAS, Leeds, MSS of the Earl of Mexborough. BL, Additional MSS 12,497, fols.429,431 and 38,599, fols.2, 55, 93. C.2/James I/S6/20. C.8/138/74. C.33/210/fo.356 and 338, part 2/fo.502. *Surtees Society*, xl (1861), 5. PRO, Wills, PROB11/294/402.)

MEXBOROUGH   Strafford and Tickhill

A village to the north-east of Rotherham which was situated on the River Don. The parish of Mexborough included the village of Ravenfield which had a dependent chapel and part of the village of Swinton; the other part was in the parish of Wath upon Dearne. 1674: 42 households in Mexborough, 19 in Denaby, 31 in Ravenfield and 38 in Swinton. 1676: 70 persons aged 16 or more in the chapelry of Ravenfield (no return for the rest of the parish).

The Reresbys of Thrybergh owned the manor of Denaby and one of the manors in Mexborough. On the eve of the Civil War these were worth respectively £249 and £120 a year. At Denaby the Reresbys mined coal.

At the height of their prosperity the Hornes of Mexborough had a landed income of some £600 a year. The most notable member of the family was Cotton Horne (c.1590-1656), an attorney who held the appointment of steward of the honour of Pontefract. He bought property in Mexborough and elsewhere. In the Civil War he supported the king but was not particularly active. His son William (1615-1679) was a public benefactor (see below). After his death the family moved to Leeds.

Thomas Westby of Ravenfield, who died in 1634, was a Catholic. After his death the Ravenfield estate, which was worth £300 a year, was purchased by George Westby and his son Thomas who may have been distant kinsmen. The new owners had strong Puritan sympathies and in the Civil War Thomas Westby (c.1612-1659) served as a member of the West Riding parliamentary committee.

Church St John: Early English.
The parish was subject to the peculiar jurisdiction of the Archdeacon of York.
The minister was a perpetual curate.
Almshouses In 1669 William Horne founded a hospital for six poor widows.
(*Memoirs of Sir John Reresby* (ed. A. Browning and others) (1991), introduction, xli. C.10/273/95. J. Fletcher Horne, 'The Hornes of Mexborough', *YAJ*, xix (1907). *YASRS*, xviii (1895), 223. C.7/82/61.)

MIDGLEY   Agbrigg and Morley

A clothing village to the west of Halifax which was situated near the River Calder. Luddenden chapel in the township of Midgley was one of the dependent chapels within the parish of Halifax. 1674: 91 households (township of Midgley).

The Farrers of Ewood Hall in Midgley owned fulling mills and coalmines. They had lived there since the 15th century but it was not until 1598 that they had acquired the manor of Midgley. Henry Farrer (c.1537-1610) did much to advance the fortunes of the family and also played a key part in the foundation of Heath Grammar School. His appetite for litigation, however, had tragic consequences for him. While engaged in a lawsuit in Westminster Hall he was stabbed by his adversary, Thomas Oldfield of Warley, and died shortly afterwards.

He left no issue and his estate in the parish of Halifax eventually descended to his nephew Henry Farrer. The new owner had interests elsewhere and in 1630 he sold this property to his brother John for £2000.

John Farrer (c.1590-1649) took up residence at Ewood Hall and appears to have renovated the Tudor building. In 1633 he entered into an agreement with Abraham Shaw, a Northowram yeoman, for the mining of coal in the wastes and commons of Hipperholme and Sowerby. Shaw was to be the working partner and the agreement set out in some detail how the charges and profits were to be shared.

In the Civil War John Farrer took the side of Parliament and was one of the members of the West Riding committee. His sons John, Henry and William all served as officers in the parliamentarian army and in 1654 the latter was made a commissioner for the removal of scandalous ministers.

In 1647 John Farrer settled the estate on William even though he was a younger son. This led the eldest son, John, to begin legal proceedings against his half-brother but they ended in failure.

By the time of his death in 1684 William Farrer had significantly increased the estate through his acquisition of the manors of Saddleworth and Wortley, near Leeds.

Church Luddenden chapel (St Mary) had been built in the 15th century but it was not until 1624 that it was properly consecrated.

(G. Dent, 'Ewood in Midgley', *Transactions of the Halifax Antiquarian Society* (1939). C.54/2834. W. Wheater (ed.), *Old Yorkshire*, Second Series (1885), 274-5. *YASRS*, ix (1890), 19.)

MIRFIELD   Agbrigg and Morley

A clothing village between Huddersfield and Dewsbury. 1674: 127 households (township of Mirfield). 1676: 200 persons aged 16 or more (parish of Mirfield).

In 1640 the West Riding magistrates were informed that Mirfield Bridge, which spanned the River Calder, was in a ruinous condition. They therefore decided that the sum of £100 should be levied on the wapentake of Agbrigg and Morley to enable the necessary repair work to be put in hand.

The Beaumont family owned considerable property in Mirfield and sometimes resided there. Their house, Castle Hall, had been built by Thomas Beaumont in the mid-16th century. In 1642 Richard Beaumont of Mirfield (who was the father of Sir Thomas Beaumont of Whitley) and five of his associates pleaded guilty to assaulting and maltreating John Hall the younger.

Robert Allenson, who became vicar of Mirfield in 1639, was ejected in 1654 by the West Riding commissioners for the removal of scandalous ministers. He was restored to the living in 1660.

Church St Mary: Norman.

School In the 17th century there was a free grammar school at Mirfield which had probably been founded in 1605.

In 1667 Richard Thorpe settled lands for the support of a schoolmaster at Mirfield.

(*YASRS*, liv (1915), 200, 348. Kirklees Metropolitan Library, Huddersfield, Whitley Beaumont MSS. A. G. Matthews, *Walker Revised* (1988), 388.)

MOOR MONKTON   Ainsty

A village to the north-west of York. The parish of Moor Monkton included the hamlet of Hessay. 1665: 39 households in Moor Monkton and 19 in Hessay. 1676: 132 persons aged 16 or more (parish of Moor Monkton).

Church All Saints: Norman.

School In 1600 it was suggested that William Raynaild who had a school at Moor Monkton might not be licensed to teach.

Principal family Slingsby of Redhouse, Moor Monkton (and Scriven Hall) (baronetcy 1638). Estate revenue: £1100 a year (1620); £1600 a year (1640); £1200 a year (1667); £1500 a year (1688). A fulling mill in Knaresborough. Number of servants: 24 (1638).

Sir Henry Slingsby (c.1560-1634) added substantially to the estate, in some cases in association with his father. Among his purchases was the manor of Scagglethorpe alias Redhouse which he acquired in 1595. In the reign of James I Redhouse superseded Scriven Hall as the family's principal seat.

In 1619 Sir Henry commissioned Francis Mayson to undertake a survey of his manor of Moor Monkton and he subsequently employed another surveyor, Solomon Swale.

He held a number of local offices of profit in the gift of the Duchy of Lancaster and valued the associated fees and leases at £500 a year. In 1615 he was stripped of these offices but five years later, after protracted litigation in the Duchy Court, he managed to recover them.

In 1633 Charles I paid a visit to Redhouse.

Sir Henry (1602-1658) inherited a flourishing estate from his father and was himself interested in the potential benefits of new methods of husbandry.

In 1638 he began to keep a diary, inspired by the example of Montaigne, and continued the practice until the beginning of 1649. In this diary he put the cost of his housekeeping at £500 a year, allowing for the rental value of the demesne lands which he farmed. He also described his experiences with a succession of drunken cooks but had words of praise for many of his servants, among them his steward Thomas Richardson, 'a man of great integrity and of indefatigable pains and industry', and his gardener Peter Clark whose 'extream labour shortened his days'.

In the Civil War he raised a regiment of volunteers for the king and fought at the battles of Marston Moor and Naseby.

In 1656 he was imprisoned at Hull as a royalist conspirator and two years later he was executed on Tower Hill. In his account of this episode Clarendon referred to his 'incorrigible fidelity to the Crown' and portrayed him as 'a gentleman of good understanding, but of a very melancholic nature, and of very few words'.

His son Sir Thomas (1636-1688) joined with Thomas Lord Fairfax at the end of 1659 when he intervened in support of General Monck.

In 1665 he entertained Prince James, Duke of York when he visited Yorkshire; and in 1670 the king appointed him constable of Scarborough Castle.

Redhouse A gabled Jacobean house situated near the River Ouse. It was built by Sir Henry Slingsby (c.1560-1634) who in 1606 let a contract for the production of 200,000 bricks and some 12,000 tiles.

During the years 1635-1641 his son Sir Henry spent £1346 on building work at Redhouse and Scriven Hall. Among the improvements at Redhouse was the construction in 1637 of the great staircase.

In 1665 Sir Thomas Slingsby was taxed on 22 hearths.

There was a medieval deer park to the south of the house.

(*YAJ*, xv, (1900), 234. YAS Library, Slingsby MSS. D. Parsons (ed.), *The Diary of Sir Henry Slingsby of Scriven, Bart.* (1836). G. Ridsdell Smith, *Without Touch of Dishonour*

(1968). Susan E. E. Pitts, 'The Slingsbys of Scriven, c.1600-1688', *Northern History*, xxxiii (1997). P. R. Newman, *Moor Monkton and its People 1600 to 1916* (Moor Monkton Village History Committee) (1982.)

MORLEY   Agbrigg and Morley

A clothing village to the south of Leeds which was situated within the parish of Batley. 1674: 111 households (township of Morley).

Church St Mary: a public chapel which according to a local tradition was leased by the patron, Thomas Earl of Sussex, to a Presbyterian congregation in 1650 and was never subsequently used by the Church of England.

In 1669 it was reported that there was a conventicle at Morley which drew large numbers of nonconformists.

Principal family Savile of Howley Hall (ennobled 1628 as Baron Savile of Pontefract (father) and Viscount Savile of Castlebar (son); Earl of Sussex 1644). Estate revenue: £3500 a year (1630); £5000 a year (1671). Iron works at Kirkstall.

Sir John Savile, Lord Savile (1556-1630) was one of Strafford's most formidable enemies. In the factional struggle which went on he set himself up as patron of the West Riding clothiers and in 1626 was named as the first alderman of Leeds. He was Comptroller of the Royal Household, 1625-1630 and Vice-President of the Council in the North, 1626-1628.

A Calvinist in his religious outlook, he had a Puritan chaplain, Anthony Nutter. In his will (1630) he named 17 servants as the recipients of legacies.

His son Thomas Lord Savile, later Earl of Sussex (1590-1658) was described by Clarendon as 'a man of an ambitious and restless nature, of parts and wit enough, but in his disposition and inclination so false that he could never be believed or depended upon'.

One of the most pressing issues following his father's death was the future of the Kirkstall iron works. In 1631 he wrote that he had carried out repairs to the forge and dams, spent at least £2000 on the provision of stock and 'sent up and Downe all the Countrey to find out workemen to make new the Bellowes'. In normal circumstances the profits amounted to over £2000 a year which represented a substantial proportion of the estate revenue. In 1646 he testified that his estate consisted 'more of stock then rent by reason of his iron works and tillage that hee managed'.

Like his father he was a fierce opponent of Strafford whom he eventually succeeded as Lord President of the Council in the North and Lord Lieutenant of Yorkshire.

After the Treaty of Berwick in 1639 he sought to encourage the Scottish rebels to dispatch an invasion force and even went so far as to forge the signatures of some of his fellow noblemen. In November 1641 the king appointed him Treasurer of the Household.

In the Civil War he vacillated between the two sides and was imprisoned first by the king and then by Parliament. Initially Howley Hall was garrisoned by the parliamentarians but in June 1643 it was seized and plundered by royalist troops under the command of the Earl of Newcastle.

With the death of James Earl of Sussex (1647-1671) the male line expired and the estate passed by inheritance to the Brudenells, Earls of Cardigan.

Howley Hall An Elizabethan mansion built by Sir Robert Savile (d.1585) and his son Sir John (1556-1630) at a cost of £30,000. Completed in 1590, it was described by William Camden as an 'exceeding neat house' and singled out by Sir Henry Slingsby the diarist as one of the largest houses in Yorkshire.

According to Thomas Earl of Sussex the Earl of Newcastle's soldiers not only took all his goods but 'did in a sort demolishe his house, to his damage above £10,000'. After the Civil War he was obliged to carry out a major works programme in order to restore the house to its former glory.

In 1674 the Brudenells were taxed on 44 hearths.

There were two parks adjoining the hall.

(M. Sheard, *Records of the Parish of Batley in the County of York* (1894). Wards 5/49. Wards 9/97/fo.579. Sheffield Archives, Wentworth Woodhouse Collection, Strafford Letters, xii, Thomas Lord Savile to Lord Wentworth, 12 September 1631. *Camden Society*, New Series, xxxi (1883). C.10/61/74. N. Scatchard, *The History of Morley* (1874). W. Smith, *The History and Antiquities of Morley* (1876). G. Wood, *The Story of Morley* (1916).)

NETHER POPPLETON   Ainsty

A village on the River Ouse in the vicinity of York. The parish of Nether Poppleton included part of the village of Upper Poppleton where there was a medieval chapel; the other part was in the parish of St Mary Bishophill Junior, York. 1665: 29 households in Nether Poppleton and 49 in Upper Poppleton. There was a ferry at Nether Poppleton.

Church St Everilda: Norman.

Principal family Hutton of Poppleton Hall. Estate revenue: £800 a year (1640).

Sir Thomas Hutton (1581-1621) was a younger son of Matthew Hutton, Archbishop of York. He acquired the manors of Upper and Nether Poppleton and had several long leases of church property which provided the family with a considerable income.

His son Richard (1613-1648) became a ward of the Crown on succeeding as a minor. His second wife was Dorothy Fairfax, a daughter of Ferdinando Lord Fairfax, whose Puritan beliefs had a profound effect on their children.

After the city of York was surrendered by the royalists in 1644 he was appointed a member of the parliamentary committee there.

Thomas Hutton (1638-1704) and his mother took in Thomas Birdsall, one of the ministers ejected after the Restoration, and employed him as their chaplain until his death in 1687. He was said to have been 'of great use in that honourable family, and to the neighbourhood, by his example, prayers, and preaching'. The family also received visits from Oliver Heywood who described Dorothy Hutton as 'a gracious woman'.

In 1663 she presented her son Charles with a set of instructions before his departure for London. Among other things, she urged him to read the Scriptures 'diligently and daily'; to attend the preaching of God's Word on the Sabbath 'and on other days if your Calling will permitt'; and to practise moderation in all things, including eating and drinking.

When the Declaration of Indulgence was issued in 1672 Thomas Hutton obtained a licence authorising him to use Poppleton Hall for nonconformist worship.

At a visitation in 1680 the churchwardens of Nether Poppleton presented Dorothy Hutton 'for not repairing to the Church till divine service be ended' and for not receiving communion at Easter; Thomas Hutton for irreverent behaviour in church, namely 'in not kneeling at the Confession and Lord's prayer nor standing up when the beliefe is said', and also for holding conventicles in the house; and Thomas Birdsall, 'reputed a nonconformist Preist', for preaching in Poppleton Hall.

Poppleton Hall In 1665 Thomas Hutton was taxed on 13 hearths.

(BL, Stowe MSS 744, fo.61. BIHR, Diocese of York, Archdeacons' Visitations, YV/CB3, 1680, City of York, fols.498-9.)

NEWBY CUM MULWITH   Claro

A sparsely populated district on the north side of the River Ure and within the parish of Ripon. 1674: five households.

Principal family Blackett of Newby Hall (baronetcy 1673). Estate revenue: £3000 a year (1682). Large-scale coalmining in Northumberland.

Edward Blackett (1649-1718) bought the manor of Newby from the Crosland family in 1678 and made it his seat. He was the eldest son of Sir William Blackett, a wealthy Newcastle merchant and colliery owner who was the first baronet of the family. In 1680 he inherited his father's title and the bulk of his estate.

Sir Edward (as he became) was a member of two Newcastle companies, the Merchant Adventurers' Company and the Hostman's Company. At Newby he took a keen interest in cattle breeding.

Newby Hall The Croslands resided at Newby and in 1674 were taxed on 12 hearths. Sir Edward Blackett, however, decided to build a completely new house and lay out the grounds in accordance with the latest fashion. The work had been completed by the time Ralph Thoresby paid a visit in 1693. In his diary he observed that he went to see 'Sir

Edward Blacket's stately house, which is indeed a most noble fabric, to which are adjoined very curious gardens, with delicate statues, and pleasant walks'.

When Celia Fiennes visited Sir Edward in 1697 she wrote that Newby Hall

> looks finely in the approach in the midst of a good parke and a River runs just by it, it stands in the middle and has two large Gardens on each side ... His house is built with brick and coyn'd with stone, with a flatt Roofe leaded and a large Cupelow in the middle ... the hall you enter is of a very good size and height, 2 dineing roomes and drawing roomes, one for the summer with a marble floore ... the house is serv'd with water by pipes into a Cistern into the garden cellars and all offices; this was the finest house I saw in Yorkshire.

(North Yorkshire County Record Office, Blackett MSS. C.6/228/10.)

NEWTON KYME   Barkston Ash

A village to the north-west of Tadcaster. The parish of Newton Kyme included the hamlet of Toulston. 1674: 28 households in Newton Kyme and Toulston. 1676: 108 persons aged 16 or more (parish).

The impropriate rectory of Newton Kyme belonged to the Fairfaxes of Denton. One of the incumbents was Henry Fairfax (1588-1665) who was a younger brother of Ferdinando Lord Fairfax and the father of Henry Lord Fairfax. During the Civil War his parsonage house was a refuge for his friends and relations on both sides of the political divide.

The Barwicks of Toulston Hall were a zealous Puritan family. After the Restoration Dame Ursula Barwick, the widow of Sir Robert Barwick, gave shelter to two nonconformist ministers, Thomas Calvert and Thomas Hardcastle.

Church St Andrew: Norman, Early English, Decorated and Perpendicular.

(B. Dale, *Yorkshire Puritanism and Early Nonconformity* (ed. T. G. Crippen) (1917), 37.)

NIDD   Claro

A small village to the north-west of Knaresborough which took its name from the River Nidd. There was no other village within the parish. 1674: 23 households (township of Nidd).

The manor belonged to the Trappes family of Nidd Hall who were mainly noted for their unswerving loyalty to the Catholic faith. Sir Francis Trappes (1570-1643), who was a barrister of Lincoln's Inn, was presented as a noncommunicant in 1604 and finally emerged as a recusant in the reign of Charles I. In 1633 his nephew Thomas Lord Wentworth, who was head of the northern commission for compounding with recusants, approached the king on his behalf. As he later explained to Secretary Coke he had requested that 'haveing twelve children, and being a Thowsand poundes in debt, his Freehold Landes not above seavenscore poundes a yeare, I might be admitted to Compound him and his eldest Sonne their Recusancy for eight poundes a yeare'. The following year Sir Francis and his son Robert were allowed to compound on this basis.

In the Civil War Robert Trappes (1599-1650) took up arms for the king and as a result his estate was sequestered.

In 1692 a seminary priest, Augustine Smithson, was serving as chaplain at Nidd Hall.
Church St Paul: Norman in origin.

In 1678 the vicarage was burnt down.

(*CRS*, ix (1911), 111 and liii (1961), 381. PRO, Exchequer, Recusant Rolls, E.377/48.)

NORMANTON   Agbrigg and Morley

A village to the north-east of Wakefield. The parish of Normanton included two other villages, Altofts and Snydal. 1674: 41 households in Normanton, 47 in Altofts and 24 in Snydal. 1676: 300 persons aged 16 or more (parish).

Altofts was the birthplace of Sir Martin Frobisher (c.1535-1594) the seaman and explorer. He bought the manor of Altofts and built a house there. His estate was settled on a kinsman, Peter Frobisher, who rapidly disposed of it and died in poverty.

The manor of Altofts was eventually acquired by Sir Arthur Ingram who proceeded to mine coal there. During the years 1636 to 1639 he was involved in a bitter dispute with Robert Hitch the vicar of Normanton. Both men were anxious to secure a lease of the impropriate tithes of Normanton which were owned by Trinity College, Cambridge. Hitch proved to be a formidable opponent but in the end he was forced to accept a compromise arrangement.

Sir Arthur also clashed with the Freestons of Brackenhill Hall in Altofts who owned a considerable amount of freehold and copyhold land there. The head of the family, Richard Freeston, was a minor who had been made a ward of the Crown. In 1638 the Court of Wards was informed that Ingram had recently enclosed Birkwood Common which (it was claimed) belonged to Brackenhill Hall and that as a result the grazing rights of the ward and his tenants had been severely curtailed. Nothing appears to have emerged from these legal proceedings but in 1641 the tenants took the law into their own hands and twice pulled down Ingram's fences.

By 1669 the Freestons had sold all their property in Altofts.

The Thimblebys of Snydal were a Catholic family who owned the manor. In 1639 James Remington, a Snydal husbandman, and his wife Grace were charged at the Pontefract quarter sessions with breaking into Snydal Hall and forcibly ejecting the owner, Charles Thimbleby.

In the Civil War the Thimblebys were zealous royalists.

Church All Saints: Decorated and Perpendicular.

School In his will (1594) Anthony Freeston founded and endowed a free school at Normanton for the teaching of 30 poor scholars of the parish.

(BL, Additional MSS 38,599, fo.93. A. F. Upton, *Sir Arthur Ingram c.1565-1642* (1961), 158-9, 191, 200-4. Wards 9/573, no pagination. C.10/161/55. *YASRS*, liv (1915), 121.)

NORTH ELMSALL   Osgoldcross

A small village in the parish of South Kirkby which was situated between Barnsley and Pontefract. 1674: 22 households (township of North Elmsall).

Principal family Wentworth of North Elmsall Hall (and Howsham Hall, East Riding) (baronetcy 1692). Estate revenue: £2200 a year (1671); £2300 a year (1683).

Sir Thomas Wentworth (1590-1650) significantly advanced the fortunes of his family through his marriage to an heiress, Mary Bamburgh. As a result of this marriage the Wentworths acquired lands at Howsham in the East Riding and property in the North Riding. In the Civil War Sir Thomas took the side of Parliament, though he appears to have been much less active than his brother Darcy.

His grandson Sir John Wentworth (1645-1671) employed Noah Ward, a Presbyterian divine, as his household chaplain. When Sir John's widow, Lady Catherine, married Heneage Finch, Earl of Winchilsea, Ward was immediately dismissed.

North Elmsall Hall An early Tudor mansion with some later additions. The main rooms listed in an inventory of 1650 included the great chamber, the dining parlour, the middle and low parlours and the gallery. There is also a reference to 'the new buldinge' which was apparently no more than a modest addition. The domestic chapel was probably a detached building.

In 1674 the house contained 22 taxable hearths.

According to the inventory of 1650 there was a park which was then being used for the grazing of sheep.

(Sheffield Archives, Wentworth Woodhouse Collection, Bright MSS 20 and 79(b). C.10/279/56. C.33/338, part 2/fo.517. A. G. Matthews, *Calamy Revised* (1934), 509.)

NORTHOWRAM
Agbrigg and Morley

A large clothing village within the parish of Halifax. 1674: 192 households.

Oliver Heywood the nonconformist divine lived for some years at Northowram after his ejection from Coley chapel. Following the Act of Toleration of 1689 he built a chapel there. We rode 'to Mr Heywood's, at Northowram, was pleased with the chapel himself lately built there for his people' (Ralph Thoresby, 1694).

Schools There was a schoolmaster at Northowram in the mid-17th century.

A free school was built on land which Joseph Hall provided about 1693. In 1697 the management of the school was vested in trustees who included Oliver Heywood.

Principal family Sunderland of High Sunderland (and Coley Hall). Estate revenue: £530 a year (1640).

The Sunderlands were new gentry who were descended from generations of clothiers.

Richard Sunderland (c.1563-1634) preferred to live at Coley Hall which he had purchased. In 1623 he and his son Abraham were required to appear before the Privy Council. This was in consequence of a petition by Millicent Conyers who alleged that Abraham was in breach of a marriage contract; in fact he was already married to Elizabeth Langdale.

Abraham Sunderland (c.1594-1644), who was a practising lawyer, usually resided at High Sunderland. In 1640 he began legal proceedings against his brothers Samuel and Peter as executors of his father's will, alleging that they had wrongfully kept possession of a personal estate worth £8000 and had refused to make over to him Coley Hall and demesne lands worth £200 a year. He was then in some financial difficulty.

In the Civil War he took up arms for the king and died in Pontefract Castle while it was under siege.

His son Langdale (1622-1698) served as a captain of horse under the command of his brother-in-law Sir Marmaduke Langdale. When compounding for his estate he claimed to be £1200 in debt. He sold the Coley and High Sunderland properties in 1654 and 1655 and settled at Ackton, near Featherstone.

High Sunderland A 15th century timber-framed house which was encased in stone by Abraham Sunderland in the early 17th century.

(Oliver Heywood, *His Autobiography, Diaries, Anecdote and Event Books* (ed. J. Horsfall Turner) (1882-5). John Lister, 'High Sunderland', *Transactions of the Halifax Antiquarian Society*, iv (1907). *Acts of the Privy Council, 1623-5*, 106,122. C.8/89/45.)

NUN MONKTON
Claro

A village to the north-west of York. There was no other village within the parish. 1674: 56 households (township of Nun Monkton).

Nun Monkton Priory, which was an establishment of Benedictine nuns, had been founded in the 12th century and dissolved in 1537. After its dissolution the church was adapted for use as a parish church.

Church St Mary: Norman and Early English.

The minister was a perpetual curate.

OTLEY   Skyrack/Claro

A market town on the River Wharfe. The extensive parish of Otley contained a considerable number of villages and hamlets, including Baildon, Bramhope, Burley in Wharfedale, Denton, Farnley and Pool which had public chapels. Bramhope, Denton and Hawksworth (with Esholt) are separately noticed. 1674: 118 households in Otley, 79 in Baildon, 71 in Burley, 47 in Farnley, 19 in Lindley, 8 in Little Timble, 35 in Menston, 35 in Newell with Clifton and 28 in Pool. 1676: 923 persons aged 16 or more (parish of Otley).

Otley is 'memorable for nothing but its situation under a huge craggy Cliff called Chevin' (William Camden).

The manor of Otley belonged to the Archbishop of York. In 1239 the Archbishop had been granted the right to hold a weekly market and an annual fair.

In August 1642 a number of parliamentarians, including the Fairfaxes, met at Otley and issued a protestation condemning the activities of the royalist party at York which they claimed were likely to bring about the introduction of an arbitrary government and 'which is the worst of all evills to beget a warre in the bowels of this County'.

In the 17th century a number of gentry families were seated at one time or another within the parish of Otley. Some appear in the separate entries for Bramhope, Denton and Hawksworth; others included Baildon of Baildon, Fawkes of Farnley and Palmes of Lindley.

During the course of the century the Baildons, the Hawksworths and the Vavasours of Weston all mined coal on the commons of Baildon.

Church All Saints: Norman, Decorated and Perpendicular.

School In his will (1602) Thomas Cave of Wakefield bequeathed £250 for a free grammar school at Otley. This sum was doubled by public subscription and in 1607 the Free Grammar School of Prince Henry was established by letters patent. In 1611 the Council in the North decreed that a schoolhouse should be built and the wealthier inhabitants of Otley entered into a bond for this purpose.

In 1652 the master of Otley School was Edward Brown who had formerly been vicar of Sheffield.

(*A Reall Protestation of Many and Very eminent persons in the County of Yorke* (1642). W. K. Jordan, *The Charities of Rural England 1480-1660* (1961), 328. Doreen E. Smith,

'Otley, A study of a Market Town During the late 17th and 18th Centuries', *YAJ*, 52 (1980). W. Paley Baildon, *Baildon and the Baildons: A History of a Yorkshire Manor and Family* (1913, 1924 and 1926).)

OWSTON   Osgoldcross

A village to the north of Doncaster. The parish of Owston included the village of Skellow. 1674: 40 households in Owston and 21 in Skellow. 1676: 167 persons aged 16 or more (parish).

For the Adams family of Owston the 17th century was a period of mixed fortune. In 1612 Philip Adams (c.1560-1623), who was a yeoman farmer, was granted a coat of arms but before the time of the Civil War the family had twice sustained a minority. On each occasion the heir was made a ward of the Crown and the wardship fines which were levied amounted to £900. William Adams (1626-1667), who succeeded his father in 1638, appears to have remained neutral in the Civil War but managed to secure a knighthood in 1665. He inherited the manor and rectory of Owston and at the height of his prosperity enjoyed an income of over £500 a year. His son and grandson, however, lived beyond their means and as a result the whole estate was lost.

In 1657 some of the inhabitants of Owston submitted a petition to the government in which they complained that although there were many families in the parish their minister was only paid £20 a year. In the light of this petition it was decided to allow him a further £40 a year.

Church All Saints: Norman, Early English, Decorated and Perpendicular.

(Wards 5/49. Wards 9/206/fo.77 and 219/40. C.33/253/fo.86. *CSP Dom, 1656-7*, 299.)

PANNAL   Claro

A village to the south-west of Knaresborough. The parish of Pannal included part of the village of Harrogate (see the entry for Knaresborough). 1674: 106 households (township of Pannal). 1676: 197 persons aged 16 or more (parish).

Church St Robert: Decorated and Perpendicular.

PENISTONE   Staincross

A hilltop village in wild moorland country to the south-west of Barnsley. The parish of Penistone included a number of villages and hamlets. 1674: 27 households in Penistone,

53 in Denby, 6 in Gunthwaite, 39 in Hunshelf, 13 in Ingbirchworth, 41 in Langsett, 23 in Oxspring and 64 in Thurlstone.

Penistone was an outpost of the clothing industry. In 1699 a market was established.

In 1602 the freeholders of Hunshelf entered into an agreement for the enclosure of the commons.

In 1627 Godfrey Bosvile of Gunthwaite Hall built a public chapel at Denby and chose as minister Charles Broxholme who was an uncompromising Puritan. He was soon in trouble with the ecclesiastical authorities and in 1632 he was suspended. He was succeeded by another Puritan, Daniel Clark, who married one of Bosvile's daughters.

During the Civil War Christopher Dickinson, who had been serving as a royalist chaplain, took over as vicar of Penistone. As recorded in the journal of Captain Adam Eyre, he met with strong opposition from the more Puritan-minded inhabitants of the parish. They promised to give him £40 if he agreed to leave but he turned down the offer. In a petition which was submitted to the Committee for Plundered Ministers it was alleged, among other things, that he was 'a common frequenter of alehouses, and of idle company, and hath beene several tymes drunk since his coming to Peniston'. The petition was referred to the West Riding committee and Dickinson was duly ejected. In 1649 Henry Swift became vicar of Penistone. After the Restoration he declined to subscribe to the Act of Uniformity but in spite of this he continued to officiate at services in the parish church.

Church St John Baptist: Early English, Decorated and Perpendicular.

In the Civil War the church was damaged by parliamentary troops.

Schools The public grammar school at Penistone had been founded in the 14th century. An inquiry conducted in 1604 revealed that the school was well endowed. In 1616 Francis Okey was described as the vicar and schoolmaster of Penistone.

At the end of the 17th century the school had 60 pupils on average.

Ralph Ward kept a school at Denby for many years. At the Restoration he was ejected.

Principal family Bosvile of Gunthwaite Hall. Estate revenue: £620 a year (1657).

Godfrey Bosvile (1596-1658) was for some years a ward of the Crown. In the reign of Charles I he and his family lived with their relatives the Grevilles in Warwickshire and the estate was left in the hands of a steward, John Shirt. In a letter addressed to Shirt in May 1642 he wrote 'The Lord direct us in our loyalty to the King and care for the safety of the Kingdome'. At the same time he was becoming increasingly exasperated over the dilatoriness of his tenants in paying their rents. In November he asked Shirt to 'send mee a note of such as are in arreare and who made default att this rent day, for I propose that if we have any law in England I will presently make Use of yt to gett my owne of them'.

In the Civil War he wholeheartedly supported the cause of Parliament both as an MP and as a colonel of a regiment of foot. His son William (1620-1662) also served as a parliamentarian officer and in 1644 was badly wounded in battle.

Godfrey Bosvile (c.1655-1714) settled at Gunthwaite after his coming of age and added considerably to the estate. It was largely through his efforts that Penistone acquired market rights.

Gunthwaite Hall A gabled house of three storeys which was probably Tudor in origin. In 1674 it had 12 taxable hearths.

Godfrey Bosvile (c.1655-1714) carried out major improvements to the hall, completing the work in 1690.

There was a park adjoining the house.

(Sheffield Archives, Spencer Stanhope MSS 60,217. R. A. Marchant, *The Puritans and the Church Courts in the Diocese of York 1560-1642* (1960), 235, 238. Surtees Society, lxv (1877), 14, 19-21, 25, 41. J. Addy, 'Penistone Grammar School 1392-1700', *YAJ*, xxxix (1956-8). Hull University Archives, Macdonald of Sleat MSS. Lady Alice Macdonald of the Isles, *The Fortunes of a Family* (1928). J. N. Dransfield, *History of Penistone* (1906).)

PONTEFRACT   Osgoldcross

An important market town and one of the most handsome in 17th century Yorkshire. The parish of Pontefract contained a number of villages and hamlets, including East Hardwick and Knottingley which had dependent chapels. The chapel at East Hardwick was founded by Stephen Cawood in 1653. Ferry Fryston was situated in two parishes: Pontefract and Ferry Fryston. 1674: 327 households in Pontefract, 61 in Ferry Fryston, 96 in Knottingley and 59 in Tanshelf. The main streets in Pontefract were Baileygate, Micklegate and Ropergate. 1676: 1600 persons aged 16 or more (parish of Pontefract).

Pontefract was both a sessions town and a parliamentary borough. It had a corporation consisting of a mayor, 12 aldermen and a recorder. Its market rights dated from 1294.

'This town is sweetly situated, and is remarkable for producing Liquorish ... in great plenty; the buildings are neat, and secured by a castle which is very stately, and strongly founded upon a rock' (William Camden).

Pontefract 'looks very finely in the approach; it's built on a hill all of stone, it's a very neate building and the streets well pitch'd [paved] and broad, the houses well built and looke more stately than any in York ... it's a fruitfull place, fine flowers and trees with all sorts of fruite, but that which is mostly intended is the increasing of Liquorish, which the gardens are all filled with' (Celia Fiennes, 1697).

In the Civil War Pontefract Castle was a major royalist stronghold. The garrison finally surrendered in July 1645 after running out of provisions. By a subterfuge the royalists seized the castle in 1648 but the parliamentarians regained possession in March 1649.

In 1645 Pontefract and Knottingley both suffered from the plague.

In 1656 Pontefract was described as a populous town which had many visitors because of the fairs and quarter sessions held there.

In 1669 it was reported that there were 30 Presbyterians, 30 Anabaptists and 80 Quakers within the parish.

Dr Nathaniel Johnston (1627-1705), who practised medicine in Pontefract, was best known for his work as a local historian. He was a friend and mentor of Ralph Thoresby.

Churches There were two large churches in Pontefract: the parish church of All Saints and the public chapel of St Giles.

All Saints: mainly Decorated and Perpendicular. Situated near the castle, the church was badly damaged during one of the sieges. In the Commonwealth period it was estimated that to restore it to its original state would cost £3000. In the event it was left as a ruin.

St Giles: Decorated. After the Civil War it replaced All Saints as a centre of worship, though it was not formally designated as the parish church until 1789.

Castle The most important royal castle in northern England. Begun in the 11th century, it had a 13th century keep and 14th century towers.

The town has a 'high and stately, famous and impregnable Castle, and Cittadell ... which for the Situation, Strength and largenesse may compare with any in this kingdome' (visitors to Pontefract, 1634).

In 1649 the castle was demolished.

Pontefract had 'a stately castle, of which now only remains the platform and stump ... but yet it is handsome because imployed to fine gardens and a bowling-green' (Thomas Baskerville, 1675).

Schools The free grammar school at Pontefract had been founded in the 13th century. In 1583 the Chancery Court of the Duchy of Lancaster assigned lands for its support and it was formally styled Queen Elizabeth's School in Pontefract. Shortly afterwards a new schoolhouse was built at the expense of the principal inhabitants.

In 1653 Stephen Cawood founded a free school at East Hardwick.

Almshouses The Hospital of St Nicholas, which had been mentioned in the Domesday Book, was largely rebuilt in the reign of Charles II. It provided accommodation for 13 poor men and women.

There was another group of almshouses which had been founded by Sir Robert Knollis and his wife in 1385. These housed 15 poor people, including two who acted as servants to the rest.

Other buildings The largest private residence in Pontefract was New Hall which had been built by Edward Talbot in 1591. The architect was Robert Smythson.

Pontefract's numerous inns included the Star and the Sun. In 1697 Celia Fiennes stayed at the Sun and wrote in her journal that 'there are many good Inns but this was a very good genteel Inn'.

(*CSP Dom, 1655-6*, 360. E.134/1656/Michaelmas 15. W. K. Jordan, *The Charities of Rural England 1480-1660* (1961), 271, 280, 302-3, 344. B. Boothroyd, *History of Pontefract* (1807). G. Fox, *The History of Pontefract, in Yorkshire* (1827). R. Holmes (ed.), *The Sieges of Pontefract Castle, 1644-1648* (1887). C. Forest, *The History and Antiquities of Knottingley* (1871).)

RASTRICK   Agbrigg and Morley

A small village and chapelry within the parish of Halifax. The chapelry also included Fixby and the two villages were linked together in the subsidy rolls. 1674: 45 households in Rastrick and 31 in Fixby. 1676: 106 persons aged 16 or more (chapelry of Rastrick).

Church St Matthew: a public chapel which had apparently been established in the 14th century. During the period 1547-1602 it no longer served as a place of worship and for some years was used as a barn. The building of a new chapel was begun in 1602 and completed the following year. John Thornhill of Fixby and John Hanson of Woodhouse both contributed money, timber and slate. Initially there were 20 seats for the congregation but this number was soon increased in response to demand.

School Before 1547 the chapel had also been used as a school and this practice was continued after the rebuilding. In his will (1621) John Hanson made provision for a modest endowment.

Principal family Thornhill of Fixby Hall. Estate revenue: £600 a year (1641); £1100 a year (1687); £1400 a year (1698). Coalmining on Old Lindley Moor. A fulling mill in Brighouse.

The Thornhills were efficient landowners but they also owed their prosperity to advantageous marriages.

In 1637 Thomas Thornhill (1585-1663) entered into an agreement with other landowners over the enclosure of some of the wastes in Rastrick. Early in the Civil War he sent one of his tenants to fight for the king, promising to give him his farm if he survived. In 1645, however, he provided a contribution of £80 to advance the cause of Parliament and he later served as a magistrate.

George Thornhill (1655-1687) died suddenly while still in his prime. Oliver Heywood the nonconformist divine wrote that he 'rode out to the moor with his man … was seized on violently with griping of guts, fel down, his body broke, dyed after they got him home … left 9 children, his wife big of the 10th'.

Fixby Hall The house was probably Elizabethan in origin. In 1674 there were 15 taxable hearths.

(J. Lister, 'Rastrick Chapel and School', *Halifax Antiquarian Society*, ii (1904-5). YAS Library, Clarke-Thornhill MSS. WYAS, Kirklees, Clarke-Thornhill MSS.)

RAWMARSH   Strafford and Tickhill

A village to the north of Rotherham. The parish of Rawmarsh contained several hamlets, including Aldwark and Kilnhurst. Aldwark is separately noticed. 1674: 72 households (township of Rawmarsh). 1676: 210 persons aged 16 or more (parish).

In 1641 three Rawmarsh labourers were found guilty of entering a close belonging to Dame Elizabeth Foljambe, the widow of Sir Francis Foljambe, and breaking down hedges and taking away the rails. At the same time the inhabitants of the parish complained to the magistrates that she had failed to pay 'diverse layes and assessments for the landes and lordeshippes of Aldewarke in the sayde parish'.

Some months later William Dodgson of Rawmarsh informed the magistrates that there was a great inequality in the way in which local taxes were levied 'because they now make all their layes and assessmentes according to the quantitie and qualitie of acres everye one occupies and enjoyes, the poorer sort being overburthened because they enjoyeing but a few acres the number of them are certainlye knowne, and the richer sort enjoyeing much the quantitye of theires cannot certainlye be knowne'. In response to this criticism the justices decided that every inhabitant of the parish should be required to deliver to the constable of Rawmarsh a true certificate of the number of acres in his occupation 'that the poore be not overburthened and the richer sort eased'.

Church St Mary: Norman in origin.

The patronage rights belonged to the Crown.

School A grammar school was established at Rawmarsh in 1618. Initially Alice Darley of Kilnhurst contributed the sum of £30 for its support and this was followed by a series of small benefactions.

In 1653 Thomas Wilson, a London clothworker with local connections, provided a building for use as a schoolhouse.

(*YASRS*, liv (1915), 265-6, 338-9. W. K. Jordan, *The Charities of Rural England 1480-1660* (1961), 332.)

RIPLEY   Claro

A village to the north-west of Knaresborough which was situated on the River Nidd. The parish of Ripley included the villages of Clint and Killinghall. 1674: 48 households in Ripley, 62 in Clint and 54 in Killinghall.

In the 17th century Ripley had a weekly market.

In 1641 a house belonging to Leonard Kendall in Killinghall was burnt down by some soldiers. His wife barely escaped with her life and it was reported that 'since that time she hath not beene perfectly in her senses'. On hearing of this episode the magistrates requested the ministers and curates in a number of West Riding wapentakes to organise collections for the relief of Kendall and his family.

Church All Saints: c.1400 with some features dating from 1567.

There is a traditional story that after the battle of Marston Moor in 1644 some parliamentarian soldiers were billeted in the church while Cromwell slept at the hall.

Schools There was a schoolmaster at Ripley in the reign of Charles II but it was not until 1702 that a free school was established there.

Principal family Ingleby of Ripley Hall (baronetcy 1642). Estate revenue: £1500 a year (1642). Lead mining at Bewerley.

At the beginning of the 17th century the Inglebys were still heavily committed to the Catholic cause, though Sir William (1549-1618) had a preference for outward conformity. After the discovery of the Gunpowder Plot the authorities sought to implicate him but without success. Among other things, they were informed that in the autumn of 1605 there had been a great meeting of Catholics at the upper lodge in Ripley Park.

His nephew Sir William Ingleby (c.1595-1652), who succeeded him, was the first Protestant head of the family. In the Civil War he took up arms for the king and fought at the battle of Marston Moor.

In contrast, his son Sir William (1621-1682) was named as a member of the West Riding parliamentary committee in 1645 and as a commissioner for ejecting scandalous, ignorant and insufficient ministers and schoolmasters in 1654. According to Ralph Thoresby he died while at prayer after attending two church services the previous day. Oliver Heywood the nonconformist divine described him as an honest magistrate who left a vast estate.

Ripley Hall Built between 1548 and 1555 in the form of a tower block. 15th century gatehouse.

The rooms listed in an inventory of 1618 included the hall, the dining parlour, the new gallery, the old and new study and the chapel. In 1674 Sir William Ingleby was taxed on 24 hearths.

A deed of 1575 refers to the old and new parks of Ripley.

(*YASRS*, liv (1915), 317-18. WYAS, Leeds, Ingilby of Ripley MSS. *YAJ*, xxxiv (1929), 182-196, 202-3.)

RIPON   Claro

A market town situated on the River Skell. The extensive parish of Ripon contained a large number of villages and hamlets, including Aldfield, Bishop Monkton, Bishop Thornton, Pateley Bridge, Sawley, Skelton and Winksley which had dependent chapels. Aldfield, Fountains and Newby cum Mulwith are separately noticed. 1674: 342 households in Ripon, 59 in Bewerley, 60 in Bishop Monkton, 99 in Bishopside (including Pateley Bridge), 36 in Bishopton, 47 in Bishop Thornton, 23 in Bridge Hewick, 16 in Copt Hewick, 71 in Dacre, 2 in Givendale, 48 in Grantley, 20 in Ingerthorpe, 44 in Markington cum Wallerthwaite, 46 in North Stainley cum Sleningford, 71 in Sawley, 21 in Sharow, 40 in Skelton, 19 in Studley Roger, 2 in Westwick and 27 in Whitcliffe cum Thorpe. The main streets of Ripon were Allhallowgate, Bondgate, Crossgate, Skellgate and Westgate.

Ripon was both a corporate town with a mayor and aldermen and a parliamentary borough. In 1665 the borough charter was formally confirmed by letters patent which also nominated the mayor, the recorder and the town clerk. The liberties of Ripon consisted of certain legal rights which had originally been granted by King Athelstan.

There were a considerable number of Catholics in the parish of Ripon: 151 persons were presented for recusancy in 1619 and 157 in 1691.

Ripon 'owes its greatness to Religion; especially to a Monastery built by Wilfred Archbishop of York' (William Camden).

Ripon is 'a faire towne, and famous for spurrs and steele bowes ... Itt haith a very large market place, where thir is twice a yeare a greate horse faire' (Life of Marmaduke Rawdon, entry for 1664). In Thomas Fuller's opinion Ripon made the best spurs in England.

Ripon is 'a pretty little Market town built of Stone ... provisions are very plentifull and cheap ... some of the Inns are very dear to Strangers that they can impose on; the town stands on a hill and there is a good large stone built Church well carved they call it a Minster ... there are two good bridges to the town' (Celia Fiennes, 1697).

In 1614 the north bridge was repaired but in 1642 it was said to be in decay.

In October 1640 the Treaty of Ripon was concluded with the Scottish rebels.

During the Civil War there was strong support for the king in Ripon and the surrounding district and in September 1642 royalist troops occupied the town. Since, however, there were no fortifications it was always vulnerable to attack and eventually it was captured by Scottish troops. In August 1645, when the royalist cause seemed doomed, George Lord Digby informed Prince Rupert that he intended to go to Ripon which was one of the most loyal towns in Yorkshire and that he had been assured that it should be possible to raise a large army in that part of the county.

In 1645 there was an outbreak of the plague in Bondgate.

Since 1320 Pateley Bridge had enjoyed the right to hold a weekly market and an annual fair.

Such families as the Inglebys of Ripley and the Proctors of Fountains mined lead on the moors and wastes of Bewerley.

Markenfield Hall, near Fountains Abbey, was a fortified manor-house which had been built in the 14th century.

Church St Wilfred: Norman, Early English, Decorated and Perpendicular.

'The town is adorn'd with a very neat Church ... having three Spire-steeples which welcome strangers to the town at a distance' (William Camden). One spire collapsed in 1615; the others were taken down in 1664.

In 1660 the church was said to have become very ruinous during 'the late ill times' and a repair programme was put in hand. The poor condition of the church was probably due more to lack of maintenance than to any damage sustained during the Civil War.

Schools There was a school at Ripon in the 14th and early 16th centuries.

In 1555 the school received a charter under the Duchy Seal when it was designated as the Free Grammar School of Queen Mary and made financially secure.

In 1604 it was reported that John Chapman, a recusant, was teaching children at Pateley Bridge cum Bishopside.

In 1695 William Hardcastle founded a school at Dacre Banks and built a schoolhouse there.

Almshouses The Hospital of St Mary Magdalen, which had been founded in the 12th century, provided accommodation for six poor women who were called sisters. The almshouses were rebuilt in 1674 by the master, Dr Richard Hooke.

Another ancient foundation was the Maison Dieu or St Anne's Hospital which housed eight poor women.

In accordance with the will of Zacharias Jepson (1672) a hospital was established for the care of ten orphan boys or sons of very poor freemen. Here they were boarded, clothed, educated and apprenticed.

(*CSP Dom, 1664-5*, 419. H. Aveling, 'The Catholic Recusants of the West Riding of Yorkshire 1558-1790', *Proceedings of the Leeds Philosophical and Literary Society, Literary and Historical Section*, x (1963), 276. *YASRS*, liv (1915), 16, 379. *CSP Dom, 1645-7*, 71. STAC8/227/6. *CSP Dom, 1660-1*, 323. E. Peacock (ed.), *A List of the Roman Catholics in the County of York in 1604* (1872), 53. E.134/16 and 17 Charles I/Hilary 14 and 17 Charles I/Easter 6.)

ROSSINGTON   Strafford and Tickhill

A village to the south-east of Doncaster. There was no other village within the parish. 1674: 33 households (township of Rossington). 1676: 120 persons aged 16 or more (parish).

The manor and park of Rossington belonged to the corporation of Doncaster which leased them out to tenants. The corporation also owned the patronage rights and in the 17th century some of the incumbents were vicars of both Doncaster and Rossington.

Church St Michael: Norman and Perpendicular.

School In 1650 William Plaxton, the Puritan vicar of Rossington who had served there since 1614, founded a school for the instruction of children of the community 'as well the poor as the rich'.

(W. K. Jordan, *The Charities of Rural England 1480-1660* (1961), 343.)

ROTHERHAM   Strafford and Tickhill

'Rotherham is a good market town well built all of stone; the Church stands high in the middle of the town and looks finely' (Celia Fiennes, 1697). The parish of Rotherham contained a number of villages and hamlets, including Greasbrough and Tinsley which had dependent chapels. Dalton was situated in two parishes: Rotherham and Thrybergh. 1674: 219 households in Rotherham, 19 in Brinsworth, 27 in Dalton, 91 in Greasbrough, 110 in Kimberworth and 49 in Tinsley. 1676: 750 persons aged 16 or more (parish).

Within the parish of Rotherham there were coalmines and iron works. In 1632 the coalmines in Kimberworth Park were said to be worth over £150 a year.

In 1636 the manors of Greasbrough and Tinsley, which then belonged to Thomas Lord Wentworth, were valued at £156 and £212 a year respectively.

In the Civil War the inhabitants of Rotherham generally favoured the cause of Parliament. The town was garrisoned by Ferdinando Lord Fairfax, captured by the royalists after heavy fighting and finally, in 1644, re-taken by the parliamentarians.

In his autobiography John Shaw, the Puritan vicar of Rotherham, recounted his experiences in the Civil War. On the outbreak of the war he and his wife fled to Hull but Sir John Hotham the governor refused to allow them to stay. Before long Shaw returned to Rotherham which, though still in parliamentarian hands, was 'very weakly' garrisoned. On 4 May 1643 the Earl of Newcastle arrived with a large army 'and when the little powder that the town had was spent' the defenders 'upon honorable terms yielded up the town'. Several of the leading parliamentarians were taken prisoner but Shaw managed to escape by hiding in the church steeple.

Church All Saints: 15th century with early 16th century features. One of the largest parish churches in Yorkshire.

The chapel on Rotherham Bridge was built towards the end of the 15th century.

School Rotherham College, founded by Thomas Rotherham in 1483, was stripped of its revenues in the reign of Henry VIII but some kind of school survived. In 1561 there was a royal decree for the reviving and continuance of Rotherham Grammar School. In 1584, however, a deed of trust was executed for the establishment and endowment of a new grammar school.

During the decade preceding the Civil War the master of this school was the celebrated Charles Hoole who was the author of a popular educational treatise called *A New Discovery* (1660).

(Sheffield Archives, Wentworth Woodhouse Collection, Strafford Letters, vol.xx (a). *Surtees Society*, lxv (1877), 135-7. W. K. Jordan, *The Charities of Rural England 1480-1660* (1961), 304-5. *YASRS*, xxviii (1903), 193, 205 ff, 211-18, 228.)

ROTHWELL — Agbrigg and Morley

A large village to the south of Leeds. The parish of Rothwell included several villages and hamlets. 1674: 286 households in Rothwell and 57 in Middleton cum Thorpe.

There were rich coal deposits in Middleton. Sir Ferdinando Leigh of Middleton Hall owned a colliery there.

William Gascoigne (1612-1644), who was the eldest son of Henry Gascoigne the squire of Thorpe on the Hill, was described by Ralph Thoresby as 'the most celebrated mathematician, not only in these parts but I believe in the world'. He specialised in the study of optics and astronomy and was the inventor of the wire micrometer which he used in his telescope. In the Civil War he took up arms for the king and died in battle.

On 29 September 1642 representatives of the Yorkshire royalists and parliamentarians entered into a treaty of neutrality at Rothwell but this proved to be very short-lived.

Early on in the Civil War Edmund Kay the vicar of Rothwell removed to Pontefract where he served as one of the chaplains who preached to the royalist troops there.

Church Holy Trinity: Perpendicular.

Prison In the later 17th century there was a prison at Rothwell whose inmates mainly consisted of debtors.

(*YASRS*, xx (1896), 100. A. G. Matthews, *Walker Revised* (1988), 394.)

ROYSTON — Staincross

A village to the north of Barnsley. The parish of Royston contained a number of villages, including Monk Bretton and Woolley which had medieval chapels. Woolley is separately noticed. 1674: 35 households in Royston, 32 in Carlton, 41 in Monk Bretton and 30 in Notton. 1676: 400 persons aged 16 or more (parish of Royston).

Monk Bretton Priory, which was an establishment of Benedictine monks, had been founded in the 12th century and dissolved in 1538. Towards the end of the 16th century Henry Talbot, a younger brother of Gilbert Earl of Shrewsbury, converted some of the priory buildings into a private residence.

Church St John Baptist: mainly Perpendicular.

School In his will (1502) John Forman, the vicar of Royston, left property for the support of a school. This was probably the same grammar school which existed in 1548 and 1583.

A public grammar school was formally established by royal patent in 1607, though it was described as an ancient foundation. The patent specified that the schoolmaster should be provided with a house and should have his salary paid out of the revenues of the Duchy of Lancaster.

Almshouses In 1654 Dame Mary Armyne, a daughter of Henry Talbot, founded a hospital at Monk Bretton. This consisted of six cottages which were allocated to poor widows.

(W. K. Jordan, *The Charities of Rural England 1480-1660* (1961), 278. B. Elliott, *Royston: People of an Ancient Parish* (1985).)

RUFFORTH Ainsty

A village to the west of York. There was no other village within the parish. 1665: 45 households (township of Rufforth). 1676: 108 persons aged 16 or more (parish).
Church All Saints: Norman.

RYTHER Barkston Ash

A village to the north-west of Selby which was situated on the south bank of the River Wharfe. 1674: 40 households. 1676: 100 persons aged 16 or more (parish).
Church All Saints: Norman, Early English and Decorated..
Principal family Robinson of Ryther Hall. Estate revenue: £570 a year (1619); £700 a year (1627).

The Robinsons had grown rich as London merchants and had bought considerable property from the Askes of Aughton, a family in terminal decline.

During the reign of James I John Robinson (1566-1619) was involved in protracted litigation relating to his Ryther estate. In 1606 he alleged that Christian Aske, who was claiming jointure lands in Ryther, had cut down 'greate trees and arbours, beinge places of pleasure'. In 1608 he brought a Star Chamber suit against a fellow squire, John Acclom, and some of his servants over their incursions into Ryther Park. He claimed that they had pulled down fences and hedges and felled a number of trees, including a giant oak which had provided shelter for both the hall and the church.

When his son John (1608-1646) was declared a ward of the Crown in 1619 it was said that many of the tenements in Ryther were 'in so great decay by reason of the long leases that have beenne made of them for lives that no tenents can be procured to inhabite them unlesse there be great costs and charges furst bestowed on them to make them tenentable'. During his minority he fell out with his stepfather, Dr Samuel Collins, accusing him of removing many of the household goods from Ryther Hall. In the Civil War he sided with Parliament and served as a member of the West Riding committee.

John Robinson (1633-1679) also engaged in litigation. In 1665 he began legal proceedings against his grandmother, Susan Collins, over the ramifications of a bequest to his late uncle James Robinson who had been formally declared a lunatic.

Ryther Hall In the Chancery suit of 1606 Christian Aske described the hall as the 'very aunciente and goodlie howse and seate of the Askes in Ryther'. John Robinson, however, related that when he first saw Ryther Hall it was 'all ruynated, wasted, fallen downe and uncovered in divers principall places' and 'verye likely in shorte tyme to be utterlie decayed and become not habitable'. Since entering into possession he had renovated the house 'to his verye greate charge'.

In 1619 the Court of Wards was informed that the hall 'is in extream ruine, and like to faull downe in many places unlesse great costs be presently bestowed in upholding the same'. The task of restoring or rebuilding the house was no doubt undertaken by John Robinson (1608-1646) after he attained his majority in 1629.

Ryther Hall had 14 taxable hearths in 1664 and 1674.

(C.2/James I/A4/56. STAC 8/250/30. Wards 5/49. Wards 9/186/fo.62; 566/197-8; and 567/fo.763. C.10/89/133.)

SADDLEWORTH   Agbrigg and Morley

The township of Saddleworth cum Quick was situated in moorland country to the south-west of Huddersfield. The chapelry of Saddleworth, which included several villages and hamlets, formed part of the parish of Rochdale in Lancashire. 1674: 245 households (township of Saddleworth cum Quick).

In a Chancery suit of 1623 Dame Elizabeth Booth, the widow of Sir William Booth of Dunham Massey in Cheshire, related that she had half the manor of Quick and the wastes and commons belonging to it as part of her jointure and that the Ramsdens of Longley, who owned the other half, had encroached on her property to the extent of causing ten houses to be built and a number of enclosures to be made. In replying to her allegations Sir John Ramsden claimed that he was the legal owner of the whole manor of Saddleworth and Quick and that he was not aware that Sir William Booth had ever been in possession of any part of the manor.

In 1640 the West Riding magistrates were informed that the king's highway over Quick Moor was 'in great decay for lack of repair'. They decided that Robert Whitehead of Quick, who had recently enclosed the common there, should be required to take on responsibility for the necessary repair work.

In 1641 some of the inhabitants of Quick complained that they were 'oppressed and overburthened in their layes and assessmentes'. In the light of their representations the justices ruled in favour of a more equitable method of apportioning charges of this nature.

(C.3/334/6. *YASRS*, liv (1915), 172, 311.)

SANDAL MAGNA   Agbrigg and Morley

A village near Wakefield. The parish of Sandal Magna included the villages of Crigglestone and Walton. At Chapelthorpe, a hamlet within the township of Crigglestone, there was a dependent chapel. West Bretton, which is separately noticed, was situated in two parishes: Sandal Magna and Silkstone. 1674: 60 households in Sandal Magna, 93 in Crigglestone and 67 in Walton cum Bretton. 1676: 774 persons aged 16 or more (parish of Sandal Magna).

In the early 17th century coal was being mined within the manor of Crigglestone.

In 1645 Crigglestone suffered from an outbreak of the plague.

Church St Helen: Norman, Decorated and Perpendicular.

Castle In 1609 it was said that in the little park of Sandal there was a ruinous building 'commonly called a castle'. In the Civil War Sandal Castle was garrisoned by royalist troops who finally surrendered in October 1645. It was then dismantled.

Schools In the early 17th century there was a private school at Chapelthorpe. This was probably kept by the curate there who had only a modest stipend.

In the mid-17th century Daniel Birt had a school at Crigglestone.

Principal family Waterton of Walton Hall. Estate revenue: £500 a year (1620); £450 a year (1660).

The Watertons lived at Walton from 1435 to 1876. In the 17th century they remained strongly attached to the Catholic religion and kept resident chaplains.

Thomas Waterton (1583-1641) was initially a Church Papist. In 1617 some pursuivants searched Walton Hall and found a considerable number of items associated with Catholic worship together with several popish books. Waterton, it was reported, took great offence at this intrusion and declared that he would now become an open Catholic and that he had a secret place in his house where he could hide a seminary priest without any fear of discovery. The following year he and his wife Bridget were convicted of recusancy. In 1619 the Privy Council informed the Lord President of the Council in the North that Bridget Waterton had recently been seduced from the established religion 'to the dainger of the rest of her houshold' and instructed him to force her to conform or, failing that, to remove her to some place of confinement. The Watertons, however, refused to compromise. In 1629 Thomas Waterton compounded for the recusancy of himself and his wife and was required to pay a rent of £80 a year.

When settling his estate in 1636 he reserved the right to dig coal in Walton but there is no evidence of mining activities.

The eldest son, Robert, died without issue in 1640. His brother Thomas then became heir to their father but during his lifetime the estate was heavily encumbered with the jointures of his mother (who had possession of Walton Hall) and his sister-in-law who remarried.

In the Civil War the Watertons supported the royalist cause and Thomas Waterton was granted a commission by the Earl of Newcastle. Sir Francis Wortley garrisoned Walton Hall for the king and was taken prisoner there in June 1644. The house was later occupied by the royalists and during the siege of Sandal Castle in 1645 came under attack from parliamentarian troops.

In 1651 a Catholic schoolmaster, John Mannering, admitted under examination that he 'doth now belong to Mr Thomas Waterton of Walton, and doeth teach his childerne'. Waterton died shortly afterwards and was succeeded by his son Thomas (1642-1704) who appears to have lived quietly and privately while remaining true to his Catholic heritage.

Walton Hall A fortified manor-house which had been crenellated in 1333. It was approached through a gatehouse.

In 1664 the house had nine taxable hearths.

(E.134/13 and 14 Charles I/Hilary 11. STAC 8/151/8. *Acts of the Privy Council, 1617-18*, 432. *Surtees Society*, xl (1861), 44-5.)

SAWLEY   Staincliffe and Ewecross

A village to the north-east of Clitheroe (Lancashire) which was extra-parochial. 1674: 74 households in Sawley cum Topside.

Sawley Abbey, which was a Cistercian establishment, had been founded in the 12th century and dissolved in 1536.

There was no church at Sawley: the nearest churches were at Bolton by Bowland and Grindleton.

SAXTON   Barkston Ash

A village between Tadcaster and Sherburn in Elmet. The parish of Saxton included the villages of Scarthingwell and Towton (where the battle of Towton Heath had been fought in 1461). 1674: 46 households in Saxton cum Scarthingwell and 18 in Towton. 1676: 236 persons aged 16 or more, including 37 recusants (parish of Saxton).

In 1645 there was an outbreak of the plague at Saxton.

Church All Saints: Norman, Early English and Perpendicular.

Principal families (1) Hungate of Saxton Hall (and Huddleston Hall) (baronetcy 1642). Estate revenue: £900 a year (1626); £1000 a year (1682).

The Hungates were a Catholic family who sometimes had a resident chaplain. In 1640 it was reported that there was a regular meeting of papists at Saxton Hall.

Sir William Hungate (1569-1634) and his wife were presented for recusancy in 1608 but he soon conformed. In 1612 he gave the Northern High Commission an undertaking that he would seek to encourage his brother Philip to follow suit.

Sir Philip Hungate (d.1652), who was a convicted recusant, inherited the estate from his brother when Sir William died without issue. In the Civil War he supported the king. His son Francis served as a royalist colonel and in 1645 fell in battle.

Sir Francis Hungate (1642-1682) related in a Chancery suit that he had been sent abroad for his better education and breeding and had only returned after the Restoration. Early in the reign of Charles II he conceived the idea of enclosing the wastes of Saxton, which amounted in his estimation to 1500 acres, and dividing them up among the principal landowners of the district. Some of the freeholders opposed the plan and this resulted in litigation.

In 1679 he was accused of being involved in a Catholic conspiracy (the Barnbow Plot) but was not brought to trial. His departure for the Continent in 1680 was probably occasioned by the persecution of Catholics.

During the late 17th century the Hungates lived mainly at Huddleston Hall, though Saxton Hall remained in their possession (see under Sherburn in Elmet).

(2) Hamond of Scarthingwell Hall. Estate revenue: £500 a year (1626); £540 a year (1700).

The Catholicism of the Hamond family often remained submerged but it was never abandoned.

Gervase Hamond (1594-1644) was made a ward of the Crown after his father's death in 1601. In June 1642 he was one of a number of disaffected magistrates who were put out of the commission of the peace but he appears to have taken no part in the Civil War.

William Hamond (1624-1697) had a recusant wife who was the widow of Francis Hungate of Saxton but he was said to be neither a royalist nor a papist. He was succeeded by his son Gervase (1651-1707) who was a convicted recusant.

Saxton Hall The ancient seat of the Hungate family. Sir Francis Hungate was taxed on 20 hearths in 1674.

Scarthingwell Hall A gabled Tudor house. In 1674 there were 17 taxable hearths. Among the rooms listed in an inventory of 1707 were the hall, the great chamber, the large dining room, the little parlour, the gallery and the best lodging.

(C.5/613/32. C.10/408/27 and 499/35. BIHR, High Commission Act Books, RVII/AB12/fo.139 and RVII/AB9/fo.2; and Court Book, RVI/25/fo.29. WYAS, Leeds, Gascoigne of Barnbow MSS, GC/E3/13. C.5/242/38,39.)

SEDBERGH   Staincliffe and Ewecross

A large village in the north-west corner of the riding. The parish of Sedbergh included the village of Dent and a number of hamlets. At Dent and Garsdale there were dependent chapels. 1674: 237 households in Sedbergh and 376 in Dent and surrounding hamlets.

Church St Andrew; Norman, Early English and Decorated.

Schools Dr Roger Lupton, who had been born in the parish, founded a chantry school at Sedbergh in 1525. The school was refounded by royal charter in 1551 as the Free Grammar School of King Edward VI in Sedbergh. In course of time it drew pupils from a wide area.

In the 17th century the masters of the school included John Mayer, Gilbert Nelson, Richard Jackson, Edward Fell and Posthumus Wharton. In 1656 Jackson was ejected by the West Riding commissioners for the removal of scandalous ministers and schoolmasters.

In 1598 Ralph Lynsey, a London vintner, left the sum of £30 with a view to endowing a free school at Dent where he had been born. Six years later a grammar school was established by letters patent.

In 1634 Thomas Dawson settled some lands for the maintenance of a schoolmaster at Garsdale and shortly afterwards a schoolhouse was built.

(W. K. Jordan, *The Charities of Rural England 1480-1660* (1961), 308-9, 329, 336. A. G. Matthews, *Walker Revised* (1988), 394. A. E. Platt, *The History of the Parish and Grammar School of Sedbergh* (1876). B. Wilson (ed.), *Sedbergh School Register 1546 to 1909* (1909). W. Thompson, *Sedbergh, Garsdale and Dent* (1910). H. L. Clarke and W. N. Weech, *History of Sedbergh School 1525-1925* (1925).)

SELBY   Barkston Ash

A market town on the River Ouse. 1674: 284 households.

A charter of 1227 had conferred the right to hold an annual fair in July and a weekly market on Wednesdays. There was a ferry for the conveyance of passengers across the Ouse.

Selby is 'a pretty, populous little town, and remarkable for Henry the first's being born in it. Here William the first, his father, built a Church in memory of St German' (William Camden).

Selby Abbey, which was a Benedictine house with a mitred abbot, had been founded in the 11th century and dissolved in 1539. After the dissolution the abbey church had been assigned the role of a public chapel. In 1619 James I granted it the status of a parish church; the minister, however, was only a perpetual curate with a stipend of £30 a year.

In 1624 the curate, Richard Smith, was suspended on account of his nonconformity. His successor, John Whitaker, was also a Puritan but he was prepared to fall into line.

During the early months of 1642 there were some disturbances while John Johnson, a controversial figure, was conducting services. At the Pontefract quarter sessions a number of men were indicted, among them Paul Hammerton who was the parish clerk and Thomas Godsey, a tanner, who was alleged to have said that 'I care not for the King nor his Lawes'. In a petition submitted to the king, who was then at York, some 200 inhabitants and parishioners of Selby claimed that Johnson was an intruder and that the lawful curate was James Wade who had been presented by the patron, Charles Walmesley of Stainer Hall. The king accepted their arguments but the West Riding magistrates informed him that Walmesley was not in fact the patron (perhaps because he was a Catholic) and that Johnson had been appointed by the Archbishop of York. Before the end of the year Paul Hammerton, who had been described as 'a man not in full orders', took over the curacy.

In December 1642 Ferdinando Lord Fairfax removed his headquarters from Tadcaster to Selby. The royalists subsequently took possession of the town but in April 1644 the garrison surrendered to the Fairfaxes.

Church St Mary and St German: Norman, Early English and Decorated.

The parish was subject to the peculiar jurisdiction of a Prebendary of York.

Part of the church, 'with half of the steeple, fell down suddenly, about 6 a clock on Sunday morning, 30 March 1690' (Edmund Gibson, 1695).

School In the mid-17th century there was a private school at Selby but the town appears to have had no public grammar school at this time.

(R. A. Marchant, *The Puritans and the Church Courts in the Diocese of York 1560-1642* (1960), 126, 280, 291-2. *YASRS*, liv (1915), 364-5, 367, 370-3. W. W. Morrell, *The History and Antiquities of Selby* (1867).)

SHEFFIELD   Strafford and Tickhill

Sheffield is 'a large market town, most noted for knives, scissors, and iron-work' (Ralph Thoresby, 1681). The parish of Sheffield contained a number of villages, including Attercliffe and Ecclesall which had dependent chapels. Attercliffe chapel was built in 1629 and consecrated in 1636. The chapel at Ecclesall had been derelict for some years but in 1622 it was renovated by the inhabitants and brought back into use. 1674: 504 households in Sheffield, 126 in Attercliffe cum Darnall, 102 in Brightside Bierlow, 136 in Ecclesall, 72 in Nether Hallam and 86 in Upper Hallam. 1676: 3000 persons aged 16 or more, including 300 Protestant dissenters (parish of Sheffield).

Sheffield had two weekly markets and two annual fairs.

According to a census of 1616 the town then had 2207 inhabitants, including 725 who were dependent on charity.

At the beginning of the 17th century the manor of Sheffield belonged to Gilbert Talbot, Earl of Shrewsbury (1553-1616). He was succeeded by his brother, Earl Edward (1561-1618) who left no issue. The Talbot estates then descended to Earl Gilbert's three daughters and their husbands. The manor of Sheffield came into the possession of the Earls of Arundel and Surrey who later became Earls and Dukes of Norfolk. In the Commonwealth period their Sheffield iron works were said to be worth £2500 or £3000 a year.

In 1624 the Company of Cutlers of Hallamshire was incorporated by Act of Parliament. The stated purpose was to provide for the good order and government of makers of knives, sickles, shears, scissors and other cutlery ware. In 1671 there were 152 iron forges within the town and many more in outlying villages.

The parish of Sheffield was a solidly Protestant area. The growth of Puritanism owed much to the leadership of Thomas Toller who was appointed vicar of Sheffield in 1598 and John Bright who succeeded him in 1635. They had a number of Puritan assistant ministers, men such as William Dawson and Stanley Gower who also served as curates of the dependent chapels.

In the Civil War the inhabitants of Sheffield were generally well disposed towards the cause of Parliament. In October 1642 a parliamentarian force arrived but in May 1643 the Earl of Newcastle captured the town without encountering any serious resistance. Although Sir William Savile was appointed governor he did not remain there long and on his departure left Major Thomas Beaumont in command. In August 1644 a parliamentarian force bombarded the castle and Beaumont surrendered.

In 1656 the inhabitants of Sheffield asked the Protector to authorise additional financial support for their minister, James Fisher, whom they described as a burning and shining light in both the town and the surrounding area. According to their petition at least 5000 people were dependent on his ministry.

During the reign of Charles II the Company of Cutlers, with the support of the local gentry, mounted a campaign against the levying of the hearth tax on iron forges.

Churches Parish church of St Peter: Norman in origin but mainly Perpendicular. The Shrewsbury chapel was built by George Talbot, Earl of Shrewsbury in the early 16th century as a burial place for his family.

Ralph Thoresby wrote in 1681 that the church was 'a handsome well-built fabric with some pretty monuments'.

A nonconformist chapel was built in Sheffield in the last decade of the 17th century.

Castle Sheffield Castle had been rebuilt in the 13th century. It was the main residence of the Talbots, Earls of Shrewsbury until the early 16th century when Sheffield Manor assumed this role but they continued to keep it in repair.

In 1647 Parliament decided that the castle should be demolished and two years later it was almost completely destroyed.

School There was a school in 1564. In his will (1603) Thomas Smith of Crowland in Lincolnshire left £30 a year for the support of a schoolmaster and usher. In a royal patent which was obtained in 1604 the school was formally constituted and named the Free Grammar School of James King of England.

In the 17th century the masters of the school included Thomas Rawson, William Whitaker and Thomas Balguy.

In 1644 Rawson, a zealous Puritan who was also the curate at Attercliffe, related that on 5 May 1643 he was 'forced to flie from the rage and fury of the Earl of Newcastle's army'.

In 1644 the schoolhouse was described as 'not habitable' and in 1648 a new building was erected.

Almshouses In his will (1616) Gilbert Earl of Shrewsbury gave direction that almshouses should be built and made provision for an endowment of £200 a year. After the Restoration his descendant Henry Earl of Norwich (later Duke of Norfolk) put the necessary work in hand and in 1673 the Earl of Shrewsbury's Hospital took in 10 poor men and 10 poor women.

In 1680 the Duke enlarged the hospital which was then able to accommodate 36 persons.

(*Calendar, Committee for Compounding*, 2474. R. A. Marchant, *The Puritans and the Church Courts in the Diocese of York 1560-1642* (1960), 38, 69-74, 229, 243, 250, 256, 270, 285-8, 318. *CSP Dom, 1656-7*, 77. A. Gatty, *Sheffield: Past and Present* (1873). Mary Walton, *Sheffield: Its Story and Its Achievements* (1948). D. Hey, *The Fiery Blades of Hallamshire. Sheffield and Its Neighbourhood 1660-1740* (1991) and *A History of Sheffield* (1998).)

SHERBURN IN ELMET   Barkston Ash

A market town to the south of Tadcaster. The parish of Sherburn contained several villages and hamlets, including Lotherton and Micklefield which had dependent chapels. 1674: 114 households in Sherburn, 10 in Huddleston cum Lumby, 21 in Micklefield, 6 in Newthorpe and 66 in South Milford.

In his poem on the travels of 'Drunken Barnaby', which was first published in 1638, Richard Braithwaite wrote

> Thence to Sherburn, dearly loved,
> And for Pinners well approved:
> Cherry-Tenths the Pastor aimeth
> More than th'Souls which he reclaimeth.

Sherburn is 'a place famous for makinge of pins, and abondance of cherries' (Life of Marmaduke Rawdon, entry for 1664).

By a royal charter of 1227 the town had the right to hold a weekly market and an annual fair.

At Huddleston there were quarries which had provided limestone for the building of York Minster.

In October 1645 a royalist force under George Lord Digby and Sir Marmaduke Langdale was heavily defeated at the battle of Sherburn.

Church All Saints: Norman, Early English and Perpendicular. The parish was subject to the peculiar jurisdiction of a Prebendary of York Minster.

School In his will (1619) Robert Hungate of Sand Hutton, a lawyer, settled lands worth some £260 a year on his nephew Sir William Hungate and his heirs for the purpose of building and maintaining a school and hospital for 24 orphan children of Sherburn and Saxton. Eventually Sir William carried out the necessary building work at Sherburn.

Principal family Hungate of Huddleston Hall (and Saxton Hall) (see under Saxton). After the Restoration the Hungates lived mainly at Huddleston.

Huddleston Hall An Elizabethan house with walls of limestone and red brick chimneys. The hearth tax returns record 11 hearths in 1664 and 13 in 1674.

The Hungates had a domestic chapel dating from the 15th century.

(Richard Braithwaite, *Drunken Barnaby's Four Journeys to the North of England* (3rd edition, 1723). C.54/2746. W. Wheater, *The History of the Parishes of Sherburn and Cawood* (2nd edition, 1882).)

SILKSTONE   Staincross

A village to the west of Barnsley. The extensive parish of Silkstone contained the town of Barnsley and a considerable number of villages and hamlets, including Cawthorne, Stainborough and parts of West Bretton and Cumberworth, all of which (like Barnsley) had medieval chapels. During the early 17th century the chapels at Cawthorne and Cumberworth were granted some parochial rights. Barnsley, Stainborough and West Bretton are separately noticed. 1674: 46 households in Silkstone, 66 in Cawthorne, 33 in Cumberworth, 41 in Dodworth, 39 in Hoyland Swaine and 46 in Thurgoland. 1676: 759 persons aged 16 or more (parish, excluding the chapelry of Barnsley).

Within the moors and commons there were substantial deposits of iron ore. In 1607 Robert Swift and Robert Greaves secured a lease of the Silkstone iron smithies together with all mines and seams in the manor of Silkstone. Subsequently, in 1618, Sir Francis Wortley of Wortley acquired an interest in a quarter part of the smithies and mines. In 1632 the Swift family brought a suit against Wortley in the Court of Exchequer, claiming that he and his agents had sabotaged the bellows of their iron mills and diverted a water course which was used for the making of iron.

The Wentworths of West Bretton bought the manor of Cawthorne in 1611 and set up iron forges there.

The Barnbys of Barnby Hall in the township of Cawthorne were a Catholic family with a dwindling estate. Thomas Barnby had an iron works known as Barnby furnace. To meet his requirement for charcoal he was obliged to purchase supplies of wood from other landowners. In 1635 he entered into an agreement with John Shewton, a Silkstone bloomer, who was to take on responsibility for the smelting process.

In the Civil War Thomas Barnby supported the royalist cause and was forced to compound for his estate.

The manor of Hoyland Swaine belonged to the Wortleys. In 1628 Sir Francis Wortley submitted a petition to the king in which he related that a number of men armed with swords, daggers and other weapons had destroyed an enclosure of his on the commons of Hoyland Swaine and wounded one of his tenants who had tried to resist them. He therefore requested that the matter should be referred to the Court of Star Chamber.

Richard Walker the vicar of Silkstone was ousted by the parliamentarians before the end of 1642. During the war his Puritan successor, John Spofford, served as a chaplain in the parliamentary army. After his ejection from the living in 1662 one of his parishioners, Robert Cotton, took him into his house.

Church All Saints: Norman, Decorated and Perpendicular.

Schools At the beginning of Charles I's reign George Burdet, a radical Puritan, was described as curate and schoolmaster of Silkstone. Some years later he migrated to New England.

There had been a grammar school at Cawthorne in the reign of Elizabeth but the endowment had been transferred to Pontefract School. In 1639 it was re-founded by a decree of the Duchy of Lancaster which laid it down that the master was to have a salary of £13 a year and that the inhabitants of Cawthorne should be responsible for maintaining the schoolhouse.

(Sheffield Archives, Wharncliffe MSS, 23, 94 and Spencer Stanhope MSS, 25(a), 35, 60278. YAS Library, Bretton Hall MSS, 53, 54. S.P.23/clxxxvii/589, 595. A. G. Matthews, *Walker Revised* (1988), 400 and *Calamy Revised* (1934), 454. BIHR, High Commission Act Books, RVI/A21/fo.371. C. T. Pratt, *History of Cawthorne* (1882).)

SKIPTON Staincliffe and Ewecross/Claro

A market town in Craven. The parish of Skipton contained a number of villages and hamlets, including Bolton which had a dependent chapel (Bolton Priory church). Beamsley was situated in two parishes: Skipton and Addingham (see the entry for

Addingham). 1674: 145 households in Skipton, 29 in Barden Forest, 34 in Draughton, 20 in Eastby, 30 in Embsay and 46 in Halton East (probably including Bolton).

Skipton is 'hid (as it were) with those steep precipices, lying quite round ... The town is pretty handsome ... and is secured by a very beautiful and strong Castle' (William Camden).

Skipton 'lies skulking among the hills, where is a stately castle' (Ralph Thoresby, 1681).

At the beginning of the Civil War Henry Earl of Cumberland garrisoned the castle for the king. In January 1643 Sir John Mallory of Studley assumed command of the garrison as governor and managed to hold out against parliamentarian attacks for three years. In December 1645 he surrendered the castle on reasonable terms.

In 1660 George Fox the Quaker leader recorded in his journal that he travelled to Skipton 'where there was a generall meeting of.....freindes out of many Countyes concerneinge ye affaires of ye Church'.

Bolton Priory, which was an establishment of Augustinian canons, had been founded in the 12th century and dissolved in 1539. The priory church had then been converted into a public chapel.

Churches Holy Trinity: Decorated and Perpendicular. Tombs of members of the Clifford family.

In the Civil War the church was damaged by cannon fire. In 1655 Lady Anne Clifford paid for the tower to be rebuilt.

In 1693 the Quakers built a meeting place in Skipton.

School Towards the end of the 15th century Peter Toller, who was Dean of Craven, established a chantry school within the parish church. The school was refounded by William Ermystead, a canon of St Paul's, in 1548 and a schoolhouse was built.

In 1655 Richard Brown, the master of Skipton Grammar School, was ejected by the West Riding commissioners for the removal of scandalous ministers and schoolmasters.

Principal family Clifford of Skipton Castle, Earls of Cumberland (and of Londesborough Hall, East Riding and Appleby and Brougham Castles, Westmorland). Estate revenue: £4500 a year (1622). Lead and coalmines in Craven. Number of servants: 25 (1674).

The Cliffords had property in Cumberland and Westmorland but their main estates were in Craven where they owned the Clifford and Percy Fees. In the early 17th century they experienced severe financial difficulties which led to the sale of land and the granting of long leases.

George the 3rd Earl (1558-1605), who was a famous privateer, was heavily in debt at the time of his death. He was succeded by his brother Francis the 4th Earl (1559-1641) who was involved in protracted litigation with his formidable niece Lady Anne Clifford (1590-1676) over the descent of the Clifford estates. He successfully resisted her claims but the episode added to his financial problems.

For some time he was at loggerheads with his son Henry. In 1622 Sir Thomas Wentworth, the future Earl of Strafford, wrote of 'his uncertaine and unstable humores'.

Henry the 5th Earl (1592-1643) served as commander in chief of the royalist forces in Yorkshire during the early stages of the Civil War. In his will (1642) he recorded his thankfulness to God 'for my education in the true Protestant religion, which I have constantly practised, abhoring all my life longe all manner of poperye and sismatticall oppinions which now threaten the ruin of the Church and State'.

With his death the male line expired. Lady Anne Clifford inherited the Clifford Fee and the Westmorland estate while Richard Earl of Cork (later Earl of Burlington) and his wife Countess Elizabeth, the only daughter of the 5th Earl, entered into possession of the Percy Fee.

In the latter part of her life Lady Anne was busily engaged in building activities in Skipton, at Barden Tower and elsewhere. After her death the estate which she left descended to the Tuftons, Earls of Thanet.

Skipton Castle The castle was Norman in origin but had largely been rebuilt in the 14th century and the early 16th century.

In 1648 and 1649 it was partly demolished by the parliamentary authorities. Lady Anne Clifford began to restore it in 1650 but it was not until 1657 that a major renovation programme was put in hand. In 1659 she noted in her diary that on her arrival at Skipton Castle she found it 'for the most part well finished and better than I expected it could have bin'.

In 1674 she was taxed on 60 hearths.

(N. Penney (ed.) *The Journal of George Fox* (1911), i, 355. A. G. Matthews, *Walker Revised* (1988), 390. *Camden Fourth Series*, 12 (1973), 139, 170, 171. W. H. Dawson, *History of Skipton* (1882). A. M. Gibbon, *The Ancient Free Grammar School of Skipton in Craven* (1947). D. J. H. Clifford (ed.), *The Diaries of Lady Anne Clifford* (1990). R. T. Spence, *Skipton Castle in the Great Civil War 1642-1645* (1991), *Lady Anne Clifford* (1997) and *Skipton Castle and Its Builders* (2002).)

SKIRCOAT Agbrigg and Morley

A clothing village within the parish of Halifax. 1674: 59 households.

School Heath Grammar School, a free school founded by royal patent in 1585 for the education of sons of the inhabitants of the parish of Halifax. The school was opened in 1600.

Principal family Savile of Copley Hall (baronetcy 1662). Estate revenue: £180 a year (1632); £1000 a year (1664). Fulling mills in Skircoat.

At the beginning of the 17th century the Saviles were a family of modest income but they would eventually profit from the marriage of Henry Savile (1578-1632) and Anne

Darcy, a sister of John Lord Darcy who died without issue in 1635. Following litigation Anne Savile secured property worth £600 a year which had belonged to her brother.

Her eldest son Thomas (1602-1642) appears to have been a man of unruly temperament. In 1641 he was twice fined by the West Riding magistrates for physical assaults carried out in Halifax. In the Civil War another son, William, took up arms for the king and was slain at Lincoln in 1644.

Thomas Savile was succeeded by his son William (1641-1661) who left no issue. The estate then passed to his cousin John Savile (1640-1689) who was travelling on the Continent at the time. In 1662 he was involved in litigation with Adam Pickhard who as the husband of Thomas Savile's widow claimed an interest in the manor of Copley.

Sir John Savile (as he became) was converted to Catholicism, no doubt through the influence of his mother who was a daughter of Sir George Palmes of Naburn. He kept a chaplain, Richard Fincham, who was arrested but later released when the authorities were persuaded that he was only a menial servant.

Following Sir John's death the estate descended to his daughter Elizabeth and through her to the Dukes of Norfolk.

Copley Hall A medieval house dating back to the 15th century or earlier. Thomas Savile carried out some improvements in the reign of Charles I.

In 1664 the hall and gatehouse were both leased to tenants.

(C.9/27/135. C.22/822/56. Wards 9/572/403,451. YAS Library, DD125. *YASRS*, liv (1915), 255.)

SLAIDBURN   Staincliffe and Ewecross

A village in the Forest of Bowland. The parish of Slaidburn, which extended to the border between Yorkshire and Lancashire, included the villages of Easington and Newton. 1674: 73 households in Slaidburn, 63 in Easington and 64 in Newton. 1676: 299 persons aged 16 or more (parish).

By a royal charter of 1294 Slaidburn had the right to hold an annual fair. In the 17th century this was primarily a cattle fair.

In 1639 the West Riding magistrates were informed that Slaidburn Bridge, which spanned the River Hodder, was 'in great decay for lack of repair'. In view of the importance of the road which it carried it was decided to treat the expenditure required as a charge on the riding as a whole.

Church St Andrew: Norman.

Schools In 1604 it was reported that there were three schoolmasters in Slaidburn: William King, Robert Boune and Christopher Tailor.

The hearth tax roll of 1674 records the existence of a schoolhouse at Easington.

(*YASRS*, liv (1915), 135, 137. E. Peacock (ed.), *A List of the Roman Catholics in the County of York in 1604* (1872), 21.)

SNAITH   Osgoldcross

A market town to the east of Pontefract which was situated near the River Aire. The extensive parish of Snaith contained a number of villages, including Airmyn, Carlton, Goole, Hook and Rawcliffe which had medieval chapels. Carlton and Cowick are separately noticed. 1674: 93 households in Snaith, 52 in Airmyn, 36 in Balne, 44 in Goole, 41 in Gowdall, 31 in Heck, 27 in Hensall, 54 in Hook, 59 in Pollington and 147 in Rawcliffe.

There had been a small Benedictine priory at Snaith which had originally been a cell of Selby Abbey. After its dissolution the priory church had become the parish church.

A number of gentry families were seated within the parish. These included major families like the Dawneys of Cowick and the Stapletons of Carlton and families with more modest estates such as the Boyntons of Rawcliffe and the Ricards of Heck.

Church St Mary: Norman in origin but with major rebuilding work in the 13th, 14th and 15th centuries.

The parish was a peculiar with its own court. The lay proprietor of the peculiar court was entitled to nominate the commissary but he carried out his functions on behalf of the ecclesiastical authorities.

Schools Nicholas Waller of Sykehouse founded a public grammar school at Snaith. In June 1623 he settled lands worth £30 a year for the support of a master and an usher and in his will (1625) he requested his executor, Edmund Yarburgh, to build a schoolhouse in a place called Scott Garth. The first three masters were George Carte, Richard Clarkson and William Clarkson.

In the reign of Charles I there was a private school at Rawcliffe. In the latter part of the century a free school was established there for the education of poor children.

Almshouses In the deed of 1623 Nicholas Waller also allocated £20 a year for the support of almshouses for 'Six poore aged or Impotent single men or widowers'. In September 1623 Roger Hilton of Hensall was admitted to the hospital 'latelie erected' by Waller.

Towards the end of the 17th century Matthew Boynton, a Puritan landowner, founded a small hospital at Rawcliffe which provided housing for four poor widows.

Principal family in Snaith Yarburgh of Snaith Hall (and Balne Hall). Estate revenue: £1500 a year (1631).

The Yarburghs had migrated from Lincolnshire in the reign of Elizabeth. They were the patrons of the living of Snaith and also owned the peculiar court.

Sir Nicholas Yarburgh (1613-1655), who was one of the first pupils at Snaith Grammar School, was made a ward of the Crown following the death of his father in 1631. Of his younger brothers Thomas became a barrister and Edmund a physician who practised at Doncaster. In the Civil War Sir Nicholas acted as a commissioner of array for the king.

His son Sir Thomas (1637-1716) inherited considerable property in Lincolnshire when the senior branch of the family expired. He and his wife, Dame Henrietta Maria, had 16 children in all. She kept a book of meditations containing quotations from such writers as George Herbert and Sir William Temple.

Snaith Hall Sir Thomas Yarburgh lived mainly at Snaith Hall until the latter part of his life when he settled in London. In the early years of Charles II's reign he appears to have carried out some building work since he was taxed on 15 hearths in 1664 and 18 in 1674.

Among the rooms listed in an inventory of 1716 were the hall, the parlour, the drawing room and 'the great room above stairs'.

(C. B. Robinson (afterwards Norcliffe), *History of the Priory and Peculiar of Snaith in the County of York* (1861). W. K. Jordan, *The Charities of Rural England 1480-1660* (1961), 270-1, 331-2. *YPRS*, lxiii (1919). C.10/99/133.)

SOUTH KIRKBY   Osgoldcross/Strafford and Tickhill

A village to the north-east of Barnsley. The parish of South Kirkby contained a number of villages and hamlets, including Skelbrooke which had a medieval chapel. North Elmsall is separately noticed. 1674: 73 households in South Kirkby, 4 in Hampole Stubbs, 13 in Skelbrooke and 38 in South Elmsall. 1676: 47 persons aged 16 or more in the chapelry of Skelbrooke (no return for the parish as a whole).

Hampole Priory, which was an establishment of Benedictine nuns, had been founded in the 12th century and dissolved in 1540. In the 17th century the manor of Hampole was in the possession of the Washington family of Adwick le Street. According to a survey of 1653 the property consisted of a capital messuage called Hampole Abbey and 597 acres of land which were worth £144 a year.

The manor of South Kirkby belonged to the Trigott family until the male line expired in the reign of Charles I. Following the death of Thomas Trigott in 1633 the estate descended to his three daughters and the property in South Kirkby was formally divided into parcels worth £120, £128 and £125 a year.

In 1639 the West Riding magistrates received a petition from the inhabitants of South Kirkby in which they claimed that 'there is great inequallitie amongst them in makeinge theire layes and assessmentes'. As a result it was decided that in future such taxes 'shall be rated and assessed proporconally and equally, according to the quantitye of acres everye one occupyeth and enjoyeth'.

In 1641 the inhabitants of Hampole Stubbs complained about the burden of local taxation and stressed that they were 'rated and assessed after the rate of a two penny towne'. The magistrates responded positively to their plea and ruled that they should be charged 'after the proporcon of a pennye towne'.

In the Civil War John Morris of South Elmsall initially served in the royalist army but later joined the parliamentarians and was made a colonel. Eventually he became disillusioned with the parliamentary cause and in 1648 he managed to seize Pontefract Castle on behalf of the king. Soon afterwards John Lambert regained possession of the castle and in 1649 Morris was captured and put to death.

George Beaumont the vicar of South Kirkby was also involved in the plan to take over Pontefract Castle. When this came to light he was tried by a council of war and suffered the same fate as his friend Morris.

At the end of the 17th century Godfrey Copley of Skelbrooke Hall, who was the last of the line, was in a desperate financial situation: he had an estate revenue of £530 a year but his debts amounted to £14,520. After his death in 1701 the manor of Skelbrooke was sold for £5600.

Church All Saints: Early English and Perpendicular.

(S.P.23/lviii/fols.65-6. Sheffield Archives, Wentworth Woodhouse Collection, Bright MSS, 82. *YASRS*, liv (1915), 117, 282-3. R. Holmes (ed.), *The Sieges of Pontefract Castle, 1644-1648* (1887). C.33/300/fols.89-90.)

SOUTH STAINLEY   Claro

A hamlet to the north-west of Knaresborough. The parish of South Stainley also included the hamlet of Cayton. 1674: 14 households in South Stainley cum Cayton.

Church St Wilfrid: medieval in origin.

Principal family Swale of South Stainley Hall (baronetcy 1660). Estate revenue: £140 a year (1630); £600 a year (1660); £500 a year (1682). Lead mining.

The Swales bought the manor and rectory of South Stainley in 1609.

Following the death of Francis Swale in 1629 his son Solomon (1610-1678) was made a ward of the Crown. In 1630 he was admitted to Gray's Inn and five years later was called to the bar.

In the Civil War he sided with the king while three of his brothers served as royalist officers.

In 1649 he purchased the estate of a kinsman, Solomon Swale, at Grinton in the North Riding where there were rich deposits of lead ore.

On 7 May 1660 he moved in the Commons that Charles II should be proclaimed as king the following day and his proposal was duly approved. For his loyalty to the Crown he was rewarded with a baronetcy.

Shortly after this he took into his house a missionary priest, Augustine Smithson, who had converted two of his sons. Smithson served for some years as his chaplain but eventually moved to Nidd Hall, the residence of the Trappes family. His successor at South Stainley Hall was another seminary priest, William Dinmore, who was there in 1692.

In 1664 Marmaduke Rawdon and two of his friends visited South Stainley Hall which was described as 'a gallant seate'. There they were 'very nobly entertaind' by Sir Solomon and his wife 'into whosse chamber after supper they were several times invited to banquetts of sweet meats' (Life of Marmaduke Rawdon).

In 1669 Sir Solomon mortgaged part of his estate and in the following years his financial difficulties became increasingly severe. As an MP he enjoyed immunity from the attentions of his creditors but in June 1678 he was expelled from the Commons when it was discovered that he was a convicted recusant. He was immediately arrested for debt and died in the King's Bench prison.

His grandson Sir Solomon (d.1733) was involved in protracted litigation with the Crown over the legal ownership of his Swaledale lead mines. As a result he died in great poverty.

South Stainley Hall A large mansion which may possibly have been Jacobean. In 1674 Sir Solomon Swale was taxed on 18 hearths.

(C.9/10/115. C.33/260/fo.778. H. Aveling, *Northern Catholics. The Catholic Recusants of the North Riding of Yorkshire 1558-1790* (1966), 349. *CRS*, ix (1911), 111, 112. C.38/235/16 November 1689. N. A. Hudleston, *Stainley and Cayton* (1956).)

SPOFFORTH   Claro

A village to the south of Knaresborough. The parish of Spofforth included the market town of Wetherby (which had a dependent chapel) and a number of villages and hamlets. Wetherby is separately noticed. 1674: 87 households in Spofforth, 58 in Follifoot, 17 in Linton, 29 in Little Ribston, 28 in Middleton cum Stockeld and 33 in Plumpton. 1676: 1100 persons aged 16 or more, including 51 recusants (parish of Spofforth).

In 1633 it was said that most of the land within the constablery of Spofforth (2200 out of 3000 acres) was owned by the Earl of Northumberland.

The parish of Spofforth was one of the more Catholic parishes within the West Riding. The survival of Catholicism was mainly due to the influence of two prominent local families, the Middletons and the Plumptons.

Church All Saints: Norman and later with a Perpendicular tower.

Castle A medieval castle or fortified house which in the early years of the 17th century was occupied by the Earl of Northumberland's steward. It was either destroyed in the Civil War or abandoned as a residence in the course of the century.

Principal families (1) Middleton of Stockeld Hall. Estate revenue: £1000 a year (1608); £1600 a year (1660).

The Middletons were one of the wealthiest Catholic families in Yorkshire.

William Middleton (c.1551-1614) was a convicted recusant. In 1612 he refused to take the oath of allegiance despite the severe penalties prescribed for the offence but was eventually pardoned. His friend Thomas Meynell wrote of him that 'he was a worthye and most memorable gentleman ... he alwaise kept a good house, and left his eldest sonne in as good estate as his father lefte him'.

His son Sir Peter (c.1586-1645), who was a Church Papist, substantially increased his estate. In 1617 Roger Dodsworth observed that he was a generous landlord who was greatly esteemed by his tenants; the tenants of neighbouring landowners who were harshly treated would often say 'God bless Sir Peter Middleton'.

In the Civil War he was largely inactive, though in September 1642 he signed a letter in which a number of Yorkshire gentlemen sought military assistance from the Earl of Newcastle. On the other hand, two of his sons, William and Matthew, served as royalist officers.

John Middleton (1652-1700), who succeeded to the estate in 1658, was presented for recusancy in 1674. His religious loyalties appear to have cost him little but in 1680 his brother Peter was imprisoned for refusing to take the oath of allegiance.

(2) Plumpton of Plumpton Hall or Tower. Estate revenue: £1000 a year (1659).

The Plumptons, who were another Catholic family, believed that they had owned the manor of Plumpton 'ever synce the Conquest'.

In 1605 it was said that Sir Edward Plumpton (1581-1659) had received a visit from Robert Winter, one of the Gunpowder Plot conspirators. In a Star Chamber case of 1631 the allegation was made that his daughter Anne had been married by a popish priest in a chamber at Plumpton Hall. He managed, however, to escape prosecution for the offence of harbouring a seminary priest.

In February 1642 there was a rumour that two pieces of ordnance had been mounted on the roof of Plumpton Hall. In the Civil War the Plumptons supported the king. Sir Edward's eldest son John, who was a royalist captain, died in 1644 as the result of wounds he received at the battle of Marston Moor.

In his will (1669) Robert Plumpton (1644-1670) related that his debts, which amounted to nearly £5000, had been occasioned by the Civil War and in particular by the sequestration of the estate; and gave direction that some of his lands should be sold.

Stockeld Hall An inventory of the Tudor mansion made in 1614 lists the main rooms as the great hall, the lower dining parlour, the high dining chamber, the chapel parlour and the gallery.

The house had 41 taxable hearths in 1674.

The Middletons had deer parks at Stockeld and Stubham.

Plumpton Hall In 1474 Sir William Plumpton obtained a licence to crenellate his mansion and enclose a park. In the reign of Henry VIII John Leland wrote that Plumpton Hall was 'a fair house of stone with 2 tourres longging to the same'.

According to a Commonwealth survey of 1653 the higher tower contained a kitchen and two larders below stairs and six chambers above and the lower tower two parlours, a dining room and three chambers. Between the towers there was a large hall together with a buttery and a cellar and two chambers upstairs.

When Sir Edward Plumpton conveyed the manor of Plumpton to his son John in 1638 it was with the proviso that he would retain possession of 'all that building called the Lowe Tower'. In 1659 his daughter Katherine fell to her death from the top of Plumpton 'high tower'.

The Plumptons were taxed on 10 hearths in 1664 and 11 in 1674.

In the 17th century the park appears to have been used for agricultural purposes.

(*YASRS*, liv (1915), 25. *CRS*, lvi (1964), 10. BL, Additional MSS 24,468, fo.138 and 32,113 (Plumpton commonplace book). BL, Egerton MSS 2574, fo.57. WYAS, Leeds, Gascoigne of Barnbow MSS, GC/E10/I. *YAJ*, xxxiv (1929). S.P.23/lviiiA/fo.425. Maureen Johnson and Bessie Maltby, 'A Seventeenth Century Recusant Family Library: Middleton of Stockeld', *YAJ*, 75 (2003).)

SPROTBOROUGH   Strafford and Tickhill

A village on the north bank of the River Don in the neighbourhood of Doncaster. The parish of Sprotborough included the hamlets of Cadeby and Newton. 1674: 26 households in Sprotborough cum Newton and 21 in Cadeby. 1676: 255 persons aged 16 or more (parish of Sprotborough).

Church St Mary: Decorated and Perpendicular.

Principal family Copley of Sprotborough Hall (baronetcy 1661). Estate revenue: £820 a year (1640); £2000 a year (1682).

Godfrey Copley (1567-1633) never married and after his death the bulk of his estate passed to a cousin, William Copley.

Godfrey Copley (1624-1678) was a royalist major in the Civil War and was later rewarded with a baronetcy. Sir John Reresby wrote of him that he was 'a fine gentleman of good credit in his country, and of excellent naturall parts, and a good justice of the peace'.

His son Sir Godfrey (c.1653-1709) was not only a politician of some standing but a man of many interests which included science, mathematics, drawing and painting. In 1691 he was elected a fellow of the Royal Society. A bequest which he left in his will was used by the Society to institute the Copley medal for scientific achievement.

Sprotborough Hall During the reign of Charles II Sir Godfrey Copley (1624-1678) drastically reduced the size of his house. There were 33 taxable hearths in 1664 but only 21 in 1674. Possibly the house was decaying.

His son built a new hall of three storeys on a different site. Ralph Thoresby, who visited him in 1703, describes it as a 'noble and spacious house' and refers to his gallery adorned with pictures by Van Dyck and other great masters, his closets with choice curiosities and his collection of mathematical instruments. In addition, he writes admiringly of the canals, woods and formal gardens with their statues and fountains.

(Wards 9/99/fols.463a and b and 464. YAS Library, Copley of Sprotborough MSS (DD38A). C.33/315/fols.597, 599.)

STAINBOROUGH   Staincross

A small village within the parish of Silkstone, near Barnsley. 1674: 23 households.

Church St James: an ancient public chapel.

School There was a school at Stainborough in the late 17th century.

Principal family Cutler of Stainborough Hall. Estate revenue: £600 a year (1640). Iron works at Stainborough.

The Cutlers lived at Stainborough for about a century.

Thomas Cutler (c.1565-1623) bought the manor for £2800 in the early part of James I's reign. In his will (1622) he gave direction that £300 should be spent on the purchase of lands for the maintenance of 'a zealous preacher of God's word for ever at Staynburgh-chapel, or some time at Barnsley, as my son Gervase Cutler shall think fit'.

Sir Gervase Cutler (1593-1645) drew up his will in March 1639 when, as lieutenant colonel of a militia regiment, he was about to go north on the king's expedition against the Scots. Among other things, he nominated a chaplain for 'my St James chappell in Stainburgh'; put it on record that his servant Thomas Denton would not be required to make recompense for the iron worth £100 'taken owte of his keepinge at the iron workes'; and made provision for Denton's son Gervase to receive a university education. In the Civil War he acted as a commissioner of array for the king, raised a considerable body of men and took the family plate, worth £1000, to Pontefract Castle where he died of a fever. According to his widow, Lady Magdalen, his personal estate to the value of £4000 was plundered by both sides in the conflict.

His son Sir Gervase (1641-1705) is said to have lived an extravagant and dissolute life. Probably it was as a result of his improvidence that the estate was sold shortly after his death.

Stainborough Hall The hall was rebuilt during the years 1670 to 1672. In 1674 there were 11 taxable hearths, as compared with 16 in 1664.

(W. K Jordan, *The Charities of Rural England 1480-1660* (1961), 377. BIHR, York Registry, will of Sir Gervase Cutler, 23 March 1638/9. S.P.23/clxxx/574, 582. J. Miller, 'Seventeenth-Century Designs for Stainborough Hall', *YAJ*, 61 (1989).)

STAINTON Strafford and Tickhill

A hamlet to the north-west of Tickhill. The parish of Stainton also included the hamlet of Hellaby. 1674: 21 households in Stainton cum Hellaby. 1676: 110 persons aged 16 or more (parish).

In the early part of the 17th century the manor of Stainton belonged to the Stanhopes of Edlington and Grimston. In 1630 Sir Edward Stanhope brought a Star Chamber suit against George French and others whom he accused of destroying enclosures on the commons of Stainton. By this time Sir Edward was in severe financial difficulties and in 1639 he sold the manor to Robert Saunderson of Sandbeck Hall.

At the Pontefract quarter sessions in April 1639 the justices were informed that there was 'great inequallitie in their layes and assessmentes in Stainton and Hellabie'. They therefore ruled that in future such taxes should be apportioned according to the quantity and quality of acres which each individual had in his possession.

In 1641 the magistrates issued a warrant for the arrest of William Roidhouse, a labourer, who was a fugitive from justice. He was said to be hiding in his house at Stainton and to have a gun which he was ready to use. In January 1642 Thomas Justice, who had recently served as constable of Stainton, was indicted for refusing to search with a hue and cry for Roidhouse, John Munforth and others who were suspected of engaging in a burglary at East Retford in Nottinghamshire.

Church St Winifred: Norman, Decorated and Perpendicular.

(*Catalogue of the Lumley MSS*, 1443, 1445, 1451, 1480, 1486, 3893. *YASRS*, liv (1915), 132, 337, 355-6.)

STANLEY Agbrigg and Morley

A village in the parish of Wakefield. In the subsidy and hearth tax rolls the entry for Stanley covers a number of villages and manor-houses, including Stanley and Wrenthorpe to the north of Wakefield and Alverthorpe and Lupset Hall to the west and south. (For Lupset Hall see under Horbury). The 1674 hearth tax return records a total of 251 households within this extensive area.

Principal families (1) Pilkington of Stanley Hall (baronetcy 1635). Estate revenue: £800 a year (1634); £600 a year (1684). Coalmining in Nether Bradley.

Thomas Pilkington of Nether Bradley (d.1611) bought the Stanley Hall estate in 1603 and took up residence there. His son Arthur (c.1591-1650) inherited considerable debts and was imprisoned for a time in York Castle at the suit of one of the creditors. He also became involved in Star Chamber suits over property rights in Stanley. When he purchased a Nova Scotia baronetcy in 1635 he was already resorting to heavy borrowing and was forced to mortgage the manor of Nether Bradley.

In the Civil War Sir Arthur took up arms for the king. All the time his financial position was growing more desperate and for the last four years of his life he was a prisoner for debt in York Castle.

His son Sir Lyon (1613-1684) was a parliamentarian officer in the army of the Earl of Essex. In 1650, however, he found himself in trouble with the Commonwealth government, apparently because of some indiscreet comments. For over a decade after his father's death he was engaged in a continuing legal battle with his creditors and others. The manor of Snapethorpe was sold and it took him some time to clear the manor of Nether Bradley of all encumbrances but in the end he managed to avoid financial ruin.

(2) Benson of Wrenthorpe Hall. Estate revenue: £1800 a year (1676).

During the early 17th century the manor of Wrenthorpe frequently changed hands. In the Commonwealth period it was bought by Robert Benson (d.1676) who was an attorney and clerk of the peace for the West Riding. After the Restoration Benson rapidly acquired a fortune as a sub-treasurer in the office of the Lord High Treasurer and built up a large estate. At his death he left a personal estate valued at £13,000.

Among the major landed families of Yorkshire he was regarded as an upstart who had few scruples. Sir John Reresby wrote of him that he was 'the most notable and formidable man for business of his time, one of noe birth' who had risen spectacularly 'but not without suspicion of great frauds and oppressions'.

His son Robert (c.1675-1731) was created Lord Bingley in 1713.

Stanley Hall A gabled Elizabethan or Jacobean mansion. In 1674 Sir Lyon Pilkington was taxed on 14 hearths.

There was a park adjoining the hall.

Wrenthorpe Hall The house was largely rebuilt by John Greenwood, a merchant, in 1612. The chosen material was brick and for this reason the house came to be known as Red Hall.

In 1674 there were 12 taxable hearths.

(C.3/284/69 and 462/20. C.5/429/86. C.8/73/82. C.10/4/125; 37/135; 55/95; and 73/82. STAC 8/216/30 and 233/24. C.33/257, part 2/fo.320; 258/fols.848-51; and 260/fo.657. C.38/208/25 January 1681/2. *Memoirs of Sir John Reresby* (ed. A. Browning and others) (1991), 90-1, 106.)

STAVELEY   Claro

A village to the north of Knaresborough. There was no other village within the parish. 1674: 32 households (township of Staveley).
Church All Saints: medieval in origin.

STONEBECK DOWN   Claro

A remote Nidderdale village or township within the parish of Kirkby Malzeard. The nearest place of worship was the public chapel at Middlesmoor which had been consecrated in 1484. 1674: 77 households.
Principal family Yorke of Gouthwaite Hall. Estate revenue: £1000 a year (1628). Lead mines. Number of servants: 17 or more (1613).

The Yorkes were a leading Catholic family in the early 17th century but in the Commonwealth period they underwent a change of religion.

Sir John Yorke (1565-1635) was a Church Papist who attended services at Middlesmoor chapel from time to time; his wife, Dame Julian, was a determined recusant; and many of his servants were said to be 'popishelie affected'.

On several occasions the authorities ordered searches to be carried out at Gouthwaite Hall. In 1614 Sir John and his wife were heavily fined in the Court of Star Chamber over a Catholic play staged at the hall which was branded as seditious. Two years later they were committed to the Fleet prison for failing to pay their fines but in February 1617 they were released.

In the course of the Star Chamber proceedings it was alleged that two secret rooms had been constructed at Gouthwaite Hall and that the family had been harbouring seminary priests.

Sir John had lead mines at Appletreewick and a smelting house at Harefield, near Pateley Bridge. To satisfy his short-term financial needs he resorted to a policy of granting leases for 3000 years or more in return for substantial entry fines.

Since he had no children he settled the estate on his nephew John Yorke who compounded for his recusancy and died in 1638. His son Sir John (1634–1663) had a Catholic guardian, Sir Ingleby Daniell, during his infancy but in 1658 he married a Protestant, Mary Norton of Richmond. During the long minority of their son Thomas (1658-1716) Lady Yorke played an important part in the affairs of the family. In 1664 she embarked on legal proceedings in defence of his property interests and in 1674 she bought the manor of Bewerley.

After the Restoration the Yorkes appear to have lived mainly at Richmond though the Gouthwaite estate remained in their possession.

Gouthwaite Hall A gabled house of two storeys. It was originally built by Peter Yorke, who died in 1589, but later enlarged by his son Sir John (1565-1635) before 1613. The latter's contribution included the hall, the great chamber and two bedrooms.

In 1674 Lady Yorke was taxed on eight hearths.

There was a park adjoining the house. In 1613 William Myers, aged 73, was keeper of the park and game.

(C. H. D. Howard, *Sir John Yorke of Nidderdale* (1939). *Catalogue of the Yorke MSS.* STAC 8/19/10. Wards 5/49. C.10/97/173 and 476/174.)

STUTTON CUM HAZLEWOOD   Barkston Ash

A township within the parish of Tadcaster which consisted of the village of Stutton and the Hazlewood Castle estate. 1674: 32 households.

Hazlewood, 'the chief seat of that particularly famous and ancient family the Vavasors' (William Camden).

It was said that the cathedrals of both York and Lincoln could be seen from Hazlewood (Edmund Gibson, 1695).

Church Hazlewood chapel: a chapel adjoining Hazlewood Castle which had been built by Sir William Vavasour following the grant of a licence in 1286. It was regarded by the church authorities as a public chapel rather than a domestic chapel.

In 1601 the Northern High Commission accepted that the Vavasours had the right to nominate the minister, subject to the approval of the Archbishop of York, but decided that Roger Wetherall, the curate then in charge, should be removed as he already had two other cures. They also ruled that in future the chapel should have churchwardens.

Principal family Vavasour of Hazlewood Castle (baronetcy 1628). Estate revenue: £800 a year (1633); £1000 a year (1660).

The Vavasours were a leading Catholic family who had a long history of recusancy and usually kept a resident chaplain.

William Vavasour (1570-1637) was noted for his great piety and wholehearted devotion to the Catholic faith. Many years before his death he became a brother of the Third Order of St Francis, 'wearing publickly the habit and cord'.

In 1612 he was sentenced to life imprisonment with forfeiture of all his lands and goods for refusing to take the oath of allegiance. From Newgate prison he submitted a petition in which he referred to his great debts and 'extraordinary charge of children'. In 1613 he was able to secure a pardon together with restitution of his property but several years elapsed before he regained his freedom.

In 1629 he and his son Henry were taken into custody. The authorities suspected (rightly) that Henry was a seminary priest but they were soon released through lack of evidence.

The eldest son, Sir Thomas (c.1590-1632), was the first baronet of the family. In 1630 he was required to pay a composition rent of £130 a year for his recusancy and that of his father and their wives. All four of his daughters became nuns.

He was succeeded by his son Sir Walter (1611-1679) who was made a ward of the Crown. His kinsman Thomas Lord Wentworth sought to persuade him to change his religion but he refused.

In the Civil War he and his brothers William and Thomas took up arms for the king. Thomas was killed at the battle of Marston Moor while Sir Walter was allowed to go over to Holland after the surrender of York.

In 1665 Sir Walter was involved in litigation with a fellow recusant, Sir Thomas Gascoigne, who he claimed had designs on the waste belonging to his manor of Hazlewood.

His son Sir Walter (1644-1713) had a chaplain, Paul Stevenson, who was described in a Catholic survey of 1692 as 'an able, witty man'.

Hazlewood Castle A medieval house which was substantially improved by Sir Thomas Vavasour in the early 17th century. He was probably responsible for the two projecting wings.

In 1674 Sir Walter Vavasour was taxed on 20 hearths. His steward, John Coolam, had two taxable hearths.

There was an ancient park belonging to Hazlewood Castle.

(BIHR, High Commission Act Books, RVII/AB19/fo.170 and AB8/fo.200. BL, Lansdowne MSS 153, fols.87, 286. Wards 5/49. C.10/118/103. *CRS*, ix (1911), 111-12.)

SWILLINGTON   Skyrack

A village near Leeds. There was no other village within the parish of Swillington. 1674: 89 households. 1676: 195 persons aged 16 or more.

In the early 17th century the manor of Swillington belonged to John Lord Darcy of Aston, then to Conyers Darcy of Hornby. For many years it was held on lease by the Dyneleys, a minor gentry family.

During the Civil War William Pickering the rector of Swillington joined the royalists at Pontefract where he preached to the troops.

Church All Hallows: Decorated and Perpendicular.

Principal family Lowther of Swillington Hall (and Preston Hall, Great Preston). Estate revenue: £1500 a year (1668); £1700 a year (1688). Coalmines in Great Preston and Swillington.

Sir William Lowther (c.1612-1688) was a Leeds woollen merchant who built up a large estate. In 1656 he bought the manors of Swillington, Great Preston and Astley from Conyers Darcy for £15,000. This transaction was followed almost immediately by litigation in which it was alleged that the property was heavily encumbered as a result of secret and fraudulent conveyances; nevertheless the deal was concluded. In the reign of Charles II there were further acquisitions, including the manor of Rothwell.

On the marriage of his son William in 1662 he settled the Swillington property on him and moved to Great Preston.

Sir William Lowther (1639-1705) was described by Abraham de la Pryme as a Presbyterian in religion. In 1692 he allowed his son William (c.1665-1729) to enter into possession of lands in Swillington worth £800 a year. The latter was created a baronet in 1715.

Swillington Hall An entry in the commonplace book of the Shann family which appears to have been inserted in 1611 contains the comment that the lordship of Swillington 'deserves A better house then it is now'.

Sir William Lowther was taxed on 13 hearths in 1664 and 15 in 1674.

During the years 1692 to 1697 William Lowther (c.1665-1729) and his wife were living in Bedfordshire and the steward, John Cockhill, was entrusted with the task of superintending a major building programme at Swillington Hall.

At the end of the 17th century Swillington Hall was a two-storeyed house of 12 bays.

(A. G. Matthews, *Walker Revised* (1988), 397. C.10/363/41 and 465/195. C.33/313/fo.326 and 330, part 1/fo.10. *Surtees Society*, liv (1870), 69. BL, Additional MSS 38,599, fo.96.)

TADCASTER   Barkston Ash/Ainsty

A market town situated on the River Wharfe between Leeds and York. The parish of Tadcaster included the township of Stutton cum Hazlewood (which is separately noticed) and the hamlets of Catterton and Oxton. 1665: 41 households in Tadcaster on the east side of the river (the Ainsty), 16 in Catterton and 19 in Oxton and Ouston. 1674: 72 households in Tadcaster on the west side of the river (Barkston Ash). 1676: 559 persons aged 16 or more, including 48 Protestant dissenters (parish).

The Wharfe flows by Tadcaster, 'a very small town; which yet I cannot but think was the same with Calcaria .... there are many Coins of Roman Emperours digged up in it .. and the platform of an old Castle still remaining, out of the ruins of which a bridge was made over the Wherf not many years ago' (William Camden).

In his poem on the travels of 'Drunken Barnaby', whch first appeared in 1638, Richard Braithwaite wrote

> Thence to Tadcaster, where stood reared
> A fair Bridge; no Flood appeared:
> Broken Pavements, Beggars waiting:
> Nothing more than Labour hating.

Tadcaster 'is a very good little town for travellers, mostly Inns and little tradesmen's houses' (Celia Fiennes, 1697). In 1639 the landlord of the Swan inn was Thomas Taylor who was also the Tadcaster postmaster. In the Civil War he was executed by the parliamentarians for taking a dispatch to Prince Rupert.

In April 1642 it was reported that the bridge at Tadcaster was in 'greate ruine and decay'. The West Riding magistrates agreed that £120 should be levied for the repair of the west end of the bridge and that it would be appropriate for the city of York and the Ainsty to bear the remainder of the cost.

In November 1642 Ferdinando Lord Fairfax made Tadcaster his command headquarters. According to one account the parliamentarians immediately embarked on preparations for its defence 'by breaking down part of the bridge and planting their ordnance upon it, and by raising a very large and strong fort upon the top of a hill'. In December the Earl of Newcastle mounted an attack from the east and Fairfax retired to Selby but in March 1644 Tadcaster was once more under parliamentarian control.

In 1645 there was an outbreak of the plague.

Church St Mary: Norman in origin but mainly Perpendicular.

In 1623 the chancel was said to be 'in great decay'.

School A free grammar school founded in 1558 by Owen Oglethorpe, Bishop of Carlisle.

Almshouses A hospital for 12 poor people which Oglethorpe also founded in 1558.

(Richard Braithwaite, *Drunken Barnaby's Four Journeys to the North of England* (3rd edition, 1723). *CSP Dom, 1660-1*, 100. *YASRS*, liv (1915), 377. *YAJ*, xv (1900), 237. H. Speight, *Two Thousand Years of Tadcaster History* (1902).)

TANKERSLEY   Strafford and Tickhill

A village between Barnsley and Wakefield. The parish of Tankersley included the larger village of Wortley. 1674: 35 households in Tankersley and 87 in Wortley which had a medieval chapel. 1676: 189 persons aged 16 or more (parish of Tankersley).

The manor of Tankersley was bought by Thomas Lord Wentworth who gave direction in 1635 that the house and park should be properly maintained and the number of deer increased to 300.

In April 1643 royalist troops routed a parliamentarian force on Tankersley Moor.

Church St Peter: Decorated.

Principal family Wortley of Wortley Hall (baronetcy 1611). Estate revenue: £2500 a year (1634); £2000 a year (1665). Iron mills in Wortley, Hunshelf, Silkstone and Wharncliffe Chase and coalmines in Barnsley.

The Wortleys had been seated at Wortley since the 12th century.

Sir Francis Wortley (1591-1652) was described by Anthony Wood as 'an ingenious gentleman' who was noted for his 'hospitality, charity and good neighbourhood'. He was the author of a number of published works, both in prose and verse, and a friend of Ben Jonson. In 1639 he received a visit from John Taylor the Water Poet who enthused about his generous hospitality in a work entitled *Part of this Summer's Travels*.

Wortley was also one of the leading industrialists in the West Riding. This was remarked upon by Roger Dodsworth who wrote that in Wharncliffe Chase he 'haith great iron workes'. During the 1630s the profits of his iron works amounted to at least £800 a year.

In 1626 he was involved in a duel and the following year he was committed to the Fleet prison for defying a Chancery decree.

Despite the enterprise he showed as a landowner he fell heavily into debt. In 1635 he conveyed the bulk of his estate, including the manor of Wortley, to his mother, Elizabeth Countess of Devonshire, in return for a cash payment of £20,000. The property was leased back to him at a rent of £1600 a year but in 1638 the Countess complained in a Chancery suit that he had defaulted.

In the Civil War he was one of the king's most ardent supporters, raising a troop of horse and garrisoning Wortley Hall. Following his capture in June 1644 he was imprisoned in the Tower of London where he remained for several years.

In his *Characters and Elegies*, which appeared in 1646, he wrote that a true English Protestant 'dares call his Sovereigne the Anointed of God .... He conceives passive obedience always due to the power of the King'.

His son Sir Francis (c.1625-1665) served as a royalist colonel and earned some notoriety by ordering the hanging of a deserter without a court martial. In 1650 he was in prison for debt. Eventually, however, he entered into possession of the property sold to his grandmother and the Nottinghamshire estate of his uncle Sir Edward Wortley.

One of the gamekeepers said of him that he was 'a little lean man, with yellowish hair; drunk very hard, and seem'd to be melancolick, and troubled in mind'. After his death Oliver Heywood the nonconformist divine wrote that he had no issue by his wife, 'he having turned her off many yeares agoe'. The estate descended to his illegitimate daughter Anne Newcomen who married Sidney Montagu, a younger son of the Earl of Sandwich, and the family then assumed the name Wortley Montagu.

Wortley Hall The house was rebuilt or substantially improved by Sir Richard Wortley (1561-1603) who completed the work in 1586. In 1674 there were 18 taxable hearths.

During the reign of Charles I a number of men were prosecuted for poaching deer in Wortley Park, the New Park at Wortley and the New Park at Hunshelf.

Roger Dodsworth noted that Wharncliffe Chase, which was within the manor of Wortley, contained red, fallow and roe deer.

(*The Earl of Strafforde's Letters and Dispatches* (ed. W. Knowler) (1739), i, 485. Sheffield Archives, Wharncliffe MSS. Anthony Wood, *Athenae Oxoniensis* (ed. P. Bliss)

(1815), iii, col.391. John Taylor, *Part of this Summer's Travels* (1640), 25-6. C.3/400/83. C.33/220/fo.310. C.38/58/28 November 1627. *Surtees Society*, lxv (1875), 282. A. J. Hopper, 'The Wortley Park Poachers', *Northern History*, xliv (2007).)

TEMPLE NEWSAM   Skyrack

A village within the parish of Whitkirk, near Leeds. 1674: 114 households.

Principal family Ingram of Temple Newsam (peerage 1661 with the title of Viscount Irwin). Estate revenue: £9000 a year (1642); £6300 a year (1660). Coalmines at Temple Newsam, Altofts, Halton and Skelton. Number of household servants: 22 (1632).

Sir Arthur Ingram (c.1565-1642) was the son of a Yorkshireman who had made his fortune as a London merchant. He was himself one of the most enterprising and acquisitive businessmen in England. In 1612 he bought the Temple Newsam estate for £12,000. By the time of his death he was the most substantial landowner in the county.

When he was in Yorkshire he usually resided in his sumptuous town house in York while his eldest son Sir Arthur (c.1596-1655) lived at Temple Newsam.

In the Civil War Sir Arthur Ingram the son was a parliamentarian who served as a member of the West Riding committee, though he does not appear to have been particularly active. In 1643, when he was sojourning in London, he complained that his estate had been 'wholly plundered' by the royalists. Later, in 1649, it was alleged that he had given assistance to the king but nothing was proved against him.

The inscription on his tomb in Whitkirk parish church refers to 'the rare endowments' of his mind and his exceptional piety.

The reduction in the estate revenue by 1660 was due partly to the sale of land and partly to the provision made for other members of the family besides the heir.

Arthur Ingram the third Viscount (1666-1702) served as Lord Lieutenant of the North Riding in the years 1699 to 1702.

Temple Newsam House A memorandum book kept by the Shann family of Methley records the first phase of the building operations undertaken by Sir Arthur Ingram the elder. 'This yere 1622 was A great parte of the new bigginge pulled down and builded up againe the next yeare at the Cost of Sir Arthure Ingram knight who had bought the lordship A little before'. The 'new begginge' was the Tudor house which was partly incorporated into Sir Arthur's palatial mansion. The building programme went on for more than a decade. In 1631 a contract was let for the supply of 150,000 bricks.

A fire which broke out in 1636 was said to have resulted in the loss of household goods to the value of £4000, though the damage to the fabric appears to have been slight.

In terms of size Temple Newsam had few rivals in Yorkshire. A hearth tax return of 1671 records that the number of hearths had recently been increased from 42 to 45.

When Sir Arthur Ingram purchased the estate there were many fallow deer in the park. By 1634, however, it had been let to a tenant for agricultural purposes.

(WYAS, Leeds, Temple Newsam MSS. C.33/259/fo.161. *Calendar, Committee for the Advance of Money*, 185,1107, 1108. BL, Additional MSS 38,559, fo.55. *The Earl of Strafforde's Letters and Dispatches* (ed. W. Knowler) (1739), i, 525. A. F. Upton, *Sir Arthur Ingram c.1565-1642* (1961).)

THORNER   Skyrack

A village to the north-east of Leeds. The parish of Thorner included the village of Shadwell and the hamlet of Scarcroft. 1674: 71 households in Thorner, 18 in Scarcroft and 31 in Shadwell. 1676: 335 persons aged 16 or more (parish).

Since 1311 Thorner had enjoyed the right to hold a weekly market and an annual fair.

In 1669 it was reported that there was a Protestant conventicle at Shadwell.

Church St Peter: Perpendicular.

THORNHILL   Agbrigg and Morley

A village to the south of Dewsbury. The parish of Thornhill contained several villages, including Flockton where a chapel was consecrated in 1699. 1674: 67 households in Thornhill, 42 in Flockton Nether, 32 in Flockton Over and 80 in Shitlington (Netherton). 1676: 600 persons aged 16 or more (parish).

Thornhill had enjoyed market rights since 1317.

In 1623 the area around Thornhill was described as a region in which coal was plentiful and wood in short supply.

Church St Michael: Perpendicular. Within the church there was the Savile family chapel with its extensive range of monuments.

Charles Greenwood, who was rector in the years 1612 to 1643, was a close friend of Strafford and a great benefactor of the parish.

Schools In his will (1642) Charles Greenwood left £500 for the founding of a free grammar school. The trustees he appointed spent £100 of this on the acquisition of a schoolhouse.

There was a school at Netherton in the reign of Charles I and one at Flockton in the reign of Charles II.

Principal family Savile of Thornhill Hall (baronetcy 1611, peerage 1668). Estate revenue: £6500 a year (1651). Coalmining in Thornhill, Brierley and Emley. Fulling mills.

The Savies, who had been seated at Thornhill since the beginning of the 15th century, were one of the richest families in Yorkshire with property in eight counties.

In 1633 Thomas Lord Wentworth (Strafford) advised his nephew Sir William Savile (1612-1644), who had been a ward of the Crown, to moderate his expenditure and avoid excess both in drinking and gaming.

In the Civil War Sir William was a royalist commander who served as governor of Sheffield, then of York where he died. In 1651 some £17,000 of the debts which he left were still unpaid.

His eldest son was George Savile, Marquess of Halifax (1633-1695), the celebrated statesman and author of *The Character of a Trimmer*.

Thornhill Hall A 15th century mansion within a moat. In 1626 the Court of Wards was informed that Dame Anne Savile had ordered 200 trees to be felled and used for 'the newe buildinge and necessary repaireinge of …..Thornehill hall and the outhouses and pales and fences thereto belongeinge'. Wentworth, however, considered that his nephew's houses, plate and furniture were not in accord with his social position.

In 1648, when the house was under siege by parliamentarian troops, there was an accidental explosion which led to a major conflagration. As a result the Savies decided to settle at Rufford in Nottinghamshire. Since references to Thornhill Hall continue to occur in the parish register from 1649 onwards it seems likely that some part of the house survived and that it was occupied by a steward, bailiff or tenant.

The Savies had deer parks at Thornhill, Brierley and Emley.

(Nottinghamshire Record Office, Savile of Rufford MSS. *The Earl of Strafforde's Letters and Dispatches* (ed. W. Knowler) (1739), i, 168-70. Wards 9/95/fols.53, 486-7. *YPRS*, 30 (1907). H. C. Foxcroft, *The Life and Letters of Sir George Savile, 1st Marquis of Halifax* (1898).)

THORNTON IN CRAVEN   Staincliffe and Ewecross

A village to the south-west of Skipton. The parish of Thornton included the hamlet of Earby. 1674: 105 households (township of Thornton). 1676: 270 persons aged 16 or more (parish of Thornton).

Thornton had market rights dating from 1300.

Thomas Drake, who served as rector of Thornton from 1623 to 1645, was a Puritan who preached without a licence. In 1632 he was suspended for a time.

Church St Oswald: Perpendicular.

School In his will (1591) Robert Windle, a clergyman, made provision for the foundation of a free grammar school for boys of his native parish of Thornton. The endowment consisted of lands worth £60 a year. The school was established at Earby in 1623 and its first master was Richard Bawden who held the appointment for many years.

Principal family Lister of Thornton Hall. Estate revenue: £1000 a year (1634); £1500 a year (1700).

Lawrence Lister (d.1609) had a recusant wife but his successors were all firm Protestants.

His son Sir William (1591-1650) was left a minor but since his lands were situated within the Percy Fee belonging to the Clifford family he escaped the financial exactions of the Court of Wards. When granting a lease of property in Thornton in 1633 he reserved to himself and his heirs the royalties of hawking, hunting and fowling during the winter season. In 1637 he made a settlement of his estate and put it on record that he had set apart 80 acres of common in Thornton for the purposes of agricultural improvement.

In the Civil War Sir William took up arms for Parliament and fought at the battle of Marston Moor. His son William (c.1612-1642) was killed at Tadcaster in December 1642 while serving as one of Sir Thomas Fairfax's officers. He was described as 'A religious and resolute gentleman whose death is much lamented'.

In 1681 the guardians of Christopher Lister (c.1662-1701) brought a Chancery suit against Richard Earl of Burlington who owned the neighbouring manor of Carleton. The Earl, they alleged, was claiming manorial rights over 300 acres within Thornton Common despite the fact that the boundary with Carleton Common was clearly marked.

The family died out in the male line in 1701.

Thornton Hall The house, which was probably Elizabethan in origin, was destroyed by royalist forces. In 1644 Parliament heard that Sir William's mansion, barns and stables had been burnt to the ground and agreed that he should be provided with a convenient house and household stuff.

Thornton Hall was never rebuilt, though the Listers remained in possession of the estate.

(R. A. Marchant, *The Puritans and the Church Courts in the Diocese of York 1560-1642* (1960), 244. YAS Library, Lister-Kaye MSS. Sheffield Archives, Wentworth Woodhouse Collection, Bright MSS 85, 86(a). W. E. Preston, 'Arthington Nunnery and Earby Grammar School', *Bradford Antiquary*, New Series, vii (1952). H. L. L. Denny, *Memorials of an Ancient House. A History of the Family of Lister or Lyster* (1913). C.3/364/41. C.10/9/53 and 483/182. C.33/304/fols.373-4.)

THORNTON IN LONSDALE   Staincliffe and Ewecross

A village in the north-west corner of the riding. The parish of Thornton in Lonsdale included the villages of Burton in Lonsdale and Ireby. (The latter was in Lancashire). 1674: 55 households in Thornton and 43 in Burton.

Since 1307 Burton had enjoyed the right to hold a weekly market and two annual fairs.

In 1640 Thornton Bridge, which spanned the River Greta, was reported to be 'in great decay'.

At the beginning of the 17th century the Redmans of Thornton Hall headed a small Catholic community. In 1604 there were 14 recusants, including Marmaduke Redman and several members of his family.

His grandson Sir John Redman (1604-1645) appears to have had no Catholic ties. In the Civil War he took up arms for the king and was eventually appointed governor of Pontefract. His eldest son William, who was a royalist captain, was with him in Pontefract Castle and lost his life during the siege in 1645.

Church St Oswald: Norman.

(*YASRS*, liv (1915), 212, 214. E. Peacock (ed.), *A List of the Roman Catholics in the County of York in 1604* (1872), 21.)

THORP ARCH   Ainsty

A village to the south-east of Wetherby which was situated on the River Wharfe. There was no other village within the parish. 1665: 44 households (township of Thorpe Arch). 1676: 148 persons aged 16 or more (parish).

Church All Saints: Norman.

School At an ecclesiastical visitation in 1637 John Lith of Thorp Arch was presented for teaching without a licence.

(*YAJ*, xv (1900), 238.)

THRYBERGH   Strafford and Tickhill

A small village on the River Don near Rotherham. The parish of Thrybergh included part of the village of Dalton; the other part was in the parish of Rotherham. 1674: 30 households in Thrybergh and 27 in Dalton. 1676: 220 persons aged 16 or more (parish of Thrybergh).

Church St Leonard: Norman, Decorated and Perpendicular.

School In the middle years of the 17th century Thomas Skeynes acted as both minister and schoolmaster at Thrybergh.

Principal family Reresby of Thrybergh Hall (baronetcy 1642). Estate revenue: £1150 a year (1629); £1200 a year (1642); £1800 a year (1689). Coalmining at Denaby and Hooton Roberts.

The Reresbys were seated at Thrybergh from the early 14th century until the beginning of the 18th century. During the early 17th century they gradually abandoned their Catholic faith.

Sir Thomas Reresby (1557-1619), who was a Church Papist, employed a recusant schoolmaster, George Eglisham, to teach his children. He had a larger estate than any of his predecessors but 'lived to sell more then he bought and left the remainder much encombred'.

His financial difficulties were mainly the result of extravagance. He rarely went to church or on any journey 'without a great many followers in blew coats and badges, and beyond the usuall number for men of his quality and fortune'.

His son Sir George (1590-1629), who was a Protestant, had 'a good Naturall witt and Judgement'. He took a keen interest in horse breeding but it proved to be unprofitable.

Sir John Reresby (1611-1646) was a man of some learning who wrote poems and essays. He also created elaborate gardens at Thrybergh Hall and introduced a wide variety of fruit and flowers. In the Civil War he decided, after some hesitation, to support the king and was eventually captured. His house was plundered by the parliamentarians.

Sir John Reresby (1634-1689) was a politician who remained loyal to James II in 1688. He is now chiefly remembered for his voluminous memoirs and his family history. His son Sir William (1669-c.1735) was a wastrel and a gamester who disposed of the whole estate and died in poverty.

Thrybergh Hall Thomas Reresby (c.1537-1587), Sir Thomas Reresby (1557-1619) and Sir John Reresby (1634-1689) all made additions and improvements to what was probably an early Tudor building.

On taking up residence in 1665 Sir John found the house in a ruinous condition. During the years 1666 to 1674 he encased some lath and plaster walls in stone, erected a tower at the west end to balance an existing one at the east end, wainscoted several rooms and painted the whole house. In addition he built new stables and a dovecote. According to the hearth tax returns the number of hearths increased from 17 in 1664 to 22 in 1674.

In 1670 he enlarged the medieval deer park. Subsequently, in 1674, he made fish ponds in the park and stocked them with tench and carp.

(BL, Additional MSS 29,440 and 29,442-3. Wards 5/49. YAS Library, MS 329 (poems and essays of Sir John Reresby, 1st baronet). WYAS, Leeds, MSS of the Earl of Mexborough. *Memoirs of Sir John Reresby* (ed. A. Browning and others) (1991). C.33/244/fo.226; 290/fo.731; 300/fo.506; and 302/fols.46-7.)

THURNSCOE Strafford and Tickhill

A small village to the east of Barnsley. There was no other village within the parish. 1674: 22 households (township of Thurnscoe). 1676: 80 persons aged 16 or more (parish).

In 1641 James Feild the constable of Thurnscoe was involved in a fight with Gilbert Waddilove, another resident of the parish. At the Doncaster quarter sessions both men were found guilty of assault, along with four Thurnscoe labourers who had assisted Feild.

Church St Helen: Norman in origin.

(*YASRS*, liv (1915), 330.)

TICKHILL   Strafford and Tickhill

A market town near the border with Nottinghamshire. The parish of Tickhill included several hamlets. 1674: 175 households in Tickhill and 10 in Stancill cum Wellingley. Tickhill consisted of three districts: Sunderland, Northgate and Westgate. 1676: 500 persons aged 16 or more (parish of Tickhill).

On the outbreak of the Civil War the royalists took possession of the town but in July 1644 the garrison in Tickhill Castle surrendered to the parliamentarians.

Church St Mary: Early English but mainly Perpendicular. One of the largest churches in the West Riding.

Castle A Norman fortress with later improvements. After the Civil War it was partly demolished.

School There was a grammar school in 1548. During the reigns of Elizabeth and James I a number of bequests were made with the aim of putting it on a sounder financial footing.

According to Roger Dodsworth £5 a year was paid by the Crown 'towards a free school'.

Almshouses Dodsworth refers to the Maison Dieu, near the church, which housed four poor people. Other medieval establishments may have fallen into disuse.

Principal family Hansby of Tickhill Castle. Estate revenue: £1000 a year (1640).

The Hansbys were a Catholic family.

Sir Ralph Hansby (1589-1643) had a large estate settled on him by his uncle Ralph Hansby of Beverley but managed to alienate him through his 'deceit and insolence'. In 1617 his uncle revoked the deed of settlement and divided the estate among his daughters. Although Sir Ralph contested this decision his eventual share of the property fell well short of his expectations.

Hansby served as bailiff to Queen Henrietta Maria of the bailiwick of Tickhill and had leases of the castle and other parts of her estate in the town. Although his first wife, Dame Jane, was a recusant he preferred to conform. After her death he married a rich widow, Elizabeth Shillito, who brought him the manor of Seacroft together with a colliery.

On the outbreak of the Civil War he garrisoned the castle on behalf of the king and acted as governor. In 1644 the Court of Wards granted the wardship and lands of his son Ralph to a parliamentarian officer, Lionel Copley.

Ralph Hansby (1632-c.1700) and his wife were presented for recusancy on several occasions during the latter part of the century. Significantly, James II appointed him as a deputy lieutenant and mayor of Doncaster.

The Hansby Residence The Hansbys lived in a substantial mansion within the curtain wall of Tickhill Castle. This was built or substantially improved by Sir Ralph Hansby.

In 1674 Ralph Hansby was taxed on 24 hearths.

(BL, Additional Charter 6275. C.8/131/102. C.10/32/62. C.22/773/11.)

TODWICK   Strafford and Tickhill

A small village to the east of Sheffield. There was no other village in the parish. 1674: 21 households (township of Todwick). 1676: 98 persons aged 16 or more (parish).

The manor of Todwick had belonged to the Wastneys family of Headon in Nottinghamshire since the 13th century. In 1677 Sir Edmund Wastneys sold it to Thomas Osborne, Earl of Danby whose family seat was at Kiveton in the same neighbourhood (see the entry for Harthill). At the end of the 17th century the manor was worth £176 a year, excluding the park.

In the early 17th century Todwick had two Puritan rectors, both of whom had been presented by the Wastneys family. Richard Hubbald, who was the minister in the years 1591 to 1623, was said to have become weary of the Church's ceremonial requirements. His successor, Thomas Hancock, who held the living until 1647, was known to the ecclesiastical authorities as a man who had a marked aversion to wearing the surplice. At the visitation of 1632 he was also accused of omitting parts of the Prayer Book services.

Church St Peter and St Paul: Norman, Decorated and Perpendicular.

(BL, Additional MSS 28,088, fo.126. R. A. Marchant, *The Puritans and the Church Courts in the Diocese of York 1560-1642* (1960), 143, 256, 304-5.)

TONG   Agbrigg and Morley

A village near Bradford and a chapelry of semi-independent status within the parish of Birstall. 1674: 81 households.

Church St James: Norman and Perpendicular. A public chapel under the patronage of the Tempest family.

Principal family Tempest of Tong Hall (baronetcy 1664). Estate revenue: £650 a year (1642); £1000 a year (1674).

Henry Tempest (1621-1658) was an infant at his father's death in 1623 and became a ward of the Crown. His mother, Katherine, soon remarried and her second husband,

Dr Henry Fairfax, who was a clergyman, assumed the role of guardian. Subsequently, in 1651, Tempest complained in a Chancery bill that Fairfax had allowed Tong Hall and the outhouses, orchards, gardens and woods to fall into 'very great ruine and decay'. The arbitrators who were appointed to look into the matter reported that there was no evidence to support this allegation but concluded that Fairfax owed the plaintiff £445 5s 0d.

In 1639 Tempest married without the consent or knowledge of his guardian. In the Civil War he took up arms for Parliament, no doubt on account of his Puritan convictions; and in the Commonwealth period he served as a magistrate and an MP for the West Riding.

In a memorandum written in 1648 he advised his eldest son to 'Oppress not thy tenants, but let them live comfortably of thy hands as thou desirest to live of their Labours, that their soules may bless thee and that it may go well with thy seed after thee. Enquire and search out diligently for a Godly Minister to preach the Gospel to thy people'.

John Tempest (1645-1693) not only acquired a baronetcy but added considerably to the estate through his marriage to an heiress.

Tong Hall According to his memorandum of 1648 Henry Tempest had 'delighted in building'. His building operations may have begun as early as 1639 when his guardian allowed him to take over most of the estate. The house which he left was nevertheless of modest size: in 1674 Sir John Tempest was taxed on eight hearths.

Sir George Tempest (1672-1745) rebuilt the house in the early years of the 18th century. In 1708 Ralph Thoresby described it as 'not yet finished'.

(WYAS, Bradford, Tempest of Tong MSS. W. Robertshaw, 'The Manor of Tong', *Bradford Antiquary*, New Series, viii (1962). BL, Additional MSS 40,670, fo.16. Wards 5/49. C.10/11/122.)

TREETON   Strafford and Tickhill

A village to the east of Sheffield. The parish of Treeton included the village of Brampton en le Morthen and part of the village of Ulley; the other part was in the parish of Aston. 1674: 44 households in Treeton, 21 in Brampton and 20 in Ulley. 1676: 286 persons aged 16 or more (parish).

Sherland Adams was the rector of both Treeton and Eyam in Derbyshire. In 1644 he was forced out of his livings, which were worth £300 a year, on account of his support for the royalist cause. After the Restoration, however, he was able to regain possession of both livings.

Church St Helen: Norman, Early English, Decorated and Perpendicular.

(A. G. Matthews, *Walker Revised* (1988), 388.)

WADWORTH   Strafford and Tickhill

A village between Doncaster and Tickhill. There was no other village within the parish of Wadworth. 1674: 63 households.

Church St John Evangelist: Norman, Early English and Perpendicular.

The parish was under peculiar jurisdiction.

Principal family Copley of Wadworth Hall. Estate revenue: £600 a year (1675).

William Copley (1575-1658) was an enterprising landowner who farmed on a considerable scale. In 1632, after taking a lease of the demesne lands of a neighbouring manor, he handed over Wadworth Hall and most of his freehold property to his son Christopher (c.1605-1664). The latter set about improving the estate by building and repairing houses for the tenants, planting orchards, hopyards and timber trees and making enclosures for development purposes. Not long before the Civil War there was a fire at Wadworth Hall which destroyed barns, stables and other outhouses and as a result he was obliged to undertake a rebuilding programme which cost him some £500.

In the Civil War Christopher Copley and his brother Lionel (1607-1675) were both heavily engaged as parliamentarian officers. Driven by Puritan fervour, they had their flags inscribed with the words 'Reformation' and 'Nay, but as a Captaine of the Hoste of the Lord am I now come'. Christopher had command of the cavalry force which defeated the royalists at the battle of Sherburn in 1645. His brother, who served as commissary general, was one of the Presbyterian MPs who were secluded in 1648 as a result of Pride's Purge. Early in the war the royalists sequestered the Wadworth estate but it was soon recovered.

During the Commonwealth period Christopher Copley was involved in a bitter financial dispute with his father and brother and went so far as to bring suits against them in the Court of Chancery. William Copley, for his part, complained that in spite of his generosity he had been badly let down when he fell heavily into debt. Ironically, Lionel Copley succeeded to the estate on the death of his brother.

In 1709 the family inherited substantial property from the Copleys of Sprotborough.

Wadworth Hall When Christopher Copley returned to Wadworth in 1644 the hall was in such a poor condition that he decided to rebuild it. The new house cost him 'at least £600'. In the reign of Charles II Lionel Copley appears to have undertaken some further building work: the hearth tax returns record 14 hearths in 1664 and 17 in 1674.

The Copleys also owned Nether Hall in Wadworth.

(C.7/418/25. C.10/55/32. C.33/261/fols.816-7.)

WAKEFIELD   Agbrigg and Morley

A town situated on the River Calder which was 'famous for its Cloath trade, largeness, neat buildings, great markets' (William Camden). The parish of Wakefield contained several villages, including Horbury which had a dependent chapel. Horbury and Stanley (with Wrenthorpe) are separately noticed. 1674: 404 households (township of Wakefield, consisting of three wards, Kirkgate, Northgate and Westgate). 1676: 2400 persons aged 16 or more, including 300 Protestant dissenters (parish of Wakefield).

Writing in the mid-17th century Thomas Fuller observed that the expression 'merry Wakefield' mystified him, though he acknowledged that the town was 'seated in a fruitful soil, and cheap country'.

Wakefield was one of the most prosperous towns in Yorkshire. Many of its inhabitants were engaged in the processes involved in the finishing of cloth produced in the neighbouring villages. In the course of the 17th century its Friday cloth market became the most important of all the West Riding wool markets.

Following a formal inquiry in 1622 a body of 16 men known as the Governors of the Poor was allocated responsibility for managing the numerous charities in the town.

There were outbreaks of the plague in 1625 and 1645.

The main bridge required frequent repairs. In 1638 the West Riding magistrates were informed of 'the great ruyne and decay of the stone bridge at Wakefield …. and the chappell adjoyneinge unto the saide bridge, which is a great staye and helpe to the same'. Accordingly it was decided that £80 should be levied within the riding for its renovation. In 1663 the cost of repairs was put at £228.

During the Civil War the town periodically changed hands. In May 1643 Sir Thomas Fairfax surprised the royalist garrison by mounting a night attack. After some fierce street fighting he emerged triumphant and took 1400 prisoners, including General George Goring. Shortly afterwards the Earl of Newcastle recaptured the town but in July 1644 it was reported that Scottish troops were quartered there.

James Lister, the Puritan vicar of Wakefield, was a royalist who preached to the troops in Pontefract Castle. He was deprived of his living by the parliamentarians but was reinstated in 1660.

In the late 17th century a coach service was in operation between Wakefield and London.

Churches All Saints: Norman, Early English, Decorated and Perpendicular. The great spire was built about 1420.

An organ which was the gift of Sir Thomas Wentworth (later Earl of Strafford) was destroyed in the Commonwealth period.

The chapel on the main bridge was built in the 14th century. In 1695 it was said to be 'much defac'd'.

In the reign of Charles II two nonconformist congregations were formed, one in Kirkgate and the other at Flanshaw Hall.

School There was a school at Wakefield as early as 1275. The Free Grammar School of Queen Elizabeth was established by royal charter in 1591 and built in 1598 on a site provided by George Savile of Haselden Hall. In 1640 Roger Dodsworth wrote that the school was 'a very beautyfull house and pleasantly situated on a piece of ground distant a bow-shoot of the north from the Church'.

In the 17th century the masters included Philip Isack, Robert Doughty and John Baskerville.

Almshouses In his will (1568) Henry Savile of Lupset Hall made provision for the building of a hospital for six poor people. Further almshouses were founded in 1580, 1647 and 1669 for a total of 25 poor men and women.

House of Correction The idea of establishing a house of correction was first conceived in 1595. In 1611 the West Riding magistrates agreed that a house of correction should be built at Wakefield for the whole riding and that £700 should be levied for that purpose. Three years later they noted that it 'hath much suppressed the number of sturdie and incorrigeable beggers and rogues and other dissolute and disordered persons within this ridding'.

The house of correction was often used as a prison as well as a workhouse. In 1669 a large number of Quakers were jailed there.

Inns There were many inns in Wakefield, among them the Golden Cock and the Horsehead, both in Westgate, the Mermaid, the Bull, the White Bear, the White Hart, the Cross Keys and the Black Swan. In 1635 Sir William Brereton lodged at the Bull and described it as 'an honest and excellent house'.

(*YAJ*, v (1877-8), 371. A. G. Matthews, *Walker Revised* (1988), 395. *YASRS*, liv (1915), 10. *Surtees Society*, cxxiv (1914), 4. M. H. Peacock, *History of the Free Grammar School of Queen Elizabeth at Wakefield* (1892). S. H. Waters, *Wakefield in the Seventeenth Century* (1933). J. W. Walker, *Wakefield: Its History and People* (1939).)

WALTON   Ainsty

A village near Tadcaster. There was no other village within the parish of Walton. 1665: 60 households. 1676: 160 persons aged 16 or more, including 26 recusants.

Church St Peter: mainly 14th century but with a Norman tower.

A new vicarage was built in 1664.

Walton Hall The original seat of the Fairfax family of Gilling Castle in the North Riding (see Gilling). It was still in use in the 17th century, though Gilling Castle was the family's principal residence. Among the rooms listed in an inventory of 1624 were the hall, the great chamber, the outer parlour and the gallery.

In 1665 Charles Viscount Fairfax was taxed on 13 hearths.
There was a park adjoining the hall.
(*Archaeologia*, xlviii (1882).)

WARMFIELD   Agbrigg and Morley/Osgoldcross

A village between Wakefield and Normanton. The parish of Warmfield included the village of Sharlston. 1674: 64 households in Warmfield and 46 in Sharlston. 1676: 331 persons aged 16 or more (parish of Warmfield).

In 1655 the vicar, Thomas Robinson, was ejected by the West Riding commissioners for the removal of scandalous ministers.

Church St Peter (Kirkthorpe): Perpendicular.

School In 1660 Dame Mary Bolles founded a grammar school whose functions included the education of 10 poor boys until they were ready to be apprenticed.

Almshouses Freeston's Hospital at Kirkthorpe was founded by John Freeston and completed in 1595. It housed seven poor men.

Principal family Stringer of Sharlston Hall. Estate revenue: £500 a year (1642). Coalmining in Sharlston and Crofton. Number of servants: 13 (1617); 20 (1640).

The Stringers were enterprising landowners who derived much of their income from direct farming and coalmining. Thomas Stringer (1586-1651) noted in his commonplace book that in 1642 he had received £337 from the sale of wheat, barley and peas.

Stringer was in Pontefract Castle when it was surrendered to the parliamentarians in 1645. Although he claimed that he had never taken up arms for the king he was imprisoned at York and required to compound for his estate. In compounding he alleged that parliamentarian troops had taken from him on several occasions money, plate and household stuff to the value of £3500 and cattle and corn worth £3700.

As he had no issue he settled the estate on his cousin Thomas Stringer of Whiston (1625-1668) who had to fight off attempts by the Commonwealth authorities to force him to compound. Another matter of concern to him was the coalmining activity of a Catholic neighbour, William Ireland of Crofton. Ireland's mines were not far from his own colliery at Sharlston and he feared that the price of coal in the area would fall so low that he could no longer make a profit. In 1655 the two men entered into a formal agreement in which Ireland undertook not to dig coal in his various manors for 21 years in return for a payment of £120 a year. In subsequent litigation Ireland complained that he could have made £230 a year from the sale of coal.

In 1664 Stringer let his delphs and mines of coal in Sharlston and Crofton, together with some other property, for seven years at a rent of £465 a year.

With the death of his son in 1681 the male line expired.

Sharlston Hall A gabled house built by the previous owners, the Flemings, in 1574.

In 1674 there were 14 taxable hearths.

(A. G. Matthews, *Walker Revised* (1988), 397. W. K. Jordan, *The Charities of Rural England 1480-1660* (1961), 279-80, 291, 346. Nottingham University Library, Galway of Serlby MSS. YAS Library, MS311 (Stringer commonplace book). *YASRS*, xviii (1895), 221. C.7/457/73.)

WARMSWORTH   Strafford and Tickhill

A village to the south-west of Doncaster. There was no other village within the parish. 1674: 29 households (township of Warmsworth). 1676: 40 persons aged 16 or more (parish).

The Bosvile family had lived at Warmsworth for several generations before their purchase of the manor in 1633. Gervase Bosvile (1571-1621) was a minor but efficient landowner who farmed on a considerable scale and engaged in piecemeal enclosure. His son Thomas succeeded him while still a minor and was made a ward of the Crown. Susan Bosvile the widow informed the Court of Wards that she had no fewer than nine children to bring up.

Thomas Bosvile (1607-1659) added substantially to the estate which he had inherited. This was probably due less to good management than to the fact that both his wives were heiresses. In the Civil War he was initially considered to be a royalist but before long he had become a member of the parliamentary committee for the West Riding.

After his death the Warmsworth estate descended to his three daughters who sold it in 1668 to John Battie of Wadworth.

George Fox the Quaker leader recorded in his journal that in 1652 he went to the steeple house (as he called it) at Warmsworth 'and they shutt ye doore of mee'. Even worse, a warrant was issued for his arrest at the instigation of Thomas Rokeby, the rector of Warmsworth. In contrast, he was able to write in 1660 that 'wee had a heavenly meetinge at Warmsworth of freindes in ye ministry and severall others'.

Eventually Warmsworth had a Quaker meeting house and burial ground.

Church St Peter: 13th century or earlier.

(Wards 5/49. WYAS, Leeds, Battie Wrightson MSS, BW/R/4. *YASRS*, ix (1890), 142-3. N. Penney (ed.), *The Journal of George Fox* (1911), i, 34, 37, 355.)

WATH UPON DEARNE   Strafford and Tickhill

A village to the north of Rotherham which was situated on the south bank of the River Dearne. The parish of Wath contained a number of villages and hamlets, including Wentworth which had a medieval chapel. There was also a medieval chapel in the village of Swinton which straddled the boundary between the parishes of Wath and Mexborough. The villages of Hoyland and Wentworth are separately noticed. 1674: 46 households in Wath, 69 in Brampton Bierlow and 38 in Swinton. 1676: 300 persons aged 16 or more (parish, but excluding the chapelry of Wentworth and possibly the chapelry of Swinton).

Since 1312 Wath had enjoyed the right to hold a weekly market and an annual fair.

Church All Saints: Norman, Early English, Decorated and Perpendicular.

School In his will (1647) Anthony Sawdrie, a clergyman, settled a rent-charge of £2 13s 4d a year which was to be paid to a schoolmaster who would teach poor children of Wath, Brampton Bierlow and Swinton. He had previously made provision for the endowment of apprenticeships for youths of the parish.

In his will (1661) Thomas Wombwell the vicar of Wath bequeathed the sum of £30 for the purpose of building a schoolhouse there. The building work was completed in 1663.

(W. K. Jordan, *The Charities of Rural England 1480-1660* (1961), 289, 342-3.)

WENTWORTH   Strafford and Tickhill

A village within the parish of Wath upon Dearne, near Rotherham. 1674: 72 households (township of Wentworth). 1676: 426 persons aged 16 or more (chapelry of Wentworth, including some neighbouring hamlets).

Church Holy Trinity: a public chapel situated in the village of Wentworth which was re-consecrated in 1491. It was largely rebuilt by William Earl of Strafford in 1684 at a cost of £700. Monuments to members of the Wentworth family of Wentworth Woodhouse.

Almshouses Almshouses for six poor men and six poor women were founded in 1697 in accordance with the will of William Earl of Strafford.

Principal family Wentworth of Wentworth Woodhouse (baronetcy 1611; ennobled with title of Viscount Wentworth 1628, then Earl of Strafford 1640). Estate revenue: £5000 a year (1619); £5700 a year (1633). Coalmines at Wentworth and Hooton Roberts. Number of servants: 50 (c.1620).

Sir William Wentworth (1562-1614) inherited one of the largest estates in Yorkshire but was involved in protracted litigation and had to make provision for a considerable number of children. In a memorandum drawn up in 1604 he urged his son Thomas to be 'just, humble, charitable, and mercifull ... moderate in all thinges and frugale in expenses'.

Sir Thomas Wentworth (1593-1641), who became Earl of Strafford shortly before his death, was one of the ablest of Crown officials in the Stuart era. As Lord Lieutenant of Yorkshire and Lord President of the Council in the North he was for a time the most powerful man in northern England and he was not slow to assert his authority in the face of opposition. As Lord Deputy of Ireland he pushed ahead with his reform programme in defiance of vested interests. During his time in Ireland he acquired substantial estates there, partly by purchase and partly by more controversial means. According to one report he gave direction before his execution that his son should surrender any right to Irish lands which had not been legally purchased.

His friend Sir George Radcliffe wrote that 'His family was great, but very orderly; prayers twice a day read by his chaplaine, an able divine, usinge the leiturgie'. As a landowner he paid close attention to matters of estate management, including the scope for improvement by enclosure. He also established a workshop at Wentworth for the manufacture of glass.

According to Radcliffe his second wife, Lady Arabella, was heavily involved in charitable work: there was no person 'in all her neighbourhood that was poore or sicke that she did not particularly take care on, dayly sendinge to them supplyes and herselfe at fit opportunityes visiting them'.

The estate descended to William Earl of Strafford (1626-1695) who appears to have inherited few of his father's qualities. In November 1642 Parliament gave him permission to go abroad and for some years he lived in France. He returned to England about the end of 1651 and having taken the oath of abjuration was able to recover his estate which had been under sequestration. During the 1650s he was in severe financial difficulties which may have been partly due to extravagance and resorted to the sale of property on a considerable scale. Although Charles II granted him a pension of £2000 a year his problems were far from over. In 1673 he told the Earl of Derby that his rents in England were rather less than £3000 a year and that his Irish rents were about the same but, on the other hand, his debts amounted to nearly £40,000. He therefore hoped for some official employment which 'may perhaps seeme almost a thing necessary to prevent my ruine'.

Wentworth Woodhouse When Sir William Wentworth succeeded his father in 1588 Wentworth Woodhouse was 'verie ruynous' and a repair programme had to be put in hand. In his memorandum of 1604 he advised his son Thomas to avoid superfluity in building. Despite this warning Strafford undertook some major building work before departing for Ireland in 1633. Writing from Wentworth Woodhouse in October 1624 he told a friend that 'I have allmost finished my this yeare's building'.

In Strafford's time Wentworth Woodhouse was a large E-shaped mansion which was surrounded by a variety of outbuildings, including stables, a coach-house, two tower blocks with lodgings, an orangery, a banqueting house and summer houses. Within the grounds there were formal gardens and a bowling green.

Willliam Earl of Strafford was taxed on 50 hearths in 1664 and 43 in 1674.

The Wentworths had deer parks at Wentworth, Gawthorpe, Kimberworth and Tankersley.

(Sheffield Archives, Wentworth Woodhouse Collection. *The Earl of Strafforde's Letters and Dispatches* (ed. W. Knowler) (1739). *Wentworth Papers 1597-1628* (ed. J. P. Cooper), *Camden Fourth Series*, 12 (1973), 9-24, 214, 319-26. C. V. Wedgwood, *Thomas Wentworth, first Earl of Strafford* (1961). BL, Additional MSS 33,589, fos.145-6. C.33/288/fo.323.)

WEST ARDSLEY   Agbrigg and Morley

See Woodkirk.

WEST BRETTON   Staincross

A hamlet to the north-west of Barnsley which was in the parish of Silkstone. 1674: 11 households (township of West Bretton).

Church St Bartholomew: a public chapel founded in the 14th century.

Principal family Wentworth of Bretton Hall (baronetcy 1664). Estate revenue: £600 a year (1630); £1000 a year (1675). Coalmine in Cumberworth Moor; iron forges at West Bretton, Bullcliff and Cawthorne.

William Wentworth (c.1604-1641) succeeded his father in 1638 but was declared a lunatic in 1640. His uncle John Wentworth had been similarly affected, though in 1615 it was said that he had been cured.

Since William left no issue the estate passed to his brother Thomas (1610-1675) who in 1643 acquired considerable property through his marriage to an heiress, Grace Popeley. During the Civil War he served as a royalist officer and was imprisoned in 1645. According to his own reckoning the financial losses which he sustained as a result of his loyalty amounted to at least £4000. After the Restoration he was rewarded first with a knighthood, then with a baronetcy. Oliver Heywood depicts him as a magistrate who was very active in the persecution of nonconformists. His funeral (which cost £1127) was attended by 4000 persons.

Bretton Hall A house which was at least partly medieval though there may also have been Tudor features. A comparison of the inventories made in 1635, 1638 and 1675 suggests that Sir Thomas Wentworth was responsible for some improvements. In 1674 he was taxed on 13 hearths. Among the principal rooms listed in 1675 are the hall, the great chamber, the dining parlour, King Henry's parlour and the little new parlour.

(YAS Library, Bretton Hall MSS. Wards 9/219/fo.3. BL, Additional MSS 4460, fo.20 and Additional Charter 58,267. *YASRS*, cxxxiv (1972).)

WESTON   Claro

A village near Otley. The parish of Weston included the village of Askwith. 1674: 29 households in Weston and 61 in Askwith. 1676: 245 persons aged 16 or more (parish of Weston).

Church All Saints: Norman and Perpendicular with a porch dated 1686.

Principal family Vavasour of Weston Hall. Estate revenue: £600 a year (1628); £600 a year (1660). Coalmining in Baildon.

Sir Mauger Vavasour (1553-1611) was an enterprising landowner who had a number of coalmines in an enclosed part of Baildon Common known as North Wood. Perhaps because of his expenditure on building he was selling land from 1602 onwards.

His son William (1581-1650) was a largely inactive royalist in the Civil War when he described himself as very aged. On the other hand, his eldest son Thomas (c.1605-1661) appeared in arms for the king.

Weston Hall A four-storeyed Elizabethan mansion built by Sir Mauger Vavasour. He was also responsible for the banqueting house in the garden.

The house had 24 taxable hearths in 1664 and 1674.

There was a park adjoining Weston Hall.

(W. P. Baildon, *Baildon and the Baildons* (1913, 1924, 1926). C.8/75/2. C.10/55/171.)

WETHERBY   Claro

A small market town on the River Wharfe which was situated in the parish of Spofforth. 1674: 66 households (township of Wetherby).

Wetherby is 'a notable trading town' (William Camden).

The bridge at Wetherby was medieval in origin. In 1614 it was reported that the pavement of the bridge was decaying because of 'the continuall travell of cole waines over the same'.

In 1645 there was an outbreak of the plague.

Church St James: a public chapel which was described in the Commonwealth period as 'of ancient erection'.

(*YASRS*, liv (1915), 17. Emily Wardman, *Wetherby: its People and Customs* (1938). R. Unwin, *Wetherby: the History of a Yorkshire Market Town* (1986).)

WHEATLEY CUM LONG SANDALL   Strafford and Tickhill

Two neighbouring hamlets within the parish of Doncaster which were linked together for administrative purposes. 1674: 14 households.

Principal families (1) Anstruther of Wheatley Hall. Estate revenue: £1500 a year (1640).

During the early 17th century the manor of Wheatley frequently changed hands. In 1636 it was bought by Sir Robert Anstruther, a Scotsman with a considerable reputation as a soldier, diplomat and antiquary.

Through his marriage to Mary Swyft in 1616 he eventually became a major landowner. Following the death of her brother Barnham Viscount Carlingford in 1635 she inherited a large estate in Yorkshire and Nottinghamshire.

Anstruther appears to have taken no part in the Civil War. After his death in 1645 his son Robert, who was then aged 15, was subjected to the attentions of the Court of Wards. When his mother died in 1652 he was finally able to enter into possession of the estate and shortly afterwards he was involved in litigation with his sisters over their marriage portions. According to Sir John Reresby he was 'very extravagant'. In London he fell in with a group of ex-officers and younger brothers with no fortunes who 'depended of him for their meat and drinke, he usually paying the reckning for the whole company whilst he had any mony'.

Within a few years he had run through his entire estate.

(2) Cooke of Wheatley Hall (baronetcy 1661). Estate revenue: £1700 a year (1658).

Brian Cooke (c.1570-1653), a Doncaster merchant, was primarily responsible for the emergence of the family as one of the most substantial gentry families in the West Riding. In the Civil War he provided the royalist forces with money, horses and arms.

His son Brian (1620-1661), who was a barrister, bought the manor of Wheatley in 1658 for £3000. He left no issue and was succeeded by his brother Sir George (1628 – 1683) whose baronetcy was granted in response to his claim that the family's loyalty to the Crown had cost them £15,000.

Sir George died unmarried and the estate passed to his brother Sir Henry (1633-c.1688) and his descendants.

Wheatley Hall In 1674 Sir George Cooke was taxed on 22 hearths.

A new house was built about 1680. This was a mansion in the classical style which was three storeys in height besides a basement.

(C.6/133/166. C.9/2/61. C.10/45/3. C.22/743/34. *Memoirs of Sir John Reresby* (ed. A. Browning and others) (1991), 4. Sheffield Archives, Cooke of Wheatley MSS.)

WHISTON   Strafford and Tickhill

A village to the south-east of Rotherham. The parish of Whiston included only part of the village; the other part was in the parish of Rotherham. 1674: 69 households (township of Whiston). 1676: 230 persons aged 16 or more (parish of Whiston).

The Stringers of Whiston were minor gentry who supported the king in the Civil War. In 1651 they inherited the estate of Thomas Stringer of Sharlston, the head of the senior branch.

Church St Mary Magdalene: Norman.

School In the reign of James I Andrew Wade was master of a school at Whiston. Subsequently he was appointed master of Sheffield Grammar School.

WHITGIFT   Osgoldcross

A village to the south-east of Howden on the south bank of the River Ouse. The parish of Whitgift contained several villages, including Swinefleet which had a dependent chapel. 1674: 35 households in Whitgift, 53 in Ousefleet, 74 in Reedness and 58 in Swinefleet.

In 1232 Whitgift had been granted the right to hold a weekly market and an annual fair; and in 1305 comparable rights had been conferred on Swinefleet.

In the 17th century there was a ferry at Whitgift which provided a means of passage across the River Ouse.

In 1638 Thomas Stephenson of Whitgift was indicted for assaulting the constable, Robert Selley, and seizing a warrant which had been issued against him. He had been accused by other residents of the parish of falsifying his accounts as an overseer of the poor and in 1640 the magistrates ordered him to pay the sum of £3 15s 4d to the current overseers.

At the same time the inhabitants of Ousefleet were complaining that the accounts of Henry Petch, who had been serving as constable there, were 'unjust, and not to be allowed of'. The justices decided that the matter should be thoroughly investigated but were subsequently informed that Petch was adopting delaying tactics.

Church St Mary Magdalene: Decorated and Perpendicular. The church is said to have been rebuilt in 1304.

The parish was subject to the peculiar jurisdiction of a Prebendary of York.

School Robert Todd, a Puritan divine, was appointed curate of Swinefleet in 1621 and over the next few years he also kept a school at Whitgift. Among the pupils educated there was his brother Andrew who was admitted to Cambridge in 1624.

(*YASRS*, liv (1915), 65, 162, 180, 181, 184-5, 197, 203-4. R. A. Marchant, *The Puritans and the Church Courts in the Diocese of York 1560-1642* (1960), 284-5.)

WHITKIRK   Skyrack

A hamlet to the east of Leeds. The parish of Whitkirk included the hamlet of Thorpe Stapleton and parts of Austhorpe, Seacroft and Temple Newsam. The other part of Austhorpe was in the parish of Garforth while Seacroft and Temple Newsam were partly in the parish of Leeds. Temple Newsam is separately noticed. 1674. 17 households in Austhorpe, 66 in Seacroft and 1 in Thorpe Stapleton. (In the hearth tax return Whitkirk was probably included in the figure of 114 households recorded for Temple Newsam). 1676: 682 persons aged 16 or more (parish).

In 1521 Thomas Lord Darcy of Temple Newsam had founded almshouses and a free grammar school at Whitkirk but these had apparently ceased to exist before the end of the 16th century.

George Shillito of Seacroft was a barrister who served as joint receiver of the honours of Tickhill, Pontefract and Wakefield. He bought the manor of Seacroft in 1605 and built a new house there. An enterprising landlord, he mined coal extensively and enclosed part of Seacroft Moor. He died without issue in 1637, having settled the estate on his wife Elizabeth who later married Sir Ralph Hansby of Tickhill.

In 1639 the West Riding magistrates gave direction that some of Shillito's coal pits on Seacroft Moor should be filled up.

The following year they were informed that the highway between Seacroft and Leeds was in 'great decay' and decided that the inhabitants of the parish of Whitkirk should be responsible for the necessary repair work.

In 1645 there was an outbreak of the plague within the parish.

In 1656 Lady Hansby sold the Seacroft estate to James Nelthorpe for £5300.

In the reign of Charles II the coalmining operations in Seacroft were the subject of litigation in the Court of Chancery. In launching these proceedings Sir Thomas Gascoigne of Barnbow related that he and Timothy Mauleverer had several coalmines, both opened and unopened, in Seacroft and that in 1672 they had come to an agreement with James Nelthorpe about the working of the mines. Nelthorpe was to bear half of the expenditure involved but in the event he had found that the charges amounted to more than the profits. Subsequently, in 1675, Sir Thomas had been assigned a half-share in a colliery which Nelthorpe owned at a rent of £50 a year.

The Cloughs of Thorpe Stapleton were minor gentry who ran into financial difficulties. In 1638 Sir Arthur Ingram bought their estate from Mauger Clough and since Thorpe Hall stood in close proximity to his Temple Newsam estate he decided to have it pulled down.

Church St Mary: Perpendicular.

Members of the Ingram family were buried in the Scargill or Temple Newsam chapel.

(W. K. Jordan, *The Charities of Rural England 1480-1660* (1961), 255, 308. R. J. Shilleto, 'The Shilletos of the West Riding of Yorkshire', *Thoresby Society*, xxvi (1924).

C.3/383/8. C.8/131/102. *YASRS*, liv (1915), 106, 191. C.33/253/fo.301. C.38/203/24 January 1679/80. BL, Harleian MSS 4630, 98. G. M. Platt and J. W. Morkill, *Records of the Parish of Whitkirk* (1892). G. E. Kirk, *The Parish Church of St Mary, Whitkirk, Leeds* (1935).)

WHIXLEY   Claro

A village to the east of Knaresborough. The parish of Whixley included the village of Green Hammerton. 1674: 76 households in Whixley and 35 in Green Hammerton.

Church St James: mainly 14th century.

Principal family Tankard of Whixley Hall. Estate revenue: £420 a year (1640); £900 a year (1700).

The Tankards bought the Whixley estate from the Bankes family in 1613.

In the Civil War Sir Richard Tankard (1608-1668) served as a major in the royalist army.

Whixley Hall Charles Tankard (d.1644) carried out considerable building work after purchasing the estate. In the reign of Charles II Christopher Tankard (1659-1705) made substantial additions to the house. When Sir Miles Stapleton of Carlton visited Whixley in 1682 a workman showed him round the new building. A two-storeyed mansion of brick.

(C.33/310/fo.483. *The Ancestor*, ii (1902), 37.)

WICKERSLEY   Strafford and Tickhill

A village to the south-east of Rotherham. There was no other village within the parish. 1674: 28 households (township of Wickersley). 1676: 98 persons aged 16 or more (parish).

In 1657 the minister, Desired Warren, rebuilt the parsonage house after a fire. According to the hearth tax roll of 1674 the new house had six hearths.

Warren appears to have been a trimmer: he served the cure without interruption from 1629 to 1667.

Church St Alban: Norman with a Perpendicular tower.

WIGHILL   Ainsty

A village to the north of Tadcaster. 1665: 47 households (township of Wighill). 1676: 119 persons aged 16 or more (parish of Wighill).

In 1600 it was reported that Christopher Thomlinson the vicar of Wighill seldom wore a surplice. A resolute nonconformist, he was deprived of his living in 1605 after refusing to subscribe to the ecclesiastical canons.

Church All Saints: Norman and Perpendicular.

Principal family Stapleton of Wighill Hall. Estate revenue: £1000 a year (1635); £1100 a year (1675).

In the 17th century the Stapleton women tended to outlive their husbands with the result that the estate was often heavily burdened with jointures.

Henry Stapleton (1574-1631) entered into possession of Wighill Hall after it had remained unoccupied for some years. Roger Dodsworth praised him for his liberal hospitality and his enlightened attitude towards his tenants: after his father's death he had allowed them to continue at their old rents without taking any fines.

His grandson Sir Miles Stapleton (1628-1669) was declared a ward of the Crown following the death of his father in 1635. Although he was a nephew of Sir Philip Stapleton, a leading parliamentarian, he took no part in the Civil War, mainly no doubt because he was a mere youth. In a Chancery case of 1657 he related that his debts were so great that he was in danger of being arrested and thrown into prison. In 1664 he was fined £500 for striking the lord mayor of York while under the influence of drink.

After the death of Henry Stapleton (1631-1674) the estate passed to his cousin Robert Stapleton, a younger son of Sir Philip Stapleton, who was a barrister of Gray's Inn. He died without issue in 1675 and was succeeded by his half-brother Henry who lived mainly in London.

Wighill Hall An Elizabethan mansion built by Sir Robert Stapleton (1548-1606). Sir Robert erected 'a fair house, or rather Palace, the model whereof he had brought out of Italy'. In the opinion of the Archbishop of York it was 'fitter for a Lord Treasurer of England then for a Knight of Yorkshire' (Sir John Harington). The house had four large towers surmounted by copper domes. In 1665 there were 15 taxable hearths.

The Stapletons had a deer park at Wighill. In 1655 Sir Miles Stapleton secured the agreement of his grandmother Mary Stapleton (who had a life interest in the manor) to the felling of timber in the park to the value of £1500 for the payment of his debts.

(*YAJ*, xv (1900), 239. R. A. Marchant, *The Puritans and the Church Courts in the Diocese of York 1560-1642* (1960), 283. H. E. Chetwynd-Stapylton, *The Stapeltons of Yorkshire* (1897). BL, Additional MSS 24,468, fo.138. Wards 5/49. C.6/136/19. C.33/262/fols.695-8.)

WISTOW   Barkston Ash

A village to the north-west of Selby. The parish of Wistow contained a number of villages, including Cawood and Monk Fryston which had medieval chapels. The chapelry of

Monk Fryston (which included Burton Salmon and Hillam) was a long way from the mother church and for that reason it had some of the characteristics of a parish. In 1642 it was described in the West Riding quarter sessions records as a parish but its church was technically a parochial chapel. 1674: 103 households in Wistow, 19 in Burton Salmon, 132 in Cawood, 41 in Hillam and 41 in Monk Fryston.

Upon the River Ouse 'stands Cawood, the castle of the Archbishops, which King Athelstan gave to the Church, as I have been told' (William Camden). The main estate in Cawood together with the castle belonged to the Archbishop of York. A ferry there provided a link between the West and East Ridings.

In April 1642 the West Riding magistrates were informed of 'the great ruine and decaye of Munckfriston cawsey.....contayninge two miles and a haulfe in length, soe that his Majesties subjects cannot passe and travaile there without daunger of their lives'. For the funding of the repair programme it was decided that the sum of £100 should be levied on the West Riding as a whole.

Cawood was a place of some importance in the Civil War. In October 1642 a parliamentarian force commanded by John Hotham seized Cawood Castle and the Archbishop, John Williams, fled for safety to Pontefract Castle. The following year the royalists put in a garrison but in 1644 the parliamentarians recaptured Cawood.

Church All Saints, Wistow: Early English, Decorated and Perpendicular.

The parish was subject to the peculiar jurisdiction of a Prebendary of York.

Castle A large gatehouse was built at Cawood Castle in the 15th century. This may possibly have been part of an extensive building programme.

In 1647 Parliament decided that the castle should be made untenable.

School In 1630 Samuel Harsnett, the Archbishop of York, settled property for the endowment of a free school at Cawood.

(E.134/18 James I/Easter 7. *YASRS*, liv (1915), 380-1. W. K. Jordan, *The Charities of Rural England 1480-1660* (1961), 335-6. W. Wheater, *The History of the Parishes of Sherburn and Cawood* (2nd edition, 1882).)

WOMBWELL   Strafford and Tickhill

A village within the parish of Darfield, near Barnsley. 1674: 78 households.

Church St Mary: a public chapel which was Saxon in origin.

Principal family Wombwell of Wombwell Hall. Estate revenue: £600 a year (1655).

The Wombwells had resided at Wombwell since the 14th century or possibly earlier. William Wombwell (c.1565-1622) frequently resorted to litigation during the reign of James I and even brought a suit against his father. According to his brother Appleton a considerable amount of land was sold to meet his legal expenses and clear the debts occasioned by his extravagance.

His son William (c.1609-1662) promised financial support for the king's forces as a signatory of the Yorkshire Engagement of February 1643 but does not appear to have been actively engaged in the Civil War. He later fell heavily into debt and his son Thomas (1632-1665) succeeded to an estate which was seriously encumbered. The family nevertheless survived the financial crisis.

Following the death of William Wombwell (1658-1695), who left no issue, the estate passed to his cousin William Wombwell of Leeds.

Wombwell Hall In 1686 Ralph Thoresby described the hall as squire Wombwell's 'ancient house'. It was a late medieval or early Tudor building.

In 1674 William Wombwell was taxed on 10 hearths.

(C.2/James I/C3/12 and W17/69. C.22/757/20. Sheffield Archives, Wentworth Woodhouse Collection, Bright MSS 185(b).)

WOMERSLEY   Osgoldcross

A village to the south-east of Pontefract. The parish of Womersley included Little Smeaton, Walden Stubbs and part of Cridling Stubbs; the other part was in the parish of Darrington. 1674: 54 households in Womersley, 11 in Cridling Stubbs, 21 in Little Smeaton and 17 in Walden Stubbs.

Since 1346 Womersley had enjoyed the right to hold a weekly market and an annual fair.

In 1640 it was reported that three tenant farmers of Womersley, William Turner, Thomas Everingham and Henry Midleton, were defying an order made by the West Riding magistrates about the method to be followed in the assessment of local taxes.

In 1641 twelve men and women of the parish were presented for recusancy. These included John Percy, who was the main landowner in Walden Stubbs, and members of his family. In the Civil War he supported the king and joined the garrison in Pontefract Castle.

In 1645 there was an outbreak of the plague in Womersley.

Church St Martin: Norman, Early English and Decorated.

(*YASRS*, liv (1915), 225-6, 246-7, 297.)

WOODKIRK   Agbrigg and Morley

A village to the north-east of Dewsbury which was also known as Woodchurch and West Ardsley. The parish of Woodkirk included the hamlet of Topcliffe. 1674: 65 households (township of Woodkirk). 1676: 200 persons aged 16 or more, including 60 Protestant dissenters (parish).

The Saviles of Howley Hall had the patronage rights in the parish of Woodkirk and during the early 17th century Anthony Nutter their Puritan chaplain often preached there. In the 1630s James Ridgeley and Samuel Newman, both nonconforming ministers, served in turn as perpetual curate at Woodkirk.

In 1619 five men were presented for refusing to kneel when receiving the bread and wine in the communion service. In 1633 the ecclesiastical authorities took action against a group of nine persons who had been engaging in separatist activities and one of them, John Reyner, was accused of holding conventicles.

Among the residents of Woodkirk was James Nayler (1618-1660) who emerged as an important figure in the sect of Quakers. In the Civil War he served in the parliamentarian army but in the republican era his religious opinions proved to be too controversial for many in the ruling party. In 1656 Parliament found him guilty of 'horrid blasphemy' and ordered him to be branded and flogged.

For many years a two-day fair had been held at Woodkirk during harvest time. In 1656, however, some of the inhabitants of the parish submitted a petition to the West Riding magistrates which called for its suppression. In support of their request they related that as a result of competition from Wakefield it no longer functioned as a cloth fair and its merchandise was now largely confined to 'peddling goods' which could be bought in the neighbouring towns. Deprived of its basic role it had become 'a tumultuous meeting of idle persons' at which lives had been lost and labourers had wasted their time when they should have been harvesting. The matter was referred to Thomas Savile, Earl of Sussex who commented that although the fair belonged to him by charter he did not consider it appropriate that private profit should take precedence over the good of the country. Accordingly the justices agreed that the fair should be discontinued.

Church St Mary: Early English.

Almshouses In 1593 Richard Greenwood, a yeoman, had founded almshouses at Woodkirk for three poor women.

(R. A. Marchant, *The Puritans and the Church Courts in the Diocese of York 1560-1642* (1960), 42-3, 108, 264, 266, 272. W. G. Bittle, *James Nayler 1618-1660: the Quaker Indicted by Parliament* (1986). *CSP Dom, 1655-6*, 264.)

WOOLLEY   Staincross

A village within the parish of Royston, near Barnsley. 1674: 53 households.

Church St Peter: mainly Perpendicular. A parochial chapel with a curate in charge. According to a Commonwealth survey there were about 160 communicants in the early 1650s.

School There was a school at Woolley in the middle years of the 17th century.

Principal family Wentworth of Woolley Hall. Estate revenue: £1250 a year (1660).

Coalmining at Woolley and Darton and on Staincross Moor.

Michael Wentworth (c.1548-1641), who bought the estate in 1599, was for many years a conforming Catholic. In 1637 he compounded for his recusancy after handing over most of his landed property to his son Sir George (1599-1660) who was a Protestant.

Sir George served as a royalist colonel in the Civil War and was involved in the defence of Wakefield and Pontefract. At his death he left no male issue and some of his manors descended to his three married daughters. His brother John (1606-1683), who was a lawyer, inherited the manor of Woolley and other property worth £750 a year and subsequently added considerably to the estate.

Woolley Hall Michael Wentworth rebuilt the house during the years 1634 and 1635. In May 1635 he was writing to Thomas Lord Wentworth from 'our new house at Wolley where I would be glade to see you before I dye'. A large building with shaped gables. According to an inventory of 1660 it contained a domestic chapel.

In 1581 the Woodruffes, who were the previous owners of the Woolley estate, had introduced a pipeline system for bringing water from Woolley Common to their house.

Christopher Saxton's survey of the manor in 1599 records the existence of a deer park. This had been enclosed about the end of the 15th century.

(Brotherton Library, University of Leeds, Wentworth of Woolley MSS. HMC, *Various Collections*, ii (Wentworth MSS). G. E. Wentworth, 'History of the Wentworths of Woolley', *YAJ*, xii (1893). J. W. Walker, 'The Manor and Church of Woolley', *YAJ*, xxvii (1924). C.22/830/31. Sheffield Archives, Wentworth Woodhouse Collection, Strafford Letters xv, Michael Wentworth to Lord Wentworth, 13 May 1635.)

WORSBOROUGH   Staincross

A village near Barnsley which was situated within the parish of Darfield.

In the Commonwealth period there were said to be about 200 communicants in the chapelry of Worsborough. 1674: 96 households.

Church St Mary: a public chapel with architectural features of various periods, Norman, Decorated and Perpendicular.

In his will (1632) John Rayney, a London draper who had been born near Worsborough, left £30 a year for the support of a lecturer.

School A public grammar school which had been in existence in the early 16th century. A schoolhouse was built in the reign of Elizabeth.

John Rayney left £13 6s 8d a year as an addition to the schoolmaster's salary.

Principal family Rockley of Rockley Hall. Estate revenue: £500 a year (1630); £700 a year (1662). Iron works at Rockley.

The family had been seated at Rockley since the 13th century or earlier.

Robert Rockley (1590-1644) was a close friend of Strafford and took on responsibility for the management of his Yorkshire estates during his absence in Ireland.

In his will (1642) he referred to his purchase of the manor of Worsborough.

In the Civil War he supported the royalist cause and two of his sons were killed while in arms for the king.

He was succeeded by his son Francis (1617-1679) who was also a royalist. He quarrelled with his mother over her jointure, borrowed heavily and was eventually imprisoned for debt. His severe financial difficulties were partly due to extensive litigation but he attributed them mainly to the efforts of his steward, William Hayford, to deprive him of his estate.

Rockley spent many years in prison and was still there at the time of his death. Despite all his tribulations the estate remained largely intact and in due course came into the possession of his daughter Catherine.

Rockley Hall The house, which stood in a secluded valley, may have been either a medieval or Tudor structure. There is no evidence of any building activity in the 17th century.

In 1674 the largest house in the Worsborough district was the mansion of Henry Edmunds which had 13 taxable hearths.

(P. J. Wallis, 'Worsborough Grammar School', *YAJ*, xxxix (1956-8). C.10/35/169; 94/135; and 483/303. C.33/267/fo.364. J. Wilkinson, *Worsborough: its Historical Associations and Rural Attractions* (1872).)

WRAGBY   Osgoldcross/Staincross

Wragby, near Wakefield, consisted of little more than a parish church. The parish of Wragby included the village of Ryhill and several hamlets. 1674: 2 households in Nostell, 29 in Ryhill and 17 in Wintersett. 1676: 350 persons aged 16 or more (parish).

The Priory of St Oswald of Nostell, which was an establishment of Augustinian canons, had been founded in the 12th century and dissolved in 1540.

Huntwick Grange was the seat of Sir Richard Saltonstall (1586-1661), one of the Puritan founders of Watertown in New England.

Church St Michael: Perpendicular. It had formerly been a priory church.

School A public grammar school which was already in existence in 1548. The schoolhouse dated from 1573.

Principal families (1) Gargrave of Nostell Priory (and Kinsley Hall). Estate revenue: £3500 a year (1612).

Sir Richard Gargrave (1573-1638) inherited a great estate following the execution of his half-brother Thomas for murder. It was said that at the height of his prosperity he could ride on his own land from Wakefield to Doncaster. He was, however, a spendthrift and a gamester and after squandering his estate he died in circumstances of abject poverty.

The manor of Nostell was sold in 1613 to William Ireland.

(2) Wolstenholme of Nostell Priory (and Seething Lane, London). Estate revenue: £3000 a year (1640).

In 1629 the Nostell Priory estate was purchased by Sir John Wolstenholme (1562-1639), a London merchant and customs farmer. The cost of the transaction was £10,000.

His son Sir John (c.1596-1670) supported the king in the Civil War and signed the Yorkshire Engagement of February 1643. As a London customs farmer he was heavily fined by Parliament and in 1646 he was declared bankrupt.

(3) Winn of Nostell Priory (and Thornton Hall, Thornton Curtis, Lincolnshire) (baronetcy 1660). Estate revenue: £2000 a year (1660); £3500 a year (1697).

The Wolstenholmes eventually recovered from their financial difficulties but in 1654 Sir John sold the manor of Nostell and the rectory of Wragby to Rowland Winn, a London merchant. He reconveyed the property to his elder brother George who was to become the first baronet of the family. On both occasions the purchase price was £11,200.

Sir George (c.1607-1667) was already a considerable landowner in Lincolnshire at the time he acquired the manor of Nostell and he continued to add to his estate.

Abraham de la Pryme relates that Sir Edmund Winn (c.1644-1694) married one of his maidservants after the death of his first wife and characterises his son Sir Rowland (1675-1722) as 'a mighty mad, proud spark, exceeding gripeing .... and a great oppressour of the poor'.

Nostell Priory Sir Thomas Gargrave (1495-1579), who bought the estate in 1566, converted part of the monastic buildings into a family residence and made it his principal seat. The rooms listed in an inventory of 1588 include the hall, the great chamber, the new great chamber, the gallery, the painted chamber and the armoury.

Immediately before the Civil War Sir John Wolstenholme the younger was undertaking major improvements to the interior. For this purpose he drew on the services of Nicholas Stone, the king's master mason, for the supply of marble chimney-pieces.

The Winns do not appear to have carried out much work before the building of a new mansion in the 18th century. The hearth tax returns for 1674 record that Sir Edmund Winn was taxed on 24 hearths.

In 1603 Sir Richard Gargrave secured a grant of free warren for Nostell Park which then contained 200 acres. In 1649 there were two parks: the Walled Park and the Red Deer Park.

(*Catalogue of the Nostell Priory MSS.* C.33/139/fo.157; 202/fo.751; 214/fo.233; and 240/fo.688. *Surtees Society*, liv (1870), 124-5. PRO, S.P.19/cxx/179 and Duchy of Lancaster, Special Commissions, DL44/442.)

Appendix

A Selection of Yorkshire Entries from a Survey of the Inns and Alehouses of England and Wales, 1686 (PRO, W.O.30/48)

	Guest beds	Stabling (number of horses)
YORK	483	800
EAST RIDING		
Beverley	182	460
Bridlington	38	75
Great Driffield	11	21
Hedon	13	31
Howden	67	58
Hull	199	349
Hunmanby	22	32
Market Weighton	20	48
NORTH RIDING		
Askrigg	34	86
Bedale	52	44
Guisborough	32	27
Helmsley	60	136
Kirkby Moorside	33	60

	Guest beds	Stabling (number of horses)
Malton	195	524
and Old Malton	10	19
Middleham	51	98
Northallerton	82	83
Pickering	16	0
Richmond	99	228
Scarborough	74	144
Stokesley	26	51
Thirsk	110	234
Whitby	40	23
Yarm	33	66
WEST RIDING		
Aberford	17	46
Barnsley	64	109
Bawtry	57	69
Boroughbridge	50	60
Bradford	29	60
Dewsbury	8	14
and Dewsbury Moor	3	4
Doncaster	206	453
Ferrybridge	34	95
Giggleswick	17	22
Halifax	130	306
Harrogate	10	10
Holmfirth	31	25
Huddersfield	29	64
Ilkley	2	6
Keighley	34	39
Knaresborough	30	60
Leeds	294	454
Otley	16	50
Pontefract	92	235
Ripon	118	422
Rotherham	63	72
Sedbergh	19	35
Selby	58	89

	Guest beds	Stabling (number of horses)
Settle	69	105
Sheffield	119	270
Sherburn in Elmet	25	55
Skipton	72	93
Snaith	31	72
Tadcaster	50	72
Wakefield	242	543
Wetherby	28	56

Select Bibliography

The Hearth Tax Returns of Charles II's Reign

Public Record Office, Exchequer, Hearth Tax Returns (E.179):
East Riding	205/504 and 514; 261/4, 5, 10 and 11
North Riding	215/451; 216/462; 261/23, 27 and 29
West Riding	210/393, 399 and 417; 262/13
York and the Ainsty	260/20.

Other Primary Sources

Anon., *The Life of Marmaduke Rawdon of York, Camden Society*, lxxxv (1863)

Aston, John, 'Diary of John Aston, 1639', *Surtees Society*, cxviii (1910)

Atkinson, J. C. (ed.), *Quarter Sessions Records, North Riding Record Society*, vols. i to vii (1884–9)

Baskerville, Thomas, 'Travels in England', Historical Manuscripts Commission, *Thirteenth Report*, Appendix, part ii (1891–3)

Braithwaite, Richard, *Drunken Barnaby's Four Journeys to the North of England* (3rd edn., 1723)

Buck, Samuel, *Samuel Buck's Yorkshire Sketchbook* (1979)

De la Pryme, Abraham, *The Diary of Abraham de la Pryme, Surtees Society*, liv (1870)

Dodsworth, Roger, *Yorkshire Church Notes, 1619–1631* (ed. J.W. Clay), *Yorkshire Archaeological Society Record Series*, xxxiv (1904)

Fiennes, Celia, *The Journeys of Celia Fiennes* (ed. C. Morris) (1949)

Firth, Sir Charles and Rait, R. S., *Acts and Ordinances of the Interregnum, 1642–1660* (1911)

Fuller, Thomas, *The Worthies of England* (ed. J. Freeman) (1952)

Gibson, Edmund, *Camden's Britannia, Newly Translated into English, With Large Additions and Improvements* (1695)
Heywood, Oliver, *Autobiography, Diaries, Anecdote and Event Books* (ed. J. Horsfall Turner) (1882–5)
Leach, A. F., *Early Yorkshire Schools, Yorkshire Archaeological Society Record Series*, xxvii (1899) and xxxiii (1903)
Legg, L. G. W. (ed.), *A Relation of a Short Survey of 26 Counties* (1904)
Lister, J. (ed.), *West Riding Sessions Records, 1611-1642, Yorkshire Archaeological Society Record Series*, liv (1915)
Purdy, J. D., *Yorkshire Hearth Tax Returns (University of Hull: Studies in Regional and Local History* Number 7) (1991)
Reresby, Sir John, *Memoirs of Sir John Reresby* (ed. A. Browning, Mary K. Geiter and W. A. Speck) (2nd edn., 1991)
Taylor, John, *Part of this Summer's Travels* (1640)
Thoresby, Ralph, *Ducatus Leodiensis* (2nd edn., 1816)
Thoresby, Ralph, *The Diary of Ralph Thoresby, FRS (1677–1724)* (ed. J. Hunter) (1830)
Turner, G. Lyon (ed.), *Original Records of Early Nonconformity under Persecution and Indulgence* (1911–14)
Wentworth, Thomas, Earl of Strafford, *The Earl of Strafforde's Letters and Dispatches* (ed. W. Knowler) (1739)
Whiteman, Anne and Clapinson, Mary (eds.), *The Compton Census of 1676: A Critical Edition* (1986).

Secondary Sources

Allen, T., *New and Complete History of the County of York* (1828–31)
Ambler, L., *The Old Halls and Manor Houses of Yorkshire* (1913)
Aveling, H., *Post Reformation Catholicism in East Yorkshire 1558–1790, East Yorkshire Local History Society*, No. 11 (1960)
Aveling, H., *The Catholic Recusants of the West Riding of Yorkshire 1558–1790, Proceedings of the Leeds Philosophical and Literary Society, Literary and Historical Section* x, part vi (1963)
Aveling, H., *Northern Catholics, The Catholic Recusants of the North Riding of Yorkshire 1558-1790* (1966)
Aveling, H., *Catholic Recusancy in the City of York, 1558–1791, Catholic Record Society*, monograph series, ii (1971)
Binns, J., *Yorkshire in the Civil Wars* (2004)
Cliffe, J. T., *The Yorkshire Gentry from the Reformation to the Civil War* (1969)
Dale, B., *Yorkshire Puritanism and Early Nonconformity* (ed. T. G. Crippen) (1917)
English, Barbara, *The Great Landowners of East Yorkshire 1530–1910* (1990)

Forster, G. C. F., *The East Riding Justices of the Peace in the Seventeenth Century*, East Yorkshire Local History Society, No. 30 (1973)
Gaunt, P., *The Cromwellian Gazetteer* (1987)
Gooder, A., *The Parliamentary Representation of the County of York 1258–1832*, ii, Yorkshire Archaeological Society Record Series, xcvi (1938)
Heaton, H., *The Yorkshire Woollen and Worsted Industries* (1920)
Henning, B. D. (ed.), *The History of Parliament: The House of Commons 1660–1690* (1983)
Hopper, A. J., 'A Directory of Parliamentarian Allegiance in Yorkshire During the Civil Wars', *Yorkshire Archaeological Journal*, lxxiii (2001)
Hunter, J., *South Yorkshire: the History and Topography of the Deanery of Doncaster* (1828)
Hunter, J., *Hallamshire: the History and Topography of the Parish of Sheffield* (1869)
Jennings, B. (ed.), *A History of Nidderdale (The Nidderdale History Group)* (1983)
Jordan, W. K., *The Charities of Rural England 1480–1660* (1961)
Lawson, J., *The Endowed Grammar Schools of East Yorkshire*, (East Yorkshire Local History Society, No. 14) (1962)
Lawton, G., *Collections Relative to Churches and Chapels within the Diocese of York* (1842)
Marchant, R. A., *The Puritans and the Church Courts in the Diocese of York 1560–1642* (1960)
Matthews, A. G., *Calamy Revised* (1934)
Matthews, A. G., *Walker Revised* (2nd edn., 1988)
McCutcheon, K. L., *Yorkshire Fairs and Markets*, Thoresby Society, xxxix (1940)
Neave, D. and Waterson, E., *Lost Houses of East Yorkshire* (1988)
Ord, J. W., *History and Antiquities of Cleveland* (1846)
Pevsner, Sir Nikolaus, *The Buildings of England: Yorkshire, the North Riding* (1966)
Pevsner, Sir Nikolaus and Neave, D., *The Buildings of England: York and the East Riding* (2nd edn., 1995)
Pevsner, Sir Nikolaus and Radcliffe, Enid, *The Buildings of England: Yorkshire, the West Riding* (2nd edn., 1967)
Poulson, G., *The History and Antiquities of the Seigniory of Holderness* (1840–1)
Raistrick, A., *Old Yorkshire Dales* (1971)
Reid, R. R., *The King's Council in the North* (1921)
Roach, J., *A Regional Study of Yorkshire Schools 1500–1820* (1998)
Roebuck, P., *Yorkshire Baronets 1640–1760* (1980)
Royal Commission on the Historical Monuments of England, *Rural Houses of West Yorkshire, 1400–1830* (Supplementary Series 8) (1986)
Sheahan, J. J., *History and Topography of the Wapentake of Claro* (1871)
Speight, H., *Lower Wharfedale* (1902)

Speight, H., *Nidderdale and the Garden of the Nidd* (1894)
Speight, H., *Nidderdale from Nun-Monkton to Whernside* (1906)
Speight, H., *Upper Wharfedale* (1900)
Victoria County History:
   A History of Yorkshire (1907, 1912, 1913)
   North Riding (1914, 1923)
   The City of York (1961)
   East Riding (1969–2002)
Waterson, E. and Meadows, P., *Lost Houses of York and the North Riding* (1990)
Waterson, E. and Meadows, P., *Lost Houses of the West Riding* (1998)
Whellan, T., *History and Topography of the City of York and the North Riding of Yorkshire* (1857, 1859)
Whitaker, T. D., *Loidis and Elmete* (1816)
Whitaker, T. D., *A History of Richmondshire, in the North Riding of the County of York* (1823)
Whitaker, T. D., *The History and Antiquities of the Deanery of Craven* (ed. A.W. Morant) (1878)
Woolrych, A. H., *Britain in Revolution 1625–1660* (2002)
Woolrych, A. H., 'Yorkshire and the Restoration', *Yorkshire Archaeological Journal*, xxxix (1958)

Index of Subjects

THERE ARE SOME subjects which occur so frequently that their inclusion in this index would have served no real purpose. Major subjects which have been excluded for this reason consist of the following: agricultural improvement (in particular enclosure); churches, schools and almshouses; clergymen and schoolteachers; Civil War operations; and outbreaks of the plague.

Alum industry 4, 77, 158, 173, 174, 197, 201, 202, 209, 241, 266, 267, 268
Architects 25, 36, 83, 146, 243, 310, 417

Bridges, building of 130, 134, 157, 171, 192, 193, 201, 202, 208, 216, 221, 231, 258, 264, 302, 320, 350, 359, 395, 401

Catholicism, strength of 6, 9, 17, 31, 48, 51, 60, 88, 92, 113, 137, 143, 152, 172, 180, 189, 194, 200, 202, 214, 231, 243, 245, 247, 255, 256, 263–4, 269, 319, 345, 384, 421, 442,
Coalmining 3–4, 141, 145, 164, 205, 223, 261, 263, 269, 283, 285, 290, 291, 295, 299, 304, 306, 309, 311, 318, 325, 331–2, 334, 343, 344, 345, 346, 349, 352, 353, 357, 359, 360, 361, 362, 365, 366, 367, 368, 371, 373, 374, 377, 380–1, 387, 390, 402, 403, 408, 410, 413, 418, 423, 424, 427, 436, 446, 450, 452, 454, 455, 458, 460, 466, 468, 470, 471, 474, 480
Coastal erosion 15, 38, 42, 63, 75, 85, 93, 94, 107, 116, 179
Cutlery manufacture 4, 431–2

Duelling 89, 141, 282, 284, 319, 453

Ferries 41, 45, 62, 67, 82, 112, 215, 324, 363, 381, 407, 430, 473, 477
Fires 11, 12, 59, 61, 94, 102, 105, 140, 141, 146, 159, 161, 178, 189, 209,

236, 253, 262, 279, 282, 300, 308, 313, 384, 410, 419, 454, 456, 457, 463, 475
Fish and fishing 2, 10, 14, 21, 30, 45, 49, 50, 66, 179, 204, 209, 228, 233–4, 241, 266, 267, 309, 363, 459
Floods 39, 140, 157, 218, 266, 271, 279, 306, 320, 348, 364, 376, 378, 379

Gaming 36, 141, 177, 239, 263, 311, 456, 459, 482

Horses and horse–racing 4, 16, 29, 40, 74, 86, 90, 108, 117, 131, 154, 177, 204, 213, 228, 253, 267, 335, 337, 421, 459
Hunting and hawking 3, 131, 194, 220, 263, 267, 363, 375, 387, 457

Inns and alehouses 4, 13, 23, 29, 71, 134, 175, 199, 259, 299, 323, 338, 339, 358, 368, 369, 401, 415, 417, 421, 452, 465, Appendix
Iron manufacture 4, 285, 395, 406, 423, 431, 432, 434–5, 445, 452–3, 470, 480

Lead mining 4, 131, 132, 134, 167, 168, 172, 207, 220, 256, 263, 306, 320, 349, 352, 366, 378, 396, 420, 421, 436, 441, 448
Lighthouses 50, 75

Manor–houses, contemporary descriptions of 36, 37, 46–7, 49, 54, 76, 83, 152, 155, 170, 192, 209, 216, 217, 256, 258, 268, 278, 279, 280, 296, 298, 303, 308, 317, 321, 336, 353, 366, 386, 388, 393, 401–

2, 407, 408–9, 411, 420, 426, 429, 440, 443, 444, 454, 459, 465, 470, 476, 482
Markets and fairs, contemporary descriptions of 21, 22, 56, 74, 90, 108, 204, 219, 228, 479
Muncipal government, developments in 9, 21–2, 204, 227, 394, 395

Petitions from local communities 20, 23, 44, 59, 70, 81–2, 125, 130–1, 134, 147, 159, 172, 175, 178, 183, 191, 195, 204, 224, 240, 241, 266, 290, 291–2, 304–5, 309, 313, 322, 323, 347, 369, 374, 382, 394, 395, 414, 415, 419, 427, 431, 432, 440, 441, 473, 479
Physicians 6, 39, 98, 113, 147, 208, 228, 244, 246, 346, 357, 371, 390, 417, 440
Poets 1–2, 4, 76, 124, 131, 133, 141, 148, 273, 291, 301, 308, 335, 350, 368, 376, 394, 398, 433, 451, 453, 459
Poor relief (excluding almshouses) 5, 16, 20, 44, 62, 69, 76, 78, 106, 116, 130–1, 136, 138, 147, 156, 161, 191, 195, 197, 198, 224, 237, 252, 294, 306, 322, 336, 357, 360, 369, 382, 396, 399, 469
Post towns and postmasters/postmistresses 13, 148, 203, 219, 252, 309, 337, 347, 452
Prisons and houses of correction 9, 13, 23, 59, 71, 226, 229, 253, 267, 390, 396, 424, 465

Roads, condition of 4, 130, 140, 147, 164, 182, 193, 257, 275, 336, 342, 345, 426, 474, 477

Scientists and scientific subjects 138, 278, 313, 333, 339, 346, 424, 444–5
Servants, establishments of 36, 48, 60, 72, 87, 143, 151, 175, 255, 260, 261, 267, 269, 285, 318, 365, 401, 404, 406, 436, 448, 454, 466, 468
Shipping 10, 18, 30, 36, 59, 69, 70, 74, 233, 266, 299
Spas 153, 233–4, 329, 389
Stewards, land 48, 102, 125, 142, 145, 170, 185, 217, 236, 261, 277, 286, 293, 296, 307, 311, 316, 318, 319, 323, 324, 363, 365, 367, 402, 405, 415, 443, 450, 451, 456, 481
Surveyors, estate 48, 91, 109, 125, 187, 217, 282, 295, 327, 393, 405, 480

Theatrical troupes 10, 143, 171, 265

Witchcraft 135, 282, 393
Woollen industry 3, 7, 8, 10, 22, 284, 285, 287, 297, 302, 304, 312, 321, 336, 342, 356–7, 372, 373, 376, 382, 387, 394, 401, 403, 404, 406, 412, 415, 437, 464

Yorkshire,
    character of the people 4, 5, 6, 10, 30, 93, 173, 186, 357
    size of population 3

Index of Persons

Acclom,
    family of 110–11
    Elizabeth 110, 111, 154
    John (d.1610) 425,
    Sir William 99, 110
Acklam, family of 92
Adams, Sherland 462
Adams of Ouston,
    family of 414
    Dame Mary 317
    Sir William 317, 414
Agar, Thomas 13
Aislabie, family of 282
Alcock, John, Bishop of Worcester 70
Aldburgh,
    family of 163
    Arthur 163, 281
Alder, William 18
Alford,
    family of 76, 118–19
    Margaret 142
Allenson, Robert 404
Alleyn, Arabella 72
Alured,
    family of 103–4
    John 59, 103–4

Anderson, George 198
Anderson of East Cowton,
    family of 159–60
Angell, Justinian 75
Anlaby, family of 47
Anne, family of 319, 370–1
Anstruther,
    family of 472
    Dame Mary 388, 472
    Sir Robert 388, 472
Appleby of Lartington,
    family of 230
Appleby of Linton upon Ouse,
    family of 217
Appleyard, family of 34
Armitage (Armytage),
    family of 362–3
Armitstead, John 351
Armyne, Dame Mary 425
Arthington,
    family of 278
    William 278, 315
Arundel and Surrey, Earl of see
    Howard, Earls and Dukes of
    Norfolk, family of
Ascham, Roger 192

Ashton, Anthony 338
Ashton, Edward 322
Aske, family of 17, 114, 425, 426
Assheton of Kirkby Hall, family of 343
Assheton of Middleton, Lancashire,
    family of 32, 343
    John 317
Aston, John 10, 312, 338, 358
Atherton, Anne 209
Atkinson, Richard 305
Atkinson, Thomas (innkeeper) 259
Atkinson, Thomas (schoolmaster) 380
Audesley, Roger, 297
Aykroyd, family of 31–2
Ayscough, Henry 41
Ayscough of Osgoodby Grange, family
    of 251–2
Ayscough of Skewsby, family of 155–6

Babthorpe, family of 51, 60–1
Bagshaw, William 291
Bagwith, Luke 267
Baildon of Baildon, family of 413
Baildon of Kippax, family of 380
Balguy, Thomas 433
Baltrus, Ralph 307
Bamburgh,
    family of 102–3
    Mary 411
    Sir William 80, 103
Bankes,
    family of 475
Barden, William 82
Barkham, Frances 297
    Sir Edward 297
Barnby, family of 435
Barrington, family of 116, 216
Barton, family of 265
Barwick, Francis 281

Barwick of Toulston,
    family of 409
    Sir Robert 56, 409
Baskerville, John 305, 465
Baskerville, Thomas 4, 10, 22, 69, 337,
    338, 389, 417
Bateson, Thomas 390
Bathurst, John 208, 228, 246
Batt, family of 304
Battie, John 467
Battison, John 368
Batty, Ellen 148
Batty, George 258
Bawden, Richard 456
Bawn, Catherine 324
Beaumont, George (merchant) 334
Beaumont, George (minister) 441
Beaumont, Godfrey 285
Beaumont of High Catton, family of
    39
Beaumont of Mirfield, family of 404
Beaumont of Whitley,
    family of 387–8, 404
    Sir Thomas 387, 404, 432
Beckwith, Christopher 185
Beckwith of Ackton, family of 345
Beckwith of Aldburgh,
    family of 157, 212
    Arthur (1615–1642) 8, 212
Beckwith of Handale Abbey, family of
    201
Bede, the Venerable 167
Beeston, Ralph 299
Beilby, family of 327–8
Belasyse (Bellasis),
    family of 151–2
    Sir Thomas, Viscount Fauconberg
    13, 150, 180
    Thomas Earl Fauconberg 132, 151,
    271

Index of Persons 497

Bell, Mark 245
Benson,
    family of 447
    Robert 326, 447
Bentinck, William, Earl of Portland 294
Bentley, Nathan 312
Berric,
    family of 346
    Richard 346, 370
Besson, Anthony 134
Best, Henry 56, 74, 86, 90, 108
Bethell of Ellerton,
    family of 43–4, 131, 132, 385
    Sir Hugh 17, 43–4
    William 385
Bethell of Rise,
    family of 97
    Sir Hugh 29, 97
Birchall, John 44
Birdsall, Thomas 408
Birt, Daniel 427
Blackett, family of 408–9
Bland,
    family of 325, 380–1
    Sir Thomas (c.1592–1653) 325, 381
Blythman, Jasper 342
Bolles, Dame Mary see Jobson, family of
Booth,
    Dame Elizabeth 426
    Sir George 306
    Sir William 426
Booth, Samuel 106
Bosvile of Braithwell, family of 314
Bosvile of Gunthwaite, family of 415–16

Bosvile of Warmsworth,
    family of 467
    Thomas 341, 467
Bouch, Anthony 301
Boune, Robert 438
Bourchier of Beningbrough Grange,
    family of 216–17
    Barrington 217, 225
    Sir John 13, 216–17, 225, 385
    Sir Ralph 77, 217
Bourchier of Hanging Grimston, family of 77–8
Bower, William (of Barnsley) 294
Bower, William (of Bridlington) 31
Bowes of Aske,
    family of 157
    Eleanor 228
Bowles, Edward 165
Boyce, Mathias 200
Boyle, Elizabeth, Countess of Burlington 83, 437
    Richard Earl of Cork and later Earl of Burlington 83, 437, 457
Boynton, Judith 219
Boynton of Barmston,
    family of 18–20, 99, 179
    Matthew 19, 234
    Sir Francis (1561–1617) 19–20, 76, 194
    Sir Francis (1619–1695) 19–20, 35, 154, 158
    Sir Matthew 18–19, 50, 129, 179
Boynton of Rawcliffe, family of 439
Brabbs, Thomas 109
Bradley, Christopher 21
Bradley, Robert 164
Bradley, Thomas 325
Bradshaw, Sir James 99

Braithwaite,
    family of 148–9
    Richard 131, 133, 141, 148, 273,
        350, 376, 433, 451
Brandling, family of 392
Brearcliffe, William 88
Brearley, Roger 355, 379
Brereton, Sir William 175, 465
Brewster, James 214
Briggs, Martin 76
Briggs, Mary 324
Briggs, William 351
Bright, John 432
Bright of Badsworth,
    family of 290–1
    Sir John 290–1, 354, 359–60
Broadley, Matthew 358
Brooke, Robert Lord see Greville,
    Robert
Brookes, family of 162–3
Brookhouse, Edmund 294
Broomhead, John 391
Brown, Edward 413
Brown, Richard 436
Browne, Sir Henry 54
Broxholme, Charles 415
Bruce, Thomas, Earl of Elgin 160
Brudenell, Earls of Cardigan, family of
    407
Bryer, Francis 288
Buck, Samuel 372
Buck, Sir John 49, 51
Buckingham, Duke of see Villiers,
    Dukes of Buckingham
Buller, James 361
Bullingham, Thomas 352
Bulmer of Leavening, family of 15
Bulmer of Marrick,
    family of 207
    William 207, 220

Burdet, George 435
Burdett, family of 334
Burgh, Roger 145
Burghley, Lord see Cecil, Lords
    Burghley and Earls of Exeter,
    family of
Burlington, Earl of see Boyle, Richard
Burnet, Gilbert 151, 203
Burnet, Thomas 153
Burton, Henry 24
Burton, Sir Thomas 321
Bushell, Daniel 63
Butler, George 44
Byerley, Robert 341

Callis, Thomas 109
Calverley of Calverley,
    family of 321
    Sir Walter 366
    Walter (1629–1691) 321, 366
Calverley of Eryholme, family of 168
Calvert, James 28
Calvert of Kiplin, family of 187–8
Camden, William passim
Campbell, James 341
Carey,
    family of,
    Henry Lord Hunsdon 328
    Henry Viscount Rochford and Earl
        of Dover 328
    John Earl of Dover 328
Carlisle, Earl of see Howard, Earls of
    Carlisle
Carre, Robert 296
Carte, George 439
Carte,
    John 360
    William 360
Carter, John 104–5
Carter, Samuel 275

Index of Persons 499

Caryer, Jennett 310
Castlehouse, Edith 343
Castley, John 305
Catlyn, John 34
Catterick, family of 245
Cave, George 114
Cave, Thomas 413
Cavendish,
    Elizabeth, Countess of Devonshire 453
    William Lord Cavendish 192
Cavendish of Welbeck, Nottinghamshire,
    Sir Charles 242–3
    William, Earl and later Marquess and Duke of Newcastle 7, 40, 53, 63, 70, 95, 101, 120, 242, 258, 292, 338, 343, 407, 428, 432, 433, 443, 452, 464
Cawood, Stephen 416, 417
Cayley, family of 144–5
Cecil, Lords Burghley and Earls of Exeter,
    family of 98, 261, 262
    Dorothy, Countess of Exeter 261
    Earl John 262
    Earl Thomas 6, 194, 261
    William Lord Burghley 50
Chaloner, Robert 390
Chaloner of Guisborough, family of 173–4
Chantrell, William 116
Chapman John (Chancery official) 137
Chapman, John (schoolmaster) 422
Chapman,
    Margery 214
    Ralph 214
Charlesworth, Richard 382
Charman, Stephen 368
Chaytor, family of 154–5

Chester, William 323
Cholmley of Brandsby, family of 141–4
Cholmley of Whitby,
    family of 143, 254, 265, 300
    Sir Henry (1609–1666) 224, 241, 268
    Sir Hugh (1600–1657) 72, 101, 175, 204, 224, 241, 266–8
    Sir Hugh (1632–1689) 158, 202, 267, 268
    Sir Richard (1580–1631) 175, 254, 267
Clapham, Thomas 336
Clapham of Beamsley,
    family of 276–7
    Elizabeth 212
    Sir Christopher 212, 276–7
Clarendon, Earl of see Hyde, Edward
Clark, Daniel 382, 415
Clark, Peter (gardener) 405
Clark, Peter (minister) 38, 116
Clark, Richard 314
Clarkson,
    Richard 439
    William 439
Clayton, Sir John 50
Clervaux, family of 154
Clifford, Earls of Cumberland,
    family of 83, 277, 323, 396, 436
    Earl Henry 83, 137, 206, 261, 436, 437
    Lady Anne Clifford 277, 436, 437
Clifton, Frances 311
Clitherow, William 144
Clough, William 263, 314
Clough of Thorpe Stapleton, family of 474
Coates, Anthony 313
Cobb, family of 92
Cochrane, Sir John 28

Cockhill, John 451
Cokayne, Sir William 78
Coke, Sir John 160, 361, 410
Collier, Jeremiah 45, 312
Collins,
    Samuel 426
    Susan 426
Collinson, Anthony 105
Comber, Thomas 249
Congreve, William 291
Constable, George 48
Constable of Burton Constable,
    family of 36–7, 57
    Dorothy 145
    Henry Viscount Dunbar 8, 13, 18, 36–7, 59
    Robert Viscount Dunbar 37, 75
Constable of Catfoss, family of 106
Constable of Caythorpe, family of 99
Constable of Everingham,
    family of 48–9
    Sir Philip 48, 91
Constable of Flamborough,
    family of 50–1, 64–5
    Sir William 19, 50–1, 64, 65, 107
Constable of Great Hatfield
    family of 106
    Christopher 106, 126
    Jane 126
Constable of Kirby Knowle, family of 189, 243
Constable of Sherburn, family of 105
Constable of Wassand,
    family of 66, 106
    Philip 89
Conyers, George 63
Conyers, Leonard 63, 199
Conyers, Millicent 412
Conyers, Roger 178
Conyers, Thomas 271

Conyers of Boulby, family of 158
Conyers of Hornby, family of 180
Conyers of Hutton Bonville, family of 138
Cooke,
    family of 472
    Brian (1620–1661) 286–7, 472
    Sir George 287, 472
Coolam, John 450
Copley of Batley, family of 298
Copley of Skelbrooke, family of 441
Copley of Sprotborough, family of 444–5
Copley of Wadworth
    family of 463
    Lionel 70, 460, 463
Cork, Earl of see Boyle, Richard
Corker, Francis 312
Cornforth, Thomas 256
Cosin,
    John Bishop of Durham 67, 141
    Mary 141
Cotton, Robert 435
Coulson, Christopher 231
Coulthurst, Henry 350
Coulton, Thomas 252
Coundon, family of 123–4
Cowling, Thomas 217
Cradock,
    Peregrina 154
    Sir Joseph 245
Crashaw, William 34–5
Crathorne, family of 120, 152–3
Craven, Sir William 320
Cressy, family of 303
Creswell, family of 92
Crewe, Nathaniel Lord, Bishop of Durham 150
Crispe, Sir Nicholas 268
Croft, Thomas 316

Croft of Stillington, family of 246
Crompton, family of 56
Cromwell,
　Mary 151
　Oliver 59, 68, 81, 114, 151, 207, 228, 233, 316, 353, 367, 395, 420, 432
　Richard 97
Crosland, George 374
Crosland of Helmsley,
　family of 408
　Sir Jordan 178
Crosse, John 374
Crossley, Jeremiah 313
Crouch, Anne 97
Crowle, George 71
Crowther, Jane 358
Culverwell, Samuel 39
Cumberland, Earl of see Clifford, Earls of Cumberland
Currer, family of 379
Curwen, Walter 363
Cutler, Sir John 360
Cutler of Stainborough, family of 445

Dakin, John 195
Dakins, Arthur 175
Dakins, Sir Arthur 159–60
Dakins of Linton, family of 126
Dalton of Swine,
　family of 113, 176
　John 104
　Robert 89
Dalton of West Hauxwell, family of 176
Danby, Earl of see Danvers, Henry, Earl of Danby
Danby, James 189
Danby of Leake, family of 200
Danby of South Cave, family of 108

Danby of Thorpe Perrow,
　family of 211, 261–2, 344
　Christopher 188, 261
　Sir Abstrupus 212, 262
　Sir Thomas (1610–1660) 56, 261–2
　Thomas 205, 262
Daniel,
　family of 75–6
　Sir Ingleby 76, 448
Danvers, Henry, Earl of Danby 156, 162
Darcy of Aston,
　family of 289
　Anne 437–8
　Elizabeth Lady Darcy 113, 289
　John Lord Darcy 75, 113, 180, 289, 450
Darcy of Hornby,
　family of 180, 289
　Conyers Lord Darcy, later Earl of Holderness 180, 450
　Sir Conyers, Lord Darcy 180, 208, 210
Darcy of Temple Newsam, Thomas Lord Darcy 474
Darke, Edith 13
Darley of Bishop Wilton, family of 27
Darley of Buttercrambe
　family of 139–40
　Elizabeth 248
　Sir Richard 139, 248
Darley of Kilnhurst, Alice 419
Dawney,
　family of 237, 330, 439
　Sir Thomas 110, 330
Dawson, Emmanuel 200
Dawson, Joseph 305
Dawson, Thomas 430
Dawson, William 432
Dealtry, family of 53

Deane, James 40
De Eland, Isabel 342
Deincourt, Robert Lord see Leake,
    Robert
De La Pole, Sir Michael 71
De La Pryme, Abraham 11, 24, 40, 67,
    69, 111, 112, 113, 163, 338, 348,
    364, 388, 451, 482
Denton,
    Gervase 445
    Thomas 445
Denton, John 248, 252
Denton, Nathan 309
Denton, William 194
Derby, Earl of see Stanley, Earls of
    Derby
Devereux, Robert, Earl of Essex 307,
    447
Devonshire, Countess of see Cavendish,
    Elizabeth
Dewsbury, William 107
Dibble, James 142
Dickinson, Christopher 415
Digby, George Lord 421, 434
Dinmore, William 442
Dockery, Stephen 57
Dockray, Robert 351
Dodgson, William 419
Dodsworth, Roger 17, 188, 204, 224,
    242, 249, 286, 307, 320, 321, 335,
    336, 340, 350, 367, 376, 379, 443,
    453, 460, 476
Dodsworth of Thornton Watlass,
    family of 257
Dolman of Badsworth,
    family of 95, 290
    John 95
    Robert 68, 290, 465

Dolman of Millington, Marmaduke 32,
    64
Doughty, Robert 465
Dover, John Earl of see Carey, family of
Drake, Thomas 456
Drayton, Michael 1
Driffield, Frances 159
Dunbar, Henry Viscount, see Constable
    of Burton Constable, family of
Duncombe, Sir Charles 178, 194
Durdent, Margaret 110
Dyneley of Bramhope, family of 315–
    16
Dyneley of Swillington, family of 450
Dyson, John 305

Eastoft,
    family of 279, 308
    John 47, 279
Eastwood, John 293
Edgar, Francis 124
Edmunds, Henry 481
Egerton, family of 162
Eglisham, George 459
Eland, William 298
Elgin, Earl of see Bruce, Thomas
Ellerker,
    family of 99
    Sir Ralph 99, 110
Ellis, Joseph 71
Ellis, Ralph 340
Ellis, Thomas 338
Ellis of Kiddal
    family of 296
    John 296, 378
Ellison, David 312
Eltoft, family of 379
Elwes, Jeremy 223
Elwyck, Hannah 398
Eratt, William 364

Ermystead, William 305, 436
Essex, Earl of see Devereux, Robert
Etherington
    family of 162
    Richard 96
Eure, Lords Eure
    family of 204–5
    Margaret 205, 262
    William Lord Eure (1529–1594) 232
    William Lord Eure (c.1579–1646) 204, 205, 331
Evelyn, John 9, 125
Everard, Hugh 369
Everingham, Thomas 478
Ewbank, George 165, 247
Ewens, Richard 349
Exeter, Earls of see Cecil, Lords Burghley and Earls of Exeter
Eynns, Thomas 62
Eyre, Adam 415
Eyre of Laughton, family of 391

Fairfax of Denton,
    family of 301, 334–6, 390, 409
    Dorothy 50, 407
    Henry 315, 409, 462
    Henry Lord Fairfax 335–6, 409
    Mary (Arthington) 278
    Mary Duchess of Buckingham 178, 308, 335
    Sir Ferdinando, Lord Fairfax 50, 70, 169, 217, 277, 285, 297, 304, 307, 311, 332, 335, 336, 343, 347, 407, 409, 413, 423, 431, 452 Sir Thomas, Lord Fairfax (1560–1640) 307, 335
    Sir Thomas, Lord Fairfax (1612–1671) 7, 8, 11, 42, 51, 111, 112, 178, 186, 239, 285, 301, 304, 308, 312–13, 335, 343, 394, 405, 413, 457, 464
Fairfax of Gilling,
    family of 168–70, 465
    Charles Viscount Fairfax 169, 170, 466
Fairfax of Steeton,
    family of 307–8
    Sir William 8, 307
Fane, Sir Francis 289, 338
Farrer,
    family of 403
    William 396, 403
Farrington, Laurence 343
Fauconberg, Thomas Lord see Belasyse (Bellasis), family of
Favill, Laurence 359
Favour, John 357
Fawcett,
    Henry 288
    William 288
Fawkes, family of 413
Feild, James 460
Fell, Edward 430
Fenwick, Charles 127
Fenwick, Mary 316
Ferrand, family of 323
Ferrers, John 297
Ferries, Thomas 71
Field, family of 339
Fielding, Robert 388
Fiennes,
    Celia passim
    William, Viscount Saye and Sele 139
Finch, Heneage, Earl of Winchelsea 411
Fincham, Richard 438
Fisher, James 432
Fitz Ralph, Ranulph 149

Fleming, family of 466
Fletcher, Christopher 245
Fletcher, Thomas 322
Flint,
    George 289
    Henry 331
    Thomas 109
Flower, family of 401
Foljambe,
    family of 283
    Dame Elizabeth 283, 419
    Sir Francis 283, 419
Forman, John 425
Forster,
    Christopher 150, 200
    Richard 150
Forster, Sir Richard 247
Foulis,
    family of 185–6
    Sir David (c.1580–1642) 184–6, 231, 232
    Sir Henry 8, 186, 232, 343
Fountayne, John 370
Fox, George 42, 107, 134, 179, 301, 436, 467
Fox, Thwaites 23
Frank, family of 322
Franke, family of 214
Frankish, Robert 35
Frankland, Richard 351
Frankland of Aldwark, family of 131–2
Frankland of Great Thirkleby, family of 251–2
Freeman,
    John 380
    William 380
Freeston,
    family of 410–11
    John 466
French, George 446

Freville, Margaret 158
Frewen, Accepted, Archbishop of York 305
Frobisher, family of 410
Fuller, Thomas 1, 4, 421, 464

Gargrave,
    family of 481–2
    Prudence 346
    Sir Richard 346, 367, 481
Garnet, John 395
Garnett, John 254
Gascoigne, Richard 314
Gascoigne of Barnbow,
    family of 274, 295–6, 319, 349
    Sir Thomas (c. 1593–1686) 295–6, 315, 349, 450, 474
Gascoigne of Gawthorpe, family of 360, 361
Gascoigne of Sedbury, Isabel 165
Gascoigne of Thorpe on the Hill, family of 424
Gate, family of 236
Gee,
    family of 22, 25–6, 39, 85
    William (d.1603) 71
Gerard, family of 141–2
Gibb, Henry 111
Gibson, Cuthbert 337
Gibson, Edmund 21, 22, 59, 66, 75, 99, 107, 173, 234, 266, 281, 310, 328, 330, 361, 431, 449
Gibson, Edward 40
Gibson of Welburn, family of 195–6
Giffard, Robert 391
Gill, Leonard 16
Girlington, family of 108
Gleadall, John 314
Gledhill, Sarah 358
Glemham, Sir Thomas 11

Godsey, Thomas 431
Goldesborough, family of 353
Goldsbrough, Richard 318
Goldsmith, George 380
Goodricke,
   family of 375
   Sir Henry 284, 375
   Sir John 13, 365, 375
Goodwin,
   Arthur 367
   Jane 367
Goring, George 464
Gower, Stanley 432
Gower of Stainsby, family of 244
Gower of Stittenham, family of 238–9
Graham of Norton Conyers, family of 260
Graham of Nunnington,
   family of 221–2
   Ranald 81, 221–2
Grantham, family of 118–19
Graver, Thomas 215
Greaves, Robert 434
Greene, Elizabeth 49
Greene, John 377
Greene of Etherdwick, family of 15
Greene of Landmoth, family of 200
Greene of Thundercliffe Grange, family of 340
Greenecall, Richard 214
Greenwood, Charles 358, 455
Greenwood, John 447
Greenwood, Richard 479
Gregory, family of 292–3
Grenville, Bernard 223
Greville, Lords Brooke,
   family of 415
   Robert 139
Grey, Nicholas 254

Griffith,
   family of 34–5
   Sir Henry (1603–1654) 18, 19, 35, 51
Grimston, family of 54–5
Gunter, John 367

Haldenby, family of 279–80
Hall, George 159
Hall, John 404
Hall, Joseph 412
Hall, Mary 237
Hall, Robert 339
Hall, William 378
Halstead, Lawrence 293
Hamerton of Hellifield Peel, family of 398
Hamerton of Purston Jaglin, family of 345
Hammerton, Paul 431
Hamond, family of 429
Hampden, John 353
Hancock, Thomas 461
Hansby of Beverley, Ralph 25–7, 460
Hansby of Tickhill
   family of 460–1
   Sir Ralph 8, 460–1, 474
Hanson, John 418
Hardcastle, Thomas 409
Hardcastle, William 422
Hardwick, Lawrence 214
Hargreaves, John 288
Harington, Sir John 476
Harper, Marmaduke 47
Harpham, Robert 85
Harris, family of 372
Harrison, Edward 304
Harrison, Francis 108
Harrison, John 395
Harrison of Acaster Selby, family of 275

Harrison of Allerthorpe,
  family of 227
  Sir Thomas 227, 329
Harsnett, Samuel, Archbishop of York 477
Hart, William 13
Harte, Sir John 150
Harwood, Thomas 244
Hastead, William 313
Hastings, Earls of Huntingdon,
  family of 242
  Earl Henry 12
  Earl Theophilus 393
  Elizabeth, Countess of Huntingdon 393
Hatfield, family of 391
Hawksmoor, Nicholas 146
Hawksworth,
  family of 365–6, 413
  Sir Richard 13, 365
Hayford, William 481
Heath, Thomas 113
Heaton, Richard 181
Hebblethwaite, family of 91, 119
Heber, Reginald 376
Heber of Marton,
  family of 400
  Thomas (1566–1633) 352
Hepworth, Thomas 286
Herbert, George 440
Hesketh, family of 62
Hewett, Sir John 328
Hewitt, Matthew 378, 397
Hewley,
  Dame Sarah 12
  Sir John 87
Heywood, Oliver 278, 291, 298, 316, 354, 365, 372, 377, 400, 408, 412, 418, 420, 453, 470
Hibbert, Henry 95

Hide, William 86
Higholme, Andrew 369
Hildesley, Sir Francis 330
Hildyard of Bishop Wilton, family of 27
Hildyard of Patrington, Sir Robert 94, 123, 128
Hildyard of Winestead, family of 22, 124–5
Hill, Edward 374
Hillary, Joseph 321
Hilton, Roger 439
Hitch, Robert 277, 355, 410
Hitch of Leathley, family of 392
Hoby of Bisham Abbey, Berkshire,
  family of 175
Hoby of Hackness,
  family of 175
  Dame Margaret 115, 175
  Sir Thomas 6, 175, 267
Hodgkinson, Henry 340
Hodgson, Francis 206
Hodgson, Phineas 106
Hodgson of Beeston, family of 299–300
Hodgson of Bramwith, Sir Thomas 381–2
Holdsworth, Francis 31
Holdsworth, Josias 305
Holgate, Robert, Archbishop of York 12, 204, 368
Hollings, Roger 401
Holme, George 338
Holme of Paul Holme, family of 94
Holmes, John 377
Holt, Thomas 310
Holtby, Richard 48
Hood, Robin 363
Hood, Thomas 68
Hooke, Richard 422

Hooke, Robert 83
Hoole, Charles 424
Hopkinson, Ellen 358
Hopton,
    family of 287
    Sir Ingram 8, 287, 347, 392
Horncastle, William 368
Horne, family of 402–3
Horseman, Gilbert 384
Hotham,
    family of 100–2, 160
    Charles 63
    Dame Katherine 80, 103
    John 8, 101, 477
    Sir John (1589–1645) 8, 16, 19, 63, 70, 80, 101, 116, 117, 124, 166, 169, 423
Housman, Francis 13
Howard, Charles, Earl of Nottingham 233
Howard, Earls and Dukes of Norfolk,
    family of 432, 438
    Henry Earl of Norwich and later Duke of Norfolk 433
    Thomas Earl of Arundel and Surrey and later Earl of Norfolk 359–60
Howard, Earls of Carlisle, family of 146
Howard, Joseph 297
Howard, Lord William of Naworth 77
Howard, Thomas, Earl of Suffolk 46
Howard of Escrick, Lords Howard, family of 46
Howett, Alice 275
Hoyle, Henry 396
Hubbald, Richard 461
Huddleston, Richard 326
Hungate, Robert 434
Hungate of North Dalton, family of 89
Hungate of Saxton and Huddleston, family of 429, 434

Hunsdon, Henry Lord see Carey, family of
Hunt, Henry 217
Hunter, Henry 254
Hunter, Robert 254
Huntingdon, Earl of see Hastings, Henry
Hustler,
    family of 129–30
    William 30, 31, 129–30
Hutchinson, James 172
Hutchinson, John 214
Hutchinson, Lucy 118
Hutchinson, William 140, 230
Hutchinson of Wykeham, family of 270–1
Hutton of Goldsborough,
    family of 353, 370–1
    Elizabeth 341, 353
    Richard 341, 353, 370
    Sir Richard (c.1594–1645) 8, 353, 389
Hutton of Marske,
    family of 122, 207, 208–9, 228
    Matthew, Archbishop of York 84, 208, 407
Hutton of Nether Poppleton,
    family of 334, 407–8
    Dame Anne 250
    Dorothy 278, 407, 408
Hyde, Edward, Earl of Clarendon 3, 43, 101, 117, 210, 335, 405, 406

Inchbald, Joseph 339
Ingleby of Lawkland, family of 326–7
Ingleby of Ripley, family of 349, 386, 420, 421
Ingram,
    family of 25, 60, 454–5, 474
    Dorothy 81

Henry Lord Irwin 25
Sir Arthur (c.1565–1642), 13, 14, 25, 182, 192, 237, 239, 364, 370, 410–11, 454–5, 474
Inman, Robert 369
Ireland,
 family of 331–2
 Elizabeth 76
 William (d.1620) 482
 William (b. 1627) 331–2, 466
Isack, Philip 465

Jackson, John 208
Jackson, Nathaniel 295
Jackson, Richard 430
Jackson, Thomas (chaplain) 282
Jackson, Thomas (servant) 79
Jackson of Hickleton, family of 309, 368–9
Jackson of Knayton, family of 200
Jaggard, Thomas 385
Jaques, family of 45
Jenison, Sir Ralph 389
Jenkins, Henry 148
Jenkinson, Josiah 396
Jepson, Zacharias 422
Jobson of Cudworth,
 family of 332
 Dame Mary (Bolles) 332, 466
Jobson of West Hauxwell, family of 176
Johnson,
 Francis 144
 Ralph 144
Johnson, John (curate of Selby) 431
Johnson, John (rector of Cherry Burton) 39
Johnson, Robert 324
Johnston, Nathaniel 371, 417
Jones, Martha 263

Jonson, Ben 453
Justice, Thomas 446

Kay, Edmund 424
Kay, Robert 343
Kaye,
 family of 285–6, 388
 Sir John (1616–1662) 285–6, 334
 Sir John (c.1641–1706) 285–6, 387
Keld, Christopher 233
Kemp, Wilfrid 125
Kempe, Richard 125
Kendall, Leonard 419–20
Kenyon, William 27
Keresforth, Thomas 294
King, William 438
Kingston, Earl of see Pierrepont, Earls of Kingston
Kirchivall, Roger 287
Kirkeby, Thomas 59
Knight, William, Bishop of Bath and Wells 195
Knight of Langold, family of 391
Knollis, Sir Robert 417
Knowles, James 398–9
Knowles, John 274
Knowles of Bilton, family of 118

Lacy, family of 54
Lambert, John 380
Lambert,
 family of 383–4
 John 65, 383–4, 400, 441
Lamplugh, Thomas, Archbishop of York 115
Langdale of Dowthorpe, Marmaduke 79, 100, 113
Langdale of Holme upon Spalding Moor,
 family of 64–5

Elizabeth 412
Marmaduke Lord Langdale 65, 70, 79
Sir Marmaduke Lord Langdale 64–5, 347, 412, 434
Langdale of Langthorpe,
  family of 79, 100
  William (1579–1645), 47, 79
Langhorn, Lancelot 167
Lascelles of Breckenbrough, family of 192
Lascelles of Stank Hall, family of 191
Lathley, Henry 63
Latimer, John Lord see Neville, John, Lord Latimer
Laud, William, Archbishop of Canterbury 16
Laughton, Edmund 391
Lawson, Godfrey 395
Lawson, Sir John 233
Lawson of Brough, family of 145–6
Laycock, William 379
Layton of Rawden, family of 356
Layton of Sexhow, family of 213, 231–2
Leake,
  Mary, Lady Deincourt 393
  Robert Lord Deincourt 393
Lechmere, Thomas 201
Lee, William 298
Leeds, family of 385–6
Legard of Anlaby, family of 16
Legard of Ganton, family of 53–4
Leigh, Sir Ferdinando 424
Leland, John 192, 245, 444
Leng, John, Bishop of Durham 254
Lenge, Hugh 184
Leppington, William 73
Lepton, family of 150
Leveson, Sir Richard 238, 239

Levitt, John 370
Lewis of Ledston,
  family of 392–3
  Sir John 392–3, 400
Lewis of Marr,
  family of 400
  Thomas 393, 400
Liddell,
  Dame Agnes 154
  Sir Francis 154
Liddell,
  Dame Catherine 291
  John 291
Lilburne, Richard 385
Lilburne, Robert 114
Lindley, Francis 311
Lindley of Leathley,
  family of 392
  Sir Henry 213
Lister, Anne 27
Lister, Anthony 351
Lister, Ingram 181
Lister, James 464
Lister, John 338
Lister, Joseph 312
Lister of Bawtry, Thomas 299
Lister of Linton Grange,
  family of 126
  Sir John 71, 126, 299
Lister of Thornton,
  family of 457
  Sir William 8, 457
  William 8, 457
Lister of Westby and Arnolds Biggin,
  family of 352
Lith, John 458
Lith (Lyeth), Thomas 131, 236
Loftus, Sir Edward 392
Londonderry, Earl of see Ridgeway, Robert

Lovell, family of 240
Lowther, Sir John 241
Lowther of Ingleton, family of 300–1
Lowther of Marske, family of 210
Lowther of Swillington, family of 450–1
Lucas, Sir Charles 358
Luddington, Robert 104
Lumley, Elizabeth, Viscountess 226, 240, 254
Lupton, Roger 430
Lyley, William 387
Lynsey, Ralph 430

Mainprice, William 81–2
Mallory,
    family of 183, 282, 349
    Sir John (c.1557–1620) 217, 282
    Sir John (1610–1656) 13, 282, 436
Maltby,
    Christopher 49
    Frances 188
Manchester, Earl of see Montagu, Edward
Mannering, John 428
Manners, Earls of Rutland, family of 102, 178
Manwaring, Edward 253
Marchant, Marmaduke 63
Margetson, James, Archbishop of Armagh, 305
Marmion, family of 264
Marsden, Henry 306, 352
Marsh, Richard 304, 357
Marshall, Elizabeth 337
Marshall, George 376
Marston, Richard 63
Martindale, Adam 7

Marvell,
    Andrew (d.1640) 124
    Andrew (1621–1678) the poet 124, 301, 308, 335, 398
Marwood,
    family of 247–8
    Margaret 163, 247
Mason (Mayson), Francis 187, 405
Mason, John 347
Mason, Robert 320
Mason, Valentine 45
Mason, William 327
Mauleverer of Allerton Mauleverer, family of 283–4
Mauleverer of Ingleby Arncliffe,
    family of 184–5, 291
    Timothy 158, 185, 474
Mauleverer of Letwell, family of 391
May, John 79
Mayer, John 430
Meare, Francis 338
Messenger, family of 349
Metcalf, Robert 200
Metcalfe, Anthony 173
Metcalfe of Bellerby, family of 244
Metcalfe of Nappa Hall, family of 134–5
Metham,
    family of 67–8, 88
    Sir Thomas 8, 67–8, 88
Meynell of Hawnby, family of 177
Meynell of North Kilvington,
    family of 254–6
    Thomas (1565–1653) 213, 228, 255, 443
    William 206
Michelburne,
    family of 16
    Mary 97

Micklethwaite
    Sir John 39
    Thomas 26, 39, 56
Micklethwaite of Swine,
    family of 113–14
    Elias 251
Middleton, Ann 13, 225
Middleton, Catherine 158
Middleton of Stansted Mountfichet,
    Essex,
    family of 113
    Constance 114
Middleton of Stockeld,
    family of 442–4
    William (c. 1551–1614) 192, 443
Midleton, Henry 478
Milbanke,
    family of 154–5
    Sir Mark (c.1630–1680) 111, 154
    Sir Mark (c.1659–1698) 154, 195
Miller, Richard 232
Milner, Jeremiah 354
Monck, George, Duke of Albemarle 97, 112, 405
Monckton of Cavil, family of 42–3
Monckton of Hodroyd,
    Elizabeth 370
    Marmaduke 346
Monson,
    Sir John 202
    Sir Robert 260
Montagu, Edward, Earl of Manchester 338
Montagu, Edward,
    Earl of Sandwich 453
    Sidney 453
Montaigne, Michel de 405
Moore, Robert 355, 356
More,
    Basil 292
    Sir Thomas 292
More of Bewick, family of 16
Morley,
    family of 223
    James 177, 223
Mornington, Giles 219
Morrice, Roger 28, 117, 186, 216
Morris, John 441
Motley,
    Henry 378, 397
    Thomas 397
Mountaigne, family of 121
Moyser,
    family of 307–8
    James 308, 371
Mulgrave, Earl of see Sheffield, family of
Munforth, John 446
Murgatroyd, family of 377
Musgrave, William 305
Musgrave of Norton Conyers, family of 259–60
Myers, William 449
Myles, Robert 207

Nalton, Francis 116
Napier, family of 236
Nayler, James 479
Neile,
    family of 138
    John 20
    Richard, Archbishop of York 7, 20, 138, 313, 356, 395
Nelson, Gilbert 430
Nelson, John 110
Nelthorpe, James 474
Nesse, Christopher 89
Nettleton, Robert 285
Nevile,
    family of 325–6

Francis (1592–1665) 278, 326
Gervase 300, 326
Neville, John, Lord Latimer 261
Newark, family of 276
Newcastle, Earl of see Cavendish of Welbeck
Newcomen, Anne 433
Newman, Samuel 479
Newstead, Christopher 138
Nicholson, Oliver 231
Noble, John 389
Noble, Michael 280
Nodding, Christopher 302
Norcliffe,
    family of 80–1, 221
    Benjamin 181
    Sir Thomas (1618–1680) 58, 80–1, 103, 221
Northropp, Richard 371
Northumberland, Earl of see Percy, Earls of Northumberland
Norton, John 119
Norton, Mary 448
Nottingham, Earl of see Howard, Charles
Nutter, Anthony 406, 479

Oddie, John 352
Ogilby, John 4
Oglethorpe, Owen, Bishop of Carlisle 452
Oglethorpe of Oglethorpe, family of 315
Okell, John 312
Okey, Francis 415
Oldfield, Thomas 403
Osbaldeston, family of 73
Osborne, George 125

Osborne of Kiveton,
    family of 361–2, 390
    Sir Edward 67, 165, 335, 361–2, 364, 391
    Sir Thomas, Earl of Danby and later Duke of Leeds 361–2, 391, 461
Otby,
    Pethuel 166
    Tristram 166
Overton, Robert 42

Page, Henry 340
Palm, Robert 324
Palmes of Lindley,
    family of 61, 413
    Douglas 112
    Mary 205
    Sir Guy 61
    William 205
Palmes of Naburn,
    family of 87
    Sir George 87, 438
    William 87, 145
Parker, family of 310
Parkin,
    Charles 230
    John 230
Parkinson, Edward 270
Parkinson, Thomas 323
Parnaby, Reynold 256
Paxton, Henry 48, 91
Payler,
    family of 32–3
    Sir Edward 32–3, 108
Paynter, George 59
Pearson, George 131
Pearson, Samuel 336
Pearson, William 189
Pecke, Francis 139
Peckett, Philip 199

Peel, Francis 293
Peirse,
    family of 137
    Richard 137, 138
Peirson, family of 84
Pembroke, Earl of see Herbert, William
Pennington, Sir William 117
Pennyman of Marske,
    family of 209–10
    Sir William 8, 209–10, 222–3
Pennyman of Ormesby,
    family of 222–3
    James 210, 222
Percehay, family of 190
Percy, Earls of Northumberland,
    family of 81, 127, 187, 245, 257, 442–3
    Earl Algernon 127
    Earl Henry 187
Percy of Scotton, family of 344
Percy of Walden Stubbs, family of 344, 478
Perkins, William 25
Perry, Andrew 166
Petch, Henry 473
Petty, Thomas 348
Phelippes, Thomas 190
Philips, John 115
Pickering, William 450
Pickhard, Adam 438
Pierrepont, Earls of Kingston,
    Henry 184
    Robert 184, 315
Pilkington, family of 446–7
Pindar, Sir Paul 209
Pinkney, George 228
Plaxton,
    John 26
    William 423
Plumpton, family of 442–4

Poole, Anne 285
Popeley, Grace 470
Portington of Barnby Dun, family of 292–3
Portington of Portington, family of 43
Powlett, Charles, Marquess of Winchester and later Duke of Bolton 207, 263
Preston, Catherine 210
Preston, Sir John 297
Proctor,
    family of 349, 421
    Sir Stephen 282, 349
Pudsay, family of 306–7
Pulleyne, family of 344
Pursglove, Robert 173
Pym, John 139, 252

Rabanke, Samuel 156
Radcliffe, Sir Edward 265
Radcliffe, Sir George 469
Ramsden,
    family of 285, 318, 374
    Rosamund 306
    Sir John 8, 285, 318, 426
    William (1558–1623) 285, 306
Rands, Richard 348
Rawdon, Marmaduke 45, 69, 199, 219, 233, 266, 312, 337, 395, 421, 434, 442
Rawson, Lawrence 395
Rawson, Thomas 433
Ray, Robert 276
Raynaild, William 404
Rayney, John 480
Read, Charles 339
Redman, Brian 327
Redman of Thornton in Lonsdale,
    family of 458
Reiner, George 398

Remington,
    Grace 411
    James 411
Remington, Thomas 326
Remington of Lund,
    family of 22, 82, 84
    Mary 30
    Sir Thomas 56, 84
Reresby,
    family of 402, 458–9
    Dame Frances 308
    Sir John (1634–1689) 11, 12, 163, 169, 260, 284, 308, 371, 375, 398, 444, 447, 459, 472
Reyner, John 479
Reynolds, Thomas 67
Ricard, family of 439
Rich, Frances, Countess of Warwick 136
Richardson, Christopher 41
Richardson, Thomas 405
Riddell, Sir Thomas 145
Ridgeley, James, 479
Ridgeway, Robert, Earl of Londonderry 332
Rimmington, James 286
Roberts, Francis 256
Robinson, Anne 235
Robinson, John 254
Robinson, Nicholas 352
Robinson, Thomas (vicar of Warmfield) 466
Robinson, Thomas (vicar of Whenby) 265
Robinson, William 71
Robinson of Allerthorpe,
    family of 227
    Thomas 147
Robinson of Deighton,
    family of 46–7
    Luke 46, 218
    Sir Arthur 46, 218
Robinson of Newby,
    family of 258–9
    William (c.1627–1643) 103, 258
Robinson of Rokeby,
    family of 229
    Matthew 147
Robinson of Ryther,
    family of 425–6
    John (1566–1619) 114, 425–6
Robinson of Thicket Hall, family of 114
Robson, George 182
Rockley,
    family of 480–1
    Francis 334, 481
    Robert 334, 481
Rodes,
    family of 353–4
    Francis 354, 369
Rogers, Edmund 294
Rogers, Ezekiel 98, 389
Rogers, Francis 385
Rogerson, Robert 164
Roidhouse, William 446
Rokeby, Thomas 467
Rokeby of Mortham,
    family of 229
    Thomas (1639–1722) 158, 229
Rokeby of Skiers Hall, family of 373
Roods, Thomas 343
Rotherham, Thomas 423
Roundell, family of 397–8
Rudston, family of 58
Rupert, Prince 11, 297, 421, 452
Rushworth, John 48
Rutland, Earl of see Manners, Edward

Ryley, Ann 324
Rymer, Ralph 141
Ryther,
    James 3, 5
    Robert 360

St Quintin,
    family of 22, 34–6
    Sir Henry 35–6, 97
Saltmarsh, Edward 192
Saltmarshe, John 120
Saltonstall, Sir Richard 481
Samwayes, Peter 137, 259
Sandys, Edwin, Archbishop of York 6, 121
Saunderson, Viscounts Castleton,
    family of 399
    Robert 446
Savile, Henry 311
Savile of Copley, family of 437–8
Savile of Howley,
    family of 4, 395, 406–7, 479
    Sir John, Lord Savile 298, 394, 406–7
    Thomas Earl of Sussex 333, 406–7, 479
Savile of Lupset,
    family of 372
    Sir John 130, 343, 372
Savile of Methley, family of 369, 401–2
Savile of Thornhill,
    family of 333, 342, 343, 372, 455–6
    Henry 465
    Sir George, Marquess of Halifax 342, 359
    Sir William 8, 11, 333, 343, 394, 432, 456
Savile of Wakefield, George 465
Sawdrie, Anthony 468
Sawer, Roger 254
Saxton,
    Christopher 1, 341, 480
    Peter 341
    Robert 393
Saxton,
    Henry 328–9
    Henry his grandson 329
Saye and Sele, Lord see Fiennes, William
Sayer,
    family of 220
    Dorothy 207, 220
    John 207, 220
Scaife,
    Luce 182
    Thomas 182
Scott, Christopher 313
Scott of Barnes Hall, family of 340
Scrimshaw, Charles 389
Scrope, Lords Scrope and Earls of Sunderland, family of 263
Scrope of Danby, family of 244, 256
Scudamore, family of 225
Scurr, Leonard 300
Seaman, John 89
Selley, Robert 473
Seton, Robert 391
Shalcrosse, Humphrey 112
Shann, family of 393, 451, 454
Sharp,
    Abraham 313
    John 313
Sharp, John, Archbishop of York 313
Sharpe, James 48, 60
Shaw, Abraham 403
Shaw, John (minister at Bolton by Bowland) 306
Shaw, John (vicar of Rotherham) 423

Sheffield, Lords Sheffield and Earls of
    Mulgrave,
    family of 202–3
    Earl Edmund (1565–1646) 12,
      202–3
    Earl John 158, 202–3, 241
Shelles, Nicholas 94
Shelton, John 77
Shepard, Thomas 139
Sherburne, family of 355
Sherrard, Daniel 208
Sherwood, Francis 52
Sherwood, William 116
Shewton, John 435
Shiercliffe, family of 340
Shiers, George 190
Shillito,
    family of 474
    Elizabeth 460, 474
Shipton,
    Matthew 241
    Richard 203
Shirt, John 415
Shrewsbury, Earls of see Talbot, Earls of
    Shrewsbury
Shute, Christopher 351
Sidney, Margaret 175
Sigsworth, Anne 171
Silverwood, Mary 324
Simpson, Henry (minister) 172
Simpson, Henry (of Great Smeaton)
    130
Simpson, Henry (of Reeth) 172
Simpson, Simon 100
Simpson, Thomas 197
Sinclair, Enoch 38
Skeynes, Thomas 458
Skipwith, family of 107
Skirlaw, Walter, Bishop of Durham 271

Slack,
    Bridget 323
    John 323
Slater, William 315
Slinger, George 276–7
Slingsby of Kippax, family of 380–1
Slingsby of Moor Monkton,
    family of 57, 390, 404–5
    Sir Henry (1602–1658) 13, 101,
      166, 205, 405, 407
    Thomas 166
Smelt,
    Luke 191
    Thomas 156–7, 220
Smelt of Kirkby Fleetham,
    family of 193
    Richard 158
Smith, Edward 52
Smith, Hugh 380
Smith, James (Catholic bishop) 270
Smith, James (vicar of Calverley) 321
Smith, Richard 431
Smith, Stephen 161
Smith, Thomas 433
Smith of Osgodby, family of 61
Smithson, Augustine 410, 442
Smithson, Francis 378
Smithson, William 190–1
Smithson of Moulton, family of 214
Smithson of Stanwick, family of 245
Smyth, William 368
Smythson,
    John 243
    Robert 25, 36, 417
Snawsell, family of 302
Sorocold, George 395
Sotheby, family of 24–5
Spence, Ferrand 324
Spencer, Mary 26
Spencer, Nathaniel 377

Spencer, Thomas 391
Spivey, John 364
Spofford, John 104, 435
Spoone, Richard 340
Sprignell, Sir Richard 330
Stacie, Anthony 391
Stanhope, Walter 366
Stanhope of Edlington and Grimston,
    family of 341–2, 386, 446
Stanley, Earls of Derby
    family of 253
    Earl James 384
    Earl William 469
Stapleton of Carlton,
    family of 136, 137, 324, 439
    Sir Miles 324, 475
    Ursula 79
Stapleton of Myton, family of 215–16
Stapleton of Warter,
    family of 117
    Sir Philip 26, 117, 476
Stapleton of Wighill,
    family of 215, 302, 476
    Henry (1574–1631) 117, 476
    Sir Miles 287, 476
Starkie, Edmund 377
Staveley, Barbara 190
Steele, Robert 29
Stephenson, Thomas 473
Stevenson, Anthony 70, 98
Stevenson, Paul 450
Steward, Zachary 201
Stillington, Robert, Bishop of Bath and
    Wells 275
Stillington, Thomas 276
Stillington of Kelfield, family of 111
Stockdale, Robert 279
Stockdale, Thomas 390
Stone, Nicholas 482
Stonehouse, Walter 333

Stoughton, Dame Mary 33
Strafford, Earl of see Wentworth of
    Wentworth Woodhouse
Stretton, Richard 308, 335
Strickland of Boynton,
    family of 27–9, 125, 133
    Ceziah 56
    Sir William (1596–1673) 28, 38,
    56, 59, 241
    Walter (d.1636) 28, 190
    Walter (d.1671) 28, 51
Strickland of Thornton Bridge,
    family of 141–2
    Sir Robert 118, 142
    Sir Thomas (1621–1694) 54, 142
Stringer, Ralph 159
Stringer of Sharlston, family of 466–7,
    473
Stringer of Whiston, family of 473
Sturdy, John 313
Sugden, Thomas 58
Sunderland of High Sunderland, then
    of Ackton,
    family of 412
    Langdale 328, 345, 412
    Samuel 396, 412
Swale, Philip 378
Swale, Solomon 282, 295, 405
Swale, William 109
Swale of South Stainley,
    family of 441–2
    Sir Solomon 379, 441–2
Swift, Henry 415
Swift, Robert 434
Swyft,
    family of 388–9
    Barnham Viscount Carlingford 388,
    472
    Mary 472
Syddall, Michael 148

Sydenham, family of 175
Sykes, Richard (cloth merchant) 396
Sykes, Richard (minister) 387
Sylvester, Edward 340
Sylvester, Matthew 291
Symkinson, Thomas 338

Tailor, Christopher 438
Talbot, Earls of Shrewsbury,
   family of 359, 432
   Earl Edward 417, 432
   Earl Gilbert 359, 424, 432, 433
   Henry 424, 425
Talbot of Bashall, family of 296–7
Talbot of Thornton le Street, family of 255
Tankard, William 164
Tankard of Arden Hall, family of 177
Tankard of Brampton,
   family of 188–9
   Thomas (1603–1663) 188–9, 281
Tankard of Whixley, family of 475
Taxter, Andrew 329
Taylor, John (schoolmaster) 374
Taylor, John, the Water Poet 4, 394, 453
Taylor, Thomas 452
Taylor, William 365
Tempest of Bolling Hall, family of 311, 312
Tempest of Broughton,
   family of 318–20
   Frances 79
Tempest of Tong, family of 461–2
Temple, Sir William 440
Tennant,
   James 89
   Richard 320, 352, 378

Theakston,
   family of 146
   Sir Richard 136
   Sir William 137, 146
Thimbleby, family of 411
Thomlinson, Christopher 476
Thomlinson, Tobias 274
Thompson of Humbleton, family of 72
Thompson of Kilham, family of 74
Thompson of Long Marston,
   family of 397–8
   Sir Henry 46, 398
Thomson, family of 321, 365–6
Thoresby, Ralph passim
Thornhill, family of 418
Thornton,
   family of 248–9
   Alice 198, 199, 233, 248–9, 361
   William (1624–1668) 233, 248–9
Thorpe, Francis 25
Thorpe, Richard 404
Thorpe of Aldbrough, family of 16
Thwaites, family of 397–8
Thweng,
   family of 241–2
   Thomasine 327
Tillotson, John, Archbishop of Canterbury 357
Tindall, family of 318
Todd,
   Andrew 473
   Robert 395, 473
Todd, Cornelius 162
Toller, Peter 436
Toller, Thomas 432
Tomkinson, Thomas 364
Topham, John 320, 383
Topham of Agglethorpe, family of 149
Towry, Robert 16

Index of Persons

Towry of Kirby Grindalythe, family of 77
Trappes, family of 410, 442
Trigott, family of 440
Trotter, family of 241–2
Troy, Ralph 238
Troy, Robert 16
Tufton, Earls of Thanet, family of 437
Tunstall, family of 135, 176, 269–70
Turner, William 478
Turner of Kirkleatham,
    family of 196–7
    John 187, 197
Twisleton, family of 316

Vanbrugh, Sir John 146
Van Dyck, Sir Anthony 445
Vane, Sir Henry 185
Vanpanie, Samuel 340
Vaughan, family of 112, 152
Vavasour, Robert 385
Vavasour of Hazlewood Castle, family of 276, 449–50
Vavasour of Spaldington, family of 31–2
Vavasour of Weston, family of 413, 471
Vermuyden, Sir Cornelius 293, 363
Villiers, Dukes of Buckingham,
    George (1592–1628) 194, 260
    George (1628–1687) 178, 194, 252, 335
Vincent of Barnbrough, family of 292
Vincent of Great Smeaton, Marmaduke 171

Waddilove, Gilbert 460
Wade, Andrew 473
Wade, James 431
Wait, Thomas 121–2
Waite, John 350
Wakefield, William 237
Walker, Obadiah 125
Walker, Richard 435
Walker, William (lawyer) 195
Walker, William (schoolmaster) 301, 351
Wall, Abraham 358
Waller, Nicholas 439
Waller, Sir William 368
Wallis, Christopher 31
Walmesley, Charles 431
Walters,
    family of 155
    Sir Robert 13, 155
Walton, Nicholas 383
Wandesford,
    family of 198–9
    Christopher 148, 198–9, 248, 261
Ward, Noah 163, 411
Ward, Ralph 415
Ward, William 55
Wardell, John 40
Warren, Desired 475
Warton,
    family of 22, 23–4, 26
    Sir Michael 23–4, 42
Warwick, Frances Countess of see Rich, Frances
Washington, family of 280, 440
Wastell, family of 235
Wastneys, family of 461
Waterhouse, Nathaniel 358
Waterton, family of 427–8
Watkinson,
    Ann 32
    William 32, 33
Watson, Thomas 132
Watts, Richard 340
Webster, John 379

Wentworth of North Elmsall,
   family of 411
   Darcy 317, 411
   Sir Thomas 317, 411
   Thomas 103, 317
Wentworth of Wentworth Woodhouse,
   family of 360, 371, 468–9
   Margaret 342
   Sir Thomas, Viscount Wentworth
   and Earl of Strafford passim
   Sir William 320, 342, 360, 380,
   468, 469
   William Earl of Strafford 360, 393,
   468, 469
Wentworth of West Bretton,
   family of 294, 369, 435, 470
   Matthew 294–5
Wentworth of Woolley,
   family of 479–80
   Anne 73
   John 281, 294, 369, 480
   Michael 334, 480
   Sir Michael 281
West, family of 391
Westby, family of 402
Westroppe,
   family of 239
   James 238
   Thomas 73, 239
Wetherald, Matthew 134
Wetherall, Roger 449
Wetherill, James 134
Wetwang, William 227
Wharton, Lords Wharton,
   family of 366–7
   Philip Lord Wharton (1613–1696)
   157, 167, 172, 366–7
   Sir Thomas 157, 167, 261, 341–2
Wharton, Posthumus 430

Wharton of Edlington,
   family of 341–2, 370
   Philip 341, 353
Wharton of Gillingwood Hall, family
   of 167–8
Wheat, Jeremy 291
Wheath, Philip 96
Whitaker, Gamaliel 382
Whitaker, John 431
Whitaker, William 433
White, family of 297
Whitehead, Robert 426
Whitelocke, Bulstrode 101
Whittacre, Robert 290
Widdrington, Sir Thomas 308
Wigglesworth, William 344
Wilcocke, William 313
Wildman, John 253
Wilkinson, John 343
Wilkinson, William 369
Wilks, John 331
Williams, John, Archbishop of York
   477
Williams, Peter 163
Willoughby, Mary 35
Wilmot, Henry Lord 284
Wilson, George 18–19, 141
Wilson, Joseph 16, 22
Wilson, Thomas (clothworker) 419
Wilson, Thomas (schoolmaster) 254
Winchester, Marquess of see Powlett,
   Charles
Windle, Robert 456
Winn, family of 482
Winter, Robert 443
Winthrop, John the younger 19
Witham of Cliffe,
   family of 206
   George 87, 206
Witham of Ledston, family of 393

Withes, family of 329
Witton, Richard 372
Wolstenholme, family of 482
Wombwell,
    family of 477–8
    Thomas (vicar of Wath) 468
Wood, Anthony 148, 453
Wood, James 368
Wood, Robert 388
Wood, Thomas (Catholic schoolmaster) 200
Wood, Thomas (Protestant schoolmaster) 313
Wood of Beeston,
    family of 299
    Elizabeth 181
    Sir John 181, 299
Wood of Kilnwick Percy, family of 76
Woodruffe, family of 480
Wooler, William 303
Wormley, Thomas 364
Wormley of Riccall,
    family of 96
    Henry 96, 110–11
Worrall, Gervase 313, 368
Worsley, family of 181
Wortley,
    family of 452–3
    Sir Francis (1591–1652) 353, 428, 434–5, 453
Wright, Ann 13
Wright, Francis 78
Wright, John 290
Wright, Rosamund 275
Wright, William 269
Wright of Ploughland,
    family of 120
    Francis 120, 153
Wycliffe, Katherine 269
Wyncope, John 329

Wyvill,
    family of 165
    Mary 212

Yarburgh,
    family of 439–40
    Edmund 322, 440
Yaxley, Charles 302
Yonge of Burn, family of 316–17
Yonge of Methley, family of 401
York of Burnsall, John 319
Yorke of Gouthwaite Hall
    family of 228, 320, 384, 448–9
    Thomas 352, 448
Young, John 189
Young,
    Richard 137
    Thomas 137